Maritime Security Law in Hybrid Warfare

Publications on Ocean Development

A SERIES OF STUDIES ON THE INTERNATIONAL, LEGAL, INSTITUTIONAL AND POLICY ASPECTS OF OCEAN DEVELOPMENT

General Editors

Alex Oude Elferink
Joanna Mossop

VOLUME 102

The titles published in this series are listed at *brill.com/pood*

Maritime Security Law in Hybrid Warfare

Edited by

Alexander Lott

BRILL | NIJHOFF

LEIDEN | BOSTON

This project received funding from the European Union's Horizon 2020 research and innovation programme under the Marie Sklodowska-Curie grant agreement No 101018998. This book reflects only the authors' view and the European Research Executive Agency is not responsible for any use that may be made of the information it contains.

Library of Congress Cataloging-in-Publication Data

Names: Lott, Alexander, editor.
Title: Maritime security law in hybrid warfare / edited by Alexander Lott
Brill.
Description: Boston, Massachusetts : Brill, 2024. | Series: Publications on ocean development, 0924-1922 ; vol 102 | Includes bibliographical references and index.
Identifiers: LCCN 2024026815 (print) | LCCN 2024026816 (ebook) | ISBN 9789004707986 (hardback) | ISBN 9789004707993 (ebook)
Subjects: LCSH: Freedom of the seas. | Hybrid warfare. | Security, International.
Classification: LCC KZA1348 .M37 2024 (print) | LCC KZA1348 (ebook) | DDC 341.6/3–dc23/eng/20240617
LC record available at https://lccn.loc.gov/2024026815
LC ebook record available at https://lccn.loc.gov/2024026816

Typeface for the Latin, Greek, and Cyrillic scripts: "Brill". See and download: brill.com/brill-typeface.

ISSN 0924-1922
ISBN 978-90-04-70798-6 (hardback)
ISBN 978-90-04-70799-3 (e-book)
DOI 10.1163/9789004707993

This book is printed on acid-free paper and produced in a sustainable manner.

Contents

Foreword

This is the essential book today for understanding maritime security law as a key element in crafting responses to hybrid threats at sea. Since the *Corfu Channel Case* at the International Court of Justice in 1949, international law, the law of the sea, and law of naval warfare have struggled to provide clear guidance for deterring and addressing hybrid threats in the maritime domain. The 1986 *Paramilitary Activities Case* and the 2003 *Oil Platforms Case* similarly proved inadequate to the task of providing guidance and relief for States under hybrid maritime assault. There is a lack of clear guidance in international law for contending with maritime threats that combine elements of conventional and irregular military forces with peacetime coercive strategies and disruptive practices, operating with synergistic effects to disorient an adversary. And yet throughout the world, from the Black Sea, the Baltic Sea, the Red Sea, to the South China Sea, States are now confronted with sophisticated, multi-dimensional and multi-domain attacks intended to erode their maritime security, and with it their political stability, economic prosperity, and national security.

"Maritime Security Law in Hybrid Warfare" systematically approaches the international law applicable to these pernicious and unconventional threats and risks, whether described as hybrid, grey zone, Fourth Generation Warfare. The task is not easy because hybrid maritime security involves cybersecurity and disinformation, crime and sabotage alongside anti-ship ballistic missile, and threats that extend from outer space to the deep seabed.

The study is authored by some of the most experienced and highly regarded experts in the field along with the rising stars. The authors form an elegant team that operates at the intersection of international law and maritime security to produce a compelling and thoughtfully coherent study that smoothly interacts with the seam between the law of the sea and the law of naval warfare. Part 1 explores the nature of hybrid warfare through the lens of maritime security law, considering the contours of hybrid attacks at sea and considerations for the use of force in self-defence and other responses, such as imposition of countermeasures. In the peacetime grey zone, the toolkit relies on the law of the sea and proposes guidelines for reducing the operating space of grey zone actors by "shedding a light" on their activities and demarcating firm positions on acceptable conduct and unacceptable threats that will produce consequences for adversaries.

This Part concludes with a detailed study on how we should draw the line between peacetime and war. Do the boundaries of classical international law still make sense in today multi-domain hybrid naval conflicts? Anna Petrig offers a three-stage inquiry to approach this vexing issue at the center of contemporary warfare at sea. First, she recommends understanding the context and making a determination of whether there is the existence of an armed conflict in international law. Second, what is the nexus between use of force during a maritime incident and the use of force during naval warfare? Third, what measures taken by States at sea amount to an attack within the meaning of the law of naval warfare? The fundamental problem she teases out is that the determination whether the law of armed conflict applies differs from land to the sea. This is the smartest and concise modeling of these distinctions I have seen and is by itself essential reading.

Part II explores questions surrounding offshore underwater infrastructure – oil pipelines and submarine communications cables that have been attacked in Europe and East Asia. This is a roadmap for thinking about what types of disruptions on the seabed constitute an armed attack in international law, and how the right of self-defence is triggered. During armed conflict at sea, what may belligerents lawfully do to protect their own critical underwater infrastructure and hold at risk those of the adversary? This part of the book contains the most sophisticated analysis in print on the Nord Stream pipeline and the Balticconnector, providing a toolkit for the law of the sea and the law of naval warfare, and how these regimes are adjacent to prescriptive and enforcement jurisdiction, civil liability, and environmental law, as well as how we should think about asymmetric responses, such as economic sanctions.

Part III turns toward hybrid threats to international navigation, such as irregular maritime migration and shipping in the Black Sea amidst the Ukraine-Russia conflict. Russia's "shadow fleet" has emerged to evade sanctions, circumventing the generally accepted international rules and standards developed by the member States of the International Maritime Organization. Dark shipping may carry as much as 20 percent of the world's oil in ships that traverse the globe, often with their automatic identification system turned off to pass unnoticed. These ships stymie traditional oceans governance and shipping regulations to serve as an economic arm of the Russian war effort and operate outside the legal obligations of flag State duties, coastal State awareness and port State control. Denmark has attempted to get a handle on such vessels transiting through the Danish Straits by focusing on its own asymmetric levers – maritime safety regulations and rules for protection of the marine environment, and associated certificates for insurance. Lacking explicit enforcement measures against foreign-flagged ships in passage through the straits, the Kingdom of Denmark is experimenting with regulatory responses that may at least reduce dark shipping in the service of Russia. To the extent these efforts prove successful, Moscow loses foreign currency from oil buyers in Asia.

This Part also contains an analysis of the distinction between *de jure* and *de facto* blockade in the context of the Black Sea. While all elements of a legal blockade may not be in place, *de facto* blockades can serve the same purpose. Furthermore, even declared exclusion zones and other war zones, as Russia has leverage in the northern Black Sea, can control shipping effectively. This section presages potential Chinese efforts to control the waters surrounding Taiwan in the event of a conflict over the island.

This study explores the relationship between threat formation and normative concepts of threats at sea against considerations of State sovereignty, the security of the European Union, and human rights law. From irregular maritime migration in the Mediterranean Sea, Part III shifts toward protection of international commerce through the Turkish Straits while Ukraine and Russia are at war. The theme of hybrid threats to international shipping implicates not just the belligerents but States relying on grain exports and the rights of neutral shipping. Against this backdrop, Turkey exercises control over the Bosporus and Dardanelles Straits pursuant to the Montreux Convention. The parameters of Turkey's governance of the straits during armed conflict at sea has effects that extend beyond the region.

Like Turkey, Japan also sits astride strategic straits, but these are subject to the conventional regime in the United Nations Convention on the Law of the Sea, limiting Japan's ability to control transit. Five strategic Japanese straits provide access for Russian and Chinese warships and submarines access to the Pacific Ocean. In October 2021, for example, a combined task force of five Chinese warships and five Russian warships sailed through Tsugaru Strait between Hokkaido and Honshu into the mid-Pacific. For decades, Japan has limited its territorial sea claim to only three nautical miles along five "designated areas" including Tsugaru Strait to ensure foreign warships, submarines, and aircraft may not exercise transit passage through the straits, which would apply shoreline-to-shoreline. This modest but effective measure unilaterally limits foreign warships to surface navigation and innocent passage except for a narrow high seas corridor through the center line, allowing Japan to maintain greater domain awareness and security of its littoral zone.

The chapter contributions and parts form a coherent study. The volume reflects a legal realism that integrates the political concept of hybrid war but is crisp and careful in maintaining the linearity and integrity of the legal analysis. In this respect, the study is essential for officials and scholars to understand the application of the law of the sea, the law of naval warfare, and other aspects of international law, such as the law of state responsibility and marine environmental law, to contemporary conflicts. Russia, Iran, and China are especially poised to generate new hybrid challenges to destabilize competitors, namely the NATO and the United States and its treaty allies in East Asia. The concept of hybrid war sits astride the firebreak between peacetime law of the sea and the law of naval warfare that applies declared war or any other armed conflict at sea. Rather than becoming fixated on the boundary between peace and war and becoming paralyzed by the hybrid nature of the attacks, these authors suggest concrete steps that States can take to become comfortable in effectively turning back such threats. The efforts to deescalate tensions and prevent war include ramping up aggressive responses that also lie below the threshold of armed conflict, such as boldly establishing safety zones around critical infrastructure at sea, as Denmark has recently done.

Responding with legal creativity is necessary but insufficient to deter or contain hybrid threats at sea, as normative factors also weigh heavily. States must better prepare the information battlespace while thinking out of the box about new legal tools in national law and international law. Some examples of such responses can be harvested from the past before the era of post-Cold War peace stripped democratic States of their resilience and confidence to develop and employ new legal concepts to advance their security. European States have begun this process, for example, with economic sanctions. The authors offer plenty of other food for thought, including better utilization of safety zones, areas to be avoided, traffic separation schemes and other devices that could be repurposed to get more out of them.

The hybrid nature of the maritime threats and challenges mean that scholars and leaders must become adept at integrating security dimensions into marine spatial planning, from internal waters to the high seas and the deep seabed. This book is an essential resource for thinking about creative development and employment of these methods.

James Kraska
Newport, Rhode Island

Illustrations

Maps

Table

Abbreviations

ADIZ	air defense identification zone
AGI	auxiliary general intelligence
AIS	automatic identification system
AP I	Protocol Additional to the Geneva Conventions of 12 August 1949, and relating to the Protection of Victims of International Armed Conflict
BCE	Before Common Era
BSGI	Black Sea Grain Initiative
CDEM	construction, design, equipment and manning
CJEU	Court of Justice of the European Union
CLC	International Convention on Civil Liability for Oil Pollution Damage
CoE	Centre of Excellence
CoH	conduct of hostilities
DPH	direct participation in hostilities
ECtHR	European Court of Human Rights
ECHR	European Convention on Human Rights
EEZ	exclusive economic zone
EIA	environmental impact assessment
EU	European Union
FUND	International Convention on the Establishment of an International Fund for Compensation for Oil Pollution Damage
GAIRS	Generally Accepted International Rules and Standards
GC II	Geneva Convention II for the Amelioration of the Condition of Wounded, Sick and Shipwrecked Members of Armed Forces at Sea
IAC	international armed conflict
ICJ	International Court of Justice
ICRC	International Committee of the Red Cross
ICTY	International Criminal Tribunal for the former Yugoslavia
IG P&I Clubs	International Group of Protection and Indemnity Clubs
IHL	international humanitarian law
IHRL	international human rights law
ILC	International Law Commission
IMO	International Maritime Organization
IOM	International Organization for Migration
ITLOS	International Tribunal for the Law of the Sea
IUMI	International Union of Marine Insurers
LOAC	law of armed conflict

LONW	law of naval warfare
LOSC	United Nations Convention on the Law of the Sea
LNTS	League of Nations Treaty Series
MARPOL	International Convention for the Prevention of Pollution from Ships
MLE	maritime law enforcement
NAFTA	North American Free Trade Agreement
NATO	North Atlantic Treaty Organization
NAVTEX	Navigational Telex
NIAC	non-international armed conflict
NM	nautical miles
NS	Nord Stream
PPP	policies, plans and programmes
SAR	search and rescue
SEA	strategic environmental assessment
SUA Protocol	Protocol of 2005 to the Convention for the Suppression of Unlawful Acts against the Safety of Maritime Navigation
TFEU	Treaty on the Functioning of the European Union
UN	United Nations
UNGA	United Nations General Assembly
UNSC	United Nations Security Council
UNTS	United Nations Treaty Series
UK	United Kingdom
US	United States of America
USS	United States Ship
USNS	United States Naval Ship
USTS	United States Treaty Series
VCLT	Vienna Convention on the Law of Treaties
WRC	Nairobi International Convention on the Removal of Wrecks
WTO	World Trade Organization
4GW	fourth generation warfare

Notes on Contributors

Dariusz Rafał Bugajski
(Captain, PhD, DSc) is graduate of the Faculty of Navigation & Naval Weapons at Polish Naval Academy as well as the Faculty of Law at the University of Gdańsk. He served as commanding officer of an Anti-submarine Warfare Naval Ship (Fast Attack Craft). Received PhD in 2001 and habilitation in international law at the Faculty of Law at Szczecin University in 2009. Member of the Maritime Law Commission of the Polish Academy of Science, the Shipbuilding Council Society, the International Society for Military Law and the Law of War, national expert of Advisory Board on the Law of the Sea (International Hydrographic Organization) and editor-in-chief of the 'International Humanitarian Law' journal. He currently is a professor of International Law and Law of the Sea at the Polish Naval Academy in Gdynia. His scientific interests include international law and security, law of the sea, international humanitarian law, strategy and history.

Stuart Casey-Maslen
is Extraordinary Professor of International Law at the University of Pretoria in South Africa where he teaches jus ad bellum, human rights law, counterterrorism law, disarmament law, and the law of armed conflict. He has a doctorate in international humanitarian law and master's degrees in international human rights law and forensic ballistics. His book on 'The Right to Life under International Law' was published by Cambridge University Press in September 2021. His books on international counterterrorism law and hybrid warfare under international law will be published in 2024.

Arne Willy Dahl
is Honorary President of the International Society for Military Law and the Law of War where he served as president in 2006–2012. He has authored 'Håndbok i militær folkerett' (handbook of military international law) and several academic articles. He is the co-editor and co-author of the 'Oslo Manual on Select Topics of the Law of Armed Conflict' (2020) and member of the Steering Committee for the revision of the San Remo Manual on International Law Applicable to Armed Conflicts at Sea. Dahl has served in many positions in the Norwegian civil service, including as a Judge Advocate General from 1989 to 2001 and from 2005 to 2014, Head of Legal office at the Chief of Defence headquarters (2001–2002) and public prosecutor at the office of the Director of Public Prosecutions (2003–2005).

Magne Frostad
is Professor of Law at the Faculty of Law, UiT the Arctic University of Norway. He studied in Norway, Sweden, England and Germany (PhD) and focuses on both domestic and international law – constitutional law, human rights, law of the sea, jus in bello, jus ad bellum, legal history and methodology. Among his publications we find a book on piracy, and he currently works on a book on naval graves.

Sofia Galani
(LLB, LLM, PhD, FHEA) is an Assistant Professor at the Panteion University of Athens and a Scientific Advisor to the Hellenic Parliament. Previously, she was a Senior Lecturer at the University of Bristol. Her research interests lie on maritime security, the law of the sea, human rights and terrorism and she has published in these areas. She is the author of 'Hostages and Human Rights: Towards a Victim-Centred Approach?' (Cambridge University Press 2021) and a co-editor (with Professor Sir Malcolm Evans) of 'Maritime Security and the Law of the Sea: Help or Hindrance?' (Edward Elgar 2020). Sofia is one of the principal contributors to the UNODC Maritime Crime: A Manual for Criminal Justice Practitioners. She sits at the Non-Executive Board of Advisors of Human Rights at Sea and is one of the authors of the Geneva Declaration of Human Rights at Sea.

Shin Kawagishi
is Professor of Public International Law at the Faculty of Humanities and Social Sciences in Shizuoka University, Japan. Prior to coming to Shizuoka University, his working experiences include an Assistant Professor of Public International Law at the Graduate School of Law in Kyoto University. He was previously a Visiting Fellow at the Max Planck Institute for Comparative Public Law and International Law in Heidelberg, Germany. He holds Doctor of Laws in 2010 and Master of Laws in 2007 respectively from the Graduate School of Law in Kyoto University. He also holds Bachelor of Laws from the Faculty of Law in Keio University in 2004. He has published on public international law, especially law on the use of force, international humanitarian law and international criminal law, in international and domestic law journals.

Timo Koivurova
is Research Professor and Director of the Arctic Centre at the University of Lapland, Finland. He has a multidisciplinary specialization in Arctic law and governance but has also conducted broader research on global law (including authoring an English-language textbook on international environmental law).

Some of his research areas include: The legal status of the indigenous peoples of the Arctic (e.g. the Sámi), regulations and politics regarding climate change in general and in the Arctic, regulating mining industry practices, the laws and politics surrounding the opening of the Arctic Ocean, the continued development of the Arctic Council as an intergovernmental forum, rapidly-changing geopolitical trends in the Arctic, both from a broader geopolitical perspective and also with a special focus on China's role in the region, and possibilities for an Arctic treaty. He has been involved as an expert in several international processes globally and in the Arctic region and has published on the above-mentioned topics extensively.

Alexander Lott

(PhD) works as a researcher at the Norwegian Centre for the Law of the Sea at UiT – The Arctic University of Norway. Alexander is also a lecturer (0.1) of administrative law at the University of Tartu, Estonia. He is the author of books 'Hybrid Threats and the Law of the Sea' (Brill 2022) and 'The Estonian Straits: Exceptions to the Strait Regime of Innocent or Transit Passage' (Brill 2018). Alexander has published widely on the law of the sea, human rights, international security law, administrative law, and environmental law. This book forms part of the Marie Skłodowska-Curie individual fellowship (2022–2024) that Alexander was awarded with by the European Commission. Prior to joining the academia, he worked as a legal adviser at the constitutional review and administrative law chambers at the Estonian Supreme Court as well as at the Ministry of Justice.

Iva Parlov

is an associate professor at the Department of Law and Governance, at the Norwegian Business School (BI). Her main research interests are within international law of the sea and international maritime law. She holds a PhD in law from the Norwegian Center for the Law of the Sea, Faculty of Law, the Arctic University of Norway. Parlov is the author of the monograph 'Coastal State Jurisdiction over Ships in Need of Assistance, Maritime Casualties and Shipwrecks' (Brill 2022). She has been continuously publishing in international journals and collected works, with a particular focus on the law of the sea and shipping.

Anna Petrig

holds the Chair of International and Public Law at the University of Basel in Switzerland. She has a PhD in the field of the law of the sea and human rights law and an LL.M. from Harvard Law School. Anna is a member of the Bar of the Canton of Berne (Switzerland) and the New York State Bar. Her broad legal experience includes work in private practice, the courts, and the Legal Division of the International Committee of the Red Cross. Anna is the author of various monographs and articles, notably pertaining to the law of the sea, transnational and international criminal law and international humanitarian law. Anna has served as Judge *ad hoc* for Switzerland on the International Tribunal for the Law of the Sea in Cases 27 and 29. She has been a member of the Swiss Delegation and CMI Delegation to the International Maritime Organization.

Henrik Ringbom
is Professor of Maritime Law and the Law of the Sea at the Åbo Akademi University in Finland and Professor II (part-time) at the Scandinavian Institute of Maritime Law at the University of Oslo. His previous work experience includes 11 years as an EU official at the European Commission and the European Maritime Safety Agency (EMSA). Prof. Ringbom has published widely in the field of European and international shipping law and environmental law.

Ulf Sverdrup
is a professor at the Department of Law and Governance, at the Norwegian Business School (BI). He was Director of the Norwegian Institute of International Affairs (NUPI) from 2011 to 2023. He holds a PhD in political science from the University of Oslo. Sverdrup led the Norwegian government-appointed commission that reviewed the implications of geopolitics for the Norwegian Government Pension Fund Global, and he was the Head of the Secretariat for the Official Norwegian Europe Review. Sverdrup has published extensively on various topics in international politics, with a particular emphasis on European affairs and Norwegian foreign policy.

Pierre Thévenin
(PhD) is a post-doctoral research fellow at the University of Tartu. He conducts research on Soviet and Russian approaches to the law of the sea.

Theresa Winkel
is a doctoral researcher at the Faculty of Law, University of Lapland. She conducts research on legal resilience and hybrid threats with a European and Arctic focus.

Table of Cases

Arbitral Tribunal Established under Annex VII of the Law of the Sea Convention

Matter of an Arbitration between Guyana and Suriname, Case 2004-04, Award of 17 September 2007.
Chagos Marine Protected Area Arbitration (Mauritius v. United Kingdom), Case 2011-03, Award of 18 March 2015.
The Arctic Sunrise Arbitration (The Netherlands v. the Russian Federation), Case 2014-02, Award on the Merits of 14 August 2015.
South China Sea Arbitration (the Philippines v. the People's Republic of China), Case No 2013-19, Award of 12 July 2016.
The 'Enrica Lexie' Incident (Italy v. India), Case 2015-28, Award of 21 May 2020.
Dispute Concerning the Detention of Ukrainian Naval Vessels and Servicemen (Ukraine v. the Russian Federation), Case No. 2019-28, Award on Preliminary Objections of 27 June 2022.

Other Arbitral Awards

Air Service Agreement of 27 March 1946 between the United States of America and France, Arbitral Award, 9 December 1978, *Reports of International Arbitral Awards*, Vol. XVIII, 417–93.
Duzgit Integrity Arbitration (Malta v. São Tomé and Príncipe), Arbitral Award, 5 September 2016, Permanent Court of Arbitration.

Committee against Torture

Fatou Sonko v. Spain (CAT/C/47/D/368/2008) of 25 November 2011.
J.H.A. v. Spain (CAT/C/41/D/323/2007) of 21 November 2008.

Court of Justice of the EU

Case C-73/07, Judgment of 16 December 2008 (Grand Chamber), EU:C:2008:727.
Case C72/22 PPU, Judgment of 30 June 2022 (First Chamber), EU:C:2022:505.

Case C348/20 P, Judgment of 12 July 2022 (Grand Chamber), EU:C:2022:548.
Case T526/19, Order of 20 May 2020 (General Court), EU:T:2020:210.
Case T-136/22, *Hamoudi v. Frontex* (pending).

European Court of Human Rights

A. and Others v. the UK (App. no. 3455/05), Judgment of 19 February 2009.
A.A. and Others v. North Macedonia (App. nos. 55798/16 and 4 others), Judgment of 5 April 2022.
Alhowais v. Hungary (App. no. 59435/17), Judgment of 3 February 2023.
Banković and Others v. Belgium and other 16 Contracting Parties (dec.) [GC] (App. no. 52207/99), Judgment of 12 December 2001.
Barseghyan v. Armenia (App. no. 17804/09), Judgment of 21 September 2021.
Denmark, Norway, Sweden and the Netherlands v. Greece, Commission Report, 1969.
Hassan and Others v. France (App. nos. 46695/10 and 54588/10), Judgment of 4 December 2014.
Hirsi Jamaa and Others v. Italy [GC] (App. No. 27765/09), Judgment of 23 February 2012.
Ireland v. the UK (App. no. 5310/71), Judgment of 18 January 1978.
Kavala v. Turkey (App. no. 28749/18), Judgment of 11 May 2020.
Khlaifia and Others v. Italy (App. no. 16483/12), Judgment of 15 December 2016.
Lawless v. Ireland (no.3) (App. no. 332/57), Judgment of 1 July 1961.
Medvedyev and Others v. France (App. no. 3394/03), Judgment of 29 March 2010.
Mehmet Hasan Altan v. Turkey, (App. no. 13237/17), Judgment of 20 March 2018.
N.D. and N.T. v. Spain [GC] (App. nos. 8675/15 and 8697/15), Judgment of 13 February 2020.
Rigopoulos v. Spain (dec.) (App. no. 37388/97), Judgment of 12 January 1999.
Safi and Others v. Greece (App. No. 5418/15), Judgment of 7 July 2022.
Sakik and Others v. Turkey (87/1996/706/898-903), Judgment of 26 November 1997.
Satakunnan Markkinapörssi Oy and Satamedia Oy v. Finland [GC] (App. no. 931/13), Judgment of 27 June 2017.
L'affaire Alkhatib et autres c. Grèce (App. no. 3566/16), Judgment of 16 January 2024.
S.S. and Others v. Italy (App. no. 21660/18) (3 May 2018 – pending).

Human Rights Committee

A.S., D.I., O.I. and G.D. v. Italy (CCPR/C/130/D/3042/2017) of 4 November 2020.

Inter-American Commission on Human Rights

The Haitian Centre for Human Rights et al. v. United States, Case 10.675, Report No. 51/96, Inter-Am.C.H.R.,OEA/Ser.L/V/II.95 Doc. 7 rev. at 550 (1997).

Inter-American Court of Human Rights

Nadege Dorzema et al v. Dominican Republic, Judgment of 24 October 2012, Series C No.251.

International Court of Justice

Corfu Channel Case (United Kingdom v. Albania), Judgment, ICJ Reports 1949, p. 4.

Military and Paramilitary Activities in and against Nicaragua (Nicaragua v. United States of America), Judgment, ICJ Reports 1986, p. 14.

Legality of the Threat or Use of Nuclear Weapons, Advisory Opinion, ICJ Reports 1996, p. 226.

Gabčikovo-Nagymaros Project (Hungary v. Slovakia), Judgment, ICJ Reports 1997, p. 7.

Case Concerning the Land and Maritime Boundary Between Cameroon and Nigeria (Cameroon v. Nigeria, Equatorial Guinea intervening), Judgment, ICJ Reports 2002, p. 303.

Oil Platforms (Islamic Republic of Iran v. United States of America), Judgment, ICJ Reports 2003, p. 161.

Legal Consequences of the Construction of a Wall in the Occupied Palestinian Territory, Advisory Opinion, ICJ Reports 2004, p. 136.

Armed Activities on the Territory of the Congo (Democratic Republic of the Congo v. Uganda), Judgment, ICJ Reports 2005, p. 168.

Application of the Convention on the Prevention and Punishment of the Crime of Genocide (Bosnia and Herzegovina v. Serbia and Montenegro), Judgment, ICJ Reports 2007, p. 43.

Case concerning Maritime Delimitation in the Black Sea (Romania v. Ukraine), Judgment, ICJ Reports 2009, p. 61.

International Criminal Tribunal for the Former Yugoslavia

Prosecutor v. Tadić (Decision) ICTY-94-1 (2 October 1995).
Prosecutor v. Kunarac, Kovac and Vukovic (Judgment) ICTY-96-23 & 23/1-A (12 June 2002).
Prosecutor v. Pavle Strugar (Judgement) IT-01-42-T (31 January 2005).

International Tribunal for the Law of the Sea

M/V 'Saiga' (No. 2) (Saint Vincent and the Grenadines v. Guinea), Judgment, ITLOS Reports 1999, p. 10.
'ARA Libertad' (Argentina v. Ghana), Provisional Measures, Order of 15 December 2012, ITLOS Reports 2012, p. 332.
M/V 'Virginia G' (Panama v. Guinea-Bissau), Judgment, ITLOS Reports 2014, p. 4.
M/V 'Norstar' (Panama v. Italy), Judgment, ITLOS Reports 2018–2019, p. 10.
Dispute Concerning the Detention of Three Ukrainian Naval Vessels (Ukraine v. Russian Federation), Provisional Measures, Order 25 May 2019, ITLOS Reports 2019, p. 283.

National Courts

US Court of Appeals for the District of Columbia, *South African Airways* v. *Elizabeth H. Dole, Secretary, U.S. Department of Transportation*, 817 F.2d 119, Judgment (24 April 1987).
Schleswig-Holsteinisches LVerfG, Urteil vom 14.09.2020 - LVerfG 3/19.
OLG Düsseldorf (25 August 2021) VI-3 Kart 211/20 (V) [2021].

Table of Treaties

(listed in a chronological order)

Treaty of Peace (Küçük Kaynarca) between the Russian Empire and the Ottoman Empire (adopted 21 July 1774), in J C Hurewitz, *Diplomacy in the Near and Middle East. A Documentary Record, 1535–1914*, Vol. I (D van Nostrand Company 1956) 54–61.

Convention Regarding the Straits: Austria, France, Great Britian, Prussia, and The Ottoman Empire, 13 July 1841, in J C Hurewitz, *Diplomacy in the Near and Middle East. A Documentary Record, 1535–1914*, Vol. I (D van Nostrand Company 1956) 123.

Declaration Respecting Maritime Law (opened for signature and entered into force on 16 April 1856) British State Papers 1856, Vol. LXI, 155–158.

Treaty between Great Britain, Austria, Belgium, France, Hanover, Mecklenburg-Schwerin, Oldenburg, Netherlands, Prussia, Russia, Sweden and Norway, and the Hanse Towns, on the one part, and Denmark, on the other part, for the Redemption of the Sound Dues (adopted 14 March 1857, entered into force 31 March 1857).

Convention for the Protection of Submarine Telegraph Cables (adopted 14 March 1884, entered into force 1 May 1888) 1901 Australian Treaty Series 1.

Hague Convention (III) relative to the Opening of Hostilities (adopted 18 October 1907, entered into force 26 January 1910) USTS 263.

Hague Convention (IV) respecting the Laws and Customs of War on Land and its annex: Regulations concerning the Laws and Customs of War on Land (opened for signature 18 October 1907, entered into force 26 January 1910) USTS 539.

Convention (V) Respecting the Rights and Duties of Neutral Powers and Persons in Case of War on Land (adopted 18 October 1907, entered into force 26 January 1910). International Peace Conference, The Hague, Official Record.

Convention (VIII) relative to the Laying of Automatic Submarine Contact Mines (opened for signature on 18 October 1907, entered into force 26 January 1910). International Peace Conference, The Hague, Official Record.

Convention (XIII) concerning the Rights and Duties of Neutral Powers in Naval War (opened for signature on 18 October 1907, entered into force 26 January 1910). International Peace Conference, The Hague, Official Record.

The Covenant of the League of Nations (adopted 28 June 1919, entered into force 10 January 1920) League of Nations – Official Journal, February 1920, pp. 3–12.

Treaty of Peace and Exchange of War Prisoners with Turkey (adopted 24 July 1923, entered into force 6 August 1924), XXVIII LNTS 12–113 (No. 701).

Convention relating to the Regime of the Straits Concluded between the British Empire, France, Italy, Bulgaria, Greece, Rumania, Soviet Russia, Yugoslavia and Turkey (adopted 24 July 1923, entered into force 6 August 1924) XXVIII LNTS 115–137 (No. 702).

Treaty for the Limitation of Naval Armament (adopted 25 March 1936, entered into force 31 December 1942) USTS No. 919.

Great Britain and Northern Ireland, Australia, Bulgaria, France, Greece, Japan, Roumania, Turkey, Union of Soviet Socialist Republics, Yugoslavia, Convention regarding the Régime of the Straits, with Annexes and Protocol (adopted 20 July 1936, entered into force 9 November 1936) 173 LNTS 213 (No. 4015).

Convention on International Civil Aviation (signed 7 December 1944, entered into force 4 April 1947) 15 UNTS 295.

Charter of the United Nations (opened for signature 26 June 1945, entered into force 24 October 1945) 1 UNTS XVI.

The Convention Regarding the Regime of Navigation on the Danube (opened for signature on 18 August 1948, entered into force 11 May 1949) 33 UNTS 181.

The North Atlantic Treaty (opened for signature 4 April 1949, entered into force 24 August 1949) 34 UNTS 243.

Convention (II) for the Amelioration of the Condition of Wounded, Sick and Shipwrecked Members of Armed Forces at Sea (adopted 12 August 1949, entered into force 21 October 1950) 75 UNTS 85.

Convention (IV) relative to the Protection of Civilian Persons in Time of War (adopted 12 August 1949, entered into force 21 October 1950) 75 UNTS 973.

European Convention for the Protection of Human Rights and Fundamental Freedoms, as amended by Protocols Nos. 11 and 14 (adopted 4 November 1950, entered into force 3 September 1953) ETS 5.

International Convention Relating to the Arrest of Seagoing Ships (adopted 10 May 1952, entered into force 24 February 1956) 439 UNTS 193.

Convention on the Territorial Sea and the Contiguous Zone (opened for signature on 29 April 1958, entered into force 10 September 1964) 516 UNTS 205.

Convention on the High Seas (opened for signature on 29 April 1958, entered into force 3 January 1963) 450 UNTS 11.

Convention on Fishing and Conservation of the Living Resources of the High Sea (opened for signature on 29 April 1958, entered into force 22 March 1966) 559 UNTS 285.

Convention on the Continental Shelf (opened for signature on 29 April 1958, entered into force 10 June 1964) 499 UNTS 311.

The Antarctic Treaty (opened for signature on 1 December 1959, entered into force 23 June 1961) 402 UNTS 71.

International Covenant on Civil and Political Rights (adopted 16 December 1966, entered into force 23 March 1976) 999 UNTS 171.

Vienna Convention on the Law of Treaties (adopted 23 May 1969, entered into force 27 January 1980) 1155 UNTS 331.

American Convention on Human Rights, 'Pact of San José' (signed 22 November 1969, entered into force 18 July 1978) 1144 UNTS 123.

International Convention Relating to Intervention on the High Seas in Cases of Oil Pollution Casualties (adopted 29 November 1969, entered into force 6 May 1975) 970 UNTS 211.

Treaty on the Prohibition of the Emplacement of Nuclear Weapons and Other Weapons of Mass Destruction on the Sea-Bed and the Ocean Floor and in the Subsoil Thereof (adopted 11 February 1971, entered into force 18 May 1972) 955 UNTS 115.

International Convention for the Prevention of Pollution from Ships (adopted 1973 (Convention), 1978 (1978 Protocol), 1997 (Protocol–Annex VI), entered into force 2 October 1983) 1340 UNTS 61, as amended.

Athens Convention relating to the Carriage of Passengers and their Luggage by Sea (adopted 13 December 1974, entered into force 28 April 1987), amended by the 2002 Protocol (adopted 1 November 2002, entered into force 23 April 2014).

International Convention for the Safety of Life At Sea (adopted 1 November 1974, entered into force 25 May 1980) 1184 UNTS 3.

Convention on the Protection of the Marine Environment of the Baltic Sea Area (opened for signature in 1974, revised in 1992, entered into force 17 January 2000) 2099 UNTS 197, 13 ILM 546 (1974).

International Convention for the Limitation of Maritime Claims (adopted 19 November 1976, entered into force 1 December 1986) 1456 UNTS 261.

Protocol Additional to the Geneva Conventions of 12 August 1949, and relating to the Protection of Victims of International Armed Conflicts (Protocol I) (adopted 8 June 1977, entered into force 7 December 1978) 1125 UNTS 3.

International Convention on Maritime Search and Rescue (adopted 27 April 1979, entered into force 22 June 1985) 1403 UNTS.

United Nations Convention on the Law of the Sea (opened for signature 10 December 1982, entered into force 16 November 1994) 1833 UNTS 3.

International Convention on Salvage (adopted 28 April 1989, entered into force 14 July 1996) 1953 UNTS 165.

Convention on Environmental Impact Assessment in a Transboundary Context (opened for signature 25 February 1991, entered into force 10 September 1997) 1989 UNTS 309.

Protocol to amend the International Convention on Civil Liability for Oil Pollution Damage (adopted 27 November 1992, entered into force 30 May 1996) 1956 UNTS 255.

Agreement on Illicit Traffic by Sea (opened for signature 31 January 1995, entered into force 1 May 2000) CETS No. 156.

Agreement for the Implementation of the Provisions of the United Nations Convention on the Law of the Sea of 10 December 1982 relating to the Conservation and Management of Straddling Fish Stocks and Highly Migratory Fish Stocks (adopted 4 August 1995, entered into force 11 December 2001) 2167 UNTS 3.

Agreement between the Republic of Finland and the Republic of Estonia on the Boundary of the Maritime Zones in the Gulf of Finland and the Northern Baltic Sea (adopted 18 October 1996, entered into force 7 January 1997) 1964 UNTS.

International Convention on Liability and Compensation for Damage in Connection with the Carriage of Hazardous and Noxious Substances by Sea (adopted 3 May 1996, not yet in force) 35 ILM 1406, as amended by the Protocol of 2010 (adopted 30 April 2010, not yet in force).

International Convention on Arrest of Ships (adopted 12 March 1999, entered into force 14 September 2011) 2797 UNTS 3.

International Convention for the Suppression of the Financing of Terrorism (adopted 9 December 1999, entered into force 10 April 2002) 2178 UNTS 197.

International Convention on Civil Liability for Bunker Oil Pollution Damage (adopted 23 March 2001, entered into force 21 November 2008) 973 UNTS 3.

Nairobi International Convention on the Removal of Wrecks (adopted 18 May 2007, entered into force 14 April 2015) 3283 UNTS, IMO doc, LEG/CONF.16/19 of 23 May 2007.

Charter of Fundamental Rights of the European Union (proclaimed 18 December 2000, entered into force 1 December 2009).

Protocol of 2005 to the Convention for the Suppression of Unlawful Acts against the Safety of Maritime Navigation (adopted 14 October 2005, entered into force 28 July 2010) IMO Doc. LEG/CONF.15/21.

Consolidated version of the Treaty on the Functioning of the European Union, OJ C 326, 26 October 2012, 47–390.

EU Council Regulation No 833/2014 of 31 July 2014 concerning restrictive measures in view of Russia's actions destabilizing the situation in Ukraine (OJ L 229 of 31 July 2014), as amended.

Initiative on the Safe Transportation of Grain and Foodstuffs from Ukrainian Ports between Ukraine, Russia, Turkey, and the United Nations (adopted 22 July 2022, entered into force 22 July 2022).

Agreement under the United Nations Convention on the Law of the Sea on the conservation and sustainable use of marine biological diversity beyond national jurisdiction (adopted 19 June 2023, not yet in force) UN Doc A/CONF.232/2023/4 of 19 June 2023.

Introduction

Alexander Lott

This book looks for answers to some of the most pressing challenges that maritime security law faces in the context of hybrid warfare. It brings together authors from various fields of international law to explore the legal intersection between naval war, military activities at sea, maritime law enforcement, and hybrid warfare. Our objective is to define the concept of hybrid warfare and establish whether it is useful for assessing the legality of a State's actions in the maritime domain.

This book provides a detailed account of some of the current challenges to maritime security law and the law of naval warfare. In my view, piracy and the so-called war on terror have now remained rather distant problems as compared to the situation that formed in the past couple of decades. These challenges shaped maritime security law throughout the past 30-or-so years when there was little great power competition at sea. As a testament to the shift in *zeitgeist*, this book makes scarce reference to terrorism, whereas the phenomenon of sabotage between States serves as one of the building blocks of this book.

Recent developments have shifted the focus of maritime security law back to challenges emanating from States, including naval warfare, military activities, the use of force at sea, and sabotage. Such developments include the Russian invasion of Ukraine (2014 and 2022) as well as the prolonged Taiwan crisis. To this may be added the armed conflict in Palestine (2023) in the context of which the Iran-backed Houthi militia has allegedly targeted mostly Israeli-linked ships on the Red Sea for pressuring Israel to a ceasefire in Gaza.[1] This armed conflict in Gaza erupted because of Hamas' mass atrocities against civilians. Months later, it escalated and triggered numerous attacks against international navigation in the Red Sea and the Bab el-Mandeb Strait. Such attacks from non-State actors that exercise control over a significant part of Palestinian and Yemeni territory are a reminder that threats of piracy and terrorism to maritime security and the applicable law are still relevant today. However, piracy and terrorism arguably no longer serve as the main determinative drivers of the development of maritime security law.

1 Patrick Wintour, 'Houthi attacks continue as US cargo ship hit in defiance of strikes on Yemen' The Guardian (15 January 2024), available at <https://www.theguardian.com/world/2024/jan/15/cargo-ship-near-yemen-reportedly-hit-by-missile-as-fears-grow-conflict-could-spread> accessed 15 January 2024.

 | DOI:10.1163/9789004707993_002

The recrudescence of great power competition at sea has raised several legal problems. Most of all, there is a need to critically assess how well is the law adapted to dealing with so-called special military operations in the course of which aggressor States manipulate the indeterminacy of the law itself to shape ambiguous norms in such a way that it helps them reach their goals. Hence the importance of clarifying norms of international law, as this anthology attempts to do. In this context, this book puts special attention to the protection of offshore critical infrastructure against acts of sabotage, the laws of blockade, and passage rights through the Danish, Japanese, and Turkish Straits.

This book comprises three parts, each of which addresses a specific research question. To ensure internal coherence in the structure of the book, the individual chapters are grouped based on the following three research questions:

1. How is hybrid naval warfare – if at all – different from naval war, military activities or law enforcement at sea and what is the threshold for the applicability of the law of naval warfare in situations that can be characterized as hybrid warfare?
2. How hybrid naval warfare impacts on the safety of objects of critical offshore infrastructure and how to increase their legal resilience?
3. How can the law of the sea and maritime security law contribute to ensuring stability in major shipping routes in hybrid warfare?

In political-military affairs, the use of the concept of hybrid warfare is well-justified. But, legally speaking, this book tests the hypothesis that States should still principally be able to classify any incidents of hybrid warfare under either the ramifications of armed conflict, or peacetime military activities or law enforcement operations at sea. Thus, in Part 1 of this book, the authors determine how hybrid naval warfare relates to the legal concepts of military activities, criminal acts, the law of the use of force, self-defence and countermeasures, as well as to armed conflict.

The work is underway both at the international and domestic levels to make the international law of the sea and its domestic implementation more resilient to hybrid warfare. As Part 2 of this anthology demonstrates, it is important to clarify some existing rules of the law of the sea relating to, for example, the protection of critical offshore infrastructure and foreign activities in the coastal State's exclusive economic zone (hereinafter EEZ). Sabotage against submarine cables and pipelines is one of the main sources of grey zone conflicts. Numerous maritime incidents in the past couple of years have raised questions about the legal resilience of critical energy or telecommunications infrastructure in the context of hybrid warfare. These problems are best exemplified by the Nord Stream explosions of September 2022 and the damaging of the submarine gas pipeline and cable of the North Atlantic Treaty Organization (hereinafter NATO) Member States Estonia and Finland in 2023. Following these incidents, the European Commission recognized that:

> In the current context of heightened risk and antagonistic man-made security threats, given the interconnected and transnational nature of these infrastructures, governments in all world regions are paying particular attention to their potential reliance on critical cables, as systemic and widespread disruptions of submarine cable communications could lead to particularly serious consequences, in case of coordinated attacks. /…/ The EU should endeavour to deepen cooperation further with NATO on resilience, including critical submarine cable infrastructures /…/.[2]

In this context, one of the topics addressed in Part 2 is the interdiction of ships suspected of being involved in sabotage against critical offshore infrastructure outside the limits of the territorial sea. This topic has implications also to Part 3 of this book which explores the implications of hybrid threats to international navigation.

In the context of international navigation, some of the most pressing challenges to maritime security law include law enforcement against non-innocent passage, discriminatory navigational restrictions, the use of force against ships and aircraft, and the legal regime of straits. Part 3 focuses on case studies that address hybrid threats in the Japanese Straits, the passage regime in the Turkish Straits in the context of the ongoing armed conflict between Russia and Ukraine, the naval blockade of Ukraine's Black Sea ports, problems related to Russia's shadow fleet (with a focus on the Danish Straits), and the instrumentalization of migration as a hybrid threat against the European Union (hereinafter EU).

This book addresses the research problem chiefly from the legal perspective, as opposed to studies in this field that have so far mostly focused on international relations and military studies. The research crosses boundaries between the various disciplines of international law, including the law of the sea, human rights law, environmental law, the law of armed conflict, and international security law. The anthology uses case studies to assess the relevant State practice and determine the interaction between, on the one hand, regional trends (incl. the Baltic Sea, the Black Sea, the Sea of Japan, the Mediterranean Sea) on maritime security and, on the other hand, the global trends in the universal application of the law of the sea.

---

2 European Commission, Commission Recommendation of 21 February 2024 on Secure and Resilient Submarine Cable Infrastructures 1, 8, available at <https://digital-strategy.ec.europa.eu/en/library/recommendation-security-and-resilience-submarine-cable-infrastructures> accessed 26 February 2024.

Hopefully, this book serves as an important source of information not only for scholars, but also for authorities and practitioners of the regions affected the most by hybrid naval warfare, such as in the South China Sea, the Persian Gulf, the Black Sea, and the Baltic Sea. It can be equally useful for other key actors in the field, including the United States, the EU, and the NATO. In addition, the pending arbitration between Ukraine and Russia in the Annex VII Arbitral Tribunal in the Dispute Concerning Coastal State Rights in the Black Sea, Sea of Azov, and Kerch Strait as well as in the Dispute Concerning the Detention of Ukrainian Naval Vessels and Servicemen highlights the relevance of this scholarly work for international courts and tribunals.

This anthology is based on selected papers presented at two scientific meetings organized by the Norwegian Centre for the Law of the Sea (hereinafter NCLOS). The workshop 'Hybrid Threats and the Law of the Sea: Interdisciplinary and Regional Perspectives' took place in Tromsø, the Arctic capital of Norway on 6 December 2022. It focused on inter-disciplinary and regional perspectives to maritime hybrid threats and was structured on case studies of the Black Sea, Japanese Straits, and the Northern Sea Route. Another theme of that workshop was the naval warfare between Russia and Ukraine and Russia's approach to the law of the sea. The inter-disciplinary workshop was followed by a conference 'Hybrid Naval Warfare through the Lens of Maritime Security Law' in Tallinn, Estonia on 11–12 May 2023.[3] The conference adopted a doctrinal approach for discussing the challenges of hybrid warfare to the law of the sea and maritime security law.

This manuscript comprises the authors' original and previously unpublished analysis. The only two exceptions are the co-authored chapter written by Timo Koivurova and Theresa Winkel as well as the one authored by Alexander Lott. The two chapters are extended versions of the authors' earlier blog posts that appeared in the NCLOS Blog and EJIL: Talk![4]

3 The full program of the Tallinn Conference on the Law of the Sea and Hybrid Warfare (LOSFARE) is available at <https://uit.no/tavla/artikkel/sub?p_document_id=799682&sub_id=799684> accessed 11 August 2023.

4 Timo Koivurova, Theresa Winkel, 'The Nord Stream Pipelines through the Lens of Law and Geopolitics' (23 June 2023) NCLOS Blog, available at <https://site.uit.no/nclos/2023/06/23/the-nord-stream-pipelines-through-the-lens-of-law-and-geopolitics/> accessed 11 August 2023. Alexander Lott, 'Attacks against Europe's Offshore Infrastructure within and beyond the Territorial Sea under Jus ad Bellum' (20 October 2023) EJIL: Talk!, available at <https://www.ejiltalk.org/attacks-against-europes-offshore-infrastructure-within-and-beyond-the-territorial-sea-under-jus-ad-bellum/> accessed 21 October 2023. Alexander Lott, 'Did an Alleged Ukrainian Attack against the Nord Stream Pipelines Violate the Law of Armed Conflict?' (21 November 2023) The NCLOS Blog, available at <https://site.uit.no/nclos/2023/11/21/did-an-alleged-ukrainian-attack-against-the-nord-stream-pipelines-violate-the-law-of-armed-conflict> accessed 28 November 2023.

PART 1

Hybrid Warfare through the Lens of Maritime Security Law

CHAPTER 1

Towards a Definition of Hybrid Warfare

Stuart Casey-Maslen, Arne Willy Dahl, Sofia Galani and Alexander Lott

Introduction

Warfare is traditionally perceived as a contest of physical resources: soldiers, weapons, etc., combined with the military skills of generals and field commanders. It was, however, pointed out already by the Prussian general Carl von Clausewitz that it is also a contest of wills – or 'moral forces'.[1]

In the field, a general may decide to retreat – or surrender – long before his military resources have been spent or destroyed, when he has lost faith in the possibility of victory in battle. This may be due to a correct assessment of the situation or be influenced by false information that has been fed to him. In a modern war, the president and/or prime minister with their cabinet may make similar decisions based on a broader range of factors, such as lack of support from friendly nations, public opinion at home, and other issues of a non-military nature. Thus, a war can be won if the perceptions of decision-makers can be influenced in a favorable direction – directly or indirectly. Enemies can even get what they want without resorting to use of armed force, in particular by employing a range of ways of manipulating minds. This is one of the key characteristics of hybrid warfare.

Grasping the contours of hybrid warfare is not an easy task and thus this chapter will seek to explore its core meaning and elements. It will first sketch the history of hybrid warfare as a concept before identifying its key features, comparing and contrasting the concept with alternative terminology that describes similar phenomena. The aim of this chapter is to provide a guide to the patchy terminology used when referring to *hybrid warfare* that will enable the reader to keep pace with the use of the various terms in this volume.

1 Carl von Clausewitz, *On war* (Wordsworth Editions Ltd 1997) 209.

 | DOI:10.1163/9789004707993_003

1 The Nature and Origin of the Concept of Hybrid Warfare

There is no internationally agreed definition of the term *hybrid warfare* in contemporary legal and military discourse.[2] Some commentators doubt if a definition of hybrid warfare would be 'adequate to multiple contexts that differ in time, space, and logic' due to the 'uniqueness of each context in which 'hybrid' manifests itself.'[3] That said, the contours of the concept and the relevance of hybrid warfare to military action in past, present, and future find significant consonance among States and commentators alike, as the contributions to this book illustrate. Moreover, the term has become 'not only a staple of national security discussions but also a household phrase in State capitals and general political discourse.'[4] As identified by Frank Hoffman, in the political discourse and strategic planning, the concept of hybrid warfare mostly serves three purposes by

- describing the dynamic nature of modern conflict,
- challenging 'conventional thinking and binary intellectual bins that have dominated the literature',
- awareness-raising in relation to risks of warfare trends.[5]

McCulloh credits the United States (hereinafter US) 2006 Quadrennial Defense Review for representing the 'watershed moment' in the shift to formally embracing the existence of the concept of hybrid threats.[6] On the other hand, that review did not explicitly refer to 'hybrid', but instead used the terminology of 'asymmetric' (threats, challenges, tactics, etc.).[7] Hence, McCulloh's

---

2 'Hybrid warfare remains a contested concept and there is no universally agreed definition of it.' Arsalan Bilal, 'Hybrid Warfare – New Threats, Complexity, and 'Trust' as the Antidote' (30 November 2021) NATO Review, available at <https://bit.ly/3bTcV5M> accessed 1 May 2023. Surprisingly, the United States Department of Defense Dictionary of Military and Associated Terms does not even contain an entry for hybrid warfare.

3 Timothy B McCulloh, 'The Inadequacy of Definition and the Utility of a Theory of Hybrid Conflict: Is the 'Hybrid Threat' New?', in Douglas C Lovelace, Jr. (ed.), *Terrorism: Commentary on Security Documents*, vol. 141: *Hybrid Warfare and the Gray Zone Threat* (Oxford University Press 2016) 59.

4 Brin Najžer, *The Hybrid Age: International Security in the Era of Hybrid Warfare* (IB Tauris 2022) 1.

5 Francis G Hoffman, 'The Hybrid Character of Modern Conflict', in Paul Brister, William H Natter, III, and Robert R Tomes (eds.), *Hybrid Warfare and Transnational Threats: Perspectives for an Era of Persistent Conflict* (Council for Emerging National Security Affairs 2011) 36–37.

6 McCulloh (n 3) 61.

7 See Quadrennial Defense Review Report (United States Department of Defense 2006) 1–113, available at <https://history.defense.gov/Portals/70/Documents/quadrennial/QDR2006.pdf?ver=2014-06-25-111017-150> accessed 16 November 2023.

reference to the 2007 maritime strategy of the US has more authority as a testament to the emergence of 'hybrid warfare' as a military term.[8]

Frank Hoffman popularized the term 'hybrid warfare' in a widely cited article for the US Potomac Institute for Policy Studies in 2007.[9] Hoffman himself credited Robert G. Walker, a lieutenant in the US Navy, with its employment a decade earlier in a thesis on the US Marine Corps as a 'hybrid force, capable of conducting operations within both the conventional and unconventional realms of warfare'.[10] Hoffman, however, coined the term *hybrid warfare* with a broader purview than Walker did, employing it to denote situations where a mix of military forces–irregular as well as regular–combine operationally with a range of non-forcible as well as forcible actions in order to achieve 'synergistic effects in the physical *and* psychological dimensions of conflict'.[11] Hybrid warfare can be employed by State and non-State actors alike[12] and it is exercised at all levels: from the tactical to the operational and the strategic.[13] Thus, consonant with the ordinary meaning of the word 'hybrid', inherent in hybrid warfare is the notion of a combination of different warriors, means and methods of warfare with a view to attaining an overall political objective.[14]

---

8 James T Conway, Gary Roughead, and Thad W Allen, 'A Cooperative Strategy for 21st Century Seapower' (2008) 61(1) Naval War College Review 1, 3. McCulloh (n 3) 64.

9 Francis G Hoffman, 'Conflict in the 21st Century: The Rise of Hybrid Wars' (Potomac Institute for Policy Studies 2007) 8, available at <https://bit.ly/3RoPnuK> accessed 1 August 2023. He had already referred to the phenomena as 'complex irregular warfare' in an article a year earlier that did not attract the same level of attention. Francis G Hoffman, 'Complex Irregular Warfare: The Next Revolution in Military Affairs' (2006) 50(3) Orbis 395–411.

10 Walker's 1998 master's thesis sought to 'assess Marine Corps hybrid operations in specific historical cases in order to rate the Marine Corps' historical performance in such roles'. See the Abstract of Robert G Walker, 'The United States Marine Corps and Special Operations', Master thesis, Naval Postgraduate School, Monterey CA 1998, available at <https://bit.ly/3sccRpN> accessed 16 November 2023. Hoffman also cites Alan Dupont's 2002 paper for the Australian National University's Strategic and Defence Studies Centre, 'Transformation Or Stagnation?: Rethinking Australia's Defence' as reflecting new thinking on hybrid warfare. Hoffman (n 9), 'Conflict in the 21st Century: The Rise of Hybrid Wars', 11. Furthermore, he credits Lt. Col William J Nemeth, USMC for his 2002 paper 'Future War and Chechnya: A Case for Hybrid Warfare', see Hoffman 2011 (n 5) 40.

11 Francis G Hoffman, 'Hybrid Warfare and Challenges' (2009) 52 Joint Force Quarterly 34–48, 36 [original emphasis].

12 Hoffman (n 9) 'Conflict in the 21st Century: The Rise of Hybrid Wars', 14.

13 Peter R Mansoor, 'Introduction', in Williamson Murray and Peter R Mansoor (eds.), *Hybrid Warfare. Fighting Complex Opponents from the Ancient World to the Present* (Cambridge University Press 2012) 3.

14 Najžer (n 4) 22.

Although the moniker – disparaged as a 'bandwagon term' by two commentators[15] – is relatively recent, most agree[16] that the 'hybrid' nature of warfare potentially dates back many centuries, if not more.[17] Mansoor, for instance, dates its 'historical pedigree' back to at least as far as the Peloponnesian War in the fifth century BCE when Athens stirred up a Helot uprising, causing its enemy, Sparta, to sue for terms fearful of a threat in its own backdoor.[18]

In a similar vein, the North Atlantic Treaty Organization (hereinafter NATO) has acknowledged that propaganda, deception, sabotage, and other non-military tactics have long been used to destabilize adversaries. Espionage, for example, has similarities with certain forms of hybrid warfare in that it seeks to be covert – to achieve its aims without revealing what is happening and who stands behind. According to the Hague Regulation IV, '[a] person can only be considered a spy when, acting clandestinely or on false pretenses, he obtains or endeavors to obtain information in the zone of operations of a belligerent, with the intention of communicating it to the hostile party.'[19] However, espionage is not aimed at influencing events directly but rather to prepare for potential future action – military or non-military.

Terrorism also seeks to influence attitudes and events and terrorist groups typically have a political agenda – in a broad sense. For example, the working definition of terrorism of the United Nations (hereinafter UN) Security Council implicitly defines terrorism, among others, as:

> Criminal acts, including against civilians, committed with the intent to cause death or serious bodily injury, or taking of hostages, *with the purpose to provoke a state of terror in the general public or in a group of*

---

15 John GLJ Jacobs and Martijn WM Kitzen, 'Hybrid Warfare', Oxford Bibliographies (Last modified 22 September 2021), available at <https://bit.ly/3ViBn2O> accessed 1 August 2023. The two authors, who nonetheless use the term as the title for their entry, cite earlier work by Thomas Mockaitis as 'an important piece of literature for understanding the history of hybrid warfare'. See Thomas R Mockaitis, 'A Hybrid War: The Indonesian Confrontation' in Thomas R Mockaitis (ed.), *British Counterinsurgency in the Post-imperial Era* (Manchester University Press 1995) 14–44.

16 Brin Najžer is thus an outlier among commentators when he asserts that hybrid warfare is a relatively new phenomenon. Najžer (n 4) IX.

17 See, e.g., the range of chapters in Murray and Mansoor (n 13). See also McCulloh (n 3) 58–59.

18 Mansoor (n 13) 3–4.

19 Art. 29 of the Convention (IV) respecting the Laws and Customs of War on Land and its annex: Regulations concerning the Laws and Customs of War on Land (opened for signature 18 October 1907, entered into force 26 January 1910) USTS 539; See also Art. 46 of the Protocol Additional to the Geneva Conventions of 12 August 1949, and relating to the Protection of Victims of International Armed Conflicts (Protocol I) (adopted 8 June 1977, entered into force 7 December 1978) 1125 UNTS 17512.

> *persons or particular persons, intimidate a population or compel a government or an international organization to do or to abstain from doing any act*, which constitute offences within the scope of and as defined in the international conventions and protocols relating to terrorism /…/.[20]

Hoffman includes terrorism in his conception of hybrid warfare,[21] but we may be more interested in hybrid warfare which is not visible – in particular, when it seeks to influence perceptions in a covert way. In contrast, terrorism seeks to achieve its aims by attracting attention through the perpetration of 'dramatic' acts.

Arguably, hybrid warfare shares more similarities with sabotage than it does with terrorism and espionage. Sabotage is also an undefined legal term,[22] but it may be understood as 'a mission (conducted via individual act or as part of a campaign) to secretly disarm, obstruct, or destroy enemy war materiel or infrastructure for military advantage.'[23] Distinct from hybrid warfare, sabotage is oriented towards a specific (para-)military mission and target (e.g. against objects of infrastructure, ships, aircraft) and as such can form part of a hybrid warfare campaign. Hybrid warfare encapsulates the essence of the broader set of methods employed by one State in its campaign against another State. Thus, hybrid warfare may manifest itself in the means of, for example, sabotage, cyberattacks, gunboat diplomacy, terrorism, propaganda, and espionage. The term *hybrid warfare* is understood here to imply a combination of regular and irregular military operations, with the addition of non-military means, aiming at influencing – sabotaging – the adversary's mind.

2 The Key Features of Hybrid Warfare

What is new about hybrid warfare in recent years, the NATO avers, is its speed, scale, and intensity. Increasing reliance on hybrid warfare has been facilitated

20 UN Resolution 1566 (2004), adopted by the Security Council at its 5053rd meeting, on 8 October 2004, S/RES/1566 (2004), para 3 [emphasis added by the authors].

21 Hoffman (n 11) 37.

22 John Tramazzo, 'Sabotage in Law: Meaning and Misunderstandings' (23 June 2023) Articles of War, available at <https://lieber.westpoint.edu/sabotage-law-meaning-misunderstandings> accessed 29 November 2023.

23 Alexander Powell, Elizabeth Yang, Annaleah Westerhaug, and Kaia Haney, 'Maritime Sabotage: Lessons Learned and Implications for Strategic Competition', Center for Naval Analyses Research Memorandum, 2021, 5, available at <https://www.cna.org/archive/CNA_Files/pdf/maritime-sabotage-lessons-learned-and-implications-for-strategic-competition.pdf> accessed 29 November 2023.

by rapid technological change and global interconnectivity.[24] Indeed, if one wonders why we are discussing hybrid warfare today, and not e.g. twenty years ago, it is reasonable to assume that the underlying cause is the growth of the Internet and our increased dependence on electronic communications which has opened opportunities for computer network attacks in a broad sense, including also anonymous influence operations via the net. Accordingly, cyber operations, especially attacks in or through cyberspace, play an important role in hybrid warfare as the concept is generally understood.

Besides the cyberspace, hybrid warfare takes place in multiple domains, such as on land, at sea, in the air, and even potentially in outer space.[25] The key feature of hybrid warfare is the planned convergence across these domains of a range of actors, their means and methods of warfare, and their performance of non-military acts. McCulloh summarizes the essence of hybrid warfare as 'a form of warfare in which one of the combatants bases its optimized force structure on the combination of all available resources – both conventional and unconventional – in a unique cultural context to produce specific, synergistic effects against a conventionally-based opponent.'[26]

Key features of hybrid warfare are usefully delineated in the International Institute for Strategic Studies' definition of the term in 2015, which reads as follows:

> The use of military and non-military tools in an integrated campaign designed to achieve surprise, seize the initiative and gain psychological as well as physical advantages utilising diplomatic means; sophisticated and rapid information, electronic and cyber operations; covert and occasionally overt military and intelligence action; and economic pressure.[27]

---

24 NATO, 'NATO's response to hybrid threats' (last updated 6 July 2023), available at <http://bit.ly/3KlVNnV> accessed 1 August 2023.

25 Hoffman (n 11) 34–35. See also Martin Murphy and Gary Schaub Jr., "Sea of Peace' or Sea of War – Russian Maritime Hybrid Warfare in the Baltic Sea' (2018) 71 Naval War College Review 123–147; Alexander Lott, *Hybrid Threats and the Law of the Sea – Use of Force and Discriminatory Navigational Restrictions in Straits* (Brill 2022); Marko Höyhtyä and Sari Uusipaavalniemi, 'The Space Domain and the Russo-Ukrainian War: Actors, Tools, and Impact' Hybrid CoE Working Paper 2023, available at <https://www.hybridcoe.fi/publications/hybrid-coe-working-paper-21-the-space-domain-and-the-russo-ukrainian-war-actors-tools-and-impact/> accessed 15 November 2023; Sascha D Bachmann and Hakan Gunneriusson, 'Hybrid Wars: The 21st-Century's New Threats to Global Peace and Security' (2015) 43(1) Scientia Militaria, South African Journal of Military Studies 77 – 98.

26 McCulloh (n 3) 71.

27 'Editor's Introduction', in *The Military Balance 2015* (International Institute for Strategic Studies 2015) 5.

The above reference to an integrated campaign echoes the NATO's use of the term 'integrated design' at the Wales Summit in September 2014.[28] As such it distinguishes hybrid warfare from other forms of asymmetric warfare.[29] Metz and Johnson have characterized asymmetric warfare in following terms:

> In the realm of military affairs and national security, asymmetry is acting, organizing, and thinking differently than opponents in order to maximize one's own advantages, exploit an opponent's weaknesses, attain the initiative, or gain greater freedom of action. It can be political-strategic, military strategic, or a combination of these. It can entail different methods, technologies, values, organizations, time perspectives, or some combination of these. It can be short-term or long-term. It can be deliberate or by default. It can be discrete or pursued in combination with symmetric approaches. It can have both psychological and physical dimensions.[30]

On the other hand, Hoffman is not satisfied with the NATO definition of hybrid warfare. He explains that:

> Hybrid warfare as a mix of methods short war has become a common interpretation and an alternative definition in Europe, where key leaders at NATO define hybrid threats as 'a wide range of overt and covert military, paramilitary, and civilian measures are employed in a highly integrated design'. The NATO version reflects a combination of methods, and emphasized an integrated and purposeful design. This is a broad definition that could explain just about all wars, which usually contain combinations of military and non-military activity in an integrated plan.

---

28 'We will ensure that NATO is able to effectively address the specific challenges posed by hybrid warfare threats, where a wide range of overt and covert military, paramilitary, and civilian measures are employed in a highly integrated design.' Wales Summit Declaration, Issued by the Heads of State and Government participating in the meeting of the North Atlantic Council in Wales, 5 September 2014, para 13, available at <https://bit.ly/41pu5eU> accessed 29 November 2023.

29 Mikael Weissmann, 'Conceptualizing and countering hybrid threats and hybrid warfare', in Mikael Weissmann, Niklas Nilsson, Björn Palmertz, and Per Thunholm (eds.), *Hybrid Warfare* (IB Tauris 2021) 61, 64.

30 Steven Metz and Douglas V Johnson II, *Asymmetry and U.S. Military Strategy: Definition, Background, and Strategic Concepts* (US Army War College 2001), quoted in Michael N Schmitt, 'Asymmetrical Warfare and International Humanitarian Law', in Wolff Heintschel von Heinegg and Volker Epping (eds.), *International Humanitarian Law Facing New Challenges: Symposium in Honour of Knut Ipsen* (Springer 2007) 13.

> In the context faced by NATO today, such activities are occurring short of armed conflict. Thus, NATO's perspective is closer conceptually to gray zone or what I call Measures Short of Armed Conflict.[31]

Instead, Hoffman places the grey zone *Measures Short of Armed Conflict* below the threshold of warfare at three different levels, i.e. irregular warfare, hybrid warfare, and conventional warfare (ranked along the level of violence).[32] Hoffman further argues that:

> Chinese conceptions of 'quasi-war' and the 'Three Warfares' which embrace legal, psychological, and information activities short of warfare, are relevant to this discussion. Recent research suggests a convergence of China and Russian tactics is occurring, emanating from Chinese interpretations of Russia's actions in the Crimea and in the cyber domain. We should expect Russia, in turn, to absorb lessons from the South China Sea, as well as other states. /…/ This gap in our understanding of the competitive space between peace and war is a shortfall in U.S. strategic culture.[33]

It is suggested that the military hegemony of the US and thus the asymmetry of the international order makes hybrid warfare especially attractive to the rivals of the US.[34] Chief among them are China and Russia. In the words of Weissmann and others: 'The fact that the combined military resources of the West remain vastly superior, certainly to those of Russia and for the time being also to those of China, has encouraged these and other actors to develop and combine other, less resource-consuming means for challenging the global hegemony of the West.'[35] Michael Schmitt has argued that, 'asymmetry hardly represents a radically new operational model, for it is in the very nature of warfare to seeks strategies, tactics, and weapons that either leverage one's own strengths (positive asymmetry) or exploit the enemy's weaknesses (negative

31 Francis G Hoffman, 'Statement before the House Armed Services Committee', in *The Evolution of Hybrid Warfare and Key Challenges* (US Government Publishing Office 2017) 40.

32 Ibid.

33 Ibid, 41.

34 Ibid, 39. Nyemann even attributes the rise of hybrid warfare to the 'success of traditional military deterrence from the West'. Dorthe B Nyemann, 'Hybrid warfare in the Baltics', in Weissmann *et al.* (n 29) 195, 199.

35 Mikael Weissmann *et al.*, 'Security Challenges in the grey zone', in Weissmann *et al.* (n 29) 1, 3.

asymmetry), or both.'[36] Hybrid or asymmetrical warfare is in this manner cast as 'a low-cost strategy with potentially high gains'.[37]

This is also confirmed by Chivvis who, in his analysis of the Russian hybrid warfare, identified its ability to economize the use force as one of its key characteristics.[38] Recognizing that Russia could not afford a protracted conventional conflict with the NATO, Moscow seeks to pursue its interests without overt use of military power wherever possible.[39] He also noted that hybrid warfare is persistent in that it breaks down the traditional delineation between war and peace as well as that it is population-centric in that Russia seeks to influence the population of target countries through information operations, proxy groups, and other influence operations.[40] Accordingly, three aims can be achieved: the capture of territory without resorting to overt or conventional military force, the creation of a pretext for overt, conventional military action and the influence of the politics and policies of countries in the West or elsewhere.[41] Hoffman remarks that these methods are well-established in the Russian practice based on the Soviet Union's legacy. In this context, Hoffman refers to George Kennan's definition of 'political warfare' as 'the employment of all the means at a nation's command, short of war.'[42]

3 Alternative Terminology

Many alternative terms exist to that of hybrid warfare, most notably 'hybrid threats', 'grey zone' conflicts, and 'fourth generation warfare' that are discussed next. Another term with similar features is 'compound warfare', a term proposed by Thomas Huber in 1996 as a descriptor for an alliance of conventional armies and irregular forces under strategic direction.[43]

---

36 Schmitt (n 30) 11.

37 Nyemann (n 34) 210.

38 Christopher S Chivvis, 'Understanding Russian 'Hybrid Warfare' and What Can Be Done about It', Testimony presented before the House Armed Services Committee on March 22, 2017, 2, available at <https://www.rand.org/pubs/testimonies/CT468.html> accessed 15 November 2023.

39 Ibid.

40 Ibid.

41 Ibid, 2–3.

42 George Kennan's policy memo for the Department of State, quoted in Hoffman (n 31) 42.

43 Thomas M Huber, 'Napoleon in Spain and Naples: Fortified Compound Warfare', in Thomas M Huber (ed.), *Compound Warfare: That Fatal Knot* (US Army Command and General Staff College Press 2002) 91–112. See also Peter R Mansoor, 'Introduction' in

Furthermore, in an essay of 1999, two Chinese officers put forward the concept of 'unrestricted warfare' that they characterized as transcending 'all boundaries and limits' and which Johnson sums up as not being 'limited to the physical, detached battlefield so the actions of war normally associated with military efforts will expand across other domains such as economics and materials resources, religion, culture, the environment, and information networks.'[44] Other less well used terms are 'ambiguous warfare', 'shadow war', 'non-linear warfare', and 'unconventional warfare'.[45] Weissmann suggests that the latter are 'more or less synonymous terms' with hybrid warfare.[46]

In the maritime domain, hybrid warfare often translates into so-called gunboat diplomacy which involves the use of force against commercial ships or sovereign immune ships falling just below the threshold of an armed conflict. The term *gunboat diplomacy* characterized the Cold War era of the second half of the twentieth century,[47] whereas it is rarely used nowadays and seems to be somewhat absorbed by new terminology.

3.1 *Hybrid Threats*

Perhaps the closest term to hybrid warfare is that of 'hybrid threats', with a threat in this context understood as 'the combination of capability, intent and opportunity'.[48] In 2010, the NATO defined a hybrid threat as 'one posed by any current or potential adversary, including State and non-State and terrorists, with the ability, whether demonstrated or likely, to simultaneously employ conventional and non-conventional means adaptively, in pursuit of their objectives'.[49] It would later refer to 'hybrid warfare threats', most notably in the 2014 Wales Summit Declaration.[50] The European Union (hereinafter EU), on the other hand, has not strictly defined 'hybrid threats' but has noted that they share the following characteristics: (a) they are a mixture of coercive

---

Murray and Mansoor (n 13) 3 note 4; and Hoffman (n 9) 'Conflict in the 21st Century: The Rise of Hybrid Wars', 20–22.

44 Richard Johnson, 'Operational Approaches to Hybrid Warfare', in Timothy McCulloh and Richard Johnson, *Hybrid Warfare* (The JSOU Press MacDill Air Force Base 2013) 57.

45 Weissmann, Nilsson *et al.* (n 35) 2.

46 Weissmann (n 29) 63.

47 See James Cable, *Gunboat Diplomacy 1919– 1991: Political Applications of Limited Naval Force* (Palgrave Macmillan, London 1994).

48 Fredrik Löjdquist 'Foreword', in Weissmann, Nilsson *et al.* (n 29) VIII.

49 NATO, 'BI-SC Input to a New NATO Capstone Concept for the Military Contribution to Countering Hybrid Threats', 25 August 2010, para 7, available at <https://bit.ly/3AikFX8> accessed 1 May 2023.

50 NATO 2014 Wales Summit Declaration (n 28) para 13.

and subversive activity, conventional and unconventional methods (i.e. diplomatic, military, economic, technological, information); (b) they are used in a coordinated manner by state or non-state actors; (c) they remain below the threshold of open organized hostilities; and (d) they seek to exploit the vulnerabilities of a target by generating ambiguity with the intention to hinder decision-making processes.[51]

In 2017, NATO and the EU agreed to create an institution supported by their respective members but independent of both international organizations to address hybrid threats. Established in Finland, the European Centre of Excellence for Countering Hybrid Threats (hereinafter Hybrid CoE) defines a hybrid threat as 'an action conducted by state or non-state actors, whose goal is to undermine or harm a target by influencing its decision-making at the local, regional, state or institutional level.'[52] Such actions, it is further stated,

> are coordinated and synchronized and deliberately target democratic states' and institutions' vulnerabilities. Activities can take place, for example, in the political, economic, military, civil or information domains. They are conducted using a wide range of means and designed to remain below the threshold of detection and attribution.[53]

Weissmann suggests that hybrid threats 'need not be active measures, but can also be passive'.[54] Hoffman, despite his close connection with 'hybrid warfare' as a concept, is also attracted by the allied label of hybrid threats, which he defined in 2014 as: 'Any adversary that simultaneously employs a tailored mix of conventional weapons, irregular tactics, terrorism, and criminal behavior in the same time and battlespace to obtain their political objectives.'[55] Seen in this light, a distinction with hybrid warfare is hard to discern. Similarly,

51 Joint Communication to the European Parliament and the Council, 'Joint Framework on countering hybrid threats: a European Union response', JOIN(2016) 18 final, 6 April 2016, 2, available at <https://eur-lex.europa.eu/legal-content/EN/TXT/PDF/?uri=CELEX:52016JC0018> accessed 1 December 2023.

52 Hybrid CoE, 'Hybrid threats as a concept', available at <https://bit.ly/45oEf2c> accessed 1 August 2023.

53 Ibid.

54 Weissmann (n 29) 63.

55 Francis G Hoffman, 'On Not-So-New Warfare: Political Warfare Vs Hybrid Threats' War on the Rocks (28 July 2014), available at <https://bit.ly/3AMrZuN> accessed 15 November 2023.

Timothy B. McCulloh seems to blend the terms 'hybrid warfare' and 'hybrid threat'. He argues that:

> A hybrid threat uniquely focuses on organizational capability and generally attempts to gain an asymmetrical advantage over purely conventional opponents within a specific environment. This advantage not only asserts itself in the realm of pure military force, but also in a more holistic manner across all the elements of national power including diplomatic, informational, military, economic, financial, intelligence, and law enforcement/legal. The advantage generates the effect of transitioning the rules of the battlefield from those of a conventional fight to those realms of a hybrid's choosing – primarily in the categories of tempo, depth, and intensity. As a result, a weaker military opponent can stand against a stronger one for an indefinite period and continue to generate effects that a more conventional opponent could not generate in the same situation.[56]

Hawken would prefer a different term to hybrid warfare altogether: 'labels like shadow wars, or the original terminology of hybrid threats, which describe the action of potentially deniable forces using irregular methods but armed with conventional firepower seem more appropriate.'[57] This appears to limit unnecessarily the operational range of action and equipment while partly potentially retaining the notion of warfare.

Nyemann, on the other hand, seeks to differentiate between *hybrid threats* and *hybrid warfare*. In the legal literature, a similar differentiation can be found. For example, Lott finds that hybrid conflict (or hybrid threat) 'can be understood as a broad term that encapsulates a combination of economic and socio-political coercion and intimidation' and argues that:

> [H]ybrid conflicts are understood to include only such military activities where the States involved abstain from the use of force against each other (e.g., passage of warships or military aircraft, military research activities, military build- up near borders, etc.). The use of force by one State against another State is indicative of the existence of a situation of hybrid warfare where it is unclear if the use of force amounts to an armed attack under Article 51 of the UN Charter.[58]

---

56 McCulloh (n 3) 58.

57 Colum Hawken, 'Q-Boats and Chaos: Hybrid War on the High Seas' The Strategy Bridge (7 December 2017), available at <https://bit.ly/3AOaQ3S> accessed 1 August 2023.

58 Lott (n 25) 17.

Nyemann considers hybrid threats as 'deniable or covert actions by an aggressor in a target State involving instruments of power such as cyberattacks (not amounting to an armed attack), information operations, economic pressure, or other unfriendly activities often performed by third-party malign non-State actors'.[59] It is true, as the Hybrid CoE implicitly recognizes, that the use of the term 'warfare' may itself be a misnomer in certain circumstances, given that situations of hybrid warfare do not necessarily cross the threshold of 'war' or an armed conflict as international law defines it.[60] It is also true, as Nyemann affirms, that: 'Ideally, States must react to hybrid threats *before* the situation evolves to a case of hybrid warfare.'[61] In a similar vein, Najžer complains that in ordinary parlance a threat is something that is yet to happen and is therefore an unsuitable alternative to hybrid warfare.[62] But the possibility of 'trouble, danger, or ruin' as the *Oxford English Dictionary* has it, certainly chimes with a burgeoning challenge to State and individual security and one that is a reflection of ongoing unhappy circumstance and action, not merely a distant menace.

There is also a perceived advantage for the attacker who remains below the legal threshold of armed conflict, perhaps with the consequence that he can 'get away with' certain hybrid operations without actually being involved in a shooting war or being held legally accountable.

3.2 *'Grey Zone' Conflicts*

Other popular terms used instead of, or in addition to, hybrid warfare include the 'grey zone', which again Hoffman uses in his writings.[63] He decries broad conceptualization of grey zone conflicts in scholarship, preferring his own:

> Those covert or illegal activities of non-traditional statecraft that are below the threshold of armed organized violence; including disruption of order, political subversion of government or non-governmental organizations, psychological operations, abuse of legal processes, and

59 Nyemann (n 34) 196.

60 See for a detailed explanation of 'war' under the law of nations: Andrew Clapham, *War* (Oxford University Press 2021). Najžer prefers an international relations definition of a 'hostile contest between states or other belligerents, carried on by degrees of coercion in order to achieve political objectives', but its breadth and lack of precision poses more questions than it answers. Najžer (n 4) 25.

61 Nyemann (n 34) 197.

62 Najžer (n 4) 38.

63 Francis G Hoffman, 'Examining Complex Forms of Conflict: Gray Zone and Hybrid Challenges' (2018) 7(4) Prism 31–47.

> financial corruption as part of an integrated design to achieve strategic advantage.[64]

Hoffman seeks to 'update our understanding' and to 'distinguish hybrid conflict' from irregular warfare, by offering a revised definition of hybrid warfare as: 'The purposeful and tailored violent application of advanced conventional military capabilities with irregular tactics, with terrorism and criminal activities, or combination of regular and irregular forces, operating as part of a common design in the same battlespace.'[65] The major distinction, he observes, 'is the addition of 'violent' to the definition to clarify its placement in the continuum, and to further distinguish it from activities short of violent conflict'.[66] That criterion relates to the degree of aggression and serves also as a useful point of departure for differentiating 'milder' hybrid threats (e.g., mass immigration, discriminatory navigational restrictions, cyberattacks, etc.) from 'violent' hybrid warfare that involves the use of force.

In contrast, Najžer is one of several who consider *hybrid warfare* and *grey zone conflicts* as synonyms.[67] Moreover, in certain US military circles, grey zone is a more popular term than hybrid (used to denote similar violent disputes), but grey zone conflict is not officially part of US military doctrine, and it is even, in the words of one commentator, a 'sometimes loathed term'.[68]

In fact, the two terms are not to be equated. Grey zone conflicts are those violent operations and clashes that occur below the threshold of armed conflict.[69] In contrast, there is no requirement that hybrid warfare occupies solely this space. While low-intensity armed violence is often a feature of hybrid warfare, that is not necessarily the case, and the two notions should not be confused. Russia's invasion of Ukraine in late February 2022 and everything that has happened since in that conflict assuredly put paid to that notion. Accordingly,

---

64 Ibid, 36.

65 Ibid, 40.

66 Ibid.

67 Najžer (n 4) 31.

68 Jed Willard, 'The US and hybrid challenges, Past, present and future', in Weissmann, Nilsson *et al.* (n 29) 157, 158.

69 Ibid. Armed conflict was defined by the International Criminal Tribunal for the former Yugoslavia (hereinafter ICTY) in 1995 as existing as a matter of international humanitarian law 'whenever there is a resort to armed force between States or protracted armed violence between governmental authorities and organized armed groups or between such groups within a State'. Prosecutor v. Tadić (Decision) ICTY-94-1 (2 October 1995), para 70.

Najžer's affirmation that hybrid warfare is always a form of 'low-level conflict' must be rejected.[70]

3.3 *Fourth Generation Warfare*

Fourth generation warfare (sometimes shortened to 4GW) is a longstanding term of military analysts. It was first proposed by William Lind and a number of serving US military officers in 1989[71] and then expanded by Thomas Hammes in 2004–2005,[72] finally being incorporated into the US Department of Defense 2006 Quadrennial Defense Review.[73] Hammes observed that 'superior political will when properly employed can defeat greater economic and military power'.[74]

In summary, 4GW holds that three generations of warfare – linear, firepower, and maneuver, respectively – have been supplanted by a complex form of insurgency that thrives in the absence or collapse of the State.[75] While it has been subject to persistent criticism on the basis of flawed analysis – Najžer calls it 'misguided'[76] – Hoffman has acknowledged that his definition of hybrid warfare built on the 4GW concept's focus on the blurring nature of conflicts to come and 'especially the blurring of war and peace'. The use of unconventional means, notably terrorism and disinformation, also characterizes 4GW (just as it does, in part, hybrid warfare).[77]

4 How Hybrid Warfare May Play Out

In warfare, one might study the combination of military and non-military means in order to achieve a desired outcome. What may be of particular interest from a legal point of view, however, is to study the use of (non-)military

70 Najžer (n 4) 29.

71 William S Lind, Keith Nightengale, John F Schmitt, Joseph W Sutton, Gary I Wilson, 'The Changing Face of War: Into the Fourth Generation' (1989) 73(10) Marine Corps Gazette 22–26.

72 Thomas X Hammes, *The Sling and the Stone: On War in the 21st Century* (Voyageur Press 2004).

73 McCulloh (n 3) 63.

74 Thomas X Hammes, 'Insurgency: Modern Warfare Evolves into a Fourth Generation' (2005) 214 Strategic Forum 1–7.

75 Najžer (n 4) 35.

76 Ibid, 36.

77 Hoffman (n 9) 'Conflict in the 21st Century: The Rise of Hybrid Wars', 18.

means or tactics that do not cross the threshold of armed conflict. This question is closely linked with identification of this threshold.

4.1 *The Threshold of Armed Conflict*

The threshold of armed conflict is important for all parties in a conflict. For attackers, an important question is not only how they can achieve their aims, but also how they can get away with an act of aggression without actually being involved in a shooting war or being held legally accountable. For defenders, the question is to find the appropriate response to an 'attack' that may or may not be above the threshold of armed conflict. Should they respond with military means, or is law enforcement measures the right reaction? The answer is likely to have military, political and legal consequences.

The threshold of armed conflict has several aspects. One is in *jus ad bellum*. An armed attack triggers the right to self-defence as a serious violation of the prohibition on the use of force against the territorial integrity or political independence of any State in the UN Charter.[78] The North Atlantic Treaty[79] also refers to the notion of armed attack, as found in Article 51 of the UN Charter, stipulating that an armed attack against one or more of Members of NATO shall be considered an attack against them all, triggering their right to individual or collective self-defence. But which acts of hybrid warfare constitute an armed attack in the sense of Article 51 of the UN Charter? Could, for example, a cyberattack qualify as an armed attack? An answer could be provided only on a case-by-case analysis. In 2022, for example, Albania's Prime Minister, Edi Rama, considered invoking Article 5 of the North Atlantic Treaty in response to cyberattacks against government networks, allegedly conducted by Iran, but eventually decided against escalating the matter.[80]

The *Tallinn Manual* is important with regard to these issues, but the forthcoming Virginia-Georgetown Manual on the *jus ad bellum* may also shed some light on these issues.[81] Similarly, considering that the instrumentalization of

78 Article 2(4) of the Charter of the United Nations (opened for signature 26 June 1945, entered into force 24 October 1945) 1 UNTS XVI.

79 The North Atlantic Treaty (opened for signature 4 April 1949, entered into force 24 August 1949) 34 UNTS 243.

80 Maggie Miller, 'Albania weighed invoking NATO's Article 5 over Iranian cyberattack' Politico (10 May 2022), available at <https://www.politico.com/news/2022/10/05/why-albania-chose-not-to-pull-the-nato-trigger-after-cyberattack-00060347> accessed 1 December 2023.

81 See 'A Manual of Jus ad Bellum Law, with Commentary: Grant year 2019', available at <https://www.srf.org/grants/a-manual-of-jus-ad-bellum-law-with-commentary> accessed 20 September 2023.

migration by certain States that direct irregular migrants to illegally cross into another State's territory in large numbers causing chaos and public disorder may be considered a breach of that State's territorial integrity as may the launch of disinformation campaigns against migrants affect a State's political independence. However, it is difficult to argue that such 'attacks' reach the threshold of Article 51 of the UN Charter for an armed attack (see *infra* Chapter 9).

The threshold of armed conflict is also relevant to the issue of application of the Geneva Conventions of 1949. The common Article 2 uses the term 'armed conflict' as trigger for the application of the conventions. It may be reasonable to assume that if there is an armed attack in the sense of Article 51, then an armed conflict will automatically follow. But one may also envision an armed conflict which has developed without a clear attacker, and where both or none of the parties invokes the right to self-defence. For example, the years 2019–2021 marked an escalation of clandestine use of force at sea by Israel and Iran against ships flying each other's flags.[82] However, Israel and Iran did not appear to invoke their right of self-defence in response to these clandestine attacks.

When do we have an armed conflict in the sense of the Geneva Conventions? It has been suggested that the threshold is crossed when one of the parties abandon the law enforcement paradigm, where you use minimum force necessary against persons that represent an imminent and local threat, as opposed to a military paradigm where you use maximum force against enemy combatant personnel irrespective of whether they constitute any threat at the moment.[83] In other words – one largely abandons the comprehensive protection of human life as afforded by human rights conventions and applies the more limited protection that applies to soldiers *hors de combat* and civilians not taking direct part in hostilities.[84]

4.2 *Tools of Hybrid Warfare*

What are the tools of hybrid warfare? A comprehensive list cannot be drawn up, since the answer depends on the imagination and resources of the parties involved. No matter what a list looks like today, some new innovative methods may see the light of day tomorrow – or may be applied under the veil of

---

82 See, e.g., Patrick Kingsley, Ronen Bergman, Farnaz Fassihi, and Eric Schmitt, 'Israel's Shadow War With Iran Moves Out to Sea' The New York Times (26 March 2021), available at <https://www.nytimes.com/2021/03/26/world/middleeast/israel-iran-shadow-war.html> accessed 10 September 2023; Lott (n 25) 117–141.

83 Arne W Dahl and Magnus Sandbu, 'The Threshold of Armed Conflict' (2006) 45(3–4) The Military Law and the Law of War Review 369.

84 Art. 51(3) of the above-referred 1977 Additional Protocol I.

darkness and recognized as such only in the aftermath. Some examples can, however, be given based on existing State practice.

One common tool is disinformation, in particular over the Internet. In war, the returns made up on each side of losses in killed and wounded are never exact, seldom truthful, and in most cases, full of intentional misrepresentations.[85] The enemy must be denied a correct impression of one's strengths and weaknesses. In peacetime, exaggerated impressions of one's military strength can be equally useful to induce a potential adversary to submit to one's will or abstain from interfering with one's plans. More subtly, disinformation concerning a particular politician can help a rival to win elections – a rival that may be more inclined to support or not to oppose one's policies. Russia is known to have spread disinformation online before the annexation of Crimea and continues to do so in Ukraine.[86] In addition, pro-Kremlin disinformation campaigns have been associated with meddling with key elections in Europe and the US.[87]

War by proxy is also a common hybrid warfare technique. China, for example, 'in the South and East China Seas, China has deployed a layered maritime force consisting of fishing vessels supported by a maritime militia backed by its recently formed China Coast Guard to conduct operations at a level of conflict below anything that justifies an armed response'.[88] China is likely to use hybrid warfare ever more persistently in the future, with rivalry in the South China Sea and animosity across the Taiwan Strait uppermost in its strategic

85 Clausewitz (n 1) Book Four, Chapter IV.

86 Ofer Fridman, *Russian 'Hybrid Warfare': Resurgence and Politicization* (Oxford University Press 2018) 101–126; Mitchell A Orenstein, *The Lands in Between Russia vs. the West and the New Politics of Hybrid War* (Oxford University Press 2019); OECD, 'Disinformation and Russia's war of aggression against Ukraine: Threats and governance responses' 3 November 2022, available at <https://www.oecd-ilibrary.org/docserver/37186bde-en.pdf?expires=1700124534&id=id&accname=guest&checksum=BEF6E3E1560ACBF825DBFB24222261B> accessed 1 December 2023.

87 Erik Brattberg and Tim Maurer, 'Five European Experiences With Russian Election Interference' (2018) Carnegie Endowment for International Peace, available at <https://www.jstor.org/stable/pdf/resrep21009.6.pdf> accessed 1 December 2023; Attila Juhász and Patrik Szicherle, 'The political effects of migration-related fake news, disinformation and conspiracy theories in Europe' (2017) Friedrich Ebert Stiftung/Political Capital, available at <https://politicalcapital.hu/pc-admin/source/documents/FES_PC_FakeNewsMigrationStudy_EN_20170607.pdf> accessed 1 December 2023.

88 Murphy and Schaub (n 25) 126. Rob McLaughlin, 'Anticipating Operational Naval Warfare Issues in International Humanitarian Law That May Arise in the Event of a Conflict in the South China Sea', in Suzannah Linton *et al.* (eds.), *Asia-Pacific Perspectives on International Humanitarian Law* (Cambridge University Press 2019) 703–716.

thinking.[89] Iran also relies on the Iranian Islamic Revolutionary Guard Corps to exercise guerrilla warfare at sea by launching sea and land anti-ship cruise missiles, missiles, mines, mini-subs and suicide boats.[90]

The instrumentalization of mass migration is another tool in States' hybrid warfare toolbox. States bordering the Mediterranean have employed mass migration as a tool to coerce or influence the EU or its Member States' policies and politics.[91] Directing large numbers of migrants to another State's borders causes not only chaos and public disorder but also internal political instability. This, combined with disinformation campaigns against migrants, has proved a valuable tool in manipulating public opinion and influencing public policies.[92]

The use of cyberattacks is widespread in hybrid warfare. Computer network attacks may bring to a halt banking systems and close down governmental services. Electricity grids can be interfered with. Trains can be brought to a halt. Navigation systems can be corrupted. At a certain point, when physical effects are brought about, the threshold of armed attack may be crossed.

In the past decade, hybrid threats to international navigation have increased. Examples include the escalation of hybrid naval warfare between Iran and Israel (especially in 2019–2022) in the Red Sea and the Arabian Sea, the alleged 2019 limpet mine attacks against tankers transiting the Strait of Hormuz as well as the incidents in 2018 and 2021 involving the use of force by Russia against, respectively, the Ukrainian and United Kingdom warships in the Black Sea. Furthermore, repeat incidents in the South China Sea involving, on the one hand, Chinese commercial and sovereign immune ships and, on the other hand, ships of other coastal States of the South China Sea as well as Western states seeking to uphold navigational rights and freedoms in the relevant area provide a long list of examples of hybrid threats to international navigation. An additional problem to international navigation emanates from State-sponsored non-State actors who operate like pirates in waters adjacent to failed States or otherwise unstable areas. This is illustrated by, for example, the suspected Houthi attacks against Israel-linked ships in the Red Sea and the

---

89 See, e.g., Gulizar Haciyakupoglu and Nichael Raska, 'China's political warfare in Taiwan', in Weissmann, Nilsson *et al.* (n 29) 173, 184–186.

90 Murphy and Schaub (n 25) 126–127.

91 Kelly M Greenhill, *Weapons of Mass Migration: Forced Displacement, Coercion, and Foreign Policy* (Cornell University Press, 2010); Christopher Chivvis, 'Hybrid War: Russian Contemporary Political Warfare' (2017) 73 Bulletin of the Atomic Scientists 316, 317–319.

92 Juhász and Szicherle (n 87).

Gulf of Aden in the wider framework of the Israeli-Hamas armed conflict that erupted in 2023.[93]

The emergence of autonomous ships brings new threats to international navigation on the horizon. Could such vessels be hacked by an unfriendly State? If so, what would the legal consequences be and what countermeasures could be taken? In the context of threats posed by cyberattacks to international navigational, additional problems arise. For example, is the sabotage of navigational aids, such as local jamming of the GPS system or taking over satellites by computer network attacks to be considered as hostilities when effected by one State against another?

Attacks against critical infrastructure serve as another means of hybrid warfare. For example, how are computer network attacks against systems controlling oil and gas rigs to be classified under international law? Can production be closed down or an uncontrolled release (blow-out) be brought in hybrid warfare about without initiating an armed conflict? In the maritime domain, attacks against critical infrastructure have been so far mostly targeted against submarine cables and pipelines (for an overview of relevant incidents in recent years, see *infra* Chapter 5.1). In this context, the sabotage against the Nord Stream and Balticconnector pipelines in the Baltic Sea in September 2022 serves as a particularly relevant example (see further *infra* Chapters 5 and 6). The targeting of submarine cables and pipelines in hybrid warfare carries several aims. It sends a message of vulnerability to the relevant coastal States in relation to their energy or telecommunications security. Furthermore, such acts of sabotage have the potential to create a supply crisis by hindering the deliveries of the relevant commodities to the market, thereby increasing the prices and laying the ground for popular unrest and destabilization of the political environment in the affected countries.

Conclusion

This chapter examined the multiple definitions of and synonyms for the term *hybrid warfare*. While there is no internationally agreed definition of *hybrid warfare*, the term is understood in this book to imply a combination of regular and irregular military operations, with the addition of non-military means, aiming at influencing the adversary's mind.

93 See, e.g., Anonymous, 'Yemen's Houthis warn ships in Red Sea to avoid Israel or face attack' The Guardian (13 December 2023), available at <https://www.theguardian.com/world/2023/dec/13/yemen-houthis-red-sea-ship-israel-attack> accessed 12 January 2024.

The concept of hybrid warfare is closely linked with the identification of the threshold of armed conflict. The methods of hybrid warfare employ such (non-)military means or tactics that are meant to remain below the threshold of armed conflict. The threshold of armed conflict is crossed when one of the parties to an incident abandons the law enforcement paradigm, where minimum force necessary is used against persons that represent an imminent and local threat, as opposed to a military paradigm where maximum force against enemy combatant personnel is employed irrespective of whether they constitute any threat.

The forms and methods of hybrid warfare as discussed in this chapter concerning security at sea demand reactions. Some in advance, in order to discourage such attacks or make them more difficult; others in response to a particular attack in progress. We need to be prepared, physically as well as politically. The legal aspects need to be charted, which is one of the principal aims of the present book.

CHAPTER 2

The Use of Force in Self-Defence and the Taking of Countermeasures in Response to Maritime Hybrid Warfare under International Law

Stuart Casey-Maslen

Introduction

This chapter considers the application of two branches of international law to adjudge the legality of State responses to hybrid warfare, particularly when wrought in the maritime environment.[1] The inter-State nature of hybrid warfare distinguishes these responses from ordinary law enforcement at sea. Applicable to the use of forcible action by States is *jus ad bellum*, which is tackled first. The foundational components of the law on inter-State use of force in contemporary international law are set forth in the 1945 Charter of the United Nations (hereinafter UN),[2] as subsequently interpreted by the International Court of Justice in its jurisprudence, in particular in its judgments on the merits in the *Nicaragua*[3] and *Oil Platforms*[4] cases.

The second branch of salient international law for adjudging responses to hybrid warfare is that governing the responsibility of States for the commission of internationally wrongful acts (i.e. violations of international law). This body of law encompasses regulation of the taking of non-forcible countermeasures, as delineated by the International Court of Justice in a contentious case from 1997,[5] with the parameters of legality subsequently articulated in greater detail

1 'Despite the obvious geographical difference, hybrid warfare or littoral guerrilla-style warfare functions in much the same fashion as land-based operations.' Tobias Burgers and Scott N Romaniuk, 'Hybrid Warriors: China's Unmanned, Guerrilla-Style Warfare in Asia's Littorals', The Diplomat (16 February 2017), available at <https://bit.ly/3NAXRKN> accessed 1 May 2023.

2 Charter of the United Nations (opened for signature 26 June 1945, entered into force 24 October 1945), Arts 2(4), 51.

3 *Military and Paramilitary Activities in and against Nicaragua* (Nicaragua v. United States of America), Merits, ICJ Reports 1986, p. 14.

4 *Oil Platforms* (*Islamic Republic of Iran v. United States of America*), Judgment, ICJ Reports 2003, p. 161.

5 *Gabčikovo-Nagymaros Project* (*Hungary/Slovakia*), Judgment, ICJ Reports 1997, p. 7.

 | DOI:10.1163/9789004707993_004

by the International Law Commission in its draft articles of 2001.[6] Determining which body of international law is applicable to a particular set of facts is not, however, without debate or dispute, as this chapter also examines.

1 The Prohibition on the Use of Force in the Maritime Environment

1.1 *The General Prohibition on Inter-State Use of Force*

The fundamental rule of *jus ad bellum* is the general prohibition on inter-State use of force, which has been the legal bedrock of the international peace and security system since 1945. Thus articulated in Article 2(4) of the UN Charter it reads in full: 'All Members shall refrain in their international relations from the threat or use of force against the territorial integrity or political independence of any state, or in any other manner inconsistent with the Purposes of the United Nations.'[7] Although the rule's codification in the Charter expressly binds only the 193 UN Member States, its formulation under customary international law applies to all States.[8]

The negotiation of the provision in 1945 and its subsequent interpretation by States, judicial authorities, and publicists have confirmed that by force is meant only 'armed force' and not also economic pressure, including

6 International Law Commission, Draft Articles on the Responsibility of States for Internationally Wrongful Acts, UN doc. A/56/10 (2001) (hereinafter, ILC Draft Articles on State Responsibility).

7 States Parties to the UN Convention on the Law of the Sea are likewise expressly obligated, when 'exercising their rights and performing their duties' under the Convention, to 'refrain from any threat or use of force against the territorial integrity or political independence of any State, or in any other manner inconsistent with the principles of international law embodied in the Charter of the United Nations'. United Nations Convention on the Law of the Sea (opened for signature 10 December 1982, entered into force 16 November 1994) 1833 UNTS 3 (hereinafter LOSC), Art 301.

8 In 1974, the UN General Assembly adopted a consensual definition of aggression in which it was generally described as 'the use of armed force by a State against the sovereignty, territorial integrity or political independence of another State, or in any other manner inconsistent with the Charter of the United Nations'. Definition of Aggression, annexed to UN General Assembly Resolution 3314 (XXIX); adopted without a vote on 14 December 1974, Art 1. The definition explicitly noted that the term 'State' was used 'without prejudice to questions of recognition or to whether a State is a member of the United Nations'. Hence, the prohibition is also applicable to the four other States as currently recognized by the UN Secretary-General based on the general practice of States: the two UN Observer States (the Holy See and the State of Palestine) and the two 'other States' (the Cook Islands and Niue).

that wrought by cyberattacks or resulting from the imposition of sanctions.[9] Misinformation, disinformation, and propaganda do not ordinarily amount to a use of force. Indeed, the International Group of Experts that elaborated the second edition of the Tallinn Manual (2.0) on the International Law Applicable to Cyber Operations in 2017 believed that the transmission of propaganda into another State is 'generally' not even a violation of sovereignty.[10] They qualified this assertion somewhat in remarking that propaganda designed to incite civil unrest in another State 'would likely violate the prohibition of intervention'.[11] Propaganda by a military vessel in transit through the territorial sea renders the passage non-innocent[12] but is not *per se* a use of force.[13]

The notion of armed force is to be appreciated in wide terms. It is not only kinetic force that is generally outlawed, such as through the firing of bullets, the dropping of bombs, or the launching of missiles, including in the maritime environment; use of biological, chemical, or radiological weapons against another State is also rendered illegal. Hence, for example, the attempted murder of a Russian military intelligence defector in Salisbury in the United Kingdom in March 2018 by Russian operatives using the chemical agent Novichok was an unlawful inter-State use of force.[14] Any use of armed force against foreign naval forces on the high seas by a State organ or agent, or other entity under its effective control, is a breach of the general *jus ad bellum* prohibition. This therefore includes the conduct of non-State actors where their actions are being directed by one State against another.

Three further elements comprise the prohibition under general international law. First, it pertains to both the threat of force and the actual employment of force, thereby potentially encompassing hybrid threats countenancing a use of force as well as hybrid warfare itself. While a 'threat of force' is not formally

9 See, e.g., James Crawford, *Brownlie's Principles of Public International Law*, 9th ed. (Oxford University Press 2019) 717; and Tom Ruys, 'The Meaning of "Force" and the Boundaries of the *Jus ad Bellum*: Are "Minimal" Uses of Force Excluded from UN Charter Article 2(4)?' (2014) 108(2) American Journal of International Law 159, 163.

10 International Group of Experts, *Tallinn Manual 2.0 on the International Law Applicable to Cyber Operations* (Cambridge University Press 2017) commentary para 29 on Rule 4.

11 Ibid.

12 According to the UN Convention on the Law of the Sea, passage is deemed to be innocent as long as it is 'not prejudicial to the peace, good order or security of the coastal State'. Innocent passage must take place in conformity with the Convention as well as with 'other rules of international law'. LOSC, Art 19(1).

13 Tallinn Manual 2.0 (n 10) commentary para 29 on Rule 4.

14 'Salisbury Incident', Statement by the United Kingdom Prime Minister (Mrs Theresa May), in *Hansard* HC Vol 637 (14 March 2018), available at <https://bit.ly/3rqxXgv> accessed 1 May 2023.

defined in international law, the notion is generally understood to encompass actions ranging from overt bellicose statements by political leaders to intimidatory acts such as unauthorized reconnaissance flights and other illicit penetration of sovereign airspace by a foreign military aircraft or of territorial waters by a foreign warship.[15] Threats may be implicit as well as explicit.[16] In its frequent articulation, the so-called 'Brownlie' formula holds that if a State declares that it will use force in conditions for which no justification for the use of force exists, then the threat is itself illegal.[17] This position was effectively endorsed by the International Court of Justice in 1996 in its *Advisory Opinion on the Threat or Use of Nuclear Weapons*.[18]

Whether passage that is not – or is no longer – innocent will also amount to an inter-State threat or use of force depends on the extent to which it engages in acts or threats of violence against the coastal State or otherwise infringes the terms of Article 2(4) of the UN Charter. A material distinction may be made between the conduct of a submarine and that of a surface warship, given that ordinary law enforcement measures more readily exist to address unlawful acts by a surface warship.[19] Under the right of innocent passage regime, submarines must sail on the surface of the territorial sea of a foreign State.[20] Thus, as Pierre Thévenin has observed, if a submarine remains under water, the threshold to determine whether it is threatening force against a coastal State may be lower than it is for surface ships. This is on the basis of the *prima facie* breach of the rules governing innocent passage. In such circumstances, the coastal State may reasonably assume that a submarine travelling under water in a foreign territorial sea is conducting unlawful activities.[21] Should a surface warship or submarine seek to mount a blockade, this would not only

15 Ian Brownlie, *International Law and the Use of Force by States* (Oxford University Press 1963) 148. In his seminal 1963 work, Brownlie leaves the door open to such acts amounting to an actual use of force and not merely a threat of force.

16 With respect to implicit threats, Annex VII Arbitral Tribunal, Matter of an Arbitration between Guyana and Suriname, Case 2004–04, Award of 17 September 2007, paras 432–439. Perhaps surprisingly, the Panel designated the rather opaque statement 'the consequences will be yours' as an overt threat to use force.

17 Brownlie (n 15) 364.

18 *Legality of the Threat or Use of Nuclear Weapons*, Advisory Opinion, ICJ Reports 1996, p. 226, para 47.

19 For further details, please see Alexander Lott, 'Maritime Security in the Baltic and Japanese Straits From the Perspective of EEZ Corridors' (2023) 54(3) Ocean Development & International Law 327, 339–340.

20 LOSC, Art 20.

21 Email from Pierre Thévenin, Faculty of Law, University of Tartu, Estonia, 4 October 2022.

be a use of force but would almost certainly also constitute an armed attack giving rise to the right to use force in self-defence.[22]

Second, only certain manifestations of force are prohibited: that which is used internationally against another State is overtly prohibited while purely domestic measures are not. The latter concerns force exercised by law enforcement agencies to enforce national criminal law, or which is engaged with a view to suppressing a domestic insurgency. More controversially, there may also be actions that engage a minimal amount of force below the threshold of Article 2(4) and corresponding customary law. In its 2016 *South China Sea Arbitration Award*, the appointed Arbitral Panel recalled a statement by China to the Philippines whereby on 10 April 2012, the Philippines had used a warship to 'harass unarmed Chinese fishermen. This is a sign of the use of force.'[23] It could also be that this was a legitimate act of law enforcement. In this regard, Olivier Corten makes a potentially useful distinction between 'military force' and 'police measures'.[24] But this only takes us so far: warships naturally may be used to conduct law enforcement on the high seas, for instance to counter piracy.[25]

Finally, to breach the terms of the general prohibition of *jus ad bellum*, force must be either directed against the territorial integrity or political independence of another State or it must be applied in any other manner inconsistent with the purposes of the UN. This element is to be interpreted in broad terms.[26] For instance, Anthony D'Amato had claimed that the Israeli Air Force bombing of an Iraqi nuclear research center at Osirak in 1981 did not affect Iraq's territorial integrity because no portion of Iraq's territory was 'taken away' from it by the bombardment.[27] This is patently incorrect. In its Resolution 487, the UN Security Council strongly condemned the military attack by Israel, which it

---

22 This may be deduced from its characterization as an act of aggression even though the two terms are not synonyms. 1974 UN Definition of Aggression (n 8) Art 3(c).

23 Annex VII Arbitral Tribunal, South China Sea Arbitration (the Philippines v. the People's Republic of China), Case No 2013-19, Award of 12 July 2016, para 790.

24 Olivier Corten, *The Law Against War. The Prohibition on the Use of Force in Contemporary International Law* (Hart 2012) 52–67.

25 And on land, military force may of course be used to defeat an insurgency and in many countries the gendarmerie – which typically falls under the Ministry of Defence and not the Ministry of Interior – are used for riot control.

26 In its first contentious case, which it judged on the merits in 1949, the International Court of Justice recalled that: 'Between independent States, respect for territorial sovereignty is an essential foundation of international relations'. *Corfu Channel Case* (*United Kingdom* v *Albania*), Judgment (Merits), ICJ Reports 1949, p. 4, 35.

27 Anthony D'Amato, 'Israel's Airstrike upon the Iraqi Nuclear Reactor' (1983) 77(3) American Journal of International Law, 584, 585.

declared was 'in clear violation' of the UN Charter and 'the norms of international conduct'.[28]

Military occupation by the armed forces of one State (or other armed groups under its effective control) of even a small portion of the territory of another, without or in breach of that latter State's consent,[29] also violates the prohibition on inter-State use of force. In the maritime environment, unauthorized construction and occupation of artificial islands by a foreign power in a State's territorial sea would certainly amount to a use of force. It does not matter for this legal determination that the occupying State firmly believes it has a solid claim to sovereignty over the territory it has forcibly occupied.[30] Thus, for instance, Argentina continues to claim its jurisdiction over the Malvinas and the existence of the dispute with the United Kingdom on this issue has long been recognized by the UN General Assembly.[31] But any renewed attempt to seize the Falkland Islands by force would violate the prohibition on inter-State use of force and once again constitute an act of aggression.[32] This would be so, even were Argentina subsequently granted sovereignty over the islands by a competent international court or tribunal.

In contrast, the unauthorized presence of foreign military vessels in the territorial sea or the exclusive economic zone is more likely to amount to a threat of force. Thus, in its 2016 *South China Sea Arbitration Award*, the Philippines accused China of a breach of Article 2(4) of the UN Charter on the basis of the unauthorized presence of Chinese Government vessels, including two Chinese Navy frigates and five Civilian Maritime Law Enforcement Agency vessels at Second Thomas Shoal, which the Philippines affirms is part of its

28 UN Security Council Resolution 487, adopted by unanimous vote in favour on 19 June 1981, operative para 2.

29 *Armed Activities on the Territory of the Congo* (*Democratic Republic of the Congo v. Uganda*), Judgment, ICJ Reports 2005, p. 168, paras 52–53.

30 Eritrea-Ethiopia Claims Commission, *Partial Award: Jus Ad Bellum – Ethiopia's Claims 1–8*, 19 December 2005, para 10; *Case Concerning the Land and Maritime Boundary Between Cameroon and Nigeria* (*Cameroon* v *Nigeria*, Equatorial Guinea intervening), Judgment, ICJ Reports 2002, p. 303, paras 314, 319.

31 See, e.g., UN General Assembly 2065 (XX), adopted on 16 December 1965 by 94 votes to 0, with 14 abstentions.

32 Thus, the UN Special Committee on Decolonization has called for 'the peaceful and negotiated settlement of the dispute over sovereignty between the two Governments', most recently in June 2022. 'Special Committee Approves Text Requesting Governments of Argentina, United Kingdom Resume Talks to Resolve Falkland Islands (Malvinas) Sovereignty Dispute', Press Release, UN doc. GA/COL/3361 (23 June 2022), available at <https://bit.ly/3RoqiRc> accessed 1 May 2023.

continental shelf.[33] Then on 28 May 2013, Major General Zhang Zhaozhong of the Chinese People's Liberation Army gave an interview on Chinese State television in which he stated that China had 'gained quite satisfactory experience about the ways to recover the islands and reefs [including Ren'ai Shoal, China's name for the Second Thomas Shoal] and defend them'.[34] This may be considered an unlawful threat of force. It was certainly taken as such by the Philippines, which transmitted a Note Verbale to China on 10 June of the same year in which it declared that it 'protests' the statements by China, which 'it cannot help but regard as threats to use force to prevent the Philippines from delivering essential supplies to its personnel at Ayungin Shoal, in violation of Article 2 of the UN Charter, and Article 301 of [LOSC]'.[35]

A clearly unlawful use of force against a State's political independence would be the assassination by an agent of another State of the head of another State or a senior State official anywhere outside the victim State's metropolitan or non-metropolitan territory. This includes hybrid action on the high seas where a non-State actor was doing a State's bidding in targeting a leading military or political figure from the victim State. Also prohibited under the terms of the general prohibition on inter-State use of force is an attack attributable to one State against the land, naval, or air forces of another which takes place outside the territory of the victim State.[36] In contrast, where it is the ability to maintain logistics systems that is affected – and thus the ability of a military to conduct and sustain military operations – the United States Department of Defense believes only that this '*might* also be considered a use of force under *jus ad bellum*'.[37]

1.2 *Responsibility for the Use of Force by Irregular Forces and Non-state Armed Groups*

It is uncontested that the actions of irregular forces engaged in hybrid warfare, including in the maritime environment, may breach the *jus ad bellum* rules

33 South China Sea Arbitration Award (n 23) paras 1117, 1118.

34 Ibid, para 1120.

35 Ibid, para 1121.

36 1974 UN Definition of Aggression (n 8) Art 3(d). See further: Independent International Fact-Finding Mission on the Conflict in Georgia, Report, Vol II (2009), 264. The drone attack against United States (hereinafter US) forces in Jordan in late January 2024, which killed and injured multiple US personnel, appears to be a clear example of hybrid warfare. See, e.g., Phil Stewart, Steve Holland and Idrees Ali, 'Three US troops killed in Jordan drone strike linked to Iran' Reuters (29 January 2024), available at <https://bit.ly/3Uh1g4w> accessed 29 January 2024.

37 US Department of Defense, *Department of Defense Law of War Manual* (Washington DC June 2015) (Updated December 2016), §16.3.1 [added emphasis].

applicable to States. The 'sending' by a State of an armed group – 'armed bands, groups, irregulars or mercenaries' in the wording of the 1974 UN Definition of Aggression – to use force against or on the territory of another State would suffice to engage the former's responsibility under international law.[38] For purposes of international responsibility, an armed group may be equated with State organs even if that status does not follow from internal law, provided that in fact the group acts in "complete dependence' on the State, of which they are ultimately merely the instrument'.[39] So too would an ostensibly non-State armed group that is operating under a foreign State's effective control.[40] It thus does not matter for the purposes of international law whether it is the State naval forces who are the perpetrators of the unlawful use of force or State agents or rather it is other actors under its effective control, such as in the form of irregular armed groups.[41]

2 The Inherent Right of Self-Defence under *Jus ad Bellum*

Being the target of an unlawful threat of force by another State allows the victim State to take non-forcible countermeasures, but not to use force. But even being subjected to an unlawful *use* of force does not necessarily give the victim State the right to use force in self-defence. Article 51 of the UN Charter, which reflects customary law, dictates that only in the event of an 'armed attack' occurring may a State exercise its inherent right of self-defence and use force in response. The differentiation of terminology – from a *use of force* in Article 2(4) to an *armed attack* in Article 51 – is both intentional and normative. But it is disputed among States precisely what constitutes an armed attack; who may

38 1974 UN Definition of Aggression (n 8) Art 3(g).

39 *Case concerning Application of the Convention on the Prevention and Punishment of the Crime of Genocide* (*Bosnia and Herzegovina* v *Serbia and Montenegro*), Judgment, ICJ Reports 2007, p. 43, para 392.

40 Nicaragua Merits Judgment (n 3) para 115.

41 Mirroring the 'little green men' of Russia present in Ukraine from 2014, retired US Navy Admiral James Stavridis has used the term 'little blue sailors' to denote individuals 'who are not exactly uniformed personnel'. These little blue sailors 'will not have any markings on their clothing, will not carry passports, and, if captured, will deny being part of any organized military'. Adm (ret) James Stavridis, 'Maritime Hybrid Warfare Is Coming', (December 2016) 142(12) US Naval Institute Proceedings, available at <https://bit.ly/3Nq0y1A> accessed 1 May 2023. Whether the targeting of foreign merchant vessels and warships by Houthi forces in late 2023 and early 2024 was an instance of hybrid warfare was, though, unsettled at the time of writing. See, e.g., Anonymous, 'UK says it thwarted Houthis' drone attack in the Red Sea' Aljazeera (28 January 2024), available at <https://bit.ly/3vTNWJh> accessed 29 January 2024.

perpetrate such an attack; and at which precise point an attack gives rise to the right of self-defence. These issues are discussed in turn.

2.1 *The Definition of an Armed Attack*

The level of violence necessary to constitute an armed attack is certainly higher than is the force whose employment is generally prohibited by one State against another.[42] As the Court observed in its Nicaragua judgment in 1986, it is necessary to distinguish 'the most grave forms of the use of force (those constituting an armed attack) from other less grave forms'.[43] Certainly, consonant with the understanding of force as 'armed' force, economic damage, for example, by use of a computer virus designed to paralyze the financial operations of a State's stock exchange or to disable the technology used to control water resources, may have a devastating impact on the victim state but preclude the right to use force in self-defence.[44]

Judge Bruno Simma described the threshold for an armed attack as one that is 'considerably high' in his separate opinion in the *Oil Platforms* case before the International Court of Justice in 2003.[45] Yet, in its judgment in that case, the Court did not exclude the 'possibility' that the mining of a single military vessel might suffice to 'bring into play' the right of self-defence.[46] This would set the bar for an armed attack quite low.[47] One may assume, however, that to meet the threshold of gravity the vessel would need to be of major military significance, such as a warship.

42 Albrecht Randelzhofer and Georg Nolte, 'Article 51', in Bruno Simma *et al.* (eds.), *The Charter of the United Nations: A Commentary*, 3rd ed. (Vol II) (Oxford University Press 2012) 1401. Yoram Dinstein, *War, Aggression and Self-defence*, 6th ed. (Cambridge University Press 2017) paras 247, 548–53.

43 Nicaragua Merits Judgment (n 3) para 191.

44 Elizabeth Wilmshurst, 'Principles of International Law on the Use of Force by States in Self-Defence', Working Paper ILP WP 05/01 (Chatham House 2005) 6.

45 Oil Platforms Merits Judgment (n 4) Separate Opinion of Judge Simma, para 12.

46 Oil Platforms Merits Judgment (n 4) para 72.

47 Other commentators prefer the term 'flexible', although this scarcely meets the demands of clarity of international legal rules. Olivier Corten, for instance, has stated that 'by not excluding the possibility that the mining of a single military vessel could be sufficient to trigger the right of self-defence, the Court made a very important statement confirming the great flexibility of the "gravity" criteria'. Olivier Corten, 'Judge Simma's Separate Opinion in the Oil Platforms Case: To What Extent are Armed 'Proportionate Defensive Measures' Admissible in Contemporary International Law', in Ulrich Fastenrath *et al.* (eds.), *From Bilateralism to Community Interest* (Oxford University Press 2011) 852. Likewise, Tom Ruys has claimed that 'the de minimis threshold should be interpreted flexibly'. Tom Ruys, *'Armed Attack' and Article 51 of the UN Charter: Evolutions in Customary Law and Practice* (Oxford University Press 2010) 143.

Indeed, correctly identifying at what point a use of force becomes an armed attack is an elusive ambition. A 'mere frontier incident' will not amount to an armed attack in the holding of the International Court of Justice in the *Nicaragua* judgment.[48] But otherwise examples of what do or do not amount to an armed attack are more forthcoming than are general indicia. Overflight of missiles across the territory of a neutral State is assuredly not an armed attack on that State.[49] Even attacks, bombardments, and the use of weapons may not in every case reach the intensity of an armed attack, in the view of Randelzhofer and Nolte. This is questionable, not least because the evidence they adduce to support this – paragraph 51 of the judgment in the *Oil Platforms* case – scarcely endorses the specifics of the claim.[50]

A cyberattack by one State on the military personnel and/or infrastructure of another may certainly amount to an armed attack on the State that has been targeted. In particular, a cyber operation that kills or seriously injures members of the armed forces, including naval forces, or destroys which or damages military objectives will assuredly be a use of force and potentially also an armed attack. This is not necessarily the case, however. Thus, the International Group of Experts that elaborated the second edition of the Tallinn Manual could not agree as to whether the 2010 Stuxnet operation that damaged hundreds of centrifuges at the Natanz nuclear facility in Iran amounted to an armed attack, although there was consensus among the members of the Group that it was a use of force.[51]

Where a cyberattack effectively disables military defenses, laying the target State open to kinetic attack without the opportunity to defend itself, the attack may similarly meet the requisite threshold.[52] But there must be certainty as to the author of the attack: mere suspicion of its originator will not suffice. And if the attacker is a non-State actor, the principle of necessity (discussed below) may dictate that other measures short of armed force, including forcible law enforcement operations, be attempted before any resort to armed force against a State deemed to be harboring that non-State actor could be lawful.

The Tallinn Manual avers that a State that provides an 'organized' armed group with malware and the training necessary to carry out operations against another State 'has engaged in a use of force against the latter so long as that

48 Nicaragua Merits Judgment (n 3) para 195.

49 Dinstein (n 42) para 569.

50 Randelzhofer and Nolte (n 42) 1410. Paragraph 51 of the judgment merely recalls the general principles referred to above as to the gravity of a use of force that amounts also to an armed attack.

51 Tallinn Manual 2.0 (n 10) commentary para 10 on Rule 71.

52 Randelzhofer and Nolte (n 42) 1419.

supply and training enabled the group to conduct cyber operations that amount to a use of force'.[53] In contrast, consistent with the holding in the *Nicaragua* case, 'merely funding a hacktivist group conducting cyber operations as part of an insurgency would not be a use of force against the State involved in the armed conflict with the insurgents'.[54] As the Tallinn Manual also affirms, acts of cyber intelligence gathering and cyber theft (even of confidential military data), as well as cyber operations that involve brief or periodic interruptions of non-essential cyber services, do not qualify as armed attacks.[55]

A use of force definitely occurs – and is generally prohibited – where it is perpetrated against the territorial integrity of another State. There is thus no requirement that the target be military in nature for a use of force to occur. The same applies to an armed attack. The question arises, however, as to whether the threshold of violence is higher in the case of civilian personnel or infrastructure in each case than it is with respect to military personnel or infrastructure. The answer would appear to be yes. According to the Tallinn Manual, a nexus between a given cyber operation and military operations 'heightens the likelihood of characterization as a use of force'.[56]

As discussed above, the mining of a single military vessel could potentially be classified as an armed attack in the view of the International Court of Justice in the *Oil Platforms* case.[57] There was no suggestion that the mining of a single merchant ship would similarly be considered an armed attack (always assuming the requisite intent and certainty as to the author of the action). That said, as Kreß has observed, the Court did not exclude the possibility that an intentional attack against a merchant vessel could amount to an armed attack.[58] One may instinctively, however, consider it far less likely. Nonetheless, Indian military strategists have suggested that an adversary could seek to disrupt

53 Tallinn Manual 2.0 (n 10) commentary para 4 on Rule 69. It is not clear why the International Group of Experts believed that the armed group must be 'organized' as this is a criterion related to *jus in bello* and not *jus ad bellum*. The Manual also does not clarify whether the International Group of Experts would require that the armed group actually go on to engage in a use of the malware for a use of force to occur.

54 Tallinn Manual 2.0 (n 10) commentary para 3 on Rule 69.

55 Ibid, commentary para 8 on Rule 71.

56 See, e.g., ibid, commentary para 9(f) on Rule 69.

57 Oil Platforms Merits Judgment (n 4) para 72.

58 Claus Kreß, 'The International Court of Justice and the "Principle of Non-Use of Force"', in Marc Weller (ed.), *The Oxford Handbook of the Use of Force in International Law* (Oxford University Press 2015) 582–83. See further on this issue Alexander Lott and Shin Kawagishi, 'The Legal Regime of the Strait of Hormuz and Attacks Against Oil Tankers: Law of the Sea and Law on the Use of Force Perspectives' (2022) 53(2–3) Ocean Development and International Law 123.

India's strategic crude oil imports by using a terrorist group to lay sea mines in maritime chokepoints like the Strait of Hormuz or Bab el-Mandeb, through which much of India's oil imports transit. The explosion of a single mine would be sufficient to disrupt shipping through the choke-point due to fear among shippers,[59] thereby potentially gaining a significant military benefit. The targeting of merchant vessels in the Red Sea by Houthi forces in late 2023 and early 2024 demonstrated the threat to global trade that hybrid warfare could engender. A tanker with links to the United Kingdom was on fire for several hours in the Gulf of Aden after being hit by a missile fired by Houthis. The targeting of MV *Marlin Luanda* on 26 January 2024 was said to be in response to 'American-British aggression'. The vessel's nominated operator is Oceonix Services Ltd, a UK-registered company.[60]

Also contentious, but more widely accepted, is the postulate that an accumulation of lesser acts of violence may, under certain circumstances, amount to an armed attack.[61] As Dinstein has observed, in its judgments on the merits in both the *Nicaragua* and *Oil Platforms* cases, the International Court of Justice opened the door to such a possibility.[62] But this issue is far from uncontroversial. Moreover, the circumstances in which small-scale attacks would be aggregated so as to constitute an armed attack appear to be limited and heavily circumscribed.[63] The Tallinn Manual suggests that a series of cyber incidents that individually fall below the threshold of an armed attack form a composite armed attack when it is the same originator (or originators acting in concert) and when aggregated the incidents meet the requisite 'scale and effects'.[64] But this does little to elucidate the circumstances under which a 'composite' armed attack has occurred.

An adversary could use a non-State armed group to target offshore oil-platforms using bomb-laden fast boats. Identifying such a threat amid a

59 Capt. (Dr) Gurpreet S Khurana, 'Maritime Dimension of Hybrid Warfare – The Indian Context', National Maritime Foundation (28 December 2017), available at <https://bit.ly/42eVJfx> accessed 1 May 2023.

60 James Gregory, 'Houthis attack British-linked tanker Marlin Luanda in Gulf of Aden' BBC (28 January 2024) available at <https://bit.ly/3SCajMr>, accessed 29 January 2024.

61 See, e.g., Tom Ruys, *'Armed Attack' and Article 51 of the UN Charter: Evolutions in Customary Law and Practice* (Cambridge University Press 2010) 174.

62 Nicaragua Merits Judgment (n 3) para 231; Oil Platforms Merits Judgment (n 4) paras 62–64. In the *Armed Activities on the Territory of the Congo* case the Court referred to a 'series of deplorable attacks' that 'could be regarded as cumulative in character'. Congo Judgment (n 29) para. 146. See also Dinstein (n 42) para 554; and Randelzhofer and Nolte (n 42) 1409 and sources cited in note 74.

63 Oil Platforms Merits Judgment (n 4) paras 122–123.

64 Tallinn Manual 2.0 (n 10) commentary para 11 on Rule 71.

dense shipping and fishing environment has always been a major challenge. Impeding maritime domain awareness through cyberattacks against coastal surveillance measures and command, control, communications and intelligence networks could precede kinetic military action. Such disruption could also precede a strike from the sea against critical littoral infrastructure, such as nuclear installations. Coastal infrastructure and assets are also susceptible to hybrid threats in the form of clandestine underwater attacks by irregular personnel trained in diving operations. Achieving even limited sub-surface maritime domain awareness is extremely challenging. Advances in underwater technology – including employing robotics – compound the threat.[65]

The war in Ukraine has had significant impacts on continental and global food security. Ukraine has traditionally been one of the world's biggest exporters of corn, wheat, and sunflower oil, flows of which largely stalled with the ports unable to be used.[66] In a debate in the UN Security Council in May 2022, the then Executive Director of the World Food Programme, David Beasley, stated: 'Failure to open those ports … will be *a declaration of war* on global food security … And it will result in famine and destabilization and mass migration around the world.'[67] Rhetoric aside, however, even where the impacts are not the indirect result of the armed conflict but a deliberate action on the part of either belligerent, this does not amount to a use of force by the party responsible against the States that are led to pay significantly higher prices for basic commodities.

But while purely economic impacts, irrespective of their severity, do not constitute a use of force, this is not the case with respect to the apparent attack

65 Khurana (n 59). Another hybrid scenario could be the deliberate disruption of the Global Undersea Communication Cable Infrastructure (GUCCI), which runs across the Indian Ocean. In December 2008, multiple accidental cable cuts in the Mediterranean Sea and the Persian Gulf resulted in widespread loss of internet connectivity across the Middle East and South Asia. India lost 50 to 60 per cent of online connectivity while Egypt lost 70 per cent.

66 Megan Durisin, Pratik Parija, and Irina Anghel, 'The $120 Billion Global Grain Trade Is Being Redrawn by Russia's War in Ukraine' Bloomberg UK (5 April 2022), available at <https://bloom.bg/3Q8ETc1> accessed 1 May 2023. Moldova obtains about 90 per cent of its grain from Ukraine. Mark A Green, 'Forty Percent of the World Food Program's Wheat Supplies Come from Ukraine' Wilson Center (2 June 2022), available at <https://bit.ly/3xh4mth> accessed 1 May 2023.

67 Briefing by David Beasley, Executive Director of the United Nations World Food Programme, on conflict and food security, UN Security Council, New York, 19 May 2022, available at <https://bit.ly/3Qgt2sl> accessed 1 May 2023.

on the Nord Stream pipelines that pass from Russia to Germany.[68] Under the UN Convention on the Law of Sea, the high seas 'shall be reserved for peaceful purposes'.[69] Given the international ownership of the pipelines,[70] their willful destruction[71] would violate the prohibition on inter-State use of force, but would not amount to an armed attack. That some of the shareholders of Nord Stream 2 AG were private companies does not alter the fact that the action was targeted against States and that the use of force was 'inconsistent with the principles of international law embodied in the Charter of the United Nations',[72] namely the peaceful settlement of disputes.[73]

At the time of writing, however, responsibility for the detonation of the pipeline had not been firmly established but intelligence from the United States indicated that it had been perpetrated by a pro-Ukrainian non-State armed group.[74] If, as that intelligence suggested, this conduct was not at the behest or

68 The Nord Stream 2 pipelines run for 1,230 kilometers from Russia through the Baltic Sea to Germany and had been due to carry billions of cubic feet of gas to Europe until Russia invaded Ukraine and Germany refused to grant the pipeline's operators a license, leaving it mothballed. Nord Stream 1 follows a similar but not identical route from Russia to Germany and had been used to ship Russian gas to Europe since 2011, until the outbreak of the Ukraine war. On 26 and 27 September 2022, there were ruptures to the two Nord Stream pipelines. Bubbles emerged on the surface of a section of the Baltic Sea between Sweden and Poland, some 23 kilometers south-east of Denmark's Bornholm Island. It was reported that pressure in the Nord Stream 2 pipeline had dropped over the course of the night of 26 September from 105 bars to 7 bars, clearly indicating a leak. Seismologists registered the equivalent of an earthquake magnitude of 1.8, triangulated to have occurred at almost exactly the same spot as the leak was bubbling to the surface.

69 Art 88, LOSC.

70 Nord Stream, 'Our Shareholders', available at <https://bit.ly/3MlihGq> accessed 12 May 2023. The State of incorporation of the Nord Stream company is Switzerland. Others suggest that it is the location of the explosions – international waters – that is key, but that is not persuasive.

71 On 28 September 2022, the Danish Minister of Defence Morten Bodskov said: 'Our assessment is ... that the breakage on the pipes is not an accident but a deliberate act.' Philip Whiteside, '"Sabotage": What we know about the Nord Stream gas leaks and who was behind them' Sky News (29 September 2022), available at <https://bit.ly/3SoKo9L> accessed 1 May 2023.

72 LOSC, Art 301.

73 UN Charter, Art 2(3).

74 Adam Entous, Julian E Barnes, and Adam Goldman, 'Intelligence Suggests Pro-Ukrainian Group Sabotaged Pipelines, U.S. Officials Say' The New York Times (7 March 2023), available at <https://www.nytimes.com/2023/03/07/us/politics/nord-stream-pipeline-sabotage-ukraine.html> accessed 1 May 2023. This was not, however, the view of the Swedish investigators. Philip Oltermann, 'State actor still main suspect behind Nord Stream sabotage, says investigator' The Guardian (6 April 2023), available at <https://bit.ly/3oYb1qL> accessed 1 May 2023.

with the prior knowledge of the Ukrainian authorities, this would mean it did not formally breach Article 2(4). Subsequently, it was revealed that the United States (hereinafter US) Central Intelligence Agency had warned Ukraine in 2022 not to blow up the pipeline following intelligence received from the Netherlands.[75] Other sources still pointed to Russia as the perpetrator.[76]

2.2 *Who May Perpetrate an Armed Attack?*

As noted above, it is unquestionably the case that an armed attack may be perpetrated against a State by an armed group that is sent to do its bidding by a foreign State. It is also accepted that where a State has effective control of a non-State armed group, the actions of the group will engage the responsibility of the controlling State. But the International Court of Justice has affirmed and reaffirmed the exacting nature of that customary law standard. The State must direct or enforce the perpetration of the salient acts, and this requirement pertains to each military (or other) operation.[77] In short, a State may advocate that an armed group 'create mayhem' against a specific State; it may even direct that this mayhem should take place in the maritime environment; and it may equip, fund, and train the group for that purpose, but without engaging its responsibility for the particular operations subsequently undertaken by that group, in the absence of specific direction or instruction. This allows considerable leeway for hybrid warfare to be wrought with plausible deniability and a considerable degree of impunity, since a forcible response by the victim State may be unlawful.[78]

With the bar set high for the right to exercise self-defence against the actions of an armed group based extraterritorially that engages in military operations against a State, a number of leading military powers have sought to bypass the apparent dictates of international law since the 9/11 attacks against the United States. Al-Qaeda was not operating under the direction or instruction of Afghanistan and its Taliban government when it launched the attacks on

75 Bruno Waterfield, 'CIA warned Ukraine not to blow up Nord Stream after Dutch tip-off' The Times (13 June 2023), available at <https://www.thetimes.co.uk/article/cia-warned-ukraine-not-to-blow-up-nord-stream-after-dutch-tip-off-378orl792> accessed 13 June 2023.

76 Gordon Corera, 'Nord Stream: Report puts Russian navy ships near pipeline blast site' BBC (3 May 2023), available at <https://bit.ly/3BfcewH> accessed 1 May 2023.

77 Nicaragua Merits Judgment (n 3) para 115; Genocide Case (n 39) paras 401, 402.

78 There may still be a violation of international law by the State that supports the non-State armed group – indeed, the International Court of Justice has held that it amounts to an unlawful threat or even use of force – but it will not give rise to the right of self-defence against the supporting State. Nicaragua Merits Judgment (n 3) para 195.

11 September 2001. A preambular paragraph in UN Security Council Resolutions 1368 and 1373 is taken by some to indicate a change in the law, allowing self-defence to an armed attack perpetrated by a non-State armed group without direction from a State.[79] But since then, the International Court of Justice has effectively rejected the notion that a non-State armed group operating on its own initiative may conduct an armed attack in the sense of Article 51 of the UN Charter.[80] This has led, according to Christian Tams, to a situation where States have been 'pressured' into admitting other, non-written, exceptions to Article 2(4) of the UN Charter.[81] Of course, this would imply that when certain States cannot do what they want to do legally, they must be permitted either to change the rules or simply to ignore them. It was always open to the United States to secure due authorization to use force against al-Qaeda in Afghanistan from the Security Council.

2.3 *When May Forcible Action in Self-Defence Begin?*

Also controversial is the point at which forcible action in self-defence may begin. Excluded is the notion of 'preventive' self-defence[82] at which vague speculation as to the possibility of an armed attack occurring at some unspecified time in the future would justify premature military action. The notion was proposed to coat the unlawful invasion of Iraq in 2003 with a veneer of legal respectability, but it failed to do so and is now debunked. Thus, the fact that an

---

79 In Resolution 1373, the Council reaffirmed the inherent right of individual or collective self-defence as recognized by the UN Charter. UN Security Council Resolution 1373 (2001), adopted by unanimous vote in favour on 28 September 2001, fourth preambular para.

80 *Legal Consequences of the Construction of a Wall in the Occupied Palestinian Territory*, Advisory Opinion, ICJ Reports 2004, p. 136, para 139. In his separate opinion to the judgment in 2005 in the *Armed Activities in the Congo* case, Judge Simma acknowledged that the Court's implicit position – and that of general international law – was that only a State could perpetrate an armed attack. Indeed, he called for that position 'urgently to be reconsidered, also by the Court'. Congo Judgment (n 29) Separate Opinion of Judge Simma, para 11. See also Shin Kawagishi, 'Clearing Uncertainties of the Jurisprudence of the ICJ on Self-Defence Against Non-State Actors' (2017) 77 Heidelberg Journal of International Law 27, 27–30.

81 Christian J Tams, 'Light Treatment of a Complex Problem: The Law of Self-Defence in the Wall Case' (2006) 16(5) The European Journal of International Law 963–978, available at <https://bit.ly/40MtTGs> accessed 1 May 2023.

82 For a thoughtful discussion of the legal issues, see Marc Weller, 'The Iraq War – 2003', in Tom Ruys and Olivier Corten (eds.), *The Use of Force in International Law: A Case-Based Approach* (Oxford University Press 2018) 639–61.

'overtly hostile State is capable of launching cyberattacks – even devastating ones – does not entitle a potential victim State to act defensively with force'.[83]

More widely accepted is the notion that an 'anticipatory' use of force in self-defence may occur in relation to an 'imminent' armed attack. The 'prevailing view' still considers Article 51 to exclude any self-defence other than in response to an armed attack that has already begun.[84] In its judgment on the merits in the *Nicaragua* case, the International Court of Justice stated that the exercise of the right to individual self-defence under customary law 'is subject to the State concerned having been the victim of an armed attack'.[85] Nevertheless, a number of commentators have argued for the right to use force in self-defence prior to an armed attack occurring, while the United States considers a 'demonstrated hostile intent' (such intent defined in turn as the threat of imminent use of force against the United States or its armed forces)[86] as sufficient to give rise to its inherent right of self-defence.[87] The Tallinn Manual shares the view that a State 'need not wait idly by as the enemy prepares to attack', affirming that the right to use force in self-defence arises if an armed attack in or through cyber space is imminent.[88] Its view of imminence appears very broad, suggesting that a threat that would manifest itself in two weeks would be sufficient to give instant rise to the right of self-defence.[89]

Ashley Deeks has defined anticipatory self-defence as the use of force in self-defence 'to halt an imminent attack' by either a State or a non-State actor.[90] The notion, she avers, requires a State to be '*virtually certain* about the time, place, author, and fact of the future attack'.[91] Many commentators optimistically rely on the exchange of letters between the American and British foreign ministers following the 1837 *Caroline* incident as evidence for a customary law doctrine of anticipatory self-defence. But as Dinstein has observed, there was nothing 'anticipatory' about the use of force against the *Caroline* steamship, as it had already been used in hostilities against the British. No less significantly, the point in dispute at the time concerned whether force could be used in

83 Tallinn Manual 2.0 (n 10) commentary para 10 on Rule 73.
84 Randelzhofer and Nolte (n 42) 1403.
85 Nicaragua Merits Judgment (n 3) para 195.
86 Judge Advocate General's Legal Center and School, *Operational Law Handbook*, 16th ed., (US Army 2016) 87.
87 Dinstein (n 42) para 580.
88 Tallinn Manual 2.0 (n 10) Rule 73 and related commentary, para 2.
89 Ibid, commentary para 6 on Rule 73.
90 Ashley S Deeks, 'Taming the Doctrine of Pre-Emption', in Weller (n 58) 661, 662.
91 Ibid, 663 [added emphasis].

self-defence on US territory without plunging Great Britain and the United States into war.[92]

Dinstein has argued instead for the notion of 'interceptive' self-defence, where it is certain that the armed attack is underway (even in a preliminary manner).[93] The cause of action must be 'irreversible', he states, if the 'legal Rubicon' is to be duly deemed to have been crossed.[94] Based on modern *jus ad bellum* rules, he would thus have allowed the United States to have destroyed the Japanese Carrier Strike Force while it was *en route* to Hawaii in December 1941, but not before it left port.[95] More debatable still is his claim that the refusal of a warship to withdraw from the territorial seas of a coastal State amounts to an incipient armed attack, which would therefore potentially justify its destruction.[96] While this may amount to a threat of force, this falls far short of the threshold set in this regard in Article 51 and customary law.

2.4 *The Regulation of the Exercise of Self-Defence*

Whenever the right to use force in self-defence exists, it is agreed that the exercise of that right must conform to two general principles: necessity and proportionality. This was affirmed by the International Court of Justice in its judgment on the merits in the *Nicaragua* case[97] and reaffirmed subsequently, including in the corresponding *Oil Platforms* case judgment.[98] Violation of either principle means that the responsible State has violated international law and has not acted in lawful self-defence.

This means that the forcible action taken ostensibly in self-defence must be necessary, and thus that no pacific alternatives reasonably exist to respond to the armed attack. Such alternatives may involve seizing the UN Security Council of the affair or referring a case against the alleged assailant to the International Court of Justice. Proportionality places a ceiling on what forcible action may be taken,[99] limiting it to repelling the military threat or driving an

92 Dinstein (n 42) para 589.
93 Ibid, para 598.
94 Ibid, para 609.
95 Ibid, paras 607, 608.
96 Ibid, para 563.
97 ICJ Nicaragua Merits Judgment (n 3) para 194.
98 Oil Platforms Merits Judgment (n 4) para 51.
99 Christine Gray, *International Law and the Use of Force*, 4th ed. (Oxford University Press 2018) 159.

invader out. Regime change is not a legitimate aim. Purely retaliatory or punitive actions are also unlawful.[100]

In its judgment in the *Oil Platforms* case, the International Court of Justice found that Operation Praying Mantis, a response by the United States to an alleged Iranian armed attack in the maritime environment, would have been disproportionate. In fact, lack of evidence for Iranian responsibility meant that no armed attack was identified, rendering the application of the two principles moot. Nonetheless, the Court made the assessment that the forcible response in self-defence would have been disproportionate on the basis that it involved, *inter alia*, the destruction of two Iranian frigates and a number of other naval vessels and aircraft, all conducted in response to the mining of a single US warship, which had been severely damaged but not sunk, and with the attack occurring without loss of life.[101]

3 The Use of Countermeasures in Response to Maritime Hybrid Warfare

Where force is used against a State, including its maritime forces or in the maritime environment, that contravenes Article 2(4) of the UN Charter and customary international law but which does not amount to an armed attack, alternative responses to a use of force must be applied.[102] Possible responses are non-forcible countermeasures, whether of a military or non-military nature, as well as acts of retorsion and reprisals.

Countermeasures are non-forcible measures taken by one State against another to stop or repair a breach of international law.[103] Ordinarily illegal acts, they are conducted not to punish the commission of a prior internationally wrongful act, but rather with a view to bringing the unlawful conduct to an end and/or in order to secure reparation for its consequences.[104] Countermeasures

---

100 Albrecht Randelzhofer, 'Article 51', in Bruno Simma (ed.), *The Charter of the United Nations: A Commentary*, 2nd ed. (Vol. 1) (Oxford University Press 2002) para 42.

101 Oil Platforms Merits Judgment (n 4) para 77.

102 Oil Platforms Merits Judgment (n 4) Separate Opinion of Judge Simma; and see Terry D Gill, 'The Forcible Protection, Affirmation and Exercise of Rights by States under Contemporary International Law' (1992) 23 Netherlands Yearbook of International Law 105–73.

103 Art 22, ILC Draft Articles on State Responsibility.

104 Commentary to Chapter II (Countermeasures), ILC Draft Articles on State Responsibility, para 1.

are therefore to be distinguished from sanctions on the basis that the latter have a punitive and 'exemplary' character.[105]

Ordinarily, countermeasures (which were generally termed *reprisals* until the late 1970s)[106] would be violative of international law. But when the measures taken are in accord with a set of conditions, they constitute a lawful form of 'self-help'.[107] Indeed, countermeasures are considered 'an important tool for States that are victims of violations of international law'.[108] But as one Indian maritime strategist has observed, responding to hybrid threats at sea is 'not an easy proposition', given that the maritime domain 'is a predominantly international medium'.[109]

Countermeasures must also be distinguished from retorsion, which is 'unfriendly' conduct that does not violate an international obligation binding the State engaging in it, even though the conduct may be a response to an internationally wrongful act.[110] That the measures taken do not contravene international law is the distinguishing feature of acts of retorsion.[111] Other differences with countermeasures are that retorsions are not necessarily temporary or reversible and (arguably) may contain a punitive element.[112] Examples of acts of retorsion are the prohibition of or limitations upon normal diplomatic relations; embargoes of various kinds; and the withdrawal of voluntary aid programs.[113]

---

105 Elisabeth Zoller, *Peacetime Unilateral Remedies: An Analysis of Countermeasures* (Transnational Publishers 1984) 106.

106 Since the International Arbitral decision in 1978 in the *Air Services Agreement* case, the term 'countermeasures' has generally been employed in international law to denote reprisals that do not involve the use of force. See *Air Service Agreement of 27 March 1946 between the United States of America and France*, Arbitral Award, 9 December 1978, *Reports of International Arbitral Awards*, Vol. XVIII, 417–93, esp. paras 80–81; and Malcolm N Shaw, *International Law*, 8th ed. (Cambridge University Press 2017) 601.

107 Crawford (n 9) 572.

108 Caroline Krass, 'Implementing Integrated Deterrence in the Cyber Domain: The Role of Lawyers', Lieber Institute (18 April 2023), available at <https://bit.ly/44nloVa> accessed 1 May 2023.

109 Khurana (n 59).

110 Commentary to Chapter II (Countermeasures), ILC Draft Articles on State Responsibility, para 3.

111 Ibid.

112 Tom Ruys, 'Sanctions, Retorsions and Countermeasures: Concepts and International Legal Framework', in Larissa van den Herik (ed.), *Research Handbook on UN Sanctions and International Law* (Edward Elgar 2017) 19–51.

113 It is uncertain whether an aid programme could be withdrawn if the effects would be to the humanitarian detriment of a population in need. The rules on countermeasures could be taken to suggest that this would not be permissible. See on this issue Paola Gaeta, Jorge

Reprisals used to be considered under international law as a forcible or non-forcible form of self-help. The term is no longer widely employed in this manner. In modern parlance, reprisals (or 'belligerent reprisals', as they often termed) are more generally associated with violent action during and in connection with an ongoing armed conflict. Belligerent reprisals concern acts that would ordinarily be unlawful – they typically amount to war crimes – but which may exceptionally be licit as a proportionate response to a prior and serious violation of international humanitarian law (hereinafter IHL). That is so, when they are conducted *primarily* with a view to returning the enemy to compliance with that body of international law.[114] Belligerent reprisals are prohibited against a wide range of targets according to general international law (in particular, military or civilian detainees) and IHL treaty provisions.

3.1 *The Form and Legality of Countermeasures*

Critical in the exercise of countermeasures is the due assessment of a prior breach of international law.[115] In practice, this is a subjective determination; under international law (and thus before a competent court or tribunal), the assessment is objective. In the *Air Services Agreement* case, the Arbitral Panel held that France was incorrect in determining that the United States had violated their mutual agreement and therefore was unentitled under international law to take countermeasures.[116]

Countermeasures may not involve the threat or use of force in violation of Article 2(4) of the UN Charter.[117] In its judgment on the merits in the *Nicaragua* case in 1986, the International Court of Justice clarified that: 'While an armed attack would give rise to an entitlement to collective self-defence, a use of force of a lesser degree of gravity cannot ... produce any entitlement to

---

E Viñuales, and Salvatore Zappalà, *Cassese's International Law*, 3rd ed. (Oxford University Press 2020) 301.

114 The International Committee of the Red Cross (hereinafter ICRC), in its treatment of reprisals, describes a belligerent reprisal as consisting of 'an action that would otherwise be unlawful but that in exceptional cases is considered lawful under international law when used as an enforcement measure in reaction to unlawful acts of an adversary.' ICRC Customary IHL Rule 145: 'Reprisals', available at <https://bit.ly/2OUWdae> accessed 1 May 2023.

115 Nigel D White and Ademola Abass, 'Countermeasures and Sanctions', in Malcolm D Evans (ed.), *International Law*, 4th ed. (Oxford University Press 2014) 537, 541.

116 *Air Service Agreement of 27 March 1946 between the United States of America and France*, Arbitral Award (9 December 1978), 446–47.

117 Crawford (n 9) 573.

take collective countermeasures involving the use of force'.[118] This categorical position was reflected in 2001 in the International Law Commission's Draft Articles on State Responsibility.[119] Action that falls below a *de minimis* threshold or which is taken for a legitimate law enforcement purpose will not amount to a prohibited use of force.

Four fundamental conditions for the lawful exercise of non-forcible countermeasures were set down by the International Court of Justice in its 1997 judgment in the *Gabčikovo-Nagymaros Project* case:

- The measure(s) must be taken in response to a previous internationally wrongful act of another State;[120]
- The measure(s) must be directed against that State;[121]
- The injured State must have called upon the culpable State to discontinue its wrongful conduct and/or to make reparation for it;[122]
- The effects of a countermeasure must be 'commensurate'[123] with the injury suffered, 'taking account of the rights in question'.[124]

Further conditions were identified by the International Law Commission in its 2001 Draft Articles on State Responsibility:

- The injured State must notify the responsible State of any decision to take countermeasures and offer to negotiate with that State;[125]
- The countermeasures may not breach obligations for the protection of fundamental human rights, obligations of a humanitarian character prohibiting (belligerent) reprisals, or other peremptory rules of international law;[126]

118 Nicaragua Merits Judgment (n 3) para 249. See further on this issue para 211.

119 Art 50(1)(a), ILC Draft Articles on State Responsibility.

120 Gabčikovo-Nagymaros Judgment (n 5) para 83. See similarly Art 49, ILC Draft Articles on State Responsibility.

121 Gabčikovo-Nagymaros Judgment (n 5) para 83.

122 Ibid, para 84.

123 In its judgment in the Nicaragua case, the Court had used the term 'proportionate'. Nicaragua Merits Judgment (n 3) para 249. See similarly Art 51, ILC Draft Articles on State Responsibility.

124 Gabčikovo-Nagymaros Judgment (n 5) para 85. See similarly Art 52, ILC Draft Articles on State Responsibility.

125 Art. 52(1)(b), ILC Draft Articles on State Responsibility. The majority, but not all, of the International Group of Experts who elaborated the second edition of the Tallinn Manual rejected the purported requirement whereby an injured State is to seek negotiations before undertaking countermeasures. Tallinn Manual 2.0 (n 10) commentary para 13 on Rule 21.

126 Art 50(1)(b), (c), and (d), ILC Draft Articles on State Responsibility.

- A State taking countermeasures is not relieved from fulfilling its obligations under any dispute settlement procedure applicable between it and the responsible State;[127]
- A State taking countermeasures must respect the inviolability of diplomatic or consular agents, premises, archives, and documents.[128]

The principle of necessity applies to the exercise of countermeasures. Thus, where the wrongful acts have ceased or the matter is pending before an international court or tribunal, countermeasures must cease (if they have already been implemented) or must not be taken.[129] This indicates that countermeasures should ordinarily be reversible.[130] In general, countermeasures must not breach the rights of third States.[131] Moreover, 'anticipatory' countermeasures are unlawful.[132] That said, an injured State is still entitled to 'take such measures as are necessary to preserve its rights'.[133]

In its judgment in the *Gabčikovo-Nagymaros Project* case, the International Court of Justice held that the unilateral assumption of control over a large amount of the waters of the Danube River by the erstwhile Czechoslovakia was disproportionate to the original offence.[134] Disproportionate measures give rise to the responsibility of the State executing them.[135]

That said, the interpretation of the principle of proportionality in relation to countermeasures is contested. Whereas the International Law Commission (hereinafter ILC) stated that the salient metric is, first and foremost, the 'injury suffered' (and most commentators concord with this position), White and Abass propose that, in order to distinguish effectively a countermeasure from a reprisal, a better approach is to consider its effectiveness in ending the unlawful act or securing due reparation.[136] Although this might be considered to

---

127 Ibid, Art 50(2)(a). It is generally – but not universally – agreed that where States have undertaken to submit a dispute to a compulsory settlement mechanism, countermeasures are not permissible until such time as the settlement mechanism has been activated. Gaeta, Viñuales, and Zappalà (n 113) 299.

128 Art 50(2)(b), ILC Draft Articles on State Responsibility.

129 Ibid, Art 53.

130 Ibid, Art 49(2) and (3); Gabčikovo-Nagymaros Judgment (n 5) para 87.

131 Gaeta, Viñuales, and Zappalà (n 113) 301.

132 Omer Y Elagab, *The Legality of Non-Forcible Counter-Measures in International Law* (Clarendon Press 1988) 63.

133 Shaw (n 106) 603.

134 Gabčikovo-Nagymaros Judgment (n 5) paras 85–87.

135 James Crawford, *The International Law Commission's Articles on State Responsibility* (Cambridge University Press 2002), 294.

136 White and Abass (n 115) 546. They receive some support in this from Gaeta *et al.* Although the latter aver that a countermeasure must not be 'grossly disproportionate in gravity

confuse necessity with proportionality, their approach is cumulatively persuasive[137] and it chimes well with the conception of proportionality *ad bellum* in the exercise of the right of self-defence. In any event, there is no stipulation in general international law that the countermeasures that are taken must concern the same obligation breached by the State that has acted wrongfully.[138]

Whether any State is entitled to take countermeasures in respect of the breach of an obligation *erga omnes* – that is to say, a peremptory norm of international law – is not settled. In the words of James Crawford, the Special Rapporteur of the ILC for the issue, the Draft Articles on State Responsibility left the matter open following 'strong reactions from many States'.[139] White and Abass find that the State and institutional practice to support an entitlement is 'inconsistent, making the drawing of any conclusions as to *opinio juris* extremely difficult, if not impossible'.[140] Nevertheless, as they observe,[141] there are a number of clear instances of relevant State practice, and ultimately they conclude such unilateral action is a 'probable' exception to a general prohibition of countermeasures, outside the realm of those endorsed by the ILC and the International Court of Justice.[142]

Notable instances of countermeasures to promote respect for *erga omnes* obligations include the suspension by the United States of treaty landing rights for South African Airways in 1986 in response to *apartheid*. In 1987, a panel of judges on the federal Court of Appeals for the District of Columbia upheld the revocation of landing rights for South African Airways pursuant to the Comprehensive Anti-Apartheid Act passed by Congress in 1986. The Court held that Congress had the authority to immediately revoke the permit and that it had intended to do so, despite the agreement between the United States and South African Airways requiring a one-year termination notice.[143] In 1998, the European Union imposed a flight ban and froze Yugoslav assets within the jurisdiction of Member States in response to the perpetration of serious violations of

and magnitude" to the wrongdoing, later in the same chapter they state that "in current international law the purpose of countermeasures must rather be seen in impelling the offender to discontinue its wrongful conduct or to make reparation for it'. Gaeta, Viñuales, and Zappalà (n 113) 302.

137 Tallinn Manual 2.0 (n 10) commentary para 4 on Rule 23.

138 Shaw (n 106) 602.

139 Crawford (n 9) 575.

140 White and Abass (n 115) 547.

141 Ibid, 548.

142 Ibid, 559.

143 US Court of Appeals for the District of Columbia, *South African Airways* v. *Elizabeth H. Dole, Secretary, U.S. Department of Transportation*, 817 F.2d 119, Judgment (24 April 1987).

international human rights law in Kosovo.[144] For a number of States, including France, Germany, and the United Kingdom, this involved a violation of their bilateral aviation agreements with the Federal Republic of Yugoslavia.[145]

3.2 *Available Countermeasures*

As noted above, under contemporary international law, countermeasures must not be forcible in nature.[146] Thus, even a naval blockade where no shot is fired is prohibited as a lawful countermeasure.[147] That they must not infringe the prohibition on inter-State use of force does not, however, mean that countermeasures may not be military in nature. Unilateral termination of a bilateral military cooperation agreement – without adequate justification under that agreement, and where the hybrid threat did not itself contravene the agreement – might be just such a countermeasure.

To date, however, most countermeasures taken under international law concern non-military measures. Thus, for instance, in the context of its *High-Fructose Corn Syrup* dispute with the United States, Mexico took countermeasures for the US breach of an obligation under the North American Free Trade Agreement (hereinafter NAFTA). An Appellate Body of the World Trade Organization (hereinafter WTO) found that the measures taken by Mexico did not conform to international law.[148] This was so, even though the effective blocking by the United States of the constitution of a NAFTA Commission – by refusing to appoint its national panel member – had 'arguably' entitled Mexico to take countermeasures under general international law.[149]

Laws and action on terrorist financing since the end of the last millennium have given the State significant powers (and duties) under international law

144 Common Position of 29 June 1998, defined by the Council on the basis of Article J.2 of the Treaty on European Union concerning a ban on flights by Yugoslav carriers between the Federal Republic of Yugoslavia and the European Community, EU doc. 98/426/CFSP, available at <https://bit.ly/3Cwl4rG> accessed 1 May 2023.

145 Elena K Proukaki, *The Problem of Enforcement in International Law: Countermeasures, the Non-Injured State and the Idea of International Community* (Routledge 2009) 192.

146 Certain members of the International Group of Experts (a minority) believed that forcible countermeasures would be lawful as long as they did not amount to an armed attack. Tallinn Manual 2.0 (n 10) commentary para 12 on Rule 22. It is extremely hard to reconcile this claim with the overwhelming majority of legal and judicial opinion.

147 Alexander Orakhelashvili, *Akehurst's Modern Introduction to International Law*, 8th ed. (Routledge 2019) 296.

148 WTO, 'DS132: Mexico – Anti-Dumping Investigation of High-Fructose Corn Syrup (HFCS) from the United States', WTO doc. WT/DS132/13 (26 November 2001).

149 Crawford (n 9) 574.

to interdict suspect transfers of funds.[150] These laws may typically be applied to prevent unauthorized non-State actors from accessing funds provided from another State for unlawful purposes. The freezing of that donor State's assets held in-country may be a lawful act of retorsion or a possible countermeasure.

Monitoring of communications with individuals and associates of non-State actors in a democratic State clearly has domestic and international human rights law implications. Again, where it is reasonably suspected that the communication may concern organized criminal activities or possible terrorist offences, the intelligence services are likely to be given a margin of discretion in interfering with the exercise of those rights.

In the discussion of countermeasures in the context of the Tallinn Manual, the experts were divided as to whether the right to privacy is to be considered as a fundamental human right and therefore excluded from a possible cyber countermeasure where the measure would ordinarily be to violate the right.[151] In the 1948 Universal Declaration of Human Rights, it was stipulated that 'No one shall be subjected to arbitrary interference with his privacy, family, home or correspondence, nor to attacks upon his honor and reputation.'[152] Despite the clear position of the institutions of the European Union and the European Court of Human Rights, the Manual argues that the right to privacy is not *per se* a fundamental human right under general international law.[153] Its exercise may be subject to constraints under domestic law, at least to the extent that these are not arbitrary in nature.[154] Further under the 1966 International Covenant on Civil and Political Rights, it is possible to derogate from full observance

150 International Convention for the Suppression of the Financing of Terrorism (adopted 9 December 1999, entered into force 10 April 2002), 2178 UNTS 197.

151 Tallinn Manual 2.0 (n 10) commentary para 4 on Rule 22.

152 Art 12, Universal Declaration of Human Rights (adopted 10 December 1948).

153 The Court of Justice of the European Union (hereinafter CJEU) has overtly termed the right to privacy as 'fundamental'. CJEU, Case C-73/07, Judgment of 16 December 2008 (Grand Chamber), EU:C:2008:727, paras 54 and 56. Furthermore, and more specifically, the European Court of Human Rights, in citing this judgment, has held that the protection of personal data is of fundamental importance to the enjoyment of the right to respect for private and family life as guaranteed by Article 8 of the European Convention on Human Rights. European Court of Human Rights, *Satakunnan Markkinapörssi Oy and Satamedia Oy v Finland* [GC], Judgment of 27 June 2017, paras 137 and 158. See also Arts 7 and 8(1) and (2), Charter of Fundamental Rights of the European Union (proclaimed 18 December 2000, entered into force 1 December 2009).

154 Art 17(1), International Covenant on Civil and Political Rights (adopted 16 December 1966, entered into force 23 March 1976) 999 UNTS 171.

of the right in 'time of public emergency which threatens the life of the nation and the existence of which is officially proclaimed'.[155]

Where a cyberattack is directed against military infrastructure or personnel but does not constitute an armed attack (whether distinctly or as a composite attack), as the Tallinn Manual affirms, a State is likely to be entitled to take countermeasures.[156] This includes hybrid action on the high seas where the offensive action against one State by an ostensibly non-State armed group is directed by another State. Countermeasures are not, though, available in response to a cyber operation conducted by a non-State actor unless, under applicable international law, the operation is attributable, in some form, to a State.[157] The countermeasure taken in response to a cyberattack may itself be cyber in nature, but it does not need to be. This is so, whenever it is conducted in response to a breach of an international legal obligation that it is owed by another State. It also does not need to target State organs, including the Ministry of Defense or the armed forces, or State cyber infrastructure, although a State must be the 'object' of the countermeasure.[158]

If the victim of a cyberattack is a private company, the right to take countermeasures vests in the relevant injured State or States. Thus, when Sony was the victim of malicious cyber operations in 2014 that were allegedly conducted by, or attributable to, North Korea, Sony was not entitled under international law to 'hack back' as a countermeasure. Instead, the right was reserved to the United States, to the extent that the cyberattack could be considered a violation of its sovereignty.[159]

Speaking in May 2022, the then United Kingdom Attorney-General set out United Kingdom policy on cyberattacks, declaring that covert cyber operations by a foreign State which 'coercively restrict or prevent the provision of essential medical services or essential energy supplies would breach the rule on non-intervention'. With respect to energy supply, she stated that prohibited cyber operations would encompass 'causing the energy supply chain to stop functioning at national level through damage or prevention of access to pipelines, interchanges, and depots; or preventing the operation of power generation infrastructure'.[160] The United Kingdom has made it clear that

155 Ibid, Art 4(1) and (2).

156 Tallinn Manual 2.0 (n 10) Rule 20.

157 Ibid, commentary para 7 on Rule 20.

158 Ibid, commentary para 6 on Rule 20.

159 Ibid, commentary paras 2 and 3 on Rule 24.

160 'International Law in Future Frontiers', Speech by the UK Attorney General, Suella Braverman, Chatham House, London (19 May 2022), available at <https://bit.ly/3KKoG8P> accessed 1 May 2023.

countermeasures are available in response to unlawful cyber operations by another State. The then Attorney-General reiterated in May 2022 that it is 'also clear that countermeasures need not be of the same character as the threat and could involve non-cyber means, where it is the right option in order to bring unlawful behavior in cyberspace to an end'.[161] She did not delineate what the countermeasures envisaged by the United Kingdom might be.

If a warship's passage through the territorial seas of a State is not, or is no longer, innocent (for instance, because it is engaged in espionage against the coastal State), countermeasures may be available. Schmitt suggests that a possible response could be to take the countermeasure of closing its territorial sea to all ships flagged in the offending State until the warship desists.[162] But given the ease of reflagging, a better approach, as proposed by Thévenin, would be to close the territorial sea also to ships registered in the foreign State or which are owned by a natural or legal person in that foreign State.[163] Other possible measures could be for the injured coastal State to deny landing rights provided for in a bilateral agreement to aircraft registered in the responsible State. It could conduct also cyber operations against private entities in the responsible State that would otherwise violate the responsible State's sovereignty.[164]

Finally, as the Tallinn Manual has observed, when a cyber operation is only one in 'a series' of ongoing actions which, according to State responsibility under international law constitute a single internationally wrongful act, countermeasures 'remain available'.[165] It cited in this regard directed denial of service attacks against the US banking system from late 2012 to early 2013, which was allegedly the work of Iranian operatives.

Conclusion

When a State is the victim of an armed attack in the maritime environment, the right to use force in self-defence in response to hybrid warfare will be available, at the least where the armed attack is attributable to a State under the rules governing State responsibility. If the sovereign decision is made to

161 Ibid.

162 Michael N Schmitt, 'Responding to Malicious or Hostile Actions under International Law', Lieber Institute White Paper (26 April 2022), available at <https://bit.ly/3qbjTqA> accessed 1 May 2023.

163 Email from Pierre Thévenin, University of Tartu, Estonia, 4 October 2022. As he notes, however, there would be an issue of proportionality to consider.

164 Schmitt (n 162).

165 Tallinn Manual 2.0 (n 10) commentary para 7 on Rule 21.

exercise that right, a range of forcible options will be lawful, subject of course to full compliance with the principles of necessity and proportionality. There is no requirement that the defensive force be used on the high seas: an attack on land or against aircraft may also be permissible. But if the International Court of Justice is correct, the targets of those attacks must be lawful military objectives under the law of armed conflict.[166] Thus, if it were the case that an intentional attack against a merchant vessel flagged to the victim State amounted to an armed attack (or were one of the cumulative incidents that amounted to an armed attack), the forcible response in self-defence could not target a merchant vessel flagged to the aggressor State (unless it were a legitimate military objective under the rules established for this purpose by the law of armed conflict).[167] Nor, ordinarily, could it lawfully target civilian objects on land or civilian aircraft.[168]

But given the relatively high threshold for an armed attack under *jus ad bellum* and the need for unequivocal attribution of responsibility to a State, in many instances there will be no right to use force in self-defence. This is as relevant to the maritime environment as it is in other domains. Non-forcible countermeasures will therefore be one of a range of possible responses to hybrid warfare along with ordinary law enforcement. The broad range of practical options that countermeasures offer – which are not limited to the maritime environment – makes them superficially attractive to a victim State. That said, strict adherence to the conditions for their exercise, as set down in the ILC's Draft Articles on State Responsibility, is critical. Otherwise, the State taking countermeasures will itself breach international law. Naturally, beyond the confines of the law, the political, military, and economic consequences and ramifications of countermeasures must always be considered.

166 Oil Platforms Merits Judgment (n 4) para 51.

167 See on this issue Steven Haines, 'Naval Warfare', in Stuart Casey-Maslen with Steven Haines, *Hague Law Interpreted: The Conduct of Hostilities under the Law of Armed Conflict* (Hart 2018) 302–303.

168 The exception would be where the vessels, aircrafts, or objects in question were deemed, by their future purpose, to make an effective contribution to military action and whose total or partial destruction, capture, or neutralization, in the circumstances ruling at the time, offered a definite military advantage. Art 52(2), Protocol Additional to the Geneva Conventions of 12 August 1949, and Relating to the Protection of Victims of International Armed Conflicts (Protocol I) (adopted 8 June 1977, entered into force 7 December 1978), 1125 UNTS 3.

CHAPTER 3

The Concept of Military Activities in the Law of the Sea and Its Implications for the Baltic Sea in a Context of Growing Threats of Hybrid Warfare

Pierre Thévenin

Introduction

Hybrid naval warfare can be defined as the activities involving the use of force located in the interstice of the concepts of law enforcement and military activities.[1] As Alexander Lott underlined, hybrid warfare thrives on the grey area between these two legal regimes.[2] In other words, hybrid naval warfare differs from both military and law enforcement activities insofar as it is characterized by its ambiguity and impermanence.

The ambiguity making hybrid naval challenging for States to handle stems from the fact that the United Nations Convention on the Law of the Sea (hereinafter LOSC) does not clearly define law-enforcement activities and military activities.[3] In addition, as exemplified by the Dispute Concerning the Detention of Ukrainian Naval Vessels and Servicemen,[4] practically speaking, the line between military activities and law enforcement operations is difficult to discern, especially when two warships are involved. In this case, the arbitral tribunal admitted the theoretical possibility for military activities to turn into law enforcement operations and vice versa.[5] The tribunal has so far recognized that confrontation between warships constitutes a military activity. However, it is yet to determine whether the boarding and arrest of Ukrainian vessels and their crew after they did not obey orders to stop amounts to a military activity

1 Alexander Lott, *Hybrid Threats and the Law of the Sea: Use of Force and Discriminatory Navigational Restrictions in Straits* (Brill Nijhoff 2022) 17.

2 Ibid, 28.

3 United Nations Convention on the Law of the Sea (opened for signature 10 December 1982, entered into force 16 November 1994) 1833 UNTS 3.

4 Annex VII Arbitral Tribunal, Dispute Concerning the Detention of Ukrainian Naval Vessels and Servicemen (Ukraine v. the Russian Federation), Case No. 2019–28.

5 Ibid, Award on Preliminary Objections of 27 June 2022, para 121.

 | DOI:10.1163/9789004707993_005

or a law enforcement operation.[6] The arbiters' caution aptly illustrates the grey areas existing between the two concepts of law enforcement and military activities.

Yet, once a determination is made regarding which framework to apply to a particular situation, hybrid naval warfare ceases to exist. Activities become governed either by the law-enforcement or military activities legal regime. In that sense, hybrid naval warfare is an ephemeral concept that does not have a legal substance of its own. Rather, it is a tool used to describe problematic activities until a legal determination can be made.

Therefore, in light of these ontological considerations, it stands to reason that clarifying the limits of the concepts of law-enforcement and military activities would help States face hybrid naval warfare activities, for it would provide them with tools to determine whether those activities are by nature military or require a law-enforcement response. This communication aims to humbly contribute to clarifying the notion of military activities in the LOSC, which remains somewhat challenging to grasp at first glance despite being widely used.

The first part of this communication briefly explains why warships are the only vessels to be able to conduct military activities at sea in peacetime before analyzing the scope and limitations of military activities in the territorial sea. The second and third parts examine the scope and limitations of military activities on the high seas and in the Exclusive Economic Zone (hereinafter EEZ), respectively. In each of these three parts, an attempt is made to analyze which military activities can be legally conducted in each of these zones. Also, the two remaining grey zones on which hybrid warfare thrives are identified. To finish, the concluding part of this communication suggests the promotion of voluntary guidelines on navigation and overflight in the Baltic Sea to clarify the concept of military activities in the region and thus reduce the number of divergent understandings of the law.

1 Monopoly of Warships on Military Activities and Their Scope and Limitations in the Territorial Sea

The first section analyses the monopoly of States on military activities at sea. This monopoly prevents or at the least significantly curtails the possibility of private military companies to lawfully conduct similar activities at sea in

6 Ibid, para 123 read in conjunction with paras 118–119.

peacetime. The second section examines the interdiction of foreign military activities in the territorial sea, while the third examines how to determine whether the actions taken by a coastal State against a warship in breach of the regime of innocent passage constitute law enforcement operations or military activities.

1.1 *Warships' Monopoly on Military Activities*

1.1.1 Immunity of Warships and the Impossibility for Private Companies to Conduct Military Activities at Sea

Contemporary international law is built on the premise that States exercise a monopoly on the use of force and violence. In humanitarian law, this monopoly is confirmed by the fact that civilians lose the protections recognized to them when they directly participate in hostilities.[7] In the law of the sea, this monopoly is enshrined in the immunities granted to warships and other government ships used for non-commercial purposes in articles 32, 95, 96 and 236 of the LOSC.[8] The fact that military activities can be exempted from the scope of compulsory dispute settlement mechanisms, should a State make a declaration to this effect, is a consequence of these immunities.[9] Moreover, a vessel should satisfy the criteria enumerated in Article 29 of the LOSC to be considered a warship. Among other things, the ship should belong to the armed forces of the State whose flag it flies; it should be placed under the command

7 Nils Melzer, *Interpretative Guidance on the Notion of Direct Participation in Hostilities under International Humanitarian Law* (ICRC 2009) 12, 20–22; Civilians are entitled to the same protections as members of the armed forces in the limited instance where *levée en masse* applies: see: ibid, 25.

8 LOSC, Articles 32, 95, 96, 236; The immunity granted to warships and other government ships on the high seas also applies in the EEZ. See: LOSC, Article 58(2) read in conjunction with Articles 95 and 96.

9 Ibid, Article 298(1)(b). Article 298(1)(b) read in conjunction with Article 297(2) and (3) allows States to exclude from the jurisdiction of the International Court of Justice, the International Tribunal for the Law of the Sea, and arbitral tribunals disputes "concerning military activities, including military activities by government vessels and aircraft engaged in non-commercial service, and disputes concerning law enforcement activities in regard to the exercise of sovereign rights or jurisdiction [concerning marine scientific research and fisheries in the exclusive economic zone]. To exclude military activities from the scope of compulsory dispute settlements States must make a declaration to that effect. Twenty-nine States have made such a declaration. See: International Tribunal for the Law of the Sea, 'Declarations made by States Parties under article 298', available at <https://www.itlos.org/en/main/jurisdiction/declarations-of-states-parties/declarations-made-by-states-parties-under-article-298/> accessed 5 October 2023.

of a duly commissioned officer and manned by a crew under regular armed forces discipline.[10]

Consequently, these observations show that only warships and other government ships can conduct military activities. Should a private military company's vessel engage in activities which would be considered military if a warship was conducting them, then it would not be granted the same immunities. In other words, these activities would not be regarded as military.

However, it does not mean that those activities would automatically and necessarily become illegal because a private military company's vessel conducts them. Rather, it does mean that such activities would fall under the scope of the LOSC. Private military company vessels would be bound by coastal States' jurisdiction regarding marine scientific research and marine environment protection in the EEZ,[11] while on the high seas, their activities would be limited by the rules enacted to fight piracy and unlawful acts against vessels established in the LOSC and other relevant instruments.[12] Effectively, these legal regimes would significantly reduce the number of activities private military companies could lawfully conduct at sea.

For instance, should a private military company wish to conduct weapons testing in the EEZ, it would need to comply with the environmental regulations established by coastal States.[13] Furthermore, it is unclear whether those activities can be undertaken under the framework of freedom of navigation recognized to other States in the EEZ.[14] Coastal States could potentially and controversially adopt an extensive interpretation of Part XIII and equate those tests to research activities which fall under the legal regime of marine scientific research and thus require private military companies to obtain their consent, which they could withhold, before their testing.[15]

At the very least, this type of hypothetical situation is likely to trigger the application of Article 59 to decide whether and to what extent the private military company could conduct weapon testing in the EEZ of a foreign State.[16] Depending on the level of interference with the coastal State's capacity to enjoy its sovereign rights, the application may constrain the private military warship

10 LOSC, Article 29.

11 Ibid, Article 56(b)(II) and (III).

12 Ibid, Articles 100 and 101; See: e.g., Convention for the Suppression of Unlawful Acts Against the Safety of Maritime Navigation (adopted on 10 March 1988, entered into force 1 March 1992) 1678 UNTS 201, Article 3(1)(a).

13 LOSC, Article 56(b)(III).

14 Ibid, Article 58 (1).

15 Ibid, Article 246 and in particular (5)(b).

16 Ibid, Article 59.

to comply with coastal State environmental legislation and perhaps obtain its consent prior to the realization of those tests.[17] This reasoning holds especially true if explosives and other noxious substances are being tested, given the fact that besides its exclusive jurisdiction to preserve the marine environment of its EEZ, the coastal State is required to prevent, reduce and control pollution from any source.[18]

Regarding intelligence-gathering operations, the private military company's vessel would be limited to laying cables and conducting surveys outside of a coastal State's territorial sea.[19]

Lastly, should a private military company's vessel conducting training exercises for its personnel and armaments interfere with other users of the sea, it is likely to be inspected on suspicion of piracy, whether in the EEZ or the high seas. Article 110 of the LOSC provides that any warship can visit a ship suspected of piracy as defined by Article 101 of the Convention.[20]

1.1.2 Activities Led by So-called 'Ghost Ships'

Over the past few months, Russian vessels have been accused of spying and attempting to sabotage windfarms and undersea communication cables in the North Sea.[21] It is believed that these ships belong to the Russian State.[22] Provided that this affirmation is true, although these ships are not warships, they enjoy

---

17 See: Satya N Nandan and Shabtai Rosenne (eds.), *United Nations Convention on the Law of the Sea 1982 – A Commentary* (Volume 2, Martinus Nijhoff 1993), 569 para 59(6)(b) [Hereinafter Virginia Commentary vol. 2]; Alexander Proelss, 'Article 59', in Alexander Proelss (ed.), *United Nations Convention on the Law of the Sea: a Commentary* (Nomos, 2017), 463 para 10. Both the Virginia commentaries and Proelss' commentary of the LOSC underline that, given the functional nature of the EEZ, the application of 59 would favour the coastal State if the right interfere with coastal State sovereign rights.

18 LOSC, Articles 56(b)(III) and 194(1) read in conjunction with Article 1(1)(4) defining pollution as *inter alia* as the "introduction by man, directly or indirectly, of substances or energy into the marine environment, including estuaries, which results or is likely to result in such deleterious effects as harm to living resources and marine life, [...] hindrance to marine activities, including fishing and other legitimate uses of the sea".

19 Ibid, Articles 79(1) and 87(c), 112.

20 Ibid, Articles 110(1) and 101.

21 See e.g: Niels Fastrup, Lisbeth Quass, Frederik H Ledegaard, 'Russiske spionskibe forbereder mulig sabotage mod havvindmøller, gasrør og strømkabler i Danmark og Norden' DR (19 April 2023), available at <https://www.dr.dk/nyheder/indland/moerklagt/afsloering-russiske-spionskibe-forbereder-mulig-sabotage-mod> accessed 1 May 2023; Gordon Corera, 'Ukraine war: The Russian ships accused of North Sea sabotage' BBC (19 April 2023), available at <https://www.bbc.com/news/world-europe-65309687> accessed 1 May 2023.

22 Fastrup, Quass, Ledegaard (n 21).

immunities recognized to other government ships used for non-commercial purposes,[23] which limits the responses a coastal State can take against them. The presence of armed guards and surveillance equipment on board these vessels does not affect their status. Coastal States can send law-enforcement vessels to control the suspected ship. Nevertheless, should the latter provide a certificate demonstrating that it is employed for non-commercial governmental purposes, coastal States' law-enforcement authorities cannot continue their inspection nor arrest the vessel by virtue of Article 96 of the LOSC.[24]

Should these vessels belong to a private company, the analysis conducted in the previous subsection regarding private military companies applies.

1.1.3 Exceptions: Activities Conducted by Warships Not Considered Military Activities

When discussing military activities and trying to understand the meaning and significance of hybrid naval warfare, it is important to underline that not all of the activities conducted by warships at sea are military by nature. At the same time, these activities do not constitute grey areas in which hybrid naval can thrive.

Passage of a warship is not considered *per se* as military activity.[25] The Convention recognizes to warships, the right to freely sail in the various maritime zones[26] and types of straits[27] it regulates, provided that said ships respect the conditions regulating the passage in question.

In addition, in zones where- and for matters regarding which the coastal State enjoys law enforcement prerogatives, activities of warships flying the flag of the coastal State designed to prevent or punish violations of its sovereign rights and jurisdiction as well as its national laws are not considered military

23 LOSC, Articles 32 and 96.

24 Ted L McDorman 'Sovereign Immune Vessels: Immunities, Responsibilities and Exemptions' in Henrik Ringbom (ed.), *Jurisdiction over Ships: Post-UNCLOS Developments in the Law of the Sea* (Brill 2015) 90; ILC, 'Draft Articles on Jurisdictional Immunities of States and Their Property, with Commentaries' (2005), draft Article 16(7) at 50 and commentary at 53 para 16.

25 Dispute Concerning the Detention of Three Ukrainian Naval Vessels (Ukraine v. Russian Federation), Provisional Measures, Order 25 May 2019, ITLOS Reports 2019, p. 283, para 68.

26 LOSC, Articles 87 (freedom of navigation in the high seas), Article 58(2) read in conjunction with Article 87 (freedom of Navigation in the EEZ), Article 17 (right of innocent passage in the territorial sea), Article 8(2) (right of innocent passage in internal waters enclosed within straight baselines previously considered territorial sea), Article 52 (right of innocent passage in archipelagic waters).

27 Ibid, Article 38 (right of transit passage), Article 45(1) (right of innocent passage through straits, where the right of transit passage does not apply).

activities, but rather law enforcement operations.[28] Such activities involve the visit of a suspected ship but also its pursuit, boarding and arrest.[29] Furthermore, the conduct of such law enforcement operations does not preclude the use of force, provided that it is necessary, proportionate and humane.[30]

Similarly, if on the high seas, a warship pursues, boards and arrests a ship engaged in piracy, slave trade, drug trafficking or illegal broadcast, its actions will not be considered military activities. Rather, it falls under the scope of law enforcement operations, as these activities are prohibited on the high seas.[31]

1.2 *Scope and Limitations of Military Activities in the Territorial Sea*

1.2.1 Interdiction of Foreign Military Activities in the Territorial Sea

Coastal States are sovereign in their territorial sea.[32] The only exception to this sovereignty is the right of innocent passage, which must be granted to foreign warships and any other ship.[33] Furthermore, under the LOSC, this right is strictly regulated. Article 19 prohibits both the conduct of foreign military activities as well as research and survey activities are banned within the territorial sea of a foreign State.[34]

This clear interdiction of military activities is explained by the fact that during the law of the sea negotiations, participants were eager to preserve their security.[35] For the same reason, the conduct of research activities

28 Ibid, Article 27(1) and (2), Article 28 (jurisdiction in the territorial sea), Article 33, Articles 303(2) (jurisdiction in the contiguous zone), Article 56(b), Article 73 (jurisdiction in the EEZ).

29 Ibid, Articles 27(2), 28(3), 33, 73(1) and 111.

30 M/V 'Saiga' (No. 2) (Saint Vincent and the Grenadines v. Guinea), Judgment, ITLOS Reports 1999, p. 10, para 155; M/V 'Virginia G' (Panama v. Guinea-Bissau), Judgment, ITLOS Reports 2014, p. 4, para 360.

31 LOSC, Article 110(1).

32 Ibid, Articles 2(1) and 2(2).

33 Ibid, Article 17.

34 Ibid, Article 19(2)(a)-(f), (j).

35 See e.g: 'Territorial Sea' Third United Nations Conference on the Law of the Sea (1973–1982) (11–22 July 1974) UN Doc A/CONF.62/C.2/SR 3 – A/CONF.62/C.2/SR.7, from 1974. During those debates, the need to strictly regulate the right of innocent passage as well as the breadth of the territorial sea to ensure the security of the featured heavily. Maritime powers tried to convince developing powers that to grant the right of innocent passage to warships was not a threat to their security, while developing States voiced opposite concerns. For an example of the position defended by maritime powers see: 'Territorial Sea Continued' Third United Nations Conference on the Law of the Sea (1973–1982) (16 July 1974) UN Doc A/CONF.62/C.2/SR.3, paras 21–23; For an example of the position defended by developing States see: 'Territorial Sea concluded' Third United Nations Conference on the Law of the Sea (1973–1982) (22 July 1974) UN Doc A/CONF.62/C.2/SR.7, para 2 (Trinidad and Tobago) On the legislative history of Article 17 and the attempts made by developing

and surveys without coastal State consent has been prohibited to avoid espionage.[36]

One exception, however, exists. If a strait used for international navigation where the right of transit passage applies is formed by the waters of a coastal State's territorial sea, then under the transit passage regime, foreign warships are allowed to launch and take onboard aircraft.[37] This exception stems from the fact that under the transit passage regime, ships can navigate in their normal mode and aircraft have the right to fly over the strait.[38] Thus, if a warship has the capacity to launch aircraft, then it can do so.

However, even in straits where the regime of transit passage does apply, surveys and research activities cannot be conducted without the consent of the strait States.[39] Similarly, the right to sail following its normal navigation mode shall not be interpreted as permission to conduct activities prejudicial to the coastal State's security.[40] Should a warship threaten a coastal State or engage in activities falling outside the perimeter of her normal mode of navigation, it would lose the protection granted by the right of transit passage.[41] At this point, the delinquent warship would no longer be deemed in transit but rather unlawfully sailing through the coastal States' territorial sea.[42] Consequently, the coastal State would have the right to apply Article 30 of the LOSC[43] and take measures discussed in the following subsection.

---

states to limit the passage of warships in their territorial sea, See: *Virginia Commentary vol. 2* (n 17), 153–155.

36 'Territorial Sea continued' Third United Nations Conference on the Law of the Sea (1973–1982) (18 July 1974) UN Doc A/CONF.62/C.2/SR.5, para 13; South Korea emphasized the need to prevent acts of foreign espionage, which could be committed under the guise of innocent passage. Although espionage is not frequently mentioned, it undoubtedly was present in the mind of the drafters when they spoke about security concerns. See also: Tommy TB Koh, 'Negotiating a New World Order for the Sea' (1984) 24 Virginia Journal of International Law 761, 773. Koh explains that fear of espionage was one of the main reasons why marine scientific research regime proved contentious during UNCLOS III.

37 LOSC, Article 39.

38 Natalie Klein, *Maritime Security and the Law of the Sea* (Oxford University Press 2011) 33–34; James Kraska and Raul 'Pete' Pedrozo, *International Maritime Security Law* (Martinus Nijhoff 2013) 222.

39 LOSC, Article 41. The use of radar, sonars and other depth-finding devices is only permitted insofar as they ensure safety of navigation or are part of the ship's normal navigation mode. See: Virginia Commentary vol. 2 (n 17), 343 para 39(10)(f).

40 LOSC, Article 39(1)(b) and (c).

41 Ibid, Article 38(3).

42 Ibid, Article 38(3) read in conjunction with Article 34(1) and 2(2); Virginia Commentary vol. 2 (n 17) 298–299 paras 34(8)(a) and 34(8)(c).

43 LOSC, Article 30.

In cases where coastal States have not established territorial seas encompassing the whole width of the Strait, like in the Viro Strait,[44] the waters beyond the territorial sea would be considered either EEZ or part of the high seas.[45] In both cases, the right of transit passage would not apply. Instead, the freedom of navigation would constitute the applicable navigational regime.[46] As is analyzed in the following parts, freedom of navigation grants foreign warships more leeway to conduct military activities.

1.2.2 Response to Warships' Non-innocent Passage: Law Enforcement or Military Activities

As examined in the previous section, actions that constitute unlawful military activities in the territorial sea of foreign States can be identified with relative ease. However, it is much more challenging to establish which actions taken by the coastal State in response to a non-innocent passage are to be considered law enforcement operations or military activities. Here lies, as far as the territorial sea is concerned, the main grey area where hybrid warfare can find fertile grounds to thrive.

The *travaux préparatoires* of the LOSC and the Convention stayed relatively silent regarding the responses a coastal State can adopt should a foreign warship contravene the right of innocent passage.[47] Article 30 of the LOSC merely prescribes that should a warship effectuate a non-innocent passage in a foreign territorial sea, the coastal State has the right to require her to cease its actions and leave its territorial sea immediately.[48] However, as Mahmoudi underlined, this provision of the LOSC is not entirely satisfactory for coastal States as it leaves them passive while a foreign warship is violating their sovereignty.[49] It is why several scholars have pushed the boundaries of the Convention on this

44 Exchange of Notes Constituting an Agreement on the Procedure to be followed in the Modification of the Limits of the Territorial Waters in the Gulf of Finland (adopted 4 May 1994, entered into force 31 July 1995) UNTS 1887; Agreement between the Republic of Finland and the Republic of Estonia on the Boundary of the Maritime Zones in the Gulf of Finland and the Northern Baltic Sea (adopted 18 October 1996, entered into force 7 January 1997) 1964 UNTS.

45 LOSC, Article 35(b).

46 Ibid, Article 36.

47 Virginia Commentary vol. 2 (n 17) 254–255.

48 LOSC, Article 30; See also: Robin Churchill, Vaughan Lowe, Amy Sanders, *The Law of the Sea*, 4th ed. (Manchester University Press 2022) 165.

49 Said Mahmoudi, 'Use of Armed Force against Suspected Foreign Submarines in the Swedish Internal Waters and Territorial Sea' (2018) 38 International Journal of Marine and Coastal Law 585, 593.

matter and have maintained that coastal States can employ a minimal amount of force to compel delinquent warships to cease their unlawful activities.

Astley and Schmitt explained that because Article 25(1) of the LOSC did not explicitly specify which steps a coastal State was allowed to take to prevent a non-innocent passage, it could use a minimum amount of force to compel the delinquent warship to stop its activities and leave the territorial sea.[50] Churchill, Lowe and Sander explain that resorting to the use of force, in this case, is warranted because even though coastal States lack enforcement jurisdiction on foreign warships, they still do exercise legislative jurisdiction, which means that coastal States have the right to take the necessary measures to ensure the respect of their laws, bar the boarding of foreign warships.[51] Moore echoes this conclusion stating that acceptable use of force to compel warships to leave the territorial sea after a non-innocent passage can include obstructing their passage with other vessels or devices but also shouldering them.[52]

The Swedish practice as well as the practice of other Baltic States of chasing and using depth charges to force Soviet and Russian submarines sailing underwater[53] to leave their territorial sea illustrates well the notion of minimal necessary use of force that coastal States can use to make a non-innocent passage stop. It also demonstrates that Baltic coastal States have been proactive when deterring foreign warships, especially submarines, in their territorial sea.[54]

However, in this context, the qualification of the coastal State actions as either military activities or law enforcement operations is particularly complex and disputed. Following the Annex VII arbitral tribunal in the Dispute Concerning the Detention of Ukrainian Naval Vessels and Servicemen, determining whether the response of a coastal State amounts to military activities partially

---

50 John Astley II and Michael N Schmitt, 'The Law of the Sea and Naval Operations' (1997) 42 Air Force Law Review 119, 131–132; Klein (n 38) 35–36; Cameron Moore, *Freedom of Navigation and the Law of the Sea: Warships, States and Use of Force* (Routledge 2021) 68–70.

51 Churchill, Lowe and Sander (n 48) 164; On the specific prohibition of boarding foreign warships see: 'ARA Libertad' (Case no. 20) (Argentina v. Ghana), Provisional Measures, Order of 15 December 2012, ITLOS Reports 2012, p. 332, para 95.

52 Moore (n 50) 68–69. Similarly, James Kraska underlines that coastal State enforcement authorities are expected to take active measures, such as navigational harassment to compel delinquent warships to leave the territorial sea. Force ought to be last resort. See: James Kraska, 'Putting Your Head in the Tiger's Mouth: Submarine Espionage in Territorial Waters' (2015) 54 Columbia Journal of Transnational Law 164, 234.

53 LOSC, Article 20: "In the territorial sea, submarines and other underwater vehicles are required to navigate on the surface and to show their flag".

54 Mahmoudi (n 49); Churchill, Lowe and Sander (n 48) 153; Lott (n 1) 147, 150–151. For a detailed discussion and comparison of the Swedish ordonnance regarding coastal law enforcement see: Kraska (n 42) 238–243.

depends on the reactions adopted by the foreign warship engaged in unlawful passage.[55] To complicate the matter further, as underlined by the arbitral tribunal, the qualification of the activities may evolve with time. What began as a law enforcement operation can turn into military activities and vice versa.[56]

Some scholars consider that if the coastal State uses potentially lethal force against a warship engaged in non-innocent passage, these actions should be considered military activities.[57] Nevertheless, other scholars accept that coastal States can conduct law enforcement operations against warships and maintain that it is possible to determine which actions constitute law enforcement operations and military activities.

To determine whether the response of the coastal State amounts to military activities or law enforcement operations, these scholars use a two-step test. Firstly, one needs to consider the type of unlawful activities the foreign warship is engaged in during her passage.[58] If she is engaged in activities that do not present a direct threat to the security of the coastal State and for which a merchant vessel can be arrested under the LOSC, such as laying down cables, conducting surveys or other activities akin to scientific research, then the coastal State response will more likely be determined as a law enforcement operation,[59] for it aims to assert its legislative jurisdiction over the delinquent warship. Nevertheless, if the foreign warship conducts military exercises or weapon testing, which could be construed as a threat of use of force against the coastal State, then the coastal State response will more likely constitute military activities rather than law enforcement.[60]

Secondly, if the foreign warship does not cease its activities after minimum use of force is applied to compel her to stop but rather engages in a stand-off

---

55 *Dispute Concerning the Detention of Ukrainian Naval Vessels* (n 4).

56 Ibid, para 121.

57 Lott (n 1) 148–149, examining the position of Ruys, in Tom Ruys, 'The Meaning of 'Force' and The Boundaries of The Jus Ad Bellum: Are 'Minimal' Uses of Force Excluded from UN Charter Article 2(4)?' (2014) 108(2) The American Journal of International Law 159, 171, 209.

58 Moore (n 50) 68; Wolff Heintschel von Heinegg, 'The Difficulties of Conflict Classification at Sea: Distinguishing Incidents at Sea from Hostilities' (2016) 98(2) International Review of the Red Cross 449, 455.

59 Drawing from Churchill, Lowe and Sanders (n 48) 164.

60 Knut Dörmann *et al.* (eds.), *Commentary on the Second Geneva Convention: Convention (II) for the Amelioration of the Condition of Wounded, Sick, and Shipwrecked Members of Armed Forces at Sea* (Cambridge University Press 2016), para 259, available at <https://ihl-databases.icrc.org/applic/ihl/ihl.nsf/Comment.xsp?action=openDocument&documentId=1A35EE65211A18AEC12581150044243A#78_B> accessed 28 April 2023; Heintschel von Heinegg (n 54) 455; Klein (n 34) 35–36.

or a confrontation, then the activities of the coastal State would also rather be considered military, as they could potentially lead to a use of force governed by the *jus in bello*.[61]

Although theoretically sound, this scholarly position supporting the conduct of law enforcement operations against foreign warships does not so far seem to be confirmed by the recent jurisprudence, which tends to favor the first approach. In the South China Sea Arbitration, the arbitral tribunal concluded that the mere presence of military vessels in the vicinity was enough to transform the attempts to arrest civilian vessels into a military activity.[62] Applying the same standard, the use of minimal force to compel a foreign warship violating innocent passage to leave the territorial sea would likely be considered a military activity.

Similarly, in its preliminary award, the arbitral tribunal settling the Dispute Concerning the Detention of Ukrainian Naval Vessels and Servicemen held that both the maneuvers conducted by the Russian Coast Guards, which included ramming,[63] to prevent Ukrainian vessels from passing through the Kerch Strait, as well as the following stand-off constituted military activities.[64] Moreover, the arbiters have yet to determine whether a law enforcement activity can end military activity.[65] If they decide that the boarding and arrest of the three Ukrainian vessels constituted a military activity rather than a law enforcement operation, the scholarly position following which law enforcement measures can be taken against a sovereign vessel will be challenging to hold, more so than it is now.

Regardless of the position one chooses regarding the possibility of conducting law enforcement operations against a warship engaged in non-innocent passage, in both cases, the onus is on the coastal State to adopt the adequate response, which in turn demands to determine with which intent a warship

61 Moore (n 50) 69 referring to Dörmann and others (n 60) para 259 footnote 68 themselves quoting: International Criminal Court, 'Situation in the Republic of Korea Article 5 Report' (June 2014), para 46. In this report, the Office of the Prosecutor discussing the sinking of South Korean Warship *Cheonan* on 26 March 2010 by North Korea underlines that the use of force between two naval vessels constitutes an armed conflict. This is confirmed by the findings of the arbitral tribunal in the dispute *Dispute Concerning the Detention of Ukrainian Naval Vessels* (n 4), para 122.

62 Annex VII Arbitral Tribunal, South China Sea Arbitration (the Philippines v. the People's Republic of China), Case No 2013–19, Award of 12 July 2016, para 1161 read in conjunction with paras 1123 and 1127.

63 *Dispute Concerning the Detention of Ukrainian Naval Vessels* (n 4), para 113.

64 Ibid, para 122.

65 Ibid, para 123.

has breached the coastal State sovereignty. Yet, ascertaining intent can be especially challenging when submarines are concerned.[66]

Determining whether a coastal State can conduct law enforcement operations against a foreign warship remains one of the main grey zones regarding military activities in the territorial sea. Furthermore, this grey zone is difficult to eradicate as it involves subjective assessment from the coastal States or *post facto* evaluation by a court, which is not helpful for coastal States having to react to this issue in real-time. In both cases, coastal States bear the responsibility to choose the appropriate response and risk a direct confrontation with the State breaching the regime of innocent passage.

2 Scope and Limitations of Military Activities on the High Seas

In this part, the first section briefly examines the UNCLOS III debates regarding the right to conduct military activities on the high seas. The second section assesses the few limitations imposed on military activities on the high seas. The third section briefly highlights the limited risk of witnessing hybrid warfare on the high seas.

This part opens the door to the third, which will be dedicated to the scope and limitations of military activities in the EEZ, where the situation is more complex given the existence of competing coastal and other States' sets of rights and obligations.

2.1 *UNCLOS III Debates Surrounding Military Activities in the High Seas*

During the UNCLOS negotiations, the issue of military activities on the high seas was hotly debated. On several occasions, a significant number of developing States tried to limit or even prohibit the conduct of military activities, while maritime powers such as the United States and the Soviet Union defended it.[67] Examples of such debate abound in the *travaux préparatoires* of the Convention.

A case in point is the debate that took place in 1976 in UNCLOS III's Plenary Commission. Several developing and non-aligned States opposed the position held by maritime powers, according to which the freedom of navigation encompassed the right to conduct military activities beyond the territorial

66 Lott (n 1) 149, quoting Ruys (n 57) 174.

67 Satya N Nandan and Shabtai Rosenne (eds.), *United Nations Convention on the Law of the Sea 1982 – A Commentary* (Volume 3, Martinus Nijhoff 1995) 88–92.

sea,[68] especially in the EEZ of foreign States.[69] Furthermore, it was claimed that the high seas should be exclusively used for peaceful purposes, which *de facto* prohibited the conduct of military operations.[70] To guarantee the interdiction of military activities, several States proposed the creation of zones of peace in various oceans.[71]

On the other end of the spectrum, maritime powers such as the United States, but also a few developing States, maintained the position that the military activities conducted on the high seas were allowed under the freedom of navigation provided that they did not breach Article 2(4) of the United Nations (hereinafter UN) Charter.[72] Furthermore, in an attempt to preserve the right to conduct military activities,[73] maritime powers argued that UNCLOS III was not an appropriate forum to discuss and negotiate on questions of peace and disarmament.[74]

From this debate emerged Article 88 of the LOSC, which merely states that 'the high seas shall be reserved for peaceful purposes'[75] and Article 301, which enshrined Article 2(4) of the United Nations Charter in the LOSC.[76]

68 'Utilisations pacifiques de l'espace océanique: zones de paix et de sécurité (suite)' Third United Nations Conference on the Law of the Sea (1973–1982) (23 April 1976) UN Doc A/CONF.62/SR.67, paras 1, 3, (Ecuador); para 28 (Madagascar); para 90 (China, accusing the USSR). [UN Doc A/CONF.62/SR.67]

69 Ibid, paras 17–18 (Madagascar); 'Utilisations pacifiques de l'espace océanique : zones de paix et de sécurité (conclusion)' Third United Nations Conference on the Law of the Sea (1973–1982) (26 April 1976) UN Doc A/CONF.62/SR.68, para 26 (Iran, presenting its own position); para 38 (Pakistan). [UN Doc A/CONF.62/SR.68]

70 UN Doc A/CONF.62/SR.67 (n 68) para 2 (Ecuador); para 28 (Madagascar); para 90 (China, accusing the USSR); UN Doc A/CONF.62/SR.68 (n 69) para 23 (Iran summarizing the main positions defended during the debate); paras 28 (Somalia); para 31 (Pakistan).

71 UN Doc A/CONF.62/SR.67 (n 68) para 5 (Ecuador); A/CONF.62/SR.68 (n 69) para 29 (Somalia).

72 UN Doc A/CONF.62/SR.67 (n 68) para 81 (USA); UN Doc A/CONF.62/SR.68 (n 69) para 19 (Philipines); para 23 (Iran summarizing the main positions defended during the debate).

73 Bernard Oxman, 'Le Régime des Navires de Guerre dans le Cadre de la Convention des Nations Unies sur le Droit de la Mer' (1982) 28 Annuaire Français de Droit International 811, 811–813; Elmar Rauch, 'Military Uses of the Oceans' (1985) 28 German Yearbook of International Law 229, 230–234; Boleslaw Adam Boczek, 'Peacetime Military Activities in the Exclusive Economic Zone of Third Countries' (1988) 19(6) Ocean Development and International Law 445, 457.

74 'Utilisations pacifiques de l'espace océanique : zones de paix et de sécurité' Third United Nations Conference on the Law of the Sea (1973–1982) (19 April 1976) UN Doc A/CONF.62/SR.66, para 3, (Peru describing the behaviour of maritime powers) UN Doc A/CONF.62/SR.67 (n 68) paras 38–40 (Soviet Union).

75 LOSC, Article 88.

76 Ibid, Article 301; Virginia Commentary, vol 3 (n 67) 90–91, para 88(7)(c).

2.2 *Interpretation of the Notion of Peaceful Uses and Peaceful Purposes: Limitations of Use of Force at Sea*

Even though a sizeable number of States advocated the total prohibition of military activities at sea based on the notions of peaceful uses and peaceful purposes of the sea, it is widely recognized that on the high seas the right to conduct military activities is only limited by Article 2(4) of the UN Charter[77] as the United States had already suggested in 1976.

In other words, very few limitations are imposed on States. Amongst them is the prohibition of aggressive acts against other ships.[78] In the same vein, damaging submarine cables is prohibited. In case of damages, companies owning the cables must be compensated.[79] Therefore, on the high seas, military activities should preferably not be conducted in areas where they risk damaging submarine cables.[80]

Furthermore, it is highly doubtful that underwater nuclear tests would be allowed on the high seas, even though the International Court of Justice did not decide on this issue.[81] This assessment is confirmed by the ever-growing importance granted to ecological issues since the Court has examined the Nuclear Weapons case. In addition, military activities in the Area are prohibited, for it is to be used exclusively for peaceful purposes.[82] The introduction of the adverb 'exclusively' in Article 141 indicates a more stringent limitation than in Articles 88 and 301.[83] Moreover, the deep seabed has historically been considered a zone where disarmament was of prime importance, as the 1971 Seabed Treaty demonstrates.[84]

---

77 See e.g: Churchill, Lowe, Sander (n 48) 378–380; Klein (n 38) 45, 54–58; Kraska and Pedrozo (n 38) 242; Boczek (n 73) 371; Virginia Commentary, vol 3 (n 67) 91 para 88(7)(c); Oxman (n 73) 815–816; *Study on the Naval Arms Race* (UN document A/40/535 1985), para 186–188; LOSC Article 301; Virginia Commentary, vol 3 (n 67) 91, para 88(7)(c); Stepan Molodtsov, 'The Exclusive Economic Zone: Legal Status and Regime of Navigation' (1986) 6 Ocean Yearbook of International Law 203, 214–216; Douglas Guilfoyle, 'The High Seas', in Don R Rothwell *et al.* (eds.), *Oxford Handbook on the Law of the Sea* (Oxford University Press 2015) 210–212; Moritaka Hayashi, 'Military and Intelligence Gathering Activities in the EEZ: Definition of Key Terms' (2005) 29 Marine Policy 123, 125–126.

78 Annex VII Arbitral Tribunal, the 'Enrica Lexie' Incident (Italy v. India), Case 2015–28, Award of 21 May 2020, paras 1071–1073.

79 Convention for the Protection of Submarine Telegraph Cables (adopted 14 March 1884, entered into force 1 May 1888), Article 2.

80 Churchill, Lowe, Sander (n 48) 376–377.

81 Klein (n 38) 50–51, 55–57; Churchill, Lowe, Sander (n 48) 379.

82 LOSC, Article 141.

83 Ibid, Article 141 read in conjunction with Articles 88 and 301.

84 Treaty on the Prohibition of the Emplacement of Nuclear Weapons and Other Weapons of Mass Destruction on the Sea-Bed and the Ocean Floor and in the Subsoil Thereof (adopted 11 February 1971, entered into force 18 May 1972) 955 UNTS 115.

In turn, when conducting military activities such as weapon testing on the high seas, it is admitted that States can establish limited security zones to ensure the safety of other users of the sea. Although, as Klein underlined, these security zones should be short-lived and geographically limited. Otherwise, they would be construed as an undue limitation to other States' high seas freedom.[85]

2.3 *Chances of Hybrid Warfare on the High Seas*

The high seas are not a zone where States can assert sovereignty nor claim sovereign rights. States cannot exercise law enforcement prerogative beyond their ships,[86] except for hot pursuit[87], which cannot be launched against sovereign vessels.

Indeed, the raison d'être of the right of hot pursuit is to visit or arrest ships in order to punish infringements of sovereign rights or violations of the coastal State's laws. Yet, warships and other government vessels enjoy immunity.[88] Thus, they cannot be legally arrested nor *a fortiori* prosecuted. The pursuit can never legally reach its prescribed end.[89] Therefore, a State launching a hot pursuit knowing beforehand that it is destined to fail or be unlawfully completed objectively starts a military activity in the form of a chase.

Consequently, the risk of witnessing hybrid warfare on the high seas is limited. Should a warship use force against another warship, then the incident would undoubtedly be considered an act of aggression regulated by the law of armed conflicts.

3 Military Activities in the EEZ

Due to its mixed legal regime, where coastal States' sovereign rights are to be balanced with the rights of other States, the EEZ is one of the prime grounds for hybrid warfare confrontation. The first section examines the various views existing towards the conduct of military activities in the EEZ. It will show that the right to conduct military activities in foreign EEZs remains contested. The second section analyses the scope and limitations of military

85 Klein (n 38) 57–60.
86 LOSC, Article 89.
87 LOSC, Article 111.
88 LOSC, Articles 95 and 96.
89 *ARA Libertad* (n 51) para 95.

activities, including intelligence-gathering operations, in this zone. It reviews whether the conduct of military activities in the EEZ is limited by the notion of 'due regard' and Article 59 of the LOSC, as maintained by Chinese scholars. Finally, following Hayashi and Klein, the second section proposes a threshold to determine the legality of military activities in the EEZ. The third section assesses the EEZs remaining grey zones that could potentially give rise to hybrid warfare. It especially focuses on the issue of surveys, as it causes significant tensions among states.

3.1 *Military Activities in the EEZ: a Disputed Issue*

Since UNCLOS III, the right to conduct military activities in foreign States' EEZ has been hotly disputed. The debate revolves around the following question: Do military activities constitute a legitimate use of the sea?

During UNCLOS III, Western States voiced their support in favor of the right to conduct military activities in foreign States' EEZs. On the 6th of December 1982, Western States made statements underlining the fact that they considered the right to conduct military activities in the EEZ of a foreign State as a part of the freedom of navigation recognized to them by Article 58 of the LOSC.[90] It was argued that such a right could not be construed as a threat to the security of the coastal State, for the Convention protected this right.[91] Furthermore, as underlined by the Italian delegate, LOSC did not grant coastal States the right to obtain prior notification for these military activities to be lawfully undertaken.[92] Moreover, in defense of this position, the United States, using the wording of Article 58.1, maintained that the right to conduct military activities and exercises constituted a legitimate and lawful use of the sea.[93]

Since 1982, the United States, through the digest of its international law practice[94] as well as the publications from the Judge Advocate General or by

90 See: 'Statements made at the 185th Plenary Meeting of UNCLOS III' (February–August 1983) UN Doc, A/CONF.62/WS/37 Addendum1 and 2 Statements made at the 185th Plenary Meeting of UNCLOS III, 240–244; These statements were made by the Federal Republic of Germany (241), France (241), Italy (241–242), the United Kingdom (243) and the United States (244).

91 Ibid, 241 (German statement).

92 Ibid, 241–242 (Italian Statement).

93 Ibid, 244 (American statement).

94 Jennifer Newstead (ed.), *Digest of the United States Practice in International Law* (US Department of State 2018) 491–492.

retired officers, have reiterated such a view.[95] Recently, both France[96] and the United Kingdom[97] have repeated similar pledges in favor of the freedom of navigation. In 2009 and 2017, the Netherlands issued two official declarations objecting to interpretations of the LOSC that it deemed erroneous. In both these documents, the Netherlands affirms that the Convention does not grant coastal States the right to prohibit foreign States from conducting military activities in their EEZ. The second sentence of the Dutch statements emphasizes that such activities are part of the freedom of navigation recognized to all States in this zone.[98]

At the same time, in contrast to Western States' views, several developing States have filed statements under Article 310 to emphasize that, in their view, the regime of the EEZ forbids foreign States from conducting military activities in this zone.

Bangladesh, Brazil, Cape Verde, Ecuador, India, Malaysia, Pakistan, Thailand and Uruguay have underlined that the EEZ legal regime does not grant other States the right to conduct military activities.[99] Some of these States maintain that such activities go against the spirit of the Convention, as they cannot be

---

95 Office of the Judge Advocate General Pacific Command (United States), 'Military Activities in the EEZ' (2021) 97 *International Law Studies*, 46; See also the publications of Raul 'Pete' Pedrozo, e.g.: 'Maintaining Freedom of Navigation and Overflight in the Exclusive Economic Zone and on the High Seas' (2020) 17 Indonesian Journal of International Law 477, 482; or J Ashley Roach and Robert W Smith, *Excessive Maritime Claims*, 3rd ed. (Martinus Nijhoff 2012) 377.

96 France, *Livre bleu: Stratégie Nationale pour la Mer et les Océans* (Bureau du Premier Ministre 2009) 2.

97 United Kingdom, *National Strategy for Maritime Security* (Secretary of State for Transport 2022) 109 endnote 22.

98 The Netherlands, 'Objections' (13 February 2009 and 27 February 2017) para B.II.2 of each declaration. The two sets of objections are identical regarding this matter, available at <https://treaties.un.org/pages/ViewDetailsIII.aspx?src=TREATY&mtdsg_no=XXI-6&chapter=21&Temp=mtdsg3&clang=_en> accessed 28 April 2023.

99 By alphabetical order: Bangladesh, 'Declarations' (14 December 2009) para 1; Brazil, 'Declaration upon Signature' (10 December 1982) paras III–IV; Brazil, 'Declaration upon Ratification' (22 December 1988) paras I–II; Cape Verde, 'Declaration made upon Signature and Confirmed upon Ratification' (10 December 1982 and 10 August 1987) para V; Ecuador, 'Declaration' (24 September 2012) para XVIII read in conjunction with paras IV and XI; India, 'Declarations' (10 December 1982) para b; Malaysia, 'Declarations' (26 August 2019) paras 2–3; Pakistan, 'Declarations' (10 December 1982) para 3; Thailand, 'Declaration' (10 December 1982) para 4; Uruguay, 'Declarations Made upon Signature and Confirmed upon Ratification' (10 December 1982 and 10 December 1992) at para D. All declarations are available at <https://treaties.un.org/pages/ViewDetailsIII.aspx?src=TREATY&mtdsg_no=XXI-6&chapter=21&Temp=mtdsg3&clang=_en, accessed 28 April 2023> accessed 28 April 2023.

considered peaceful.[100] Others argue that conducting military activities in the EEZ threatens the security and territorial integrity of the coastal State, hence the need to limit them.[101] Regardless of the argumentation used by all these States, it is interesting to point out that they especially condemn the use of weapons and explosives.[102]

It is important to note that proponents of the freedom of navigation have officially disputed the statements issued by this group of States. It was argued that the limitations Bangladesh and other States are trying to impose on the freedom of navigation constitute, for all intents and purposes, reservations to the LOSC, which in turn constitutes a violation of the Convention itself.[103]

Although China did not issue a declaration when signing nor ratifying the LOSC,[104] Beijing counts amongst the staunchest opponents to the conduct of military activities in the EEZ. To defend its position, China and Chinese scholars are relying, like the other States wishing to curtail foreign military activities in the EEZ, on the notion of 'due regard' and peaceful purposes. Indeed, China claims that foreign military activities in the EEZ are incompatible with these notions.[105]

In contrast with other States, however, China also uses Article 59 of the LOSC and the so-called rule of residual rights to claim that coastal States have the right to limit the conduct of foreign military activities in their EEZ. It is the

100 See: Brazil, Declaration upon Signature (n 99) para III; Brazil, Declaration upon Ratification (n 99) para I; Cape Verde (n 99) para V; Malaysia (n 99) para. 2; Thailand (n 99), para 4; Uruguay (n 99) para D.

101 Brazil, Declaration upon Signature (n 99) para III; Brazil, Declaration upon Ratification (n 99) para I; Cape Verde (n 99) para V; Ecuador (n 99) para XVIII; Malaysia (n 99) para 2; Thailand (n 99) para 4; Uruguay (n 99) para D.

102 Cape Verde (n 99) para V; Brazil Declaration upon Signature (n 99) para IV; India, Declarations (n 99) para b; Malaysia (n 99) para 3; Pakistan (n 99) para III.

103 See e.g: Germany, 'Objections with Regard to the Declaration made by Ecuador upon Accession' (21 October 2013); Italy, 'Objections with Regard to the Declaration made by Ecuador upon Accession' (23 October 2013), available at <https://treaties.un.org/pages/ViewDetailsIII.aspx?src=TREATY&mtdsg_no=XXI-6&chapter=21&Temp=mtdsg3&clang=_en, accessed 28 April 2023> accessed 28 April 2023.

104 UN Division for Ocean Affairs and the Law of the Sea, 'Law of the Sea Bulletin no 107' (2022), 3, available at <https://www.un.org/Depts/los/doalos_publications/LOSBulletins/bulletinpdf/LOS-Bulletin107-web.pdf> accessed 28 April 2023.

105 Ren Xiaofeng and Cheng Xizhong, 'A Chinese Perspective' (2005) 29 Marine Policy 139, 141–142; Li Guangyi, Wan Binhua and Zhu Hongjie, 'On the Rights and Obligations of Military Activities in the Exclusive Economic Zone' (2011) 13 China Oceans Law Review 148, 154–155; Moritaka Hayashi, 'Military Activities in the Exclusive Economic Zones of Foreign Coastal States' (2012) 27 The International Journal of Marine and Coastal Law 785, 801.

Chinese view that Article 59 applies not only to the distribution of resources in the EEZ but also to solving outstanding issues in the EEZ regimes, such as the issue of foreign military activities.[106] Chinese scholars use this article to argue that since the freedom of navigation in the EEZ does not expressly authorize the conduct of military activities, the legality of these activities should be determined against the interests of the coastal State.[107] According to them, the security interests of the coastal States must weigh more than the freedom of navigation recognized to other States.[108] For this reason, China defends a ban on all foreign military activities in the EEZ of a coastal State conducted without its permission.[109]

In total, it is reported that 21 States limit the right of foreign States to conduct military operations, exercises, and maneuvers in the EEZ.[110]

3.2 *Scope and Limitations of Military Activities in the EEZ*

3.2.1 The Meaning of 'Due Regard' and Its Impact on Military Activities

The EEZs legal regime is unique, for it is a zone where exclusive coastal States' sovereign rights cohabit with the rights and freedoms recognized to other States.[111] Those competing sets of rights are balanced by the obligation to show due regard for the rights and duties of coastal and other States, respectively.[112]

The notion of 'due regard for the rights and duties of the coastal State' enshrined in Article 58(3) of the LOSC relates to the obligation of other States not to hinder the coastal State's capacity to enjoy their sovereign rights in the EEZ nor engage in activities that could inflict damages on the living and non-living resources.[113] Similarly, other States must not encroach upon the coastal

106 Ren Xiaofeng and Cheng Xizhong (n 105) 144.

107 Ibid.

108 Ibid.

109 Li Guangyi, Wan Binhua and Zhu Hongjie (n 105) 158, 165.

110 James Kraska, 'Intelligence Collection and the International Law of the Sea' (2022) 99 International Law Studies 602, 612; Roach and Smith (n 95), 379–391; Those countries are: Bangladesh, Brazil, Burma (Myanmar), Cambodia, Cape Verde, China, Ecuador, India, Indonesia, Iran, Kenya, Malaysia, Maldives, Nicaragua, North Korea, Pakistan, Philippines, Portugal, Thailand, Uruguay, and Vietnam. Legislations of these countries limiting military activities in the EEZ can be consulted at <https://www.jag.navy.mil/organization/code_10_mcrm.htm> accessed 28 April 2023.

111 LOSC, Articles 56 and 58.

112 Ibid, Article 56(2) and 58(3).

113 Virginia Commentary vol. 2 (n 17) para 58(10)(e); Hayashi (n 77) 132–133.

State's jurisdiction over artificial islands, structures and other installations.[114] Although less discussed, the obligation of 'due regard for the rights and duties of other States' contained in Article 56(2) regards coastal States' obligation not to unduly interfere nor create obstacles to international navigation.[115]

Furthermore, despite the efforts of the Third World, it is generally understood that the notion of due regard mentioned in Article 58(3) does not include the obligation to respect the security interests of the coastal State.[116] Otherwise, as Kraska emphasizes, it would mean that in the EEZ, the freedom of navigation recognized to warships would fall prey to the political interests and arbitrary decisions of coastal States.[117] Attard and Van Dyke are more reserved, however. In their opinion, the vague formulation of Article 58(3) betrays the fact that developing States were uneasy and unwilling to accept the conduct of military activities in the EEZ of foreign States rather than the exclusion of coastal State's security interests from the notion of due regard.[118] This observation is further validated by the declarations made during the signature of the LOSC in 1982 and the limited but not insignificant number of States that prohibited foreign military activities in their EEZ.[119]

Similarly, the notion of due regard is not to be understood as modifying the meaning of peaceful uses and peaceful purposes in such a way as to ban the conduct of military activities in the EEZ. As on the high seas, military activities are deemed lawful, provided they do not violate Article 2(4) of the UN Charter.[120]

In conclusion, according to the obligation of due regard for both the rights and duties of coastal and other States, military activities are lawful in the EEZ of foreign States, for they stem from the warships' freedom of navigation.

114 Virginia Commentary vol. 3 (n 67) 565, para 58(10)(c); Hayashi (n 77) 132–133.

115 Virginia Commentary vol. 3 (n 67) 543–544, para 56(11)(f), read in conjunction with para 58(10)(e). According to the commentators, in their EEZ, coastal States cannot adopt laws and regulations that exceed their scope of the rights and granted to them under part V of LOSC.

116 Hayashi (n 77) 132–133; Raul 'Pete' Pedrozo, 'Military Activities in the Exclusive Economic Zone: East Asia Focus' (2014) 90 International Law Studies 514, 533.

117 Kraska (n 110) 607.

118 Jon M Van Dyke, 'Military Ships and Planes Operating in the Exclusive Economic Zone of Another Country' (2004) 28 Marine Policy 29, 31–32; David Attard, *The Exclusive Economic Zone in International Law* (Clarendon Press 1987) 68.

119 George V Galdorisi and Alan G Kaufman, 'Military Activities in the Exclusive Economic Zone: Preventing Uncertainty and Defusing Conflict' (2002) 32 California Western International Law Journal 253, 284–290.

120 See e.g: Oxman (n 73) 826–27; Rauch (n 73) 241–242; Stepan Molodtsov (n 77) 214–216; Hayashi (n 77) 125–126; Klein (n 38) 50–51. Churchill, Vaughan and Sander (n 48) 281–284.

However, they should not prevent coastal States from enjoying their sovereign rights nor cause harm to natural resources contained in the EEZ.[121]

3.2.2 Article 59 and Its Impact on Military Activities in the EEZ

Article 59 of the LOSC is a mechanism to solve conflicts of rights that may arise between coastal and other States in the EEZ. When a dispute over competing interests and unattributed rights arises between coastal and other States, the Convention provides that the dispute ought to be resolved on the basis of equity, taking into account relevant circumstances, the interests of each party to the dispute, and the interests of the international community as a whole.[122]

Chinese scholars have recently relied on this article to maintain that the right to conduct military activities in the EEZ should be limited by the need to respect coastal States' security interests.[123] However, their position seems not to be supported by the *travaux préparatoires* of the Convention. The authors of the Virginia commentaries affirm that Article 59 should be understood considering the functional nature of the EEZ. In disputes revolving around the exploration and exploitation of resources, Article 59 should protect the rights of coastal States over the freedoms granted to other States. Symmetrically, in disputes that do not involve resources, Article 59 should favor the interests of other States and the international community over the sovereign rights of coastal States.[124]

Flowing from these elements, as mentioned earlier, it is impossible to support the claim made by Chinese scholars. The protection of coastal States' security interests is not a sovereign right guaranteed by LOSC. On the contrary, the right to conduct military activities in the EEZ, as a right stemming from the freedom of navigation, is.[125]

3.2.3 Threshold to Determine the Legality of Military Activities in the EEZ

Flowing from the previous sections, in the EEZ, only two limits can be imposed on foreign military activities: the need to respect Article 2(4) of the UN Charter and the obligation to respect the sovereign rights of the coastal States. In practical terms, following Hayashi and Klein, it means that the use of explosives

121 Hayashi (n 77) 133; Klein (n 38) 48.

122 LOSC, Article 59.

123 Xiaofeng and Xizhong (n 105) 144–145.

124 Virginia Commentary vol. 2 (n 17) para 59(6)(b), 569. Churchill, Vaughan and Sander (n 48) 292–293 corroborate the analysis conducted by the authors of the Virginia Commentary.

125 LOSC, Article 58(2) read in conjunction with Article 88 which does not preclude the conduct of military activities.

as well as weapons testing that could harm the marine environment and, therefore, hinder the coastal State's capacity to enjoy its sovereign rights are to be prohibited.[126] Furthermore, it could include the possibility of forbidding the use of electronic and cyber weapons if their use would interfere with the coastal States' capacity to enjoy their sovereign rights.[127]

On the other hand, military activities such as training exercises without explosives, the launching of aircraft or the installation of military cables are allowed in the EEZ, for they are lawful uses of the sea[128] that respect both the concept of peaceful purposes of the sea and the sovereign rights of the coastal States.

The idea that in foreign EEZs, military activities involving the use of explosives and other noxious substances are to be prohibited is further corroborated by the LOSC's marine scientific research regime. According to Article 246(5)(b), a coastal State can withhold its consent if a research project involves the use of explosives and other noxious substances that could harm the marine environment.[129] Reasoning by analogy, given that explosives and other toxic substances would have the same effect on the marine environment regardless of their use for military or research purposes, it seems reasonable that military activities involving the use of said substances should not take place in the EEZ of foreign States, for had they been used in the course of research activities they would not have been allowed by the coastal State.

Regarding the specific issue of intelligence-gathering operations, Papastravridis contends that the threshold identified by Hayashi and Klein can be used to determine their legality.[130] Thus, intelligence operations conducted in preparation for an armed attack against the coastal State are prohibited.[131] Similarly, operations aiming to gain information for the economic benefit of a foreign State should be considered unlawful. For instance, conducting surveys to locate oil and gas wells would be deemed illegal.[132]

126 Hayashi (n 77) 129; Klein (n 38) 49–51, 60–61; Galdorisi and Kaufman (n 119) 279. See also: Astley and Schmitt (n 50) 137.

127 Klein (n 38) 50–51.

128 LOSC, Article 58(1).

129 Ibid, Article 246(5)(b).

130 Efthymios Papastavridis, 'Intelligence Gathering in the Exclusive Economic Zone' (2017) 93 International Law Studies 446, 471–473. Papastravridis' finding echoes the conclusion reached by other scholars that intelligence-gathering operations are lawful in the EEZ of foreign States; See e.g: Rauch (n 52) 252. Kraska (n 110) 607–610.

131 Papastavridis (n 130) 472.

132 Ibid.

At last, the threshold upheld by Hayashi and Klein appears to be corroborated by the Annex VII Arbitral Tribunal in the *Chagos Case* and *South China Sea Case*. Examining the meaning of Article 56(2) and 58(3) of the LOSC, respectively, the Tribunals concluded that the obligation of due regard does not impose a universal obligation to avoid any impairment of coastal States' rights. Rather, the extent of the due regard requirement depends on a three-variable equation. The legality of an action should be measured against the anticipated impairment suffered by the coastal State, the nature and importance of said activity for the other State, and whether the activity in question could be conducted elsewhere or in a different manner.[133]

Applying this equation to the case of military activities leads to the result found by Hayashi and Klein. Using explosives and weapons in foreign EEZs would lead to impairments of coastal States' sovereign rights that outweigh the necessity of conducting military activities in the EEZ, especially given the fact that the same activity can be led on the high seas, where they would not negatively affect coastal States' sovereign rights. Symmetrically, using the same formula, in the case of military activities conducted without weapons and explosives, the importance of the freedom of navigation outweighs the infringements on coastal States' sovereign rights.

3.3 *EEZs Grey Zones and Risks of Hybrid Warfare*

3.3.1 Law Enforcement or Military Activities against Warships Interfering with Coastal States' Sovereign Rights in the EEZ

The first grey area existing in the EEZ is similar to the one existing in the territorial sea. It concerns the qualification of the coastal States' actions in response to an infringement of their sovereign rights resulting from foreign military activities. Do these responses amount to military activities or law enforcement operations?

Although coastal States enjoy law enforcement prerogatives to preserve their sovereign rights in an EEZ,[134] the possibility of conducting law enforcement operations against foreign warships interfering with coastal States' sovereign

133 Annex VII Arbitral Tribunal, Chagos Marine Protected Area Arbitration (Mauritius v. United Kingdom), Case 2011-03, Award of 18 March 2015, para 519; *South China Sea Arbitration* (n 62) para 742. In 1997, Astley and Schmitt also suggested a similar idea. They deemed that if a military activity potentially interfering with coastal States' sovereign rights could be conducted elsewhere it should be. See: Astley and Schmitt (n 50) 137.

134 LOSC, Article 73.

rights seems unconvincing. Indeed, the grounds on which coastal States can exercise their jurisdiction are much more limited than in the territorial sea. In addition, if military activities in a foreign territorial sea are clearly prohibited in the LOSC, it is not the case in the EEZ. The LOSC does not expressly limit the right to conduct military activities in this zone. Although founded in law, the abovementioned limitations constitute scholarly arguments to guide States' actions. They are not binding and have not been endorsed by States. Thus, should a coastal State use force against a foreign warship to protect its sovereign rights, this use of force will likely be interpreted as a military activity against a sovereign vessel and would meet the threshold required to start an armed conflict.

3.3.2 Surveys: an Endangered Military Activity

The second grey area existing in the EEZ pertains to the conduct of surveys. Surveys can be both hydrographic and military[135] and are often conducted by warships or other government vessels.

States, as well as scholars, are divided on this issue. The Western States, chiefly the United States and the United Kingdom, consider surveys as activities governed by the freedom of navigation regime.[136]

In support of this position, it is argued that surveys are vital to ensure the safety of navigation and, therefore, should not be regulated by LOSC's marine scientific research regime, which grants coastal discretion to prohibit them in their EEZ.[137] Furthermore, it is argued that surveys shall not be governed by the

135 Roach and Smith define hydrographic surveys as surveys conducted "to obtain information for the making of navigational charts and the safety of navigation, and includes determination of one or more of several classes of data in coastal or relatively shallow areas – depth of water, configuration and nature of the natural bottom, directions and force of currents, heights and times of tides and water stages, and hazards of navigation – for the production of nautical charts and similar products to support safety of navigation." Meanwhile, military surveys are broadly defined as "activities undertaken in the ocean and coastal waters involving marine data collection (whether or not classified) for military purposes, and can include oceanographic, marine geological, geophysical, chemical, biological and acoustic data." See: Roach and Smith (n 95) 436–437.

136 Roach and Smith (n 95) 437; Van Dyke (n 118) 34; Papastavridis (n 130) 452; Kraska (n 110) 606; *The Commander's Handbook on the Law of Naval Operations* (US Department of the Navy 2022) paras 2–14.

137 Raul 'Pete' Pedrozo, 'Preserving Navigational Rights and Freedoms: The Right to Conduct Military Activities in China's Exclusive Economic Zone' (2010) 9(1) Chinese Journal of International Law 9, 12–13; Sam Bateman, 'Hydrographic Surveying in the EEZ: Differences and Overlaps with Marine Scientific Research' (2005) 29 Marine Policy 163, 165 (quoting Alfred HA Soons, *Marine Scientific Research and the Law of the Sea* (Kluwer 1982) 125, 157).

LOSC's marine scientific research regime, for in the Convention, the drafters have always distinguished between surveys and other research activities.[138]

On the other hand, States like India and, more importantly, China maintains that surveys should be considered a scientific activity like any other. Therefore, coastal States should consent to surveys taking place in their EEZ before their conduct.[139] Tellingly, under Chinese law, surveys require the prior consent of the State to be lawfully conducted.[140] Beijing explained that its decision to regulate survey activities was motivated by security concerns and the desire to prevent espionage against the Chinese State.[141]

Scholars such as Bateman and Klein have also challenged the specificity of surveys vis-à-vis other research activities. Klein noticed that under both the regime of innocent passage and transit passage, surveying activities are prohibited unless the coastal State's consent has been previously granted.[142] These observations lead her to believe that surveying activities are not necessary for the safety of navigation of the ship conducting them. Consequently, surveys should not be considered as other internationally lawful uses of the sea related to the freedom of navigation mentioned in Article 58.1 of the LOSC.[143] Instead, following this reasoning, military surveys should be governed by the marine scientific research regime.[144]

In addition, Bateman underlined that although surveys are important for the safety of navigation, they also collect commercially and strategically valuable data on the seabed of coastal States. Regulating them using the LOSC's marine scientific research regime would, therefore, ensure that these surveys benefit both the international community and the coastal States whose economic development would likely benefit from such surveys.[145] Incidentally, Bateman's and Klein's arguments reinforce the idea defended in 2005 by Estonia that surveys conducted by sovereign vessels to prepare the laying of pipelines should be governed by the marine scientific research regime rather than the freedom of navigation one.[146]

Regardless of the position one adopts regarding this debate, the mere fact that two points of view exist regarding the nature of surveys creates risks of

---

138 Kraska and Pedrozo (n 38) 284–285.
139 Van Dyke (n 118) 34; Hayashi (n 105) 795, 797–798.
140 Hayashi (n 105) 798–799.
141 Ibid.
142 LOSC, Articles 19(2)(j), 40.
143 Ibid, Article 58(1).
144 Klein (n 38) 223.
145 Bateman (n 137) 169–170; Klein (n 38) 223 (quoting Bateman (n 137) 169–170).
146 Lott (n 1) 212–213.

hybrid warfare. If a coastal State tries to stop a foreign warship from conducting surveys using force, it could degenerate into an armed confrontation. The 2005 incident involving the Russian research vessel *Pjotr Kotsov* and the Estonian Coast Guard aptly illustrates the risks generated by such events.[147]

In this type of situation, exemplified by the 2005 incident, the main factor inducing risks of confrontation is the assessment of the intent or goal with which research vessels conduct surveys. On the one hand, research vessels may narrowly consider their actions as surveys undertaken to ensure the safety of navigation. On the other, coastal States may consider those surveys as the initial step towards the completion of a larger marine scientific research project, such as the building of the North Stream pipeline in the case of the 2005 incident. The crux of the issue is that it is challenging to know with certainty to what end foreign research vessels are conducting surveys. To avoid an immediate escalation of tensions, the coastal can ask research vessels suspected of carrying out unlawful marine scientific research activities the type and purpose of their activity. The question then becomes, can the coastal State trust the veracity of the answer given by suspected research vessels? The answer to this question largely depends on the nature of the coastal and flag States' relations. Eventually, the coastal State will bear the burden of deciding which actions to take vis-à-vis suspected infringements of the marine scientific regime and will have to bear the cost of being mistaken.

To further complicate the matter, as the scholarly debate briefly summarized above shows, both coastal and flag States would have juridical arguments at their disposal to defend their positions in front of courts. Once again, without the intervention of a court or tribunal, this grey zone seems difficult to dissipate as it stems from two different interpretations of the LOSC.

However, to finish, it must be noted that considering *prima facie* all surveys as research activities regulated by Part XIII of the LOSC inherently poses risks to the warships' freedom of navigation. Indeed, due to the difficulty of knowing whether a warship is conducting a survey and to what end it is conducting it when it sails around the world, coastal States could use this argument to impose requirements such as prior notification or authorization on the navigation of foreign warships in the EEZ. Such blanket requirements would deprive the warships of the right to carry out surveys necessary to ensure the safety of navigation or, at the worst, simple passage, which are protected under the LOSC under the freedom of navigation regime.[148]

---

147 Ibid.

148 LOSC, Article 58(1).

Conclusion

Hybrid naval warfare is better understood as a transitory phenomenon that is dependent on grey areas between the concepts of law enforcement and military activities. Thus, because the concept of military activities is overall clear and does not accept many areas of uncertainty, creating a legal concept of hybrid warfare seems superfluous at this point in time.

From the analysis conducted in this communication, it appears that the concept of military activities in the LOSC, after all, is clearer than it appears at first glance. It designates the activities conducted by a warship, which are neither passage nor law enforcement activities. Furthermore, the limitations imposed on military activities within the various maritime zones are also overwhelmingly clear. In the territorial sea, military activities are banned. Elsewhere, they are allowed provided that they do not breach Article 2(4) of the UN Charter and, where applicable, pay due regard to the sovereign rights of the coastal States.

Only two grey areas related to the concept of military activities remain to be clarified. The first concerns whether coastal States' actions in response to unlawful military activities in their territorial sea constitute law enforcement operations or military activity. This grey area is arduous to dissipate as this assessment depends not only on the actions taken by coastal States but also on the actions taken by the delinquent State. In the EEZ, the situation is more straightforward. Limited coastal State jurisdiction in this zone implies that most of the activities conducted against a delinquent foreign warship would be considered military.

The second area where the LOSC is unclear regards surveys. As mentioned above, two competing interpretations of the Convention exist on this matter. One considers that surveys are activities regulated by the freedom of navigation regime, while the other maintains that surveys are a type of research activity. Furthermore, these two interpretations are not mutually exclusive. The assessment of the nature of surveys as either an activity regulated by the freedom of navigation or marine scientific research regime is goal-dependent. Without trust and good faith, and importantly without the intervention of a judicial body, it seems impossible to clarify this issue. In turn, it means that incidents potentially leading to a confrontation between coastal and flag States are bound to occur.

In conclusion, stemming from these observations, creating a legal concept of hybrid warfare appears superfluous as it would not clarify the grey areas around the concept of military activities.

Given its semi-enclosed nature, the number of coastal States bordering it, and the current level of tension due to the war in Ukraine, it is likely that foreign military activities will take place in the EEZ of the Baltic Sea coastal States. Similarly, based on contemporary Russian practice, it is likely that illegal incursions in the territorial sea and sovereign airspace of coastal States will occur again.[149]

Thus, Baltic States could clarify their positions regarding the remaining grey areas identified in this communication to prevent tensions from rising further and deter actions leading to hybrid warfare. To do so, they could promote guidelines regarding navigation and overflight in the Baltic Sea similar to the ones developed in the early 2000s in the Asia-Pacific region by experts from China, Japan, Russia and the United States on the same issue.[150]

These Asian guidelines were drafted after a series of naval incidents in the Pacific in a context not too dissimilar to the current Baltic situation. The propositions they contain were designed to clarify the military activities warships were allowed to conduct in the EEZ of foreign States to decrease tensions. Moreover, they also dealt with the issue of surveys and the use of electronic systems that could be operated to conduct intelligence-gathering operations.[151] Furthermore, these guidelines follow the same spirit as the formula advanced by Hayashi and Klein. They are built on the premise that coastal States' sovereign rights should be respected and not interfered with, while at the same time, freedom of navigation should be preserved.[152]

Promoting a regional understanding of the concept of military activities at the Baltic level would contribute to reducing the tensions created by the risks of naval incidents stemming from divergent interpretations of the law. In turn, promoting such a regional understanding of military activities would obviate the need to develop a legal concept of hybrid warfare that would add a layer of complexity to the law of the sea, which does not need it.

---

149 Lott (n 1) 147–154.

150 Mark J Valencia and Kazumine Akimoto, 'Guidelines for Navigation and Overflight in the Exclusive Economic Zone' (2006) 30 Marine Policy 704, 707.

151 Sam Bateman, 'Prospective Guidelines for Navigation and Overflight in the Exclusive Economic Zone' (2005) 144 Maritime Studies 17, 19–20, 26–27.

152 Ibid, 21, 25–26.

CHAPTER 4

Use of Force in Hybrid Naval Warfare Contexts: Applicability of the Law Enforcement or Conduct of Hostilities Rules?

Anna Petrig

Introduction: a Myriad of Thresholds Separating the Peacetime from the Wartime Legal Regime

Historically, international law rests on a rather categorical distinction between peace and war. Consequently, it offers a discrete set of rules for both states of affairs between nations: the law of peace and the law of war.[1] Today, it is widely accepted that these two bodies of law are not hermetically sealed off from each other but instead characterised by a certain degree of permeability.[2] The divide between war and peace has thus been watered down in contemporary international law but has not become irrelevant. Indeed, various commentators stress its lasting significance.[3] The distinction between the normal and

1 Carsten Stahn, 'Jus Post Bellum: Mapping the Discipline(s)' (2007) 23(2) American University International Law Review 311, 316. Since the term 'law of war' is used here in contrast to the 'law of peace', it is understood broadly, not only including the *jus in bello* in the sense of the law of armed conflict (hereinafter LOAC) but also other bodies of law, notably prize law, the law of neutrality and the *jus ad bellum*. For a similarly broad definition, see, e.g., US, Department of Defense, Office of the General Counsel, *Department of Defense Law of War Manual* (June 2015, Updated July 2023) para 1.3.

2 Evidence is abundant. Anecdotally, it may be pointed to the fact that even some of the LOAC rules apply in peacetime: Marco Sassòli, *International Humanitarian Law: Rules, Controversies, and Solutions to Problems Arising in Warfare* (2nd edn, Edward Elgar Publishing 2024) 205. As regards the maritime domain, the law of the sea is not entirely displaced once a situation amounts to an armed conflict, which triggers the applicability of the law of naval warfare (hereinafter LONW), but remains relevant in various respects. For example, the law of the sea rules defining the maritime zones are vital in describing the regions of operations under the LONW; see, e.g., San Remo Manual on International Law Applicable to Armed Conflicts at Sea (12 June 1994) (hereinafter San Remo Manual), Part II.

3 See, e.g., Dino Kritsiotis, 'War and Armed Conflict', in Rain Liivoja and Tim McCormack (eds.), *Routledge Handbook of the Law of Armed Conflict* (Routledge 2016) 5, writing that the 'fragmentation between war and peace' occurs at the 'very core' of international law, amounting to the '*summa divisio* of the discipline'; Aurel Sari, *Blurred Lines: Hybrid Threats*

DOI:10.1163/9789004707993_006

exceptional condition in international affairs[4] remains relevant because the concept of war, despite its archaic touch, continues to 'affect [...] the application of law'.[5] Broadly speaking, the 'idea of war often operates to legitimate something that would otherwise be illegal'.[6] The law of armed conflict (hereinafter LOAC) is paradigmatic in this regard as it allows under certain conditions to lawfully kill and destroy,[7] thus making legal '[b]ehaviour that international law would ordinarily condemn and regard as impermissible'.[8] In this sense, the rules belonging to the wartime paradigm are generally more permissive than those belonging to the peacetime regime.[9]

The vexing problem is that no single bright line separates the peacetime from the wartime legal regime. Instead, a myriad of thresholds defines the applicability of entire bodies of law or specific rules designed to govern matters pertaining to the exceptional state of affairs between nations. To begin with, there are the various thresholds belonging to the *jus ad bellum*: 'threat to the peace, breach of the peace, or act of aggression',[10] 'use of force'[11] and 'armed attack'[12]. The list becomes even longer if we consider *jus in bello* thresholds, such as 'declared war' and 'armed conflict'[13] or 'attacks'[14]. Treaties belonging to the law of neutrality refer to yet other thresholds to define their scope of application, notably 'naval war'[15] and 'war on land'[16]. Roaming the legal terrain

and the Politics of International Law (Hybrid CoE January 2018) 3, stating that 'the dividing line between peace and war remains key to the contemporary international legal system'.

4 Sari, Blurred Lines (n 3) 3.

5 Andrew Clapham, *War* (Oxford University Press 2021) Preface v.

6 Ibid.

7 Ibid.

8 Kritsiotis (n 3) 7.

9 See, e.g., Section 1.3 as regards the use of force specifically.

10 Charter of the United Nations (signed 26 June 1945, entered into force 24 October 1945) XV UNCIO 335 (hereinafter UN Charter), Art 39.

11 Ibid, Art 2(4).

12 Ibid, Art 51.

13 Geneva Convention II for the Amelioration of the Condition of Wounded, Sick and Shipwrecked Members of Armed Forces at Sea (adopted 12 August 1949, entered into force 21 October 1950) 75 UNTS 85 (hereinafter GC II), Art 2.

14 Protocol Additional to the Geneva Conventions of 12 August 1949, and relating to the Protection of Victims of International Armed Conflicts (Protocol I) (adopted 8 June 1977, entered into force 7 December 1978) 1125 UNTS 3 (hereinafter AP I), Art 49.

15 Convention (XIII) concerning the Rights and Duties of Neutral Powers in Naval War (adopted 18 October 1907, entered into force 26 January 1910), title and preamble.

16 Convention (V) Respecting the Rights and Duties of Neutral Powers and Persons in Case of War on Land (adopted 18 October 1907, entered into force 26 January 1910), title and preamble.

where peace and war border each other thus implies passing different checkpoints at different places, each having its distinct, sometimes unclear, criteria for letting someone through – rather than crossing one official border check between peace and war by simply pulling one's passport. Overall, identifying the applicable law has become an intricate and complex endeavour: not only has the number of thresholds multiplied in the post-World War II international legal order, but the meaning of most thresholds remains unclear, if not disputed.[17]

A hallmark of hybrid (naval) wars is that they are not only fought on land, sea and air but regularly extend to the information, cyber and – of importance here – legal domains.[18] In the latter, where 'lawfare' is conducted,[19] the exploitation of the complexity and uncertainty of legal thresholds separating the peacetime from the wartime legal rules is a common tactic.[20] Hybrid adversaries engage in conduct that either remains just below the thresholds triggering the more permissive wartime rules, or is hard to assess in terms of whether it reached a given threshold. This strips a law-compliant state – or one that exercises 'interpretive forbearance' and opts to apply the more restrictive peacetime rules despite the applicability of wartime rules[21] – from the possibility of relying on the more permissive wartime rules. By 'instrumentalizing

---

17 See Aurel Sari, 'Hybrid Warfare, Law, and the Fulda Gap', in Winston S Williams and Christopher M Ford (eds.), *Complex Battlespaces: The Law of Armed Conflict and the Dynamics of Modern Warfare* (Oxford University Press 2018) 175–179.

18 See, e.g., Sari, Blurred Lines (n 3) 5, arguing that 'law is a domain of competition, just like the land, maritime, air, information and cyber domains are'.

19 See, e.g., Andres B Munoz Mosquera and Sascha Dov Bachmann, 'Lawfare in Hybrid Wars: The 21st Century Warfare' (2016) 7 Journal of International Humanitarian Legal Studies 63–87.

20 Hitoshi Nasu, 'Challenges of Hybrid Warfare to the Implementation of International Humanitarian Law in the Asia-Pacific', in Suzannah Linton, Tim McCormack and Sandesh Sivakumaran (eds.), *Asia-Pacific Perspectives on International Humanitarian Law* (Cambridge University Press 2019) 230.

21 Rob McLaughlin, 'Anticipating Operational Naval Warfare Issues in International Humanitarian Law That May Arise in the Event of a Conflict in the South China Sea', in Suzannah Linton, Tim McCormack and Sandesh Sivakumaran (eds.), *Asia-Pacific Perspectives on International Humanitarian Law* (Cambridge University Press 2019) 710, uses this term to denote situations in which an incident at sea amounts to an armed conflict, and thus renders the LONW applicable, but in which the targeted state chooses, for political or diplomatic reasons, *not* to rely on the more permissive LONW authorisations and instead to respond to the incident by having recourse to the less far-reaching peacetime law authorisations.

legal thresholds',[22] hybrid adversaries thus create an 'asymmetrical legal environment' operating in their favour.[23]

The following example, which pertains to one of the *jus ad bellum* thresholds, is instructive in this respect. According to Article 51 of the United Nations (hereinafter UN) Charter, the right to individual and collective self-defence is only triggered by an 'armed attack', a threshold which not every 'use of force' prohibited under Article 2(4) of the UN Charter fulfils.[24] These different thresholds – 'armed attack' and 'use of force' – create an 'operational sweet spot'[25] for a hybrid adversary. By using force that is prohibited by Article 2(4) of the UN Charter but does not meet the threshold of an armed attack, it denies the target state the possibility to forcibly respond in self-defence.[26] Similarly, the collective security guarantee of Article 5 of the North Atlantic Treaty Organization (hereinafter NATO) Treaty takes effect only if a member of the alliance becomes a victim of an 'armed attack'.[27] Using force that remains just below this intensity level, a hybrid adversary may advance its interest without risking a forcible response from NATO.[28]

Of interest in this chapter are, however, not the *jus ad bellum* but rather the *jus in bello* thresholds, concretely the one triggering the applicability of the law of naval warfare (hereinafter LONW) – a set of rules specifically designed to regulate armed conflicts at sea. Incidents in various world regions make it rather plain that hybrid adversaries also understand how to exploit this threshold by engaging in conduct that is difficult to assess in terms of LONW applicability. The Kerch Strait incident is a case in point. It 'demonstrates how adept Russia is at exploiting the seam between the contending peacetime and

22 Sari, Hybrid Warfare (n 17) 163; Alexander Lott, *Hybrid Threats and the Law of the Sea* (Brill Nijhoff 2022) 16 ('hybrid warfare takes advantage of the grey zone between the laws of peace and war').

23 Sari, Hybrid Warfare (n 17) 163–164; see also Munoz Mosquera and Bachmann (n 19) 74.

24 But note that the US conflates the notions of 'armed attack' and 'use of force', while acknowledging the differing view: US, Office of the General Counsel of the Department of Defense (n 1) para 1.11.5.2 (Use of Force Versus Armed Attack): 'The United States has long taken the position that the inherent right of self-defense potentially applies against any illegal use of force. Others, however, would be inclined to draw more of a distinction between "armed attacks" and uses of force that do not give rise to the right to use force in self-defense.'

25 Sari, Hybrid Warfare (n 17) 180.

26 Ibid; see also Lott (n 22) 17–18, 23 and 245.

27 North Atlantic Treaty (opened for signature 4 April 1949, entered into force 24 August 1949) 34 UNTS 243 (hereinafter NATO Treaty).

28 Sari, Blurred Lines (n 3) 3; Sari, Hybrid Warfare (n 17) 186–187.

wartime legal dimensions of the Crimea conflict',[29] notably cloaking the question of the applicable law in uncertainty.[30] Incidents involving the Chinese maritime militia are a further, notorious example where an adversary taps into the fine line separating tension and harassment subject to the peacetime rules from an incident qualifying as an armed conflict at sea and triggering the more permissive LOAC authorisations.[31]

It is against this background that the author of the present chapter has chosen to contribute with some reflections to the second research question underlying the present book: '[W]hat is the threshold for the applicability of the law of naval warfare in situations that can be characterised as hybrid warfare?'[32] Bearing in mind the word limit, the complexity of the enquiry, and the fact that the applicability questions *inter alia* depend on the rule(s) in question, a narrow focus has been chosen for this chapter. It considers the use of force against or involving ships in hybrid naval warfare contexts and analyses when such use of force is governed by the more permissive conduct of hostilities rules of the law of naval warfare (hereinafter LONW CoH rules)[33] rather than the more restrictive maritime law enforcement rules (hereinafter MLE rules).

To answer this question, the chapter proceeds as follows. After this introduction, it will be demonstrated that the decision to use force under MLE or LONW CoH rules is consequential. While the principles limiting the use of force – necessity, proportionality and precaution – sound very similar under both sets of rules, their content is markedly different. As will be shown, the

29 James Kraska, 'The Kerch Strait Incident: Law of the Sea or Law of Naval Warfare?' (3 December 2018) EJIL: Talk!, available at <www.ejiltalk.org/the-kerch-strait-incident-law-of-the-sea-or-law-of-naval-warfare/> accessed 30 March 2024, 6.

30 Kraska, ibid, e.g., argues that the incident is governed by the LONW. By contrast, in *Dispute Concerning the Detention of Three Ukrainian Naval Vessels* (Ukraine v. Russian Federation), Provisional Measures, Order 25 May 2019, ITLOS Reports 2019, p. 283, the Tribunal understood the incident as one concerning the interpretation and application of the United Nations Law of the Sea Convention. But see Declaration of Judge Lijnzaad, ibid, 330, in which she explains that she has voted for the Order, 'but with a certain reluctance as to the Tribunal's considerations about the law that may be applicable to this case' (para 1) and in which she expresses concerns 'whether the current matter is truly a dispute concerning the interpretation and application of the Convention, or whether other rules of international law, for which the Tribunal may not have jurisdiction, are at issue' (para 5), thus insinuating that the matter may be governed by the LONW.

31 See, e.g., McLaughlin, South China Sea (n 21) 707–710.

32 See the introductory chapter of the present book.

33 On the exact scope of the present analysis and the fact that the term 'conduct of hostilities rules' is too broad in light of it but used for the sake of simplicity, see *infra* n 72.

conditions for the lawfulness of the use of force are relatively more permissive under the LONW CoH rules (allowing for proactive, first resort use of force against legitimate targets) as compared to the MLE rules (allowing only for reactive, last resort use of force).[34] As a result, the question of the applicability of the LONW CoH versus MLE rules has 'a significant impact on the legality of the use of force under international law' (Section 1).[35]

The chapter's core is devoted to the issue of thresholds, that is, to the question of when the LONW CoH rules are applicable to a given incident at sea involving the use of force. It is posited that answering it requires a three-prong enquiry, which starts with the rather obvious threshold question as to whether the general situation of violence in which the incident occurs amounts to an armed conflict. If so, the applicability of the entire LONW regime is, in principle, activated for a given context ('context applicability').[36] However, the analysis must not stop here since not every incident occurring in the geographical or temporal context of an armed conflict at sea is indeed covered by the LONW, but only those featuring a sufficient link – or nexus – with the armed conflict.[37] Neither shoplifting on dry land nor armed robbery at sea is, if unrelated to the armed conflict, governed by the LOAC and the LONW, respectively – which are bodies of law developed specifically to address the specificities of armed conflict and therefore do not provide appropriate rules for issues beyond it.[38] Thus, the second threshold question is whether a specific incident features a sufficient nexus with the armed conflict at sea ('incident applicability').[39] If so, in a third step, it must be assessed whether the measure in question amounts to an attack, for only then will the LONW CoH rules be applicable[40] ('measure applicability'). Indeed, under the LONW, belligerent measures are not limited to attacks but may consist, for example, of control measures, such as the right of visit and search of neutral vessels or the right to inspect specially protected

34 In detail see *infra* Section 1.3.

35 Elvina Pothelet, 'Searching for the "Nexus": A Proposal to Refine the Scope of Applicability of International Humanitarian Law and War Crimes Law' (PhD thesis, University of Geneva 2021) 369.

36 Pothelet uses the terms 'regime applicability', 'macro-applicability' and 'context applicability' to refer to the first threshold that must be met in order to apply the shore-based LOAC. Ibid, 13.

37 For shore-based LOAC: see Sassòli, IHL 2024 (n 2) 220 in general; and Pothelet (n 35) 370–371 as regards use of force specifically.

38 Sassòli, IHL 2024 (n 2) 220.

39 In the context of shore-based LOAC, Pothelet (n 35) 13 refers to 'case applicability' or 'micro-applicability' to denote this second threshold.

40 James Kraska and others, *Newport Manual on the Law of Naval Warfare* (US Naval War College 2023) 130.

enemy vessels.[41] Taking LONW measures that do not qualify as an attack may also imply the use of force, which is, however, not governed by the LONW CoH rules.[42] In sum, the applicability of the LONW CoH rules requires that three thresholds are met: the situation of violence must amount to an 'armed conflict', the incident provoking the use of force must feature the requisite 'nexus' with the armed conflict, and the forcible measure taken must amount to an 'attack' (Section 2).

In the next Section, it will be demonstrated that the doctrinal and practical debates so far have largely focused on whether a given situation of violence amounts to an armed conflict, forming the first threshold requirement. Even if these debates feature a palpable land bias, analyses of the notion of armed conflict at sea have become more frequent in recent years as there is a renewed interest in the LONW in light of actual and potential conflicts with a maritime dimension. By contrast, the second threshold requirement – the nexus – has received far less attention, even in the rich qualification debate centring around shore-based armed conflicts, which is surprising as the thorniest applicability issues arise at this very level.[43] In 2019, Marco Sassòli noted that 'the contours of the nexus requirement for the applicability of IHL [International Humanitarian Law] remain totally unexplored in IHL scholarship'.[44] Meanwhile, the excellent study of Elvina Pothelet has addressed this doctrinal gap in an important way[45] – yet only regarding the shore-based LOAC. It is posited and argued that due to the 'rule-exceptionalism' of the LONW – a term used by Rob McLaughlin to refer to rules of the LONW, which are peculiar in that they deviate from the LOAC as applicable on land[46] – the territorially

41 See San Remo Manual, Part V, entitled 'Measures Short of Attack: Interception, Visit, Search, Diversion and Capture'; Wolff Heintschel von Heinegg, 'The Difficulties of Conflict Classification at Sea: Distinguishing Incidents at Sea from Hostilities' (2016) 98(2) International Review of the Red Cross 449, 462; Kraska and others, Newport Manual (n 40) 37 and 131–132.

42 Gloria Gaggioli, 'The Use of Force in Armed Conflicts Conduct of Hostilities, Law Enforcement, and Self-Defense', in Winston S Williams and Christopher M Ford (eds.), *Complex Battlespaces: The Law of Armed Conflict and the Dynamics of Modern Warfare* (Oxford University Press 2018) 61, 69, referring to the example of blockade enforcement.

43 Pothelet (n 35) 4; she argues that this is a result of the fact that the LOAC applicability at the context-level is rather widely defined.

44 Marco Sassòli, *International Humanitarian Law: Rules, Controversies, and Solutions to Problems Arising in Warfare* (Edward Elgar Publishing 2019) 201.

45 Pothelet (n 35); as per Sassòli, IHL 2024 (n 2) 222, she remains the 'scholar who most thoroughly analysed the nexus' so far.

46 Robert McLaughlin, 'Active Resistance by Merchant Vessel Crews During International Armed Conflict is Not "Direct Participation in Hostilities"' (2022) 99 International Law Studies 284, 289; see also Sassòli, IHL 2024 (n 2) 430, referring to the 'the sometimes

informed findings regarding the nexus cannot be directly transposed to the LONW (Section 3).

In the final Section, it is concluded that there is a need to further explore and refine the threshold criteria for the applicability of the LONW and, specifically, to develop a maritime-specific theory of nexus.

1 Applicability of MLE or LONW CoH Rules: a Consequential Decision

Under both the MLE and the LONW CoH rules,[47] the use of force is not prohibited but regulated. However, as will be shown in the following Section, the two sets of rules regulate it in markedly different ways.[48] Since the LONW CoH rules are generally more permissive than the MLE rules, the 'choice of the applicable paradigm may have significant legal and humanitarian consequences'.[49]

1.1 *Use of Force in MLE: Instances and Legal Framework*

In a maritime law enforcement context, the projection of force may be necessary for various purposes, notably to compel a vessel to navigate to or away from a certain place; to stop and board it; to defend against criminal suspects; or to seize, destroy and sink a ship.[50] The use of force in policing operations at sea is primarily governed by domestic law, notably administrative and criminal law,[51] which has to comply with international law on the matter.

To identify international rules on the use of force in MLE operations, one intuitively turns to the law of the sea and, specifically, the United Nations

---

astonishing (…) rules' of the LONW; and Sassòli, IHL 2019 (n 44) 400, pointing to the 'distinctive features and surprising rules' of LONW when seen from the viewpoint of shore-based LOAC.

47 This chapter rests on the idea that the use of force under international law is governed by only two paradigms, which are the MLE and LONW CoH rules, and that the use of force in self-defence is not a third paradigm comprising further authorisation; arguing this way Gaggioli (n 42) 105–106.

48 Pothelet (n 35) 369.

49 Nils Melzer and Etienne Kuster, *International Humanitarian Law: A Comprehensive Introduction* (International Committee of the Red Cross 2016) 30.

50 Cameron Moore, 'The Use of Force', in Robin Warner and Stuart Kaye (eds.), *Routledge Handbook of Maritime Regulation and Enforcement* (Routledge 2015) 28.

51 Matteo Tondini, 'The Use of Force in the Course of Maritime Law Enforcement Operations' (2017) 4(2) Journal on the Use of Force and International Law 253, 255.

Convention on the Law of the Sea (hereinafter LOSC).[52] Yet, surprisingly, the 'Constitution for the Oceans' is silent on the matter,[53] as are most other treaties authorising enforcement measures against delinquent vessels. The 1995 Fish Stock Agreement[54] and the 2005 SUA Protocol[55] – and, on a regional level, the 1995 Agreement on Illicit Traffic by Sea of the Council of Europe[56] – are exceptions in this respect as they comprise provisions limiting the use of force. However, their respective scope of application remains narrow.[57] The UN Security Council Resolutions authorising enforcement measures against ships engaged in maritime crime equally lack explicit guidance on the use of force.[58] More recent resolutions, at least, tend to stipulate that 'applicable international

52 United Nations Convention on the Law of the Sea (opened for signature 10 December 1982, entered into force 16 November 1994) 1833 UNTS 3.

53 This was no oversight. Ivan Shearer, who attended the LOSC negotiations as a delegate, explains this gap by 'a disinclination' during the Third UN Conference on the Law of the Sea 'to discuss such distasteful matters' (Ivan Shearer, 'The Development of International Law with Respect to the Law Enforcement Roles of Navies and Coast Guards in Peacetime' (1998) 71 International Law Studies 429, 440) and also by the prevailing perception among delegates that 'customary international law already governed the exercise of force' sufficiently (Ivan Shearer, 'Problems of Jurisdiction and Law Enforcement Against Delinquent Vessels' (1986) 35(2) International and Comparative Law Quarterly 320, 341). On the latter argument, see also David H Anderson, 'Some Aspects of the Use of Force in Maritime Law Enforcement', in Nerina Boschiero and others (eds.), *International Courts and the Development of International Law* (TMC Asser Press 2013) 233, 234, who identifies policing at sea and the use of force as one of the matters not governed by the LOSC, which, according to its preamble, 'continue to be governed by the rules and principles of general international law'.

54 Agreement for the Implementation of the Provisions of the United Nations Convention on the Law of the Sea of 10 December 1982 relating to the Conservation and Management of Straddling Fish Stocks and Highly Migratory Fish Stocks (adopted 4 August 1995, entered into force 11 December 2001) 2167 UNTS 3, Art 22(1)(f).

55 Protocol of 2005 to the Convention for the Suppression of Unlawful Acts against the Safety of Maritime Navigation (adopted 14 October 2005, entered into force 28 July 2010) IMO Doc. LEG/CONF.15/21, Art 8*bis*(9).

56 Agreement on Illicit Traffic by Sea, implementing Article 17 of the United Nations Convention against Illicit Traffic in Narcotic Drugs and Psychotropic Substances (opened for signature 31 January 1995, entered into force 1 May 2000) CETS No. 156, Art 12(1)(d).

57 The provisions only apply if enforcement measures authorised in the respective treaty against suspects engaging in offences defined in the respective treaty are taken.

58 E.g., resolutions on piracy and armed robbery at sea, human trafficking and smuggling of migrants, and the enforcement of embargos relating to arms, weapons of mass destruction and other objects.

human rights law' must be observed when taking enforcement action at sea, thus indirectly constraining the use of force in MLE.[59]

In light of this, it is mainly in international human rights law (hereinafter IHRL) rather than in the law of the sea or transnational maritime criminal law where limitations of the use of force are to be found.[60] The right to life, enshrined in all major universal and regional IHRL treaties and amounting to customary international law,[61] is of primordial importance in this respect.[62] The case law of the European Court of Human Rights (hereinafter ECtHR) on the right to life and use of force and related doctrine is an extremely rich source. While most cases indeed relate to policing on land, and may thus not necessarily be transposable one-to-one to policing at sea with its distinct features,[63] the body of maritime-specific case law on the use of force is slowly growing.[64] This IHRL-specific case law is supplemented by judicial pronouncement on the use of force by courts and tribunals belonging to the LOSC dispute settlement mechanisms. The International Tribunal for the Law of the Sea (hereinafter ITLOS), in its seminal *M/V 'Saiga' (No. 2)* case, generically referred to 'international law' as a source from which it inferred the principles on the use of force

---

59 Anna Petrig, 'The Role Accorded to Human Rights in Security Council Maritime Resolutions', in Kiara Neri (ed.), *Le Conseil de sécurité des Nations Unies et la mer – The United Nations Security Council and the Sea* (Editoriale Scientifica 2018) 51–53 (initial silence on the compliance of enforcement measures with IHRL), 53–55 (mooring authorised enforcement powers to IHRL) and 69 (summary).

60 On the important role IHRL plays in light of the relative silence of the law of the sea and transnational maritime criminal law on the protection of suspects at sea, see Anna Petrig, 'Human Rights and Law Enforcement at Sea', in Ruxandra-Laura Boşilcă, Susana Ferreira and Barry J Ryan (eds.), *Routledge Handbook of Maritime Security* (Routledge 2022) 153–164.

61 International Covenant on Civil and Political Rights (adopted 16 December 1966, entered into force 23 March 1976) 999 UNTS 171, Art 6; Convention for the Protection of Human Rights and Fundamental Freedoms (signed 4 November 1950, entered into force 3 September 1953) CETS No. 5, Art 2; African Charter on Human and Peoples' Rights (adopted 27 June 1981, entered into force 21 October 1986) 1520 UNTS 217, Art 4; American Convention on Human Rights, 'Pact of San José' (signed 22 November 1969, entered into force 18 July 1978) 1144 UNTS 123, Art 4.

62 Efthymios D Papastavridis, 'The Use of Force at Sea in the 21st Century: Some Reflections on the Proper Legal Framework(s)' (2015) 2(1) The Journal of Territorial and Maritime Studies 119, 134. Limits on the use of force do not only flow from the right to life but also from the right to property; the latter is, however, less discussed in doctrine.

63 On the differences see Tondini (n 51) 254 and 259.

64 See most recently ECtHR, *L'affaire Alkhatib et autres c. Grèce* (App. no. 3566/16), Judgment of 16 January 2024.

in MLE,[65] rather than to IHRL.[66] Overall, there is a high degree of convergence regarding the substance of the principles on the use of force, which are necessity, proportionality, and precaution,[67] as developed by courts and tribunals deciding IHRL and LOSC disputes, respectively. These principles, which apply regardless of the maritime zone in which force is used during policing operations,[68] will be explained and contrasted to the similarly named principles under the LONW CoH rules once we have contextualised the latter.

1.2 *Use of Force under the LONW CoH: Instances and Legal Framework*

The LONW rests on three pillars. The first consists of the LOAC rules, which can be split into those regulating the conduct of hostilities at sea (in this chapter referred to as the LONW CoH rules) and those protecting certain persons at sea;[69] the second is prize law; and the third is maritime neutrality law.[70] As the present chapter focuses on the use of force as part of hostilities at sea, only the first pillar of the LONW is relevant. Within it, the analysis is limited to the CoH rules relevant for attacks against targets on, under and above the sea, at

---

65 Which is applicable by virtue of the LOSC, Art 293.

66 *M/V 'Saiga' (No. 2)* (Saint Vincent and the Grenadines v. Guinea), Judgment, ITLOS Reports 1999, p. 10, para 155. In light of this, Tullio Scovazzi, 'ITLOS and Jurisdiction over Ships', in Henrik Ringbom (ed.), *Jurisdiction over Ships: Post-UNCLOS Developments in the Law of the Sea* (Brill Nijhoff 2015) 382–404, 395, suggested that 'Perhaps the ITLOS, making a step further, could have pointed out that the relevant rules of customary international law are found in international human rights law, and in particular in the rules on the human right to life.' In the *Arctic Sunrise Arbitration* (The Netherlands v. the Russian Federation), Case 2014-02, Award on the Merits of 14 August 2015, para 198, the Tribunal held that it may, 'pursuant to Article 293, have regard to the extent necessary to rules of customary international law, *including international human rights standards*, (…) in order to assist in the interpretation and application of the Convention's provisions that authorise the arrest or detention of a vessel and persons' (emphasis added); at stake in this case was, however, not the right to life, but other rights, notably the right to liberty.

67 For a shore-based context, see Stuart Casey-Maslen, *Use of Force in Law Enforcement and the Right to Life the Role of the Human Rights Council*, Academy In-Brief No. 6 (Geneva Academy of International Humanitarian Law and Human Rights 2016) 6; for the maritime context, see Tondini (n 51) 266. The terminology to denote the first two principles is not always consistent; 'necessity' is sometimes referred to as 'unavoidability' and 'proportionate' as 'reasonable and necessary' (see, e.g., *M/V 'SAIGA' (No. 2)* (n 66) para 155). However, the content is similar; see, e.g., Douglas Guilfoyle, *Shipping Interdiction and the Law of the Sea* (Cambridge University Press 2009) 281, arguing that the words 'the minimum reasonably necessary' and 'proportionate' essentially denote the same standard.

68 Tondini (n 51) 256.

69 In the San Remo Manual, they are referred to as 'international humanitarian law', see Rule 13(a).

70 Kraska and others, Newport Manual (n 40) 1 and 84.

the exclusion of rules governing attacks from the sea against targets on land.[71] Although too broad a term in light of the limited scope of the present analysis, we refer to these rules as LONW CoH rules.[72]

The applicability of the century-old 1907 Hague Conventions to targeting *at* sea, in addition to targeting objectives on land *from* the sea,[73] and the LONW rules' applicability in current times,[74] are issues that must not be answered for the present chapter. This is because there is a 'general agreement that the basic principles underlying contemporary international humanitarian law [on the conduct of hostilities on shore] are equally applicable'[75] to the conduct of hostilities at sea as a matter of customary international law.[76] Indeed, the principles of distinction, proportionality and precaution apply as such across warfighting domains, including at sea.[77] Yet, this should not belie the fact that some

71 The rules applying to 'attacks from the sea (…) against objectives on land' are excluded as shore-based LOAC rules apply to them; this accrues from AP I, Art 49(3) and customary international law; see Sassòli, IHL 2024 (n 2) 431.

72 The term 'conduct of hostilities' is too broad in light of the scope of the present chapter for several reasons. First, CoH rules not only comprise targeting law (methods) but also weapons law (means) (Sassòli, IHL 2024 (n 2) 31), which is not analysed here. Second, CoH rules govern all methods and means of warfare, also those not amounting to an attack; e.g., declaring and establishing a blockade under the LONW does not by itself constitute an attack (Kraska and others, Newport Manual (n 40) 131); this chapter, however, only deals with attacks. Third, the CoH rules also cover attacks from the sea of targets on land, which are excluded here. Nevertheless, the term 'conduct of hostilities rules' (CoH rules) is used in the present chapter; not only for the sake of simplicity, but also because it is common in practice and doctrine to contrast the 'law enforcement paradigm' with the 'conduct of hostilities paradigm'; see, e.g., Gloria Gaggioli (n 42).

73 On this distinction and the respective applicable sources, see Kraska and others, Newport Manual (n 40) 134.

74 See, e.g, Sassòli, IHL 2024 (n 2) 432, stating that with the exception of the GC II, 'treaties applicable to naval warfare are more than 100 years old, and it is not clear whether their rules still apply'.

75 Wolff Heintschel von Heinegg, 'Maritime Warfare', in Andrew Clapham and Paola Gaeta (eds.), *The Oxford Handbook of International Law in Armed Conflict* (Oxford University Press 2014) 150, opening phrase of section '3 The Legal Framework Applicable to the Conduct of Hostilities at Sea', 'A. Basic principles applicable to naval warfare'.

76 This also accrues from the San Remo Manual, see, e.g., Rule 38 (no unlimited right to choose methods and means of warfare), Rule 39 (principle of distinction), Rule 40 (definition of military objective), Rule 41 (attacks must be limited to military objectives), Rule 42 (superfluous injury/unnecessary suffering; prohibition of indiscriminate attacks), Rule 43 (no quarter), Rule 46 (precautions/proportionality in attack).

77 Sassòli, IHL 2024 (n 2) 431, stating that distinction, proportionality and precaution 'largely apply, with some particularities, to naval warfare'; see also Kraska and others, Newport

major legal differences exist between land and naval warfare. A notable difference for the present chapter is that the LONW CoH rules are platform-centric rather than person-centric.[78] While under land-based CoH rules, the *person's* status or conduct is crucial in determining whether he or she is a legitimate target, in the LONW, the status and conduct of the *vessel* is generally decisive – the person disappears behind the ship, so to speak.[79] Later in this chapter, we will dive deeper into this 'rule-exceptionalism' – or 'distinctive features and surprising rules'[80] – of the LONW.

1.3 *Principles Governing the Use of Force: Similar Names, Different Content*

The principles governing the use of force sound quite similar under both the MLE and LONW CoH paradigms. Yet, as will be demonstrated in what follows, their content differs considerably.[81]

Our analysis starts with the principle of necessity, which operates differently under the two paradigms. Under the law enforcement paradigm, 'absolute' or 'strict' necessity has three main facets. First, the use of force must be a last resort (*ultima ratio*); force must only be applied when 'strictly necessary'[82] or 'strictly unavoidable'[83]. Use of force must thus remain 'exceptional'[84] and officials must, as far as possible, apply non-violent means to achieve compliance,[85] such as 'persuasion, negotiation, and mediation, backed by the inherent authority of a law enforcement official who is acting on behalf of the state'[86]. Second, force must only be used to pursue a legitimate aim, namely 'in self-defence or defence of others against the imminent threat of death

Manual (n 40) 86 (distinction and proportionality; but note that they understand proportionality as a 'basic rule' of the LONW rather than a principle) and 156 (precaution).

78 Kraska and others, Newport Manual (n 40) 84.

79 McLaughlin, DPH (n 46) 291, writes on merchant mariners specifically that they 'are generally tarred with the status brush of their vessel, as opposed to their status being determined based on their individually attributed conduct'.

80 Sassòli, IHL 2019 (n 44) 400.

81 Gaggioli (n 42) 69.

82 Code of Conduct for Law Enforcement Officials (adopted by General Assembly Resolution 34/169 of 17 December 1979) (hereinafter UN Code of Conduct for Law Enforcement Officials), Art 3.

83 Basic Principles on the Use of Force and Firearms by Law Enforcement Officials (adopted 7 September 1990 by the Eighth United Nations Congress on the Prevention of Crime and the Treatment of Offenders) ST/HR/1/Rev.6 (Vol. I/Part 1) 351 (hereinafter Basic Principles on the Use of Force), Principle 9.

84 UN Code of Conduct for Law Enforcement Officials, Art 3, Commentary.

85 Basic Principles on the Use of Force, Principle 4.

86 Casey-Maslen (n 67) 7.

or serious injury, to prevent the perpetration of a particularly serious crime involving grave threat to life, to arrest a person presenting such a danger and resisting their authority, or to prevent his or her escape'.[87] Third, where the use of force is unavoidable, only the minimum amount necessary must be used. Therefore, even a potentially violent suspect must, whenever this is reasonably possible, be arrested rather than killed,[88] and the amount of force 'must be in keeping with the level of resistance offered'.[89] This essentially calls for a graduated law enforcement response.[90]

The applicability of the principle of necessity, including the aforesaid three elements, to maritime law enforcement has been confirmed by international courts and tribunals, notably by the ITLOS in the *M/V 'Saiga' (No. 2)* case. Concerning the use of force to obtain the arrest of suspects on board a ship used for the commission of a crime – a legitimate aim provided a respective enforcement authorisation exists under international law[91] – the Tribunal held that 'international law (…) requires that the use of force must be avoided as far as possible',[92] which testifies to the *ultima ratio* character of the use of force at sea.[93] ITLOS further affirmed the need for a graduated law enforcement response by stating that '[t]he normal practice used to stop a ship at sea is first to give an auditory or visual signal to stop, using internationally recognised signals. Where this does not succeed, a variety of actions may be taken, including the firing of shots across the bows of the ship. It is only after the appropriate actions fail that the pursuing vessel may, as a last resort, use force.'[94]

Under the conduct of hostilities paradigm, by contrast, the use of force against lawful targets is presumed. In land warfare, it is not prohibited to use lethal force as a first resort based on the status (e.g. a combatant) or conduct of the person (e.g. a civilian directly participating in hostilities), even if these persons do not pose an imminent threat to life at the moment of the attack.[95]

---

87 Basic Principles on the Use of Force, Principle 9.

88 Casey-Maslen (n 67) 7–8.

89 IACtHR, *Nadege Dorzema et al. v. Dominican Republic*, Judgment of 24 October 2012, Series C No. 251, para 85(III).

90 Gaggioli (n 42) 70.

91 See *Arctic Sunrise Arbitration* (n 66) para 222, where the Tribunal makes the lawfulness of a MLE measure dependent on the availability of a legal basis in international law and the respect of the principles of necessity and proportionality.

92 *M/V 'SAIGA' (No. 2)* (n 66) para 155.

93 This accrues from a joint reading of ibid, paras 155 and 156.

94 Ibid, para 156.

95 ICRC, *The Use of Force in Armed Conflicts: Interplay between the Conduct of Hostilities and Law Enforcement Paradigms* (expert meeting report prepared and edited by Gloria Gaggioli; International Committee of the Red Cross November 2013) 8.

In the conduct of hostilities at sea, it is equally permissible to use force as a first resort. In addition, the following rule exceptionalism under the LONW accentuates the difference between the law enforcement and conduct of hostilities paradigms: the LONW is, as mentioned, concerned with the 'conduct and status of platforms rather than people'.[96] For the assessment of which targets are lawful, this implies that it is not the status or conduct of persons on board a vessel but rather the status and conduct of the vessel as such that is generally decisive. If the vessel is a military objective,[97] it can be lawfully attacked; as per the traditional view, the principle of distinction does not account for civilians on board.[98] Under the LONW CoH rules, persons on board a ship share, as a rule, the fate of the vessel.

To sum up, key differences exist under the MLE and LONW CoH paradigms as regards the question of whether force can be lawfully used. In MLE, this is only permissible as a last resort and in a reactive way, for example, to arrest a person suspected of having committed or about to commit a maritime crime or in a situation of self-defence or defence of others arising during the boarding of a suspect ship. In assessing whether force can be used, the person against whom force is displayed is in the focus, and lawfulness depends on whether a concrete and imminent risk for the life and limb of others emanates from the targeted person. By contrast, under the CoH paradigm, force can be used as a first resort and proactively if the target is a lawful one. In assessing the latter, it is not the person but rather the vessel on board which the person finds himself or herself, which is generally determinative.[99]

With this, we turn to the principle of proportionality, the content of which also differs under the two paradigms despite being labelled similarly. In the law enforcement context, the proportionality principle requires balancing the risk posed by the individual to enforcers and others with the potential harm done to that individual and bystanders.[100] Essentially, the principle 'protects

96 McLaughlin, DPH (n 46) 290; see also 291; Kraska and others, Newport Manual (n 40) 92.

97 Which vessels qualify as military objectives is not discussed here; but see the relevant rules in the San Remo Manual, e.g., Rule 40 (general definition of a military objective), Rule 51 (hospital ships) and Rule 60 (enemy merchant vessels).

98 Kraska and others, Newport Manual (n 40) 92; consequently, civilians on board a targetable platform are not considered collateral damage and are not considered in the assessment of the proportionality of the attack; see *infra* n 108.

99 On the differences between reactive use of force under MLE and proactive use of force under LONW CoH authorisations at the example of the Houthi rebel violence in the Red Sea, see Rob McLaughlin, 'Houthi Operations in the Red Sea and LOAC?' (8 January 2024) Lieber Institute West Point, available at <https://lieber.westpoint.edu/houthi-operations-red-sea-loac/> accessed 30 March 2024.

100 ICRC, The Use of Force (n 95) 8.

the lives of everyone'.[101] Further, it requires a 'strict' assessment, meaning that if the suspect is not posing an imminent threat of death or serious injury, the use of (potentially) lethal force is disproportionate; moreover, death or injury of bystanders must be avoided as far as possible.[102] The principle of proportionality applies to both policing on land and at sea.[103]

Under the conduct of hostilities paradigm, the principle of proportionality protects surrounding civilians and civilian objects – rather than the target per se as would be the case under the law enforcement paradigm – from injury and damage that is excessive in relation to the concrete and direct military advantage.[104] The risk of excessive collateral damage resulting from hostilities at sea is generally much lower than the one emanating from attacks against targets on land, where the presence of civilian persons and objects is much more likely,[105] especially in urban areas where warfare is increasingly conducted[106]. In addition to this factual difference between shore and sea, there is also a legal one. As per the traditional view, under the platform – rather than person-centric LONW CoH rules,[107] the crew and companies of a targetable vessel do not need to be subjected to any proportionality assessment, even if all or some of them are civilians.[108] In other words, '[t]he civilian crew are not considered collateral damage – while embarked they are targetable with, and share the fate of, their ship just as a naval crew would'.[109] Whether the principle of proportionality applies at least to passengers on board a merchant vessel liable to attack remains a controversial issue.[110]

This brief comparison evidences the marked differences between the principle of proportionality under the MLE and LONW CoH paradigms, respectively. Under the MLE rules, it protects everyone's life, including the life of the person against whom force may be used. Persons are at the very core of the

101 Gaggioli (n 42) 70.

102 Ibid, 67 and 70.

103 On the applicability at sea, see *Arctic Sunrise Arbitration* (n 66) para 222.

104 ICRC, The Use of Force (n 95) 8. As per Kraska and others, Newport Manual (n 40) 154, the content of AP I, Art 51(5)(b) – a provision governing land-based attacks and attacks from the sea against targets on land – also applies to attacks at sea as a matter of customary international law.

105 Kraska and others, Newport Manual (n 40) 154; but see 154–155 for real-life examples where collateral damage has been caused in the context of the conduct of hostilities at sea (whether it has been excessive is not assessed).

106 Sassòli, IHL 2024 (n 2) 389–390.

107 See *supra* n 78 and 96 and respective text.

108 Kraska and others, Newport Manual (n 40) 154; McLaughlin, DPH (n 46) 291.

109 McLaughlin, DPH (n 46) 291.

110 Kraska and others, Newport Manual (n 40) 155.

assessment of whether the use of force is proportionate. Under the LONW CoH rules, by contrast, the target as such is not covered by the principle; what is more, civilian persons on board a targetable vessel are generally not considered in the proportionality assessment.

Finally, there are also notable differences regarding the principle of precaution. Under the law enforcement paradigm, all precautions must be taken to avoid the use of force as such.[111] This principle 'acts as a precursor to the principles of necessity and proportionality'[112] and aims at minimising, to the greatest extent possible, injury or death. This aim can notably be realised by adopting an adequate legal and administrative framework governing the use of force; training officials in the use of non-lethal methods to accomplish their goals; equipping them with means that allow for a differentiated use of force; and planning and controlling law enforcement operations in a way that preserves the right to life to the greatest extent possible.[113] The applicability of this principle to enforcement operations taking place at sea has most recently been confirmed by the ECtHR.[114]

Under the LONW CoH rules, the principle of precaution does not require one to avoid the use of force as such to the greatest extent possible but merely to avoid excessive incidental civilian harm and injury. The principle is thus geared towards target verification and identification as well as avoidance of excessive incidental harm.[115] Whether under the LONW CoH rules, the more or less demanding standard (all 'feasible' versus all 'reasonable' measures that must be taken) applies,[116] can be left open for present purposes, for it accrues sufficiently from the above that the principle of proportionality has a different content under the MLE and LONW CoH rules.

In conclusion, even though the principles governing the use of force are labelled similarly under the law enforcement and conduct of hostilities paradigms, this cursory overview has demonstrated that they considerably differ in content both as regards the actual use of force and preventive measures to

111 Gaggioli (n 42) 70–71.

112 Casey-Maslen (n 67) 9.

113 ICRC, The Use of Force (n 95) 43.

114 *L'affaire Alkhatib et autres c. Grèce* (n 64) paras 126 ff and 133 ff.

115 See AP I, Art 57(4); San Remo Manual, Rule 46 and related commentary in Louise Doswald-Beck (ed.), *San Remo Manual on International Law Applicable to Armed Conflicts at Sea* (Cambridge University Press 1995) 123–124.

116 The San Remo Manual, Rule 46 adopts the 'feasible' standard. Kraska and others, Newport Manual (n 40) 158, argue for the 'reasonable' standard.

take.[117] Broadly speaking, the MLE paradigm is, compared with the LONW CoH paradigm, not only more person-centric but also more restrictive[118]. This is not surprising because, as mentioned earlier, the applicability of the LOAC makes certain conduct that is normally outlawed perfectly lawful. The use of deadly force is paradigmatic in this respect. It confirms Clapham's observation that 'the concept of war affects the application of law' and that '[t]he idea of war often operates to legitimate something that would otherwise be illegal'.[119] In light of this, the determination that a given use of force against a ship is not governed by the MLE but rather by the LONW CoH rules is consequential.[120] At the same time, deciding whether the LONW CoH rules are applicable to a given incident – which involves a three-prong enquiry to which we turn next – is not easy at all.[121]

2 The Applicability of the LONW CoH Rules: a Three-Prong Enquiry

As posited in the introduction, a three-prong enquiry is necessary to determine whether the LONW CoH rules are applicable to an incident involving the use of force at sea.[122] First, it must be ascertained whether the situation of violence, in which an incident involving a ship occurs, or an isolated incident at sea, amounts to an armed conflict. If so, the LONW regime is applicable as such to this situation (context applicability). Second, the LONW does not govern all events occurring in this context but only those featuring a sufficient link with the armed conflict in question. In other words, a nexus must exist between an incident involving a ship and the armed conflict (incident applicability). Third, only if the measure taken against the ship qualifies as an attack in the sense of the LONW will the LONW CoH rules discussed above be applicable (measure applicability). If all three thresholds, presented in the following Section, are met, the use of force against or involving ships is governed by the more permissive LONW CoH rules rather than the MLE rules.

117 In addition, major differences exist in terms of obligations that apply after the execution of an operation involving force, notably regarding the obligation to conduct an effective investigation; see ICRC, The Use of Force (n 95) 49–51.
118 Gaggioli (n 42) 65.
119 Clapham (n 5) Preface v.
120 ICRC, The Use of Force (n 95) 1.
121 Confirming the intricate nature of the threshold question: ICRC, The Use of Force (n 95) 1.
122 See text relating to *supra* n 36–42.

2.1 *Context Applicability: Existence of an Armed Conflict*

The LONW in its entirety – meaning all three pillars, which are the LOAC rules, prize law and maritime neutrality law – only applies if a situation of violence reaches the threshold of an international armed conflict (hereinafter IAC).[123] The first pillar of the LONW, the LOAC rules, even apply in non-international armed conflict (hereinafter NIAC) at sea, which is not the case for the other two pillars.[124] However, NIACs will not be considered any further here.

Treaty law does not offer a definition of the concept of IAC. The Second Geneva Convention of 1949, for instance, solely refers to an 'armed conflict which may arise between two or more of the High Contracting Parties', that is, between two or more states. Absent a definition in law, the legal contours of the concept have been sketched out by State practice, doctrine and judicial interpretation.[125] As regards the latter, the definition of the ICTY provided in the *Tadić* case has become the one generally recognised as authoritative,[126] including in the context of IACs with a maritime dimension[127]. As per the *Tadić* case, 'an [international] armed conflict exists whenever there is a resort to armed force between States'.[128] In light of the tendency of hybrid adversaries to deny the existence of an IAC and/or their involvement in such,[129] it is important to remember that the determination of whether this threshold is met does not depend on the views of the parties involved, but solely on the prevailing facts on the ground.[130]

---

123 Kraska and others, Newport Manual (n 40) 18. Similarly to the shore-based LOAC rules (see *supra* n 2), some of the LONW LOAC-rules already apply in peacetime; see ICRC, *Commentary on the Second Geneva Convention: Convention (II) for the Amelioration of the Condition of Wounded, Sick, and Shipwrecked Members of Armed Forces at Sea* (Cambridge University Press 2017), Art 2, paras 221–222. Since we are only concerned with the first pillar, the LOAC rules, where the threshold of IAC seems to be widely accepted, the position of some states that maritime neutrality law only applies in case of (declared) war is not further discussed here; see on this Kraska and others, Newport Manual (n 40) 19.

124 Kraska and others, Newport Manual (n 40) 18.

125 ICRC-Commentary GC II (n 123), Art 2, paras 239–240.

126 This has been affirmed, e.g., in ICC, The Office of the Prosecutor, *Situation in the Republic of Korea: Article 5 Report* (June 2014) para 44.

127 ICC, *Situation in the Republic of South Korea* (n 126) para 43; ICRC-Commentary GC II (n 123), Art 2, para 240; Kraska and others, Newport Manual (n 40) 20.

128 *Prosecutor v. Tadic* (Decision) ICTY-94-1 (2 October 1995) para 70.

129 Lott (n 22) 23; Borys Kormych and Tetyana Malyarenko, 'From Gray Zone to Conventional Warfare: The Russia-Ukraine Conflict in the *Black Sea*' (2022) 34(7) Small Wars & Insurgencies 1, 19.

130 ICRC-Commentary GC II (n 123), Art 2, paras 233–235; Kraska and others, Newport Manual (n 40) 20.

The first element of the *Tadić* IAC definition – 'between States' – requires that the resort to armed force involves two or more states.[131] While a plurality of actors is necessary, the definition covers not only the situation where the use of force by one state is met with armed resistance by the targeted state but also the unilateral use of force to which, for whatever reason, no forcible response follows.[132] Further, it does not matter whether *de jure* organs (be it the navy, the coast guard or any other state organ) or *de facto* organs use force; even the conduct of private persons is covered if the state exercises overall control over the non-state actors in question.[133] The force must not be directed against another state's armed forces; rather, it suffices that its territory (including its territorial or archipelagic waters), population, or military or civilian infrastructure comes under attack.[134] Yet, it remains unclear whether the use of force against a merchant ship qualifies as a use of force against the flag state if the incident does not happen in that state's territorial or archipelagic waters.[135]

The second element of the *Tadić* IAC definition – 'resort to armed force' – covers the use of any means or method having the potential to cause death, injury, physical damage, or destruction, including those specific to the maritime context, such as the use of torpedoes, naval mines and unmanned vessel or the establishment of a naval blockade.[136] Importantly, it is not required that harm actually results from resorting to the armed force.[137] Further, per the prevailing view, there is no intensity requirement, that is, 'no element of scale'[138] applying for so long as there is a resort to armed force between states. To use the words of Pictet, '[i]t makes no difference how long the conflict lasts, or how much slaughter takes place'.[139] Indeed, in the maritime context, it is not

131 Ibid, paras 241–243.

132 Ibid, para 245; Kraska and others, Newport Manual (n 40) 21.

133 Kraska and others, Newport Manual (n 40) 22–23.

134 ICRC-Commentary GC II (n 123), Art 2, para 246.

135 Kraska and others, Newport Manual (n 40) 24. For a discussion of whether this scenario could amount to an 'armed attack' in the meaning of the UN Charter, Art 51, see Martin Fink, 'Protecting Commercial Shipping with Strikes into Yemen: Do Attacks Against Merchant Shipping Trigger the Right of Self-Defence?' (26 January 2024) EJIL:Talk!, available at <www.ejiltalk.org/protecting-commercial-shipping-with-strikes-into-yemen-do-attacks-against-merchant-shipping-trigger-the-right-of-self-defence/> accessed 30 March 2024. If so, the threshold of IAC is generally fulfilled (see McLaughlin, South China Sea (n 21) 707); but it may even be fulfilled if the threshold of an 'armed attack' is not reached.

136 Kraska and others, Newport Manual (n 40) 21.

137 Ibid.

138 ICC, *Situation in the Republic of South Korea* (n 126), paras 10 and 45.

139 Jean Pictet (ed.), *Commentary on the Second Geneva Convention: Convention (II) for the Amelioration of the Condition of Wounded, Sick, and Shipwrecked Members of Armed Forces at Sea* (International Committee of the Red Cross 1960) 28.

unusual to see 'short, sharp, localised and "done" in a day' IACs.[140] The sinking of the *Cheonan*, a South Korean warship, by a torpedo launched from a North Korean submarine on 26 March 2010, which resulted in the death of nearly fifty navy sailors, is a classic example.[141]

Whether the *Tadić* definition of the IAC – 'resort to armed force between States' – is fulfilled in a given case tends to be a rather straightforward determination if traditional actors, means, and methods are involved, that is if naval forces confront each other. Yet, determining whether certain conduct reaches the threshold of an IAC becomes an intricate task if states rely on proxies to engage in aggressive or physically coercive action against another state's ship; deploy non-naval vessels to do so; and/or rely on non-traditional means and methods to engage in violent acts – which are the very hallmark of hybrid naval wars.[142] In the South China Sea, for instance, confrontations involving ostensibly 'civilian' ships, most notably fishing vessels, are not a rare occurrence.[143] Relying on proxies, such as 'maritime militias', provides the hybrid adversary with 'an effective attribution veil'[144] because it will often be difficult to demonstrate that they are either *de facto* state organs or private actors acting under the overall control of a state. This, however, is necessary because only the use of force attributable to a state can trigger an IAC.[145]

The focus so far has been on temporally and geographically limited incidents at sea *triggering* the existence of an IAC. In these cases, the difficulty lies in drawing the, sometimes fine, line between harassment and tension on the one hand and a resort to armed force by a state amounting to an IAC on the other. However, there is also the situation where an IAC undisputedly *exists* and in the context of which an incident at sea occurs. The Kerch Strait incident would belong to this latter scenario. While in the first scenario, the

140 McLaughlin, South China Sea (n 21) 703.

141 ICC, *Situation in the Republic of South Korea* (n 126), para 7. See McLaughlin, South China Sea (n 21) 703, for two further examples of one-day IACs at sea, which both took place in 1998, one involving the US and Iran, the other China and Vietnam.

142 On the use of non-traditional actors, means and methods, and the ensuing difficulties for determining whether an armed conflict exists, see Heintschel von Heinegg, Conflict Classification (n 41) 452–453 (in general); Lott (n 22) 20 (regarding contexts of hybrid naval warfare); and McLaughlin, South China Sea (n 21) 707–710 (regarding the South China Sea region specifically).

143 McLaughlin, South China Sea (n 21) 704 and 716.

144 Ibid, 706; this is just one advantage of this tactic, for others see 705–706: deploying large numbers of 'civilian' vessels makes it more difficult for the adversary to maintain situational awareness; is a very cheap force multiplier; and obfuscates the status of these vessels under the LOAC, creating uncertainty as to whether they are lawful targets.

145 See Nasu (n 20) 225.

context and incident applicability collapse (if the incident at sea amounts to an IAC and triggers the applicability of the LONW, it *per se* features a sufficient nexus with the armed conflict), it must for the latter situation be established that the incident features a sufficient link with the IAC for it to be governed by the LONW. This nexus requirement is discussed next.

2.2 *Incident Applicability: Nexus between Use of Force Incident and Armed Conflict*

Suppose a given situation amounts to an armed conflict, through which the regime of the LONW becomes applicable as such. In that case, a question arises as to which events – here, which incidents involving the use of force against ships – are governed by the LONW CoH rules rather than the MLE rules. As mentioned earlier, the LONW does not govern all acts occurring in the spatio-temporal framework of an armed conflict but only those featuring a sufficient link – or *nexus* – with it.[146]

Sometimes, it is obvious that there is a sufficient nexus between a particular incident and an armed conflict.[147] For example, in the ongoing IAC between Russia and Ukraine, the sinking of a Russian warship by a Ukrainian naval drone is an incident involving the use of force against a ship where the nexus between the conduct and the conflict seems palpably obvious.[148] Sometimes, it is equally obvious that incidents involving the use of force against ships do *not* feature a nexus with an armed conflict raging in the respective region. For example, in 2010–2011, violence against merchant ships in the form of hijackings was thriving off the coast of Somalia. Although Somalia was experiencing

146 Elvina Pothelet, 'Life in Rebel Territory: Is Everything War?' (20 May 2020) Armed Groups and International Law, available at <www.armedgroups-internationallaw.org/2020/05/20/life-in-rebel-territory-is-everything-war/> accessed 30 March 2024; Pothelet (n 35) 5; Sassòli, IHL 2024 (n 2) 220; see also text belonging to *supra* n 39.

147 See Pothelet (n 35) 4 who argues in a land-based context, that the applicability of the LOAC to specific events is not always 'open to doubt' and that there are 'many events related to the core of the conflict that are unmistakably covered' by the LOAC.

148 In recent months, Ukraine has sunk several Russian warships using the Magura V5, a relatively small, uncrewed, remote-controlled boat with a reach of 800 km and capable of carrying a payload of 250 kg; see Abdujalil Abdurasulov, 'Ukraine War: The Sea Drones Keeping Russia's Warships at Bay' BBC (12 March 2024), available at <www.bbc.com/news/world-europe-68528761> accessed 30 March 2024; Abdujalil Abdurasulov, 'Ukraine War: The Sea Drones Keeping Russia's Warships at Bay' BBC (12 March 2024), available at <www.bbc.com/news/world-europe-68528761> accessed 30 March 2024; and Pjotr Sauer, 'Russia Reportedly Fires Navy Chief After Ukraine's Attacks on Black Sea Fleet' The Guardian (13 March 2024), available at <www.theguardian.com/world/2024/mar/13/russia-reportedly-fires-navy-chief-attacks-black-sea-fleet-ukraine> accessed 30 March 2024.

several armed conflicts during these years, there was general agreement that these incidents were not acts of war but criminal acts qualifying as armed robbery at sea or piracy, and thus to be met by a law enforcement response subject to the MLE rules on the use of force.[149]

While many cases are clear-cut, there are also borderline cases. Particularly in hybrid naval war contexts, events occur that – at least at first glance – do not relate 'to the core of the conflict'[150] but rather appear peripherical to it. In such cases, therefore, it is difficult to determine whether these events are sufficiently connected with the surrounding conflict in order to be governed by the LONW.[151] The Kerch Strait incident, which happened in 2018 and thus at a time when an IAC between the Russian Federation and Ukraine existed, is paradigmatic in this regard. To this day, it is controversially discussed as to whether the incident features a sufficient link with the armed conflict that would subject it to the LONW.[152] Equally challenging to assess are the acts of violence committed by Houthi rebels since 2017, such as the use of remote-controlled crafts filled with explosives to inflict harm on other ships. Whether these are criminal acts,[153] or whether (some of them) are acts of war governed by the LONW because they have a sufficient nexus with an armed conflict is an intricate question.[154]

149 Even in this clear situation, there was initially a moment of confusion about the applicable legal framework. In one of its first resolutions authorising enforcement measures to counter armed robbery at sea and piracy, the UN Security Council decided that the authorised measures 'shall be undertaken consistent with applicable international humanitarian and human rights law' (UNSC Res 1851 (16 December 2008) UN Doc S/RES/1851 para 6). The reference to 'international humanitarian law' (i.e., LOAC) raised some doubts about the applicable legal framework. However, the word 'applicable' suggests that the UN Security Council did not declare the LOAC to be, in fact, applicable but rather referred to its potential applicability. For a detailed analysis on why the LOAC is not applicable in countering Somali-based piracy at sea and on land, see Robin Geiß and Anna Petrig, *Piracy and Armed Robbery at Sea: The Legal Framework for Counter-Piracy Operations in Somalia and the Gulf of Aden* (Oxford University Press 2011) 132–136.

150 Pothelet (n 35) 4.

151 See *supra* n 20–23 on how hybrid adversaries deliberately engage in conduct that is just below a certain threshold (here: the applicability of the LONW to a given incident) or is difficult to assess in terms of whether it has reached it.

152 See *supra* n 30.

153 The use of remotely controlled rather than crewed vessels to inflict harm to other ships complicates the assessment of whether these acts constitute piracy or SUA offences; see on this Anna Petrig, 'Autonomous Offender Ships and International Maritime Security Law' in Henrik Ringbom, Erik Røsæg and Trond Solvang (eds.), *Autonomous Ships and the Law* (Routledge 2021) 23–55.

154 On whether an armed conflict between Houthis and other states (e.g., Israel) can be construed at all, see McLaughlin, Houthi Operations (n 99). Even if there is one or several

Despite the importance of the concept of nexus in determining whether borderline incidents have a close enough link with an armed conflict and are thus subjected to the LOAC, it has remained under-researched and under-theorised in LOAC doctrine.[155] Commentators, State practice, and international bodies have occasionally mentioned the nexus requirement.[156] Most often, this has occurred in the context of the use of force, that is, as a criterion for distinguishing acts of hostilities subject to the LOAC from other uses of force.[157] For the longest time, however, the concept existed as 'a logical intuition more than a strictly defined legal requirement'.[158] It was not until Pothelet's study that the concept of nexus was elevated from an 'intuitive idea'[159] to a legal concept with fairly clear contours.[160]

In her study, she first *conceptualises* the nexus, clarifying that it is a legal requirement for the LOAC applicability. She further considers how it relates to the war crimes jurisprudence (where nexus considerations are part and parcel of the doctrinal discussion) and how it fits into the overall framework governing the applicability of the LOAC.[161] In essence, she argues that the nexus is neither an additional nor an alternative requirement to the LOAC applicability. Instead, it is an aspect of the five applicability criteria for the LOAC, namely, that an event is only governed by the LOAC if it falls within its material, geographical, temporal as well as the active and passive personal scope of application.[162] Since the scope of application differs from rule to rule, there is not one single nexus, but the definition of the nexus requirements depends on the rule in question.[163] However, this does not lead to a hyper-fragmentation of the conditions of LOAC applicability, as there are, according to Pothelet, two

armed conflicts, it must be determined for each incident whether it features a sufficient link with an armed conflict.

155 See Pothelet (n 35) 92 and 497.

156 For an overview of mentions of the nexus as a condition for the applicability of the LOAC, see ibid, 99–102; for an overview of commentators who invoke the nexus as a limiting factor in the context of a broad interpretation of the geographical scope of applicability of the LOAC, see 102–109.

157 Ibid, 99–100.

158 Ibid, 108.

159 Ibid, 99.

160 See also *supra* n 45 on the fact that Pothelet's study remains the only in-depth analysis of the nexus to date; Sassòli, IHL 2024 (n 2) 222 states that the several pages he devotes to the concept of nexus in his latest LOAC treatise 'are nearly exclusively based' on Pothelet's findings.

161 Pothelet (n 35) Part I.

162 Ibid, 123, 163–164, 174–175 and 500; see also Sassòli, IHL 2024 (n 2) 221.

163 Pothelet (n 35) 173–174; Pothelet, Life in Rebel Territory (n 146).

'dominant' types of nexus: the passive personal and the material. This follows from the object and purpose of the LOAC rules, which is either to protect conflict-affected persons (passive personal nexus: a link between a person in need of protection and an armed conflict) or to regulate conflict-related conduct (material nexus: a link between the conduct in question and an armed conflict), or a combination thereof.[164] Of our interest is the material nexus since we enquire into the question of when an incident involving the use of force against a ship – and thus a certain conduct – is sufficiently linked to an armed conflict to warrant the applicability of the LONW CoH rules rather than the MLE rules.

Building on this conceptualisation, Pothelet then *defined* the content of the nexus for selected sets of rules,[165] including the CoH rules.[166] Her excellent and detailed analysis of the nexus, as a requisite to render the CoH rules applicable to a particular incident involving the use of force, relates to land-based LOAC.[167] However, due to the LONW 'rule-exceptionalism', shore-based interpretations of LOAC concepts cannot necessarily be transposed to the LONW.[168] As will be shown in Section 3, this holds (at least in part) true for the definition of the nexus as a prerequisite to render the CoH rules applicable to a particular incident of use of force. Before discussing this specific aspect of the 'incident applicability' of the LONW, we briefly present the third and final threshold requirement, 'measure applicability'.

2.3 *Measure Applicability: Measure Amounts to an Attack*

Even if the LONW is applicable as such to a given situation of violence because it amounts to an armed conflict (context applicability) and a specific incident occurring in this context features a sufficient link with the surrounding conflict and is thus governed by the LONW (incident applicability), the LONW CoH rules are only applicable if the measure taken against the ship amounts to an attack (measure applicability).[169] The fact that the CoH rules apply only to attacks also holds true for shore-based CoH rules.[170]

164 Pothelet (n 35) 175–176 and 501–503.
165 Ibid, Part II.
166 Ibid, Chapter 5.
167 Ibid, Chapter 5, Section III.
168 Arguing in this way in the context of the land-based concept of 'direct participation in hostilities', which cannot be imported into the LONW: McLaughlin, DPH (n 46) 290.
169 See also text belonging to *supra* n 40–42.
170 Sassòli, IHL 2024 (n 2) 375.

Under the LONW, belligerent measures are not limited to attacks. Attacks are indeed just one of the belligerent acts that the LONW foresees.[171] Next to the right to conduct hostilities,[172] the LONW authorises a series of other measures against ships and their crew.[173] According to the Newport Manual, they include 'the right to visit, search, and diversion of enemy and neutral vessels; the right of capture; the right to inspect specially protected enemy vessels (e.g., hospital ships); the right to control neutral vessels (…) in the immediate vicinity of naval operations; the right to establish and enforce a blockade; the right to establish and enforce exclusion zones; the right to demand the surrender of enemy military personnel; and the right to undertake convoy operations'.[174] Taking these measures may also necessitate the use of force. However, since these measures do not qualify as attacks, the use of force is not governed by the CoH rules, which apply only to attacks.[175] And the LONW rules are silent on the type and amount of force that may be used in such situations – as is the case with the land-based LOAC rules, which provide for the use of force outside the context of hostilities.[176] Broadly speaking, the standard is similar to the MLE standard and, thus, less permissive than the LONW CoH standard.[177]

While it is clear that the LONW CoH rules only apply to attacks, determining whether a concrete measure amounts to an attack involves at least two difficulties. First, there is no treaty law definition of the concept of 'attack' in the LONW, unlike for attacks conducted on or against targets on land.[178] And, as we will see in short, the definitions offered in soft law instruments and

171 Heintschel von Heinegg, Conflict Classification (n 41) 462.

172 On the fact that the concept of 'conduct of hostilities' is broader than that of 'attacks', see *supra* n 72.

173 See San Remo Manual, Part V, entitled 'Measures Short of Attack: Interception, Visit, Search, Diversion and Capture'; Kraska and others, Newport Manual (n 40) 37 and 131–132.

174 Kraska and others, Newport Manual (n 40) 37.

175 Gaggioli (n 42) 69 while referring to the example of blockade enforcement.

176 On LOAC rules on the use of force outside hostilities, see Pothelet (n 35) 373–376; an example is the duty of the occupying power to maintain public order and safety, which implies that it may use force to enforce the law.

177 While some commentators argue that, in such cases, the law enforcement rules (as shaped by IHRL) as such govern the use of force, the interaction between IHRL and LOAC may be more complex. For example, it may be argued that the respective LOAC rules on the use of force outside the conduct of hostilities must be interpreted in light of IHRL (systemic integration), which leads to a similar result in terms of the applicable standard (one akin to the law enforcement standard) but differs methodologically and in terms of accountability. See Pothelet (n 35) 375–376 for an interesting discussion of this issue, which cannot be developed further here given the limited word count.

178 AP I, Art 49(1).

doctrine differ from each other with regard to key aspects.[179] Second, we have seen that belligerent measures other than attacks regularly consist of control measures. While taking these measures as such does not amount to an attack, a ship resisting them may be lawfully attacked. For instance, the declaration, establishment and enforcement of a blockade does not amount to an attack; however, a vessel resisting blockade enforcement measures can be lawfully attacked.[180] To provide another example, visit, search and capture under prize law do not constitute an attack. However, if the vessel subjected to these measures offers a certain degree of resistance, it becomes liable to attack.[181] The crucial question then becomes what type of resistance turns the vessel into a military objective and allows the belligerent, which initially solely engaged in LONW control measures, to attack a neutral or enemy vessel – in which case the use of force is subject to the much more permissible LONW CoH rules.

To denote this threshold, the San Remo Manual refers variedly to 'actively resisting visit, search or capture',[182] to 'intentionally and clearly resist visit, search or capture'[183] and to 'clearly resist capture'[184]. Whether these different wordings imply different standards is not explained in the Manual's commentary. The Newport Manual does not provide much guidance either on when the threshold of 'active resistance' is crossed; it solely states that the determination 'is a question of fact in each circumstance'.[185] Given the consequential nature of the decision of whether a belligerent is authorised to engage in an attack and thus to rely on the permissive CoH rules, the determination should be governed by precise criteria allowing for a principled approach.

The circumstances that render a vessel liable to attack – namely, actively resisting control measures – would not turn an object in land warfare into a military one. As Sassòli puts it, 'those circumstances could at best raise suspicion and may justify the use of force according to a law enforcement paradigm'.[186] This is a further LONW 'rule-exceptionalism' that makes it hard – if not impossible – to transfer land-based theories in relation to the applicability of the

179 See below Section 3.3.
180 Kraska and others, Newport Manual (n 40) 131.
181 Ibid, 132.
182 San Remo Manual, Rule 60(e) applying to enemy merchant vessels.
183 Ibid, Rule 67(a) applying to neutral merchant vessels.
184 Ibid, Rule 98 applying to merchant vessels suspected of breaching a blockade.
185 Kraska and others, Newport Manual (n 40) 174; anecdotally, they state that '[f]iring upon the blockade force or continuing to attempt to breach the blockade' and 'attempting to ram an enforcing belligerent warship' amount to active resistance.
186 Sassòli, IHL 2024 (n 2) 437.

CoH rules to the maritime context. This problem will be explained further in the next Section.

3 Nexus for CoH Rules: LONW 'Rule Exceptionalism' Does Not Allow Transposing Shore-Based Theories

The nexus requirement has received hardly any attention in the LONW doctrine. By contrast, for shore-based LOAC rules, the study of Pothelet offers rather detailed guidance on how the use of force must be linked to an ongoing armed conflict to justify the applicability of the CoH rules.[187] However, the criteria to distinguish an act of hostility that renders the CoH rules applicable from another type of use of force are hardly transposable to the naval warfare context because of the specificities and exceptional rules of the LONW. This will be demonstrated in this Section. First, it will be explained that the war crimes jurisprudence already provides limited guidance for determining the applicability of CoH rules ashore, but even less for the LONW CoH rules. Second, it will be shown that the notion of attack is crucial in determining the material scope of applicability – and thus the nexus – of the CoH rules on land. Yet, for the LONW CoH rules, this concept does not have the same guiding function because there is neither a uniform definition of it nor a clear understanding of when a belligerent can engage in an attack. Third, we will see that on land, the concept of direct participation in hostilities (hereinafter DPH) – in particular, one of its definitional elements, the belligerent nexus – has clarified when a forcible act amounts to a hostile act. However, in the vessel-centric rather than person-centric LONW, the notion of DPH geared towards a person's conduct is misplaced and largely inapplicable. Overall, the terrestrially informed definition of the nexus for the CoH rules is hardly helpful for determining the applicability of the LONW CoH rules.

3.1 *War Crime Nexus: Exceedingly Low Threshold and Missing Maritime Dimension*

We have seen that two dominant types of nexus requirements exist for determining the LOAC applicability: the passive personal nexus (designating the link between a person in need of protection and an armed conflict) and the material nexus (describing the link between a particular conduct and an armed conflict). For CoH rules, the latter type of nexus is relevant.[188] Since war

187 Pothelet (n 35) Chapter 5, Section III.

188 See text belonging to *supra* n 161–164; ibid, 256 and 502.

crimes courts have understood the nexus as a link between a conduct and a conflict,[189] and because the LOAC nexus is identical to the war crimes nexus[190], it is possible to rely on the war crimes case law for defining the LOAC nexus.[191] As regards the war crimes jurisprudence, the ICTY's definition of the nexus in the *Kunarac* case has been widely endorsed by domestic and international courts alike and has become the most authoritative one.[192]

The ICTY has described the nexus in the following terms in the *Kunarac* case: '[w]hat ultimately distinguishes a war crime from a purely domestic offence is that a war crime is shaped by or dependent upon the environment – the armed conflict – in which it is committed. (…) The armed conflict need not have been causal to the commission of the crime, but the existence of an armed conflict must, at a minimum, have played a substantial part in the perpetrator's ability to commit it, his decision to commit it, the manner in which it was committed *or* the purpose for which it was committed. Hence, if it can be established, as in the present case, that the perpetrator acted in furtherance of or under the guise of the armed conflict, it would be sufficient to conclude that his acts were closely related to the armed conflict.'[193] Essentially, a conduct is sufficiently linked with a conflict – and thus governed by the LOAC – if the conduct either serves a conflict-related *purpose* (the perpetrator 'acted in furtherance of' the conflict) or if, at least, the conduct is *enabled* by the conflict (the perpetrator 'acted under the guise of' the conflict).[194]

The latter nexus-test sets the bar 'exceedingly low'.[195] It is essentially enough that the conflict creates the conditions making the conduct possible, that is, that the conflict 'has an impact on the actual occurrence of the conduct rather than on the reason why it occurred'.[196] The 'conduct enabled by the conflict'-test is satisfied if the conflict offers the means (such as weapons or means of coercion), the opportunity or simply a facilitative environment to engage in the conduct in question.[197] The latter refers to situations where, as

189 Ibid, 502.

190 Ibid, 499.

191 Ibid, 502.

192 Ibid; for her detailed analysis of the war crimes jurisprudence on the nexus before and after the *Kunarac* case, see Chapter 4, Section B.

193 *Prosecutor v. Kunarac, Kovac and Vukovic* (Judgment) ICTY-96-23 & 23/1-A (12 June 2002) para 58 (emphasis added to point to the disjunctive nature of the test: the conflict providing the purpose is only one possibility to pass the nexus test).

194 See Pothelet (n 35) 256 noting that these two tests reflect the war crimes jurisprudence more generally (with variations in detail, of course).

195 Ibid, 219, 225, 471, 497 and 502.

196 Ibid, 274.

197 Ibid, 275–276.

a result of the conflict, security has been undermined and law enforcement is weak or non-existent, possibly coupled with an increased social acceptance of violence and crime.[198] If it indeed sufficed to establish a nexus (and thus the LOAC applicability) if the perpetrator was able to commit the crime because of a conflict-related enforcement vacuum and situation of lawlessness, a great deal of maritime crime, which often thrives in waters adjacent to conflict-affected regions, would routinely turn into acts of war. The *modus operandi* of Somali-based pirates, for instance, was possible but for the enforcement gap, which resulted from the armed conflict waged in the country for decades. Indeed, hijacking ships and anchoring them in Somali ports until ransom is paid is only possible in a 'facilitative environment', that is, one where no effective port authorities, coast guard or navy prevent and suppress such conduct. The link between the conduct and the conflict is far too tenuous to warrant the applicability of the CoH rules – both on land and at sea, and the 'conduct enabled by the conflict'-test of the *Kunarac* case should be rejected.[199]

Instead, one should rely on the second, more demanding *Kunarac* nexus test – the one requiring that the conduct serves a conflict-related purpose – to establish the applicability of the CoH rules. The purpose of the conduct is the reason *why* the person engages in the conduct; the aim, objective or goal one seeks to achieve with his or her conduct.[200] A conduct is 'conflict-related' if, in the context of a conflict, it aims at serving a belligerent to the detriment of its adversary.[201] Essentially, in the *Kunarac* case language, the 'perpetrator acted in furtherance of' the armed conflict.[202] Thereby, the conduct can either aim at harming the adversary (hostile conduct) or at supporting a belligerent's own capacity to overcome its adversary (favourable conduct).[203]

For some types of LOAC rules, the war crimes jurisprudence offers useful guidance for establishing when particular conduct features a conflict-related purpose; this is, for instance, the case for the rules protecting persons in the power of the enemy from certain treatment. However, as regards CoH rules,

198 Ibid, 285.

199 For the land, see ibid, 502–503, who argues that the test would lead to absurd results; e.g., a 'civilian taking advantage of the chaotic security situation created by the conflict to kill his neighbour' would pass the test and not commit an ordinary murder but a war crime.

200 See ibid, 258–260 where she explains the difference between purpose and intent.

201 Ibid, 286, 326, 482 and 503.

202 *Prosecutor v. Kunarac, Kovac and Vukovic* (Judgment) ICTY-96-23 & 23/1-A (12 June 2002) para 58.

203 Pothelet (n 35) 262.

this jurisprudence is much less developed,[204] and, consequently, provides relatively little guidance.[205] For the naval context, the war crimes jurisprudence is an even less valuable source. While the concept of war crimes is not foreign to the LONW[206] – among the war crimes likely to occur at sea are serious violations of CoH rules (such as an attack of a protected vessel)[207] – it is embryonic compared to the land. There are no clearly defined offence definitions[208] and – except for cases relating to events during or before World War II – jurisprudence in relation to hostilities at sea is virtually non-existent.[209] The land-based case law pertaining to CoH rules, in turn, cannot necessarily be transposed to the sea as the LONW CoH rules differ in various ways from those relevant to land-based targeting.[210] As a result, certain conduct that amounts to a war crime in land warfare would not be unlawful under the LONW.[211]

Overall, the war crimes jurisprudence is of limited usefulness for defining the nexus for the CoH rules on land because of the exceedingly low threshold of the 'conduct enabled by the conflict'-test of the *Kunarac* case and the relatively little case law concretising for the CoH rules when conduct has a conflict-related purpose. These reasons hold even more true for the CoH rules under the LONW. In light of the limited value of the war crimes case law, Pothelet argues that the better source for guidance on the nexus for CoH rules is the LOAC treaty rules – most notably the notion of attack, which defines

204 That there is much less case law on CoH rules has to do with the 'particular difficulties' to establish violations of targeting law (CoH rules); it is comparatively easier to establish violations of rules protecting people in the power of the enemy: see Sassòli, IHL 2024 (n 2) 29–30.

205 Pothelet (n 35) 295 and 368.

206 See, e.g., Kraska and others, Newport Manual (n 40) 12–17 discussing war crimes at sea.

207 Ibid, 13.

208 As per Natalino Ronzitti (ed.), *The Law of Naval Warfare: A Collection of Agreements and Documents with Commentaries* (Martinus Nijhoff Publishers 1988) 2 the absence of elaborated secondary rules has to do with the fact that the content of the primary rules is not sufficiently clear: 'The crisis of the law of naval warfare has rendered less certain the content of rules by which belligerents are to abide. This is a critical issue which makes it difficult to develop an up-to-date doctrine on sanctions for breaches of the law of naval warfare. In effect, a theory of crimes of war and reprisals cannot be properly elaborated, unless there is a common agreement on the content of the rules and the importance of the values they embody.'

209 As most cases pertained to targeting of objects on land from sea; see, e.g., the ICTY's cases on the shelling of the old town of Dubrovnik, which was partly done from sea: *Prosecutor v. Pavle Strugar* (Judgement) IT-01-42-T (31 January 2005) paras 49, 62 and 66.

210 See Section 1.2.

211 Kraska and others, Newport Manual (n 40) 14.

the material scope of applicability (and thus the nexus) for the CoH rules.[212] However, as alluded to earlier and explained further below, the notion of attack is not very well delineated in the LONW and may thus not offer the same guidance in determining the nexus.

3.2 *Notion of Attack: Different and Unclear Meaning in the* LONW

We have seen that the tightest form of nexus between a conduct and a conflict exists when the former serves a conflict-related purpose. This implies that a use of force is only governed by the CoH rules if its purpose is conflict-related, that is, if it aims at harming the enemy.[213] That attacks serve a conflict-related purpose is intuitive – they are neither a side effect nor incidental to a conflict, but rather the 'essence of warfare' and thus intrinsically linked with it.[214] This intuition is confirmed by treaty law; Article 49(1) of AP I states that an attack 'means acts of violence against the adversary, whether in offence or in defence'.

According to Pothelet, the use of the term 'adversary' in the definition of attack is crucial as it emphasises that its target is the adverse party to the conflict. If a belligerent uses force, what matters is that the target was attacked *because* it is associated with the enemy; it is the very affiliation of the target with the adversary that motivates the use of force. The 'wording chosen for this definition strongly suggests that the *purpose* of an attack is to aim at, to harm the enemy in the conflict'.[215] If conduct aims at harming the enemy, the purpose of the conduct is conflict-related, and the more demanding form of nexus of the *Kunarac* test is fulfilled.

However, in the LONW, the authoritative definition of the term 'attack' lacks precisely this element. According to Rule 13(b) of the San Remo Manual, 'attack means an act of violence, whether in offence or in defence'. Hence, there is no mention that the act must be directed 'against the adversary' – which is no oversight but rather due to the LONW 'rule-exceptionalism' explained above: while in land warfare, acts of violence are only carried out against the enemy, in naval warfare it is, in limited situations, lawful to carry out acts of violence against neutral ships, notably if they actively resist control measures authorised under the LONW.[216] It has already been mentioned that there is uncertainty as to what kind and level of resistance of a ship turns it into a military

212 Pothelet (n 35) 295 and 368.
213 See text relating to *supra* n 200–203; ibid, 382.
214 Ibid, 385.
215 Ibid, 383.
216 See text relating to *supra* n 180–181.

objective, thus clearing the way for subjecting it to an attack.[217] Not only this but also the fact that some authors define the attack similarly to Article 49(1) of AP I[218] – according to which it must be directed 'against the adversary' – blurs the notion of attack under the LONW.

Overall, the notion of attack provides clear guidance on the applicability of the shore-based CoH rules. The same cannot be said for the LONW, as the concept of attack lacks clear contours.

3.3 *No Guidance from the DPH Concept: DPH Does Not Exist under LONW*

To buttress her finding that the nexus requirement for the LOAC CoH rules consists of a conflict-related purpose, Pothelet relies on the concept of DPH, or rather, how it is interpreted.[219] The notion is helpful because acts amounting to DPH are a form of acts of hostilities; thus, the concept of DPH also, to some extent, clarifies what an act of hostility is. Lawyers who interpreted the notion of DPH therefore contributed to answering the question of when the use of force is sufficiently connected to an armed conflict to amount to an act of hostility and thus being governed by the CoH rules.[220]

Despite the central place of the concept of DPH in LOAC,[221] it is not defined in treaty law. Rather, it has been interpreted through doctrine and practice, notably by the International Committee of the Red Cross (hereinafter ICRC). According to the latter, an act qualifies as DPH if it crosses a certain threshold of harm, is causal for the harm and features a 'belligerent nexus', meaning that 'the act must be specifically designed to directly cause the required threshold of harm in support of a party to the conflict and to the detriment of another'.[222] We will not dive any deeper into that notion because – unlike in a land-based setting – it is not a valuable source to define when a use of force amounts to an act of hostility. This is due to the simple reason that the concept of DPH is foreign to the LONW, which is another LONW 'rule-exceptionalism'. This is mainly a

217 See *supra* n 182–185.

218 Kraska and others, Newport Manual (n 40) 131 state: 'For purposes of the law of naval warfare, an attack is an act of violence against the adversary, whether in offense or defense.'

219 Pothelet (n 35) 385.

220 Ibid.

221 Civilians are protected from attacks 'unless and for such time as they take a direct part in hostilities': AP I, Art 51(3).

222 ICRC, Interpretive Guidance on the Notion of Direct Participation in Hostilities (report written by Nils Melzer; International Committee of the Red Cross May 2009) 46.

reflection of the fact that the LONW is vessel-centric rather than person-centric.[223] It is not the conduct of members of the civilian crew of merchant ships that matters, but rather the conduct of the vessel.[224] Active resistance by merchant vessel crew is not DPH; in case of capture, they are generally accorded prisoner of war status and are not prosecuted for the fact of offering resistance or even engaging in hostile acts.[225]

This is a further example demonstrating that the most valuable sources for clarifying the nexus requirement in the context of land-based CoH rules cannot necessarily be imported into the LONW because of the specificities of its CoH rules. This is not surprising if we remember that the definition of the nexus is rule-dependent.[226] Since the LONW CoH rules differ from the shore-based CoH rules, we must not rely on terrestrially informed definitions of the nexus but rather elaborate a maritime-specific theory of when the use of force has a conflict-related purpose and is thus governed by the LONW CoH rules. Only this way will the threshold of applicability of the LONW CoH rules become clearer.

Conclusion: Clarifying Rigid Legal Thresholds to Respond to a Fluid Threat

This chapter contributed with reflections to the second research question underlying the present book: '[W]hat is the threshold for the applicability of the law of naval warfare in situations that can be characterised as hybrid warfare?' The answer to this question proved more complex than anticipated for the following reasons.

First, there is not one single threshold for the applicability of the LONW. Rather, the scope of applicability must be defined for each rule – or set of

223 For a comprehensive analysis on why active resistance by merchant vessel crews in IACs does not constitute DPH (except, arguably, for passengers on board merchant vessels), see McLaughlin, DPH (n 46).

224 See text relating to *supra* n 180–186 on *vessel* actively resisting control measures of the LONW, which renders the *vessel* liable to attack; see also text relating to *supra* n 98 on the fact that the principle of distinction under the LONW CoH rules does not account for civilian on board and *supra* n 108 on the fact that the principle of proportionality, as per the prevailing view, does not apply to civilian crew (but arguably to passengers).

225 McLaughlin, DPH (n 46) 305 (regarding enemy civilian merchant mariners) and 317 (regarding neutral civilian merchant mariners).

226 See text relating to *supra* n 163.

rules – separately. It is against this background that a narrow focus has been chosen for this chapter, solely enquiring into the applicability of the LONW CoH rules to incidents involving ships.

Second, other than often assumed, the applicability question is not solved by determining that a certain situation of violence amounts to an armed conflict. Crossing this threshold only means that the LOAC is applicable as such to a given context ('context applicability'). Yet, not every event occurring in the geographical-temporal context of an armed conflict is indeed governed by the LOAC, but only events sufficiently linked with it. Therefore, it is necessary to answer a second threshold question, namely whether the incident in question features a sufficient nexus in order to be governed by the LONW ('incident applicability').[227] But we cannot stop there. The LONW foresees the use of force outside hostilities (e.g., in the course of control measures), which is not governed by the CoH rules. Hence, we must, in a third and final step, ascertain whether the specific use of force amounts to an attack, which triggers the applicability of the LONW CoH rules ('measure applicability').

Third, none of the three key notions of this three-prong enquiry – armed conflict, nexus and attack – features clear contours. While the notion of 'armed conflict at sea' has received some more attention in recent years, the nexus has been widely neglected and the notion of attack has not been sufficiently scrutinised either.

Fourth and finally, the notion of nexus has – including for the CoH rules – recently been explored in an in-depth study by Pothelet, which greatly added to its clarification. However, due to the LONW 'rule-exceptionalism', the analysis pertaining to shore-based LOAC cannot be transposed as such to the LONW CoH rules.

In light of this, the question of the threshold for the LONW applicability cannot be conclusively answered here. Rather, further research is necessary to clarify this consequential threshold question. However, at least one thing can be said with confidence: the threshold for the applicability of the more permissive LONW CoH rules, rather than the MLE rules, is – and should remain – the same for all incidents involving ships, whether occurring in a so-called hybrid naval warfare context or not. While the concept of hybrid naval warfare is a useful analytical lens to understand the phenomenon of 'a combination of regular and irregular military operations, with the addition of non-military means, aiming at influencing – sabotaging – the adversary's mind',[228] it also carries a certain risk.

---

227 In the situation where an incident involving a ship *triggers* the IAC, the context and incident applicability collapse; see final paragraph of Section 2.1.

228 This is how the term 'hybrid warfare' is understood in the present book; see *supra* Chapter 1.

At the very beginning of this chapter, we argued that the 'idea of war often operates to legitimate something that would otherwise be illegal'.[229] The fact that the notion of 'hybrid naval war' invokes this very idea of war could be wrongly used to legitimise the recourse to the more permissive LONW CoH rules, even if inapplicable in a given case. Whether the LONW CoH rules govern an incident at sea is, and must remain, a matter of legal thresholds – and not a matter of rhetoric.

229 Clapham (n 5) Preface v.

PART 2

The Legal Resilience of Critical Offshore Infrastructure to Hybrid Warfare

CHAPTER 5

The Protection of Critical Undersea Infrastructure within and beyond the Limits of the Territorial Sea under the *Jus ad Bellum* and *Jus in Bello*

Alexander Lott

Introduction

Numerous incidents in Europe and the Asia-Pacific regions have recently damaged critical offshore infrastructure. Damage to cables, pipelines, and other sea installations mostly occurs due to human errors and natural phenomena.[1] However, critical offshore infrastructure is also increasingly being intentionally damaged by State or non-State actors. Attacks against offshore pipelines and cables as well as windfarms cause problems for the energy sector, whereas the cutting of submarine cables that account for approximately 98 % of intercontinental data flows implies also disruptions in Internet services.

Throughout the years, submarine cables in the Taiwan Strait have been frequently injured, at times leaving the local islanders disconnected from the Internet.[2] More unexpectedly, in April 2021, a fiber-optic cable connecting Norway's Svalbard archipelago and the mainland of northern Norway was cut, and a long section of the cable was removed. The Norwegian authorities found the lost section of the cable at the end of 2021 lying on the seafloor of the Norwegian exclusive economic zone (hereinafter EEZ) many kilometers

1 For example, in June 2023, an important submarine fiber optic cable off the coast of Alaska was cut presumably due to an ice scouring event. It affected internet and cellular services in Alaska and took months to repair. See Ava White, 'As frustration grows, Quintillion extends timeline for restoring Western Alaska internet service' KTOO (26 July 2023), available at <https://www.ktoo.org/2023/07/26/as-frustration-grows-quintillion-extends-timeline-for-restoring-western-alaska-internet-service/> accessed 27 August 2023.

2 Huang Tzu-ti, 'Taiwan undersea cable cuts linked to Chinese vessels' Taiwan News (17 February 2023), available at <https://www.taiwannews.com.tw/en/news/4812970> accessed 27 August 2023; Joe Brock, 'U.S. and China wage war beneath the waves – over internet cables' Reuters (24 March 2023), available at <https://www.reuters.com/investigates/special-report/us-china-tech-cables/> accessed 27 August 2023.

 | DOI:10.1163/9789004707993_007

away from its original location.[3] In January 2022, another cable connecting the mainland coast of Norway with Svalbard was damaged.[4]

On 19 October 2022, at least three fiber-optic cables that reportedly connect Marseille to Lyon, Milan, and Barcelona were cut off the French coast.[5] The following morning, a cable connecting the British Shetland Islands to the rest of the United Kingdom's communications system was cut in two sections – as a result of which, the Shetland Islands briefly lost telephone and Internet services.[6] A Russian research ship was spotted near the cables when they were cut supposedly due to a fishing trawler's activity in the area.[7] A couple of weeks before that incident, a cable connecting the Shetland Islands and the Danish Faroe Islands was broken.[8]

In September 2022, explosions partly destroyed the Nord Stream pipelines in the Danish and Swedish EEZs. The Swedish investigators have characterized these explosions as an act of sabotage.[9] A year later, on 8 October 2023 (at 01:20

3 Thomas Newdick, 'Norwegian Undersea Surveillance Network Had Its Cables Mysteriously Cut' The Drive (11 November 2021), available at <https://www.thedrive.com/the-war-zone/43094/norwegian-undersea-surveillance-network-had-its-cables-mysteriously-cut> accessed 27 August 2023; Lisbeth Kirk, 'Mysterious Atlantic cable cuts linked to Russian fishing vessels' EUobserver (26 October 2022), available at <https://euobserver.com/nordics/156342> accessed 27 August 2023.

4 Thomas Nilsen, 'Disruption at one of two undersea cables to Svalbard' The Barents Observer (9 January 2022), available at <https://thebarentsobserver.com/en/arctic/2022/01/disruption-one-two-undersea-optical-cables-svalbard> accessed 27 August 2023.

5 Anonymous, 'Fibre optic cable sabotage causes global internet slowdown' The Brussels Times (25 October 2022), available at <https://www.brusselstimes.com/311704/fibre-optic-cable-sabotage-causes-global-internet-slowdown> accessed 27 August 2023.

6 Anonymous, 'Damaged cable leaves Shetland cut off from mainland' BBC News (20 October 2022), available at <https://www.bbc.com/news/uk-scotland-north-east-orkney-shetland-63326102> accessed 27 August 2023.

7 Edward Stringer, 'Putin knows that undersea cables are the west's Achilles heel' Financial Times (4 November 2022), available at <https://www.ft.com/content/0ddc5b48-b255-401b-8e9f-8660f4eab37b> accessed 27 August 2023; Severin Carrell, 'Shetland loses telephone and internet services after subsea cable cut' The Guardian (20 October 2022), available at <https://www.theguardian.com/uk-news/2022/oct/20/shetland-loses-telephone-internet-services-subsea-cable-damaged> accessed 27 August 2023.

8 Youri van Logchem, 'Protecting Submarine Cables: Two Submarine Telecommunication Cables Break off the Shetland Coast' (15 November 2022) The Institute of International Shipping & Trade Law (IISTL) Blog, available at <https://iistl.blog/2022/11/15/protecting-submarine-cables-two-submarine-telecommunication-cables-break-off-the-shetland-coast/> accessed 27 August 2023.

9 Anna Ringstrom and Terje Solsvik, 'Nord Stream leaks confirmed as sabotage, Sweden says' Reuters (18 November 2022), available at <https://www.reuters.com/world/europe/traces-explosives-found-nord-stream-pipelines-sweden-says-2022-11-18/> accessed 27 August 2023; Stine Jacobsen, ''Powerful explosions' behind Nord Stream leaks, Danish police say' Reuters

local time),[10] a potential act of sabotage resulted in the partial destruction of a concrete-coated submarine gas pipeline (jointly owned by Estonian and Finnish companies) in the Finnish part of the EEZ corridor in the Viro Strait that is located between Estonia and Finland in the Gulf of Finland. In addition, in the Estonian part of the narrow EEZ corridor, a telecommunications cable linking the two States had been cut and another submarine telecommunications cable linking Estonia and Sweden was severed in the Estonian EEZ.[11] At 00:30 local time, that is about an hour before the Balticconnector was injured, the Russian submarine cable Baltika was cut in the Finnish EEZ close to the Balticconnector pipeline (on the Balticconnector incident, see also *infra* Chapter 6).[12]

In February 2024, allegedly the Houthi militia that is engaged in a protracted non-international armed conflict in Yemen cut in the Red Sea four submarine telecommunications cables that connect Europe and Asia, which led to disruptions in Internet services especially in the coastal States of the Persian Gulf and India.[13] The above-referred suspected acts of sabotage, especially that of October 2023 against the submarine cables in the northern Baltic Sea appear

(18 October 2022), available at <https://www.reuters.com/world/europe/danish-police-say-powerful-explosions-behind-nord-stream-leaks-2022-10-18/> accessed 27 August 2023.

10 Mihkel Kärmas, 'Balticconnector case more sabotage than an accident, experts say' ERR News (16 February 2024), available at <https://news.err.ee/1609255413/balticconnector-case-more-sabotage-than-an-accident-experts-say> accessed 21 February 2024; Kathryn Armstrong and Vishala Sri-Pathma, 'Finland investigates suspected sabotage of Balticconnector gas pipeline' BBC News (10 October 2023), available at <https://www.bbc.com/news/world-europe-67070389> accessed 17 October 2023.

11 Miranda Bryant, 'Sweden says undersea telecoms link to Estonia damaged' The Guardian (17 October 2023), available at <https://www.theguardian.com/world/2023/oct/17/telecoms-cable-between-sweden-and-estonia-damaged-sweden-says> accessed 17 October 2023; Andrew Whyte, Barbara Oja, 'Sabotage investigated as one possible Estonia-Sweden cable breakage cause', ERR News (19 October 2023), available at <https://news.err.ee/1609137785/sabotage-investigated-as-one-possible-estonia-sweden-cable-breakage-cause> accessed 19 October 2023.

12 Mark Gerassimenko and Karl Kivil, 'Peskov: Kremlil pole andmeid sidekaabli kahjustamise kohta' ERR Uudised (7 November 2023), available at <https://www.err.ee/1609157492/peskov-kremlil-pole-andmeid-sidekaabli-kahjustamise-kohta> accessed 8 November 2023.

13 Assaf Gilead, 'Houthis hit submarine communications cables' Globes (26 February 2024), available at <https://en.globes.co.il/en/article-houthis-hit-underwater-communications-cables-1001472165?fbclid=IwAR1meM7jYK3MVKTsEbUGA_tZiCRVFmgJGTOaAgmySOBCoJdnA4UryJo5h4E> accessed 28 February 2024; Khitam Al Amir, 'Internet disruptions in GCC states: Did Al Houthi militants blow up Red Sea cables?' Gulf News (27 February 2024), available at <https://gulfnews.com/world/gulf/yemen/us-special-envoy-says-iranian-hezbollah-operatives-in-yemen-aiding-houthi-attacks-1.101327634> accessed 27 February 2024.

to have served as the main trigger for the European Commission to conclude a roadmap (recommendation) for increasing the protection of the submarine cables against hybrid threats faced by the European Union (hereinafter EU).[14]

This chapter addresses the question of how hybrid naval warfare impacts the safety of objects of critical offshore infrastructure and how to increase their legal resilience. This study explains the regimes of *jus ad bellum* and *jus in bello* applicable to protecting critical offshore infrastructure in the territorial sea and areas subject to the high seas freedoms. It addresses the threshold subject of whether suspected acts of sabotage against critical offshore infrastructure can be considered as an 'armed attack' which could give rise to action taken in self-defence. The chapter then considers against which State armed attack can be regarded as having been committed, and in particular, whether the coastal State can be regarded as the victim of the attack. This last question is important because the coastal State does not possess territorial sovereignty over the EEZ, nor does that State necessarily have jurisdiction over or indeed a link to all infrastructure located there.

This chapter makes use of, among other incidents, the case study of the Nord Stream explosions of September 2022 and, to a lesser extent, the damaging of the submarine gas pipeline and cables of the North Atlantic Treaty Organization (hereinafter NATO) Member States Estonia and Finland in 2023. In the literature to date, these explosions have been explored from the peacetime and *jus ad bellum* perspectives.[15] This chapter demonstrates that the legality of the Nord Stream explosions can be assessed from the perspective of the law of armed conflict and debates the question whether an alleged Ukrainian attack against the Nord Stream pipelines violated the law of armed conflict in the wider framework of the ongoing international armed conflict between Russia and Ukraine. It examines the legal qualification of the Nord Stream pipelines as a legitimate military objective and the environmental considerations pertaining to the sabotage against these pipelines.

---

14 European Commission, Commission Recommendation of 21 February 2024 on Secure and Resilient Submarine Cable Infrastructures, available at <https://digital-strategy.ec.europa.eu/en/library/recommendation-security-and-resilience-submarine-cable-infrastructures> accessed 27 February 2024; Foo Yun Chee, 'EU should upgrade submarine cable infrastructure with state aid, paper says' Reuters (19 February 2024), available at <https://www.reuters.com/technology/eu-should-upgrade-submarine-cable-infrastructure-with-state-aid-paper-says-2024-02-19/> accessed 21 February 2024.

15 Danae Azaria and Geir Ulfstein, 'Are sabotage of submarine pipelines an 'armed attack' triggering a right to self-defence?' EJIL: Talk! (18 October 2022), available at <https://www.ejiltalk.org/are-sabotage-of-submarine-pipelines-an-armed-attack-triggering-a-right-to-self-defence> accessed 27 August 2023.

While this chapter does not focus on peacetime protection of submarine cables and pipelines from non-State actors,[16] it nonetheless first debates the use and role of safety zones around submarine cables and pipelines as a potential measure for preventing the breaking or injury of submarine critical offshore infrastructure due to acts of sabotage at the first place.

1 The Establishment of Safety Zones or Routing Measures around Submarine Cables and Pipelines

The above-referred incidents demonstrate that European coastal States need to consider whether it is possible to establish safety zones under Article 60(4) of the United Nations Convention on the Law of the Sea[17] (hereinafter LOSC or Convention) around important objects of offshore infrastructure located in the EEZ. The said article stipulates that the coastal State may, where necessary, establish reasonable safety zones around such artificial islands, installations and structures in which it may take appropriate measures to ensure the safety both of navigation and of the artificial islands, installations and structures. According to Article 60(5) of the LOSC, safety zones can be up to 500 m wide, unless authorized differently by generally accepted international standards or by the International Maritime Organization (hereinafter IMO).

States that are keen on protecting the freedom of navigation in the EEZ (including anchoring) tend to interpret Article 60(4) of the LOSC in a way that prevents the establishment of safety zones around submarine cables and pipelines. For example, the Ministry of Labor and Social Affairs of Norway can establish safety zones around and above subsea facilities with the exception of pipelines and cables, since, according to Norway's interpretation of the international law of the sea, safety zones are not permitted around such objects as they do not qualify under the definition of facilities.[18]

---

16 On peacetime protection of submarine cables against non-State actors, see Douglas Guilfoyle, Tamsin Phillipa Paige and Rob McLaughlin, 'The Final Frontier of Cyberspace: The Seabed beyond National Jurisdiction and the Protection of Submarine Cables' (2022) 71 International & Comparative Law Quarterly 657, 662–675; Douglas Burnett, Tara Davenport, and Robert Beckman (eds.), *Submarine Cables – The Handbook of Law and Policy* (Brill 2013).

17 United Nations Convention on the Law of the Sea (opened for signature 10 December 1982, entered into force 16 November 1994) 1833 UNTS 3.

18 See Norway's position and guideline for § 53 Establishment of safety zones for subsea facilities of the Regulations relating to health, safety and the environment in the petroleum activities and at certain onshore facilities, adopted 12 February 2010, entered into

According to this view, submarine cables and pipelines are excluded from the scope of Article 60(4) of the LOSC. This provision refers to the possibility of establishing safety zones around artificial islands, installations and structures. The terms 'installations' and 'structures' are left undefined in the Convention, but they are commonly presumed to include such objects that are related to the coastal State's sovereign rights for the purpose of exploring and exploiting, conserving and managing the natural resources in the EEZ (Art 56(1)(a) of the LOSC), e.g. offshore oil or gas rigs and windfarms. Andreone has found that,

> Looking, then, at oil, gas, or renewable energy platforms, the extent of the enforcement powers of coastal States over these items has recently caused concern and, in particular, the matters of their protection and of their environmental impact are likely to lead to significant developments in the EEZ legal regime.[19]

In addition, Article 60(1)(b) of the LOSC refers explicitly to the possibility that the installations and structures in relation to which the coastal State is entitled to establish safety zones may also have 'other economic purposes' as compared to those mentioned in Article 56 of the LOSC. They may even include such 'installations and structures which may interfere with the exercise of the rights of the coastal State in the [EEZ]' (Art 60(1)(c) of the LOSC).

Alternatively, the coastal State may establish routing measures in the EEZ, including areas to be avoided and no anchoring areas (on the routing measures, see also *infra* Chapter 6). The routing measures in the EEZ would have to be first adopted by the IMO. However, the routing measures would likely not be as effective in the protection of critical undersea infrastructure as the safety zones since the legal framework applicable to routing measures (unlike the safety zones) does not permit the coastal State to significantly broaden the reach of her enforcement jurisdiction in the relevant parts of the EEZ against foreign ships.

The IMO routing measures are dependent on the coastal State's 'usual' enforcement jurisdiction in relation to her maritime zones as stipulated in

---

force 1 January 2011, available at <https://www.ptil.no/en/regulations/all-acts/the-framework-regulations3/VIII/53/?expandGuideline=true&hideParagraph=true> accessed 17 October 2023. Churchill, Lowe, and Sander note that, in the context of safety zones, Norway herself has also used a dynamic interpretation of the LOSC. Robin Churchill, Vaughan Lowe, and Amy Sander, *The law of the sea* (4th ed., Manchester University Press 2022) 242.

19 Gemma Andreone, 'The Exclusive Economic Zone', in Donald R Rothwell, Alex G Oude Elferink, Karen N Scott and Tim Stephens, *The Oxford Handbook of The Law of the Sea* (Oxford University Press 2015) 172.

the LOSC. While the routing measures can be considered as the 'applicable international rules and standards' within the meaning of Article 220(3) of the LOSC, the coastal State's measures in response to violations of these rules and standards are limited under the said provision to the right of the coastal State to 'require the vessel to give information regarding its identity and port of registry, its last and its next port of call and other relevant information required to establish whether a violation has occurred.' The coastal State may adopt more effective measures, such as the inspection and detention of a foreign ship, only in cases where the ship has caused substantial or major damage or such threat to the marine environment or related interests of the coastal State because of a violation of the routing measures (see Art 220(5–7) of the LOSC). Therefore, the measures provided under the LOSC in response to violations of the routing measures are *ex post* reactive, rather than preventive as in the case of the safety zones.

In the safety zone, the coastal State can take measures to track movements as well as ensure swift enforcement against any violations. Harrison explains that:

> Such safety zones would permit a coastal state to prohibit free navigation in the designated areas for the purposes of ensuring the safety of offshore operations. However, the Convention is ambiguous as to what precise measures may be taken to enforce laws and regulations adopted under these powers. /…/ It is clear from Article 60(4) that the coastal state does not have complete discretion in determining whether to exercise its enforcement powers.[20]

Kaye argues that, in the safety zone, the coastal State has rights 'analogous to those possessed in internal waters, as entry into the safety zone is prohibited without the authorization of the coastal State.'[21] In support of this, Kaye refers to Article 60(6) of the LOSC, which nonetheless does not include any explicit reference to the permit-based passage regime in a safety zone.[22] According to Kaye, one may argue that 'jurisdiction within the safety zone is not dissimilar

20 James Harrison, 'Safeguards against Excessive Enforcement Measures in the Exclusive Economic Zone – Law and Practice', in Henrik Ringbom (ed.), *Jurisdiction over Ships – Post-UNCLOS Developments in the Law of the Sea* (Brill 2015), 224–225.

21 Stuart Kaye, 'A Zonal Approach to Regulation', in Robin Warner and Stuart Kaye, *Routledge Handbook of Maritime Regulation and Enforcement* (Routledge 2016) 12.

22 Article 60(6) of the LOSC stipulates that: 'All ships must respect these safety zones and shall comply with generally accepted international standards regarding navigation in the vicinity of artificial islands, installations, structures and safety zones.'

to that of a State utilizing port State control, as failure to comply with the State's rules could mean exclusion from the safety zone.'[23] Be that as it may, the potential establishment of safety zones around submarine cables and pipelines in the EEZ as debated in this chapter would not imply the prohibition of (freedom of) navigation in the relevant area.

Instead, the discussion here is limited to the question of whether the coastal State may prohibit the stopping and anchoring of ships in the safety zone for the protection of critical underwater infrastructure. It is acknowledged here that the imposition of such safety zones around submarine cables and pipelines that might not fall under the legal category of 'installations and structures' under the terms of Article 60(4) of the LOSC is, legally speaking, a controversial measure. But, unlike the introduction of a permit-based passage regime in a safety zone, the establishment of safety zones around submarine cables and pipelines in the EEZ would not severely impede the freedom of navigation in the EEZ as a prohibition of navigation in these safety zones is not necessary, nor conceivable, for securing the safety of submarine cables and pipelines that often cross long distances.

The resolution of the IMO on safety zones does not specify what enforcement measures the coastal State may adopt in response to violations of the safety zone regime, but makes it clear that every coastal State 'should take action in accordance with international law and, where it considers necessary, notify the flag State of the infringement allegedly committed by a vessel flying its flag and provide available factual evidence to substantiate the allegation'.[24] Harrison argues that the coastal State's appropriate enforcement measures 'may include the power to arrest a vessel' in response to violations of the regime of a particular safety zone.[25]

This view is supported by the relevant case law. In the Arctic Sunrise case, the Annex VII Arbitral Tribunal found that the reference to 'appropriate measures to ensure the safety both of navigation and of the artificial islands, installations and structures' in Article 60(4) of the LOSC, 'allows the coastal State to take, in the safety zone, appropriate measures in the nature of the enactment of laws or regulations, and of the enforcement of such laws and regulations, provided that such measures are aimed at ensuring the safety of both navigation and the

23 Ibid.

24 IMO Resolution A.671(16), Annex, para. 3.1.

25 Harrison (n 20) 226.

artificial islands, installations, or structures.'[26] The Annex VII Arbitral Tribunal found that such rights 'go beyond' the coastal State's rights in the EEZ at large.[27]

According to Oude Elferink, whereas the Annex VII Arbitral Tribunal confirmed that the coastal State has the right to board and arrest a ship due to violations of the safety zone, the Tribunal rather focused on 'whether the Russian Federation had effected the arrest after a hot pursuit from the safety zone' under Article 111 of the LOSC.[28] The Tribunal raised the question of 'whether the pursuit of the Arctic Sunrise remained uninterrupted from the time of the first stop order until the boarding of the Arctic Sunrise /.../ some 36 hours later' and answered it negatively.[29] Thus, at the heart of the arbitral proceedings were questions related to the hot pursuit, rather than the safety zone.

Under the Danish legislation, safety zones appear to be established around submarine cables and pipelines also in the Danish EEZ. It is prohibited for ships to anchor, without urgent necessity, in the 400-metres-wide safety zones around submarine cables and pipelines and where, in a situation of urgent necessity, a ship has anchored in a safety zone around a cable or pipeline, then the master of the ship is obliged to immediately inform the Admiral Danish Fleet of the anchoring.[30] The Danish approach to the establishment of safety zones around submarine cables and pipelines also in the EEZ has important ramifications for increasing legal resilience of offshore infrastructure against hybrid warfare.[31] In particular, in relatively small seas such as the Baltic Sea, the establishment and monitoring of safety zones in the EEZ could be complemented with rapid law enforcement against suspected violations of the infrastructure protection regime in the safety zones. For example, if Estonia and

26 Annex VII Arbitral Tribunal, The Arctic Sunrise Arbitration (The Netherlands v. the Russian Federation), Case 2014-02, Award on the Merits of 14 August 2015, para 211.

27 Ibid.

28 Alex G Oude Elferink, 'The Russian Federation and the Arctic Sunrise Case: Hot Pursuit and Other Issues under the LOSC' (2016) 92 International Law Studies, 381, 383.

29 Annex VII Arbitral Tribunal, The Arctic Sunrise Case (n 26), Award on Merits, para 269. See also Oude Elferink (n 28) 395–397.

30 Sections 1 and 2 of the Order no. 939 on the protection of submarine cables and submarine pipelines, adopted 27 November 1992, entered into force 1 January 1993, available at <https://dma.dk/Media/637792377883187147/Order%20on%20the%20protection%20of%20submarine%20cables%20and%20pipelines.pdf> accessed 17 October 2023; See also the Danish Offshore Safety Act of 6 February 2018, available at <https://offshore.at.dk/en/regulations/the-offshore-safety-act/#10> accessed 17 October 2023. A reply of 18 October 2023 to the present author's information request from Mr. Jakob Nick Bøgeby Levring of the Danish Energy Agency, on file with the author.

31 For Australia's and New Zealand's practice in establishing cable protection safety zones outside the limits of the territorial sea, see Guilfoyle, Paige and McLaughlin (n 16) 665.

Finland had put such measures in place, then the Russian commercial ship *SVG Flot* could likely not have remained in the vicinity of the Balticconnector pipeline and the Estonian-Finnish submarine cable three days in a row in October 2023 when the pipeline and cable were damaged.[32]

The Danish approach to establishing safety zones around submarine cables and pipelines in an EEZ appears to be based on a liberal interpretation of Article 60(4) of the LOSC. It may also provide an example of a dynamic interpretation of Article 60(1) of the LOSC since, according to a more restrictive view, most submarine pipelines and cables are not necessarily covered by the said provision, as discussed above. One might argue that the systemic interpretation of the Convention and the careful balance struck between the high seas freedoms and coastal State's sovereign rights in the EEZ does not permit such a dynamic interpretation of the said provisions to the extent that they would permit the establishment of safety zones in the EEZ around cables and pipelines. However, in the view of the present author, this matter is comparable to the one concerning the establishment of air defense identification zones (hereinafter ADIZ) and the impact of ADIZ on the high seas freedom of overflight. The aim of both ADIZs and safety zones is the same, i.e. to increase the coastal State's security at the expense of high seas freedoms.

Many States have established an ADIZ that extends beyond their sovereign airspace,[33] and within which, according to Annex 15 to the Convention on International Civil Aviation, 'aircraft are required to comply with special identification and/or reporting procedures additional to those related to the provision of air traffic services'.[34] The referred treaty is applicable only to civil aircraft and not to State aircraft. In the airspace above the EEZ and the high seas, the freedom of overflight applies (Arts 58(1) and 87(1)(b) of the LOSC). The impact of the ADIZ-specific identification and reporting procedures on the freedom of overflight is comparable to the impact of safety zones to the

32 See Karl Kivil *et al.*, 'Russian cargo ship spent weekend in vicinity of Balticconnector pipeline leak' ERR News (11 October 2023), available at <https://news.err.ee/1609128785/russian-cargo-ship-spent-weekend-in-vicinity-of-balticconnector-pipeline-leak> accessed 16 October 2023.

33 Bangladesh, Canada, China, Cuba, Iceland, India, Indonesia, Iran, Japan, Republic of Korea, Myanmar, Pakistan, Panama, the Philippines, Taiwan, Thailand, and the United States. Jinyuan Su, 'Is the Establishment of Air Defence Identification Zones Outside National Airspace in Accordance with International Law?' (2021) 32(4) European Journal of International Law 1309, 1310.

34 Annex 15 to the Convention on International Civil Aviation (16th ed.), International Civil Aviation Organization, Montréal 2018, Chapter 1, 1–2. Convention on International Civil Aviation (signed 7 December 1944, entered into force 4 April 1947) 15 UNTS 295.

freedom of navigation in an EEZ. Both zones serve the same purpose, i.e. the protection of coastal State's security interests in the relevant area.

For example, the United States uses relatively strict peacetime measures in response to a violation of the legal regime established within the limits of an ADIZ:

> Failure by an aircraft to identify itself once it enters an ADIZ does not, of itself, entitle the declaring State to use force against that aircraft, although it may subject the aircraft to interception. Depending on the circumstances, a persistent failure to comply with instructions may be evidence that the aircraft, in fact, poses a threat to the declaring State.[35]

These measures in the ADIZ are applied in relation to civil aircraft. State aircraft are usually not being intercepted even if they have failed to properly report about their entry into the ADIZ. However, in some cases, such as China's measures under the East China ADIZ, both State and civil aircraft are targeted.[36]

The safety zone in an EEZ is narrow, whereas an ADIZ may cover vast areas of airspace above an EEZ. There is no clear legal basis for the establishment of an ADIZ outside the coastal State's sovereign airspace under international law and, according to the US guidelines, '[t]he legal basis for a State to establish an ADIZ is its right to establish conditions and procedures for entry into its national airspace.'[37] By contrast, safety zones in an EEZ are firmly included within the LOSC 'toolbox'. If the international law of the sea tolerates the practice of States in establishing ADIZs outside their sovereign airspace which is not supported by a clear legal basis in the treaty law (especially where the ADIZ is applied in respect of State aircraft) and the prohibition of passage in safety zones established for the protection of installations and structures, then there might be also room for tolerating the use of safety zones for the prohibition of anchoring and stopping around submarine cables and pipelines in the EEZ.

As discussed above, they are all controversial measures from a legal point of view. Their legality is intertwined with developments in State practice and *opinio juris* which might embrace a dynamic interpretation of the existing law or, if necessary, effectuate a change of law. In the context of the rise of hybrid

35 Department of Defense Law of War Manual (United States Office of General Counsel of the Department of Defense 2015, updated 2023) 938.

36 Donald R Rothwell, Tim Stephens, *The International Law of the Sea* (3rd ed., Hart 2023) 336.

37 Jinyuan Su, 'The Practice of States on Air Defense Identification Zones: Geographical Scope, Object of Identification, and Identification Measures' (2020) 18(4) Chinese Journal of International Law 812, 812–813; Department of Defense Law of War Manual (n 35), 937.

warfare and the targeting of submarine cables and pipelines, there appears to be a need for such a dynamic interpretation of Article 60 of the LOSC on safety zones in the EEZ. The establishment of safety zones provides an effective measure for the coastal States to address a legal gap in the LOSC in relation to the protection of submarine cables and pipelines outside the limits of the territorial sea against acts of sabotage.

In the next chapter, the implications of such sabotage from the *jus ad bellum* perspective are examined.

2 The Protection of Critical Offshore Infrastructure under *Jus ad Bellum*

2.1 *Implications of the Nord Stream Explosions*

The response of the Danish Prime Minister to the Nord Stream explosions illustrates the importance of legal resilience of critical infrastructure located in EEZ against the unlawful use of force. The Danish Prime Minister made it clear that the attacks against the Nord Stream pipelines were not attacks against Denmark – as the explosions of the pipelines occurred in international waters and not in the Danish territorial sea.[38]

The Nord Stream explosion sites were close to the outer limits of the Danish and Swedish territorial sea and next to major shipping routes. If these acts of sabotage had occurred in the territorial sea of Germany, Denmark, or Russia (the pipelines do not cross the territorial sea of Sweden and Finland), they would have likely amounted to an armed attack, thus triggering the right of self-defence under Article 51 of the United Nations (hereinafter UN) Charter.[39] The Secretary General of the NATO, Mr. Jens Stoltenberg, commented in the aftermath of the Nord Stream explosions that an attack on critical offshore infrastructure can trigger collective self-defence under Article 5 of the North Atlantic Treaty.[40]

---

38 Anonymous, 'Denmark, Sweden view Nord Stream leaks as 'sabotage'' Deutsche Welle (27 September 2022), available at <https://www.dw.com/en/denmark-sweden-view-nord-stream-pipeline-leaks-as-deliberate-actions/a-63251217> accessed 27 August 2023.

39 Charter of the United Nations (opened for signature 26 June 1945, entered into force 24 October 1945) 1 UNTS XVI.

40 Katya Adler, 'A journey to the site of the Nord Stream explosions' BBC News (18 November 2022), available at <https://www.bbc.com/news/world-63636181> accessed 27 August 2023; The North Atlantic Treaty (opened for signature 4 April 1949, entered into force 24 August 1949) 34 UNTS 243.

2.2 *Does a Use of Force against Critical Offshore Infrastructure Amount to an Armed Attack also beyond the Limits of the Territorial Sea?*

Guilfoyle, Paige, and McLaughlin have found that, depending on the scale and effects of cutting a submarine cable for a coastal State, such acts can be categorized as an armed attack (without differentiating between where the attack took place). They argue that if the intentional severing of a submarine cable causes long-term disruption to services in the region, it would be difficult to characterize the act 'as anything other than an armed attack'.[41] The further discussion in this chapter bases itself on this view.

In the view of the present author, sabotage against critical offshore infrastructure outside the sovereign territory of a coastal State can potentially also amount to an armed attack, thus triggering the right of self-defence under Article 51 of the UN Charter. For example, it is doubtful that Denmark would continue to draw a line between an armed attack and less grave uses of force on the basis of the outer limits of its territorial sea if explosions targeted, for example, the German-Danish immersed tunnel in the EEZ corridor of the Femern Strait (Fehmarnbelt).[42] Unlike many other submarine tunnels that are tunneled through the continental shelf, the Femern Strait's road and rail tunnel is constructed on the seabed by laying premade concrete sections of the tunnel to a trench on the seabed. Notably, the tunnel to the extent that it is located outside the territorial sea of the coastal State does not form part of the coastal State's territory. The State Constitutional Court of Schleswig-Holstein has found that:

> Taking possession of the seabed through the construction of the tunnel does not result in an occupation in the sense of territorial title under international law. The tunnel is a structure in the continental shelf. The area in question remains part of the continental shelf and does

---

41 Guilfoyle, Paige and McLaughlin (n 16) 679.

42 See section 1 of the Proclamation by the Government of the Federal Republic of Germany concerning the extension of the breadth of the German territorial sea, adopted 11 November 1994, entered into force 1 January 1995, available at <http://www.un.org/depts/los/LEGISLATIONANDTREATIES/PDFFILES/deu_1994_territorial_proclamation.pdf> accessed 27 August 2023. See section 6(2) of the Danish *Bekendtgørelse om Danmarks eksklusive økonomiske zone* (Executive Order on Denmark's exclusive economic zone), adopted 24 June 1996, entered into force 1 July 1996, available at <https://www.retsinformation.dk/eli/lta/1996/584> accessed 27 August 2023); See Femern Belt Development, 'Femern Belt Link – the world's longest immersed tunnel' Femern A/S, available at <https://www.femern.info/en/femern-belt-link-worlds-longest-immersed-tunnel> accessed 27 August 2023.

> not become the sovereign territory of the coastal State. This does not exclude, but on the contrary entails, that the coastal State exercises the necessary sovereign powers to regulate all affairs regarding the tunnel and in the tunnel in its continental shelf. These sovereign powers, which are functionally restricted to the construction and operation of the tunnel, including legislative competence, result from the right of the coastal State to construct it.[43]

Yet if the unlawful use of force in an EEZ or on the continental shelf against underwater tunnels, windfarms, cables, pipelines, platforms, or other objects of critical infrastructure causes significant damage and especially where the unlawful use of force results in the loss of human life, the coastal State can invoke the right of self-defence under Article 51 of the UN Charter. However, for that right to be lawfully invoked, it must be the case that the incident was a deliberate attack and not a mere accident.[44]

Similar to attacks against tunnels, cables, or pipelines, the unlawful use of force against offshore windfarms in a coastal State's EEZ at least has the potential to amount to an armed attack under Article 51 of the UN Charter if it causes significant damage to the coastal State, especially if it leads to massive power outages in the coastal State's population. It is common for offshore windfarms to be located in a coastal State's EEZ. One may wonder how likely would it be if numerous explosions would target, for example, the Danish windfarms that are located next to Bornholm Island and in the vicinity of where the Nord Stream explosions occurred, that Denmark would still claim that it does not consider such use of force to amount to an attack against Denmark as the explosions occurred in international waters.

The classification of the use of force as an armed attack under Article 51 of the UN Charter depends *inter alia* on the perpetrator of the operation, the distinction being made mostly on the basis of whether the perpetrator is a State organ or a non-State actor.[45] The International Court of Justice (hereinafter

43 Excerpts from Schleswig-Holsteinisches LVerfG, Urteil vom 14.09.2020 - LVerfG 3/19 as translated by the Centre for Maritime Law of the National University of Singapore, available at <https://cmlcmidatabase.org/schleswig-holstein-lverfg-319> accessed 27 August 2023.

44 Compare with the 'scale and effects' test, in *Oil Platforms* (*Islamic Republic of Iran v. United States of America*), Judgment, ICJ Reports 2003, p. 161, paras 51–64.

45 *Military and Paramilitary Activities in and against Nicaragua* (Nicaragua v. United States of America), Merits, ICJ Reports 1986, p. 14, para 195; *Armed Activities on the Territory of the Congo* (Democratic Republic of the Congo v. Uganda), Judgment, ICJ Reports 2005, p. 168, para 146; General Assembly Resolution 29/3314, adopted 14 December 1974, Annex

ICJ) has clearly made this distinction by limiting the right of self-defence to attacks conducted by one State against another State.[46] Notably, State practice (e.g., the response by the United States and its allies to the acts of terror of 11 September 2001) demonstrates more flexibility in categorizing attacks by non-State actors as an armed attack. Claiming another State's responsibility for an intentionally clandestine use of force (sabotage) in the marine environment which is suitable for concealing any evidence about the origin of the attack, is not an easy task for the victim State that needs to bear the burden of proof.

2.3 *Which State May Invoke the Right of Self-Defence in Response to Attacks against Offshore Infrastructure?*

In addition, the coastal State needs to establish a direct link with the targeted infrastructure so that the attack against the infrastructure can be equated with an attack on that State.[47] Establishing a direct link with the targeted infrastructure is complicated if the location of attack against the critical infrastructure falls outside the limits of the coastal State's territorial sea since offshore infrastructure is not subject to flag State jurisdiction (unlike ships). With the main exception of military cables,[48] offshore infrastructure is usually not owned by the coastal State, but instead by private companies.

Article 60(2) of the LOSC stipulates that the coastal State has exclusive jurisdiction over installations and structures in its EEZ, whereas the coastal State's jurisdiction is more narrowly construed under the Convention in respect of submarine cables and pipelines (Art 79(2) and (4) of the LOSC). For example, the Iranian oil platforms against which the United States used force in the Persian Gulf, were located beyond the outer limit of Iran's territorial sea and within its EEZ and upon its continental shelf. Nonetheless, one might argue that Iran was entitled to use force in self-defence in response to this attack.[49]

By contrast, in an EEZ and on the continental shelf, third States have the freedom to lay submarine cables and pipelines (Articles 58(1), 79(1), and 87(1)(c) of the LOSC). Hence, as the targeted cables or pipelines in the coastal State's

---

'Definition of Aggression', Art 3(g); See Olivier Corten, *The Law Against War: The Prohibition on the Use of Force in Contemporary International Law*, 2nd ed. (Hart 2021) 105.

46 *Legal Consequences of the Construction of a Wall in the Occupied Palestinian Territory*, Advisory Opinion, ICJ Reports 2004, p. 136, para 139.

47 Oil Platforms Case, Judgment (n 44) para 64.

48 On submarine military cables, see J Ashley Roach, *Military Cables*, in Burnett, Beckman, Davenport (n 16) 339–349.

49 Stuart Kaye, 'International Measures to Protect Oil Platforms, Pipelines, and Submarine Cables from Attack' (2007) 31(2) Tulane Maritime Law Journal 377, 414; Oil Platforms Case, Judgment (n 44) para 82.

EEZ or continental shelf 'might have no connection with the coastal State',[50] the unlawful use of force against these objects does not *prima facie* breach the coastal State's sovereign interests. Nor does it suffice for a State to claim the right of self-defence in response to an attack against a submarine cable or pipeline based solely (as opposed to also owning the object) on the fact that the landfall of the targeted cable or pipeline is located within its territory or under its jurisdiction. If the opposite was true, then it could lead to a paradoxical situation where, for example, Estonia could claim the right of self-defence based on the fact that the Russian landfall of the damaged Nord Stream 2 pipelines on the Kurgalsky Peninsula is located in an area which, according to the Estonian State Borders Act, is 'part of Estonia not under the jurisdiction of Estonia' due to a dispute over the land boundary between Estonia and Russia.[51]

It would be possible to establish a direct link with the targeted underwater pipeline or cable if the destruction caused significant damage to the population of the coastal State (e.g., substantial loss of human life, significant disruption of critical services such as internet connection or electrical grid). In addition, as suggested by Azaria and Ulfstein, arguably another relevant factor for determining whether a particular State is entitled to invoke the right of self-defence might be the incorporation of the company that owns the targeted submarine pipeline or cable in the State claiming self-defence.[52]

In this context, parallels can be drawn with operations in cyberspace. For example, Germany has stated that it concurs with the view expressed in Rule 71 of the Tallinn Manual 2.0 which proves that '[a] State that is the target of a cyber operation that rises to the level of an armed attack may exercise its inherent right of self-defence. Whether a cyber operation constitutes an armed attack depends on its scale and effects.'[53] France has stated that she reaffirms:

---

50 Ibid, 418.

51 *Riigipiiri seadus* (State Borders Act), Section 22(1), adopted 30 June 1994, entered into force 31 July 1994, available at <https://www.riigiteataja.ee/en/eli/508022023002/consolide> accessed 27 August 2023; On the border dispute, see Lauri Mälksoo, 'Which Continuity: The Tartu Peace Treaty of 2 February 1920, the Estonian–Russian Border Treaties of 18 May 2005, and the Legal Debate about Estonia's Status in International Law' (2005) 43(4) Archiv des Völkerrechts 513–524; For a map depicting the course of the Estonian land boundary along the 1920 Tartu Peace Treaty lines and the route of the Nord Stream 2 in the relevant area, see Alexander Lott, 'Nord Streami plahvatused ja Eesti keskkonnajulgeolek' ERR Uudised (28 September 2022), available at <https://www.err.ee/1608730792/alexander-lott-nord-streami-plahvatused-ja-eesti-keskkonnajulgeolek> accessed 27 August 2023. For the location of the Nord Stream 2 landfall near the Narva River, see Google Maps 'Nordstream 2', available at <https://goo.gl/maps/5Ep3a6jLYyxWgToW7> accessed 27 August 2023.

52 Azaria and Ulfstein (n 15).

53 Cyber Law Toolkit, 'National position of Germany (2021)', available at <https://cyberlaw.ccdcoe.org/wiki/National_position_of_Germany_(2021)#Self-defence_and_armed

> [T]hat a cyberattack may constitute an armed attack within the meaning of Article 51 of the United Nations Charter, if it is of a scale and severity comparable to those resulting from the use of physical force. In the light of these criteria, the question of whether a cyberattack constitutes armed aggression will be examined on a case-by-case basis having regard to the specific circumstances. A cyberattack could be categorised as an armed attack if it caused substantial loss of life or considerable physical or economic damage. That would be the case of an operation in cyberspace that caused a failure of critical infrastructure with significant consequences or consequences liable to paralyse whole swathes of the country's activity, trigger technological or ecological disasters and claim numerous victims. In such an event, the effects of the operation would be similar to those that would result from the use of conventional weapons.[54]

If the State invoking the right of self-defence under Article 51 of the UN Charter meets the above-referred criteria, then its use of force against an appropriate military target of another State is subject to the limitations set by the principles of necessity and proportionality and the corpus of the law of armed conflict.[55] The grounds for and limitations applicable to conducting attacks against critical offshore infrastructure in the course of an international armed conflict are examined next.

3 Attacks against Critical Offshore Infrastructure under *Jus in Bello*

Under the LOSC, foreign military activities in an EEZ are permitted to the extent that they do not amount to threat or use of force against the territorial integrity or political independence of any State and are consistent with the principles of international law embodied in the UN Charter (see Articles 88 and 301). At the same time, foreign military activities are prohibited in the

_attack> accessed 27 August 2023. Michael N Schmitt (ed.), *Tallinn Manual 2.0 on the International Law Applicable to Cyber Operations* (Cambridge University Press 2017) Rule 71.

54 Cyber Law Toolkit, 'National position of France (2019)', available at <https://cyberlaw.ccdcoe.org/wiki/National_position_of_France_(2019)#Self-defence,_armed_attack_and_use_of_force> accessed 27 August 2023.

55 Military and Paramilitary Activities in and against Nicaragua (n 45) para 176. *Legality of the Threat or Use of Nuclear Weapons*, Advisory Opinion, ICJ Reports 1996, p. 226, paras 41–42; Oil Platforms Case, Judgment (n 44) para 76; On the principles of necessity and proportionality, see Chris O'Meara, *Necessity and Proportionality and the Right of Self-Defence in International Law* (Oxford University Press 2021).

territorial sea (e.g., Articles 2 and 19(2)(a–c) of the LOSC). This follows from the coastal State's sovereignty over its territorial sea, based on which international humanitarian law and *jus in bello* (both terms used here interchangeably to cover the same) also distinguish between the protection standards of offshore critical infrastructure – predicated on whether they are located within or outside the limits of a neutral State's territorial sea. The need to respect neutral territory is the main exception to the agnosticism of international humanitarian law regarding the differentiation between various maritime zones.

3.1 *Attacks against Cables within and beyond Neutral Waters*

For example, it is prohibited to conduct any belligerent acts and target, within the limits of the territorial sea of a neutral State (neutral waters), such submarine cables or pipelines that connect the territories of a belligerent and a neutral State.[56] Presumably, the prohibition to target submarine cables or pipelines in neutral waters applies even if both landfalls of a submarine cable or pipeline are located at a point held by the enemy. By contrast, in the territorial sea of a belligerent State, such submarine cables that connect the territories of a belligerent and a neutral State can be targeted.

In principle, belligerent acts against critical offshore infrastructure can be conducted outside neutral waters. According to McLaughlin, Paige, and Guilfoyle, cables that connect two points of the territories of a belligerent 'may be cut at any point, including in the high seas',[57] but that 'the high seas cutting of cables connecting a belligerent and a neutral is permissible so long as the cable has become a military objective.'[58]

Even such infrastructure objects that do not exclusively serve the belligerents might, in situations of military necessity and where they act as military objectives,[59] serve as lawful military objectives during an armed conflict provided that they are located outside the limits of a neutral State's territorial sea. The

56 Rule 15 of the San Remo Manual on International Law Applicable to Armed Conflicts at Sea, 12 June 1994, available at <https://www.icrc.org/en/doc/resources/documents/article/other/57jmsu.htm> accessed 27 August 2023. See also Wolff Heintschel von Heinegg, 'The Law of Armed Conflict at Sea', in Dieter Fleck (ed.), *The Handbook of International Humanitarian Law*, 2nd ed. (Oxford University Press 2009) 475, 515.

57 Guilfoyle, Paige and McLaughlin (n 16) 687.

58 Ibid, 689.

59 Rule 40 of the San Remo Manual (n 56). On submarine cables as military objectives, see Rob McLaughlin, Tamsin Paige, Douglas Guilfoyle 'Submarine Communication Cables and the Law of Armed Conflict: Some Enduring Uncertainties, and Some Proposals, as to Characterization' (2022) 27(3) Journal of Conflict and Security Law 297, 326–327.

Tallinn Manual 2.0 supports such a conclusion in relation to submarine cables.[60] In this context, McLaughlin, Paige, and Guilfoyle comment that:

> [T]he Tallinn Manual 2.0 reiterates the 1995 consensus that cables may be targeted on the same basis as any other object. The Tallinn Manual 2.0 thus did not expressly address the older and seemingly discounted idea that attacks on neutral cables could only be legitimate if a higher threshold–one of 'absolute necessity' – was met. That was, we humbly submit, a missed opportunity. There was in the old law the germ of recognition that the centrality of cables to international life meant a higher standard of protection should apply. We argue that idea has become only more pressing in an age where data cables are now the backbone of cyberspace.[61]

It is debatable whether there exist such neutral cables that could be granted a higher standard of protection under the law of naval warfare. Kraska observes that the idea of a neutral submarine cable has mostly lost its practical purpose.[62] This is because, as Burnett explains, 'the concept of a neutral cable is meaningless in terms of modern submarine cable usage, interconnectivity between cable systems, and diverse opaque cable ownership structures.'[63] Kraska has found that 'states may expect that adversaries' plans to disrupt international submarine cables during naval warfare are limited only by their national laws and their imagination.'[64] Based on a careful examination of State practice in World War I and II, Burnett came to the same conclusion.[65] Furthermore, Kraska notes that, 'the technology of the global cable system, and customary law reflected in state practice, suggest that belligerent states would use or even destroy neutral submarine cables during armed conflict'.[66]

---

60 Tallinn Manual 2.0 (n 53) 556. On submarine cables as military objectives, see also James Kraska, Raul 'Pete' Pedrozo, *Disruptive Technology and the Law of Naval Warfare* (Oxford University Press 2022) 194–195.

61 McLaughlin, Paige and Guilfoyle (n 59) 319.

62 James Kraska, 'The Law of Maritime Neutrality and Submarine Cables' (29 July 2020) EJIL Talk!, available at <https://www.ejiltalk.org/the-law-of-maritime-neutrality-and-submarine-cables/> accessed 27 August 2023.

63 Douglas R Burnett, 'Submarine Cable Security and International Law' (2021) 97 International Law Studies 1660, 1674.

64 James Kraska, 'Submarine Cables in the Law of Naval Warfare' (10 July 2020) Lawfare, available at <https://www.lawfareblog.com/submarine-cables-law-naval-warfare> accessed 27 August 2023.

65 Burnett (n 63) 1673. See also McLaughlin, Paige and Guilfoyle (n 53) 308–312.

66 Kraska (n 62).

Kraska and Pedrozo have reached the conclusion that the law of neutrality does not protect neutral cables outside the limits of the territorial sea of a neutral State (neutral waters) 'from destruction by belligerents nor prevents belligerents from using neutral cable infrastructure for cyberattacks against another belligerent.'[67] They explain that:

> The automatic routing of cable traffic (done instantly and without human decision) in today's global submarine cable systems means that belligerents engaged in cyberattack are unable to avoid neutral cables. It is virtually impossible to direct (or restrict) a cyberattack through a particular cable, which means that cyber operations are likely to use submarine cables owned or operated by neutral states. At the same time, neutral states are absolved of their traditional obligation under the law of neutrality to ensure that their cables are not (mis)used by a belligerent when communications travels through cables located in the neutral state.[68]

Yet it is submitted here that the concept of neutral submarine cables has not lost its practical purpose. For example, from the perspective of Russia as a belligerent State in the context of its armed conflict with Ukraine, the submarine cables that connect Estonia to Finland and Sweden are considered as neutral cables insofar as Estonia, Finland, and Sweden are not in an armed conflict with Russia. The damages to the submarine cables on the night of 7/8 October 2023 occurred in the Estonian EEZ, thereby falling outside the limits of neutral waters. They resulted in a situation where two out of seven (of which two connect Estonia and Sweden and five link Estonia and Finland) telecommunications submarine cables that serve as the backbone of Estonia's 'digital society' were cut/damaged. The only land telecommunications cable connects Estonia to the rest of the world via Latvia and Lithuania. These submarine communications cables connect neutral States in the context of Russia's on-going war of aggression against Ukraine and serve their domestic Internet use.

3.2 *Attacks against Pipelines in a Neutral State's EEZ: Case Study of the Nord Stream*

The use of force against submarine pipelines and submarine cables must conform to the law of armed conflict, including the rules on distinction and

67 Kraska and Pedrozo (n 60) 196–197.

68 Ibid, 197.

proportionality.[69] In this context, the use of force against the Nord Stream pipelines in the wider framework of the ongoing international armed conflict between Russia and Ukraine serves as a useful case study. According to Nordic States' investigative media reports, three Russian sovereign immune vessels were in the relevant maritime area before the Nord Stream explosions of September 2022.[70] The reason for their presence in that area remains unclear. Russian research vessels are known for mapping the locations of Western European critical offshore infrastructure in the North Sea and Russia has allegedly systemically made preparations to sabotage wind farms and communication cables in Europe.[71]

Still, from the perspective of *jus ad bellum* and *jus in bello*, it is significant that preliminary Western intelligence reports have emerged about a purportedly pro-Ukrainian group of six divers conducting the sabotage against the Nord Stream pipelines, whereas the Ukrainian Government denies any involvement in such an alleged operation.[72] Nonetheless, a joint report by the Washington Post and Der Spiegel reached the unequivocal conclusion that:

> A senior Ukrainian military officer with deep ties to the country's intelligence services played a central role in the bombing of the Nord Stream

---

69 Rule 68 of Yoram Dinstein and Arne Willy Dahl (eds.), *The Oslo Manual on Select Topics of the Law of Armed Conflict: Rules and Commentary* (Springer 2020) 62–63.

70 Gordon Corera, 'Nord Stream: Report puts Russian navy ships near pipeline blast site' BBC News (3 May 2023), available at <https://www.bbc.com/news/world-europe-65461401> accessed 27 August 2023.

71 Gordon Corera, 'Ukraine war: The Russian ships accused of North Sea sabotage' BBC News (19 April 2023), available at <https://www.bbc.com/news/world-europe-65309687> accessed 27 August 2023.

72 See Dan Sabbagh, Philip Oltermann, and Lorenzo Tondo, 'Officials believe pro-Ukraine group may have sabotaged Nord Stream – reports' The Guardian (8 March 2023), available at <https://www.theguardian.com/world/2023/mar/07/officials-believe-pro-ukraine-group-sabotage-nord-stream-pipelines> accessed 27 August 2023. See also Andrew Roth, 'Biden 'knew of Ukrainian plan to attack Nord Stream' three months before explosion' The Guardian (6 June 2023), available at <https://www.theguardian.com/business/2023/jun/06/biden-knew-of-plan-to-attack-nord-stream-three-months-before-explosion> accessed 27 August 2023. Paul Ronzheimer, Gabriel Gavin, and Victor Jack, 'Zelenskyy denies Ukraine involvement in Nord Stream pipeline blasts' Politico (7 June 2023), available at <https://www.politico.eu/article/zelenskyy-denies-ukraine-involvement-in-nord-stream-pipeline-blasts/> accessed 27 August 2023. In February 2024, the Swedish prosecutors ended their investigation into the Nord Stream explosions due to lack of jurisdiction, whereas parallel investigations in Denmark and Germany continue. Andrew Roth, 'Sweden to drop inquiry into Nord Stream pipeline explosions' The Guardian (7 February 2024), available at <https://www.theguardian.com/business/2024/feb/07/sweden-drop-inquiry-nord-stream-pipeline-explosions> accessed 7 February 2024.

> natural gas pipelines last year, according to officials in Ukraine and elsewhere in Europe, as well as other people knowledgeable about the details of the covert operation. /…/ Chervinsky did not act alone, and he did not plan the operation, according to the people familiar with his role, which has not been previously reported. The officer took orders from more senior Ukrainian officials, who ultimately reported to Gen. Valery Zaluzhny, Ukraine's highest-ranking military officer, said people familiar with how the operation was carried out.[73]

International law recognizes different standards for attribution depending on whether an act is governed by the law of armed conflict or not. Even if Ukraine (e.g., its armed forces) exercised overall control over the alleged divers' mission by way of financing and provision of training, logistics, and weapons to the divers, then based on the case law of the ICJ, such sabotage appears not to amount to a potential armed attack attributable to Ukraine against the coastal States (Denmark and Sweden) in whose maritime zones the explosions occurred in terms of Article 51 of the UN Charter absent Ukraine's effective control over the operation.[74] Article 8 of the ILC Draft Articles on Responsibility of States for Internationally Wrongful Acts provides that '[t]he conduct of a person or group of persons shall be considered an act of a State under international law if the person or group of persons is in fact acting on the instructions of, or under the direction or control of, that State in carrying out the conduct.'[75] Even if Ukraine's involvement in the attack against the Nord Stream pipelines was confirmed, it would still need to be verified that Ukraine exercised effective control over the likely unmarked group of divers who allegedly conducted the sabotage against the Nord Stream pipelines.

Yet, in the context of an armed conflict, the attribution standards are more flexible. The ICJ has noted that 'the ICTY [the International Criminal Tribunal for the former Yugoslavia] presented the 'overall control' test as equally applicable under the law of State responsibility for the purpose of determining /…/ when a State is responsible for acts committed by paramilitary units,

73 Shane Harris and Isabelle Khurshudyan, 'Ukrainian military officer coordinated Nord Stream pipeline attack' The Washington Post (11 November 2023), available at <https://www.washingtonpost.com/national-security/2023/11/11/nordstream-bombing-ukraine-chervinsky/> accessed 13 November 2023.

74 Military and Paramilitary Activities in and against Nicaragua (n 45) paras 115, 195, 230.

75 International Law Commission, *Draft articles on Responsibility of States for Internationally Wrongful Acts, with commentaries* (United Nations 2008) 47.

armed forces which are not among its official organs.'[76] Thus, it appears that, according to the rules of the law of armed conflict, it would suffice to invoke Ukraine's responsibility for the alleged activities of a group of divers that hypothetically conducted the sabotage against the predominantly Russian-owned and Russian-controlled Nord Stream pipelines if Ukraine exercised overall control over their actions.

As examined above, under customary international law as reflected in Rule 15 of the San Remo Manual, it is not permissible to carry out an attack against critical offshore infrastructure within the limits of a neutral State's territorial sea.[77] By contrast, if pipelines belonging to a belligerent State were injured in an EEZ/a continental shelf of a third State, then such use of force might be in conformity with the law of armed conflict even if the pipelines land in a neutral State.[78]

Rule 68 of the Oslo Manual provides that: 'During an armed conflict, submarine pipelines and high voltage cables exclusively serving one or more Belligerent States may – if it is militarily necessary – be seized or destroyed subject to the applicable principles and rules of LOAC [the Law of Armed Conflict], in particular distinction, proportionality and the obligation to take feasible precautions.'[79] Yet this concerns such submarine cables and pipelines that serve *exclusively* belligerent(s).[80] The Nord Stream pipelines transported gas from the belligerent State Russia to the neutral State Germany. Thus, the pipelines did not serve exclusively a belligerent State but also a neutral State.

Furthermore, at the time of attacks the Nord Stream pipelines likely served as civilian objects. Civilian objects, categorized as all objects that are not military objectives, cannot be the object of attack or reprisals.[81] Article 52(2) of

---

76 *Application of the Convention on the Prevention and Punishment of the Crime of Genocide* (Bosnia and Herzegovina v. Serbia and Montenegro), Judgment, ICJ Reports 2007, p. 43, para 404.

77 This has implications for debates on the establishment or abolition of EEZ corridors in international straits. See Alexander Lott, 'Maritime Security in the Baltic and Japanese Straits from the Perspective of EEZ Corridors' (2023) 54(3) Ocean Development & International Law 327–348.

78 On the qualification of neutrality of States providing aid to Ukraine in deterring the Russia's war of aggression, see, e.g., Michael N Schmitt, '"Strict" Versus "Qualified" Neutrality' (22 March 2023) Articles of War, available at <https://lieber.westpoint.edu/strict-versus-qualified-neutrality/> accessed 27 August 2023.

79 The Oslo Manual (n 69) 62.

80 Ibid.

81 Art. 52(1) of the Protocol Additional to the Geneva Conventions of 12 August 1949, and relating to the Protection of Victims of International Armed Conflicts (Protocol I) (adopted 8 June 1977, entered into force 7 December 1978) 1125 UNTS 17512.

Protocol I stipulates that attacks need to be limited strictly to military objectives and, in so far as objects are concerned, military objectives are limited to those objects which by their nature, location, purpose, or use make an effective contribution to military action and whose total or partial destruction, capture or neutralization, in the circumstances ruling at the time, offers a definite military advantage. Schmitt explains that:

> An effective contribution is one that in fact contributes to the enemy's military action. The contribution need not be great, but the object must be of a kind that is militarily useful to the enemy in the circumstances. A definite military advantage is one that is more than 'potential or indeterminate'.[82]

According to Article 49(3) of the Protocol I, the above-referred provision (Art 52(2)) does not affect the rules of international law applicable in armed conflict at sea or in the air. However, Article 52(2) of Protocol I is widely considered as reflective of customary international law applicable also at sea.[83] In this context, it is questionable whether the Nord Stream pipelines could have served as military objectives in the context of the ongoing international armed conflict between Russia and Ukraine.

The pipelines indirectly contributed to the belligerent State's war efforts because of Russia's revenues from the sale of natural gas to the European market. Thus, it could be argued that the Nord Stream pipelines could be seen as civilian objects contributing to a belligerent State's war-sustaining effort, thereby potentially making it a legitimate military objective. The Newport Manual states that: 'In this view, enemy export of certain goods, like crude oil, renders a vessel a military objective because the enemy earns revenue that contributes to its war-fighting effort.'[84] If commercial ships exporting a belligerent State's crude oil may fall under this category, then there appears to be no reason why natural gas pipelines that are controlled and owned by a belligerent State-run company (e.g., Gazprom) could not be treated equally as a military objective due to their contribution to a belligerent State's war-sustaining effort.

---

82 Michael N Schmitt, 'International Humanitarian Law and the Conduct of Hostilities', in Ben Saul and Dapo Akande (eds.), *The Oxford Guide to International Humanitarian Law* (Oxford 2020) 164.

83 The definition of military objectives in Rule 40 of the San Remo Manual is a verbatim copy of Article 52(2) of Protocol I. See also James Kraska, Raul 'Pete' Pedrozo *et al.*, *Newport Manual on the Law of Naval Warfare* (US Naval War College 2023) 136.

84 Ibid, 138.

However, the Newport Manual clarifies that most States do not subscribe to the view that military objectives include civilian objects contributing to a belligerent State's war-sustaining effort.[85] Thus, the United States' interpretation as reflected in the Newport Manual is not widely supported under Protocol I. The United States Commander's Handbook states that:

> To be a military objective does not require the attack of the object provides immediate tactical or operational gains or the object makes an effective contribution to a specific military operation. Rather, the object's effective contribution to the warfighting or war-sustaining capability of an opposing force is sufficient. Although terms such as warfighting, war-supporting, and war-sustaining are not explicitly reflected in the Additional Protocol I definition of 'military objective,' the United States has interpreted the military objective definition to include these concepts. Commanders participating in coalition operations should be aware that some allies and partners do not believe objects that provide war-sustaining objects are military objectives.[86]

In addition, the flow of natural gas from Russia to Germany had stopped by the time the Nord Stream pipelines were injured.[87] Thus, at the time of the attack, the pipelines were not exporting commodities and did not contribute to the war-sustaining efforts of Russia. Hence, it is highly doubtful if the Nord Stream pipelines could have served as a lawful military target in the context of the ongoing international armed conflict in Europe – even if, hypothetically, the attack had been carried out by one belligerent State against another belligerent State.

---

85 Ibid. On reluctance in the NATO to referring to war-sustaining objects as military objectives, see Schmitt (n 82) 163.

86 The Commander's Handbook on the Law of Naval Operations (US Navy, US Marine Corps, US Coast Guard, Norfolk, 2022) 8–4.

87 Gerald Traufetter, 'Bundesregierung stoppt umstrittene Gaspipeline Nord Stream 2' Der Spiegel (22 February 2022), available at <https://www.spiegel.de/wirtschaft/reaktion-auf-russische-aggression-robert-habeck-stoppt-nord-stream-2-a-bd78bdc1-dfb2-4662-865e-5fa4796b1076> accessed 27 August 2023. Alex Lawson, 'Nord Stream 1: Gazprom announces indefinite shutdown of pipeline' The Guardian (2 September 2022), available at <https://www.theguardian.com/business/2022/sep/02/nord-stream-1-gazprom-announces-indefinite-shutdown-of-pipeline> accessed 27 August 2023.

3.3 *Environmental Considerations*

An attack on a submarine pipeline has a detrimental effect on the marine environment. States have a duty to prevent such effects in peace time, but does this obligation apply also in an armed conflict?

According to Rule 34 of the San Remo Manual, belligerent States need to comply with the overall rules of the law of armed conflict at sea when conducting hostile actions in a neutral State's EEZ or on its continental shelf. Belligerent States must meet the requirement of due regard for the rights and duties of the coastal State, *inter alia*, for the exploration and exploitation of the economic resources of the EEZ and the continental shelf and the protection and preservation of the marine environment (on the meaning of 'due regard' and its impact on military activities, see *supra* subchapter 3.2.1 of Chapter 3).[88] An EEZ and a continental shelf are areas in which the coastal State is entitled, pursuant to Articles 56, 60(1–2), 77 and 80 of the LOSC, to exercise sovereign rights in relation to economic activities, whereas most belligerent acts against installations, artificial islands, tunnels, windfarms, etc., presumably infringe the coastal State's sovereign rights in the area, including by way of potentially negatively impacting the marine environment and the exploitation of resources. In the context of the due regard requirement, belligerent States need to exercise restraint ('take care') when contemplating carrying out attacks against offshore critical infrastructure located in the EEZ or on the continental shelf of a neutral coastal State.[89]

If critical offshore infrastructure is damaged in a neutral State's EEZ or on its continental shelf, then precautions need to be taken to ensure due regard for the protection and preservation of the marine environment.[90] In the Nuclear Weapons Case, the ICJ found that '[t]he existence of the general obligation of States to ensure that activities within their jurisdiction and control respect the environment of other States or of areas beyond national control is now part of the corpus of international law relating to the environment.'[91] The ICJ found that environmental considerations need to be taken into account in the implementation of the law of armed conflict.[92] According to Koppe, this suggests 'the existence of a general duty of care for the environment.'[93] Compliance

88 See also Bernard H Oxman, 'The Principle of Due Regard', in *The Contribution of the International Tribunal for the Law of the Sea to the Rule of Law: 1996–2016* (Brill 2017) 108–117.

89 See Rule 37 of the San Remo Manual (n 56).

90 Ibid, Rule 35.

91 Legality of the Threat or Use of Nuclear Weapons (n 55) para 29.

92 Ibid, para 32.

93 Erik Koppe, *The Use of Nuclear Weapons and the Protection of the Environment during International Armed Conflict* (Hart 2008) 255.

with this obligation is particularly relevant in relation to acts of sabotage against submarine oil or gas pipelines.

Rule 44 of the San Remo Manual, widely considered reflective of customary international law,[94] prohibits any damage arising to the marine environment if such use of force is not justified by military necessity. In this context, it is doubtful if the use of force against the Nord Stream pipelines was conducted with due regard for the natural environment. This act of sabotage posed a significant danger to the marine environment in many respects:

– Underwater explosions often cause fatal noise pollution for marine mammals even many kilometers away from the epicenter of the explosion,[95] and the area of the Nord Stream explosions is known as the habitat area of the critically endangered Baltic Sea population of harbor porpoise;[96]
– The explosions resulted in heavy gas leakage and supposedly the world's heaviest methane emission event to date;[97]
– In the context of the precautionary principle which, as found by a summary of practice on Rule 44 of the San Remo Manual,[98] is relevant also in an armed conflict, the explosions at least had the potential to disturb the seabed to the extent that toxic seabed sediments were suddenly released to the water column. These toxic chemicals might not be limited only to

94 International Humanitarian Law Databases, 'Rule 44. Due Regard for the Natural Environment in Military Operations', in Louise Doswald-Beck, Jean-Marie Henckaerts *et al.*, *ICRC's study on customary international humanitarian law*, available at <https://ihl-databases.icrc.org/en/customary-ihl/v1/rule44> accessed 27 August 2023. Cymie R Payne, 'Protection of the Natural Environment', in Saul and Akande (n 82) 219.

95 Erik M Salomons *et al.*, 'Noise of underwater explosions in the North Sea. A comparison of experimental data and model predictions' (2021) 149(3) The Journal of the Acoustical Society of America 1878, 1886. Alexander M von Benda-Beckmann *et al.*, 'Assessing the Impact of Underwater Clearance of Unexploded Ordnance on Harbour Porpoises (Phocoena phocoena) in the Southern North Sea' (2015) 41(4) Aquatic Mammals 503, 503.

96 HELCOM, Map and data service, 'Biodiversity: Harbour porpoise', available at <https://maps.helcom.fi/website/mapservice> accessed 10 October 2023.

97 International Methane Emissions Observatory, 'Estimate of total methane emissions from the Nord Stream gas leak incident' (2023) UN environment programme 2–3, available at <https://wedocs.unep.org/bitstream/handle/20.500.11822/41838/methane_NordStream_gas_leak.pdf?sequence=3&isAllowed=y> accessed 27 August 2023. Sophie Loran and Kamilia Lahrichi, 'UNEP finds Nord Stream gas leak may be the highest methane emission event, but still a drop in the ocean' UN environment programme (20 February 2023), available at <https://www.unep.org/technical-highlight/unep-finds-nord-stream-gas-leak-may-be-highest-methane-emission-event-still> accessed 27 August 2023.

98 ICRC, Rule 44 (n 94).

agricultural and other industrial activities.[99] The explosions could break heavily corroded Second World War-era containers full of chemical warfare agents. This would have caused a sudden release of toxins into the marine environment.

Notably, one of the main dumping sites of containers laden with chemical warfare agents is located on the bottom of the seafloor east of Bornholm Island, close to the Nord Stream explosion sites.[100] It is estimated that approximately 30,000 to 50,000 tons of chemical weapons (gross weight) were dumped northeast of Bornholm Island after the Second World War and that some unmapped containers were thrown overboard randomly *en route* to the main dumping site.[101] In 2009, a representative of the Organisation for the Prohibition of Chemical Weapons estimated that at least 32,000 tons of chemical weapons were dumped east of Bornholm Island.[102] This is problematic given that the strong explosions could have damaged some containers of chemical warfare agents that might have been initially deemed to be at a safe distance when the submarine pipelines were laid on the seabed.

Conclusion

Submarine cables and pipelines located in an EEZ or the high seas are extremely vulnerable to hybrid warfare at sea. The practice of Denmark demonstrates that it is possible to establish effective safety zones around submarine cables and pipelines in an EEZ, especially where the EEZs of coastal States are relatively narrow, as in the Baltic Sea.

This chapter argues that the legal resilience of critical offshore infrastructure in the face of sabotage could be further increased if States would not draw a clear legal boundary between attacks within or beyond the outer limits of the territorial sea. An attack against the coastal State's underwater road or rail tunnel, wind farm, oil or gas platform, or submarine pipelines and cables may have equally grave consequences for the coastal State if carried out in the EEZ or on the continental shelf instead of its territorial sea. Hence, sabotage against

99 Hans Sanderson *et al.*, 'Environmental impact of sabotage of the Nord Stream pipelines' (2023) Research Square 4–12.

100 See, e.g., Paula Vanninen *et al.*, 'Exposure status of sea-dumped chemical warfare agents in the Baltic Sea' (2020) 161 Marine Environmental Research 1, 2.

101 Per O Granbom, 'Dumped Chemical Ammunition in the Baltic: A Rejoinder' (1994) 25 Security Dialogue 105, 109.

102 See Grant Dawson, *International Law and Sea-Dumped Chemical Weapons* (Oxford University Press 2023) 19.

critical offshore infrastructure may amount to an armed attack if conducted not only within, but also outside the sovereign territory of a coastal State. Offshore infrastructure in an EEZ or on the continental shelf falls under the jurisdiction of the coastal State, whereas this is not the case on the high seas.

If the unlawful use of force in an EEZ or on the continental shelf, for example, against underwater tunnels or platforms results in significant damage to the coastal State or the loss of human life, then there seems to be sufficient grounds for invoking the right of self-defence under Article 51 of the UN Charter. For this, the coastal State also needs to supply persuasive evidence that another State is responsible for the attack, and it needs to establish a direct link with the targeted infrastructure so that the attack against the infrastructure can be equated with an attack on that State.

It is easier to establish a direct link with the damaged or destroyed object if the location of the attack is within, rather than outside the limits of the coastal State's territorial sea given that offshore infrastructure is not subject to flag State jurisdiction (unlike ships). The use of force under the right of self-defence needs to be aimed at an appropriate military target. The use of force needs to conform with the law of armed conflict, in particular the principles of necessity and proportionality.

During an international armed conflict, the protection standards of offshore critical infrastructure differ depending on whether the object is located within or outside the limits of a neutral State's territorial sea. Conducting military operations within the limits of a neutral State's territorial sea is prohibited. By contrast, even such cables and pipelines that do not exclusively serve belligerent States might, in situations of military necessity, serve as lawful military targets in areas where the high seas freedoms apply. Furthermore, under the *jus in bello*, the use of force against cables or pipelines in an EEZ or on a continental shelf might be lawful even if the cables or pipelines land in a neutral State – provided that rules of the law of armed conflict, including the rules on distinction and proportionality are satisfied.

However, belligerent States must meet the requirement of due regard for the rights and duties of the coastal State, *inter alia*, for the exploration and exploitation of the economic resources of the EEZ and the continental shelf and the protection and preservation of the marine environment. Furthermore, based on the Balticconnector incident, it was argued that the concept of neutral submarine cables has not lost its practical purpose and that granting them a higher standard of protection under the law of naval warfare would be possible.

This chapter demonstrated that the legality of the Nord Stream explosions can be assessed not only from the perspective of peacetime rules and *jus ad bellum*, but also in the context of the *jus in bello*. In the context of an armed conflict, the attribution standards are more flexible than in peace time. It would suffice that a belligerent State exercises overall control over a group of persons by way of financing and provision of training, logistics, and weapons for invoking that State's responsibility for the relevant acts. In case Ukraine as a belligerent State exercised overall control over the group of divers that allegedly conducted the Nord Stream explosions, it would *prima facie* imply Ukraine's responsibility for the sabotage against the Nord Stream pipelines.

Nonetheless, it is doubtful that the Nord Stream pipelines could have served as a military objective even in the context of the armed conflict between Russia and Ukraine. It was also established that the Nord Stream pipelines likely did not serve as a civilian object that contributes to a belligerent State's war-sustaining effort from the perspective of the ongoing international armed conflict in Europe, given that the flow of natural gas from Russia to Germany had stopped by the time the attacks were launched against the Nord Stream pipelines in September 2022. Nor did the perpetrators of the attack give due regard for the protection and preservation of the Baltic Sea marine environment. Based on these reasons, it appears that an attack allegedly attributable to Ukraine against the Nord Stream pipelines was not in conformity with the law of armed conflict.

CHAPTER 6

Sabotage of Critical Offshore Infrastructure: a Case Study of the Balticconnector Incident

Henrik Ringbom and Alexander Lott

Introduction

The Hong Kong-registered and Chinese-owned container ship *NewNew Polar Bear* is suspected of having been involved in damaging the Balticconnector gas pipeline and submarine cables in the exclusive economic zone (hereinafter EEZ) and continental shelf of Estonia and Finland on her way to a port of Russia in the Gulf of Finland on the night of 7/8 October 2023. During the voyage, the *NewNew Polar Bear* crossed the Balticconnector pipeline and the Estonian-Swedish, Russian, and Estonian-Finnish submarine cables that all sustained damage during that night. The *NewNew Polar Bear* crossed the Balticconnector pipeline at the time of seismic activity near the pipeline while being accompanied by a Russian nuclear-powered container ship, the *Sevmorput*.[1] In addition, the Russian merchant ship *SVG Flot* was spotted spending three days, including the day when the cable and the pipeline were damaged, in the relevant maritime area.[2]

1 Mihkel Kärmas, 'Balticconnector case more sabotage than an accident, experts say' ERR News (16 February 2024), available at <https://news.err.ee/1609255413/balticconnector-case-more-sabotage-than-an-accident-experts-say> accessed 21 February 2024; Atle Staalesen, 'Runaway ship Newnew Polar Bear, suspected of sabotage in Baltic Sea, is sailing into Russian Arctic waters' The Barents Observer (26 October 2023), available at <https://thebarentsobserver.com/en/security/2023/10/runaway-ship-newnew-polar-bear-suspected-sabotage-baltic-sea-sailing-russian-arctic> accessed 27 October 2023; Andrius Sytas and Anne Kauranen, 'Three Baltic pipe and cable incidents 'are related', Estonia says' Reuters (27 October 2023), available at <https://www.reuters.com/world/europe/three-baltic-pipe-cable-incidents-are-related-estonia-says-2023-10-27> accessed 27 October 2023; See also Mirjam Mäekivi and Marcus Turovski, 'Chinese vessel even nearer to Balticconnector pipeline at time of leak' ERR News (17 October 2023), available at <https://news.err.ee/1609134998/chinese-vessel-even-nearer-to-Balticconnector-pipeline-at-time-of-leak> accessed 19 October 2023.

2 Karl Kivil, Marcus Turovski, Helen Wright, 'Russian cargo ship spent weekend in vicinity of Balticconnector pipeline leak' ERR News (11 October 2023), available at <https://news.err.ee/1609128785/russian-cargo-ship-spent-weekend-in-vicinity-of-Balticconnector-pipeline-leak> accessed 11 October 2023.

 | DOI:10.1163/9789004707993_008

The main focus of the investigation into the damage caused to the submarine pipeline in Finland's waters is on the Hong Kong-flagged cargo ship *NewNew Polar Bear*. It is possible that this ship damaged the offshore infrastructure of Estonia and Finland with its anchor.[3] The *NewNew Polar Bear* left the Baltic Sea and reached China's port of Tianjin in December 2023 after crossing the Northern Sea Route. Upon its return from Russia, the ship first had to sail through the Finnish and Swedish EEZs. This chapter asks if Finland was entitled to board the *NewNew Polar Bear* while in its EEZ and arrest the ship?

Against this background, the broader aim of this chapter is to assess the legal situation of critical offshore infrastructure in the context of hybrid naval warfare (see *supra* Chapter 1) by identifying various means at the coastal State's disposal to take enforcement measures against a foreign ship suspected of having damaged a submarine pipeline. The focus of this chapter is accordingly on submarine pipelines, but it includes some discussion on submarine cables too, to the extent it is relevant for the overall discussion of the chapter. As illustrated below, the coastal State's options for interdicting a ship outside the territorial sea differ significantly depending on whether the suspected ship damaged a cable or a pipeline.

The legal framework applicable to interdicting a ship suspected of injuring a submarine cable or pipeline outside the limits of the territorial sea is complicated and, arguably, includes legal gaps. The starting point of this chapter is that potential gaps and imperfections in the legal framework usually are more easily identified if departure is taken in a particular concrete case. Our point of departure and case study is the Balticconnector incident, and our assumption is that a coastal State's jurisdiction in that case was considerably more multifaceted than the Finnish authorities have explained in their public statements.

1 The Context

The Finnish Border Guard made radio contact with the *NewNew Polar Bear* in the Gulf of Finland on its return journey westwards following a stay in St Petersburg. However, the vessel did not cooperate with the Finnish authorities. Finland's National Bureau of Investigation, investigating the damage to the Balticconnector pipeline, commented that Finland was constantly on alert in this situation and was ready to intervene if the ship had entered the Finnish territorial sea. However, it noted that Finland had no right to take any

3 Kärmas (n 1); Staalesen (n 1).

law enforcement measures against the *NewNew Polar Bear,* such as boarding, inspection, and arrest of the vessel.[4] Hence the Finnish coastal authorities eventually did not take any enforcement action against the vessel, reportedly since they lacked jurisdiction to do so, as the vessel did not enter Finland's territorial sea.

In general, the legal grounds for law enforcement measures against a foreign ship are broader in the territorial sea. However, this paper seeks to argue that Finland had legal arguments and remedies to take some enforcement measures even in its EEZ against the *NewNew Polar Bear* which was suspected of sabotaging pipelines on the Finnish continental shelf.

A contributing reason for the black-and-white response by the Finnish authorities is presumably that the relevant Finnish legislation (essentially the Penal Code (39/1889),[5] the Act on the EEZ (2004/1058) and the Act on certain underwater cables and pipelines (1965/145)[6] make a stricter distinction between the territorial sea and the EEZ than international law does when it comes to jurisdiction over matters related to pipelines. However, the focus of this paper is on international law, which, as hypothesized here, provides greater prescriptive and enforcement jurisdiction in the present case.

The injuring of the pipeline and the Estonian, Finnish, Swedish, and Russian submarine cables on the night of 7/8 October 2023 did not lead to any significant disruptions in critical services in the relevant coastal States. Nonetheless, Finland, Sweden, and Estonia reacted to these incidents as a matter of grave concern. Finland's president Mr. Sauli Niinistö commented that: 'It is likely that the damage to both the gas pipeline and the [Estonian-Finnish] communication cable is the result of external activity.'[7] On 18 December 2023,

---

4 Arni Alandi, 'Location of Balticconnector in exclusive economic zone limits investigation' ERR News (31 October 2023), available at <https://news.err.ee/1609150024/location-of-Baltic connector-in-exclusive-economic-zone-limits-investigation> accessed 3 November 2023.

5 Under section 1 of the Finnish Penal Code the general scope of applicability is limited to crimes committed «in Finland». Its applicability with respect to crimes committed in the Finnish EEZ is to be addressed according to Act 2004/1058 on the EEZ and Act 1672/2009 on Environmental Protection in Maritime Transport.

6 Along with the adoption of the Finnish EEZ in 2004, the geographical scope of Act 1965/145 on certain underwater cables and pipelines was extended to the EEZ (section 1). However, the same section of the amended act clarifies that it only applies to cables and pipelines beyond the limits of the territorial sea with respect to ships flying a Finnish flag, Finnish citizens or Finnish corporations. Finland has no separate act for the continental shelf.

7 Jon Henley and Jillian Ambrose, 'Undersea pipeline damage appears to be deliberate, says Finland' The Guardian (10 October 2023), available at <https://www.theguardian.com /world/2023/oct/10/undersea-pipeline-damage-appears-to-be-deliberate-says-finland> accessed 10 October 2023.

the European Commission agreed to provide 800.000€ in emergency financial support to Finland from the European Union's (hereinafter the EU) Internal Security Fund for securing the incident area and investigating the disruption of the pipeline.[8]

The Secretary General of the North Atlantic Treaty Organization (hereinafter the NATO), Mr. Jens Stoltenberg, made it clear that if the incidents were 'proven to be an attack on NATO critical infrastructure ... it will be met by a united and determined response from NATO'.[9] A few days later, Prime Minister Rishi Sunak announced that, in 2024, the United Kingdom will deploy over 20,000 soldiers to northern Europe (16,000 soldiers to Norway and Estonia alone) complemented with eight Royal Navy ships, 25 fighter jets and an aviation task force to deter hybrid activities and protect critical infrastructure in the region.[10]

Russia has a long track record in mapping the vulnerabilities of the critical offshore infrastructure of the NATO member States in the Baltic Sea and North Sea. However, a Russian submarine cable Baltika was also injured on the night of 7/8 October 2023. The laying of the 1115-km-long communications cable Baltika on the seabed of the Gulf of Finland and the Baltic Sea was completed in 2021 to ensure the security and uninterrupted operation of Internet communications in Kaliningrad (see Map 6.1).[11]

---

8 See e.g. European Commission, 'The Commission provides emergency funding to Finland in relation to the damage of the Balticconnector pipeline' Press Release (18 December 2023), available at <https://energy.ec.europa.eu/news/commission-provides-emergency-funding-finland-relation-damage-Balticconnector-pipeline-2023-12-18_en> accessed 20 December 2023.

9 Jon Henley, 'Finland says 'state actor' not ruled out in mystery of damaged Baltic gas pipeline' The Guardian (12 October 2023), available at <https://www.theguardian.com/world/2023/oct/12/finland-says-state-actor-not-ruled-out-in-mystery-of-damaged-baltic-gas-pipeline> accessed 12 October 2023.

10 The UK Prime Minister's Office, 'PM accelerates military support to Northern Europe following visit to Sweden' Press Release (13 October 2023), available at <https://www.gov.uk/government/news/pm-accelerates-military-support-to-northern-europe-following-visit-to-sweden> accessed 15 October 2023.

11 Mark Gerassimenko and Karl Kivil, 'Peskov: Kremlil pole andmeid sidekaabli kahjustamise kohta' ERR Uudised (7 November 2023), available at <https://www.err.ee/1609157492/peskov-kremlil-pole-andmeid-sidekaabli-kahjustamise-kohta> accessed 8 November 2023; Anonymous, 'Rostelecom PVOLS Kingisepp – Kaliningrad', TAdviser, available at <https://tadviser.com/index.php/Product:Rostelecom_PVOLS_Kingisepp_-_Kaliningrad> accessed 27 August 2023; See also 'Kaliningrad Cable', Submarine Cable Map, available at <https://www.submarinecablemap.com/submarine-cable/kaliningrad-cable> accessed 27 August 2023.

MAP 6.1 The Estonian, Finnish, Swedish, and Russian submarine cables and the Balticconnector pipeline that all sustained damage in the Northern Baltic Sea on the night of 7 to 8 October 2023. The dark grey lines in the Baltic Sea depict the submarine cables and the Balticconnector pipeline. The original map has been converted to black and white. The approximate locations of the incidents (in red color) and the names have been inserted by the authors. The map serves an illustrative purpose only.
SOURCE OF THE BASE MAP: SUBMARINE CABLE MAP, AVAILABLE AT <HTTPS://WWW.SUBMARINECABLEMAP.COM> ACCESSED 27 SEPTEMBER 2023.

In the EEZ corridor of the Gulf of Finland established by Finland and Estonia in 1994 by voluntarily limiting the outer limits of their territorial sea at the entrance to the Gulf of Finland,[12] the Baltika Cable runs through the Finnish

12 Exchange of Notes Constituting an Agreement on the Procedure to be followed in the Modification of the Limits of the Territorial Waters in the Gulf of Finland (adopted 4 May 1994, entered into force 31 July 1995) UNTS 1887.

EEZ and on its continental shelf.[13] The Baltika Cable is owned by the Russian company Rostelecom, which is, in turn, controlled by the Russian State. It serves as the only telecommunications cable linking the Kaliningrad exclave to mainland Russia that does not cross the territories of Russia's neighboring States (due to the existence of the EEZ corridor in the Gulf of Finland). The land communications cables between Kaliningrad exclave and Russia proper cross Lithuania and Poland that border Kaliningrad. In this context, the damaging of the Russian Baltika submarine cable demonstrates Russia's vulnerability to sabotage against (offshore) energy infrastructure in respect to its strategically important Baltic Sea exclave of Kaliningrad that is isolated from the rest of the Russian mainland territory.

In the growing body of legal literature on the peacetime protection of submarine cables and pipelines,[14] there appears to be a common understanding that this framework includes certain weaknesses. The broader legal starting point of this paper is that coastal States' enforcement rights and duties with respect to activities by foreign ships impacting their cables and pipelines in the EEZ/continental shelf is not clearly regulated in the United Nations Convention on the Law of the Sea[15] (hereinafter LOSC or Convention). Yet, according to the preamble of the Convention, it is designed to settle 'all issues relating to the law of the sea' and address all usages of the oceans. Thus, regulatory gaps need to be filled through interpretation.

Two main approaches to coastal States' enforcement jurisdiction over suspected sabotage of pipelines in their EEZ and continental shelf may be identified: one may take the position that in the absence of specific enforcement provisions in the LOSC, there is no right for coastal States to take enforcement action in the EEZ; or one may take the view that the absence of such explicit jurisdiction means that such jurisdiction must be construed based on the Convention's provisions and international law more generally in light of the overall context.

---

13 'Gulf of Finland', Navionics Chart Viewer, available at <https://webapp.navionics.com/#boating@6&key=kdfkJsizvC> accessed 27 August 2023.

14 On peacetime protection of submarine cables against non-State actors, see Douglas Guilfoyle, Tamsin Phillipa Paige and Rob McLaughlin, 'The Final Frontier of Cyberspace: The Seabed beyond National Jurisdiction and the Protection of Submarine Cables' (2022) 71 International & Comparative Law Quarterly 657, 662–675; Douglas Burnett, Tara Davenport, and Robert Beckman (eds.), *Submarine Cables – The Handbook of Law and Policy* (Brill 2013).

15 United Nations Convention on the Law of the Sea (opened for signature 10 December 1982, entered into force 16 November 1994) 1833 UNTS 3.

Neither approach is self-evident, but since the matter here relates to a new type of threat that was not in the minds of the drafters of the LOSC, the latter approach, based on a dynamic and contextual interpretation of the LOSC, appears to be justifiable. The targeting of pipelines and cables as a means of conducting hybrid warfare has increasingly shifted the safety concerns relating to cables and pipelines from a mainly private concern (operator's economic interest in preventing damage to the cable or pipeline) towards a public (security and environmental) concern for States.[16]

All States concerned with the Balticconnector incident are parties to the LOSC. Under Article 31(1) of the 1969 Vienna Convention[17] on the law of treaties, the general rule of interpretation is that a treaty shall be interpreted 'in good faith in accordance with the ordinary meaning to be given to the terms of the treaty in their context and in the light of its object and purpose.' The context is to be established on the basis of the text and preamble of the treaty and other treaty relations (Article 31(2) of the 1969 Vienna Convention). Moreover, account shall be taken of, *inter alia*, 'any subsequent practice in the application of the treaty which establishes the agreement of the parties regarding its interpretation' and 'any relevant rules of international law applicable in the relations between the parties' (Article 31(3) of the 1969 Vienna Convention). Supplementary means of interpretation, including assessing the preparatory works, may be resorted to under Article 32 of the 1969 Vienna Convention to determine the meaning, when interpretation under the main rule 'leaves the meaning ambiguous or obscure' or 'leads to a result which is manifestly absurd or unreasonable.'

The LOSC seeks to establish a legal order for the oceans, covering according to its preamble, 'all issues relating to the law of the sea'. Like any treaty, it is based on the premise that the rights and obligations are undertaken in good faith, and it specifically provides that rights, jurisdictions and freedoms provided in the Convention shall be exercised 'in a manner which would not constitute an abuse of right.' (Article 300 of the LOSC). Under its preamble, the

16 In order to clarify the legal framework for cables and pipelines, the International Law Association established a Committee in 2018 to examine, *inter alia*, 'whether international regulation of submarine communications cables, power cables and pipelines warrant different treatment beyond that set out in UNCLOS'. See mandate of the Committee in <https://www.ila-hq.org/en_GB/documents/mandate-1> accessed on 19 January 2024. The Committee has not yet produced its final report, but the second interim report from 2022 is available at <https://www.ila-hq.org/en_GB/documents/submar-3> accessed on 19 January 2024.

17 Vienna Convention on the Law of Treaties (adopted 23 May 1969, entered into force 27 January 1980) 1155 UNTS 331.

Convention is guided by 'a spirit of mutual understanding and cooperation' and a desire to establish 'with due regard for the sovereignty of all States, a legal order for the seas and oceans which will facilitate international communication and will promote the peaceful uses of the seas and oceans ...'

Under this starting point, it seems clear that the overall interests underlying the LOSC heavily favor the interests of States who seek to have their undersea infrastructure intact; it is difficult to find anything in the text of the Convention or in its underlying object and purpose that would protect actors or States that seek to abuse the provisions of the LOSC for carrying out sabotage activities at sea, or to protect ships that may reasonably be suspected to be involved in such activities from further investigation.

More generally, the object and purpose of the LOSC regime was to establish a durable and all-encompassing legal regime for the oceans. This favors a dynamic interpretation of the Convention against the background of the arrival of new types of threats and activities that were not – directly, at least – conceived by the drafters of the Convention, such as State-supported sabotage activities by commercial ships. The increasing feature of such activities and threats in practice arguably justifies a flexible reading of the enforcement in favor of States seeking to counteract such activities whether undertaken by commercial or government-owned ships.

2 Law of the Sea Considerations on Prescriptive and Enforcement Jurisdiction

The EEZ is a functional 'compromise' zone. For some issues, the zone is subject to exclusive coastal State jurisdiction, for others, it resembles rather the high seas, where freedom of navigation applies, and jurisdiction mainly rests with the flag State. In other words, whether the coastal State has jurisdiction in the EEZ depends on the subject matter concerned. Furthermore, one may differentiate between the various categories of jurisdiction in the EEZ. In the words of Guilfoyle, '[t]he EEZ constitutes a patchwork of 'sovereign power' (including enforcement jurisdiction) over some subject matters and mere 'jurisdiction' (not necessarily extending to enforcement) over others.'[18]

Nonetheless, not even navigational freedoms imply the absence of rules or obligations. First, Article 88 of the LOSC provides that '[t]he high seas shall be reserved for peaceful purposes' and Article 58(2) makes that applicable to the

18 Douglas Guilfoyle, *Shipping Interdiction and the Law of the Sea* (Cambridge University Press 2009) 19.

EEZ. Second, flag States must ensure that ships, as a minimum, comply with generally accepted international rules on safety, environmental protection etc. (Article 94 of the LOSC). Third, there is a general duty for States to exercise navigational freedoms with 'due regard' for the interests of other States, including coastal States (Articles 87(2), 56(2) of the LOSC).[19]

2.1 *Prescriptive Jurisdiction*

The jurisdiction of Finland to lay pipelines in its EEZ and on its continental shelf is not in question. It follows from the general right of all States to lay cables and pipelines under LOSC Articles 58(1) and 79(1) and is further emphasized by coastal States' powers to place certain conditions on other States' pipelines in their continental shelf/EEZ under Article 79(2) and (3) of the LOSC. In addition, Article 79(4) safeguards the right of the coastal State to establish conditions for pipelines entering its territory or territorial sea, as well as its jurisdiction over cables and pipelines serving other lawful activities in the continental shelf, such as the exploration and exploitation of resources or the operation of artificial islands, installations or structures. Furthermore, any activity which involves drilling in the EEZ, e.g. for the laying of the Balticconnector pipeline, is subject to the *exclusive* jurisdiction of the coastal State under Article 81 of the LOSC. Article 246(5) of the LOSC on marine scientific research further underlines this, by acknowledging a right for coastal States to withhold research permits in the EEZ, e.g. if the research involves explosives, drilling or marine pollution.

The jurisdiction of coastal States to establish safety zones in an EEZ close to such pipelines is less clear (Art 60(4) of the LOSC, see also *supra* Chapter 5.1). The coastal State's jurisdiction in respect of such pipelines is obviously not as wide as the right governing installations, structures etc., where a safety zone of 500 meters can be established unilaterally, nor as wide as the jurisdiction over

19 The reciprocal duty of due regard does not as such involve a priority between different interests and must accordingly be analysed on a case-by-case basis. See para 519 of Annex VII Arbitral Tribunal, Chagos Marine Protected Area Arbitration (Mauritius v. United Kingdom), Case 2011-03, Award of 18 March 2015 where it is found that, "the extent of the regard required by the Convention will depend on the nature of the rights held by [the other State], their importance, the extent of the anticipated impairment, the nature and importance of the activities contemplated by the [coastal State], and the availability of alternative approaches. In the majority of cases, this assessment will necessarily involve at least some consultation with the right-holding State." See also the Annex VII Arbitral Tribunal, the "Enrica Lexie" Incident (Italy v. India), Case 2015-28, Award of 21 May 2020, paras 973–975; Robin Churchill, Vaughan Lowe, and Amy Sander, *The law of the sea* (4th ed., Manchester University Press 2022) 287–291.

cables and pipelines that serve such installations (e.g., oil or gas platforms) and can be considered as integral parts of such installations of the coastal State under Article 79(4) of the LOSC.[20] But at least the International Maritime Organization (hereinafter the IMO) could establish such zones, at the request of Finland and Estonia, through its routing measures, based on the jurisdiction of those States over the cable in question.

2.2 *Enforcement Jurisdiction*

However, in the case of the Balticconnector incident it is not the prescriptive right, which is at issue, but the jurisdiction to take *enforcement* measures against ships suspected to be engaged in unlawful activities. Both types of jurisdiction are required for taking enforcement measures at sea. Coastal State enforcement jurisdiction linked to pipelines is not specifically regulated in the LOSC.

Article 113 of the LOSC makes it clear that the intentional or negligent damaging of pipelines or cables beneath *the high seas* is unlawful. The offence does not presuppose actual damage of the pipeline, as it extends to 'conduct calculated or likely to result in such breaking or injury'. However, the article places enforcement jurisdiction with the flag State. This may be natural in view of the origin of Article 113 of the LOSC pre-dating the EEZ,[21] but nevertheless creates an uncertainty in view of the extended prescriptive rights that coastal States have been granted with respect to pipelines in their EEZ and continental shelf (which clearly exceed their jurisdiction with respect to pipelines on the high seas).

As far as enforcement on the high seas is concerned, Guilfoyle has summarized that, '[a] state's public vessels may interdict a non-national vessel on the high seas in one of three cases: where the flag state consents; where a permissive rule of general international law allows the interdiction; or where the vessel is without nationality (i.e. stateless).'[22]

The *NewNew Polar Bear* was not stateless as she sails under the flag of Hong Kong. To the extent of the authors' knowledge, Finland had not sought the flag State's (Hong Kong/China) consent for boarding the ship in the Baltic Sea. It is possible, even though not necessarily likely, that the flag State might have

20 See also the Annex VII Arbitral Tribunal, Arctic Sunrise Arbitration (the Netherlands v. the Russian Federation), Award of 14 August 2015, paras 211 and 244; Churchill, Lowe, and Sander (n 19) 269.

21 See Douglas R Burnett, 'Submarine Cable Security and International Law' (2021) 97 International Law Studies 1660, 1671.

22 Guilfoyle (n 18) 339.

given Finland the permission to board the vessel. Guilfoyle has explained that, '[c]ommonly, permission to search does not encompass permission to seize, and if evidence of prohibited conduct is found further disposition instructions must be sought from the flag state before further enforcement action is taken against the vessel, its cargo or persons aboard.'[23] Therefore, if Finland had sought to seize or arrest the ship, it would have had to file additional requests to the flag State.

Under Article 110(1) of the LOSC, officials can board a ship on the high seas in the event that this ship engages in piracy, slave trade, broadcasts illegal broadcasts or has no nationality. None of these grounds were relevant in relation to the *NewNew Polar Bear* incident. Furthermore, Guilfoyle notes that:

> [H]igh seas jurisdiction to enforce is only generally granted over piracy and unauthorized broadcasting, and the latter only in a qualified form. All UNCLOS parties are also obliged individually to 'prevent and punish' the use of their flag vessels in the slave trade, but there is no general duty of cooperation to this end, let alone universal high seas enforcement jurisdiction.[24]

As a starting point, the enforcement rules for the high seas apply to the EEZ as well, insofar as they are not incompatible with the rules for the EEZ (Article 58(2) of the LOSC). Guilfoyle accordingly concludes in relation to law enforcement measures on the high seas or in the EEZ that '[i]f there is not flag-State consent given in advance to interdicting a flag vessel in international waters, or a specific exception allowing the interdiction, it will be prohibited as a use of force.'[25] As regards pipelines incidents it was already noted that no specific enforcement jurisdiction is provided for coastal States with respect to pipelines in their EEZ and continental shelf, but that coastal States' prescriptive jurisdiction in these areas clearly exceeds their jurisdiction with respect to pipelines on the high seas. More generally, it is clear that enforcement jurisdiction in the EEZ offers more grounds for interfering with foreign ships than is the case on the high seas. The question is whether such considerations may be given any significance when seeking to establish coastal States' enforcement jurisdiction with respect to pipelines incidents in their EEZ or continental shelf.

The only two violations in the EEZ that are covered by specific coastal State enforcement jurisdiction are vessel-source pollution (Articles 220 and 221 of

23 Ibid, 341.
24 Ibid, 23.
25 Ibid, 277.

the LOSC) and enforcement linked to natural resources (in essence, fishing vessels) under Article 73(1) of the LOSC. Enforcement jurisdiction against ships suspected of polluting the marine environment is carefully differentiated, depending on the nature of the threat, the significance of the pollution and the strength of the evidence. By way of contrast, jurisdiction with respect to fishing vessels is very broad, including the right to board, detain and arrest the fishing vessel if it is necessary to ensure compliance with the national fisheries rules.

The enforcement jurisdiction over foreign (merchant) ships suspected of being involved in marine pollution is based on the jurisdiction of coastal States over environmental protection in their EEZ (Article 56(1)(b)(III) of the LOSC), while the broader enforcement powers over foreign fishing vessels derive from the sovereign rights that coastal States have over living and non-living resources in the EEZ (Article 56(1)(a) of the LOSC). Pipelines are not specifically mentioned in the list of coastal State competences in the EEZ, but jurisdiction nevertheless follows from the reference in Article 56(1)(c) to 'other rights and duties provided for in this Convention', in combination with some of the articles referred to in the next subchapter.

Based on this starting point, some potential jurisdictional bases for taking enforcement action against the *NewNew Polar Bear* are identified below, mainly to demonstrate that the Finnish authorities' argument that action could not be taken as the vessel stayed in the EEZ, was unduly cautious. The considerations below may be applied separately or cumulatively.

3 Potential Jurisdictional Bases

3.1 *Jurisdiction over Ships Polluting the Marine Environment*

The only explicit enforcement jurisdiction against commercial ships on the EEZ which is specifically regulated in the LOSC relates to marine pollution. A first option is thus to base jurisdiction on the pollution caused by the damaged pipeline.

It is well-known that natural gas leakages may cause significant damage both to marine life and to the atmosphere.[26] The damaging of submarine oil or gas pipelines likely has an impact on the living resources in the EEZ at varying levels depending on the scale of oil or gas leaks as well as the location of

26 DNV Recommended Practice, DNV-RP-F107 Risk Assessment of Pipeline Protection (2010), 32–34; Alexander Proelß, 'Pipelines and Protected Areas' in Richard Caddell and D Rhidian Thomas (eds.), *Shipping, Law and the Marine Environment in the 21st Century* (Lawtext 2013) 276.

the leaks and their vicinity to living resources. Still, the leaks may not have a notable effect on the living resources in the relevant EEZ. In particular, this might be the case for the leakage of natural gas into the marine environment, while the leakage of oil to the marine environment tends to have a greater impact on the living organisms.

The environmental risks of pipelines are acknowledged in the LOSC, e.g. in the distinction made between cables and pipelines on the continental shelf in Article 79(2) of the LOSC, permitting the coastal State to 'take reasonable measures for … the exploitation of its natural resources and the prevention, reduction and control of pollution from pipelines'. It is not further clarified what such reasonable measures might consist of, but arguably the word 'control' implies at least some jurisdiction to take enforcement measures against ships suspected of being involved in causing such pollution.

This type of pollution is clearly included in the definition of pollution of the marine environment in Article 1(4) and hence covered by Part XII of the LOSC, under which all States have an obligation to protect and preserve the marine environment (Article 192 of the LOSC) and 'shall take, individually or jointly as appropriate, all measures consistent with this Convention that are necessary to prevent, reduce and control pollution of the marine environment from any source' (Article 194(1) of the LOSC).

3.1.1 Article 220

In the case of vessel-source pollution, more specific rules are laid down in Articles 211 and 217–221 of the LOSC, with Article 220(3–6) specifically dealing with enforcement jurisdiction over foreign ships on the EEZ. Article 220(3) of the LOSC stipulates that where there are clear grounds for believing that a vessel navigating in the EEZ or the territorial sea of a State has, in the EEZ, committed a violation of applicable international rules and standards for the prevention, reduction and control of pollution from vessels or laws and regulations of that State conforming and giving effect to such rules and standards, that State may require the vessel to give information regarding its identity and port of registry, its last and its next port of call and other relevant information required to establish whether a violation has occurred. Furthermore, where there are clear grounds for believing that a vessel navigating in the EEZ or the territorial sea of a State has, in the EEZ, committed such a violation resulting in a substantial discharge causing or threatening significant pollution of the marine environment, that State may undertake physical inspection of the vessel for matters relating to the violation (Art 220(5) of the LOSC). The preconditions for such inspection are that the vessel has refused to give information or if the information supplied by the vessel is 'manifestly at variance with the evident factual situation and if the circumstances of the case justify such inspection'. Also, if the provisions of Article 220(3–6) of the LOSC had been applied, Finland could have required the vessel in question to give 'other relevant information required to establish whether a violation has occurred' (220(3) of the LOSC).

James Kraska has found in relation to Article 220(5) that, 'the flag state, the vessel, and the coastal state are likely to disagree on the weight of the evidence, yet the objective test of the evidence in UNCLOS seems to tilt in practice toward the coastal state to make the determination.'[27] Kraska further comments that:

> Coastal states have jurisdiction in the EEZ with regard to 'protection and preservation of the marine environment. /…/ In the territorial sea or EEZ, coastal states may undertake physical inspection in cases where there are 'clear grounds' for believing that a violation of national laws that reflect international standards has occurred, and that are 'resulting in a substantial discharge causing or threatening significant pollution of the marine environment.' This test is as vague as the checklist that applies to ships 'navigating' in the territorial sea. In particular, the temporal or chronological elements are unclear because of the 'ing' verbs – may the coastal state act only if the violation is currently or actively resulting or causing or threatening pollution, or may it act much later, such as after the ship already has departed the EEZ and the threat is no longer unfolding? In either case, the authority of the coastal state to conduct a physical inspection is qualified in that it is done 'if the vessel has refused to give information or if the information supplied by the vessel is manifestly at variance with the evident factual situation and if the circumstances of the case justify such inspection.' This provision along introduces three more decision points for the coastal state: (1) has the ship refused to provide information?; (2) is the information inconsistent with evident facts?; and (3) do the circumstances justify an inspection? Given the subjective nature of the test, reasonable interpretations that are in conflict may be applied in good faith.[28]

In particularly severe cases of pollution impact (and clear evidence) the ship could be detained and subject to legal measures under Article 220(6) of the LOSC.

---

27 James Kraska, 'Excessive Coastal State Jurisdiction', in Henrik Ringbom (ed.), *Jurisdiction over Ships – Post-UNCLOS Developments in the Law of the Sea* (Brill 2015) 188–189.

28 Ibid, 189–190.

However, these enforcement rules have traditionally been applied with respect to pollution from the ship itself (as is indicated in the title of Article 211 of the LOSC), rather than to other forms of pollution caused by the vessel. The wording of Article 220(3) of the LOSC does not in itself clarify whether it may also extend to pollution caused by pipelines damaged by a ship. The underlined text below leaves open the possibility that national laws cover a wider spectrum of pollution sources, provided they have an international basis.

> Where there are clear grounds for believing that a vessel navigating in the exclusive economic zone ... has, in the exclusive economic zone, committed a violation of applicable international rules and standards for the prevention, reduction and control of pollution from vessels *or laws and regulations of that State conforming and giving effect to such rules and standards*, that State may require the vessel to give information regarding its identity and port of registry, its last and its next port of call and other relevant information required to establish whether a violation has occurred.

A duty to adopt such laws may be read into Article 214 of the LOSC, under which States 'shall adopt laws and regulations and take other measures necessary to implement applicable international rules and standards established through competent international organizations or diplomatic conference to prevent, reduce and control pollution of the marine environment arising from or in connection with seabed activities subject to their jurisdiction'.

Similarly, in respect of pollution caused by dumping, coastal States shall enforce applicable international rules and standards 'with regard to dumping within its territorial sea or its exclusive economic zone or onto its continental shelf' (Article 216(1)(a) of the LOSC). As far as is known, however, there are currently no international rules regulating gas releases into the marine environment.

3.1.2 Article 221

A more wide-reaching jurisdiction can be based on Article 221 of the LOSC, and the underlying Intervention Convention,[29] which offers coastal States a very broad enforcement jurisdiction to take measures against ships in cases

29 International Convention Relating to Intervention on the High Seas in Cases of Oil Pollution Casualties (adopted 29 November 1969, entered into force 6 May 1975) 970 UNTS 211.

of imminent 'maritime casualties'.[30] This article includes powers to arrest the ship, even beyond the territorial sea, if the environmental risks so require. As opposed to earlier proposals in the drafting of the LOSC, which covered marine incidents more generally, the wording of Article 221 of the LOSC limits the range of casualties covered to those involving ships, through its definition of 'maritime casualty'. However, since the Balticconnector pipeline incident is closely related to the nautical activities of the ship in question, it may still fall within the scope of the Article, as is indicated by the inclusion of 'other incident of navigation' to the definition of 'maritime casualty' and the underlined words below.

1. Nothing in this Part shall prejudice the right of States, pursuant to international law, both customary and conventional, to take and enforce measures beyond the territorial sea proportionate to the actual or threatened damage to protect their coastline or related interests, including fishing, from pollution or threat of pollution following upon a maritime casualty *or acts relating to such a casualty*, which may reasonably be expected to result in major harmful consequences.
2. For the purposes of this article, 'maritime casualty' means a collision of vessels, stranding or other incident of navigation, or other occurrence on board a vessel or external to it resulting in material damage or imminent threat of material damage to a vessel or cargo.

The article, however, which is a maritime version of the doctrine of necessity, is usually considered to require a high threshold of damage to the coastline or its resources.

3.1.3 Natural Resources

It may also be noted that Article 73(1) of the LOSC extends to measures for the purpose of preventing damage to any marine living resources in the EEZ.

> The coastal State may, in the exercise of its sovereign rights to explore, exploit, conserve and manage the living resources in the exclusive economic zone, take such measures, including boarding, inspection, arrest and judicial proceedings, as may be necessary to ensure compliance with the laws and regulations adopted by it in conformity with this Convention.

30 A protocol adopted in 1973, extended the main rules of the Intervention Convention, which were limited to pollution or threat of pollution by oil, to casualties involving other substances by oil.

Article 73(1) of the LOSC does not specifically link the damage to the living resources to the fishing vessel itself, which leaves open the prospect that the damage to the living resources could stem from oil and gas leaks from pipelines, provided there is a link to the ship in question. As demonstrated by the Balticconnector incident, the pipelines may be damaged by a ship's anchor, while the Nord Stream explosions of 2022 resulted from explosives attached to the pipelines by divers operating from a ship.

The use of the enforcement measures listed in Article 73(1) of the LOSC is subject to the criterion of necessity. Harrison notes that,

> This necessity standard is central to determining the balance between coastal state rights and the interests of other states. The inclusion of this phrase means that the enforcement actions of the coastal state are subject to some scrutiny by an international court or tribunal. /…/ At the outset, it must be remarked that the term 'necessary' is open-ended.[31]

Harrison concludes, with reference to case law, that 'coastal states should not be found in violation of Article 73(1) unless their actions can be shown to be arbitrary or patently unreasonable or exercised in bad faith.'[32] For avoiding this, the coastal State is required to provide at least some evidence of an offence that triggers the relevant enforcement actions under Article 73(1) of the LOSC.[33] Harrison illustrates this with the following example:

> [I]f a foreign fishing vessel is merely navigating through the EEZ, it is arguable that a coastal state should have to show some evidence that an offence has been committed before exercising any enforcement powers over that vessel. This would be the case even in the case of an inspection of the vessel, as inspection itself amounts to an interference with the freedom of navigation being exercised by the vessel. In this context, it is also appropriate to impose a minimum evidential threshold on the coastal state to prevent it from abusing its enforcement powers. Yet, in both situations, the evidential threshold should not be set too high. Doing so, would undermine the sovereign rights of the coastal state.[34]

31 James Harrison, 'Safeguards against Excessive Enforcement Measures in the Exclusive Economic Zone – Law and Practice', in Ringbom (n 27) 220.

32 Ibid, 221.

33 Ibid.

34 Ibid, 221–222.

The damaging of a submarine gas pipeline which is in operation may have an impact on marine living organisms, since a considerable amount of natural gas enters the marine environment leading to environmental damage.[35] Hence, to the extent the damage of the pipeline would affect living resources in the EEZ, it is possible to argue that the coastal State's sovereign rights over those resources could justify action based on Article 73(1) of the LOSC, including inspection, arrest, and starting judicial proceedings. In that situation, the coastal State would thus have an additional basis on which to enforce its laws in the EEZ in respect of a ship suspected of polluting the marine environment. It must be acknowledged, though, that Article 73(1) of the LOSC is drafted with jurisdiction over fisheries in mind and that it is not intended to extend to damage to living resources caused by other marine activities.[36]

3.1.4 Summary

The LOSC does not provide an explicit jurisdiction to investigate ships involved in pollution caused by damaged pipelines on the EEZ. However, the pollution caused by a damaged pipeline is clearly covered under the general environmental jurisdiction of coastal States in their EEZ and by the general rights and obligations in the Convention relating to the protection of the marine environment. To the extent that this type of pollution is caused by ships, e.g. through anchoring maneuvers, there are good grounds for treating the environmental damage as analogous to pollution emanating from the ship itself, which would imply that the enforcement jurisdiction against suspected ships is linked to the level of (potential) damage and the level of evidence linking the pollution to the ship. The latter consideration implies a right and duty of the coastal State to find out the facts relating to the ship and, hence, to undertake physical inspection of the ship, if other means of establishing basic facts are not helpful.

While not conclusive, this brief overview indicates that by focusing on the jurisdiction that coastal States have over the marine environment in their EEZ, Finland could have argued in favor of having some jurisdiction against the suspected ship based on the environmental impact of the damage to the Balticconnector pipeline. The potential measures include a physical inspection of the ship to find out more about its whereabouts, but even such enforcement

---

35 On the level of impact required for environmental damage, see Karen Hulme, *War Torn Environment: Interpreting The Legal Threshold* (Martinus Nijhoff 2004) 30–39.

36 In the M/V "Virginia G" (Panama/Guinea-Bissau), Judgment, ITLOS Reports 2014, p. 4, the ITLOS accepted to include bunkering vessels serving fishing vessels in the EEZ under the scope of Article 73, but also established that "the principle of reasonableness applies generally to measures under Article 73" (para 270).

measures as the arrest of the ship could be justified under international law. Causing damage to natural living resources could be subject to far-reaching enforcement jurisdiction of the coastal State, based on Article 221 of the LOSC and possibly – by analogy – Article 73(1) on marine living resources.

3.2 *Enforcement Rules with Respect to Damaging a Submarine Pipeline*

Another way to argue in favor of the coastal State jurisdiction over the *NewNew Polar Bear*-type of situation focuses on the (suspected) breach of the pipeline as such, rather than its incidental consequences.

3.2.1 Article 113

Article 113 of the LOSC requires every State to adopt the laws and regulations necessary to make the willful or negligent breaking or injury of a submarine cable or pipeline a punishable offense. This provision also applies to conduct calculated or likely to result in such breaking or injury. Thus, Article 113 of the LOSC sets the jurisdictional background in relation to the severing of a submarine cable or pipeline and makes it clear that the intentional cutting of submarine cables or injuring of submarine pipelines is illegal. It is subject to criminal liability if carried out both within and beyond the limits of the territorial sea of the coastal State.

In this context, the question arises as to whether Article 113 of the LOSC *per se* could be considered as an exception permitting the interdiction of a foreign ship on the high seas and in the EEZ? Currently, the dominant view appears to hold that Article 113 does not provide for universal jurisdiction in the Balticconnector incident type of cases as it offers no explicit enforcement jurisdiction for States other than the flag State.

Heintschel von Heinegg has pointed out that Articles 113–115 of the LOSC neither require nor prohibit the exercise of universal jurisdiction in respect of attacks against submarine cables or pipelines and thus not only the flag State or State of nationality, but other States as well may exercise their jurisdiction in response to such attacks.[37] On that basis, in support of a position that a Baltic Sea coastal State could have boarded the *NewNew Polar Bear*, one might potentially refer to Article 113 of the LOSC arguing that it enables the exercise of universal jurisdiction in respect of attacks against submarine cables or pipelines.

---

37 Wolff Heintschel von Heinegg, 'Protecting Critical Submarine Cyber Infrastructure: Legal Status and Protection of Submarine Communications Cables under International Law', in Katharina Ziolkowski (ed.), *Peacetime Regime for State Activities in Cyberspace* (NATO CCD COE Publication 2013) 291, 311.

In this context, a comparison can be made with Article 10 of the 1884 Paris Convention for the Protection of Submarine Cables Outside the Territorial Sea[38] that allows to board a ship outside the territorial sea and question the crew about the suspected breaking or damaging of a submarine cable. Beckman distils from Article 110 of the LOSC an explicit recognition that, 'additional reasons for exercising the right to board foreign flagged ships may be established by treaty.'[39] In this context, Article 10 of the 1884 Convention has special relevance as an additional permissive rule of general international law that would allow the interdiction of a ship suspected of damaging a submarine cable on the high seas.[40]

However, there are some limitations. Kraska and Pedrozo note that while the 1884 Convention prohibits the breaking or injury of submarine cable through willful or culpable negligence, this 'does not apply, however, to situation of accidental damage, such as by fishers.'[41] Yet it does not appear that the damage to the Balticconnector pipeline was caused by accident. In this connection, the Estonian Defense Minister Mr. Hanno Pevkur has commented that, 'if the ship's anchor hangs free for over 185 kilometers, it is hard to believe that it is an accident.'[42] This position is shared by experts who conducted simulations on the impact of the dragging of the anchor on the likely course divergences.[43]

---

38 Convention for the Protection of Submarine Telegraph Cables 1884 (adopted 14 March 1884, entered into force 1 May 1888) 1901 Australian Treaty Series 1.

39 Robert Beckman, 'Protecting Submarine Cables from Intentional Damage', in Burnett, Davenport, and Beckman (n 14) 281, 286.

40 Notably, while the 1884 Paris Convention applies to the protection of submarine cables, most of its provisions have been incorporated into the LOSC in a way that the provisions apply in parallel to submarine pipelines as well. Article 10 of the 1884 Convention could be seen as an exception in this context.

41 James Kraska and Raul 'Pete' Pedrozo, *Disruptive Technology and the Law of Naval Warfare* (Oxford University Press 2022) 182. Article 113 of the LOSC does not apply to such a situation either.

42 Heini Pitkänen, 'Viron puolustusministeri: Kaasuputkivaurioihin yhdistetty kiinalaisalus veti ankkuriaan satoja kilometrejä pitkin merenpohjaa' Helsingin Sanomat (24 November 2023), available at <https://www.hs.fi/ulkomaat/art-2000010015226.html> accessed 12 December 2023; See also Rebekka Salmela, 'Merikapteeni: On mahdollista, että kiinalaisalus veti ankkuriaan satoja kilometrejä merenpohjassa' Helsingin Sanomat (26 November 2023), available at <https://www.hs.fi/kotimaa/art-2000010017239.html> accessed 12 December 2023.

43 Malte Humpert, 'Northern Sea Route Saw Seven Containership Voyages in 2023, Including Controversial Trip by Chinese Container Ship' High North News (21 December 2023), available at <https://www.highnorthnews.com/en/northern-sea-route-saw-seven-containership-voyages-2023-including-controversial-trip-chinese> accessed 22 December 2023.

It has been noted in literature that the focus on flag State enforcement for this type of crimes may be appropriate for accidental damage but is clearly unsatisfactory to deal with the type of intentional sabotage-like conduct that is suspected in the case of the *NewNew Polar Bear*.[44] In cases such as the Balticconnector incident where one of the States involved either as a flag State of a ship suspected of damaging a submarine cable or pipeline or as the interdicting State is a non-State party to the 1884 Convention, the boarding of the ship by a State non-party to the 1884 Convention (e.g., Estonia or Finland) might be possible provided that the above-discussed dynamic interpretation of Article 113 of the LOSC is adopted, thereby permitting universal jurisdiction in respect of such incidents.

Alternatively, in relation to submarine cables (though not necessarily pipelines), one might argue in support of Article 10 of the 1884 Convention forming part of customary international law. Kraska maintains that:

> While Article 10 of the 1884 treaty specifies that warships and other government vessels have a right to verify the nationality of a merchant vessel if it is suspected of having broken a submarine cable, this provision is a departure from the concept of exclusive flag state jurisdiction over ships, as embodied in Article 92 of the LOSC. Still, it is also possible to suggest that Article 10 persists even now by virtue of Article 30 of the 1958 [high seas] convention, which states that prior agreements already in force shall continue. Thus, the rule that states may approach and visit merchant vessels to investigate cut or damaged cables may still apply to states party to the 1884 convention and the 1958 convention, or perhaps more broadly under customary international law.[45]

Davenport has found that:

> [T]here is some merit in the argument that warships of all States should have the right to board vessels suspected of intentionally breaking a cable. For example, Article X of the 1884 Cable Convention allows warships to require the master of a vessel suspected of having broken a cable to provide documentation to show the ship's nationality and thereinafter

44 Stuart Kaye, 'International Measures to Protect Oil Platforms, Pipelines and Submarine Cables from Attack' (2007) 31(2) Tulane Maritime Law Journal 377, 422.

45 James Kraska, 'Submarine Cables in the Law of Naval Warfare' (10 July 2020) Lawfare, available at <https://www.lawfareblog.com/submarine-cables-law-naval-warfare> accessed 27 November 2023.

> to make a report to the flag state. This provides an effective deterrent to prospective attacks.[46]

Still, it is unclear whether Article 10 of the 1884 Convention is part of customary international law, not least because the practice of States in boarding a foreign ship based on the said provision is limited and, arguably, because Article 10 was not included in the LOSC (unlike the other provisions of the 1884 Convention). McLaughlin, Paige, and Guilfoyle comment that:

> At least one such inspection occurred when in 1959 a US warship investigating a break in an Atlantic cable off Newfoundland 'boarded the Soviet trawler *Novorossiisk* and minuted its papers'. The Paris Convention, however, provided only for 'visitation on the high seas, not for arrest or even for search.' Its practical utility is further hampered by its low level of ratification having only 36 parties.[47]

Kraska and Pedrozo take the view that the 1884 Convention does not allow for the arrest of the ship and her crew.[48] However, they comment that in the above-referred 1959 incident where the United States Navy suspected the Soviet ship of cutting five submarine cables, since *Novorossiisk* had been 'in the immediate vicinity of all five cable breaks at the time the lines were cut', the ship was subject to a 70-minutes-long 'investigation' by a United States Navy officer and four enlisted sailors.[49]

3.2.2 An Enforcement Gap in the EEZ?

The key question here is whether the presence of the pipeline in the Finnish EEZ and on its continental shelf, combined with other circumstances (including co-ownership of the pipeline and its role as a domestically important energy object) tying the cable to Finnish interests, could amount to establishing a jurisdictional link to Finland, strong enough to authorize enforcement measures in the EEZ.

The main rule of Article 113 of the LOSC extends to pipelines damaged in the EEZ of other States as well.[50] It follows *a fortiori* from the jurisdictional system

46 Tara Davenport, 'Submarine Cables, Cybersecurity and International Law: An Intersectional Analysis' (2015) 24 Catholic University Journal of Law and Technology 57, 84–85.

47 McLaughlin, Paige, and Guilfoyle (n 14) 663.

48 Kraska and Pedrozo (n 41) 182.

49 Ibid, 182–183.

50 The origin of the article is to be found in Article 27 of the 1958 High Seas Convention, which in turn was inspired by Article 2 of the 1884 Convention.

set up by the Convention, and more explicitly from its Article 58(2), 'insofar as [Article 113 and other high seas articles] are not incompatible with [Part V of the LOSC, on the EEZ].' The damaging of pipelines also breaches the duty of States to exercise the navigational rights in the EEZ with due regard for the interests of the coastal States.[51] It was already noted that coastal States have a clear prescriptive right to lay cables and pipelines in their EEZ/continental shelf and that some of the jurisdictional rights of the coastal State apply only in relation to the laying of pipelines, but not *vis-à-vis* cables. In particular, Article 79(2) of the LOSC acknowledges the right of the coastal State to 'take reasonable measures for the exploration of the continental shelf, the exploitation of its natural resources and the prevention, reduction and control of pollution from pipelines'. In addition, the delineation of the course of the pipeline, but not the cable, is subject to the consent of the coastal State (Article 79(3) of the LOSC). If anything, therefore, a systematic approach to the LOSC favors more enforcement jurisdiction for coastal States with respect to pipelines on its continental shelf than with respect to cables.

More generally, too, assuming that a ship was deliberately involved in sabotaging a submarine cable or pipeline and that the enforcement authorities were on the scene and caught the ship red-handed on the high seas or in the EEZ, it seems intuitively obvious that the suspected ship would have to submit itself to some enforcement jurisdiction. This follows also from more general duties to cooperate in the LOSC referred to in the introductory section above, and the prohibition of abuse of rights. It would simply defeat the purpose of the LOSC, and international law more generally, if a ship were free to engage in illegal activities that are blatantly against the interest of the majority of States in protecting submarine critical infrastructure and especially those of the coastal State in its own EEZ, without offering the State which suffers considerable damage from the act of sabotage any opportunity to intervene. If that assumption is correct, a certain jurisdiction to find out whether a violation of the international rules has actually taken place follows logically, even in the absence of a clear enforcement provision to that effect in the LOSC.

What also speaks in favor of the coastal State's jurisdiction in the case of the Balticconnector incident is the direct impact of the damaged pipeline to Finland, given that the damaged pipeline enters its own territory. This establishes several links in terms of the effects, including that the interruption of gas supplies due to the damage was directly felt by Finland, the economic damage affected Finnish companies owning and operating the pipeline, and

---

51 See *supra* n 19.

the general security implications of a damaged (critical) marine infrastructure affected Finland. Article 79(4) of the LOSC acknowledges additional jurisdiction for coastal States 'to establish conditions for cables and pipelines entering its territory or territorial sea', but it is not certain whether this provision can be read as strengthening coastal States' jurisdiction over such cables and pipelines *beyond* the territorial sea.[52]

3.2.3 Article 59

Alternatively, the regulatory gap with respect to the enforcement jurisdiction in respect of damaged pipelines in the EEZ may be approached by means of Article 59 of the LOSC, which is specifically designed to deal with this type of 'residual rights'-conflicts in the EEZ that are not specifically addressed in the LOSC. Article 59 stipulates that:

> In cases where this Convention does not attribute rights or jurisdiction to the coastal State or to other States within the exclusive economic zone, and a conflict arises between the interests of the coastal State and any other State or States, the conflict should be resolved on the basis of equity and in the light of all the relevant circumstances, taking into account the respective importance of the interests involved to the parties as well as to the international community as a whole.

While the wording of this article does not indicate a presumption in favor of coastal or other States, it seems obvious that willfully damaging another State's gas pipeline would score very low on this balancing of interests, compared to the interest of the coastal State and the 'international community as a whole'. The flag State's only available counterargument, the freedom of navigation that applies in the EEZ, would seem to be of limited weight in the context of the Balticconnector incident, in view of the severe allegations against one or two individual ships in that particular case and, hence, the limited effects on navigation in the zone more generally.

The balance required to ensure that coastal States do not abuse enforcement jurisdiction on the EEZ suggests that enforcement jurisdiction should be linked to the level of evidence against the ship in question. That, in turn, speaks in favor of enabling a relatively light jurisdiction of the coastal State to search the suspected ship for the purpose of obtaining evidence. The exercise of the jurisdiction could further be limited to situations where the true

52 See also Dorota Englender, 'Article 79', in Alexander Proelss (ed.), *United Nations Convention on the Law of the Sea (UNCLOS): A Commentary* (C.H. Beck/Hart/Nomos 2017) 627, referring to somewhat diverging views of Beckman and Burnett *et al.*

circumstances cannot be established by flag State cooperation or direct communication with the ship, i.e. where the alternative means of finding out the facts were very limited.

However, it should be noted that Article 59 of the LOSC by its nature is more helpful in settling disputes *ex post*, e.g. in courts, than offering concrete guidance in a specific ongoing enforcement situation. To date, there seems to be very little, if any, practice on Article 59 in case law in general,[53] and none of relevance for the Balticconnector case at hand. On the other hand, clarification of the more precise meaning of the formula laid out in Article 59 of the LOSC will not be achieved if States do not test the boundaries of their enforcement jurisdiction in response to suspected acts of sabotage, possibly even when lacking an explicit legal basis for taking enforcement measures in response to a supposedly grey zone methods of aggression.

3.2.4 Safeguards

If Finland had taken measures to visit the *NewNew Polar Bear*, it would in any case have had to comply with a number of safeguards that are listed in section 7 of Part XII of the LOSC, including the duty to use clearly marked government ships for the purpose, to avoid adverse consequences, prompt release subject to reasonable security, liability for excessive measures (Articles 224–232 of the LOSC). For example, Article 225 of the LOSC stipulates that: 'In the exercise under this Convention of their powers of enforcement against foreign vessels, States shall not endanger the safety of navigation or otherwise create any hazard to a vessel, or bring it to an unsafe port or anchorage, or expose the marine environment to an unreasonable risk.'

The safeguards include rules on how to conduct investigations and various obligations to exercise caution in doing so. While the safeguards feature in the environmental part of the Convention, it is often considered that they apply to enforcement measures against commercial ships more generally.[54] Moreover, the International Tribunal for the Law of the Sea (hereinafter ITLOS) has held that:

> [A]lthough the Convention does not contain express provisions on the use of force in the arrest of ships, international law, which is applicable by virtue of Article 293 of the Convention, requires that the use of force

---

53 The article was referred to by both parties, but not found applicable, in the 'Enrica Lexie' award (n 19) at paras 908–910.

54 See e.g. Vasco Becker-Weinberg, 'Section 7 Safeguards' in Alexander Proelss (ed.), *United Nations Convention on the Law of the Sea (UNCLOS): A Commentary* (C.H. Beck/Hart/Nomos 2017) 1528–1529.

> must be avoided as far as possible and, where use of force is unavoidable, it must not go beyond what is reasonable and necessary in the circumstances.[55]

These so-called 'Saiga principles' are generally recognized as forming part of customary international law and have been reiterated in more recent case law.[56] In the *M/V 'SAIGA' (No. 2) Case*, the ITLOS further stated that: 'It is a well-established rule of international law that a State which suffers damage as a result of an internationally wrongful act by another State is entitled to obtain reparation for the damage suffered from the State which committed the wrongful act'.[57]

A potentially relevant detail among the enforcement safeguards is found in Article 228 of the LOSC, which secures the priority of flag States to take enforcement measures for its vessels for pollution violations committed beyond the territorial sea of other States. However, that priority does not apply if the proceedings relate to a case of major damage to the coastal State, or if 'the flag State in question has repeatedly disregarded its obligation to enforce effectively the applicable international rules and standards in respect of violations committed by its vessels.' The same reasoning could be extended by analogy to other types of enforcement measures. In the present case this would mean that States that have a bad record of respecting the integrity of other States' marine infrastructure in international waters gradually would be less confident that the primacy of flag State jurisdiction protects them from legal action by other States.

3.2.5 Summary

Most activities for which LOSC provides for prescriptive coastal State jurisdiction in the EEZ are matched with specific enforcement jurisdiction over ships suspected of those activities. This applies to ship-source pollution and fisheries, but also to pollution resulting from dumping and other sources. With respect to damage to pipelines, this is not the case. The deliberate damaging of pipelines is only addressed in the high seas context and here jurisdiction is left

55 M/V "Saiga" (No. 2) (Saint Vincent and the Grenadines v. Guinea), Judgment, ITLOS Reports 1999, p. 10, para 155.

56 See Annex VII Arbitral Tribunal, Matter of an Arbitration between Guyana and Suriname, Case 2004-04, Award of 17 September 2007, para 445; Arctic Sunrise award of 14 August 2015 (n 20) para 222.

57 This is also reflected in Article 232 of the LOSC. See also M/V "SAIGA" (No. 2) Case (n 55) para 170; recalled also in M/V "Virginia G" (n 35) para 428; M/V "Norstar" (Panama v. Italy), Judgment, ITLOS Reports 2018–2019, p. 10, para 316.

with the flag State, though not necessarily exclusively. The undisputed right of the coastal State to lay pipelines and to monitor and control their integrity and safety on their continental shelf (Article 79 of the LOSC), combined with the equally clear legal condemnation of the damaging of such pipelines in Article 113 of the LOSC and in international law more generally, is not matched with a single explicit enforcement provision.

While this gap may not have been a major problem as long as incidents involving damage to pipelines were few and far between and mostly handled by means of civil claims by the party suffering the (economic) damage from the incident, the increasing tendency of State actors to target pipelines and cables as a means of hybrid attacks and sabotage emphasizes the importance and urgency of closing this gap that coastal States and 'pipeline States' increasingly face.

The significant interests of the coastal State over pipelines in its EEZ and continental shelf arguably justify a broader jurisdiction than what the explicit regulatory framework currently provides. Justifications may be found in the comprehensive nature of the LOSC itself, which invites to a systematic approach for interpreting regulatory gaps[58] but also in the specific balancing of interests which is inherent in the reciprocal due regard obligations in Articles 87(2), 56(2) of the LOSC and in the balancing formula of Article 59. The reasons underlying such 'gap-filling' may also be sought in its negotiation history. The Convention was not drafted with intentional government-supported sabotage actions in mind and its enforcement scheme does not consider the prospect that a flag State specifically abuses navigational rights granted in the Convention to damage lawfully established critical infrastructure in coastal States' maritime zones.

New types of hybrid activities inflict potentially severe damage at many levels for coastal States, which needs to be part of the balancing of interests. Those activities, moreover, specifically consist of abuses of opportunities offered by the current legal system and are based on the premise that other States constrain their responses by complying with that same legal framework. All these considerations justify a dynamic interpretation of the rules, in light of the altered circumstances and novel challenges.

It should be added, however, that the argument favoring increased enforcement powers of coastal States in this kind of situation is a cautious one, based

58 See also Kristina Siig, Birgit Feldtmann, Fenella M W Billing, 'Introduction to UNCLOS 1982 as a System of Regulation', in Kristina Siig, Birgit Feldtmann, Fenella M W Billing (eds.), *The United Nations Convention on the Law of the Sea: A System of Regulation* (Routledge 2023).

on a variety of applicable principles relating to the avoidance of excessive force and safeguarding the navigational interests of the ship in question, as provided in the LOSC safeguards and elsewhere.

4 Enforcement Options Based on Collaboration with other States

If the above-referred opportunities were not considered to represent sufficient jurisdictional bases to act on ships passing through Finland's EEZ, there are other less intrusive mechanisms to secure enforcement. The examples below presume close collaboration between the Finnish authorities and other States. Press reports do not include information on whether any such collaboration initiatives have been taken on the part of Finland, and there is no reason to speculate on that issue here. Yet the mere availability of these options of collaboration between Finland's neighboring States adds to the overall impression that the Finnish authorities were not without remedies to take action against the *NewNew Polar Bear,* even if the ship did not enter Finnish territorial waters.

First, Finland could have requested permission by the flag State to board the ship for the necessary fact-finding exercises on the way back from St Petersburg. The ship's stay in St Petersburg for a few days before returning to the Finnish EEZ would have given Finnish authorities ample time to seek this type of agreement from the flag State.

Second, the practice of asking subsequent ports of assistance in investigations is widespread in the field of safety investigations and specifically foreseen in Article 218(2–4) of the LOSC in terms of pollution violations. Finland had the right to ask subsequent port States to examine the ship's log in detail and interview its crew. Finland made such a request to the Chinese authorities and when the *NewNew Polar Bear* arrived in China's port in December 2023, the Chinese, Finnish, and Estonian authorities were reportedly supposed to jointly investigate the ship, whereas by February next year attempts to establish contact with the owners of the ship had failed.[59] However, by that time, over two months had passed from the Balticconnector incident. On her return voyage to China, the ship appears to have made only stops in Russian ports.

59 Claudia Chiappa and Pierre Emmanuel Ngendakumana, 'Finland: We 'trust' China will help probe Baltic Sea pipeline damage' Politico (8 December 2023), available at <https://www.politico.eu/article/finland-we-trust-china-help-probe-baltic-sea-pipeline-damage> accessed 22 December 2023; Marko Tooming, 'Kilk: et Estlink 2 lõhuti pahatahtlikult, on 99,99 protsenti välistatud' ERR Uudised (6 February 2024), available at <https://www.err.ee/1609245246/kilk-et-estlink-2-lohuti-pahatahtlikult-on-99-99-protsenti-valistatud> accessed 7 February 2024.

Third, Finland could have requested other Baltic Sea coastal States, especially Sweden, to investigate the whereabouts of the *NewNew Polar Bear* and potential options for boarding and inspecting the ship at the time when she was leaving the Gulf of Finland and the Baltic Sea proper via the Danish Straits. Reportedly, the ship crossed the Danish Straits in the middle of October 2023, approximately a week after the Balticconnector incident in the Gulf of Finland.

Presumably, the *NewNew Polar Bear* used the EEZ corridors established in the Kattegat and, if relevant, in the Bornholmsgat, and Fehmarnbelt prior to and after crossing the Danish Straits proper, i.e. the Great Belt, Little Belt, and Øresund.[60] This would have enabled her to avoid entering the territorial sea of the coastal State(s) in parts of the maritime area that are not subject to the special passage regime providing an exception from the applicability of the transit passage regime in the Danish Straits proper under the 1857 Copenhagen Convention in combination with Article 35(c) of the LOSC.[61] In any case, according to Article 1(1) of the 1857 Copenhagen Treaty, no ship transiting the Great Belt, Little Belt, or Øresund cannot, 'under any pretext whatsoever, be subject, when crossing the Sound or the Belts, to detention or any hindrance'. This does not preclude Denmark exercising prescriptive jurisdiction but means that enforcement might be possible only outside the Danish Straits proper.[62]

---

60 For the location of the EEZ corridors in the Danish Straits, see the map in Energistyrelsen, 'Figur 1. Kort over 33 områder med aktive ansøgte ÅD-projekter', 3 March 2023, available at <https://ens.dk/sites/ens.dk/files/Vindmoller_hav/bilag_1_oversigt_over_aad-ansoegninger.pdf> accessed 11 October 2023. It is unclear whether the ship crossed the Great Belt or the Øresund for exiting the Baltic Sea. If the *NewNew Polar Bear* left the Baltic Sea via the Øresund, she might have sailed through the Swedish part of the strait, i.e. in the Swedish territorial sea. This chapter does not investigate this matter in any greater detail for length reasons, but it needs to be briefly clarified that even though the *NewNew Polar Bear* would have entered the Swedish territorial sea after the Swedish-owned cable had sustained damage, it might have been still possible for Sweden to board and inspect the ship in its territorial sea similar to Finland's right in its maritime area to board and inspect the same ship in relation to the suspected sabotage of the Balticconnector pipeline.

61 Treaty between Great Britain, Austria, Belgium, France, Hanover, Mecklenburg-Schwerin, Oldenburg, Netherlands, Prussia, Russia, Sweden and Norway, and the Hanse Towns, on the one part, and Denmark, on the other part, for the Redemption of the Sound Dues (adopted 14 March 1857, entered into force 31 March 1857). United Nations Treaty Collection, United Nations Convention on the Law of the Sea: Declarations made upon signature, ratification, accession or succession or anytime thereinafter, Denmark's declaration upon the ratification of the LOSC on 16 November 2004; Sweden's declaration upon signing the LOSC on 10 December 1982 and ratifying it on 25 June 1996. Both available at <https://treaties.un.org/pages/ViewDetailsIII.aspx?src=TREATY&mtdsg_no=XXI-6&chapter=21&Temp=mtdsg3&clang=_en#EndDec> accessed 10 December 2023.

62 Alex G Oude Elferink, 'The Regime of Passage through the Danish Straits' (2000) 15(4) The International Journal of Marine and Coastal Law 555, 562.

Hence, while Denmark and Sweden have prescriptive jurisdiction over the Great Belt, Little Belt, and Øresund, they appear to lack enforcement jurisdiction under the terms of the 1857 Convention over ships in passage (including the *NewNew Polar Bear*) either entering or leaving the Baltic Sea in these three straits. Nonetheless, the Kattegat includes a long EEZ corridor as the only route of exit or entry in respect of the Baltic Sea in which Denmark and Sweden can enforce their laws, but only to the limited extent permitted under the LOSC.

The role of Sweden is particularly interesting from the perspective of the potential interdiction of the *NewNew Polar Bear* in the Baltic Sea, given that Sweden is a party (whereas Estonia and Finland are not) to the 1884 Convention. It is submitted here that Sweden as a party to the 1884 Convention could have boarded the Hong Kong-flagged *NewNew Polar Bear* that is believed to have damaged the Balticconnector gas pipeline and submarine cables in the Baltic Sea, including the Swedish-owned cable EE-S1 linking Estonia and Sweden, based on Article 10 of the 1884 Convention discussed above (see section 3.2.1).

China (in relation to the flag State of Hong Kong) is not a State party to the 1884 Convention. Nonetheless, Sweden as a State party to the 1884 Convention appears to have had the right to board the Hong Kong-flagged *NewNew Polar Bear*. In this context, the central question is whether the right of visit, as stipulated in Article 10 of the 1884 Convention, is dependent on the nationality of the ship that is suspected of damaging a cable or whether that provision provides for an exception to the principle of treaty law according to which a treaty binds only its States parties. Article 10 provides that when boarding a vessel, the officers of one of the High Contracting Parties,

> [M]ay demand from the captain or master the production of the official documents proving the nationality of the said vessel. The fact of such document having been exhibited shall then be endorsed upon it immediately. Further, formal statements of the facts may be prepared by the said officers, whatever may be the nationality of the vessel incriminated.

Thus, one of the aims of the right of visit is enabling the verification of the nationality of the ship in question. Papastavridis explains with reference to Gilbert Gidel's 1932 book *Le droit international public de la mer* that since Article 10 of the 1884 Convention 'stipulated that warships of all signatory powers have a right to stop and verify the nationality of merchant ships of all nations' and thus '[a]s it was drafted to apply to also *vis-à-vis* third states, the interference on the high seas was limited to the right of approach and *d'enquête de pavillon*, which, however, involved the right to board, but not to search the vessel.'[63] (emphasis added) Hence, the right of visit (short of enforcement measures) under Article 10 of the 1884 Convention is independent of the nationality of the ship as (non-)party flag State vessel that is suspected of damaging a cable.

The 1884 Convention criminalizes damaging of cables 'wilfully or through culpable negligence' on the high seas, without barring additional civil actions (Article 2). Legal actions shall be taken by courts 'of the country to which the vessel on board of which the infraction has been committed belongs', i.e. the flag State or, if that cannot be carried out, a State that has penal jurisdiction under other applicable national or international law (Article 8).

Any enforcement measures against the *NewNew Polar Bear* under the 1884 Convention would have required, on Sweden's part, a will and interest in asserting her coastal State's rights by means of a somewhat progressive development of the law of the sea through the creation of new State practice, since the Balticconnector incident demonstrates that States parties to the 1884 Convention appear to be oblivious in respect of the right of visit as stipulated in Article 10.

The next subchapter debates the validity of a potential dynamic interpretation of international law, based on which one could potentially argue that Estonia, Finland, and Sweden were entitled to board and inspect the *NewNew Polar Bear* based on a claim of necessity.

5 General International Law Considerations

Assuming that it was established that the *NewNew Polar Bear* had been engaged in willfully sabotaging the Balticconnector pipeline, at the order of a State,[64] it is clear that a whole new set of additional rules would come into play, also affecting the rights of coastal States to take measures against the ship in question. For example, the right of States to exercise self-defence under Article 51 of

63 Efthymios Papastavridis, *The Interception of Vessels on the High Seas, Contemporary Challenges to the Legal Order of the Oceans* (Hart 2013) 34. According to Art 2(1)(h) of the Vienna Convention on the Law of Treaties, "third State" means a State not a party to the treaty.

64 The fact that the damage was undertaken by non-State actors, such as a commercial ship in this case is not necessarily ruling out an armed attack, see *supra* Chapter 5. On other difficulties linked to proving that an armed attack against a particular State, and the different tests involved, relating to scale and effect, see *Oil Platforms* (*Islamic Republic of Iran v. United States of America*), Judgment, ICJ Reports 2003, p. 161, paras 51–64.

the United Nations (hereinafter UN) Charter raises questions with respect to how concepts such as 'armed' attack' and necessity and proportionality could play out in this context. Hybrid attacks may also raise issues belonging to the law of naval warfare, providing for a different enforcement regime altogether. An analysis of those rules was undertaken in *supra* Chapter 5 and will not be repeated here, in view of the many uncertainties relating to the facts of the Balticconnector incident.

An analysis of the rules of State responsibility also brings the discussion well beyond the law of the sea, but as was already noted, the LOSC accepts in its preamble that it does not operate in a vacuum and that issues not regulated in it continue to be governed by the rules and principles of general international law. Under the 2001 Draft Articles on State Responsibility,[65] a conduct which may otherwise be wrongful in a variety of situations, including if the matter relates to countermeasures to another wrongful act, may be justified under the doctrine of necessity. The doctrine of necessity in international law is outlined in Article 25 of the 2001 Draft Articles on State Responsibility, which expresses its scope in negative terms:

1. Necessity may not be invoked by a State as a ground for precluding the wrongfulness of an act not in conformity with an international obligation of that State unless the act:
   a. is the only way for the State to safeguard an essential interest against a grave and imminent peril; and
   b. does not seriously impair an essential interest of the State or States towards which the obligation exists, or of the international community as a whole.
2. In any case, necessity may not be invoked by a State as a ground for precluding wrongfulness if:
   a. the international obligation in question excludes the possibility of invoking necessity; or
   b. the State has contributed to the situation of necessity.

The formulation clearly leaves scope for applying the doctrine of necessity in the *NewNew Polar Bear*-type of incident, given that the focus is on a particular ship, rather than the right of navigation more generally and that other forms of enforcement measures based on direct collaboration with the ship and other States may leave immediate enforcement measures as the only remaining way to 'safeguard an essential interest against a grave and imminent peril'. A similar argument may thus be raised in respect of the coastal State's right to take

65 International Law Commission, *Draft Articles on Responsibility of States for Internationally Wrongful Acts, with commentaries* (United Nations 2008).

enforcement measures in response to a suspected act of sabotage against submarine cables outside the limits of the territorial sea. When a foreign-flagged ship abuses rights or freedoms in the coastal State's maritime area and threatens to cause significant harm to the coastal State, then the coastal State should have the right to intervene, even in the absence of an explicit right to do so in any of the applicable legal rules.

6 On the Role of Civil Liability Rules

Complementing the rules of State responsibility discussed above, there is a series of rules relating to the civil liability for damage caused, which may also have a bearing on the enforcement opportunities against suspected ships in a *NewNew Polar Bear*-type of situation.[66] These rules can also usefully be divided between environmental liability rules and other liability rules.

The main international civil liability convention for dealing with damage by hazardous and noxious substances, including gases, caused by ships, the so-called HNS Convention,[67] is not applicable to this type of incidents, as it only covers hazardous and noxious substances carried *on board* the ship.[68] Instead, the civil liability of the owner and operator of the ship will be based on the regular tort liability regime for shipowners, which is not internationally harmonized and thus mainly based on national rules.

In Finland, the starting point is the Tort Act (Act 412/1974), which establishes a fault-based liability system, which covers personal injury, property damage and, in certain conditions, pure economic losses.[69] However, the Tort Act does not apply if liability is subject to special rules adopted in law or contract.[70] As regards ship operations, the starting point for liability rules in Finland – and in all Nordic States applying a virtually identical legislation on this point, Chapter 7, section 1 of the Maritime Code (Act 1994/674). Under

66 See also Peter Wetterstein, 'Subsea Gas Pipelines in the Baltic Sea Area – Civil Liability Issues', in Henrik Ringbom (ed.), *Regulatory Gaps in Baltic Sea Governance: Selected Issues* (Springer 2018).

67 International Convention on Liability and Compensation for Damage in Connection with the Carriage of Hazardous and Noxious Substances by Sea (adopted 3 May 1996, not yet in force) 35 ILM 1406, as amended by the Protocol of 2010 (adopted 30 April 2010, not yet in force).

68 HNS Convention, Article 1(5).

69 One of the requisites for compensating economic losses in Chapter 5 section 1 of the Tort Act is that the loss was caused by a criminal act.

70 Tort Act, Chapter 1, section 1.

this main rule the shipowner ('laivanisäntä', 'redare', could also be translated to 'ship operator') is vicariously liable for loss or damage that the master, crew member or pilot causes through fault or neglect in the performance of their duties, but also for errors committed by other persons performing work in the service of the ship. In the Water Act (Act 587/2011), a fault-based liability is placed with ships owners causing economic losses to third parties.[71] There is little doubt, therefore, that the owner of the *NewNew Polar Bear* would be liable to compensate for the damage caused to the Balticconnector pipeline if the incident could be linked to the activities of the ship. The scope of the compensable damage would be regulated by the Tort Act (or Water Act), but the owner would still be entitled to limit the liability according to Chapter 9 of the Maritime Code, based on the size of the ship, unless the claimant can prove that damage resulted from the liable person's 'personal act or omission, committed with the intent to cause such damage, or recklessly with knowledge that such damage was likely to occur'.[72]

In addition, certain Finnish laws relating to environmental impairment liability, which provide a strict liability regime for damage caused by ships to fixed installations (as opposed to movable ships) in the EEZ/continental shelf would apply to this event. Notably, under section 1 of the Environmental Damage Act (Act 737/1994), environmental damage caused by pollution of water and air, but also other disturbances, such as heating or smell, is to be compensated. Compensation extends beyond injury and property damage, to pure economic losses, if they are not insignificant, up to a 'reasonable amount'[73] and to reasonable restoration costs.[74] Damage caused by a criminal act is always compensated.[75] The liability rests with the operator, i.e. the person who carries out the activity that causes the environmental damage.[76] At the EU level, Directive 2004/35 on environmental liability, obliges operators of identified activities to bear the costs for preventive and remedial actions in cases of environmental damage, including damage to species and habitats in the EEZ.[77] It could be

71 Water Act, Chapter 13, section 4.

72 The wording of Maritime Code, Chapter 9, section 4 matches that of Article 4 of the 1976 International Convention for the Limitation of Maritime Claims (adopted 19 November 1976, entered into force 1 December 1986) 1456 UNTS 261, as subsequently amended.

73 Environmental Damage Act, section 5(2).

74 Ibid, section 6.

75 Ibid, section 5(1).

76 Ibid, section 7.

77 Directive 2004/35/EC of the European Parliament and of the Council of 21 April 2004 on environmental liability with regard to the prevention and remedying of environmental damage, Official Journal of the European Union 2004 L 143/56, Article 2(1).

applicable for this type of cases, and, if so, the standard of care required would depend on the nature of the activity that caused the damage.[78]

Both economic losses and environmental damage emanating from the damage could, in other words, justify the institution of civil proceedings against the suspected ship, by the State as well as by private actors, notably the owner or operator of the Balticconnector pipeline (such as Gasgrid Finland and Estonia's Elering). Civil claims offer the opportunity to arrest the ship (or even one of its sister ships) in a suitable jurisdiction, under the applicable arrest rules, in order to ensure sufficient financial security to cover the claims.[79]

Such actions are normally undertaken with respect to ships in ports, but the port State jurisdiction for the purpose of exercising civil liability over ships in the EEZ is not regulated in the LOSC. With respect to pollution, Article 229 of the LOSC only provides that:

> Nothing in this Convention affects the institution of civil proceedings in respect of any claim for loss or damage resulting from pollution of the marine environment.

The only article in the LOSC that specifically addresses civil enforcement jurisdiction with respect to foreign ships is Article 28, which is limited to the territorial sea.

While civil law actions on behalf of the State or those who have suffered economic losses from the incident does not in itself generate independent enforcement rights over ships in the EEZ, a pending civil law claim on environmental liability would add to the relevance and reasonableness claim for further enquiries of the suspected ship's earlier whereabouts.

---

78 Ibid, Article 3(1) and Annex III.

79 Ship arrest is a well-known method of securing maritime claims, which requires a decision by a local court. None of the parties involved in the Balticconnector incident have ratified the International Convention Relating to the Arrest of Seagoing Ships (adopted 10 May 1952, entered into force 24 February 1956) 439 UNTS 193. Estonia has ratified the 1999 International Convention on Arrest of Ships (adopted 12 March 1999, entered into force 14 September 2011) 2797 UNTS 3. Finland signed it subject to ratification in 2000 but has not ratified it. Russia and China are not parties to either convention. The maritime claims that can be secured by arrest by courts under Article 1 of the 1999 Convention include: 'loss or damage caused by the operation of the ship' and environmental damage and threat thereof.

Conclusion

It is suggested here that the significant interests of the coastal State over pipelines in its EEZ/continental shelf justify a broader jurisdiction than what the explicit regulatory framework currently provides. Part of the reasons for that proposition originate in the text of the Convention itself, such as the due regard obligations, the prohibition of abuse of rights and the written indication of certain control rights of coastal States over pipelines in their EEZ/continental shelf and in Article 59 of the LOSC.

Other reasons may be found by closely analyzing the architecture of the Convention. On the one hand, the Convention firmly establishes the criminality of damaging cables and pipelines on the high seas. On the other hand, the Convention suggests that enforcement rights in the EEZ are broader than those on the high seas and that enforcement with respect to pipelines in the EEZ are broader than the corresponding jurisdiction with respect to cables. The environmental risks linked to damaged pipelines also justify drawing analogies to pollution and environmental damage caused by the ship itself.

Historic considerations also support a flexible interpretation, as the Convention was not drafted with the scenario of intentional government-supported sabotage actions in mind. Its enforcement scheme does not consider the prospect that a flag State specifically abuses navigational rights granted in the Convention with the purpose of damaging lawfully established critical infrastructure in the coastal State's maritime area.

The most important reason for the openness towards a dynamic interpretation of the enforcement jurisdiction of coastal States in incidents similar to the one discussed in this chapter relates to the change of State practice in recent years. The tendency of State actors to deliberately target pipelines and cables as a means of hybrid warfare against other States significantly changes the nature of the balance between the coastal State and the ship and its flag State, as drafted in the Convention. Such attacks against subsea infrastructure deliberately target legal grey zones and their success specifically depends on the caution exercised by victim States in not taking actions which are not specifically authorized in the relevant international conventions.

Therefore, a cautious response may even promote hybrid warfare of this nature in the future. Conversely, the contention that coastal States remain without a remedy to take measures against a ship that is (reasonably suspected of being) engaged in sabotaging its critical energy infrastructure seems difficult to defend, both in view of the object and purpose of the Convention and in light of a number of general rules of international law, such as the doctrine of necessity, the duty to act in good faith and the general observance of an international legal order in the first place. In the specific case of the Balticconnector incident, emphasizing the coastal States' interest is further justified by the importance of the coastal State interests at stake and the very direct impact of the damage to Estonia and Finland, both to the States as such and to the companies co-owning and co-operating the Balticconnector pipeline.

It would clearly have been easier for the Finnish authorities to identify enforcement jurisdiction, had the *NewNew Polar Bear* entered the Finnish territorial sea on its way back from St Petersburg. Yet, this chapter has sought to show that even a more active enforcement role could have been justifiable under international law. The main alternatives include:

- prior agreement with the ship's flag State to authorize a fact-finding visit and potential further measures as discussed in section 4;
- basing the jurisdiction on the environmental impact of the suspected event as discussed in section 3.1 with one or more of the relevant sub-options discussed therein;
- basing the jurisdiction on a progressive interpretation of States' jurisdiction for this type of situations, as explored in section 3.2, possibly in combination with other rules of general international law, as discussed in sections 5–6; or
- a collaboration with port States along the ship's route or with other coastal States, such as Sweden, whose jurisdiction over the *NewNew Polar Bear* could have been established based on, for example, the 1884 Convention (section 4).

For commercial parties suffering damage, the existing maritime law regime offers opportunities to secure financial claims by means of arrest if the suspected ship (or its sister ship) is targeted for the purpose. However, the shipowner's liability will normally be limited to relatively modest amounts linked to the size of the ship, unless willful misconduct can be proven. And even if the intent or required recklessness on behalf of the owner could be proven, it may well be that the ship's third party insurance is capped at the maximum under the global limitation regime.

In the longer term, the coastal States which seek to avoid finding themselves in a similar situation to that of the Finnish authorities in the case of the Balticconnector incident should consider adopting precautionary measures, reflecting some of the jurisdictional opportunities identified above. The list of potential measures below is not exhaustive and is provided in no particular order of priority.

- The coastal State's domestic legislation could be amended to reflect the flexibility of international law in this area. As was noted, Finnish national enforcement laws make a sharp distinction between maritime areas within and beyond its territorial sea, which reduces the opportunity to make use of jurisdictional grey zones as identified in this chapter under international law.

- Pipelines could be better monitored and surveyed, both at the surface and through technology on or near the pipeline. The jurisdiction of the coastal State to install monitoring equipment on its own pipelines on the continental shelf is not controversial under the law of the sea and could potentially be a valuable source of information (and proof) in future instances of pipeline damages. In the context of sabotage against critical undersea infrastructure, this could increase the coastal State's maritime domain awareness and preparedness for rapid enforcement against suspected acts of sabotage.
- Each coastal State confronted with hybrid warfare should consider, as a first step, making the fullest use of the zonal approach of the LOSC, first and foremost by way of establishing the maritime zones that enable to broaden the jurisdictional reach of the coastal State and thereby narrowing down the room of maneuver for grey zone activities at sea. It is possible to establish further navigational restrictions near pipelines, as discussed in the previous chapter of this book. The jurisdiction of Estonia and Finland to impose such restrictions unilaterally or bilaterally beyond their territorial seas is limited by the reference to international rules as a maximum ceiling in Article 211(5) and (6) of the LOSC, though with a theoretical jurisdictional opportunity offered by Article 211(6)(c). However, routing measures of various severity, e.g. ranging from non-anchoring zones to full scale mandatory areas to be avoided, can be adopted internationally through the 'competent international organization', i.e. the IMO. Such international endorsement of the measures would also have the consequence that the measures would qualify as 'applicable' international rules and standards, within the meaning of the limited enforcement provisions in, *inter alia*, Articles 220, 226 and 228 of the LOSC.
- Continued development of regional and global soft and hard law instruments to make sure response capabilities match the threats of today, and hence to reduce the advantage currently offered to States that specifically seek to abuse gaps in the legal system while expecting that others will follow them. For example, the development of new treaty law could grant universal enforcement jurisdiction in respect of ships suspected of damaging submarine pipelines or cables outside the limits of the territorial sea similar to the universal jurisdiction granted over piracy and unauthorized broadcasting under the LOSC.
- Based on the analysis above, it is clear that the interdiction of foreign-flagged ships suspected of having inflicted damage to a pipeline outside the limits of the territorial sea is an area of law which includes many legal gaps that need to be overcome, either by way of a dynamic interpretation of the relevant LOSC provisions or by way of developing new treaty law. The more

coastal States manage to close such grey areas, the less room there is for hybrid attacks and warfare on undersea infrastructure that is of critical importance for all States from the perspective of electricity, gas and oil, and telecommunications networks.

– In the hope of increasing the legal resilience of offshore critical infrastructure in the Gulf of Finland, there have been proposals to abolish the EEZ corridor which is established in the middle of the Gulf mainly in the interests of the east-west navigation. The Balticconnector incident occurred in the EEZ corridor. The more such presumed acts of sabotage take place in the EEZ corridor, the more Finland and Estonia will be tempted to extend the outer limits of their territorial sea to the maximum limit under Article 3 of the LOSC (12 nautical miles), so that the central part of the Gulf of Finland would be completely covered by the territorial sea, with the effect that the international corridor would disappear. This measure could somewhat strengthen jurisdiction over the pipelines (see *supra* Chapter 5), including for carrying out an investigation into a presumed act of sabotage because such an incident would then occur in the territory of the coastal State. However, as the investigations into the Nord Stream explosions have shown,[80] the main criteria for being able to successfully conclude an investigation into a submarine pipeline incident is not only whether the coastal State's citizens or territory was involved in conducting the operation, but also whether the coastal State's interests (including security) were damaged. In the case of the Balticconnector incident, the coastal State's (Finland's) interests were clearly damaged and thus the location of the presumed act of sabotage outside the limits of Finland's territorial sea can hardly serve as a reason for dropping the inquiry. Furthermore, the potential abolishment of the EEZ corridor would not help to establish jurisdiction over ships navigating in the Gulf and would not provide additional enforcement jurisdiction with respect to ships suspected of damaging pipelines in the area. In view of the presence of the EEZ (previously high seas) area north of Gogland Island (Suursaari) in the eastern part of the Gulf of Finland, the measure would have the effect that much of the Gulf of Finland could qualify as a strait

80 Swedish Prosecution Authority, 'The prosecutor closes the Swedish investigation concerning gross sabotage against Nord Stream' Press Release (7 February 2024), available (together with the laconic official decision in Swedish) at <https://www.aklagare.se/en/media/press-releases/2024/february/the-prosecutor-closes-the-swedish-investigation-concerning-gross-sabotage-against-nord-stream/> accessed 7 February 2024; Laura Gozzi, 'Nord Stream: Denmark closes investigation into pipeline blast' BBC (26 February 2024), available at <https://www.bbc.com/news/world-europe-68401870> accessed 27 February 2024.

subject to the rules of transit passage under Article 37 of the LOSC. This, in turn, would grant freedoms of navigation and overflight not only within the limits of the EEZ corridor in the middle of the Gulf of Finland where these freedoms currently apply, but in the entire maritime area of the Gulf of Finland (as measured either from the baselines or coasts of the two coastal States). Such a broadening of the freedom of navigation and overflight in the Gulf of Finland would hardly serve the interests of Estonia and Finland.

– The rapidly changing frequency and means of State-sponsored interference with offshore infrastructure may also require a policy shift in the approach by authorities to enforcement actions. Expecting a specific legal basis for any enforcement action is unlikely to be a useful strategy against hybrid warfare, which by definition targets grey zones in the legal system. A more daring and less formalistic approach to enforcement jurisdiction provides a useful means of testing the legal limits and may even prove to be a way to develop international law in this field, while awaiting further treaty developments. Proportionate enforcement measures against a few individual suspected offenders are not likely to challenge the regulatory regime as a whole, and if the legality of the enforcement action were to end up being assessed by an international court or tribunal, it would provide an even better opportunity to clarify the boundaries of international law faced with rapidly changing threats and challenges.

CHAPTER 7

The Nord Stream Pipelines from the Viewpoint of Law and Geopolitics

Timo Koivurova and Theresa Winkel

Introduction

Over the last two decades, the Nord Stream pipeline project in the Baltic Sea has sparked the probably most contentious debate in decades on European energy security in the face of a rapidly deteriorating geopolitical landscape in the region. With the first ideas emerging as early as the mid-1990s, a basic agreement on the construction of the pipeline project was signed in September 2005 by the Russian and European energy companies. Two months later, the Nord Stream consortium, comprised of the subsidiary of Russian majority shareholder Gazprom (Gazprom international projects North 1 LLC; 51%), along with two German energy companies, E.ON Ruhrgas AG (24.5%) and BASF/Wintershall AG (24.5%), set up the North European Gas Pipeline Co. (NEGP), which as of 2007 became to be known as Nord Stream AG.[1] The Swiss-based company would manage the first of the two projects that we refer to as 'Nord Stream 1'.

The Nord Stream Extension project or the Nord Stream 2 was, for a variety of reasons that we explore below, developed by a different company, also based in Switzerland (Nord Stream 2 AG). As Gazprom, a Russian state-owned corporation, was the main driver in both companies through its subsidiary, it is justifiable to say that these Nord Stream projects were developed in concert. Although it is common to speak of Nord Stream 1 and 2 as the two pipelines, both projects in fact comprise two lines each (Nord Stream 1 A and B and Nord Stream 2 A and B). Nord Stream 1 came on stream in 2011 and 2012, while Nord Stream 2 was very close to completion before the Russian invasion of Ukraine on 24 February 2022.

Both projects, especially the Nord Stream 2, were controversial from the very beginning. From the early stages, the Nord Stream pipelines have been

1 Gazprom, 'Nord Stream: Historical Background' Press Release (15 January 2008), available at <https://web.archive.org/web/20080115091142/http://www.gazprom.com/eng/articles/article22901.shtml> accessed 5 March 2023.

 DOI:10.1163/9789004707993_009

regarded as a bilateral venture between Germany and Russia. The European countries were divided in their positions: while the Western states, including the Netherlands, France, the United Kingdom (hereinafter UK) and Germany focused more on the economic nature of the project,[2] Poland and the Baltic states warned about the geopolitical implications. As a first point of criticism, there would be increased energy dependence with Russia (while these states preferred to continue land transit via the Polish and Ukrainian territories rather than circumventing the two countries, which would further reduce Russian reliance on them for gas exports to Europe[3]). Second, from the Ukrainian perspective, if Russia no longer needed the energy infrastructure of its neighbor, there would be little leverage to defend against Russian aggression and maintain Ukraine's territorial integrity.[4] In contrast, the German ruling coalition had a clear economic and political interest in seeing the Nord Stream project completed: the project did not only fit into the planned German exit from coal and nuclear power, but also presented a cheaper alternative to importing expensive liquefied natural gas from North America. Retrospectively, the pipelines can be considered a centerpiece of the Russian strategy to weaken Ukraine, as German President Frank-Walter Steinmeier recently admitted his regret for the long support of the projects.[5] Though the German position drastically changed with the Russian invasion in February 2022, early warnings from neighboring states had been dismissed.[6] Early on with the Nord Stream 1 discussions, the former Polish defense minister Radek Sikorski went so far to

2 Frank Umbach, 'Commercial Project or Strategic Disorientation? The Controversial Nord Stream 2 Gas Pipeline' Bundesakademie für Sicherheitspolitik (19 January 2018), available at <https://www.baks.bund.de/en/working-papers/2018/commercial-project-or-strategic-disorientation-the-controversial-nord-stream-2> accessed 13 September 2023.

3 Ben Cahill and Leslie Palti-Guzman, 'The Role of Gas in Ukraine's Energy Future' CSIS (13 January 2023), available at <https://www.csis.org/analysis/role-gas-ukraines-energy-future> accessed 6 September 2023.

4 Dylan Carter, 'Why Nord Stream 2 Is Centerpiece of Ukraine Crisis with Russia (EXPLAINER)' The Kyiv Independent (13 December 2021), available at <https://kyivindependent.com/why-nord-stream-2-is-centerpiece-of-ukraine-crisis-with-russia-explainer/> accessed 7 September 2023.

5 Andreas Rinke, Thomas Escritt, and Alex Richardson, 'I Got Putin Wrong, Says Chastened German President' Reuters (4 April 2022), available at <https://www.reuters.com/world/europe/i-got-putin-wrong-says-chastened-german-president-2022-04-04/> accessed 7 September 2023.

6 As well as warnings from foreign security specialists: Edward Lucas had warned the German government of Russian hybrid warfare tactics already in 2010, see Edward Lucas, 'Why Germany Has Learned the Wrong Lessons From History' Foreign Policy (27 December 2022), available at <https://foreignpolicy.com/2022/12/27/germany-russia-ukraine-war-scholz-zeitenwende-history-geopolitics/> accessed 13 September 2023.

compare the pipeline to the 1939 Molotov-Ribbentrop pact, named after the Soviet and German foreign ministers who divided Poland in a secret protocol.[7] According to the Polish minister, Russia would be in the position to cut off Poland and Belarus without losing access to Russia's most profitable European export market (i.e. Germany). But also the European Union (hereinafter EU) energy commissioner Andris Piebalgs backed the criticism of Germany's unilateral approach to Russia.[8] Fears were not unfounded as Gazprom had repeatedly blackmailed various states in the period between 2003 and 2007, including Estonia, Latvia, Lithuania, Ukraine and Belarus, to either comply with their conditions or face a reduction in gas supplies.[9] In 2010, the perspective on the role of law and on the entire Nord Stream projects changes when we consult the views of various security experts, including Edward Lucas (warning the German government of Russian hybrid warfare tactics in 2010) and Robert L. Larsson (Swedish Defense Research Agency; emphasizing in a 2008 briefing paper to the European Parliament that Nord Stream gives Russia an excuse to act assertively with its armed forces in the Baltic region).[10] Since the beginning of Nord Stream 1, they have warned that the Baltic Sea gas pipelines are not only a commercial project for Russia.

Regardless, the project plannings went ahead and Nord Stream 1 encountered little challenges, probably also because it was included in the EU list of Trans-European Energy Network Guidelines and also its designation as a project of European interest.[11] The Nord Stream extension project started immediately after its predecessor, sealed with an agreement between Gazprom and the European partners in 2015 and following not long after the Crimean crisis. The political opposition grew stronger and geopolitical concerns amongst the parties of origin were expressed by Sweden. Meanwhile, Finland remained mostly neutral and Denmark was significantly more hesitant in its decision-making

7 Mark Beunderman, 'Poland Compares German-Russian Pipeline to Nazi-Soviet Pact' EUobserver (2 May 2006), available at <https://euobserver.com/world/21486> accessed 5 March 2023.

8 Ibid.

9 Anonymous, 'FACTBOX: Russian Oil and Gas as Political Weapon?' Reuters (2 May 2007), available at <https://www.reuters.com/article/us-russia-estonia-energy-idUSL0211261020070502> accessed 6 September 2023.

10 Lucas (n 6), Robert L Larsson, 'Security Implications of the Nord Stream Project' EP Briefing Paper (European Parliament, 2008) 13, available at <https://www.europarl.europa.eu/meetdocs/2004_2009/documents/dv/afet_01042008_security/afet_01042008_securityen.pdf> accessed 7 September 2023.

11 Decision No 1364/2006/EC laying down guidelines for trans-European energy networks and repealing Decision 96/391/EC and Decision No 1229/2003/EC, OJ 2006 L 262/1, Art 8.

process, causing delays in the construction phase.[12] Sweden's skepticism on Russian energy dependence was notably influenced by the visit of (at that time) US Vice-President Joe Biden in 2016.[13] Another concern in Sweden was the abuse of the project for intelligence gathering purposes in the Baltic Sea, especially concerning air, surface and sub-surface activities around Estonia, Finland, Sweden and Denmark.[14] As experts with the Swedish Defense Research Agency pointed out, the pipeline could accommodate hydro-acoustic systems and sonars, 'electronic eyes and ears', that could be used for monitoring and informing Russian intelligence agencies.[15] Despite the existing concerns, the Swedish government refused to actively block the project through its national laws (and rather favored stopping it at the EU political level).[16]

In this article, we intend to critically explore, first, the application and role of law to the Nord Stream projects in how the projects were taken forward. Given the controversial nature of (especially) Nord Stream 2, there have been a great number of legal arguments and procedures invoked to halt the project. Yet, we will first explain the main rules that were applied to the construction and laying of the Nord Stream pipelines, namely the national environmental impact assessment (hereinafter EIA) and permit procedures and transboundary EIA that was organized under the Espoo Convention on Environmental Impact Assessment in a Transboundary Context (hereinafter Espoo Convention) and the United Nations Convention on the Law of the Sea (hereinafter LOSC).[17] It was these rules that were most clearly applicable to the Nord Stream projects, even if legal challenges for the Nord Stream 2 increased heavily after the 2014 Crimean annexation by Russia. It is useful to take up these other legal challenges as we chronologically go through the evolution of Nord Stream 2.

12 See the outline of the Danish process in section 2 of the present article; Justyna Gotkowska and Piotr Szymański, 'The Nordic Countries on Nord Stream 2: Between Scepticism and Neutrality' (2016) 223 OSW Centre for Eastern Studies, available at <https://www.osw.waw.pl/en/publikacje/osw-commentary/2016-10-12/nordic-countries-nord-stream-2-between-scepticism-and> accessed 19 December 2022.

13 Mikael Oscarsson, 'Nordstream 2 Interpellation 2015/16:753' Sveriges Riksdag (8 August 2016), available at <https://www.riksdagen.se/sv/dokument-lagar/dokument/interpellationsdebatt/nordstream-2_H310753> accessed 5 March 2023.

14 Larsson (n 10).

15 Ibid, 13.

16 Gotkowska *et al.* (n 12).

17 United Nations Convention on the Law of the Sea (opened for signature 10 December 1982, entered into force 16 November 1994) 1833 UNTS 3; Convention on Environmental Impact Assessment in a Transboundary Context (opened for signature 25 February 1991, entered into force 10 September 1997) 1989 UNTS 309, Art 2 (1).

We will also be making conclusions as to whether the law could have been applied differently to the Nord Stream cases. For instance, already at the beginning of Nord Stream 1, the Secretariat of the Espoo Convention proposed that mega-projects such as Nord Stream 1 should have been scrutinized also from the viewpoint of their geopolitical implications. We will also reflect on the role of law in general in having these Nord Stream projects approved since, without the Russian invasion of Ukraine, it seemed at the time that Nord Stream 2 would have also been completed.

Considering the changed dynamics between East-West relations, the destruction of the pipelines and environmental injuries,[18] new questions arise. In particular with a view to the law and legal procedures that were crucial in having the Nord Stream project accepted, one may wonder whether we could have interpreted and applied the law differently. Second, and finally, it is also important to ask whether law, and international law in particular, can and should be able to counter the challenges of mega-projects like Nord Streams. If it can convincingly be argued that the Putin's regime in Russia has consciously developed the Nord Streams from the beginning of 2000's, we will also have to ask how resilient the law is when it is fully instrumentalized in pursuit of a long-term goal by an autocratic actor. It is therefore important to conclude with an opinion on whether a change in approach as to how we manage critical infrastructures is needed.

1 Nord Stream 1

Even if there was already a heightened sense of concern when Nord Stream 1 (hereinafter NS1) was proposed, it is fair to say that the resistance was still at a low level in comparison to the second pipeline project, Nord Stream 2

18 See recent studies surrounding the impact of the Nord Stream explosions on marine life and the climate, Hans Sanderson, Michał Czub, Sven Koschinski *et al.*, 'Environmental Impact of Sabotage of the Nord Stream Pipelines' (2023) Preprint (Version 1), available at Research Square <https://doi.org/10.21203/rs.3.rs-2564820/v1> accessed 10 October 2023; Thomas Dahlgren, Bastien Queste, and Olof Lönnehed, 'Methane from Nord Stream Has Spread Far from the Leaks' University of Gothenburg (11 December 2022), available at <https://www.gu.se/en/news/methane-from-nord-stream-has-spread-far-from-the-leaks> accessed 10 October 2023; see also announcement in 2023 as the single largest methane emission event, UNEP, 'UNEP Finds Nord Stream Gas Leak May Be the Highest Methane Emission Event, but Still a Drop in the Ocean' UN Environment Programme (20 February 2023), available at <http://www.unep.org/technical-highlight/unep-finds-nord-stream-gas-leak-may-be-highest-methane-emission-event-still> accessed 5 March 2023.

(hereinafter NS2). This manifests itself in the way the applicable legal rules and procedures were undertaken with relative ease. It is of much importance here to explore how the law was applied in the first project, even if we won't do a detailed analysis, given that some of the issues have already been analyzed elsewhere.[19] Particular emphasis will be on whether it was indeed the case that only certain specific national and international legal rules were applicable to the NS1, including the freedoms guaranteed under LOSC and procedural rules according to the Espoo Convention. This is of great relevance as the NS2 procedure followed in the footsteps of NS1, so it was crucial how the relevant officials reasoned as to why certain international and national legal rules were seen as applicable to the NS1.

Before examining the relevant legal rules, it is important to recap what was the original plan by the Nord Stream AG company for transmitting natural gas via a pipeline from Russia to Germany. The proposal in 2005 was to have submarine pipelines from the Vyborg region to cross Finland's and Sweden's exclusive economic zones (hereinafter EEZ) before entering the EEZ and territorial waters of Denmark and finally landing in Greifswald Germany.

1.1 *The Main Rules and Procedures Applicable to the Nord Stream 1 Project*

One of the fundamental international legal frameworks that applied to the NS1 was the LOSC. According to the LOSC, some of the previous high seas freedoms are preserved in the EEZ – a new zone that had emerged in the course of the Third United Nations Conference on the Law of the Sea. According to Article 58:

> 1. In the exclusive economic zone, all States, whether coastal or land-locked, enjoy, subject to the relevant provisions of this Convention, the freedoms referred to in article 87 of navigation and overflight and of the laying of submarine cables and pipelines, and other internationally lawful uses of the sea related to these freedoms, such as those associated with the operation of ships, aircraft and submarine cables and pipelines, and compatible with the other provisions of this Convention.[20]

---

19 Timo Koivurova, Ismo Pölönen, 'Transboundary Environmental Impact Assessment in the Case of the Baltic Sea Gas Pipeline' (2010) 25 The International Journal of Marine and Coastal Law 151.

20 LOSC (n 17) Art 58 (1) (emphasis added).

Hence, laying of submarine pipelines is a right or freedom that is reserved to states in other states' EEZs. As submarine pipelines are laid down on continental shelves, Article 79 of LOSC provides more specific regulation on submarine cables and pipelines on the continental shelf:

1. All States are entitled to lay submarine cables and pipelines on the continental shelf, in accordance with the provisions of this article.
2. Subject to its right to take reasonable measures for the exploration of the continental shelf, the exploitation of its natural resources and the prevention, reduction and control of pollution from pipelines, the coastal State may not impede the laying or maintenance of such cables or pipelines.
3. The delineation of the course for the laying of such pipelines on the continental shelf is subject to the consent of the coastal State.

It follows that Article 58 and 79 of LOSC gave the Swiss company the right to lay a pipeline within the EEZs and continental shelves, as intended with the routing through the EEZs of Finland and Sweden. However, the same right did not apply to the sections of the pipeline that would cross the territorial sea of the coastal states and remained under the full sovereignty of Russia, Denmark and Germany.

Another crucial international legal framework that was applied to the project was the Espoo Convention. This was the case as it applies to the types of pipelines as that proposed to transmit natural gas from Russia to Germany. In particular, the Convention requires that 'The Parties shall, either individually or jointly, take all appropriate and effective measures to prevent, reduce and control significant adverse transboundary environmental impact from proposed activities'.[21] The provision continues to specify that the origin state shall 'ensure that in accordance with the provisions of this Convention an environmental impact assessment is undertaken prior to a decision to authorize or undertake a proposed activity listed in Appendix I that is likely to cause a significant adverse transboundary impact'.[22] In addition, 'The Party of origin shall, consistent with the provisions of this Convention, ensure that affected Parties are notified of a proposed activity listed in Appendix I that is likely to cause a significant adverse transboundary impact'.[23]

It was clear from the outset that such a large-scale natural gas pipeline would likely cause significant transboundary impacts, also impacting potentially all the littoral states of the Baltic Sea. For this reason, the responsible

21 Espoo Convention (n 17), Art 2 (1).
22 Ibid, Art 2 (3).
23 Ibid, Art 2 (4).

Espoo officials from the four states and Russia (which was not an Espoo party, but had agreed to apply the Espoo Convention to this project, as much as permitted by its national legislation) commenced mutual meetings to think how this highly complex project was supposed to be administered.

Hence, from the international legal viewpoint, at least two issues seemed clear at the beginning of NS1. First, the Swiss company had a right to apply for national permits for constructing a pipeline to traverse from Russia to Germany via the EEZs of Finland and Sweden, and EEZ and territorial sea of Denmark. This right stems from the applicable legal framework, the LOSC, and it does start from the premise that the coastal states, in this case Finland and Sweden, have a legal obligation to allow the laying of the pipeline, provided that the environmental risks are manageable. Second, they also have a right to determine the routing of the pipeline in their EEZ. As the pipeline was planned to operate also in the territorial seas of three states, these states have a right to decide whether it can proceed or not, on the basis of their national legislation. From the practical viewpoint, this was relevant for Denmark, being the only transit state in between Russia and Germany, in whose territorial seas the pipeline was envisaged to operate.

Second, it also seemed clear that the Espoo Convention was supposed to apply to NS1, given that the likely environmental impacts of the project were seen as significant, and these would likely have an impact in all the littoral states of the Baltic Sea. Yet, even if the relevant rules seemed fairly clear from the very beginning, this did not mean that there were no alternative framings of how the NS1 should be managed.[24] These are important issues, since, as mentioned above, the way the rules were applied for NS1 were in principle also applied for the NS2.

There were two main challenging issues at the beginning: could another international legal framework be more suitable for administering the NS1 process? And in what way should the Espoo Convention be interpreted to apply to this extremely complex multi-jurisdictional proposed activity? At the very start, there was an idea within the Baltic Marine Environment Protection Commission that perhaps it could have a role in administering the NS1 process. After all, the Helsinki Convention on the Protection of the Marine Environment of the Baltic Sea Area,[25] by which the Helsinki Commission was founded, is a

24 David Langlet, 'Nord Stream, the Environment and the Law: Disentangling a Multijurisdictional Energy Project' (2013) 59 Scandinavian Studies in Law 80–108.

25 Convention on the Protection of the Marine Environment of the Baltic Sea Area (opened for signature in 1974, revised in 1992, entered into force 17 January 2000) 2099 UNTS 197.

legal treaty to which all the littoral states of the Baltic Sea are parties, including Russia. The Helsinki Commission even established a working-group to examine its role in handling the NS1. The Helsinki Convention also has a provision on EIAs.[26]

Yet, when reading Article 7 of the Helsinki Convention it becomes clear that the provision does not provide any legal obligations for the parties to commence EIAs or transboundary EIAs. Rather, the Convention requires the contracting states that are already undertaking a transboundary EIA, e.g. on the basis of the Espoo Convention, to notify the Commission and other parties of such a case. Therefore, the Helsinki Convention does not establish independent legal obligations to carry out a transboundary EIA and was not applicable to this proposed activity.[27]

Perhaps most conspicuously, the Secretariat of the Espoo Convention took up the idea via a 2009 discussion paper, as to whether we should adopt a more ambitious way in applying the Espoo Convention to these complex large-scale projects, 'such as large-scale energy project concerning several countries might be the routing of a gas pipeline'.[28] The paper was prepared at the request of the European Commission and specifically intended to outline the challenges in applying the Espoo Convention to major infrastructure projects and propose possible solutions. It was evident that the Secretariat's paper was advancing a view that the transboundary EIA should have been implemented differently from how it was carried out by the parties of origin, as the paper was published in 2009 when the Espoo process had already been in progress from 2005. The Secretariat's paper first identifies what the strategic element is:

> 12. For the purpose of the present analysis, the strategic dimension will be related to political influences, strategic views, and the connections between the activity and policies, plans and programmes (PPP) or other projects. In general terms, any activity has to some extent a strategic dimension; only those in which the strategic dimension is predominant, however, will be considered to be complex activities here.

---

26 Ibid, Art 7.

27 It should also be noted that LOSC guidance on EIA is, even if legally binding, too unspecific to provide a framework for carrying out a transboundary EIA.

28 United Nations Economic Commission for Europe, 'Large-Scale Transboundary Projects: Application of the Convention to complex activities' (2 March 2009), UN Doc ECE/MP.EIA/WG.1/2009/4, para 13.

Then, the paper identifies why Nord Stream types of projects should be dealt differently:

> 13. An example of the strategic dimension for a large-scale energy project concerning several countries might be the routing of a gas pipeline. Geopolitical issues, economic interests and relations between Parties could influence the pipeline route, thus diminishing the alternatives considered in the EIA. In addition, the pipeline project could significantly influence the regional energy market, affecting countries' energy and climate policies and strategies. Finally, a large energy project could also make regional integration more difficult if there is no consensus among affected Parties. All these aspects form parts of the project's strategic dimension.

The desired solution of the Secretariat is to have such complex projects assessed via the strategic environmental assessment:

> 14. The strategic dimension of a planned activity would ideally be considered in the strategic environmental assessment (SEA) of the PPP, which sets the framework for the activity. Here an EIA might examine the compatibility of the planned activity, including decisions taken in early planning, with the PPP and with other projects. However, in practice, a complex activity might not be planned on the basis of a PPP, or if it is, the PPP might not be subject to SEA. Complex projects might arise from an informal or non-statutory process, i.e. not following an established planning scheme of PPP. In this case, the strategic dimension of complex projects is best analysed at the EIA stage.

Interestingly, the Secretariat is of a view that project's geopolitical, energy policy and climate policy impacts could be examined in this SEA stage, even if also in its view, the 'strategic dimension [...] is not generally included within the framework of EIA'.[29] However, for the Secretariat, 'the Convention does not stop Parties from assessing strategic issues within EIA'.[30]

It is important to examine this argument very carefully as this is from the Espoo Convention's Secretariat, which should know how the Espoo Convention should be applied in different circumstances, also in the case of the Nord Stream proposal. By the time the discussion paper was issued, in 2009, the

29 Ibid, para 16.

30 Ibid.

actual transboundary EIA procedure had already progressed quite far. However, the veiled criticism of the Secretariat in the discussion paper is important to tackle here, as it would suggest that the transboundary EIA procedure was undertaken in, perhaps not faulty manner, but at least not in as ambitious manner as it could have been. Beyond the veiled Nord Stream criticism, the paper provides recommendations for future guidance regarding the procedural and methodological issues of applying the Convention to complex activities.

First off, the Secretariat does advance the deep connection between the SEA and EIA procedures and the relevance of first conducting SEA, which would guide also the making of individual project-level EIA. The first problematic aspect is that the SEA protocol to the Espoo Convention only entered into force in 2010, after the transboundary EIA of the Nord Stream proposal, but also after the release of the discussion paper. Perhaps more to the point, it is difficult to envisage how the origin states who were in charge of organizing the Espoo procedure would have come to assess all these geopolitical, energy and climate implications of this project, as the Secretariat seems to suggest. Strategic environmental assessment does not cover all these 'strategic' dimensions of a plan, project or program, but it rather requires the government in preparing these PPP's to also evaluate rigorously the environmental and health impacts of a government program or policy. The concept of SEA does not include e.g. evaluating geopolitical implications of a larger policy document. This also brings to the fore the question as to what type of policy document could have been evaluated as a necessary precondition to the more specific transboundary EIA. It should be one that would be jointly decided by the five origin states or then even the nine littoral states of the Baltic Sea as they were the ones who would be impacted by the Nord Stream project.

It seems clear, thus, that there were no legal obligations for the origin states to commence such a procedure, before the obligatory steps with the Espoo Convention. But, as the Secretariat suggests, 'the Convention does not stop Parties from assessing strategic issues within EIA'.[31] Even if the origin states were not legally obligated to assess strategic issues, could they have still requested these from the Nord Stream company at the beginning of the procedure. From the viewpoint of the Espoo Convention alone, it seems fair to suggest that the origin states can conduct a more comprehensive assessment of the impacts of a pipeline that is meant to cross the entire Baltic Sea. The Espoo Convention does allow the parties to take more ambitious approaches in the way they apply the Espoo Convention.

31 UN Doc ECE/MP.EIA/WG.1/2009/4 (n 28) para 16.

Yet, even if this possibility exists for the origin states, who have to actually process the pipeline via their domestic legal systems, it does not seem that this could have actually been undertaken under realistic circumstances. First of all, as Russia is one of the origin states – and had agreed to apply the Convention even if it is not a party – it is difficult to think that it and Germany would have any incentive to be part of an endeavor to conduct joint governmental evaluations of Nord Streams geopolitical, energy and climate implications. Also, who would have made the final decision on the permissibility of the Nord Stream pipeline? It is unimaginable to think that these origin states would have created an ad hoc separate final decision-making on the Nord Stream, where this geopolitical and other policy level evaluations could have been used. The Espoo Convention relies on origin states as states that need to process the environmental impacts of a proposed activity, also with regard to the neighboring states' environment. It is ultimately the domestic EIA procedures and permitting procedures that will need to be triggered to receive consents to construct a submarine pipeline, and these systems cannot use information about the geopolitical or energy implications of the Nord Stream project, but only of its environmental impacts.

It seems clear that the Swiss Nord Stream company had a legal right to apply for permits to construct the different segments of the submarine pipeline in all of the five domestic legal systems. From this viewpoint, it is difficult to argue that the Espoo contact points could have requested the company to complete a variety of different studies related to geopolitics, energy and climate policies. It is also arguable that even if they could have commissioned such studies by themselves, which was politically inconceivable, it is difficult to see how these could have been used anywhere. If the states would have just argued that there are too many obstacles to go ahead with the project, because of various geopolitical and other concerns, the company could have still gone ahead and applied for the permits from various national legal systems; after all, it had a right to apply for the permit to construct a submarine pipeline, and at least for the portions of EEZ, it also had a presumptive right to lay down the pipelines under LOSC.

This also explains why the four Espoo Convention origin states and Russia agreed to apply the Espoo Convention to the Nord Stream project, but in a way whereby they would synchronize the workings of their domestic legal systems and the Espoo Convention. The project discussions started already in 2005 (and the whole project was developed throughout 1990's with the pipeline routes investigated via a feasibility study during 1997 and 1998) between the five origin states (Russia, Finland, Sweden, Germany, Denmark), with the idea to plan the project in such a way that international co-ordination meetings would ensure that the company produces an assessment of the entire impacts of the proposed natural gas pipeline. Important was also to make sure that the various origin states' domestic legal EIA and permitting procedures would be working together with the international aspects of the project, in a way that all the potentially affected states were able to comment on both the scope of the impact assessment studies but also the final Espoo report and the individual country environmental impact statements. This was a very complicated undertaking, given that all the five origin states were also potentially affected states. Hence, they needed to evaluate the impacts of the proposed project within the segment that traverses their EEZ/territorial sea, but also make sure that the impacts from a neighboring state did not cause significant impacts. In brief, as this procedure has been studied elsewhere more carefully, the following took place:

1. Notification was sent to all the nine Baltic Sea countries as potentially affected states of the proposed pipeline, together with the project information document that contained detailed information of the project and its potential environmental impacts in the entire route. It was the international co-ordination meetings by the five origin states that were making sure that this document was of high enough quality. This document was also translated to all the nine languages. This also marks the time when the national EIA systems are triggered in operation, and further are open to the potentially affected states and their publics.
2. Draft EIA report was sent to informal commenting to all the nine Baltic states in November 2008, and after comments and adjustments, the final Espoo report was released in March 2009. At this stage, also the national environmental impact statements for various separate segments of the pipeline were opened for international and public consultations and the EIA procedures were completed by mid-2019.
3. In 2009 and 2010 the various legal permits for constructing the submarine pipeline were obtained from the five origin states, which enabled the actual construction to commence, and the two pipelines were completed by 2011 and 2012, respectively.

Even if there were already security and other concerns during NS1, it is fair to say that the legal procedures were undertaken smoothly. The only real obstacle occurred during the Finnish EIA process, in which Finnish authorities requested the company to examine the Estonian side of the EEZ, as it seemed environmentally more justified (due to more even ground) than the Finnish side. The company observed this request from the Finnish officials and applied for a permit to conduct seabed surveys at the Estonian side of the EEZ. However, the Estonian government refused to issue the permit, based on the argument that these would qualify as marine scientific research.[32] As the coastal state needs to consent to any marine scientific research in its EEZ, this became quite a dilemma to solve.[33]

2 Nord Stream 2

Nord Stream AG started to prepare an extension of the NS1 quite early. They presented the project information document in March 2013,[34] which then kick-started the notifications from the origin states to all the potentially affected states in April 2013. National EIA systems were commenced to not only evaluate impacts of the project to the portion that runs in their jurisdiction, but also the transboundary impacts. When the Finnish EIA started to organize public hearings based on the scoping document, these were open not only to Finnish stakeholders, but to all potentially affected states. Hence, the first stage of national and international EIA procedures was processed but then Russia invaded and annexed Crimea and commenced supporting hostilities in Eastern Ukraine in 2014. It was this series of events that explains why the national and transboundary EIA procedures came to a pause, some officials thinking that the Nord Stream 2 will end at this point.[35]

During 2014, there were various restrictive measures and sanctions from the EU, European countries and North America targeted at Russia and Russian actors, due to the events in Ukraine. This obviously had an impact on the Nord Stream 2 as well, given that the majority shareholder is the Russian state-owned company Gazprom. Another serious blow to the NS2 was the proceedings instigated by the Polish competition agency UOKiK. While the first pipeline 'extension' project was carried out by Nord Stream AG comprised of the Nord Stream consortium, a new company was initially set up in 2015 to manage the second pipeline project – first known as New European Pipeline AG and including the

32 The Estonian Government Office, 'Valitsus otsustas kabinetinõupidamisel mitte rahuldada Nord Stream AG taotlust mereuuringuteks Eesti majandusvööndis' Press Release (6 December 2012), available at <https://www.valitsus.ee/uudised/valitsus-otsustas-kabinetinoupidamisel-mitte-rahuldada-nord-stream-ag-taotlust> accessed 7 September 2023.

33 For further discussion, see Alexander Lott, *Hybrid Threats and the Law of the Sea – Use of Force and Discriminatory Navigational Restrictions in Straits* (Brill 2022) 205–219; Langlet (n 24).

34 Nord Stream AG, 'Nord Stream Extension Project Information Document' (2013).

35 Interview by Timo Koivurova of Finnish officials (17 February 2023).

majority shareholder Gazprom and its European partners (BASF / Wintershall, E.ON, Shell, OMV and ENGIE).[36]

36 BASF, 'Gazprom, BASF, E.ON, ENGIE, OMV and Shell Sign Shareholders' Agreement on the Nord Stream 2 Project' Press Release BASF (4 September 2015), available at <https://www.basf.com/global/en/media/news-releases/2015/09/p-15-334.html> accessed 11 September 2023; note that the Polish competition authority raised concerns that a joint venture responsible for the construction of Nord Stream 2 gas pipeline would undermine competition. The energy companies requested a clearance of concentration in late 2015 (which was later rejected by the President of the Polish competition agency UOKiK). Rather than acting as shareholders, as it was previously the case with Nord Stream AG, Gazprom became the sole shareholder of the new project company Nord Stream 2 AG. The European partners acted as lenders and committed themselves to provide long-term financing for fifty percent of the total cost of the project (estimated in 2017 at €9.5 billion). However, when the European Commission in 2018 fell clear of imposing a fine on Gazprom in its competition case based on abuse of dominance in the EU gas market (and only asked for commitments in amending business operations), the Polish competition authority took matters into its own hands and imposed the world's largest competition fine at that time, 29 billion złoty (about €6.5 billion) and another 234 million złoty against the five European energy companies. Despite the strong Polish opposition, Gazprom and the project sponsors won the appeal against the Polish competition agency UOKiK in November 2022 and were able to avoid the penalty payment. Poland's Court of Competition and Consumer Protection reasoned that the competition authority went beyond its competence by assessing the effects on the economy and whether the investors tried to circumvent the law. See Anonymous, 'UPDATE 2-Polish Anti-Monopoly Office Says Nord Stream 2 Threatens Competition' Reuters (22 July 2016), available at <https://www.reuters.com/article/poland-gas-nordstream-idUSL8N1A825Z> accessed 11 September 2023; ENGIE, 'Nord Stream 2 AG and European energy companies sign financing agreements' Press Release (24 April 2017), available at <https://en.newsroom.engie.com/assets/nord-stream-2-ag-and-european-energy-companies-sign-financing-agreements-63bf-314df.html?dl=1#:~:text=Nord%20Stream%202%20AG%20signed,to%20be%20%E2%82%AC9.5%20billion> accessed 7 September 2023. It should be noted though that the lenders quit their financing following the invasion in February 2022, with Shell being the first and Uniper being the latest firm to write off its financial contribution, Shell, 'Shell Intends to Exit Equity Partnerships Held with Gazprom Entities' Press Release (28 February 2022), available at <https://www.shell.com/media/news-and-media-releases/2022/shell-intends-to-exit-equity-partnerships-held-with-gazprom-entities.html> accessed 7 September 2023; see also Christoph Steitz, Victoria Waldersee and Victoria Waldersee, 'Germany's Uniper Joins Peers in Writing down Loan to Nord Stream 2' Reuters (7 March 2022), available at <https://www.reuters.com/markets/europe/germanys-uniper-record-full-impairment-loss-nord-stream-2-loan-2022-03-07/> accessed 7 September 2023; America Hernandez and Thibault Larger, 'Poland Hits Gazprom with the World's Largest Competition Fine' POLITICO (7 October 2020), available at <https://www.politico.eu/article/poland-hits-gazprom-with-world-largest-competition-fine> accessed 7 September 2023; Alicja Ptak, 'Gazprom Wins Appeal against Huge Nord Stream 2 Antitrust Fine in Poland' Notes from Poland (22 November 2022), available at <https://notesfrompoland

With the Nord Stream 2 AG and sponsorship arrangements in 2017, the company continued with the already initiated national and international EIA procedures. It was able to complete the full Espoo report by April 2017[37] and the parties of origin were able to commence the stage of public consultations on 6 April 2017 from the actual reports of the predicted impacts, nationally and in the transboundary context. In Finland, the Espoo report together with national environmental impact statement were open for public hearings during 7 April to 5 June 2017. Yet, from this stage onwards, the procedure became more complicated for the Nord Stream 2 project, in particular for the portions pertaining to Denmark and Germany. Meanwhile, Finland's and Sweden's EIA and permitting processes progressed in similar manner. The national EIA and transboundary EIA procedure was cleared and the government go-ahead was reached for both countries at about the same time in April 2018. Despite numerous appeals, Finland's supreme administrative court turned them down on 19 August 2019, which meant that the NS2 was cleared to be constructed in Finland's EEZ.

2.1 *The Impact of the Amendment to the Danish Continental Shelf Act*

The first concrete obstacle, that changed the way the transboundary EIA procedures were meant to function, emerged when Denmark, a transit country where the pipeline also traverses its territorial sea, decided to amend its Continental Shelf Act[38] (effective from the beginning of 2018). This gave the Danish Ministry for Foreign Affairs additional rights to recommend where infrastructure projects demanded inspection beyond that provided by the Danish Energy Agency, including considerations of foreign policy, national security or military interests. For this reason, Nord Stream 2 AG could not rely anymore on the plan to have the pipeline traverse through the territorial sea of Denmark, so that it started to examine alternative routings beyond the territorial sea. Based on the seabed surveys, the company arrived at two alternative routings by August 2018. In March 2019, the Danish Energy Agency requested the company to assess a third routing option.[39] Nord Stream 2 AG submitted its

---

.com/2022/11/22/gazprom-wins-appeal-against-huge-nord-stream-2-antitrust-fine-in-poland/> accessed 11 September 2023.

37 Nord Stream 2 AG, Ramboll, 'Espoo Report' (2017).

38 Bekendtgørelse af lov om kontinentalsoklen og visse rørledningsanlæg på søterritoriet 2018 ('Continental Shelf Act').

39 Teis Jensen and Stine Jacobsen, 'Denmark Asks Nord Stream 2 to Assess Third Route Option for Gas Pipeline' Reuters (28 March 2019), available at <https://www.reuters.com/article/us-gazprom-nordstream-2-denmark-idUSKCN1R916S> accessed 12 September 2023.

third application and an EIA on 15 April 2019, with the route running through Denmark's Southeastern EEZ.[40] Subsequently, in May 2019, the Danish Energy Agency was able to commence public participation of the EIA report of this routing. All these different submissions for routing also resulted in notifications to the potentially affected states. Finally, in October 2019, the Danish Energy Agency issued a permit for construction in the Danish EEZ, with a total of 34 conditions and a limited time window of four weeks to file complaints.[41]

Russia immediately welcomed the approval; Russian Foreign Minister Sergey Lavrov was quoted in the Russian news agency outlet TASS that 'commercial projects should be free from any politicization and should not become hostages to geopolitical games'.[42] At that time, also the German government viewed the pipeline as a primarily commercial project and important for strengthening European energy security.[43] However, the conditional Danish permit required Nord Stream 2 AG to comply with specific equipment requirements for pipelaying vessels, including a preliminary investigation prior to pipelaying, use of a remotely operated vessel (ROV), dynamic positioning of the pipelaying vessel and application of the conventional S-laying technique.[44]

Construction of the Danish section began in December 2019 and was due to be completed by mid-January 2020, with each of the two pipelines reaching a total length of 147km. However, the threat of US sanctions significantly complicated the pipelaying progress. The Allseas ship (a Swiss company contracted for NS2 construction) named *Pioneering Spirit* ceased its activities at the end of 2019,[45] despite only a minor part remaining to be laid in the Danish EEZ.[46]

---

40 Danish Energy Agency, 'New Nord Stream 2 Application for Two Southern Route Options' Energistyrelsen (2 May 2022), available at <https://ens.dk/en/press/new-nord-stream-2-application-two-southern-route-options> accessed 12 September 2023; see also Nord Stream 2 AG, Ramboll, 'Nord Stream 2 Construction Permit Application Summary, Denmark, South-Eastern Route' (2019).

41 Danish Energy Agency, 'Tilladelse til Nord Stream 2 naturgasrørledningerne i Østersøen' Energistyrelsen (30 October 2019), available at <https://ens.dk/ansvarsomraader/olie-gas/offentliggoerelser-om-olie-gas/tilladelse-til-nord-stream-2> accessed 12 September 2023.

42 Anonymous, 'Lavrov Calls Denmark's Nord Stream 2 Decision "Responsible Approach"' TASS (31 October 2019), available at <https://tass.com/politics/1086317> accessed 8 September 2023.

43 Umbach (n 2).

44 Danish Energy Agency (n 41).

45 Allseas, 'Allseas suspends Nord Stream 2 pipelay activities' Press Release (21 December 2019), available at <https://allseas.com/wp-content/uploads/2019/12/2019-1221-Media-statement-Allseas-discontinues-Nord-Stream-2-pipelay.pdf> accessed 8 September 2023.

46 The pipeline was reported to be 94% complete, see Nastassia Astrasheuskaya, 'Russia to Go It Alone on Construction of Nord Stream 2 Pipeline' Financial Times (28 January

The drop out required the willingness of other companies to operate despite the threat of sanctions, while also fulfilling the logistical and technical requirements. In spring 2020, the *Akademik Cherskiy* and *Fortuna* took over pipelaying activities, although with a slower pace than the *Pioneering Spirit*. Notably, only the *Akademik Cherskiy* was equipped with dynamic positioning system similar to the Allseas ship, while *Fortuna* was an anchored-based vessel that would not have fulfilled the Danish requirements. Following another delay, the Danish Energy Agency issued an amended construction permit in July 2020, confirming the request to employ an anchoring vessel. Construction was further delayed due to fish spawning, lasting until end of September 2020 and ultimately longer than notified in the permit. Considering the combined threat of US sanctions, the imposed cessation and changing weather conditions, no construction progress was made in all of 2020, but pipelaying only resumed in February 2021. The first line of NS2 saw successful completion a few months later in June 2021, about one and a half years after the desired completion date.

Nord Stream 2 AG accused the Danish government of deliberately delaying permit approval to prevent the project.[47] The Danish position towards the project is said to have been influenced by geopolitical and environmental considerations, as well as normative impetus from liberal democratic politics. Wood and Henke have argued that rather than intentionally delaying construction progress, the processes and decisions would form part of an independent legal system in a rule of law state (which ultimately issued the permit for NS2 despite existing concerns).[48] Indeed, the legal processes have been followed without obvious signs of abuse. Yet, the circumstances were such that Denmark held a more influential card in its hand compared to its neighbors based on the initial routing through its territorial sea. It was among the last to issue its permit and the incidental timing allowed the EU institutions to amend the Gas Directive (discussed later on) while construction was not yet completed. This ultimately caused further delays for Nord Stream 2 and with the German certification process through changes in EU energy law. It is not unreasonable to assume that the growing political opposition following Russian aggression

2020), available at <https://www.ft.com/content/a0f1b83c-41b4-11ea-bdb5-169ba7be433d> accessed 13 October 2023.

47 Anonymous, 'Nord Stream 2 Says Denmark Tries to Delay Pipeline as It Seeks Third Route Option' Reuters (15 April 2019), available at <https://www.reuters.com/article/us-gazprom-nordstream-2-denmark/nord-stream-2-says-denmark-tries-to-delay-pipeline-as-it-seeks-third-route-option-idUSKCN1RR15F> accessed 28 March 2023.

48 Steve Wood and Otto Henke, 'Denmark and Nord Stream 2: A Small State's Role in Global Energy Politics' (2021) 148 Energy Policy 111991.

influenced the implementation and uses of the law, both on Danish domestic level (within the allowed window of LOSC) and European.

2.2 *The Impact of US Sanctions*

Aside from the Danish procedural delays, further hindrances were caused by the series of US sanctions that placed a temporary strain on US-German foreign relations. It is a well-known fact that the pipeline had long been opposed by the US government out of security concerns (both Trump and the Biden administration).[49] In July 2021, the two allied countries had finally reached a compromise and issued a joint statement on support for Ukraine and European energy security.[50] They affirmed their shared determination to hold Russia accountable for its aggression and malign activities by imposing costs via sanctions and other tools. The statement further specified that, if Russia was to misuse any pipeline as an energy weapon, including Nord Stream 2, Germany would take action at the national level and press for effective measures at regional European level.[51] Measures in question could include sanctions in the energy and/or in other economically relevant sectors. Nonetheless, the statement does not provide more clarity into how an energy weapon abuse would be judged. As some experts had argued, the pipeline was already weaponized at that time considering Russia's influence on Europe's energy crisis while suggesting an expedited certification process as a solution to soaring gas prices.[52] However, at least for Germany the joint statement would remain of declaratory nature up to the point of the Russian invasion into Ukraine, when the German certification process was halted.

2.3 *The Impact of the EU Gas Directive Amendment*

While construction was delayed during the Danish permit process and companies were dropping out due to the threat of US sanctions, another obstacle for

49 Though US energy interests and exports were argued to play a role as well, see Umbach (n 2).

50 US Department of State, 'Joint Statement of the United States and Germany on Support for Ukraine, European Energy Security, and Our Climate Goals' Press Release (21 July 2021), available at <https://www.state.gov/joint-statement-of-the-united-states-and-germany-on-support-for-ukraine-european-energy-security-and-our-climate-goals/> accessed 31 March 2023.

51 Ibid.

52 Zachary Basu, 'Germany Urges Congress Not to Sanction Nord Stream 2, Calling It a "Victory for Putin"' AXIOS (28 November 2021), available at <https://www.axios.com/2021/11/28/germany-nord-stream-sanctions-congress-ukraine> accessed 31 March 2023.

NS2 emerged with the 2019 amendment of the EU Gas Directive.[53] The amendment clarified a discussion around the applicability of EU law to import pipelines (to and from third countries), such as Nord Stream, which depended on the classification of the pipeline as either an interconnector or transmission pipeline.[54] Nord Stream 2 was said to be the only pipeline that faced 'retroactive' application of the amendment, which was heavily disputed by the company (although the pipeline was not yet in operation at that time, but argued to be close to completion).[55] With the clarified unbundling requirement for gas pipelines entering the EU from third countries (like Russia), Nord Stream 2 would have to make sure that ownership and operation of the pipeline would be kept separately. From the perspective of EU law, this requirement would ensure increased competition, benefits for the consumer and prevent potential conflicts of interest, given that the gas supplier would be prevented from controlling the infrastructure that transports its gas to the EU. Notably, Nord Stream 1 was exempt from the unbundling requirement as it was already in operation before the amendment to the Third Energy Package, as well as its status as interconnector rather than a direct supplier (supplying gas to the German gas transmission system rather than having direct access to EU customers).

The changes in legislation led Nord Stream 2 AG to litigate before German and, eventually, EU courts. As EU directives require transposition into national law with the aim to be achieved and thereby ensuring harmonization across member states, Germany had to either pass new laws or amend existing ones in order to fulfill the Directive's objective. Under the new German law, Nord Stream 2 was required to transfer ownership of the pipeline to a German subsidiary and obtain an operating license in order to be compliant.[56]

---

53 Council and European Parliament Directive 2019/692 of 17 April 2019 amending Directive 2009/73/EC concerning common rules for the internal market in natural gas (2009) OJ L 211.

54 See discussion by Kim Talus and Alan Riley with opposing views on the classification of the pipeline, in Kim Talus, 'Application of EU Energy and Certain National Laws of Baltic Sea Countries to the Nord Stream 2 Pipeline Project' (2017) 10 The Journal of World Energy Law & Business 30; See also a confidential letter drafted by the Legal Service of the European Commission dated 2017 arguing that Nord Stream 2 is neither a transmission pipeline nor an interconnector for the purposes of the Gas Market Directive and that the TEP does not intend to bind authorities of third countries, in European Commission, 'Request pursuant to the Framework agreement – Nord Stream 2' POLITICO (letter dated 12 September 2017 in Brussels), available at <https://www.politico.eu/wp-content/uploads/2017/09/NS2-SPOLITICO-17091912000.pdf> accessed 13 October 2023.

55 Case C348/20 P, Judgment of 12 July 2022 (Grand Chamber), EU:C:2022:548, para 17.

56 German Energy Industry Act (EnWG) [2019].

This would only be the case if the subsidiary transferred 'essential assets and human resources' under German jurisdiction.[57] Since that was not the case, the *Bundesnetzagentur*, Germany's energy regulator, suspended the certification process in November 2021.[58]

With regard to the role of the law in the Nord Stream 2 case, the Gas Directive amendment and subsequent mandatory changes in German law show the impact that EU legislation had in slowing down the construction progress, despite the German eagerness to see the project completed. From the start, it was clear that the unbundling requirements contained in the Third Energy Package interfered with the German interests to obtain a cheaper gas source with Nord Stream, compared to the alternative of importing expensive liquefied natural gas from North America. The Nord Stream deal would have also been in line with the planned German exit from coal and nuclear power and was strongly defended by the ruling coalition.[59]

The new unbundling conditions would intend to prevent Gazprom's potential dominance of the EU gas market by unbundling suppliers from operators to ensure fair competition. Even though the amendment to the Gas Directive allowed for derogations under specific circumstances,[60] when NS2 AG sought a derogation in 2020, the German Federal Network Agency rejected the application.[61]

---

57 Bundesnetzagentur, 'Verfahren Zur Zertifizierung Der Nord Stream 2 Vorläufig Ausgesetzt' Press Release (16 November 2021), available at <https://www.bundesnetzagentur.de/SharedDocs/Pressemitteilungen/DE/2021/20211116_NOS2.html> accessed 13 September 2023.

58 Ibid.

59 The black-red government coalition of CDU/CSU and SPD at that time sought to limit political interference with the project as much as possible, even implying certain control over decisions of independent German agencies in a 2015 meeting between Sigmar Gabriel and Vladimir Putin. Following German government elections, the same coalition was elected to power and the politicians at first aimed to block the 2019 revision of the EU Gas Directive that ran contrary to German commercial interests. Only following a compromise with the French government did Germany vote in favor of the amendment in the Council, which was widely argued to oppose goals of the European Energy Union, see Anca Gurzu, 'France and Germany Split over Nord Stream 2 Pipeline' POLITICO (7 February 2019), available at <https://www.politico.eu/article/france-and-germany-split-over-nord-stream-2-pipeline-russian-gas-regulation/> accessed 28 March 2023; Anonymous, 'Germany, France Compromise on Nord Stream 2' DW (8 February 2019), available at <https://www.dw.com/en/eu-adopts-french-german-compromise-on-nord-stream-2-pipeline-to-russia/a-47429195> accessed 13 September 2023.

60 EU Directive 2019/692 (n 53), see preamble and Art 49 (a) clarifying the conditions for derogations in relation to transmission lines to and from third countries.

61 Bundesnetzagentur, 'No Derogation from Regulation for Nord Stream 2' Press Release (15 May 2020), available at <https://www.bundesnetzagentur.de/SharedDocs/Pressemitteilungen/EN/2020/20200515_NordStream2.html> accessed 13 September 2023.

The main reason for rejection was the factual circumstances, namely that the pipeline had not seen completion before 23 May 2019 (the date that the amending directive entered into force).[62] NS2 AG insisted that the line had already been completed from an economic point of view. At that time, irreversible investment decisions for the project would have already been made or were already being implemented and around two-thirds of the pipeline had already been built when the EU Gas Directive was amended.[63] Regardless, the court agreed with the authorities on the point that it was not fully constructed at the time and was therefore not completed within the meaning of the law.[64]

Nord Stream 2 AG subsequently took the case to the EU General Court, seeking to annul the amendment to the Gas Directive, but ultimately being dismissed by the Court. The judges found that the company was not directly concerned by the amending directive.[65] However, the judgment was criticized for confusing 'direct concern' with the EU concept of 'direct effect'.[66] After appealing the decision, the Court of Justice of the European Union overturned the previous judgement that was considered an error of law, and saw the company being individually concerned by the effects of the Directive.[67] Within two years of legal proceedings, Nord Stream 2 was successful with achieving partial admissibility of its claim.[68]

Conclusion

The CJEU judgement from July 2022 came after a significant turn of events following the Russian invasion into Ukraine earlier in February that year. While the German certification process was already delayed based on the new unbundling requirements, it was now the full-scale invasion that caused the

62 Ibid.

63 Gary Hornby, 'German Court Rejects Russian Nord Stream 2's Appeal for Derogation' S&P Global (25 August 2021), available at <https://www.spglobal.com/commodityinsights/en/market-insights/latest-news/natural-gas/082521-german-court-rejects-russian-nord-stream-2s-appeal-for-derogation> accessed 13 September 2023.

64 OLG Düsseldorf (25 August 2021) VI-3 Kart 211/20 (V) [2021].

65 Case T-526/19, Order of 20 May 2020 (General Court), EU:T:2020:210.

66 Case C348/20 P *Nord Stream 2 AG v Parliament and Council* [2022] CMLR, Opinion of Advocate General Bobek, paras 35ff.

67 Case C348/20 P (n 55).

68 Meanwhile, Nord Stream 2 also started arbitration proceedings against the EU under the Energy Charter Treaty. Despite Russia not having ratified the Energy Charter Treaty, Switzerland, being the domicile of Nord Stream 2 AG, is indeed a contracting party.

government to take a radical change in foreign policy, further away from any potential cooperation with Russia on these projects.[69]

With the recent explosions in September 2022, that rendered both pipelines inoperable and resulted in the single largest methane emission event,[70] we can categorize the Nord Stream projects as failures from economic and environmental standpoints. But also from a political and security perspective, we have come to understand that our western societies and politicians miscalculated the threat emanating from the strategic thinking of the Russian government. Despite earlier warning signs, such as previous gas manipulations in the Baltics, Belarus and Ukraine,[71] the view of Western European states was largely influenced by the German *Ostpolitik*, which aimed for stable relations with the East through the creation of economic ties.[72] It is clear now that this approach towards Russia demonstrated a shortage of foresight and strategic depth[73] and negated the impact that the Nord Stream project could have on European security.

Overall, the legal proceedings have proven the prevalence of the rule of law with decisions being made independent of the changing political climate following the Crimean annexation. Considering the Danish amendment of its Continental Shelf Act, but also the EU Gas Directive amendment and its application to NS2, the law has certainly played a role in delaying the project. Despite the obstacles faced by the company, the law and due process have been respected, which is important for the integrity of our own societal norms. At the same time, it can be observed how the law enabled the Nord Stream project to proceed and facilitate the strategic objectives of a hybrid actor, where energy matters turned into a tool of manipulation, all while being veiled as an economic project. A purely environmental perspective in energy matters, as occurred during the Nord Stream EIA process, even runs the risk of

69 Sarah Marsh, Madeline Chambers and Sarah Marsh, 'Germany Freezes Nord Stream 2 Gas Project as Ukraine Crisis Deepens' Reuters (22 February 2022), available at <https://www.reuters.com/business/energy/germanys-scholz-halts-nord-stream-2-certification-2022-02-22/> accessed 29 March 2023.

70 UNEP (n 18).

71 Reuters (n 9); see also Ukrainian Research Institute Harvard University, 'Europe's Gas Crisis and Russian Energy Politics: Experts Respond', available at <https://huri.harvard.edu/tcup-commentary/europes-gas-crisis-russian-energy-politics> accessed 11 September 2023.

72 Stefan Meister, 'Nord Stream 2: The Dead-End of Germany's Ostpolitik' Berlin Policy Journal – Blog (20 February 2019), available at <https://berlinpolicyjournal.com/nord-stream-2-the-dead-end-of-germanys-ostpolitik/> accessed 11 January 2024.

73 Ibid.

effectively contributing to conflict.[74] Awareness is now increasing around this type of hybrid strategies, where actors resort to a range of non-military, unconventional means that formally comply with the law, yet exploit vulnerabilities where desired. The pipelines then served a dual purpose from a Russian perspective – the implementation of an economically attractive project, yet also key in strengthening Russian geopolitical influence across the region.

With the first objective in mind, to examine whether the law was correctly interpreted and applied to the Nord Stream pipelines, it can be concluded that the law, in particular the important role of international law, was applied in a good manner to the Nord Stream projects. Even beyond that, the approach and assessment of the environmental consequences and impacts of the pipeline in all its segments raised a high standard. The overall administration of these projects was carried out by the five origin states in a community approach and based on the international rules that dictated how the EIA's and permits needed to be received. In fact, it can also be said that international law, with regard to the LOSC and the Espoo Convention, if taken literally, gave little room for interpretation. Their application was clear and, in the spirit of good faith under international law, they provided the Nord Stream companies with sufficient predictability for construction. It is also important to emphasize the vast impact that the law had in legitimating these projects. Even when Russia openly challenged the European security architecture at the end of 2021, it still seemed that the Nord Stream 2 project would have seen its completion until the very end.

Another crucial aspect is to understand that, all in all, it is not possible to completely dissociate law and legal procedures from the general geopolitical stances that the relevant states had over Russia. Especially at the start of the projects, the law found itself in a geopolitical environment that enabled it to function based on legal values, such as providing predictability to the relevant parties. With the current circumstances, where we experience a full overturn of the geopolitical environment but continuing with the same laws in place, it is reasonable to assume that few would argue in favor of constructing the Nord Stream pipelines.

This demonstrates the impact of the prevailing geopolitical environment at that time and the fact that, even though the law has been applied in a good manner to the projects, it could not prevent its abuse as an instrument of geopolitics by the Russian regime. Whether we can then see the role of law in a

74 Frédéric G Sourgens, 'Energy Lessons from the Ukraine Crisis' EJIL: Talk! (24 February 2022), available at <https://www.ejiltalk.org/energy-lessons-from-the-ukraine-crisis/> accessed 13 September 2023.

different light when we study the Nord Stream projects from the viewpoint of the security concerns. We can clearly see how international law is struggling to cope with the challenges posed by hybrid actors. It can be noted that the Russian invasion in Ukraine from 2022 onwards and the failed Nord Stream projects have demonstrated the naivety of the West in terms of its foreign policy towards Russia in general and the integrity of its critical infrastructures. This is why in the recent timeframe, important regulatory revisions are in progress to increase resilience to threats within the EU, including those emanating from large infrastructure projects.

Looking back, it is difficult to say with full certainty how the Nord Stream projects evolved from the viewpoint of the strategies of all the relevant countries and polities involved considering the various interpretations. However, it is clear at least for the security community that the alleged purely economic nature of Nord Stream was doubtful from the start (and despite arguments in favor of security of gas supply and climate change considerations). Scholars had been pointing out the risks of building such long-term infrastructure across the Baltic Sea, also recalling the past evidence showing how Russia had used its energy to influence policy throughout the 1990s.

It is true that the project company was constructed in such a way that it seemed to be a private undertaking based in Switzerland, yet the influence of Gazprom, as a Russian state-owned company, has all along been behind the project. There is little doubt that Russian leadership would refrain from wielding its influence through its energy companies. As previously explored, security experts in Sweden had raised early concerns about how Russia could use the pipeline for spying activities, including the monitoring of NATO vessel movements, and justify an increase in its own military activities in the Baltic Sea. Nord Stream 2 brought even more controversy, adding concerns about how Russia could decrease the importance of existing land pipelines transiting through Ukraine and Poland and become a centerpiece of its Ukraine strategy leading up to the invasion in February 2022.

As some analysts had argued, if Russia was indeed pursuing a long-term strategic objective with the Nord Stream pipelines and intending to increase its geopolitical influence over the EU, Europe and the Baltic Sea, these concerns may offer us a new perspective on the role of law. We have also seen in the analysis of the EIA and construction process that international law was clearly one of the main legitimating forces of the pipeline project, steering us towards discussing mostly environmental aspects.

Today, with the knowledge we have about the cynical abuse of international law to legitimize the Crimean annexation and its full-scale invasion in Ukraine, paired with the profile that security experts had been drawing about the Putin regime from the beginning, it is remarkable that the construction of the Nord Stream pipelines could proceed to this extent. From this viewpoint, it could be argued that Russia was nearly able to fulfill its geopolitical objectives based on a clever, yet cynical manipulation of the law. Further, the law can be seen as a reflection of the geopolitical environments that were prevailing and were, particularly from the perspective of the German process, naïve to believe in a purely economic nature of the project. It remains questionable to what extent German politicians had considered the risks with a changing geopolitical landscape in mind. It appears that the monetary prospect of obtaining cheaper energy resources far outweighed the daunting prospect of potential security risks. Ultimately, the Nord Stream cases are showing us the challenges that liberal-democratic societies have with autocratic polities and the need to develop realistic means to manage these, also in law and legal procedures, which is already underway.

These challenges exacerbate in situations where there is division between cooperating states. From the beginning, European governments disagreed over Nord Stream 2 and the potential security implications. It is therefore imperative to develop greater cohesion on a regional level to map critical infrastructure projects that could seriously impact regional security. In a time of increasingly unconventional measures taken by hybrid actors, strong cooperation and information exchange is a prerequisite for the prevention and coordinated response to similar threats. A significant step into that direction is the closer cooperation between the NATO and the EU in security and defense policies, including the creation of a joint task force on resilience and critical infrastructure discussed in early 2023. As the President of the European Commission, Ursula von der Leyen, stated in the joint press conference, '[t]he Nord Stream sabotage has shown that we need to take more responsibility for the security of our network infrastructure. There too, we are aware that the individual countries are responsible for the security of this infrastructure. And for sure, we will not share vulnerabilities. But following best practices, experiences, this is a field where we can work closer together and where we will intensify the cooperation.'[75]

This is clearly the right direction in terms of law and policy developments. The European Commission is now accelerating initiatives on improving the resilience of European critical infrastructure, including a 5-point plan, as well

75 Ursula von der Leyen, 'Statement by the President: EU-NATO Cooperation' (10 January 2023), available at <https://ec.europa.eu/commission/presscorner/detail/en/statement_23_121> accessed 13 September 2023.

as new and updated legislation.[76] Building resilience is not only crucial when it comes to energy and infrastructure projects, but also in various other civilian domains, including the legal domain itself that can be abused for strategic purposes.[77] The lessons that we have learned with Baltic Sea gas pipelines have prompted us to come up with stronger strategies to counter security challenges that critical infrastructures pose.

---

76 Proposal for a Council recommendation on a coordinated approach by the Union to strengthen the resilience of critical infrastructure COM/2022/551 [2022].

77 Aurel Sari, 'Blurred Lines: Hybrid Threats and the Politics of International Law' (Hybrid CoE 2018) Strategic Analysis 4; This practice has become known as 'Hadesian lawfare', which means the law is being weaponized in a manner that distorts the fundamental principles of the international legal order, see Waseem A Qureshi, 'Lawfare: The Weaponization of International Law' (2019) 42 Houston Journal of International Law 39.

PART 3

Hybrid Threats to International Navigation

CHAPTER 8

The Emerging 'Shadow Fleet' as a Maritime Security and Ocean Governance Challenge

Iva Parlov and Ulf Sverdrup

Introduction

The Russian Oil Price Cap regime that entered into force in 2022 (hereinafter also the Sanction Regime) has triggered significant changes in international shipping. During a short period of time, a sizeable 'shadow fleet' (also known as 'dark fleet') has emerged. According to some estimates, close to 20 percent of the international oil trade is currently transported by this fleet.[1] The emergence of the shadow fleet might have implications far beyond limiting the effectiveness of the sanctions on Russia. Indeed, it raises important concerns regarding safety at sea and a wide range of maritime security issues, while increasing the risk of environmental damage. Given the scale and significance of the shadow fleet, and the protracted nature of Russian aggression in Ukraine, this development has led to long-term concerns about some of the foundational building blocks of global ocean governance, and the future legal and economic order, which is mostly visible in the context of liability insurance.

The commercial pressure in normal circumstances ensures that almost all ships have reputable liability insurance in place,[2] typically from a member of

1 There has been a certain climb in numbers over the last year. According to some sources (report from January 2024), close to one fifth of the global crude oil tanker fleet is in the shadow fleet, with no cover from the International Group of P&I Clubs. See Elisabeth Braw for Atlantic Council, 'Russia's growing dark fleet: Risks for the global maritime order', Issue brief January 2024, available at <https://www.atlanticcouncil.org/in-depth-research-reports/issue-brief/russias-growing-dark-fleet-risks-for-the-global-maritime-order/> accessed 16 February 2024. In March 2023, CNN reported about 10 percent of the shadow fleet among large tankers and warned that the numbers are growing. See CNN, 'A mysterious fleet is helping Russia ship oil around the world. And it's growing' (1 March 2023), available at <https://edition.cnn.com/2023/03/01/business/russia-oil-shadow-fleet/index.html> accessed 16 February 2024.

2 Purchase of new or second-hand ships is regularly dependent on terms and conditions of ship finance. Banks normally require clean papers and a valuable ship as a collateral/mortgage, and consequently also insurance from reputable companies. For more see Erik Røsæg and Henrik Ringbom, 'Liability and Compensation with Regard to Places of Refuge', Study No. EMSA/RES/001-2004, Report of 12 October 2004, 15. See also Nicholas Gaskell and Craig Forrest, *The Law of Wreck* (Informa 2019) 381 and 386.

 | DOI:10.1163/9789004707993_010

an International Group of P&I Clubs (hereinafter IG or IG P&I Clubs).[3] Concerned with socio-economic and environmental risks posed by shipping, States have relied on this practice extensively, not least because an adequate liability and compensation regime forms a critical pillar of ocean governance, and goes hand-in-hand with technical and environmental standards developed through, among others, the International Maritime Organization (hereinafter IMO).

Indeed, the IMO has been working for decades on improving shipping standards for the prevention of incidents and pollution at sea. These advancements have arisen through the adoption of a comprehensive set of 'generally accepted international rules and standards' (hereinafter GAIRS), such as the replacement of a single hull with a double hull for oil tankers, standards for safe and environmentally sound ship-to-ship transfers, etc.[4] As far as liability issues are concerned, the year 1969 saw a critical moment when the IMO adopted the International Convention on Civil Liability for Oil Pollution Damage (hereinafter CLC). This was the first international treaty addressing liability and compensation for victims of vessel-source pollution. A suite of similar IMO conventions followed in the post-CLC era, all collectively referred to as the IMO liability and compensation regime.[5]

---

3 In fact, there has always been an understanding that the International Group of P&I Clubs provides liability cover to more than 90 percent of the world's ocean-going tonnage. See the official web site of the Group, available at <https://www.igpandi.org/> accessed 16 February 2024.

4 Following the *Erica* incident, the single hull requirement was replaced by the double hull requirement under the 1992 amendments to the International Convention for the Prevention of Pollution from Ships (hereinafter MARPOL). The original text of MARPOL was adopted in 1973, 1340 UNTS 61, and was further amended by the Protocol of 1978, 1340 UNTS 61, and by the Protocol of 1997, 1340 UNTS 61, as further amended. For ship-to-ship transfers of particular relevance is chapter 8, Annex I of MARPOL, as well as chapter V, regulations 19 and 19-1 of the 1974 International Convention for the Safety of Life at Sea (SOLAS) (adopted 1 November 1974, entered into force 25 May 1980) 1184 UNTS 2, as amended.

5 The 2001 International Convention on Civil Liability for Bunker Oil Pollution Damage (hereinafter the Bunker Convention) (adopted 23 March 2001, entered into force 21 November 2008) 973 UNTS 3; The International Convention on Liability and Compensation for Damage in Connection with the Carriage of Hazardous and Noxious Substances by Sea (hereinafter the HNS Convention), originally adopted in 1996 and amended by the 2010 Protocol, but not yet in force. Another relevant convention is the 2007 Nairobi International Convention on the Removal of Wrecks (hereinafter the WRC) (adopted18 May 2007, entered into force 14 April 2015) and the 1974 Athens Convention relating to the Carriage of Passengers and their Luggage by Sea (hereinafter PAL) (adopted 13 December 1974, entered into force 28 April 1987), amended by the 2002 Protocol (adopted 1 November 2002, entered into force 23 April 2014). The IMO liability and compensation conventions to a large extent use the same form and language. See, for example, Article VII(8) of the CLC, Article 12(8) of the HNS, Article

The strength of the actual implementation and enforcement of the IMO liability and compensation regime lies in the well-tested system of prompt and effective compensation for victims of pollution, through strict liability imposed on the shipowner, backed with compulsory liability insurance (typically P&I insurance) and direct action against the insurer.[6] Particularly reassuring in this respect are the verification processes and payment done through the IG of P&I Clubs, which are globally known for their visibility, reputation and financial stability.[7]

However, this system is now being challenged by a rapid transformation in global shipping. As a reaction to the Russian Oil Price Cap Regime introduced in 2022, a strong growth of the so-called 'dark' or 'shadow' fleet has emerged to evade sanctions imposed by the West.[8] As warned at the IMO on several occasions, the last one being the Assembly Resolution A.1192(33) adopted in December 2023, the maritime industry is faced with significant challenges as the 'shadow' vessels navigate under no adequate liability insurance. These are typically substandard ships that are engaged in unsafe and environmentally problematic ship-to-ship operations on the high seas, with their automatic identification system (hereinafter AIS) turned off.[9] Fraudulent registrations and

7(10) of the Bunker Convention, Article 12(10) of the WRC. For more see Nicholas Gaskell, 'Decision Making and the Legal Committee of the International Maritime Organization' (2003) 18(2) The International Journal of Marine and Coastal Law 155, 165.

6 Donald Rothwell and Tim Stephens, *The International Law of the Sea* (Bloomsbury 2016) 393.

7 See Iva Parlov, *Coastal State Jurisdiction over Ships in Need of Assistance, Maritime Casualties and Shipwrecks* (Brill 2022) 206. See also the official website of the International Group of P&I Clubs (n 3). Based on the vessel's IMO number and/or name one can easily access information on a P&I entry. The same system is embraced by the individual members of the IG through their own web sites.

8 Jonathan Yerushalmy and Haylena Krishnamoorthy, 'How a burnt out, abandoned ship reveals the secrets of a shadow tanker network' The Guardian (18 September 2023), available at <https://www.theguardian.com/business/2023/sep/18/how-a-burnt-out-abandoned-ship-reveals-the-secrets-of-a-shadow-tanker-network> accessed 16 February 2024.

9 See IMO Doc, A 33/Res.1192 of 11 December 2023, 'Urging Member States and All Relevant Stakeholders to Promote Actions to Prevent Illegal Operations in the Maritime Sector by the "Dark Fleet" or the "Shadow Fleet"'; A 33/13/2 of 30 October 2023, 'Consideration of the Reports and Recommendations of the Marine Environment Protection Committee' 2–3; LEG 110/5 of 16 January 2023, 'Consequences and concerns for the global liability and compensation regime relating to the increase in ship-to-ship transfers in the open ocean' submitted by Australia, Canada and United States. See also Lloyd's List, 'Denmark leaves position unclear on inspecting sanctions-busting Russian tankers' (20 November 2023), available at <https://lloydslist.com/LL1147324/Denmark-leaves-position-unclear-on-inspecting-sanctions-busting-Russian-tankers> accessed 16 February 2024.

fraudulent ship registries are also of great concern.[10] In other words, the shadow fleet vessels pose a threat to maritime safety and security, towards the marine environment.[11] Whereas the shadow fleet practice is not a new phenomenon (similar reactions occurred during sanctions against Iran and Venezuela in the past), the scale, number and tonnage of ships associated with the current practice are significant, and seem to be on the rise, which is cause for concern.[12] Data is admittedly not yet systematic and fully reliable, but some estimations can nonetheless be discerned. Close to one-fifth of oil tankers operates as a 'shadow fleet'. Moreover, according to Lloyd's List, the IG coverage for the global tonnage of tankers fell around 10 percent – from 87 (as of 20 February 2022) to 79 (as of 7 February 2024).[13]

Against this backdrop and taking the perspective of both international law and geopolitics, this chapter investigates the implications of the emerging shadow fleet practice for ocean governance, and further asks whether and how the law of the sea can contribute to ensuring stability in major shipping routes in hybrid warfare. The chapter starts with providing an understanding of the Sanction Regime, the practice associated with shadow fleet, and the risks thereby posed. Then the chapter continues with a discussion on the legal and political challenges stemming from this development, and investigates the solutions thereto provided, including in the form of rights

10 IMO Doc, LEG 111/6 of 16 January 2024, 'Measures to prevent unlawful practices associated with the fraudulent registration and fraudulent registries of ships'.

11 Allianz, 'Safety and Shipping Review 2023', available at <https://commercial.allianz.com/content/dam/onemarketing/commercial/commercial/reports/AGCS-Safety-Shipping-Review-2023.pdf> accessed 16 February 2024.

12 Compared to Iranian oil, Russian oil is more attractive to shadow fleet due to (i) higher rates on the freight market and (ii) smoother operation, along with (iii) a less strict sanction regime. As reported by a tanker analysist, and published by Financial Times, the premium for Russian oil trade in February 2023 was 50 percent higher, and at times even more than 100 percent higher, than in normal circumstances. In addition, 'waiting time' spent on loading/unloading is not as long as with Iranian oil, which makes the entire operation smoother. Finally, the sanction regime is not as strict as the one imposed on Iranian oil trade. All that shipowners and operators need to do is to show that they did not know that Russian oil was practically sold above the price cap. See Chris Cook and David Sheppard, 'Iran's "ghost fleet" switches into Russian oil', Financial Times (7 February 2023), available at <https://www.ft.com/content/955389bf-d01b-4acb-bd15-b764425a8a18> accessed 25 February 2024. As reported by Windward, shadow fleet that was first associated only with Iranian and Venezuelan sanctions was small in size and 'did not significantly impact non-sanctioned trade'. See Windward, 'Illuminating Russia's Shadow Fleet', available at <https://windward.ai/knowledge-base/illuminating-russias-shadow-fleet/> accessed 16 February 2024.

13 See Lloyd's List, available at <https://lloydslist.com/> accessed 16 February 2024.

and obligations of States acting in different capacities – flag, coastal and port States. Although the current international regime provides a few obvious legal and political routes for constraining the shadow fleet, this chapter argues that important steps could and should be made, not least in strengthening the procedural rules imposed on flag States for ensuring that they only register vessels in possession of *adequate* marine insurance. The structure of the main discussion in this chapter follows the public/private divide between (i) the law of the sea issues related to pure jurisdictional rights and obligations of States, as envisaged under the 1982 United Nations Convention on the Law of the Sea[14] (hereinafter LOSC); and (ii) international maritime law issues, and specifically issues related to liability insurance, as referred to in the LOSC in general terms and as further developed under the IMO's mandate.

1 The Russian Oil Price Cap Regime and the 'Shadow (Dark) Fleet' Practice

2.1 *The Russian Oil Price Cap Regime*

As a result of Russia's aggression towards Ukraine, the Sanction Regime came into place on 5 December 2022. The purpose of the regime is to prohibit the transport, and thereto related insurance service, of Russian oil traded above a certain price cap, which was initially set at USD 60 per barrel, with the possibility to be adjusted depending on market developments.[15] This regime was introduced by G7 and its coalition partners (European Union (hereinafter EU) and Australia) to reduce Russia's revenues, and thereby weakening its capacity to continue war in Ukraine, while simultaneously aiming to retain Russian oil on the world market to keep prices down.[16]

The regime essentially requires the shipping industry to take its due diligence to ensure that the price of crude oil does not go beyond the set price cap. The nature and scope of the due diligence vary depending on the proximity of

14 United Nations Convention on the Law of the Sea (opened for signature 10 December 1982, entered into force 16 November 1994) 1833 UNTS 3.

15 EU Council Regulation No 833/2014 of 31 July 2014 concerning restrictive measures in view of Russia's actions destabilizing the situation in Ukraine (OJ L 229 of 31 July 2014), as amended.

16 Ibid. For a short overview, see also Skuld News (5 December 2022), available at <https://www.skuld.com/topics/legal/sanctions/russia/the-price-cap-on-russian-oil-and-petroleum-products/#:~:text=On%205%20February%202023%20the%20Price%20Cap%20Scheme,products%20traded%20at%20a%20discount%20to%20crude%20oil> accessed 16 February 2024.

a certain party to a given contract of sale. As shipowners and their P&I insurers are considered parties without direct access to price information, their due diligence obligation equates to the obtainment of a commitment from their counter parties that no Russian oil will be purchased above the price cap. This commitment is then witnessed through an attestation contained either in a stand-alone document, or as an integral part of the contract. In circumstances where there are reasonable grounds to believe that such attestation is false and/or that, after the voyage has already commenced, Russian oil is sold at the greater amount than the price cap, P&I insurers are required to withdraw their cover.

For example, the marine insurance company GARD, a member of IG, formulated this as follows:

> The Club shall not indemnify an Assured against any liabilities, costs or expenses where the provision of cover, the payment of any claim, or the provision of any benefit in respect of those liabilities, *may expose the Club to risk of violation of the price cap policy*. In the event the Club determines that a violation of the price cap policy has taken place, *the Club may immediately terminate* the policy and *will have no liability* whatsoever under the policy beyond what is permitted by applicable law.[17]

Along the same lines, by way of a circular, the IMO issued a set of guidelines according to which the flag State 'should ensure that it cancels the certificate in accordance with the [IMO] conventions if or when they receive notification of termination of the insurance or other financial security'.[18]

Even though the sanction regime is clearly defined and consistently designed, it has proven difficult to enforce and implement in practice. Whereas the regime has mostly worked for those covered by the IG, it has been observed that a large portion of the Russian oil is sold above the price cap and transported by the shadow fleet without possessing IG cover. As such, the emergence of the shadow fleet can be viewed as an unintended and unexpected effect of the sanction regime.

When the price cap was initially set, there were concerns that it might lead to the re-registering of the fleet, although it was not considered to be a very likely development. It was, for instance, argued that Russia probably

17 GARD P&I Member Circular No 18/2023 of February 2024, Annex A, point 4, available at <https://www.gard.no/Content/36665094/cache=20240502112839/MemberCircular_18_2023.pdf> accessed 16 February 2024.

18 IMO Doc, LEG.1/Circ.12 of 7 April 2022, 'Guidance on the Impact of the Situation in the Black Sea and the Sea of Azov on Insurance or other Financial Security Certificates'.

would find it challenging to build up a 'shadow fleet' rapidly enough in the near term, partly due to the fact that Western ships are financed through loans from banks requiring adequate insurance.[19] However, the shadow fleet problem did eventually emerge. Indeed, others were concerned at an early stage, and argued that the sanctions triggered a fundamental fragmentation of the market for Russian oil and the emergence of new patterns in shipping and transport.[20] They also observed that a significant share of Russian oil was sold above USD 60 per barrel, calling for more rigorous inspection and auditing of transactions.

1.2 *The Shadow (Dark) Fleet Practice*

As indicated in the introduction, the shadow fleet denotes, among others, vessels engaged in illegal trade of Russian oil to circumvent sanctions imposed by the West, simultaneously evading compliance with safety and environmental standards, and avoiding insurance screenings and costs. These vessels typically navigate without adequate liability insurance or other financial security.[21] As one commentator describes: 'the little piece of paper a dark ship may have that says it's insured is not worth the paper it's written on'.[22] This is disturbing as the shadow fleet practice poses serious risks to maritime safety and significantly increases the risk of oil spills. [23] A large part of the fleet consists of old ships that operate under unclear ownership structures, characterized by substandard maintenance.[24] They are also known for changing their name and flag quite regularly, as well as navigating with automatic identification system (AIS) turned off, not least to engage in unsafe, environmentally problematic or illegal ship-to-ship transfers on the high seas without being detected.[25] As observed by Lloyd's List, '[f]ake recognized organisations, fraudulent insurance entities, sham company

19 Simon Johnson, Lukasz Rachel, Catherine Wolfram, 'Design and implementation of the price cap on Russian oil exports' (2023) 51(4) Journal of Comparative Economics 1244–1252, available at <https://doi.org/10.1016/j.jce.2023.06.001> accessed 16 February 2024.

20 Tania Babina *et al.*, 'Assessing the Impact of International Sanctions on Russian Oil Exports' (23 February 2023), available at <https://ssrn.com/abstract=4366337> accessed 16 February 2024.

21 See, e.g., IMO Doc, A 33/13/2 (n 9) 2–3.

22 Simon Lockwood, a maritime executive with the insurance broker WTW, as referred to by Braw (n 1).

23 See, e.g., IMO Doc, LEG.1/Circ.12 (n 18).

24 See IMO Doc, A 33/13/2 (n 9) 2–3.

25 See ibid. A significant number of ship-to-ship transfers has been observed off the coast of Morocco and Greece. See Braw (n 1).

registrations and vessel numbering – these are all on the rise'.[26] Particularly worrying is the estimation that one-fifth of the global crude oil tanker fleet counts for the shadow fleet.[27] According to Winward, a maritime risk management and maritime domain awareness company, the 'shadow' fleet continued to grow in 2023, and was estimated to include over 1,800 vessels.[28] These ships attempt to evade detection, sanctions, and regulations, and many are likely engaged in various illegal operations. Winward reported that they registered more than 600,000 AIS signal losses, and that the ships were involved in more than 48,600 tanker-to-tanker operations. It has also been reported that vessel traffic in the Baltic Sea shows significant alterations since Russia's invasion of Ukraine – from an average of 662 to an average of 955 journeys made by crude oil tankers per month.[29] These tankers seemed to grow in deadweight tonnage as well – from 60,354,000 to 92,043,000 metric tons. What is mostly worrying is the significantly elevated average age of tankers departing from Kaliningrad, which has surged from 15.4 to 29.3 years.[30]

As warned at the IMO, the global maritime industry is put through considerable challenges due to the proliferation of the shadow fleet,[31] and thereby increased risk of oil spills and collisions. The gravity of the problem has been well demonstrated in practice. Allianz reports that 'there were at least eight groundings, collisions or near misses involving tankers carrying sanctioned oil products in 2022 – the same number as in the previous three years combined'.[32] To give one example, in May 2023 the 26-years old oil tanker *Pablo* caught fire off the Malaysian coast.[33] This tanker, flying a flag of Gabon, was already set to be sold as scrap when it was at the age of 21. However, due to 'a sudden surge

---

26 Lloyd's List, 'The good, the bad and the ugly: the flagging standards of flag states' (26 January 2024), available at <https://www.lloydslist.com/LL1148077/The-good-the-bad-and-the-ugly-the-flagging-standards-of-flag-states> accessed 16 February 2024.

27 Braw (n 1).

28 Windward, Windward Q4 Trade Patterns & Risk Insights Report, available at <https://windward.ai/blog/windward-q4-risk-report/?submissionGuid=7e57ede8-6ae6-4519-9b27-90f88fcb11b0> accessed 16 February 2024.

29 Braw (n 1).

30 Ibid.

31 See IMO Doc, A 33/13/2 (n 9) 2–3. See also IUMI Press release (19 September 2023), available at <https://iumi.com/news/press-releases/a-positive-year-for-hull-underwriters-but-change-is-on-the-horizon-say-iumi#:~:text=At%20the%20IMO%2C%20the%20Legal%20Committee%20noted%20that,increasing%20the%20risk%20of%20oil%20spills%20and%20collisions> accessed 16 February 2024.

32 Allianz (n 11).

33 See Maritime Executive, 'Fire on "Shadow" Tanker off Malaysia is Extinguished, Search Continues' (2 May 2023), available at <https://maritime-executive.com/article/fire-on-shadow-tanker-off-malaysia-is-extinguished-search-continues> accessed 16 February 2024.

in demand for older – and cheaper – oil tankers', its demolition was cancelled.[34] The International Union of Marine Insurers (hereinafter IUMI) reports that salvors were not able to board the vessel because this ship was part of a shadow fleet.[35]

Luckily, the *Pablo* was free of cargo at the time of incident, but the question does arise as to what happens when a fully laden tanker under a reputable P&I insurance collides with a shadow fleet tanker?[36] There are some warnings indicating that incidents like *Pablo* are all too likely to happen again.[37]

To sum up, even if systematic and comprehensive data is yet lacking, these developments indicate that the emergence of shadow fleet constitutes a serious maritime security risk. A large share of global oil is currently being shipped on vessels without adequate and well-tested insurance; these ships might be substandard, and many are frequently engaged in unsafe and environmentally problematic ship-to-ship transfers, with AIS turned off. Each vessel might in itself represent a serious risk, but more importantly, the scale, scope and global nature of the entire shadow fleet constitutes a significant systemic risk for the existing maritime governance. The shadow fleet threatens more than 50 plus years of global regulatory efforts to make shipping safe, secure and environmentally sound, and to ensure prompt and adequate compensation of victims of vessel-source pollution.

2 States' Rights and Obligations under the Law of the Sea

Under the LOSC, flag States are provided with a set of rights and obligations to ensure maritime safety and environmental protection; while port and coastal States are provided with rights to protect their interests from shipping-related risks and, at times, obligations to not interfere with navigational rights. In the

---

34 Yerushalmy and Krishnamoorthy (n 8).

35 IUMI Press release (19 September 2023), available at <https://iumi.com/news/press-releases/a-positive-year-for-hull-underwriters-but-change-is-on-the-horizon-say-iumi#:~:text=At%20the%20IMO%2C%20the%20Legal%20Committee%20noted%20that,increasing%20the%20risk%20of%20oil%20spills%20and%20collisions> accessed 16 February 2024.

36 Allianz (n 11). Some of the issues that arise in relation to the shadow fleet practice concern the polluter-pays principle (shipowners of the shadow fleet are not identifiable; their insurance non-existing or inadequate) and the balance between the payment contributors (the shadow fleet increased the burden on tax payers and the exposure of the FUND Convention vis-à-vis CLC). For a brief overview, see IMO Doc, LEG 110/5 of 16 January 2023, submission by Australia, Canada and United States.

37 Yerushalmy and Krishnamoorthy (n 8).

same vein, States are obliged to cooperate in matters of liability and compensation, including marine insurance. In the next few sections, rights and obligations of States are discussed in greater detail: first, in the context of State jurisdiction over safety and environmental standards in general, and then more specifically in the context of marine insurance. These two aspects combined are seen by the authors as the key pillars of good ocean governance in the shipping sector.

2.1 *Flag States*

It is a well-established rule that vessels engaged in international voyages, at any point in time, are subject to flag State jurisdiction and control, with the obligation of the flag State to ensure *effective* jurisdiction and control in administrative, technical and social matters over its vessels.[38] It is also a well-known rule that there must exist a *genuine* link between the ship and the flag.[39] However, both 'effectiveness' nor 'genuineness' are defined any further. What is rather clear is that the flag State has the responsibility to determine the requirements of entry for allowing ships into its registry.[40] However, there are again no international criteria imposed on the flag State on the process of ship registration. The proposal in 1986 for the adoption of an international treaty on ship registration (the 1986 United Nations Ship Registration Convention) failed to gain the necessary support among States.[41] Simultaneously, the competitiveness on the market caused the phenomenon of 'flags of convenience', the main characteristic of which is a service-minded philosophy,[42] the reason why some flags of convenience have been criticized for substandard shipping.

As a 'competent international organization' for shipping, IMO has a special responsibility under the LOSC to facilitate the development of international rules and standards, to ensure maritime safety and environmental protection. These rules and standards are important for the prohibition of substandard shipping. They strike a balance between the need to protect and preserve the marine environment, while ensuring shipping does not become prohibitively expensive. Some of these rules and standards may later qualify as 'generally

38 LOSC, Articles 91 and 94.

39 LOSC, Article 91.

40 LOSC, Article 91.

41 See briefly in Robin Churchill and Christopher Hedley, 'The Meaning of the "Genuine Link" Requirement in Relation to the Nationality of Ships' (2000) International Transport Workers' Federation.

42 See, e.g., Shuo Ma, *Economics of Maritime Business* (Routledge 2021) 278.

accepted international rules and standards' (GAIRS), becoming applicable to all States.[43]

When imposing the obligation on flag States to ensure effective exercise of jurisdiction and control over their vessels, the LOSC in specific terms demands that flag States ensure that vessels flying their flag comply with GAIRS as a *regulatory minimum* (Article 94 of the LOSC), to avoid substandard shipping.[44] The primary responsibility for enforcing GAIRS thus rests with each individual flag State. This relates to both vessel-source pollution and maritime safety standards.

As far as safety is concerned, every flag State is obliged to take measures necessary to ensure that vessels flying their flag are *inter alia* seaworthy and have on board equipment and instruments appropriate for safe navigation.[45] In this respect, 'each State is required to conform to generally accepted international regulations, procedures and practices [GAIRS] and to take any steps which may be necessary to secure their observance'.[46] Regarding the matter of vessel-source pollution, flag States are again responsible for enforcement of GAIRS, including approval of operations Plan for ship-to-ship transfers of oil under MARPOL.[47] Port States are concurrently given the authority to exercise control over foreign vessels entering their ports to ensure that GAIRS are followed through.[48] It is precisely port State control that caused many flags of convenience to remedy the perceived disrepute by ensuring better compliance with IMO standards.[49] In fact, many flags of convenience are now outperforming traditional registries in this respect.[50] *Many*, however, is not to say *all*. There are still several States with no political will to impose their sovereignty on vessels flying their flag and States without resources, capacities, and traditions to make adequate inquiries before deciding to register a vessel with their registry. This may indeed be attractive to those involved in illegal activities and may

---

43 Erik J Molenaar, *Coastal State Jurisdiction over Vessel-Source Pollution* (Kluwer Law International 1998) 183. See also Robin Churchill, 'The 1982 United Nations Convention on the Law of the Sea', in Donald Rothwell *et al.* (eds.), *The Oxford Handbook of the Law of the Sea* (Oxford University Press 2015) 31. The third States-effect of GAIRS has been confirmed in jurisprudence. See South China Sea Arbitration (the Philippines v. the People's Republic of China), Case No 2013-19, Award of 12 July 2016, para 1083.

44 For more on the regulatory minimum/maximum see Molenaar (n 43) 151.

45 LOSC, Article 94(3)(a) and (b).

46 LOSC, Article 94(5).

47 LOSC, Article 217; MARPOL, Annex 1, Chapter 8, Regulation 41.

48 LOSC, Article 218.

49 Ma (n 42) 281.

50 Paris MoU, White List, available at <https://parismou.org/Statistics%26Current-Lists/white-grey-and-black-list> accessed 16 February 2024. See also Shuo Ma, *Economics of Maritime Business* (Routledge 2021) 281.

even result in fraudulent documentation, eventually being presented to ports that may have no capacity to perform thorough investigations on possible frauds.[51] The IMO has already taken initiatives to prevent unlawful practices of fraudulent registrations and fraudulent registries of ships, by encouraging States to, *inter alia*, (i) strengthen collaboration between themselves and with the relevant stakeholders; (ii) invest in technologies that would enable better detection of frauds; (iii) promote greater transparency and information sharing; and (iv) invest in education and training of port officers, among other practices.[52] Although all laudable measures, these practices are arguably not sufficient to tackle the bigger picture. As will be demonstrated later in this chapter, fraudulent behavior is only one part of the problem. Another aspect lies in the fact that certain behaviors reflect an inadequately robust regulatory framework and are not illegal per se.

Compared to flag and port States, powers vested in coastal States are rather limited, but nonetheless still exist. In principle, they are subject to restrictions, the stringency of which depends on (i) the location of the vessel and (ii) the nature and significance of the violation in question. These are discussed in the following section.

To sum up, under the law of the sea, flag States have always had regulatory and enforcement jurisdiction over their vessels, regardless of vessel location. Flag States are obliged to ensure that their vessels comply with GAIRS, as a regulatory minimum to prevent substandard shipping, and, consequently, to ensure maritime safety and environmental protection. There needs to be a genuine link between the flag State and the ship, and the flag State is obliged to ensure effective jurisdiction and control in administrative, technical and social matters over its vessels (Article 94(1) of the LOSC). In this respect, the law of the sea does offer solutions to the problem of a substandard shadow fleet. However, these solutions do not prevent inadequate or sloppy inspections and verifications, especially given the lack of specifically agreed upon due diligence to be followed by the flag State in the process of ship registration and verifications of financial security.

51 On fraudulent registration and fraudulent registries see IMO Doc, LEG 111/6 (n 10) Annex, para 98. In its submission to the IMO in January 2023, China reported on problems in practice, such as the difficulty 'for the flag State to verify the authenticity of the documents of registration cancellation' and thus 'ships might use "false documents" to change their flag registration'. See IMO Doc, LEG 110/6/2 of 16 January 2023, submission of China, 2.

52 IMO Doc, LEG 111/6 (n 10) Annex, para 100.

2.2 *Rights and Obligations of States other than the Flag State*

2.2.1 Port Entry

The International Court of Justice (hereinafter ICJ) long ago held that: 'it is by virtue of its sovereignty that the coastal State may regulate access to its ports'.[53] There is indeed no general right to access ports and thus any entry to a foreign port is simply considered a 'benefit'.[54] Unless prohibited under a special bilateral or multilateral treaty,[55] the port State may at any point in time deny a benefit to which no ship has a special right. Also, the port State could prohibit the entry of substandard vessels engaged in illegal transfer of Russian oil; however, the problem is that these vessels may engage in illegal activities while on the high seas (with AIS turned off), avoiding necessary screenings and inspections. To some extent, problematic could also be the legal basis for extra-territorial jurisdiction due to its unclear content and status in international law. At the same time, it has been convincingly argued that port States are increasingly showing interest in expanding their jurisdictional powers through ex-post enforcement, rather than being physically present on the high seas. The convenience in this respect is that intruding ex-post enforcement with navigation is insignificant. As found by Ringbom:

> The denial of market-related benefits as a vehicle for exercising jurisdiction over events taking place on the high seas has been used in fisheries regulation for decades. A well-established example is the prohibition to land catches that have been unlawfully caught on the high seas. In commercial shipping, State practice is less widespread, but in particular since the turn of the Millennium, there have been examples of port States conditioning access to their ports of vessels based on their conduct beyond the State's own coastal waters.[56]

---

53 *Military and Paramilitary Activities in and against Nicaragua* (Nicaragua v. United States of America), Merits, ICJ Reports 1986, p. 14, para 213. See also Robin Churchill and Vaughan Lowe, *The Law of the Sea* (3rd edition, Manchester University Press 1999) 61.

54 Vaughan Lowe, 'The Right of Entry into Maritime Ports in International Law' (1977) 14 San Diego Law Review 597–622; Anthony Morrison, *Places of Refuge for Ships in Distress* (Martinus Nijhoff Publishers 2012) 73.

55 The behavior of the port State is at any time subject to the general principles of international law (e.g., non-discrimination, good faith and reasonableness) as well as to specific treaty obligations (bilateral or multilateral). This applies to both regulatory and enforcement jurisdiction.

56 Henrik Ringbom, 'Ships in ABNJ – Broadening Jurisdictional Opportunities for Non-flag States', in Vito de Lucia, Alex Oude Elferink, Lan Ngoc Nguyen (eds.), *International Law and Marine Areas beyond National Jurisdiction: Reflections on Justice, Space, Knowledge and Power* (Brill 2022) 335. As referred to by Ringbom, see also Arron N Honniball,

As far as the LOSC is concerned, apart from echoing the ICJ judgement in few instances, it makes little mention of ports.[57] For example, in matters of protection and preservation of the marine environment (Part XII of the LOSC), Article 211(3) makes it explicit that the port State has the right to establish particular requirements for the prevention, reduction and control of pollution of the marine environment as a condition for the entry of foreign ships into its ports or internal waters. In this respect, measures that can be adopted by port States are not necessarily constrained by standards adopted at the IMO. To some extent, the port State may devise unilateral regulations (port States may also act in concert, as EU Members normally do), which is not always the case within the regime applicable in the territorial sea,[58] and even less so in the exclusive economic zone (hereinafter EEZ).[59] The basic jurisdictional reasoning for the port State's actions against foreign vessels comes from the full territorial sovereignty and is further strengthened by the principle of protection.

In conclusion, port States have significant rights to effectively enforce Russian Oil Price Cap regime for environmental reasons. However, not all ports have the same political will, or capacity or resources to deal with this issue. It is important to note what has been displayed in media: previously most of the crude oil tankers transiting the Baltic Sea were bound for ports in United States (hereinafter U.S.) or EU ports as a (final) destination; however, these vessels are now mostly headed towards ports in India and China, both of which are not part of the Sanction Regime.[60] Nonetheless, waters of the EU and U.S. are potentially being used for "passage" purpose only, prompting further discussion in the following sections regarding the rights and obligations of coastal States under the passage regimes.

Extraterritorial Port State Measures: The Basis and Limits of Unilateral Port State Jurisdiction to Combat Illegal, Unreported and Unregulated Fishing (PhD Thesis, Utrecht University 2019) chapters 6 and 7; Bevan Marten, 'Port State Jurisdiction over Vessel Information: Territoriality, Extra Territoriality and the Future of Shipping Regulation' (2016) 31 International Journal of Marine and Coastal Law 470; Sophia Kopela, 'Port-State Jurisdiction, Extraterritoriality, and the Protection of Global Commons' (2016) 47 Ocean Development & International Law 96–97.

57 See Churchill and Lowe (n 53) 61.

58 LOSC, Article 211(4). This provision needs to be read together with Article 21(2) of the LOSC, which requires GAIRS in relation to the CDEM standards.

59 LOSC, Article 211(5).

60 Windward (n 12).

2.2.2 The Passage Regimes

Passage regimes under the LOSC offer significant protection to unimpeded navigation through the territorial sea of coastal States, as well as in straits used for international navigation. Even though coastal States enjoy territorial sovereignty in these waters, their jurisdictional rights are significantly restricted.

2.2.2.1 *Innocent Passage*

As a point of departure, under Article 24(1) of the LOSC the coastal State is obliged to refrain from hampering, denying or impairing the innocent passage of foreign ships navigating through its territorial sea. Nonetheless, Article 21(1) of the LOSC does allow the coastal State 'to adopt laws and regulations' that address innocent passage as such, for purposes such as safety of navigation, the preservation of the marine environment, the prevention, reduction and control of vessel-source pollution, etc. As far as construction, design, equipment and manning standards (hereinafter CDEM standards) are concerned, the coastal State cannot regulate any further than giving effect to the IMO standards, i.e., GAIRS,[61] which should suffice since GAIRS aim at preventing substandard ships in the first place. The coastal State's powers under Article 21(1) of the LOSC are in any event not confined to CDEM standards. Indeed, the regulatory powers of the coastal State are rather broad.[62] To what extent the coastal State has enforcement powers is more debatable.

'To adopt' laws and regulations is not synonymous 'to enforcing' them. One approach is to narrowly interpret Article 21 so that enforcement is allowed only to the extent explicitly regulated under the LOSC itself (addressed below). Otherwise, the coastal State could risk hampering, denying or impairing the innocent passage, and thus violating Article 24(1) of the LOSC. On the contrary, it can be argued that the jurisdiction of coastal State is not explicitly excluded in cases not mentioned in the LOSC and therefore may be implicitly deduced from the principle of territorial sovereignty. However, this argument gets less convincing when considering the sensitivity of the regime that protects navigational interests, which among others is reflected in (i) the prohibition under Article 24 of the LOSC (the explicit obligation of the coastal State not to hamper, deny or impair the innocent passage of foreign vessels), and (ii) the fact that the LOSC itself does use the term 'to adopt and enforce' elsewhere in the Convention (Article 234 of the LOSC in respect of navigation in

61 LOSC, Article 21(2).

62 For more on the broad coastal State regulatory jurisdiction in the territorial sea, see Molenaar (n 43) 203–204; Henrik Ringbom, *The EU Maritime Safety Policy and International Law* (Martinus Nijhoff 2008) 441.

ice-conditions). In practice, depending on the nature of a given measure (i.e., intrusiveness of navigational interests), for measures not explicitly mentioned in the LOSC States generally seek the consensus at the IMO to ensure their actions obtain approval of the global community, thereby (implicitly) ensuring no breach of the innocent passage obligation (Article 24(1) of the LOSC).[63] This is often the case regarding enforcement of safety measures adopted as associated protective measures in particularly sensitive sea areas.[64]

The enforcement powers of the coastal State are explicitly allowed under Article 221 (maritime casualties, which will be addressed below) and Article 220 of the LOSC. According to Article 220, the coastal State is allowed to physically inspect a vessel when there are 'clear grounds' to believe that a vessel navigating in the territorial sea has violated GAIRS, or laws and regulations adopted in accordance with the LOSC for the purpose of prevention, reduction and control of vessel-source pollution. Unless, for example, evidence is collected from a drone which shows that the vessel is engaged in unlawful discharge of oil or clear evidence shows that the vessel is indeed substandard, it could be hard to argue that the conditions for physical inspection under Article 220 of the LOSC are fulfilled. Merely stating that the vessel violated regulations by turning off its AIS is insufficient. As pointed out at the IMO, these circumstances 'may warrant further investigation' but 'may not be *determinative* of

63 Given that the coastal State is at all times obliged not to hamper innocent passage, Oxman argues that the coastal State may risk violating this obligation if the coastal State ignores or goes against the IMO's recommendation or does not even ask for it. Conversely, the coastal State is in a strong position when it implements the IMO recommendations. See Bernard H Oxman, 'Environmental Protection in Archipelagic Waters and International Straits: The Role of the International Maritime Organization' (1995) 10(4) The International Journal of Marine and Coastal Law 467–469.

64 Australia, for example, sought the approval of the IMO for mandatory pilotage in its territorial sea, in particular in the Great Barrier Reef Particularly Sensitive Sea Area (PSSA), but the approval came in the form of recommendatory pilotage. In the words of Rothwell, '[i]n the absence of international recognition by a body such as the IMO that the waters of the territorial sea were either particularly hazardous or particularly sensitive thereby requiring the services of a pilot to ensure safe passage, compulsory pilotage enforced by way of coastal State laws and regulations would be considered to hamper innocent passage'. See Donald Rothwell, 'UNCLOS Navigational Regimes and Their Significance for the South China Sea', in Shicun Wu, Mark Valencia and Nong Hong (eds.), *UN Convention on the Law of the Sea and the South China Sea* (Routledge 2015) 157. See also the analysis provided by Roberts on the New Zealand's approach to seeking the approval of the IMO for the areas to be avoided (ATBA) in the territorial sea of New Zealand. See Julian Roberts, *Marine Environment Protection and Biodiversity Conservation: The Application and Future Development of the IMO's Particularly Sensitive Sea Area Concept* (Springer 2007) 122–126.

illegal activity'.[65] In some circumstances, turning off AIS is normal and lawful, e.g., when necessary to avoid piracy. Detention of a foreign vessel is subject to even stricter conditions as there needs to be 'evidence that so warrants', along with the 'clear grounds' that there was a violation in the first place. For the sake of investigation, there is nothing preventing the coastal State from inquiring with the vessel and/or the flag State to detect potential non-compliance with GAIRS. Both the flag State and the shipowner share a vested interest in ensuring the vessel's safety and preventing pollution, thus mitigating the potential liability for the shipowner. The 'clear grounds' by which the coastal State can argue regarding a violation of GAIRS remains ambiguous, but this is partly necessary as it remains dependent on particular circumstances of each individual case. Nonetheless, it is worth noting that the coastal State is not obliged to wait until an incident, let alone pollution, occurs to exercise its right of inspection. This is not the aim of Article 220.

Therefore, for the purpose of ensuring safety of navigation and environmental protection, the coastal State may regulate innocent passage, but arguably cannot inspect ships in such passage or attempt to enforce intrusive measures, unless a maritime casualty has already occurred (Article 221 of the LOSC as will be addressed below), or there are *clear* grounds to believe that GAIRS (or other laws and regulations adopted in accordance with the LOSC for the purpose of prevention, reduction, and control of vessel-source pollution) have been violated. It is not immediately clear how these rights translate to the IMO liability and compensation regime, including marine insurance, and will be further explored later in this chapter. At this stage, it is important to underscore that the coastal State is prohibited from regulating passage for commercial purposes, let alone exercising enforcement jurisdiction in this regard. Yet, for the regime of innocent passage to apply, the ship must be both 'innocent' and in 'passage'.

The coastal State has the right to take all the necessary steps in its territorial sea 'to prevent passage which is not innocent' (Article 25(1) of the LOSC). For example, this would allow the coastal State to inspect, detain and even expel the ship from its waters. The requirement of 'innocence' is articulated in Article 19 of the LOSC, which stipulates that passage is innocent 'so long as it is not prejudicial to the peace, good order or security of the coastal State' (paragraph 1). Article 19 continues to clarify that passage is to be considered 'non-innocent' if a foreign ship 'engages in any of the [...] activities' listed thereinafter, such as an act of 'willful and serious pollution' and 'any other activity not having a direct bearing on passage' (paragraph 2).

65 See IMO Doc, A 33/13/2 (n 9) 2–3.

Ship-to-ship transfer of oil for trade purposes is not an activity that has a direct bearing on passage and hence the ship would have lost its innocence by engaging in such an activity, unless the activity is done in accordance with MARPOL. It would have also not been in 'passage'. Under the LOSC, a foreign vessel in passage is allowed to stop and anchor only in exceptional scenarios: (i) when stopping and anchoring is 'incidental to ordinary navigation'; (ii) in cases of *force majeure* or distress; and (iii) when stopping and anchoring is needed for the purpose of rendering assistance to persons, ships or aircraft in danger or distress.[66] Halting and anchoring for oil transfer for commercial purposes does not meet any of the three exceptions,[67] which opens for coastal State enforcement jurisdiction.

At the same time, nothing prevents a vessel from engaging in a ship-to-ship transfer on the high seas where the freedom of navigation applies;[68] this is indeed how the shadow fleet operates.

2.2.2.2 *Transit Passage*

Transit passage applies in straits used for international navigation. It is similar to the freedom of navigation regime, offering greater protection to navigational interests than the protection offered under the innocent passage regime. Among others, this is evident in the right of submarines to navigate submerged[69] while in the restricted coastal State regulatory and enforcement jurisdiction.[70] According to Article 44 of the LOSC, no State is allowed to

66 LOSC, Article 18(2).

67 On this point see the *Duzgit Integrity Arbitration* (Malta v. São Tomé and Príncipe), Arbitral Award, 5 September 2016, Permanent Court of Arbitration, paras 234–236.

68 LOSC, Articles 87 and 58(2).

69 See Article 39(1)(c) of the LOSC.

70 According to the LOSC, States bordering straits may only adopt laws and regulations concerning the safety of navigation and the regulation of maritime traffic as provided explicitly in Article 41 (sea lanes and traffic separations schemes) and in relation to the prevention, reduction and control of pollution, by giving effect to *applicable international regulations* regarding the *discharge* of oil, oily wastes and other noxious substances in the strait, and with regards fishing vessels. See Article 42 of the LOSC. It is worthwhile mentioning the controversies in the example of the Torres Strait, where Australia again sought the approval of the IMO for compulsory pilotage, but eventually got a recommendation only, due to a strong opposition from US and Singapore. See IMO Doc, MEPC 133(53) of 22 July 2005, 'Designation of the Torres Straits as an Extension of the Great Barrier Reef Particularly Sensitive Sea Area'. Legally speaking, compulsory pilotage in straits used for international navigation does not seem to find the support in the LOSC, nor does there seem to be a general support among States in this respect. Probably best captured in the words of Beckman, '[i]f one or more maritime states challenge before an international court or arbitral tribunal Australia's regulations on compulsory pilotage, the chances are good that the challenge will succeed. This would create an authoritative precedent on the extent of the powers of littoral states under UNCLOS to regulate ships exercising the

hamper transit passage applied in straits used for international navigation, unless allowed under a special regime.

2.2.2.3 *Special Regimes: the Example of the Danish Straits*

Geographically, the Danish Straits are an important point in the shipment of Russian oil. It is estimated that nearly 2 million barrels of crude oil are being shipped through the Danish Straits daily.[71] In October and early November 2023, several tankers carrying Russian oil were seen transiting Danish waters without a P&I cover from an IG Member; some even stopped and anchored for a certain period of time (e.g., MV *Vela Rain* anchored for more than 30 hours).[72]

Due to the environmental risks and concerns regarding the effectiveness of the sanctions, EU Member States are finding ways to cope with the shadow fleet practice. In the case of Denmark, it is not surprising that authorities have been suggested to stop, search and "block" tankers suspected of circumventing sanctions as they pass through Danish Straits en route from the Baltic ports.[73] According to Lloyds, Denmark expressed its readiness to conduct inspections on oil tankers passing through the Danish Straits that 'might be breaching international maritime regulations on *safety* or *insurance*', yet only upon the

---

right of transit passage in straits used for international navigation'. See Robert Beckman, 'PSSAs and Transit Passage – Australia's Pilotage System in the Torres Strait Challenges the IMO and UNCLOS' (2007) 38(4) Ocean Development & International Law 351. Practically speaking, however, vessels do seem to comply with Australian regulations on pilotage, regardless of whether they proceed to an Australian port or not. See Donald Anton, 'Making or Breaking the International Law of Transit Passage: Meeting Environmental and Safety Challenges in the Torres Strait with Compulsory Pilotage' in David Caron and Nilufer Oral (eds.), *Navigating Straits: Challenges for International Law* (Brill 2014) 79. The ultimate compliance goal is therefore achieved, but the legal controversy remains, and it stays relevant for any future attempt other States may wish to pursue in similar situations. Whereas it is hard to speculate on why there is a good compliance with recommendatory regulations despite the legal controversy, one may nonetheless assume that vessels do not want to compromise on safety issues in the first place, and consequently also on liability for pollution, along with the fact that the IMO did recognize the particularly sensitive character of the sea area of the Torres Strait and the fact that vessels want to avoid any potential delays on their voyage not to experience negative commercial and legal (contract-based) consequences.

71 Henry Foy, Richard Milne and David Sheppard, 'Denmark Could Block Russian Oil Tankers from Reaching Markets' Financial Times (15 November 2023), available at <https://www.ft.com/content/6409ed38-73f4-46b3-b0f1-649c5e5b79db?accessToken=zwAGEPJLJjhwkc9kCe04c_RGs9Ow8WScXlt52w.MEYCIQDKbHGXkcOvH760AyPdhAUm190YmVRdXCjJAJlCfTgTFAIhAPeScivwPsXhTLnZI9zzQPLYT5L2t4HsFY4-YxNH2G_R&sharetype=gift&token=fbf9b113-d0dc-4513-8ab6-c9d3de5ba29a> accessed 16 February 2024.

72 Lloyd's List (n 9).

73 Foy, Milne, Sheppard (n 71).

receival of applicable information indicating a breach of regulations in the Straits.[74]

Although the Danish Straits are used for international navigation, these straits are excluded from the application of the transit passage regime as regulated under Article 35(c) of the LOSC due to the special regime developed based on the 1857 Copenhagen Treaty.[75] However, it is altogether unclear which regime does apply in the Danish Straits. This is particularly relevant for issues not explicitly regulated under the Copenhagen Treaty.[76]

The Copenhagen Treaty does not identify the nature of the specific legal regime applicable in the Danish Straits; however, Article I stipulates that Denmark is prohibited from exercising enforcement jurisdiction over ships 'in passage', i.e., no ship shall be subject to any detention or hindrance (see further *supra* Chapter 6.4), thus protecting navigational interests. At the same time, the purpose of the Copenhagen Treaty is to prevent Denmark from charging fees to vessels that are in passage, or those that must stop and anchor due to *force majeure* or commercial reasons.[77] In principle, there is nothing in the Copenhagen Treaty preventing Denmark to adopt laws and regulations to address maritime safety and environmental protection as such. These issues are not targeted through the Copenhagen Treaty.

In its accession to the LOSC, Denmark declared as follows:

> It is the position of the Government of the Kingdom of Denmark that the exception from the transit passage regime provided for in article 35(c) of the Convention applies to the specific regime in the Danish straits (the Great Belt, the Little Belt and the Danish part of the Sound), which has developed on the basis of the Copenhagen Treaty of 1857. The present legal regime of the Danish straits will therefore remain unchanged.[78]

---

74 Lloyd's List (n 9).

75 Treaty between Great Britain, Austria, Belgium, France, Hanover, Mecklenburg-Schwerin, Oldenburg, Netherlands, Prussia, Russia, Sweden and Norway, and the Hanse Towns, on the one part, and Denmark, on the other part, for the Redemption of the Sound Dues (adopted 14 March 1857, entered into force 31 March 1857).

76 Alex G Oude Elferink, 'The Regime of Passage through the Danish Straits' (2000) The International Journal of Marine and Coastal Law 560.

77 See Article 1 of the 1857 Copenhagen Treaty, available at <https://www.retsinformation.dk/eli/retsinfo/1857/21000> accessed 16 February 2024.

78 Declaration of Denmark to LOSC, available at <https://treaties.un.org/Pages/ViewDetailsIII.aspx?src=TREATY&mtdsg_no=XXI-6&chapter=21&Temp=mtdsg3&clang=_en#EndDec> accessed 16 February 2024.

With this declaration, Denmark was clearly seeking to exempt the Danish Straits from the transit passage regime outlined by the LOSC. This suggests that Denmark considers the regime applicable in the Danish Straits more advantageous to its interests than if the regime of transit passage under the LOSC were to apply. As far as warships are concerned, the U.S. considers the regime to be either transit passage or passage subject to freedom of navigation.[79] The significance lies in the enforcement powers of the coastal State, which are subject to more restrictions under the transit passage and freedom of navigation regime than, for example, under the innocent passage regime. Yet, warships are to be distinguished from commercial vessels, but State practice does not provide enough guidance on the general perception of the nature of the legal regime applicable in the Danish Straits. Perhaps it is a variation between transit and innocent passage. In any event, even if one could argue that the regime applicable in the Danish Straits is more favorable to Denmark than the regime of transit passage under the LOSC, this does not infer that the Danish Straits are subject to Denmark's full territorial sovereignty. In other words, there is no indication that the legal regime applicable in the Danish Straits would grant Denmark unilateral enforcement powers for *safety* or *insurance* matters; such authority is neither conferred by the Copenhagen Treaty, nor by the innocent or transit passage regimes. It is worth noting that the discussion on insurance is forthcoming in this chapter.

2.2.3 Exclusive Economic Zone, High Seas and At-Sea Enforcement

In the EEZ and on the high seas, the coastal state lacks territorial sovereignty, with its jurisdictional powers being more restricted than in the territorial sea. Regulatory powers are only available for environmental reasons; enforcement under Article 221 of the LOSC (right of intervention into maritime casualties) and under Article 220 of the LOSC, the latter being subject to even stricter conditions than in the territorial sea. In particular, the coastal State would only have the enforcement powers if there are 'clear grounds' for believing that the vessel violated GAIRS for the prevention, reduction and control of vessel source pollution. Even then, the coastal State would only be allowed to gather information regarding the vessel's identity, port of registry, its preceding and subsequent port of call and any other relevant details necessary to determine if a violation has occurred.[80] In other words (and as mentioned earlier with

79 Oude Elferink (n 76) 565.

80 LOSC, Article 220(3). For more see James Kraska, 'Excessive Coastal State Jurisdiction', in Henrik Ringbom (ed.), *Jurisdiction over Ships – Post-UNCLOS Developments in the Law of the Sea* (Brill 2015) 188–190.

regard to the territorial sea), a vessel who has turned off its AIS does not give sufficient grounds for the coastal State to exercise enforcement jurisdiction, but may merit further investigation to detect whether there has been a violation of GAIRS for the purpose of prevention, reduction and control of pollution.

In principle, on the high seas and in the EEZ vessels are free to navigate, stop, anchor and perform commercial ship-to-ship transfers without being interrupted by a non-flag State. Thus, at-sea enforcement on the high seas remains in the hands of flag States. However, at-sea enforcement is to be distinguished from the ex-post enforcement. As observed in scholarship and indicated earlier, the post-LOSC practice demonstrates 'the shift from physical at sea enforcement measures on the high seas towards ex-post enforcement measures relying on other jurisdictional bases than those specifically provided for in [the LOSC]'.[81] In this respect, jurisdiction over foreign vessels is mostly sought through port State jurisdiction. The core issue, however, lies in the fact that the shadow fleet avoids ports that are inconvenient to their operations and those willing to enforce Western sanctions.

2.2.4 Maritime Casualties

Maritime casualties can be catastrophic. The core element of preventing maritime casualties from occurring in the first place lies in the GAIRS system. As previously mentioned, the lack of a reputable third-party verification system for security and safety can hamper the prevention of maritime casualties from occurring. The reason why maritime casualties are brought to discussion in this chapter is the fact that, once a maritime casualty occurs, the coastal State has the right of intervention for the purpose of *prevention* of *pollution* (even though not for the purpose of *prevention* of a *maritime casualty*). The right of intervention (at-sea enforcement) allows the coastal State to take any measures necessary to protect its national interests from pollution, or a threat thereof.[82] Discussion in this section therefore revolves around the question of *when* the coastal State is allowed to intervene *to prevent pollution.*

---

81 Ringbom (n 56) 318.

82 This argument is not obvious for the territorial sea as LOSC explicitly recognizes the right of intervention in marine areas *beyond* the territorial sea, whereas Article 19, which applies *within* the territorial sea, speaks of non-innocent passage in cases of certain 'activities'. It is ambiguous as to whether an event that does not qualify as an 'activity', such as a maritime casualty, may be considered 'non-innocent'. The wording of Article 19(2) of the LOSC suggests that nothing but the activity makes a passage 'non-innocent'. However, as argued elsewhere, the word 'act' or 'activity' should in the context of 'innocence'/ 'non-innocence' be interpreted as 'event', rather than 'activity'. In other words, if

The right of intervention beyond the territorial sea (see *supra* Chapter 6) is regulated under Article 221 of the LOSC where a maritime casualty is defined as:

> a collision of ships, stranding or other incident of navigation, *or other occurrence on board a ship or external to it* resulting in material damage or *imminent threat* of material damage to a ship or cargo.[83]

According to the definition contained in the LOSC, there is no need for pollution to occur and for the ship to be damaged for it to be treated as a casualty or for the right of intervention to be triggered – a threat thereof suffices. However, such a threat must be *imminent* and must be caused by *an occurrence on board the ship or external to it*, if not specifically by collision, stranding or other incident of navigation.

The risk of maritime casualties is increasing. On the one hand, piracy and weaponization of shipping increases the likelihood for casualties and external occurrences that could cause damage to a ship. As demonstrated through the attacks in the Red Sea, shipping is vulnerable to security threats – increasing the risk of casualties for all types of vessels.[84] On the other hand, the increased number of vessels in the shadow fleet sailing with AIS turned off and making all efforts to lack the transparency in itself is a risk and will likely increase the risk of casualties. It is often portrayed in media that multiple switches of flag, name, class and registered owners are all signs of a substandard ship that is bound to cause an accident.[85] Intuitively, this conclusion is understandable, considering such vessels typically lack coverage under IG, and those insured by non-IG insurers have been historically 'overrepresented among vessels that are detained or otherwise appear to be substandard'.[86] It is still unclear whether

---

a ship runs into a maritime casualty, such a ship can be considered non-innocent, even though it is not really engaged in any 'activity'. For this argument see Parlov (n 7) 188–189.

83 This definition is essentially borrowed from Article II of the 1969 International Convention Relating to Intervention on the High Seas in Cases of Oil Pollution Casualties (the Intervention Convention).

84 See press release by the International Chamber of Shipping (ICS), available at <https://www.ics-shipping.org/statement/international-chamber-of-shipping-statement-on-the-red-sea-ship-attacks/> accessed 16 February 2024; See also Financial Times, 'Shipping companies avoid Red Sea after Houthi attacks', available at <https://www.ft.com/content/3f5d2519-94cb-4f37-9049-4e0e936212e2?shareType=nongift> accessed 16 February 2024.

85 Lloyd's List, 'Dark fleet tanker Pablo changed flags six days before fatal casualty' (2 May 2023), available at <https://lloydslist.com/LL1144944/Dark-fleet-tanker-Pablo-changed-flags-six-days-before-fatal-casualty> accessed 16 February 2024.

86 See IMO doc, LEG 76/WP.1 of 13 October 1997, 1 and Annex.

this is adequate grounds to assert that the shadow fleet represents an *imminent* threat of a vessel being damaged.

In the *Gabcikovo-Nagymaros Project* Case, the Court held that 'the mere apprehension of a possible 'peril' could not suffice'.[87] According to the Court, the term 'imminence' is synonymous to the terms 'immediacy' or 'proximity' and 'goes *far beyond* the concept of "possibility"'. In the scale of possible-probable-highly probable, 'imminent' would thus correspond to 'highly probable', rather than just 'probable'.[88] Moreover, in the words of the Court, even though the term 'imminence' goes 'far beyond the concept of "possibility"', this 'does not exclude' the possibility that a peril:

> appearing in the long term might be held to be 'imminent' as soon as it is established, at the relevant point in time, that the realization of that peril, however far off it might be, is not thereby any less certain and inevitable.[89]

Given the exceptional character of the right of intervention, the term 'imminence' tends to be interpreted restrictively, which is also implied in the IMO's Resolution where States acknowledged that ships in the shadow fleet pose a 'real and high risk of incident' but failed to mention anything about the risk of being 'particularly' high to allude to 'imminence' and the right of intervention.[90] However, this still does not explain where the imminence lies.

Learning from the experience, in the case of the *Amoco Cadiz*, salvors were too late in preventing the accident,[91] which led to France proposing that the word 'imminent' be removed from the definition of a maritime casualty.[92] The proposal ultimately found no support among States.[93] Nonetheless, the key point of the *Amoco Cadiz* lies in the fact that salvors were engaged in the entire process and had opportunity to board the *Amoco Cadiz* earlier, although they did not. In the case of the shadow fleet, salvors know that they will not

87 The *Gabcikovo-Nagymaros Project* Case (Hungary v. Slovakia), Judgment of 25 September 1997, ICJ Reports 1997, 7, para 54.

88 Parlov (n 7) 94.

89 The *Gabcikovo-Nagymaros Project* Case (n 87) para 54.

90 See IMO Doc, A 33/13/2 (n 9) 2–3.

91 See IMO doc, LEG 75/6/1 of 14 February 1997, 6–7. See Samir Mankabady, *The International Maritime Organization, Volume II* (Croom Helm 1987) 209.

92 Parlov (n 7) 153.

93 Imminent threat of a 'vessel being damaged' is to be distinguished from imminent threat of a 'damage to the coastline and related interests'. The latter is a condition under the 1969 Intervention Convention, but arguably does not form a condition under Article 221 of the LOSC and customary international law. See Parlov (n 7) 154.

be paid for their work and are therefore not boarding the vessel, increasing the risk of pollution. This fact, combined with environmental trends, e.g., the precautionary approach, could speak of imminence being satisfied, especially when the territorial sovereignty forms the key legal basis for the coastal State's protection. Moreover, the 2007 Nairobi International Convention on the Removal of Wrecks (hereinafter WRC) gives the coastal State the right of intervention when a ship 'is about, or may reasonably be expected, to sink or to strand, where effective measures to assist the ship or any property in danger are not already being taken'.[94] As argued elsewhere, the term 'effective' preserves the right of the coastal State to decide on whether salvage is producing effective results.[95] If it is clear that salvage will not take place, although under normal circumstances the salvors would in fact assist the vessel, the coastal State is in a better position to intervene at an earlier stage. It is also not to be forgotten that the definition of a maritime casualty (and hence the condition of imminence) in Article 221 of the LOSC is tailored for the marine area beyond the territorial sea. The 1989 Salvage Convention, which applies regardless of a maritime zone, does not refer to the condition of imminence when mentioning the coastal State's customary right of intervention.[96] On the other hand, the WRC does require imminent threat for a maritime casualty to occur. Yet, its application within the territorial sea remains optional (Article 3(2) of the WRC) and not many States have in fact opted for it.[97]

The threshold for the right of intervention to be invoked is also dependent on the gravity of the pollution risk. Beyond the territorial sea the rule is clear in that there must be a risk of 'major harmful consequences'.[98] The exact meaning of this term is short of clarity due to the absence of specific criteria to guide the assessment, but it is arguably not difficult to meet such a criteria when the vessel is loaded with oil, especially in narrow and congested areas. What is more problematic is that one needs to wait for an occurrence of a maritime casualty to trigger the right of intervention. In other words, the right of intervention cannot be invoked to prevent a maritime casualty as such; rather, this is where effectively implemented GAIRS plays a critical role.

94 WRC, Article 2(1) and Article 1(4).

95 Parlov (n 7) 170.

96 See Article 9 of the International Convention on Salvage (the Salvage Convention) (adopted 28 April 1989, entered into force 14 July 1996) 1953 UNTS 165.

97 Only 22 States opted for the extended application of the WRC. See IMO Doc, Status of IMO Treaties, 556, available at <https://wwwcdn.imo.org/localresources/en/About/Conventions/StatusOfConventions/Status%202024.pdf>.

98 LOSC, Article 221.

2.2.5 Initiatives Taken at the IMO

In December 2023, the IMO Assembly adopted resolution A.1192(33) 'urging member States and all relevant stakeholders to promote actions to prevent illegal operations in the maritime sector by the "dark fleet" or "shadow fleet"'.[99] States are primarily encouraged to effectively implement GAIRS, particularly in relation to ship-to-ship transfers and enhancing reporting on illegal activities. Flag, coastal, and port States are all called to exercise their respective jurisdictional rights and obligations to prevent or punish, as the case may be, any breach of GAIRS.[100] However, as discussed in this chapter, the real problem with shadow fleet boils down to the lack of resources and capacities on the side of flag States, and to some extent also port States, to implement the existing legal framework. The absence of a robust due diligence system imposed on flag States is in this respect problematic. Moreover, jurisdictional constraints on coastal States and those bordering straits, due to strong protection of navigational rights, exacerbates the problem.

The scope and content of GAIRS in relation to marine insurance remains ambiguous as it is not particularly dealt with under the LOSC, meriting further examination in light of the IMO liability and compensation regime, interpreted alongside some general provisions of the LOSC. In any event, States are ultimately liable for damage or loss caused by enforcement measures which are prohibited or deemed excessive, depending on the available information and what is reasonably necessary in a given situation (Article 232 of the LOSC). This is particularly relevant in instances where the LOSC is ambiguous on the conditions allowing for the exercise of coastal State jurisdiction, such as with regard marine insurance, as well as the terms 'clear grounds' (Article 220) and '*occurrence on board a ship or external to it* resulting in material damage or *imminent threat* of material damage to a ship or cargo' (the threshold for intervention under Article 221 of the LOSC or Article 2(1), read together with Article 1(4) of the WRC). The general applicability of the principle of proportionality within the territorial sea, however, is controversial.[101]

What remains to be further explored is the regulatory framework for marine insurance, where the LOSC is to be interpreted in conjunction with the IMO liability and compensation regime.

99 See IMO Doc, A 33/Res.1192 (n 9).

100 See IMO Doc, A 33/13/2 (n 9).

101 See James Harrison, 'Patrolling the Boundaries of Coastal State Enforcement Powers: The Interpretation and Application of LOSC Safeguards Relating to the Arrest of Foreign-Flagged Ships' (2018) 42 L'Observateur des Nations Unies 117, 117–143; Henrik Ringbom, 'Legalizing Autonomous Ships', in Aldo Chircop *et al.* (eds.), *Ocean Yearbook* (Brill Nijhoff 2020) 453.

3 Marine Insurance and the Law of the Sea

As indicated earlier, flag States are responsible for compliance and enforcement of GAIRS to address vessel-source pollution.[102] In the same vein, Article 94(3) of the LOSC imposes an obligation on the flag State to take measures necessary to ensure safety at sea. There should be no better safety risk assessment than that provided by a verified and reputable insurer. After all, it is in the interest of the insurer that the risk of a casualty, and consequently the shipowner's liability for pollution, does not materialize. This explains the indirect purpose of the IMO liability and compensation conventions, i.e., to provide incentive to ensure maritime safety is not compromised. This also explains why flag States may want to 'offload' their tasks to insurers: if a reputable insurer provides insurance, it strongly indicates the ship's safety. In turn, ship safety leads to safety of life and protection and preservation of the marine environment. Therefore, it could be argued that demanding a ship (including a shadow fleet vessel) to be 'insured' is essentially part of the safety requirement. However, the primary purpose of the liability and compensation regime is to protect victims through prompt and effective compensation, rather than safety of ships. A ship may well be safe, even when not insured against liability claims.

As previously mentioned, coastal States are allowed to regulate passage of foreign ships through their waters, and may enforce inspections when there are 'clear grounds' to believe that the vessel violated GAIRS, or laws and regulations regarding vessel-source pollution in accordance with the LOSC (Article 220). The IMO liability and compensation conventions are indeed adopted in accordance with the LOSC; however, this regime does not focus on prevention, reduction and control of vessel-source pollution.

It was mentioned earlier in this chapter that there exists a potential argument for the coastal State to exercise enforcement jurisdiction, based on its territorial sovereignty, even when this is not explicitly provided for under the LOSC. However, there are a few arguments to support the conclusion that the coastal State does not have jurisdiction in relation to marine insurance. First, the coastal State must at any point in time ensure that it does not hamper, deny or impair innocent passage (Article 24 of the LOSC) or transit passage (Article 44 of the LOSC).[103] Second, the lack of coastal State jurisdiction in relation to

102 LOSC, Article 217.

103 This explains the tendency of seeking the approval of the IMO when coastal States wish to adopt enforcement measures not explicitly addressed under the LOSC, even though these measures would apply in the territorial sea. See *supra* n 64 and n 70. The preparatory work of the WRC reveals that the US strongly argued against imposing compulsory insurance

marine insurance is implied in the way the IMO liability and compensation conventions are drafted. It suffices to give an example of the WRC, which in Article 12(12) prescribes that:

> each State Party shall ensure, under its national law, that insurance or other security to the extent required by paragraph 1 is in force in respect of any ship of 300 gross tonnage and above, *wherever registered*, entering or leaving a *port* in its territory, or arriving at or leaving from an *offshore facility* in its territorial sea.[104]

Thus, it is presumed that coastal States are not asserting jurisdiction over the IMO requirements concerning compulsory insurance (or similar financial guarantee) while the vessel is in passage through the territorial sea without entering a port of the coastal State or arriving at or departing from an offshore facility in the territorial sea.[105] This is also implied in the 2023 IMO Assembly's Resolution where flag, coastal, and port States are encouraged to exercise their respective jurisdiction powers to address the problem with shadow fleet. No insurance is mentioned in relation to coastal State jurisdiction, but only in relation to ports whose role here is non-controversial.[106]

Here it is also important to explain the relevance of Article 235(2) of the LOSC and the way it arguably separates the regime of marine insurance from the previously discussed system of GAIRS where the coastal States do have a certain role regarding State jurisdiction. Namely, Article 235(2) of the LOSC is focused on '*damage* caused by pollution' and the system of *compensation* for victims, and explicitly addresses marine insurance in the following way:

---

requirements on ships flying a flag of a non-State party. See IMO doc, LEG/CONF.16/18 of 17 May 2007, 1 and LEG/CONF.16/6 of 1 March 2007. The view of the US was expressed in the following words: 'The draft wreck removal convention would authorize coastal States to impose financial costs on foreign shipowners not as a condition of port entry, which is not a coastal State authority provided under customary international law. (Several IMO conventions have been elaborated to fill that gap, most recently the Bunkers Convention)'. See IMO Doc, LEG/CONF.16/7 of 15 March 2007, para 5.

104 The same is prescribed in CLC, Article VII(11), the Bunkers Convention, Article 7(12), HNS Convention, Article 12(11).

105 The same conclusion is implied in the IMO Doc, A 33/13/2 (n 9) 2–3. Under the legislation of the UK, the compulsory insurance requirements in relation to foreign ships are limited to port entry. See the UK Merchant Shipping Act 1995, Section 192A ('Compulsory insurance or security').

106 IMO Doc, A 33/Res.1192 (n 99).

> States shall ensure that recourse is available *in accordance with their legal systems* for *prompt* and *adequate compensation* or other relief in respect of *damage* caused by pollution of the marine environment by natural or juridical persons under their jurisdiction.

Paragraph 3 of Article 235 continues:

> With the objective of assuring prompt and adequate compensation in respect of all damage caused by pollution of the marine environment, States *shall cooperate* in the implementation of existing international law and the further development of international law relating to responsibility and liability for the assessment of and compensation for damage and the settlement of related disputes, as well as, *where appropriate*, development of *criteria and procedures* for payment of adequate compensation, such as *compulsory insurance or compensation funds*.

In clear contrast to the system of GAIRS, no flag State is obliged under Article 235 of the LOSC to impose on their vessels the IMO liability and compensation regime as a *regulatory minimum* to prevent, reduce and control vessel-source pollution, nor is the coastal State given any jurisdictional rights in this respect. All that Article 235 does is imposing a rather soft obligation for States 'to cooperate', 'where appropriate', in developing 'criteria and procedures for payment of adequate compensation, such as *compulsory insurance or compensation funds*'. States did fulfil their obligation to cooperate by adopting the IMO conventions on liability and compensation in the first place. However, it is questionable whether the current set of criteria and procedures under the IMO liability and compensation regime is indeed 'adequate', as elaborated below.

4 Marine Insurance and the IMO Liability and Compensation Regime

4.1 *A "Warranty" of Prompt and Effective Compensation for Victims of Vessel-Source Pollution*

In 1967, the catastrophe of the *Torrey Canyon* marked a critical point in developing international law on liability and compensation for victims of vessel-source pollution. The consequences of this casualty were no doubt disastrous, heavily polluting both British and French coastlines, and impacting local economies (tourism and fishing industry), livelihood of local communities, and marine life.[107] As a matter of urgency, the IMO Council conveyed an extraordinary session during which an *ad hoc* Legal Committee was established to prepare, among others, the work for what soon became the 1969 International Convention on Civil Liability for Oil Pollution Damage (hereinafter CLC), with a clear ambition to establish a system that would ensure that victims of vessel-source pollution get compensated 'promptly' and 'adequately'.[108] The goal was set to be achieved through strict liability imposed on the shipowner, backed with compulsory insurance (typically P&I insurance) and direct action against the insurer, typically a member of an IG P&I Club. This 'regime' has successfully withstood the test of time, as clearly supported by the adoption of liability and compensation conventions in the post-CLC era. These conventions essentially mirror the wording of the CLC by using a 'boilerplate text',[109] particularly concerning compulsory insurance.[110] As the majority of the global fleet is insured via IG of P&I Clubs, States rely quite heavily on this regime when allowing foreign vessels to enter their ports and sail through their waters to facilitate international trade, while maintaining maritime safety and environmental protection. Even in situations where ships need a place of refuge (refuge for ship/cargo, rather than for humans), coastal States are often willing to surrender their sovereignty if there is a proper insurance in place.[111]

However, according to Lloyd's, nearly 70 percent of the shadow fleet does not have reputable P&I cover and are mostly 'relying on institutions that have never been tested in international law'.[112] The pivotal issue remains: where does the primary regulatory gap or challenge lie in this regard?

4.2 *The Primary Responsibility of the Flag State and the Lawfulness of a Non-IG Insurance*

The primary responsibility under the IMO liability and compensation regime is placed on the flag State. In concrete terms, the flag State is obliged to demand that

---

107 Michael M'Gonigle and Mark Zacher, *Pollution, Politics, and International Law* (University of California Press 1979) 36; Patrick Griggs, '"Torrey Canyon", 45 Years On: Have We Solved All the Problems?', in Baris Soyer and Andrew Tettenborn (eds.), *Pollution at Sea: Law and Liability* (Informa 2012).

108 Thereby avoiding problems with single-ship companies and bankruptcy.

109 Gaskell (n 5) 165.

110 As displayed in media, the insurance certificate obtainable under the IMO liability and compensation conventions is part of a standardized system that has proven to be well-tested and undisputed in practice. For the same perception in media, see Safety4Sea, available at <https://safety4sea.com/norway-ratifies-first-the-2010-hns-convention/>.

111 Parlov (n 7) 205–215.

112 Lloyd's List (n 26).

vessels under its flag possess an adequate marine insurance.[113] In this respect, the flag State has the option to accept marine insurance '*or*' in fact 'other financial security, such as the guarantee of a bank or *similar* financial institution'.[114]

Under normal circumstances, where most ships have insurance of an IG P&I member, it is typical that a 'Blue Card' is first issued by an IG P&I insurer as a warranty that a ship is adequately insured. Then, a 'certificate of insurance' is issued by the vessel's flag State to confirm the adequacy of the 'Blue Card', a mechanism that has proven to be undisputed in practice as implied in the fact that the IMO encourages States to accept 'Blue Cards' from members of the IG P&I Clubs.[115] Regarding the providers of financial security other than IG Members, the IMO is not entirely dismissive, but does encourage States to have a special verification process to adequately validate '*financial standing and solvency*' of such providers.[116] This could be, for example, through audited financial statements from the previous three years, the rating held by an independent and internationally recognized rating agency, etc.[117] At the same time, the IMO guidelines are adopted in the form of a circular – clearly with a non-legally binding effect. In the same vein, the language used in these guidelines is hortatory ('State parties *should*'). In all, this indicates that no flag State is in breach of international law by adhering to a non-Blue Card mechanism – accepting financial security from providers other than an IG P&I Club, without going through a robust verification system. As a corollary obligation, the non-flag States must not infringe/must respect the right of the flag State.

If another State party to a specific IMO liability and compensation convention has doubts regarding the insurers capability to fulfill its obligations under the IMO liability and compensation regime, that State may demand consultations with the flag State that issued the certificate of insurance.[118] It should not be problematic that the primary responsibility to ensure compliance with the IMO liability and compensation conventions depends on the flag

113 See, e.g., CLC, Article VII; the Bunkers Convention, Article 7; HNS, Article 12; WRC, Article 12.

114 See, e.g., WRC, Article 12. The exact wording varies depending on the convention, but the substance is essentially the same.

115 IMO Doc, IMO Circular Letter No. 3464 of 2 July 2014, 'Guidelines for Accepting Insurance Companies, Financial Security Providers and the International Group of Protection and Indemnity Associations (P&I Clubs)', Annex, 1. These Guidelines might undergo updates later in 2024. This chapter, however, reflects research done until February 2024.

116 Ibid.

117 Ibid.

118 See, e.g., CLC, Article VII(7); the Bunkers Convention, Article 7(9); HNS, Article 12(7); WRC, Article 12(9).

State; however, the problem arises when the flag State has little or no capacity (financial and administrative resources) to undertake thorough (if any) screenings and inspection concerning the adequacy of the financial security and its providers, which is mostly the case with open registries, also known as flags of convenience. The shadow fleet vessels are indeed registered with such flags. It seems Gabon is now the 'destination of choice' for the shadow fleet vessels.[119] Its registry doubled in size during the first half of 2023 and almost 100 percent of vessels registered under Gabon are considered 'high risk' vessels.[120] The *Pablo*, for example, was flying a flag of Gabon.[121] According to the Lloyd's List:

> Gabon-flagged tankers in sanctioned oil trades now account for the vast majority of the 140 plus ships that Gabon now flags. But the Gabonese registry is not operated out of Gabon – it is controlled from Dubai.[122]

Other flags of convenience attracting shadow fleet are, for example, Cameroon, Liberia and Panama.[123] Cameroon is on the blacklist of the Paris Memorandum of Understanding (Paris MoU), classified as a 'very high risk' flag.[124] Eswatini seems to be taking on registration part, without even being a member of the IMO, i.e., without showing any real interest in shipping.[125]

To sum up, the governance system could cope well at the systemic level as long as most of the fleet is insured through a well-established/reputable insurance system. However, the lax interpretation and implementation of the obligations following from the applicable legal regime (to ensure that vessels possess 'adequate' financial security) becomes much more of a pressing problem as the growing share of the shadow fleet is not covered by such a system. Simply put: if 99 percent of the fleet were covered by transparent, reputable and financially stable insurers, such as IG, it would not constitute a global

119 TradeWinds, 'As dark fleet sails into lax flags, more cracks emerge in shipping's international safety order' (21 February 2023), available at <https://www.tradewindsnews.com/opinion/as-dark-fleet-sails-into-lax-flags-more-cracks-emerge-in-shipping-s-international-safety-order/2-1-1407776> accessed 16 February 2024. See also Braw (n 1).

120 Braw (n 1).

121 Maritime Executive (n 33).

122 Lloyd's List (n 26).

123 Windward (n 12).

124 Paris MoU, Black List, available at <https://parismou.org/Statistics%26Current-Lists/white-grey-and-black-list> accessed 16 February 2024.

125 Lloyd's List, 'Sanctioned ships briefly find a new home as Eswatini enters the flagging business' (26 January 2024), available at <https://lloydslist.com/LL1148076/Sanctioned-ships-briefly-find-a-new-home-as-Eswatini-enters-the-flagging-business> accessed 16 February 2024.

concern; and the lack of a robust due diligence procedure imposed on the flag State would not be of much concern in practice. However, if the percentage drops to 75–79 percent, which some estimates show to be the case, or even potentially to 50 percent, the pressure on the flag States should proportionally increase. In a well-established system where the flag States may offload the risk to P&I Clubs members of the IG, the good ocean governance would be possible. If IG is no longer playing this role, the flag States should be held accountable for their part. Again, the LOSC does oblige flag States to effectively exercise their jurisdiction and control in *administrative*, technical and social matters over its vessels. Moreover, States are obliged to cooperate, *where appropriate*, in developing criteria and procedures for payment of 'adequate' compensation, such as compulsory insurance. The shadow fleet underscores the 'appropriate' opportunity for States to cooperate on building a more robust due diligence system. This system would ensure robust verification of insurers (or other providers of financial security) to validate financial stability and solvency.

It is noteworthy to point out that sanctions have earlier in history also triggered significant disruptions in marine insurance. In 1914, Europe went to war. At the time, Britain introduced a blockade of Germany, and step-by-step, they added new dimensions and measures, including a blacklist of shipping.[126] In 1916, the British Clubs, the leading insurers at the time, informed their members that claims would no longer be paid if vessels carried goods to British enemies or the cargo was consigned to a British enemy subject. For instance, when the British identified a company trading with Germany, it was denied insurance by Lloyd's of London, which dominated the market for maritime insurance at the time. Britain also offered "green cards" to neutral shipping companies that allowed British cargo control in distant ports, and threatened to seize vessels sailing to Germany without control. The American government did not support this regime, leading to the establishment of their own insurance club in February 1917 called the 'American Club', which enabled them to sail to Germany and avoid the sanctions.[127] It is, however, unclear if American vessels sailed to Germany under coverage of the American Club. As we know, the U.S. soon declared war on Germany in April 1917, and the U.S. then aligned

126 For a history of the Blockade see Christian Götter, 'From a Militarily to a Politically Enforced Instrument: The Development of the Allied Blockade during the First World War' (2021) 1(26) Les Cahiers Sirice 59–71, available at <https://www.cairn.info/revue-les-cahiers-sirice-2021-1-page-59.htm> accessed 16 February 2024.

127 For a history of the American Club, see Richard Blodgett, *The American Club: A Centennial History* (Corporate History.net 2016), available at <https://d7a3216312da6f8c5faa-a6c4a22c6d23d8694e5e3f94c3d57dde.ssl.cf2.rackcdn.com/fc77f310208811e7b38287e21760dab6_American-Club-book-by-CorporateHistory-2016.pdf> accessed 16 February 2024.

itself with the British system. Most of the fleet in the American Club migrated back to the British Clubs within a decade, but the American Club has lasted for more than a hundred years.

Hence, sanction regimes have previously triggered the establishment of alternative and competing insurance systems. In 2024, it is indeed difficult to predict the future. The large shadow fleet represents a considerable reputational challenge to the whole shipping industry and to shipping insurance. It is unclear how and to what extent the shadow fleet vessels and the emerging industry surrounding these vessels, including financial actors, agents, and the insurance industry, will affect the future of the maritime industry and the future governance regime. At this point, we can imagine different alternatives. One potential outcome is further fragmentation and decreased transparency of the shipping industry. This could entail the proliferation of numerous regional and local insurance actors operating under different industry standards and rules, and compounded by poor third-party verification system. Such a development will undermine the entire set of global efforts of the last fifty plus years to eradicate sub-standard shipping in all aspects. Alternatively, we can imagine a gradual integration and consolidation of the whole (or large parts) of the shadow fleet, eventually leading to the establishment of an alternative club organizing large parts of the shadow fleet. If so, the different clubs will compete on standards, price, and requirements. Perhaps in the future, we might witness segments of the global fleet obtaining a 'blue card' issued by the established IG members, while others hold a 'red card' issued by a future Shadow Fleet Club. Perhaps the industry could eventually find an equilibrium or a mode of mutual recognition of the two, or we could observe the onset of a more radical division or decoupling of shipping.

Conclusion

The global community has witnessed over 50 years of significant efforts to make shipping safer and oceans cleaner. Through the development of (i) technical and environmental standards and (ii) liability and compensation regime, the IMO has shown remarkable efforts in making the topic of vessel-source pollution a rather sporadic part in the contemporary debates on any new regulatory developments. However, the rise of the shadow fleet triggers a warning and brings to attention the weaknesses of the current international legal regime. To evade sanctions from the West, Russian oil is now transported by a sizeable shadow fleet, which includes vessels that lack adequate insurance, avoid commercial screenings and tend to engage in unsafe and environmentally problematic ship-to-ship transfers on the high seas, with AIS switched off. These are often substandard vessels.

As demonstrated in this chapter, according to the law of the sea, the primary responsibility for maritime safety and vessel-source pollution lies with the flag States. Port States, on the other hand, have significant jurisdictional powers to prohibit port entry to substandard vessels, although subject to the general principle of non-discrimination. Moreover, they have the right to control and inspect foreign vessels to ensure no substandard shipping is tolerated. However, not all ports show sufficient political will to undertake such inspections, and some ports do not have the capacity or resources to undertake proper inspections. The shadow fleet vessels indeed use those ports – they tend to be heading towards India, China, and other States that are not part of the Sanction Regime. They do, however, use the EU waters mostly for passage purposes, where coastal States have some jurisdictional powers, but these are rather limited and at times unclear in their nature and scope. Whereas the regulatory powers are broad, the enforcement remains subject to significant restrictions due to a strong protection of navigational rights. When a vessel has turned off its AIS, it is difficult to prove a breach of environmental regulations and the threshold for intervention is at times short of clarity. Testing the waters here can be 'tricky' since States are liable for damage or loss caused by prohibited or excessive measures under international law, although the general applicability of the principle of proportionality in the territorial sea is unsettled in international law, yet the obligation not to hamper, deny or impair passage rights persists. At the same time, it must not be forgotten that the coastal State is not obliged to wait for pollution to happen before the coastal State is allowed to take measures of protection. This has never been the purpose of the LOSC.

Whereas the initiatives taken at the IMO may solve part of the problem, they are arguably insufficient. Flag States, apart from being the primarily responsible for adopting and enforcing GAIRS to prevent substandard shipping without being obliged to follow a robust due diligence in the process of ship registration, also wield considerable (although arguably not absolute) discretion in accepting financial security from non-IG members to ensure prompt and effective compensation of victims of pollution. Article 94(1) of the LOSC obliges flag States to *effectively* exercise their jurisdiction and control in *administrative*, technical and social matters over their vessels. Article 235 of the LOSC further underscores the obligation for States to cooperate 'where appropriate' in developing 'criteria and procedures for payment of adequate compensation, such as compulsory insurance or compensation funds', which States have done so by adopting the IMO liability and compensation conventions. However, these conventions do not specify any verification processes to be implemented by the flag State in ensuring financial stability, visibility and reputation of the provider of financial security. It appears that almost 70 percent of the shadow fleet, accounting for roughly 20 percent of the world tanker fleet, lacks reputable P&I cover. Instead, it uses institutions that have neither been tested in international law, nor in their financial strength, nor in their capacity to act promptly if an accident should occur. The IMO has shown efforts in encouraging flag States to accept "Blue Cards" from members of IG P&I Clubs, or other reputable companies, and to revoke certificates of insurance when sanction violations are obvious. However, these encouragements were issued in the form of circulars – with no legally binding effect.

The fact that the flag State retains the primary responsibility to ensure compliance with the IMO liability and compensation conventions should not in and of itself be problematic. In fact, this is where the reputable P&I Clubs (such as IG) have stepped in with their own 'screenings' and inspections, to ensure sufficient standards are met. The problem becomes more acute and pressing as the shadow fleet has grown to such a scale and scope, reputable P&I Clubs retract due to the sanction regime, and flag States lack capacity, financial and administrative resources to undertake inspections and commercial screenings regarding financial security provided to its vessels. This scenario is mostly the case with some flags of convenience – flags that attract shadow fleet vessels, some operated by private entities and some not even members of the IMO, and hence with no genuine interest in regulation of shipping.

The law is therefore in some respects insufficient in providing adequate tools for effectively enforcing the Sanction Regime on shadow fleet, thereby hindering effects to maintain stability in major shipping routes during hybrid warfare. The insufficiencies mainly stem from (i) the lack of a robust due diligence for ship registration, in relation to both fraudulent registrations and inadequate financial screenings of providers of financial security, and (ii) the partial lack of coastal State enforcement jurisdiction over foreign vessels in passage regimes, which, however, is a reflection of a carefully struck balance in the LOSC that should be preserved as such.

What is then the future we want for the oceans we need?[128] The IMO liability and compensation regime has withstood the test of time, and the efforts

128 This question borrows from the idea 'the ocean we need for the future we want', a narrative that explains the reason for the increasing climate change risks and degradation of biodiversity beyond national jurisdiction being firmly on top of the agenda of the global regulators. Between 30 November and 13 December 2023, more than 150 United Nations'

the IMO made in this respect are clearly present. However, the shadow fleet practice demonstrates the lack of efficiency in the contemporary context where shipping is proving to be very vulnerable to security risks. Indeed, some flag States show no political will to adhere to the IG or similar (reputable) liability cover; some States have no adequate capacity to do the necessary verifications in this respect.

There is uncertainty whether the shadow fleet presents a temporary exception in that 'normality' will soon be restored, or if we are facing a more permanent structural shift. The protracted nature of Russia's war, the recurrent undermining of a rules-based order and 'western led order' by Russia and China, and the numerous attempts by emerging economies to make themselves become robust and resilient towards potential future Western sanctions, along with attempts to establish alternative orders and organizations, like BRICS, the Belt and Road Initiative, might point in the direction that smooth re-integration into the established system is probably not so likely. Although the shadow fleet represents a significant share of the shipping industry, perhaps we have not yet crossed the threshold for full disintegration of the current system.

The momentum at the United Nations is rather clear: States are increasingly assuming a protective role in safeguarding the environment against the threats posed by climate change, biodiversity and pollution. The adoption of the international agreement on the conservation and sustainable use of marine biological diversity[129] is perhaps a prime example in this regard. Unfortunately, rather than moving towards sustainable use and management of the oceans, the shadow fleet practice forces us to confront the longstanding, yet now significant, issue of flags of convenience. To prevent the breakdown of existing maritime governance system, the IMO could and should encourage States to adopt a more robust due diligence regime. This regime should provide clear procedural steps to be followed for screening the financial strength of providers offering financial security to vessels carrying oil and dangerous

Member States participated in the COP28 UN Climate Change Conference in Dubai, the United Arab Emirates. The participants concluded, among others, on the necessity to speed up the transition away from fossil fuels. For outcomes of the conference see United Nations Climate Change forum, available at <https://unfccc.int/cop28/outcomes> accessed 16 February 2024.

129 Agreement under the United Nations Convention on the Law of the Sea on the conservation and sustainable use of marine biological diversity beyond national jurisdiction (adopted 19 June 2023, not yet in force) UN Doc A/CONF.232/2023/4 of 19 June 2023.

cargo, probably along the robust procedures for ship registration that would in general terms improve vessels' compliance with IMO safety and environmental standards.[130] In Article 235, the LOSC does oblige States to cooperate 'where appropriate', in developing 'criteria and procedures for payment of adequate compensation, such as compulsory insurance or compensation funds'. The shadow fleet seems to present the 'where appropriate' opportunity for States to take bolder cooperative actions regarding financial security within the IMO liability and compensation regime.

---

130 This is indeed already advocated at the IMO with regard to fraudulent ship registrations and fraudulent registries of ships. See IMO Doc, LEG 111/6 (n 10) para 99.

CHAPTER 9

The Instrumentalization of Migration as a Hybrid Threat against the EU: Can Human Rights Become 'Hybrid' Too?

Sofia Galani

Introduction

'Let's call it what it is: [the instrumentalization of migrants] is a hybrid attack to destabilise Europe'.[1] With this phrase, in her 2021 State of the Union address, the President of the European Commission, Ursula von der Leyen, openly expressed the view that the 'weaponization' of migrants by neighboring States is considered a hybrid threat by the European Union (hereinafter EU) and is treated as such. The statement came in response to the pressure the EU experienced at its borders caused by the President of Belarus, Alexander Lukashenko, who intentionally directed thousands of migrants to illegally cross into the EU via Belarus, in retaliation for the EU sanctions imposed on Belarus, following the 2020 fraudulent presidential elections and brutal crackdowns on human rights and the rule of law.[2] The EU Member States responded to this threat by border closures and pushbacks, forcing thousands of migrants to remain in limbo.[3] This is not the first time a State neighboring the EU instrumentalizes

1 2021 State of the Union Address by President von der Leyen (15 September 2021), available at <https://ec.europa.eu/commission/presscorner/detail/en/SPEECH_21_4701> accessed 20 November 2023.

2 Joint Communication to the European Parliament, the Council, the European Economic and Social Committee and the Committee of the Regions, Responding to state-sponsored instrumentalisation of migrants at the EU external border, JOIN(2021) 32 final, 23 November 2021 1–2, available at <https://eur-lex.europa.eu/legal-content/EN/ALL/?uri=JOIN%3A2021%3A32%3AFIN> accessed 21 November 2023; Paul Dallison, 'Lukashenko on Migrants: "They're Not Coming to My Country, They're Going to Yours' *Politico* (19 November 2021), available at <https://www.politico.eu/article/alexander-lukashenko-migrants-belarus-poland-border/> accessed 21 November 2023; Piotr Lubinski, 'Hybrid Warfare or Hybrid Threat – The Weaponization of Migration as an Example of the Use of Lawfare – Case Study of Poland' (2022) 51 Polish Political Science Yearbook, 43.

3 Poland, for example, has been found in breach of its human rights obligations under the European Convention on Human Rights for the treatment of migrants in its borders with Belarus in several cases. See *D.A. and Others v Poland* (App. no. 51246/17), judgment of 22 November

 | DOI:10.1163/9789004707993_011

migrants against the EU.[4] States, such as Greece and Spain, have had similar experiences and are now considering the instrumentalization of migration a threat to their territorial and political integrity, responding to it with harsh anti-migration policies that raise serious human rights questions.[5]

But, what is a 'hybrid threat'?[6] The EU has not adopted a fixed definition of 'hybrid threats' and finds a flexible definition more suitable for adapting to their evolving nature.[7] It considers, however, that hybrid threats share some common characteristics that include: their aim 'to capture the mixture of coercive and subversive activity, conventional and unconventional methods (i.e. diplomatic, military, economic, technological), which can be used in a coordinated manner by state or non-state actors to achieve specific objectives while remaining below the threshold of formally declared warfare'; their 'emphasis on exploiting the vulnerabilities of the target and on generating ambiguity to hinder decision-making processes'; and their vehicles 'to control the political narrative or to radicalize, recruit and direct proxy actors' are

---

2021; *M.K. and Others v Poland* (App. nos. 40503/17, 42902/17 and 43643/17), judgment of 23 July 2020 and the interim measures in *R.A. and Others v Poland* (App. no. 42120/21), 28 September 2021.

4 For the instrumentalization of migration in general, see Kelly M Greenhill, *Weapons of Mass Migration: Forced Displacement, Coercion, and Foreign Policy* (Cornell University Press 2010). See also Kelly Mitchell, 'Migration-Based Hybrid Warfare on Europe's Externalized Borders: Case Studies on Morocco and Belarus in 2021' Yale University (29 April 2022), available at <https://politicalscience.yale.edu/sites/default/files/keiran_mitchell.pdf > accessed 21 November 2023; Julia Himmrich, 'A "Hybrid Threat"? European Militaries and Migration' Dahrendorf Forum (2 March 2018) 12–14, available at <https://www.dahrendorf-forum.eu/publications/europe_military_migration/> accessed 21 November 2023; Nina Miholjcic, 'Migration as an Instrument of Modern Political Warfare: Cases of Turkey, Morocco and Belarus' Jean Monnet Network on EU Law Enforcement Working Paper Series No. 11/22, available at <https://jmn-eulen.nl/wp-content/uploads/sites/575/2022/05/WP-Series-No.-12-22-Migration-as-an-Instrument-of-Modern-Political-Warfare-Cases-of-Turkey-Morocco-and-Belarus-Miholjcic.pdf> accessed 21 November 2023; Ioannis P Sotiropoulos, 'The Mass Migration as a Hybrid Threat to European Security' Policy Paper Series (June 2020), available at <https://cceia.unic.ac.cy/wp-content/uploads/Policy-Paper_5-2020.pdf> accessed 21 November 2023; Yurii Punda, Vitalii Shevchuk and Viljar Veebel, 'Is the European Migrant Crisis Another Stage of Hybrid War?' (2019) 13 Estonian Journal of Military Studies 116; Viljar Veebel, 'Is the European Migration Crisis Caused by Russian Hybrid Warfare?' (2020) 13 Journal of Politics and Law 44.

5 Mariana Gkliati, 'Let's Call It What It Is: Hybrid Threats and Instrumentalisation as the Evolution of Securitisation in Migration Management' (2023) 8(1) European Papers 561, 565–570. See also the discussion in Section 1.

6 For a detailed discussion on the meaning of hybrid warfare, see Chapter 1 of this volume.

7 Joint Framework on Countering Hybrid Threats – A European Union Response, JOIN(2016) 18 final, 6 April 2016, 2, available at <https://eur-lex.europa.eu/legal-content/EN/TXT/?uri=CELEX%3A52016JC0018> accessed 21 November 2023.

massive disinformation campaigns and social media.[8] According to the EU, the state-sponsored instrumentalization of people for political ends meets these criteria and is now considered '[a] particularly cruel form of hybrid threat' that '[has] the intention of destabilising or undermining society and key institutions, and [has] the effect of putting citizens at risk'.[9]

Despite the seemingly clear stance of the EU on the matter, it is imperative to evaluate how a primarily humanitarian issue – migration – has transformed into a hybrid threat and what this approach entails for the protection of the human rights of migrants. Bearing in mind that sea crossings are more challenging for the EU to control and more dangerous for migrants to survive, this paper will focus on seaborn migration, but some of the findings are of relevance to the instrumentalization of migrants and their human rights on land too.[10] Section 1 will provide a background into instances in which the EU has been threatened or flooded with large numbers of migrants entering the EU on board boats. Then, it will examine why migration, and in particular seaborn migration, is perceived as a 'threat' by the EU as well as its hybrid nature. The analysis will show that although some EU Member States equate mass migration to a threat to their sovereignty and territorial integrity, the threshold of conventional war is not reached. This means that the instrumentalization of migration generates a 'grey zone', blurring the rules applicable to the EU responses.[11] While the EU Member States have never responded with a full-scale attack against the States that direct migrants to illegally cross into their territory, they have increasingly militarized their responses to migration, ignoring their impact on the human rights of migrants. Over the last years, we have witnessed a shift from search and rescue (hereinafter SAR) operations in the Mediterranean Sea to maritime law enforcement, increased border surveillance and externalization of border controls, all aimed at deterring migrants from reaching Europe at a significant human cost.[12] The narrative of the

8 Ibid.

9 JOIN(2021) 32 final (n 2) 1.

10 In this paper, the term 'migration' will be used to refer to mixed migration flows that include migrants, refugees and asylum-seekers.

11 For the ability of hybrid warfare to generate 'grey zones', see Frank G Hoffman, '"Hybrid Threats": Neither Omnipotent Nor Unbeatable' (2010) 54 (3) *Orbis* 441, 441–455; Aurel Sari, 'Legal Resilience in an Era of Gray Zone Conflicts and Hybrid Threats' ECIL Working Paper 2019/1, available at <https://law.exeter.ac.uk/media/universityofexeter/collegeofsocialsciencesandinternationalstudies/lawimages/research/Sari_-_Legal_Resilience_ECIL_WP_2019-1.pdf> accessed 21 November 2023.

12 Mariagiulia Giuffre and Violeta Moreno-Lax, 'The Rise of Consensual Containment: From Contactless Control to Contactless Responsibility for Migratory Flows', in Sing J Sativinder (ed.), *Research Handbook on International Refugee Law* (Elgar 2019); Daniel Ghezelbash,

instrumentalization of migration as a hybrid threat has created 'a sense that human rights too can become "hybrid" and therefore suspended under these supposedly exceptional "hybrid" circumstances'.[13]

Against this backdrop, this paper will argue that, regardless of whether migration is treated as a hybrid threat, States remain bound by their human rights obligations towards migrants. The 'grey zone' generated by hybrid threats concerns the applicable rules to the responses of States, i.e. whether the law of armed conflict applies or not, rather than the application of human rights (which would continue to apply even in armed conflict).[14] This means that no exceptions or derogation rules arise out of this 'grey zone' that would permit States to deviate from their human rights obligations under international law. Section 2 will reinforce this point by explaining that maritime law enforcement comes with strict human rights safeguards that cannot be sidelined even if mass migration is considered a hybrid threat. In addition to the human rights obligations EU Member States have at sea, the EU should find the right means to protect migrants from being 'weaponized' once on land. As such, Section 3 will turn to explain that building the EU's legal resilience will remain problematic unless the protection of the human rights of migrants is incorporated into the measures adopted against the instrumentalization of migrants.

1 The Instrumentalization of Migration against the EU

In the last decades, the EU has been swamped, or threatened to be swamped, with large flows of migrants on several occasions that 'points to a developing trend in the tactics of Europe's peripheral authoritarian states'.[15] To counter

---

Violeta Moreno-Lax, Natalie Klein, and Brian Opeskin, 'Securitization of Search and Rescue at Sea: The Response to Boat Migration in the Mediterranean and Offshore Australia' (2018) 67 (2) International and Comparative Law Quarterly 315, 315–351; Peter Roberts, 'The Militarisation of Migration: From Triton to Sofia: Assessing the Credibility of the EU's Naval Interventions Against Migrant Smuggling in the Mediterranean', in Tuesday Reitano *et al.* (eds.), *Militarised Responses to Transnational Organised Crime* (Palgrave Macmillan 2018).

13 Daria Krivonos, '"Hybrid" Human Rights? How Speaking of "Hybrid Warfare" Masks the Violence of EU borders beyond Belarus' Raster.Fi (21 November 2021), available at <https://raster.fi/2021/11/24/hybrid-human-rights-how-speaking-of-hybrid-warfare-masks-the-violence-of-eu-borders-beyond-belarus/> accessed 21 November 2023.

14 Gerd Oberleitner, *Human Rights in Armed Conflict – Law, Practice, Policy* (Cambridge University Press 2015) 52–190; Noam Lubell, 'Challenges in Applying Human Rights Law to Armed Conflict' (2015) 87 International Review of the Red Cross 737–754.

15 Mitchell (n 4) 17.

these threats, the EU and its Member States have adopted measures that raise major questions about their compatibility with human rights.[16] While this paper is not aimed at evaluating the EU's migration policies, a brief discussion of how authoritarian States have instrumentalized mass migration and how the EU Member States responded to this tactic is needed to pave the way for elaborating on why migration is now perceived as a hybrid threat by the EU and, in turn, how this has affected the human rights of migrants.

To begin with, in 2010, Gaddafi threatened that Europe 'could turn into Africa' as millions of Africans were awaiting in Libya to reach Europe.[17] To stop 'Europe's invasion' by African migrants, he pushed for a EUR 5 billion cash deal.[18] Following Gaddafi's overthrow, the situation became only worse as Libya descended into a near-failed State unable to control its borders.[19] To control the large numbers of migrants leaving Libya for Italy and Malta, both States entered into bilateral memorandums with Libya agreeing to provide training and capacity building (through EU funds) to the Libyan Coast Guard.[20] In practice, this support is aimed at enabling the Libyan Coast Guard to interdict migrant boats and return them to Libya.[21] The treatment of migrants, however, both during the interception operations and upon their return to Libya have alarmed the international community as there is growing evidence of not only severe human rights violations but also of crimes against humanity.[22]

---

16 See, for example, n 12.

17 Anonymous, 'Gaddafi Wants EU Cash to Stop African Migrants' BBC (31 August 2010), available at <https://www.bbc.com/news/world-europe-11139345> accessed 21 November 2023.

18 Ian Traynor, 'EU Keen to Strike Deal with Muammar Gaddafi on Immigration' The Guardian (1 September 2010), available at <https://www.theguardian.com/world/2010/sep/01/eu-muammar-gaddafi-immigration> accessed 21 November 2023.

19 Sofia Galani, 'Tensions and Cooperation in Realizing Maritime Security in the Mediterranean Sea: The Examples of Maritime Terrorism and Irregular Migration' (2021) 31 Italian Yearbook of International Law 91, 96.

20 The two memoranda are available at <https://eumigrationlawblog.eu/wp-content/uploads/2017/10/MEMORANDUM_translation_finalversion.doc.pdf> and at <https://www.statewatch.org/media/documents/news/2020/jun/malta-libya-mou-immigration.pdf> accessed 21 November 2023.

21 Marina Mancini, 'Italy's New Migration Control Policy: Stemming the Flow of Migrants from Libya Without Regard for Their Human Rights' (2018) 27 Italian Yearbook of International Law 259, 260–268.

22 OHCHR, '"Detained and Dehumanised": Report on Human Rights Abuses against Migrants in Libya' (13 December 2016), available at <https://www.ohchr.org/sites/default/files/Documents/Countries/LY/DetainedAndDehumanised_en.pdf> accessed 21 November 2023; OHCHR, 'Lethal Disregard: Search and Rescue and the Protection of Migrants in the Central Mediterranean Sea' (May 2021), available at <https://www.ohchr.org/sites

In a similar vein, in 2016, Erdogan threatened to 'open the gates' to thousands of migrants who wanted to reach the EU via Turkey.[23] Earlier that year, Turkey had pushed the EU for a bilateral agreement by which it committed to preventing migrants from crossing into Europe as well as to receiving back those who had crossed illegally into Greece in return for EUR 6 billion in aid, visa-free travel for Turkish nationals and accelerated EU membership talks.[24] Three years later, Erdogan again threatened to flood Europe with migrants. Shortly after his statement, thousands of migrants tried to cross the Evros border to enter Greece.[25] In an unprecedent move, Greece suspended the reception of asylum applications, a move that lacked a legal basis both under EU and international law, forcing hundreds of migrants to remain stuck in the border in dire conditions.[26] The Evros border crisis was followed by numerous migrant incidents in the Aegean Sea that led to the launch of Rapid Border Intervention by Frontex.[27] The instrumentalization of migration has remained high on Turkey's agenda as it serves managing the EU's criticism of its foreign policy and ongoing derogation from the rule of law.[28] Inevitably, Greece keeps being confronted with large flows of migrants to which it often responds with

/default/files/Documents/Issues/Migration/OHCHR-thematic-report-SAR-protection-at-sea.pdf> accessed 21 November 2023; Report of the Independent Fact-Finding Mission on Libya (A/HRC/52/83) (3 March 2023).

23 Safak Timur and Rod Nordland, 'Erdogan Threatens to Let Migrant Flood into Europe Resume' The New York Times (25 November 2016), available at <https://www.nytimes.com/2016/11/25/world/europe/turkey-recep-tayyip-erdogan-migrants-european-union.html> accessed 21 November 2023.

24 EU-Turkey Statement, 18 March 2016, available at <https://www.consilium.europa.eu/en/press/press-releases/2016/03/18/eu-turkey-statement/> accessed 21 November 2023.

25 Bethan McKernan and Daniel Boffey, 'Greece and Bulgaria Crack Down on Turkish Borders as Refugees Arrive' The Guardian (28 February 2020), available at <https://www.theguardian.com/world/2020/feb/28/tensions-rise-between-turkey-and-russia-after-killing-of-troops-in-syria> accessed 21 November 2023.

26 UNHCR statement on the situation at the Turkey-EU border (2 March 2020), available at <https://www.unhcr.org/news/press/2020/3/5e5d08ad4/unhcr-statement-situation-turkey-eu-border.html> accessed 4 April 2023.

27 'Frontex to Launch Rapid Border Intervention at Greece's External Borders', available at <https://www.frontex.europa.eu/media-centre/news/news-release/frontex-to-launch-rapid-border-intervention-at-greece-s-external-borders-NL8HaC> accessed 20 November 2023. See also the pending complaint of *Hamoudi v Frontex* (Case T-136/22) before the Court of Justice of the EU that concerns, among others, the incompatibility of Rapid Border Intervention with human rights.

28 Miholjcic (n 4) 3–5; Key findings of the 2022 Report on Turkey, 12 October 2022, available at <https://ec.europa.eu/commission/presscorner/detail/en/country_22_6088> accessed 4 April 2023.

questionable practices.[29] Greece considers that the instrumentalization of migrants has 'escalated the phenomenon to a hybrid nature threat, directly affecting the EU internal stability [and] climaxed the situation to the dimension of an offence against Greece's national security, which necessitate[s] to be counter-addressed as such'.[30]

Morocco has also instrumentalized migration against Spain. In 2021, at least 6,000 migrants crossed from Morocco into Ceuta, a Spanish enclave, with the encouragement of Moroccan border guards.[31] The following days scenes of chaos and violence between the Spanish forces and migrants emerged.[32] It was reported that Morocco provoked the incident as a reaction to Spain's decision to offer Covid-19 treatment to Brahim Ghali, a Sahrawi politician and key figure in the struggle of the Sahrawi people for self-determination.[33] To contain the uncontrolled numbers of migrants reaching Spain, the latter was forced into negotiations with Morocco that concluded with the Spanish recognition of Morocco's plan for autonomy for Western Sahara.[34] The move signaled Spain's departure from its long-standing official position of neutrality on the matter.[35] This has not been the sole incident in which large numbers of migrants sought to cross illegally into the Spanish enclaves, Ceuta and Melilla, which Spain perceives as 'attacks on its territory'.[36] In 2022, upon Spain's proposal, the NATO

29 *Safi and Others v Greece* (App. No. 5418/15), judgment of 7 July 2022; Niamh Keady-Tabbal and Itamar Mann, 'Weaponizing Rescue: Law and the Materiality of Migration Management in the Aegean' (2023) 36 (1) Leiden Journal of International Law 61–82.

30 Letter from Ioannis Plakiotakis (Hellenic Republic Ministry of Maritime Affairs and Insular Policy) to Fabrice Leggeri (Frontex Executive Director) Ref: ORD/FDU/TUHO/3115/2020, available at <https://www.statewatch.org/media/1941/greece-2.pdf> accessed 21 November 2023.

31 Ashifa Kassam, 'Spain Accuses Morocco of "Show of Disrespect" for EU in Migrant Row' The Guardian (19 May 2021), available at <https://www.theguardian.com/world/2021/may/19/spain-accused-of-summary-deportations-as-thousands-sent-back-to-morocco> accessed 21 November 2023.

32 Ibid.

33 Anonymous, 'Western Sahara Leader's Treatment in Spain Angers Morocco' Reuters (18 May 2021), available at <https://www.reuters.com/world/western-sahara-leaders-treatment-spain-angers-morocco-2021-05-18/> accessed 21 November 2023; Miholjcic (n 4) 6.

34 Mitchell (n 4) 19.

35 Ibid. See also Anonymous, 'Western Sahara: Why Spain is now Endorsing the Moroccan Autonomy Plan' Modern Diplomacy (24 March 2022), available at <https://moderndiplomacy.eu/2022/03/24/western-sahara-why-spain-is-now-endorsing-the-moroccan-autonomy-plan/> accessed 21 November 2023.

36 Anonymous, 'Spain Calls Deadly Migrant Rush An "Attack" on Its Territory' France 24 (25 June 2022), available at <https://www.france24.com/en/africa/20220625-18-migrants

underlined in its Strategic Concept the impact of migration, as a hybrid threat, on human and state security, underscoring the decisiveness of the Spain to treat irregular migration as such.[37]

Russia has not openly threatened the EU with flows of migrants. The study of Russia's interventions in Syria shows that following its involvement in the conflict, large numbers of refugees left Syria.[38] However, no direct causal link can be established between Russia's intervention in Syria and the large waves of refugees, as there were more factors that forced Syrians to leave their homes.[39] Similarly, while it was inevitable that Russia's invasion in Ukraine would cause large flows of refugees, Russia's agenda in Ukraine was greater than just inundating the EU with refugees.[40] Still, Russia has systematically exploited the large numbers of Syrian and Ukrainian refugees by launching disinformation campaigns.[41] These include fake news, fabrication of criminal statistics with a view to presenting migrants as the main culprits, and the spread of misleading content about the failures of European governments to tackle irregular migration.[42] Pro-Kremlin disinformation campaigns against migrants vilify them and exacerbate hate crimes, discrimination, islamophobia

-die-in-mass-attempt-to-enter-spain-s-enclave-melilla-in-marocco> accessed 21 November 2023.

37 Belén Carreño, 'Spain Wants NATO to Flag Migration as "Hybrid Threat" in Policy Roadmap, Says Foreign Minister" Reuters (8 June 2022), available at <https://www.reuters.com/world/europe/spain-wants-nato-flag-migration-hybrid-threat-policy-roadmap-says-foreign-2022-06-08/> accessed 21 November 2023; NATO Strategic Concept, adopted by the Heads of State and Government at the NATO Summit in Madrid, 29 June 2022, 3, available at <https://www.nato.int/nato_static_fl2014/assets/pdf/2022/6/pdf/290622-strategic-concept.pdf> accessed 21 November 2023.

38 Punda, Shevchuk and Veebel (n 4) 123–126; Veebel (n 4) 48–49.

39 Ibid.

40 Punda *et al.*, ibid, 126–129; Veebel, ibid, 49–50.

41 W Lance Bennett and Steven Livingston, 'The Disinformation Order: Disruptive Communication and the Decline of Democratic Institutions' (2018) 33(2) European Journal of Communication 122–139; Antonios Nestoras, 'How the Kremlin is Manipulating the Refugee Crisis: Russian Disinformation as a Threat to European Security' Institute of European Democrats Research Paper (January 2019), available at <https://www.iedonline.eu/download/2019/IED-Research-Paper-Russia-as-a-security-provider_January2019.pdf> accessed 21 November 2023.

42 Christopher S Chivvis, 'Understanding Russian 'Hybrid Warfare' and What Can Be Done about It', Testimony presented before the House Armed Services Committee on March 22, 2017, 2, available at <https://www.rand.org/pubs/testimonies/CT468.html> accessed 15 November 2023; Attila Juhasz and Patrik Szicherle, 'The Political Effects of Migration-Related Fake News, Disinformation and Conspiracy Theories in Europe', Friedrich Ebert Stifüng (2017) 9–22, available at <https://politicalcapital.hu/pc-admin/source/documents/FES_PC_FakeNewsMigrationStudy_EN_20170607.pdf> accessed 21 November 2023.

and social exclusion, while also causing significant political turbulence and instability within the EU.[43]

1.1 *Why Does the EU Perceive Mass Migration as a Threat?*

The securitization of migration is not a new phenomenon.[44] The rise of migration as a security issue is linked with the end of Cold War.[45] Nonetheless, it was the excessively high numbers of migrants trying to reach the EU over the past few years that embedded migration as a security issue in European politics, institutional practices, and the population's conscience. Large migrant flows are believed to infringe upon a State's sovereignty, territorial integrity, national security, economic and social stability.[46] Mass migration is considered responsible for altering the homogeneity of population and weakening the national tradition and cultural identity of a nation.[47] It is also believed to create political and financial difficulties for welfare States that may no longer be in a position to deliver their socio-economic policies in the same way as before the influx of migrants.[48] Economic instability along with a rise in poverty, additional pressure on public services, unemployment and a rise in racist or xenophobic sentiments result in 'reifying migration as a force which endangers the good life in west European societies'.[49] The economic and social upheaval caused by mass migration, inevitably, influences politics and decision-making. There have been several occasions that election results were influenced by the impact of mass migration, mostly by benefiting far right candidates.[50] Angela Merkel's losses, for example, in the regional elections of

43 Judit Szakacs and Eva Bognar, 'The Impact of Disinformation Campaigns about Migrants and Minority Groups in the EU' European Parliament (2021) 21–26, available at <https://www.europarl.europa.eu/RegData/etudes/IDAN/2021/653641/EXPO_IDA(2021)653641_EN.pdf> accessed 21 November 2023.

44 Ole Waever, Barry Buzan, Morten Kelstrup and Pierre Lemaitre, *Identity, Migration and the New Security Agenda in Europe* (Pinter 1993); Ole Waever, 'European Security Identities' (1996) 34(1) Journal of Common Market Studies 103–132.

45 Jef Huysmans and Vicki Squire, 'Migration and Security', in Myriam D Cavelty and Thierry Balzacq (eds.), *Handbook of Security Studies* (Routledge 2009) 1.

46 Mitchell (n 4) 1.

47 Jef Huysmans, 'The European Union and the Securitization of Migration' (2000) 38(5) Journal of Common Market Studies 751, 757–758.

48 Ibid, 767–770.

49 Ibid, 752.

50 Anthony Edo *et al.*, 'Immigration and electoral support for the far-left and the far-right' (2019) European Economic Review 99; Chrysovalantis Vasilakis, 'Massive Migration and Elections: Evidence from the Refugee Crisis in Greece' (2018) 56(3) International Migration 28.

2016 were mainly attributed to her pro-Syrian migration stance,[51] while the Brexit vote result was linked with the migration crisis in Europe.[52]

Besides, irregular migration is considered a threat because it is associated with other illegal activities, such as smuggling of migrants, human trafficking, and terrorism. Migrant smuggling affects the sovereignty of States as it violates the entry requirements of a State.[53] The violation of border security in combination with the involvement of criminal organized groups in these activities results in conflating irregular migration with transnational crimes.[54] As a result, States tend to focus on the criminal nature of these activities, dismissing the rights of those smuggled, such as the right to asylum.[55] This appears to be a standard approach of the EU that, in its security documents, places more emphasis on the criminal nature of these activities than on the risks faced by victims.[56]

In addition, a rise in terrorist attacks in Europe has been associated with irregular migration as the EU Member States have struggled to do background checks on each person entering their country.[57] The border controls and checks as well as the building of fences across land borders have enabled the EU Member States to control the numbers of illegal entries. The situation, however, seems uncontrollable at sea, where borders exist only on nautical charts. The figures demonstrate the large scale of the problem. At the beginning of 2023,

51 Kate Conolly, 'Angela Merkel Defends Immigration Policy after Election Blow' The Guardian (7 September 2016), available at <https://www.theguardian.com/world/2016/sep/07/angela-merkel-defends-german-immigration-policy-elections-afd> accessed 21 November 2023.

52 William Outhwaite, 'Migration Crisis and "Brexit"', in Cecilia Menjivar *et al.* (eds.) *The Oxford Handbook of Migration Crises* (Oxford University Press 2019) 93; Paul Taggart and Aleks Szczerbiak, 'Putting Brexit into Perspective: The Effect of the Eurozone and Migration Crises and Brexit on Euroscepticism in European States' (2018) 25(8) Journal of European Public Policy 1194.

53 UNODC, Global Study on Smuggling of Migrants 2018, available at <https://www.unodc.org/documents/data-and-analysis/glosom/GLOSOM_2018_web_small.pdf> accessed 21 November 2023.

54 Ibid; Europol Support to Fight Migrant Smuggling: A Valued Partner but Insufficient of Data Resources and Result Management (2021), available at <https://www.eca.europa.eu/Lists/ECADocuments/SR21_19/SR_migrant_smuggling_EN.pdf> accessed 21 November 2023.

55 Himmrich (n 4) 12–14.

56 JOIN(2021) 32 final (n 2) JOIN(2016) 18 final (n 7) 14.

57 Marc Helbling and Daniel Meierrieks, 'Terrorism and Migration: An Overview' (2022) 52(2) British Journal of Political Science 977; Enzo Nussio, Vincenzo Bove and Bridget Steele, 'The Consequences of Terrorism on Migration Attitudes across Europe' (2019) 75 Political Geography 102047.

for example, the International Organization for Migration (hereinafter IOM) recorded 21,407 arrivals of migrants in Europe of whom only 1,300 arrived by land compared to 21,107 who arrived by sea.[58] Although there has not been sufficient data to connect the dots between the smuggling of migrants, the transfer of terrorists and the terrorists attacks on European soil,[59] the large flows of migrants have inevitably alarmed European States, especially following the fall of the Islamic State and the return of Foreign Terrorist Fighters to Europe.[60]

1.2 *Why Does the EU Perceive Mass Migration as a Hybrid Threat?*

Despite the impact of mass migration on the sovereignty of host States, it cannot be considered a conventional military threat that would justify the employment of traditional military means in response. In contrast, the manipulation of large migration flows as a threat against the EU matches the characteristics of hybrid threats namely that (a) they are a mixture of coercive and subversive activity, conventional and unconventional methods (i.e. diplomatic, military, economic, technological, information) (b) they are used in a coordinated manner by state or non-state actors (c) they remain below the threshold of open organized hostilities (d) they seek to exploit the vulnerabilities of a target by generating ambiguity with the intention to hinder decision-making processes.[61]

Let us now lay out how mass migration fits within these criteria. Encouraging or facilitating large flows of migrants to gather near the borders of an EU Member State or illegally cross into its territory requires no military action. In the instances described above, the sending States did not even employ violent means. It is usually between the host States and migrants that violence erupts, destabilizing public order. Furthermore, although the sending States are involved in directing the flows of migrants, they are not directly involved in their smuggling. The smuggling of migrants remains a primarily non-state actors' business.[62] This is particularly the case in the Mediterranean Sea where migrants cannot cross into the EU on their own means and rely on criminal organized groups to transfer them to Europe. In this case, the large flows of migrants can hardly be attributed to a State, creating ambiguity

58 IOM Europe (6 March 2023), available at <https://dtm.iom.int/europe/arrivals> accessed 21 November 2023.

59 Europol and INTERPOL, Migrant Smuggling Networks, Joint Europol-INTERPOL Report (May 2016), 12, available at <https://www.europol.europa.eu/cms/sites/default/files/documents/ep-ip_report_executive_summary.pdf> accessed 21 November 2023.

60 Galani (n 19) 102–103.

61 JOIN(2016) 18 final (n 7) 2.

62 UNODC (n 53) 67–104. See also, Hybrid CoE, 'Hybrid Threats as a Concept', available at <https://www.hybridcoe.fi/hybrid-threats-as-a-phenomenon/> accessed 4 April 2023.

as to who is responsible for their smuggling. The instrumentalization of mass migration is also aimed at unconventional and vulnerable targets. In the case of the EU, it has been used to influence its politics, policies and decision-making without overt confrontation, while the EU's vulnerability lies in the lack of a common and coherent migration policy and its inability to effectively regulate its cyberspace.[63] The lack of a common migration policy has become the target of disinformation campaigns that promote anti-immigration and far right sentiments, manipulating the public to demand the cessation of free movement within the EU, one of its underlying values.[64]

Overall, it becomes evident that while mass migration causes significant challenges for the EU Member States, the threat of mass migration does not reach the threshold of a conventional armed attack, and this explains why the EU considers that the instrumentalization of migration is employed by authoritarian regimes to undermine the EU's shared democratic values and polarize societies for their own purposes.[65]

2 The Instrumentalization of Migration and Human Rights at Sea

It is worth noting upfront that the protection of human rights at sea is not an easy issue to address. While it is now broadly accepted that human rights apply at sea as they do on land,[66] the obligations of States and the exercise of jurisdiction at sea are determined both by the international law of the sea and human rights law, not always without frictions between the two of them.[67] Petrig has aptly pointed out that 'not only has the law of the sea been in large part human rights blind, but human rights law has until very recently suffered from serious

63 Himmrich (n 4) 20–21; Kelly Greenhill, 'Migration as a Weapon in Theory and in Practice' (2016) Military Review 23, 26; Nicolas Mazzucchi, 'AI-Based Technologies in Hybrid Conflict: The Future of Influence Operations' Hybrid CoE Paper 14 (June 2022), available at <https://www.hybridcoe.fi/wp-content/uploads/2022/06/20220623-Hybrid-CoE-Paper-14-AI-based-technologies-WEB.pdf> accessed 21 November 2023.

64 Juhasz and Szicherle (n 42) 8.

65 EU External Action, Countering Hybrid Threats (31 March 2022), available at <https://www.eeas.europa.eu/eeas/countering-hybrid-threats_en> accessed 4 April 2023.

66 Geneva Declaration on Human Rights at Sea (2022) 4, available at <https://www.humanrightsatsea.org/sites/default/files/media-files/2022-02/GDHRAS_Jan_2022_Final_online_version_sp%20%281%29.pdf> accessed 21 November 2023.

67 Irini Papanicolopulu, *International Law and the Protection of People at Sea* (Oxford University Press 2018); Natalie Klein, 'Geneva Declaration on Human Rights at Sea: An Endeavor to Connect Law of the Sea and International Human Rights Law' (2022) 53(2–3) Ocean Development & International Law 1.

sea blindness'.[68] This means that the law of the sea was not developed in a way that could accommodate the needs of persons at sea, while human rights treaties were designed with a land context in mind, letting the application of human rights at sea fall through the cracks. Despite these challenges, there have been significant efforts to push the recognition and protection of human rights at sea forward, and the narrative of seaborn migration as a hybrid threat should not be employed to counter these developments or open up for exceptions to the application of human rights at sea.[69]

2.1 *The Application of Human Rights at Sea*

As noted, the maxim that human rights apply at sea as they do on land is now widely accepted. This does not mean that the application of human rights may not be adjusted to give due consideration to the special nature of the maritime environment. In *Rigopoulos v Spain*, for example, the European Court of Human Rights (hereinafter ECtHR) acknowledged that 'a period of sixteen days was not incompatible with the notion of 'promptness' as required under article 5 (3) of the European Convention on Human Rights (hereinafter ECHR)[70] in view of the 'wholly exceptional circumstances' that were involved therein'.[71] The 'wholly exceptional circumstances' arose from the fact that the transfer of the applicant from the high seas, where he had been arrested, to a Spanish port required a journey longer than it would normally require for an on-land transfer.[72] Nonetheless, in acknowledging the existence of 'wholly exceptional circumstances', the ECtHR did not intend to create any exceptions to the application of human rights at sea. Instead, it aimed to reinforce that States remain bound by their human rights obligations, although in a more nuanced manner that would not put an unbearable burden on them when discharging their obligations at sea. Such circumstances are not established in the context of

68 House of Lords, International Relations and Defence Committee, 'UNCLOS: The Law of the Sea in the 21st Century (1 March 2022) 49, available at <https://committees.parliament.uk/publications/9005/documents/159002/default/> accessed 21 November 2023.

69 Steven Haines, 'Developing Human Rights at Sea' (2021) 35(1) Ocean Yearbook 18; Sofia Galani, 'Port Closures and Persons at Sea in International Law' (2021) 70 International and Comparative Law Quarterly 605; Sofia Galani, 'Assessing Maritime Security and Human Rights: The Role of the EU and its Member States in the Protection of Human Rights in the Maritime Domain' (2020) 35 International Journal of Marine and Coastal Law 325.

70 European Convention for the Protection of Human Rights and Fundamental Freedoms, as amended by Protocols Nos. 11 and 14 (opened for signature 4 November 1950, entered into force 3 September 1953) ETS 5.

71 *Rigopoulos v Spain* (dec.) (App. no. 37388/97), ECHR 1999-II. See also *Medvedyev and Others v France* (App. no. 3394/03), judgment of 29 March 2010, paras 131–134.

72 Ibid.

mass migration, be it treated as a hybrid threat or not, as it is the large number of migrants that pose challenges to States rather than the unique nature of the maritime environment. This does not mean that States have an obligation to rescue every migrant at sea. The obligation to rescue lives at sea remains one of means not of result.[73] What this means is that the narrative of mass migration as a hybrid threat does not establish any 'wholly exceptional circumstances' that would release States from their obligation to take all reasonable measures to protect the human rights of migrants.

This then begs the question of whether the influx of migrants could refine the human rights obligations of States. The ECtHR has answered this question in the negative. While it has acknowledged that the large number of migrants poses challenges to the efforts of European States to manage their borders, it has rejected the possibility that this could justify recourse to practices which are incompatible with the Convention.[74] This reinforces the point that even if the instrumentalization of mass migration is perceived as a hybrid threat, States remain bound by their human rights obligations. On the other hand, the number of migrants crossing illegally into a State's territory has been taken into account to restrict the application of article 4 of Protocol No. 4.[75] This has happened in cases where, according to the ECtHR, migrants deliberately took advantage of their large numbers in order to create a disruptive situation and cross the border of a State illegally instead of accessing the legal points of entry that a State has put in place to manage irregular migration.[76] The migrants' own conduct has thus been considered a ground for a State to deny entry to its territory even to asylum-seekers.[77] It would be extremely difficult, however, for such circumstances to be established at sea where no genuine and effective access to means of legal entry can be put in place, even if one goes as far as

---

73 *Safi and Others v Greece* (n 29) para 157.

74 *Khlaifia and Others v Italy* (App. no. 16483/12), judgment of 15 December 2016, para 241; *N.D. and N.T. v Spain* [GC] (Application nos 8675/15 and 8697/15), judgment of 13 February 2020, paras 169–170.

75 Ibid.

76 *Khlaifia and Others v Italy*, ibid, para 240; *N.D. and N.T. v Spain*, ibid, paras 200–201; *A.A. and Others v North Macedonia* (App. nos. 55798/16 and 4 others), judgment of 5 April 2022, paras 114–115. For a critique of the ECtHR's approach on the matter see Giulia Ciliberto, 'A Brand-New Exclusionary Clause to the Prohibition of Collective Expulsion of Aliens: The Applicant's Own Conduct in N.D. and N.T. v Spain' (2021) 21(1) Human Rights Law Review 203.

77 *A.A. and Others v North*, ibid, para 117.

arguing that migrants become culpable by over-boarding unseaworthy boats which forces States to come to their rescue.[78]

Finally, it should be examined whether derogation rules apply at sea, permitting States to depart from their human rights obligations in the context of mass migration. On the pretext of migration being a hybrid threat, certain EU Member States have declared a state of emergency to legitimize derogations from their fundamental rights obligations.[79] Article 72 of the Treaty on the Functioning of the EU (hereinafter TFEU) allows States to depart from their obligation to implement 'a common policy on asylum, immigration and external border control, based on solidarity between Member States, which is fair towards third-country nationals (article 67 (2) of the TFEU)' if justified by the need to maintain law and order and to safeguard internal security.[80] However, the Court of Justice of the EU (hereinafter CJEU), has ruled that derogations from EU law in the name of public security demand 'a threat to the functioning of institutions and essential public services and the survival of the population, as well as the risk of a serious disturbance to foreign relations or to peaceful coexistence of nations, or a risk to military interests'.[81] Accordingly, the CJEU has found that the exceptional situation of an influx of migrants is not capable on its own of triggering article 72 of the TFEU.[82]

Equally strict has been the ECtHR when it comes to derogations from the ECHR based on Article 15 (1) of the ECHR. The latter provides that '[i]n time of war or other public emergency threatening the life of the nation any High Contracting Party may take measures derogating from its obligations under [the] Convention to the extent strictly required by the exigencies of the situation, provided that such measures are not inconsistent with its other obligations under international law.' A 'public emergency threatening the life of the nation' has been interpreted to refer to 'an exceptional situation of crisis or emergency which affects the whole population and constitutes a threat to the organized life of the community of which the State is composed'.[83] Indeed, as discussed

---

78 Recommendation by the Council of Europe Commissioner for Human Rights, 'Pushed Beyond the Limits Four Areas for Urgent Action to End Human Rights Violations at Europe's Borders' (April 2022), 29, available at <https://www.coe.int/en/web/commissioner/-/pushed-beyond-the-limits-urgent-action-needed-to-stop-push-back-at-europe-s-borders> accessed 21 November 2023.

79 Gkliati (n 5) 565–567.

80 Consolidated version of the TFEU OJ C 326, 26.10.2012, 47–390.

81 CJEU, Case C72/22 PPU, Judgment of 30 June 2022 (First Chamber), EU:C:2022:505, para 88.

82 Ibid, para 92.

83 *Lawless v Ireland (no.3)* (App. no. 332/57), judgment of 1 July 1961, para 28.

earlier, the influx of migrants is understood to affect national security, social stability, and the way of living of Europeans. Nonetheless, in public emergencies that fall within the scope of article 15 of the ECHR, the normal measures and restrictions provided for by the Convention are inadequate to maintain public order and safety.[84] This shows that in spite of the perceived impacts of mass migration on a State's security and stability, one would go too far to argue that the crisis or risks arising from the influx of migrants cannot be managed on the basis of the normal measures and restrictions available to States by the Convention. In practice, several States have triggered article 15 in response to various threats, but not in response to large flows of migrants.[85]

Furthermore, the application of article 15 of the ECHR has never been tested at sea. Article 15 can be triggered when a crisis concerns only part of the territory of a State but still threatens the life of the entire nation.[86] Accordingly, a State could argue that the emergency concerns its territorial waters and derogate from protecting the human rights of the large numbers of migrants crossing illegally into its territorial waters.[87] There are, however, two important restrictions that would make the application of article 15 to the territorial waters of a State with regards to migrants' rights almost impossible. The first concerns the obligation of States not to adopt measures incompatible with their obligations under international law, and States bear significant obligations in the maritime domain under the international law of the sea. With reference to the issue of migrants discussed here, States have a duty to render assistance to any person found at sea in danger of being lost and, individually or in cooperation with

84 *Denmark, Norway, Sweden and the Netherlands v Greece*, Commission Report, 1969, para 153.

85 See, for example, *Ireland v the UK* (App. no. 5310/71), judgment of 18 January 1978, paras 205, 212 (terrorism); *A. and Others v the UK* (App. no. 3455/05), judgment of 19 February 2009, para 181 (terrorism); *Mehmet Hasan Altan v Turkey*, (App. no. 13237/17), judgment of 20 March 2018, paras 91–93 (military coup); *Kavala v Turkey* (App. no. 28749/18), judgment of 11 May 2020, para 88 (military coup). See also a full list of the States that derogated from the ECHR in response to the Covid-19 pandemic, available at <https://www.coe.int/en/web/conventions/derogations-covid-19> accessed 21 November 2023.

86 *Sakik and Others v Turkey* (87/1996/706/898-903), judgment of 26 November 1997, para 39; *Barseghyan v Armenia* (Application no. 17804/09), judgment of 21 September 2021, para 36.

87 According to article 2 of the 1982 United Nations Convention on the Law of the Sea (hereinafter LOSC), 'the sovereignty of a coastal State extends, beyond its land territory and internal waters and, in the case of an archipelagic State, its archipelagic waters, to an adjacent belt of sea, described as the territorial sea' which means that a coastal State can prescribe and enforce human rights standards within its territorial waters. United Nations Convention on the Law of the Sea (opened for signature 10 December 1982, entered into force 16 November 1994) 1833 UNTS 3.

other States, to develop SAR services to ensure that assistance is rendered to any person in distress at sea.[88] States would therefore not be allowed to adopt measures that restrict the application of the ECHR while being inconsistent with their obligations under the international law of the sea. The second restriction arises from article 15 (2) that provides that no derogation can be made in respect of article 2, except in respect of deaths resulting from lawful acts of war, and articles 3, 4 (1) and 7. In the context of seaborn migration, the right to life and the freedom from torture or inhuman or degrading treatment are arguably the most affected rights.[89] As a result, States cannot lawfully derogate from the protection of these rights even on the ground of the crisis or emergency caused by the instrumentalization of mass migration. Finally, it should be stressed that there are no bespoke rules in international law of the sea that provide for circumstances that would justify limiting the application of human rights at sea.[90]

2.2 *Human Rights Jurisdiction at Sea*

Having established that the large flows of migrants arriving to European waters on boats and the challenges they pose to the EU Member States do not constitute grounds for restricting the application of human rights at sea, we ought to understand when States exercise jurisdiction for the purposes of protecting human rights. This is particularly relevant to our discussion, because, as discussed earlier, the EU and its Member States have externalized border controls or shifted the responsibility of rescuing migrants to other States. The narrative of mass migration as a hybrid threat has facilitated this approach as it reinforces the perception that migration is a security issue that needs to be dealt with outside the EU borders.

The issue of jurisdiction is considerably straightforward when migrants are in ports or within the territorial sea of a State. The sovereignty of a coastal State extends to its internal waters and territorial sea and thus States have to uphold human rights.[91] In *Safi and Others v Greece*, where a fishing boat carrying migrants sank within the territorial waters of Greece and near the coasts of the Greek island Farmakonisi, no jurisdiction issue was raised and Greece

88 LOSC, Art 98; International Convention for the Safety of Life At Sea (adopted 1 November 1974, entered into force 25 May 1980) 1184 UNTS 3, Regulation 15; International Convention on Maritime Search and Rescue (adopted 27 April 1979, entered into force 22 June 1985) 1403 UNTS, Chapter 2.

89 Galani (2021) (n 69) 608–612.

90 Geneva Declaration on Human Rights at Sea (n 66) 4.

91 Article 2 of the LOSC.

was found in breach of article 2 for the lack of an effective SAR operation.[92] In *Alhowais v Hungary*, in which a Syrian migrant died while trying to reach Hungary via the Tisza River, Hungary was found in breach of its article 2 obligations for failing to implement an operational SAR plan that could ensure that the life of those trying to cross the border were protected.[93]

Jurisdictional questions become more complex on the high seas where it needs to be assessed whether States exercise extraterritorial human rights jurisdiction. Under article 94 of LOSC, vessels on the high seas are subject to the exclusive jurisdiction of flag States. In line with the principle of exclusive flag State jurisdiction, the ECtHR has stressed that the ECHR applies on board vessels that fly the flag of a Contracting Party.[94] In *Hirsi Jamaa and Others v Italy*, the ECtHR found that the interception of migrants and their transfer onto Italian military ships for the purpose of returning them to Libya brought them within Italy's jurisdiction for the purposes of article 1 of the ECHR.[95] This underpinned the conclusion that Italy had violated articles 3, 4 of Protocol No. 4 and 13 of the ECHR. Previously, the Inter-American Commission on Human Rights had also found that the interception of Haitian migrants on the high seas and their immediate return to Haitian authorities had violated several rights protected under the American Declaration of the Rights and Duties of Man.[96] Equally, in *Hassan and Others v France*, the ECtHR had no difficulty in finding that Somali pirates arrested and detained on a board a frigate were within France's jurisdiction.[97] In such cases, States are considered to exercise *de jure* effective control.

There is also emerging consensus by human rights courts and bodies that States exercise extraterritorial human rights jurisdiction when they exercise *de facto* effective control over persons intercepted or deprived of their liberty at sea. In *Medvedyev v France*, France was found to exercise jurisdiction over the crew of a Cambodian-flagged vessel who had been arrested for drug trafficking offences, although the suspects were not transferred to the French

92 *Safi and Others v Greece* (n 29) paras 129–167.

93 *Alhowais v Hungary* (App. no. 59435/17), judgment of 3 February 2023, paras 135–145.

94 *Banković and Others v Belgium and other 16 Contracting Parties* (dec.) [GC] (Appl. no. 52207/99) ECHR 2001-XII, para 59.

95 *Hirsi Jamaa and Others v Italy* [GC] (App. No. 27765/09), judgment of 23 February 2012.

96 *The Haitian Centre for Human Rights et al. v. United States*, Case 10.675, Report No. 51/96, Inter-Am.C.H.R., OEA/Ser.L/V/II.95 Doc. 7 rev. at 550 (1997); Inter-American Commission on Human Rights, American Declaration of the Rights and Duties of Man, 2 May 1948.

97 *Hassan and Others v France* (App. nos 46695/10 and 54588/10), judgment of 4 December 2014.

warship but remained on board their vessel guarded by French agents.[98] The Committee against Torture has also found that for as long as State agents keep migrants under their control for the purposes of identification or repatriation, they bring them within their jurisdiction and have to respect and protect their human rights, regardless of whether they keep migrants on board a vessel on government service or a private vessel.[99]

European States are fully aware of these obligations, and this is why they have been increasingly avoiding coming into contact with migrants at sea. It seems, however, that as States become more innovative in avoiding their human rights obligations, so does the interpretation of human rights law. The views of the Human Rights Committee in *A.S., D.I., O.I. and G.D. v Italy* clearly point to that direction.[100] The complaint concerned the response, or better put the lack of response, on behalf of Italy to a distress call received by a boat in distress in the Maltese SAR region. Italy informed Malta of the distress call and did not send any help to migrants until Malta requested it to do so and when it was too late. In fact, Italy also ordered an Italian warship, the *ITS Libra*, that was near the shipwreck to move away from it instead of coming to its rescue. The Human Rights Committee found that:[101]

> in the particular circumstances of the case, a special relationship of dependency had been established between the individuals on the vessel in distress and Italy. That relationship comprised factual elements – in particular, the initial contact made by the vessel in distress with the Italian rescue centre, the close proximity of the *ITS Libra* to the vessel in distress and the ongoing involvement of the Italian rescue centre in the rescue operation – and relevant legal obligations incurred by Italy under the international law of the sea [...].

The Committee also underlined that 'the individuals on the vessel in distress were directly affected by the decisions taken by the Italian authorities in a manner that was reasonably foreseeable in the light of the relevant legal obligations of Italy'.[102] Given the lack of direct contact between Italy

98 *Medvedyev and Others v France* (n 71).

99 *J.H.A. v. Spain* (CAT/C/41/D/323/2007) (21 November 2008); *Fatou Sonko v Spain* (CAT/C/47/D/368/2008) (25 November 2011).

100 *A.S., D.I., O.I. and G.D. v Italy* (CCPR/C/130/D/3042/2017) (4 November 2020).

101 Ibid, para 7.8.

102 Ibid.

and the victims, it was not an easy task for the Human Rights Committee to substantiate that the victims came within the jurisdiction of Italy that had clearly disregarded several of its international law obligations. This 'special relationship of dependency' based on the facts combined with the foreseeable consequences of Italy's omissions points to a new direction where States may be found to exercise extraterritorial jurisdiction even when they establish 'contactless' control over the victims.[103] The facts of the complaint as well as the views of the Human Rights Committee, which were met with strong dissent by some of its members and mixed reactions by scholars, accurately demonstrate the battle between the struggle of migrants for survival and the efforts of European States to manage mass migration that takes place almost daily in the Mediterranean Sea.[104] The conclusion is that no matter how challenging European States find managing large numbers of migrants, they are not relieved from their obligation to protect the human rights of migrants. At the time of writing, another significant case is pending before the ECtHR. It concerns the compatibility of a pullback operation, meaning the interception of migrants by the Libyan coastguard, upon information received by the Italian Maritime Rescue Coordination Centre, and their return to Libya where several of them faced serious human rights violations, including being detained in inhumane conditions and tortured.[105] While we cannot be certain whether the ECtHR will follow the direction set by the Human Rights Committee or take a different one, the comments of the Council of Europe Commissioner for Human Rights in her intervention highlight the fact that Italy knew or ought to have

---

103 Mariagiuilia Giuffre, 'A Functional-Impact Model of Jurisdiction: Extraterritoriality before of the European Court of Human Rights' (2021) 82 QIL, Zoom-in 53, 72–77.

104 See, for example, the Joint Opinion of Committee Members Yuval Shany, Christof Heyns and Photini Pazartzis (dissenting). See also Aphrodite Papachristodoulou, 'The Recognition of a Right to be Rescued at Sea in International Law' (2022) 35 Leiden Journal of International Law 337, 354–356; Silvia Dimitrova, 'Rethinking 'Jurisdiction' in International Human Rights Law in Rescue Operations at Sea in the Light of AS and Others v Italy and AS and Others v Malta: A New Right to be Rescued at Sea?' (2023) 56(1) Israel Law Review 120; Malcolm D Evans and Sofia Galani, 'The Views of the Human Rights Committee in A.S., D.I., O.I. and G.D. v Italy and the Right to Life at Sea' University of Bristol Law School Blog (31 May 2021), available at <https://legalresearch.blogs.bris.ac.uk/2021/05/> accessed 21 November 2023.

105 *S.S. and Others v Italy* (App. no. 21660/18) (3 May 2018). See also Violeta Moreno-Lax, 'The Architecture of Functional Jurisdiction: Unpacking Contactless Control – On Public Powers, S.S. and Others v. Italy, and the "Operational Model' (2020) 21(3) German Law Journal 385.

known that migrants returned to Libya are subjected to human rights violations,[106] arguing that the victims were within Italy's jurisdiction even if Italy never established any actual contact with them.

3 Legal Resilience at the EU Level

Hybrid threats, including the instrumentalization of migration, have been high on the agenda of the EU that has developed a counter-hybrid threats policy revolving around four pillars of action: situational awareness, resilience, response and cooperation.[107] The EU's resilience concept refers to its ability 'to prevent, withstand and recover from crises,' originating from hybrid threats as well as its efforts to support the resilience building of its neighbors.[108] Resilience includes building legal resilience which refers to the capacity of EU law and the domestic law of Member States to cope with the harms caused by hybrid threats.[109] According to Sari, building legal resilience in response to hybrid threats requires a strategic approach which contains several strands, such as a better understanding of the legal threat landscape, using law to build societal resilience, boosting legal preparedness and capacity building to develop a coherent approach among the EU, NATO and the Members States.[110] While evaluating the overall strategy of the EU to counter hybrid threats falls outside the scope of this chapter, this section will proceed by discussing how the EU could move forward to best build legal resilience in response to the instrumentalization of migration as a hybrid threat, underlying the importance of incorporating the human rights of migrants in its responses.

To begin with, the EU needs to study more the threats posed by migration and the 'grey zone' the latter generates that, arguably, renders EU law and policies inapplicable or vulnerable. In light of the current developments, it

106 Third party intervention by the Council of Europe Commissioner for Human Rights under Article 36, paragraph 3, of the European Convention on Human Rights, Application No. 21660/18, S.S. *and others v Italy* (CommDH(2019)29) (15 November 2019), 9.

107 Countering Hybrid Threats – Factsheet (March 2022), available at <https://defence-industry-space.ec.europa.eu/system/files/2022-03/Factsheet%20-%20Countering%20Hybrid%20Threats.pdf> accessed 4 April 2023.

108 Ibid.

109 Aurel Sari, 'Hybrid Threats and the Law: Building Legal Resilience' Hybrid CoE Research Report 3 (2021) 31, available at <https://www.hybridcoe.fi/wp-content/uploads/2021/10/20211104_Hybrid_CoE_Research_Report_3_Hybrid_threats_and_the_law_WEB.pdf> accessed 4 April 2023.

110 Ibid, 34–35.

remains unclear why the narrative of mass migration as a hybrid threat has led to the 'hybridization' of human rights. There seems to be no legal justification for the restriction of the application of human rights law which comes in stark contrast to the EU's proposition that its responses to hybrid threats should be guided by the rule of law, the universality and indivisibility of human rights and respect for the principles of the United Nations Charter and international law.[111] By departing from its own values and principles to tackle hybrid threats, the EU undermines the rule of law on its own accord.

Furthermore, the EU's efforts to build cyberspace resilience should acquire a sharp focus on protecting EU citizens from disinformation campaigns and fake news concerning migrants.[112] An EU study has shown that 97 per cent of EU citizens have been exposed to fake news, 38 per cent of whom on a daily basis, demonstrating the large scale of the problem.[113] These include anti-propaganda campaigns launched by Russia aimed at exploiting the sensitivity of irregular migration. The impact of disinformation campaigns targeting migrants is two-fold. On the one hand, it disrupts the unity and effective governance of the EU. This is because a large number of EU citizens can no longer participate in democratic processes with informed decisions but are instead misguided by anti-immigrant and xenophobic sentiments that seek to alter the EU values, such as the freedom of movement.[114] On the other hand, disinformation campaigns further victimize migrants by subjecting them to hate crimes, discrimination, islamophobia and social exclusion.[115] It thus becomes evident that unless the EU adopts adequate measures to effectively regulate cyberspace with a view to tackle anti-immigration propaganda, migration will continue to be used as a hybrid threat against the EU.

Finally, the EU needs to build a resilience bridge with the countries neighboring the Mediterranean Sea, and especially Turkey. It is now well-established that these countries have become key sources of hybrid aggression, as is that

111 Article 21 of the Treaty of the EU (26 October 2012) (C326/13). See also JOIN(2016) 18 final (n 7) 2.

112 Directive (EU) 2016/1148 of the European Parliament and of the Council of 6 July 2016 concerning measures for a high common level of security of network and information systems across the Union [2016] OJ L 194/1; Joint Communication to the European Parliament and the Council, Resilience, Deterrence and Defence: Building strong cybersecurity for the EU (13 September 2017) JOIN(2017) 450 final, available at <https://eur-lex.europa.eu/legal-content/en/ALL/?uri=CELEX%3A52017JC0450> accessed 21 November 2023.

113 Synopsis Report of the Public Consultation on Fake News and Online Disinformation (26 April 2018) 7, available at <https://digital-strategy.ec.europa.eu/en/library/synopsis-report-public-consultation-fake-news-and-online-disinformation> accessed 21 November 2023.

114 Juhasz and Szicherle (n 42) 4.

115 Szakacs and Bognar (n 43) 21–26.

the countries in the Mediterranean region are so interrelated in terms of their maritime security that it becomes almost impossible for the EU to effectively address irregular migration, unless it cooperates with the countries in the region.[116] Turkey will remain a destabilizing actor in the region for as long as it is able to threaten the EU with migrants. The EU-Turkey agreement on migration has only given an advantage to Turkey to, every now and then, blackmail the EU with large flows of migrants while ignoring their human rights. The EU thus needs to consider other legal tools, such as accession talks, to keep Turkey in line. Better cooperation with Turkey may be facilitated through the closer collaboration that has been forged between the EU and NATO on the front of hybrid threats, including irregular migration.[117] NATO has also been witnessing Turkey undermining its values.[118] 'One of NATO's greatest strengths is the fact that membership is based on protecting and honoring the sovereignty and independence of all members',[119] a principle that Turkey has been consistently violating by instrumentalizing migration against other NATO members. The EU and NATO are therefore presented with a challenging, yet unique opportunity to adopt a comprehensive approach that would build a resilience bridge with Turkey and, as a result, counter hybrid threats, such as migration, that originate from its own partners or members, while also preventing it from 'weaponizing' innocent people for political ends.[120]

Conclusion

The instrumentalization of migration has emerged as a major hybrid threat against the EU. This paper demonstrated that authoritarian States have been instrumentalizing mass migration to disrupt the governance, politics, and policies of the EU. All this can be achieved without overt confrontation, direct

116 Galani (n 19) 91–115.

117 Antonia Maria Sarantaki, 'Frontex & NATO: A New Partnership in the Making' (January 2019) ELIAMEP Working Paper No 100/2019, available at <https://www.eliamep.gr/wp-content/uploads/2019/02/100_2018_-WORKING-PAPER-_Antonia-Maria-Sarantaki.pdf> accessed 21 November 2023.

118 Ruud Van Dijka and Stanley R Sloan, 'NATO's Inherent Dilemma: Strategic Imperatives vs. Value Foundations' (2020) 43 (6–7) Journal of Strategic Studies 1014.

119 Ibid, 1034.

120 Chris Kremidas-Courtney, 'Building a Comprehensive Approach to Countering Hybrid Threats in the Black Sea and Mediterranean Regions' NATO Maritime Security, 5, available at <https://nmiotc.nato.int/wp-content/uploads/2020/02/Building-a-Comprehensive-Approach-to-Countering-Hybrid-Threats-in-the-Black-Sea-and-Mediterranean-Regions-by-Chris-Kremidas-Courtney.pdf> accessed 21 November 2023.

involvement of State actors or reaching the threshold of armed hostilities, but by exploiting the EU's vulnerabilities, mainly the lack of a common migration policy and effective regulation of its cyberspace. The EU is fully aware of these challenges, and this is why it keeps militarizing its responses to mass migration, especially in the Mediterranean Sea where it is impossible to control the illegal entries of thousands of migrants. This is unsurprising, given that the instrumentalization of migration targets the sovereignty and territorial integrity of European States.

Yet, as explained, the instrumentalization of migration worsens the situation of migrants both because their journey to the EU becomes riskier and because, upon their arrival in the EU, they become the target of vile disinformation campaigns. This stresses the importance of not 'hybridizing' human rights even if migration is perceived as a hybrid threat. In this chapter, it was demonstrated that the instrumentalization of migration does not create any exceptions that would permit European States to deviate from their human rights obligations towards migrants arriving to the EU on boats. In contrast, it was explained that neither the uniqueness of the maritime environment nor the large numbers of migrants or the externalization of border controls at sea create any exceptional conditions upon which derogation from human rights is permitted. This makes explicit the need for the EU to build its legal resilience in response to mass migration as a hybrid threat, but as explained, this cannot be achieved unless the human rights of migrants are incorporated in its efforts. Only in this way, the EU will be able to better respond to the instrumentalization of migration as a hybrid threat, while also upholding its human rights values and the rule of law.

CHAPTER 10

Naval Blockade of Ukraine's Black Sea Ports in the Light of International Law

Dariusz Rafał Bugajski

Introduction

The shores and the waters of the Black Sea and the Sea of Azov are the places where some of the longest roads in the world meet, one maritime, and the second, overland. From the Sea of Azov, it is a distance of 4500 km to the Strait of Gibraltar by sea, and 6500 km to the Yellow Sea, by land.[1] However, from a legal point of view, the overland road has been divided into different sovereignties, and all transport of goods and movement of people are under the full control of land powers. Contrary to that, the entire maritime route, even within territorial waters, is governed by the concept of navigational rights and freedoms under international law.

The Russian military aggression against Ukraine and various hybrid actions in Europe once again emphasize the importance of shipping and critical infrastructure such as seaports for neutral States and belligerents. Russia and Ukraine are considered as the world's breadbaskets. Russia is the world's top wheat exporter, accounting for 24%, Ukraine is fifth, at 9%.[2] Ukraine was also a major exporter of corn (16% of world exports),[3] and sunflower seed oil (42% of world exports).[4] Due to the decline of the metallurgy industry, Ukraine's prior main export category, as a result of the war in Donbas which began in 2014, agricultural products accounted for Ukraine's largest export category, and nowadays during the ongoing war is the main source of financial resources for

1 Dariusz R Bugajski, *Navigational Rights and Freedoms in the International Law and Practice* (Akademia Marynarki Wojennej 2021) 216.

2 Food and Agriculture Organization of the United Nations web site, available at <www.fao.org/faostat/en/> accessed 15 January 2024.

3 IndexMundi web site, available at <www.indexmundi.com/agriculture/?commodity=corn> accessed 22 December 2023.

4 IndexMundi web site, available at <www.indexmundi.com/agriculture/?commodity=sunflowerseed-oil&graph=production> accessed 22 December 2023.

 | DOI:10.1163/9789004707993_012

the Ukrainian budget apart from foreign aid.[5] That is why Russians are constantly stealing grain in occupied territories and their ports, destroying grain storage by any available means in unoccupied territories, or preventing export from Ukrainian ports of the remaining grain.[6] These actions are intended to disrupt the global food market, particularly the agricultural sectors in countries supporting Ukraine, with the aim of diminishing their support.[7]

Considering the current course of armed, political, and legal activities and their impact on the development of the law of naval warfare, it is important to seek answers to questions regarding how the law of the sea and the law of international security can contribute to ensuring stability on the sea lanes of communication in hybrid warfare. The naval blockade is a centuries-old institution of naval warfare.[8] The question is if Russia's right to employ a naval blockade outweigh the rights of neutral States to trade with a belligerent?

This chapter is confined to analyzing the legality of the Russian naval blockade in the north-western part of the Black Sea under international humanitarian law and the 1982 United Nations Convention on the Law of the Sea (hereinafter LOSC)[9] after 24 February 2022. This is because previous incidents during the decade-long conflict, such as the seizure of Ukrainian ships in the Kerch Strait in 2018,[10] and the restriction of navigation in the Kerch Strait and

5 The Observatory of Economic Complexity web site, available at <https://oec.world/en/profile/country/ukr> accessed 15 March 2023.

6 Global Rights Compliance, 'New report reveals large-scale, organized Russian plan to systematically pillage Ukraine's grain, using proceeds to fund occupation and illegal war', available at <https://globalrightscompliance.com/2023/11/16/new-report-reveals-large-scale-organised-russian-plan-to-systematically-pillage-ukraines-grain-using-proceeds-to-fund-occupation-and-illegal-war/> accessed 15 March 2024.

7 Specific strategies Russia could employ to target U.S. wheat production can be organized into four categories of attack: cyberattacks targeting grain storage and transport infrastructure, restricting fertilizer exports to U.S. and/or global markets, manipulating international wheat markets, agricultural biowarfare. Karl A Scheuerman, 'Weaponizing Wheat: How Strategic Competition With Russia Could Threaten American Food Security', Joint Force Quarterly 111, October 2023, available at <https://ndupress.ndu.edu/JFQ/Joint-Force-Quarterly-111/Article/Article/3569549/weaponizing-wheat-how-strategic-competition-with-russia-could-threaten-american/> accessed 22 January 2024.

8 Presumably, the first naval blockade was declared by the Dutch in 1584. Wolff Heintschel von Heinegg, 'Naval Blockade' (2000) 75 International Law Studies 203, 205.

9 United Nations Convention on the Law of the Sea (opened for signature 10 December 1982, entered into force 16 November 1994) 1833 UNTS 3.

10 James Kraska, 'The Kerch Strait Incident: Law of the Sea or Law of Naval Warfare?' (2018) EJIL: Talk! Blog of the European Journal of International Law, available at <www.ejiltalk.org/the-kerch-strait-incident-law-of-the-sea-or-law-of-naval-warfare/> accessed 25 January 2024.

the Sea of Azov, have already been extensively discussed from the perspective of international law.[11] Additionally, until 24 February 2022, Russian aggression against Ukraine was limited both territorially and in the size of the forces. The Sea of Azov was omitted in the latest stage of the conflict because shortly after 24 February 2022, Russian forces seized control of all ports and the entire coastline of the Sea of Azov.[12]

This chapter consists of a review of the current stage of warfare in the Black Sea and of an analysis of the legal concept of naval blockade and other restrictions imposed on navigation in the Black Sea by Russia. This is supplemented with remarks on the applicability of the concept of hybrid warfare to the methods employed in the war in the Black Sea.

At present, Ukrainian ports may be divided into three categories, namely, those which are occupied (Mariupol, Berdyansk, Kerch and Sevastopol), those which are on the frontline (Kherson and Mykolaiv), and ports of the Big Odesa which are in Ukrainian hands (Chornomorsk, Odesa and Pivdennyi). Only the last group is operational and was used under the Black Sea Grain Initiative (hereinafter BSGI).[13] The BSGI was a temporary arrangement, and it was under constant threat of being attacked. Since the BSGI was established, ships laden with grain and other foodstuff had left three Ukrainian ports of Big Odesa. There is also another group of minor harbors in Ukrainian hands, including those in the Danube Delta on the border with Romania: Ust-Danube (Kilia and Ochakiv arm mouth), Izmail (Kilia arm), and Reni (maritime Danube),[14] which

11 Alexander Lott, *Hybrid Threats and the Law of the Sea. Use of Force and Discriminatory Navigational Restrictions in Straits* (Brill Nijhoff 2022) 39–86; Raul 'Pete' Pedrozo, 'Russia-Ukraine Conflict: The War at Sea' (2023) 100 International Law Studies 1; Shani Friedman 'To Blockade or not to Blockade? The Legal Status of Russia's Suspension of Shipping in the Sea of Azov' (2024) Israel Law Review 1.

12 Elena Becatoros, Oleksandr Stashevskyi, and Ciaran McQuillan, 'Russia claims to have taken full control of Mariupol' AP News (21 May 2022), available at <https://apnews.com/article/russia-ukraine-kyiv-prisoners-of-war-71d0dfb842caaaad30b92671637c1f3b> accessed 14 March 2024.

13 Initiative on the Safe Transportation of Grain and Foodstuffs from Ukrainian Ports between Ukraine, Russia, Turkey, and the United Nations (adopted 22 July 2022, entered into force 22 July 2022). Technically there were two agreements one signed on behalf of Ukraine (Minister of Infrastructure) and Turkey (Minister of Defense) and an identical document with the only difference being the replacement of the Ukrainian signature by the signature of the Russian Minister of Defense. Both were also signed for the United Nations by the Secretary-General, available at <www.un.org/sites/un2.un.org/files/black_sea_grain_initiative_full_text.pdf> accessed 24 October 2023, and at <www.un.org/en/black-sea-grain-initiative/update-15-july-2023> accessed 24 October 2023.

14 Export volumes via alternative routes reached their maximum at the beginning of 2023 and had been fixed at the following monthly rates: road transport 0.6–0.7 million tons; rail

are handy for the transport of grain providing a safe navigational channel under the right of innocent passage through the territorial sea of neutral Romania and Bulgaria to the Turkish Straits. An armed attack by Russia against objects in a foreign territorial sea, especially against navigation would be regarded as a violation of the sovereignty of the coastal nation.[15]

The Danube Delta ports can be used to transport goods directly to Western Europe through the neutral waters of the Danube River without a risk of being attacked.[16] The law of neutrality also regulates the use of nearby Romanian ports.[17] Transportation between the Romanian ports and neighboring Ukraine is possible by land.[18]

In light of the above, questions may arise regarding, firstly, the scope of navigation to and through neutral waters. The second issue is the matter of navigation through the territorial sea and exclusive economic zone (hereinafter EEZ) of Ukraine, which could have been subject to lawful wartime actions, including a blockade. Therefore, it needs to be determined whether the Russian actions amounted to a blockade and whether it was in accordance with international law. If so, what were the temporal and geographical boundaries of this blockade? Finally, apart from strictly military domain, did the Russian blockade had any aspects of a hybrid nature?

---

transport 1.1–1.3; small ports on the Danube 1.3–1.5. Nevertheless, it is important to realize, that the ongoing construction of grain terminals in the ports of Ismail and Reni, simplification of export rules and procedures, introduction of electronic queues at the borders, and creation of dry ports in the western regions should increase Ukraine's grain exports in 2023. 'AussenWirtschaftBranchenreport Ukraine' Aussenwirtschaftscenter Kyjiw (April 2023), 55, available at <www.go-international.at/export-know-how/branchenreports/ukraine-io-agrar.pdf> accessed 1 December 2023.

15 Bugajski (n 1) 85.

16 Pedrozo (n 11) 16.

17 The nearby ports include the largest Romanian maritime port of Constanța and the second-largest maritime and inland port of Braila on the Danube River.

18 The Romanian section of the Danube between Braila and Sulina mouth is also termed maritime Danube as this section is navigable by river-sea vessels and sea-going vessels. 170 km long, this river section is maintained by the Romanian River Administration of the Lower Danube for vessels with a maximum draught of 7.32 meters. 'The Manual on Danube Navigation is a project within the scope of the BMVIT Action Programme for the Danube until 2022' Viadonau 2019, 50, available at <www.viadonau.org/fileadmin/user_upload/Manual_on_Danube_Navigation.pdf> accessed 15 December 2023.

TABLE 10.1 Navigation to Ukrainian ports since 24 February 2022

	Danube river ports	The ports of big Odesa, the Black Sea grain initiative ports (unoccupied)	Ports not operational for Ukraine (occupied or on the frontline)
Ports (from West to East)	Reni, Izmail, Ust-Danube	Chornomorsk, Odesa, Pivdennyi (formelyYuzhny)	Mykolaiv, Kherson, Sevastopol, Kerch, Berdyansk, Mariupol
Legal status of waters on the direct way to ports	Internal waters and territorial waters of neutral nations	Territorial waters of Ukraine and international waters	Territorial waters of Ukraine and international waters
The navigational regime of access	Free navigation on the maritime Danube (Sulina) and innocent passage	Freedom of navigation	occupied
Regions of operations	Neutral waters	Naval warfare zone (territorial waters of belligerents and international waters)	occupied
Wartime transshipments of grain, monthly (million tons)	1.1 (Oct. 2022) 1.45 (Feb. 2023)	4.13 (Oct. 2022) 3.35 (Feb. 2023)	-

SOURCE: DARIUSZ RAFAŁ BUGAJSKI. TRANSSHIPMENTS FROM: 'AUSSENWIRTSCHAFTBRANCHEN REPORT UKRAINE' AUSSENWIRTSCHAFTSCENTER KYJIW (APRIL 2023), 55, AVAILABLE AT <WWW.GO-INTERNATIONAL.AT/EXPORT-KNOW-HOW/BRANCHENREPORTS/UKRAINE-IO-AGRAR.PDF> ACCESSED 1 DECEMBER 2023.

1 Naval Blockade, Freedom of the Seas, and Military Activity at Sea

1.1 *The Legal Regime Applicable to Blockades*

The classical meaning of naval blockade encompasses the interception by sea of the approaches to the coasts or ports of an enemy, with the purpose of cutting off all his overseas communications. It should be emphasized that its object is not only to stop the importation of supplies but to prevent export as well.[19] In practice, sometimes there is confusion over how to distinguish 'blockade' from 'contraband'. Despite both being methods used for economic warfare at sea[20] the distinction between 'naval blockade' and 'contraband', lies chiefly in the fact that in the latter case, goods are liable to seizure only if they are included on the contraband lists, and are intended to be imported to the territory under enemy control.[21] In the case of 'blockade' of an enemy's coast or any of his ports, all merchant vessels, and all cargoes, of whatever nationality, may be subject to confiscation. The character of the cargo or ship, and its flag or ownership, are irrelevant. It is enough that a ship is endeavoring to enter or leave a blockaded area to be captured by the blockading forces.[22]

It must be emphasized that as long as neutral flagged vessels or airplanes are navigated outside the range of operations of the forces conducting the effective blockade, and as long as they do not carry contraband or act in a way that makes them open to attack, 'the freedoms and rights of navigation and overflight supersede the belligerents' interests in a comprehensive prohibition of the imports of their respective enemies'.[23] Moreover, neutral States may continue to trade with belligerents but it does not give them the right to access the blockaded ports of the belligerents.[24]

Any action of armed forces to interrupt another country's communication at sea, is equal to the use of force, but does not necessarily involve armed struggle.[25] That is because of the simple fact that 90% of the total world trade exchange is facilitated by sea, and every country is dependent on it. When there is no armed struggle, then the blockade may be called a 'pacific blockade' as a blockade exercised by a great power for the purpose of bringing pressure to bear on a weaker State without actual armed conflict.[26] That it is an act of war, is undeniable. It can only be employed as a measure of coercion by maritime powers that are able to bring into action such vastly superior forces to those of the blockaded State.[27] The concept of 'peaceful blockade' does not apply

19 Constantine J Colombos, *The International Law of the Sea* (Longmans 1951) 539.

20 Martin Fink, 'The ever-existing "crisis" of the law of naval warfare' (2022) 104 International Review of the Red Cross 1971, 1974.

21 Ibid.

22 Colombos (n 19).

23 Heinegg (n 8) 216.

24 Kraska (n 10) 558.

25 Andrzej Makowski, 'The Mavi Marmara Incident and the Modern Law of Armed Conflict at Sea' (2013) 2(7) The Israel Journal of Foreign Affairs 75, 75.

26 Walter R Thomas, 'Pacific Blockade: A Lost Opportunity of the 1930's?' (1980) 62 International Law Studies 197, 197–200.

27 Thomas Barclay, 'Pacific Blockade' (1911) Encyclopedia Britannica 20.

to the armed conflict between Russia and Ukraine.[28] Furthermore, nowadays, the acceptance of a 'peaceful blockade' is not justified in the light of the United Nations (hereinafter UN) Charter because a naval blockade must always be classified as a use of armed force, even if its execution does not lead to armed combat. In any case, however, if it is not authorized by the UN Security Council under Article 42 of the UN Charter or if it is not conducted in self-defence, then it is illegal.[29]

The naval blockade is a customary concept described chiefly in the 1856 Paris Declaration,[30] which is accepted as customary law,[31] and the 1909 London Declaration on Naval Warfare.[32] Although the London Declaration has never been enforced, its provisions have been observed during armed conflict and it is generally regarded as customary international law.[33] In light of international law, a naval blockade as a method of naval warfare to be legally valid requires two criteria, including one based on law and the other based on fact. The legal requirement of a blockade, including its interruption, suspension, and resumption, provides for the declaration (publicity) and notification (to the belligerents and the neutral States) of the completion of the commencement, duration, coordinates of the blockade zone and the date by which neutral ships may leave the blockaded coast (period of grace).[34] The legal effect of a blockade creates an obligation of respect. However, this only occurs when the factual requirement is met by deploying sufficient forces to

28 See James F McNulty, 'Blockade: Evolution and Expectation' (1980) 62 International Law Studies 172, 184.

29 Nigel D White, 'From Korea to Kuwait: The Legal Basis of United Nations' Military Action' (1998) 20(3) The International History Review 597.

30 Declaration Respecting Maritime Law (opened for signature and entered into force on 16 April 1856), British State Papers 1856, Vol. LXI, 155–158.

31 Virtually all States acceded to the Paris Declaration. The United States, which aimed at a complete exemption of private property from capture at sea, withheld its formal adherence, its amendment not having been accepted by all the Powers. In 1861, at the beginning of the Civil War, the United States announced nevertheless that it would respect the principles of the Declaration for the duration of the hostilities and the same equally, in 1898 during the war against Spain. Declaration Respecting Maritime Law (adopted on 16 April 1856), available at <https://ihl-databases.icrc.org/en/ihl-treaties/paris-decl-1856?activeTab=undefined> accessed 30 November 2023.

32 Declaration concerning the Laws of Naval War (opened for signature on 26 February 1909, not entered into force). Due to its rejection by the British House of Lords, the Declaration was not ratified by any signatory. Source Dietrich Schindler and Jiri Toman, *The Laws of Armed Conflicts* (Martinus Nijhoff 1988) 845–856.

33 Robert W Tucker, *The Law of War and Neutrality at Sea* (US Naval War College 1957) 285; Heinegg (n 8) 209.

34 Heinegg (n 8) 214.

provide real effectiveness to the blockade. Effectiveness means that the belligerent forces must be sufficiently powerful to prevent access to the enemy coastline or ports.[35] Theoretically, a blockade may also be enforced by purely cyber means.[36] Effectiveness is a question of fact to be determined, for example, by a prize court.[37] In addition, blockades must be enforced impartially among flags of all nations.[38] Warships and neutral vessels in distress may enter and leave a blockaded area.[39]

Finally, the old question has arisen again, also in this war, and that is how the use of naval mines or other means (e.g., artillery) may have contributed to the effectiveness of the blockade.[40] A blockade may be maintained by military aircraft, submarines, or an offshore missile battery and artillery if such weapons can be utilized in a discriminatory fashion, and even by naval mines. However, a blockade may be rendered effective by the placement of naval mines, but not exclusively.[41] This prohibition does not follow from Article 2 of the 1907 Hague Convention VIII, for it is nearly impossible to prove that the mines have been laid 'for the sole purpose of intercepting commercial navigation.'[42]

Nonetheless, despite using sufficient forces and means, the effectiveness of a blockade is never complete in practice and it does not require complete enforcement success.[43] Therefore, the question arises as to what is the threshold of effectiveness? An example is the blockade of the Polish coast by Germany in September 1939, which was successful because the German Navy outnumbered the Polish Navy. Moreover, the most modern Polish destroyers were sent to the United Kingdom before the war, and the political layout of the borders meant that a narrow Polish 'corridor' of land with only ports was

---

35 Louise Doswald-Beck (ed.), *San Remo Manual on International Law Applicable to Armed Conflicts at Sea* (Cambridge University Press 1995) 177, Rule 95.

36 International Group of Experts, *Tallinn Manual 2.0 on the International Law Applicable to Cyber Operations* (Cambridge University Press 2017) Rule 67.

37 The 1909 London Declaration on Naval Warfare stated that the determination of effectiveness was in any case reserved to the competent (international or national) prize court. Heinegg (n 8) 208.

38 James Kraska, Raul 'Pete' Pedrozo *et al.*, *Newport Manual on the Law of Naval Warfare* (US Naval War College 2023) 122.

39 Ibid.

40 Ibid, 121.

41 Heinegg (n 8) 215.

42 Article 2. 'It is forbidden to lay automatic contact mines off the coast and ports of the enemy, with the sole object of intercepting commercial shipping.' Convention (VIII) relative to the Laying of Automatic Submarine Contact Mines (opened for signature on 18 October 1907, entered into force 26 January 1910).

43 Newport Manual (38) 121.

surrounded on both sides by German territory. However, even in this case, the blockade was not totally effective. Some smaller boats and ships managed to circumvent the blockade on their way to neutral ports.[44]

In a naval blockade, the distance and deployment of the armed forces depends on the legal status of maritime areas, freedom of the high seas, and rights of navigation. At the same time, access to the ports of neutral countries must not be hindered and the blockade must be limited to ports or coastal areas occupied or under the control of the enemy.[45] Merchant vessels violating the blockade may be detained, and vessels that defy the blockade may be attacked. The blockade cannot be selective, i.e., it cannot apply to ships of selected flag States. In any case, a blockade is prohibited if its purpose is to starve or undermine the livelihood of the civilian population, or if civilian casualties are or may be disproportionate to the expected military gain (principle of proportionality).[46] Where a blockaded community is at risk of famine or disease, food and/or medical supplies must be adequately routed, with control, provided that they are distributed by an impartial humanitarian organization.[47]

1.2 *The Relevance of the Law of the Sea in Armed Conflicts and the Law of Neutrality*

Navigational rights and freedoms are designed in the interest of the entire international community and due to this fact, among others, these rights cannot be suspended by neutral States on the ground that two or more States are at war with each other. Therefore, these freedoms and rights are fully applicable not only in a time of peace but also in a time of armed conflict at sea, ensuring the free movement of navies and international trade (right of innocent passage, right of transit passage and right of archipelagic sea lanes passage), as well as of air forces (right of transit passage and archipelagic sea lanes passage) of belligerents within the borders of neutral States (in territorial waters and airspace above these waters).[48]

The 1958 Geneva Conventions of the Law of the Sea[49] and the LOSC contain clauses providing for the use of the sea in accordance with the principles of

---

44 Dariusz R Bugajski, *The Polish Naval Academy: In the Centenary of Regaining Access to the Sea* (Akademia Marynarki Wojennej 2019) 29–34, 45.

45 Heinegg (n 8) 212.

46 Ibid, 213.

47 Rule 103 of the 1994 San Remo Manual, see Doswald-Beck (n 35) 180.

48 Ibid, 12–14, Rules 23–35.

49 Convention on the Territorial Sea and the Contiguous Zone (opened for signature on 29 April 1958, entered into force 10 September 1964) 516 UNTS 205; Convention on the High Seas (opened for signature on 29 April 1958, entered into force 3 January 1963) 450

those conventions, as well as in accordance with the principles contained in 'other rules of international law'. In particular, the following articles should be indicated: Article 87(1) of the LOSC, Article 1(2) of the 1958 First Geneva Convention on the Territorial Sea and the Contiguous Zone, and Article 2 of the 1958 Second Geneva Convention on the High Seas. There is a common agreement that the phrase 'other rules' refers, among other things, to international law on armed conflicts.[50] An apparent contradiction appears when comparing this rule with Article 88 of the LOSC, which reserves the use of the high seas 'for peaceful purposes only'. This contradiction disappears when one realizes that the latter provision does not imply a restriction or exclusion of military activities on the high seas but is primarily a consequence of the prohibition of the use of force and the threat of the use of force in international relations, as provided for in Article 2(4) of the UN Charter. The confirmation is explicitly stated in Article 301 of the LOSC, which provides that, 'in the exercise of their rights and obligations, states (...) shall refrain from threatening or using force with regard to the territorial integrity or political independence of another state, or acting in any other manner inconsistent with the principles of international law contained in the Charter of the United Nations.'[51] Let us be reminded that the term 'peaceful use' used in the 1959 Antarctic Treaty[52] meant demilitarization and neutralization and thus, in practice, an almost total prohibition of military activities. In the case of the LOSC, the reservation of the use of the high seas for peaceful purposes is interpreted in the relevant legal literature, differently from the Antarctic Treaty, as prohibiting the threat or use of force or, by inversion, as permitting any non-aggressive military action on the high seas.[53]

UNTS 11; Convention on Fishing and Conservation of the Living Resources of the High Sea (opened for signature on 29 April 1958, entered into force 22 March 1966) 559 UNTS 285; Convention on the Continental Shelf, and (opened for signature on 29 April 1958, entered into force 10 June 1964) 499 UNTS 311.

50 George K Walker, 'Oceans Law, the Maritime Environment, and Law of Naval Warfare' (1996) 69 International Law Studies, 190.

51 Article 301 of the LOSC; Rules 10 and 36 of the 1994 San Remo Manual, see Doswald-Beck (n 35) 82, 110–111.

52 The Antarctic Treaty (opened for signature on 1 December 1959, entered into force 23 June 1961) 402 UNTS 71.

53 Satya N Nandan and Shabtai Rosenne (eds.), *United Nations Convention on the Law of the Sea. A Commentary vol. III* (Brill Nijhoff 1995) 91; Rüdiger Wolfrum, 'Military Activities on the High Seas: What are the Impacts of the U.N. Convention on the Law of the Sea?', in Michael Schmitt and Leslie Green (eds.), *The Law of Armed Conflict: Into the Next Millenium* (US Naval War College 1998) 501.

Therefore, the application of the LOSC standards also goes beyond peacetime. It provides an opportunity to expect certain behavior from countries during crisis and armed conflicts.[54] In this context, the law of the sea and international security law contribute to ensuring stability in major shipping routes during peacetime, wartime, and hybrid warfare. How? It is enough to recall for instance the right of neutrality, the spatial scope of a neutral territory, as well as the rights of passage through the territorial waters of a neutral State.[55] The LOSC defines the maximum breadth of the territorial sea which forms in an armed conflict the neutral waters of a neutral State. In addition, the convention explicitly provides the right of innocent passage, the right of transit passage through straits used for international navigation,[56] as well as the right of archipelagic sea lanes passage in neutral waters for the forces of the belligerents. It should be added that the right of innocent passage in neutral waters can be fully exercised by warships of the belligerents. Such a solution is provided not only by the LOSC, but also above all the law of war.[57] Therefore, the belligerents may use the territorial sea of neutral States for navigation purposes exclusively under a right of innocent passage.

Access to the Turkish Straits is strategically important for both parties (see further *infra* Chapter 11). Ukraine relies on access to the Turkish Straits through the territorial sea of Romania and Bulgaria. Surprisingly, Russian sovereign immune vessels have been utilizing Turkish waters since at least mid-2023. For example, Russian government ships (auxiliaries), the *Lady Mariia* and the *Baltic Leader*, took a route through the Turkish territorial sea along its northern shores to the vicinity of Sinop in northern Turkey in February 2024. This route likely enables the Russian ships to be protected against an Ukrainian attack.[58] Additionally, in the 1907 Hague Convention (XIII) on Neutral Powers in Naval

54 William L Schachte Jr., 'International Straits and Navigational Freedoms' (1993) 24(2) Ocean Development & International Law 179ff.

55 Convention (XIII) concerning the Rights and Duties of Neutral Powers in Naval War (opened for signature on 18 October 1907, entered into force 26 January 1910), Article 10: 'The neutrality of a Power is not affected by the mere passage through its territorial waters of war-ships or prizes belonging to belligerents'.

56 cf Akira Mayama, 'The Influence of the Straits Transit Regime on the Law of Neutrality At Sea' (1995) 26(1) Ocean Development and International Law 1–30.

57 Rules 20 and 21 of the 1994 San Remo Manual, see Doswald-Beck (n 35) 99–101.

58 Both auxiliaries (Ro-Ro Cargo Ships), the *Lady Mariia* and the *Baltic Leader* flying the Russian flag, transited the Bosporus from Tartus (Syria) to Novorossijsk after delivering military cargo. Auxiliary vessels are vessels, other than warships, that are owned by or under the exclusive control of the armed forces. They are civilian objects, unless and in the course of acting in a supporting capacity for the armed forces. Then they can be attacked. The Commander's Handbook on the Law of Naval Operations (US Navy, US Marine

War that was a codification of customary law at the time, belligerent warships were allowed to moor in ports or on the roadsteads of neutral States under the consent of the coastal State without violating its neutrality.[59]

The customary freedom of the high seas in the context of military use of the high seas is the same as freedoms confirmed by the LOSC. These freedoms include the freedom of the high seas (freedom of navigation, of overflight and of laying submarine cables and pipelines), and operational freedoms, such as the conduct of exercises and maneuvers by various naval and air forces, group-maneuvering and anchoring, intelligence collection and reconnaissance, provisioning, non-combatant use of weapons, placing military installations on the sea and on the seabed, hydrographic surveys, and other peaceful military activities.[60] Operational freedoms in international waters, especially in the EEZ, being only part of customary law are at the same time modified in conflict with the treaty powers of coastal States.[61]

1.3 *Ukraine's Use of the Rights and Freedoms Recognized by the LOSC*

As mentioned above, concerning political geography, navigation to and from unoccupied Ukrainian ports may proceed according to two different legal principles (see *supra* Map 10.1). Firstly, navigation to and from the main Ukrainian ports of Big Odesa that remain continuously under Ukraine's control is subject to the laws of naval warfare. Secondly, navigation from the Ukrainian ports at the mouth of the Danube may proceed through neutral inland waters on the Danube River according to the 1948 Convention Regarding the Regime of Navigation on the Danube,[62] and through the territorial sea of neighboring

---

Corps, US Coast Guard 2022), 2–3; Marine Traffic website, available at <www.marinetraffic.com/en/ais/home/centerx:35.5/centery:43.9/zoom:7> accessed 26 February 2024.

59 For example, the Polish submarine ORP 'Orzeł' took advantage of the right to shelter in a neutral port on September 15, 1939, by entering the Estonian capital Tallinn. The next day, at the insistence of the Germans and Russians, Estonian military authorities boarded the ship, interned the crew, confiscated all the navigation aids and maps, and commenced dismantling all the armaments. On September 17, ORP 'Orzeł' escaped and continued to patrol the Baltic Sea. They took the decision to join the United Kingdom when they arrived on October 14. Bugajski 2019 (n 44) 30, 33.

60 Charles E Pirtle, 'Military Uses of Ocean Space and the Law of the Sea in the New Millennium' (2000) 31(1) Ocean Development and International Law 7, 8; Said Mahmoudi, 'Foreign Military Activities in the Swedish Economic Zone' (1996) 11(3) The International Journal of Marine and Coastal Law 365, 374–378.

61 The Commander's Handbook (n 58) 2–14.

62 The Convention Regarding the Regime of Navigation on the Danube, signed at Belgrade (opened for signature on 18 August 1948, entered into force 11 May 1949) 33 UNTS 181. Currently, navigation is governed by the Danube Commission dating to the 1856 Paris Conferences, which established for the first time an international regime to safeguard

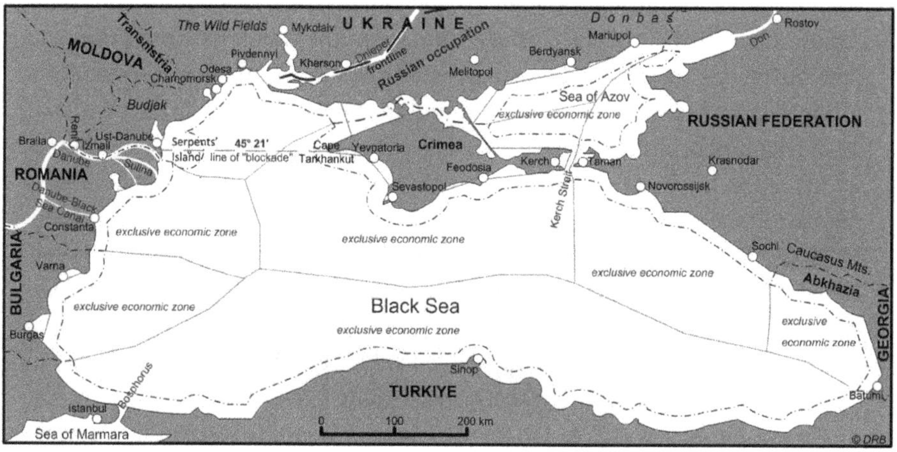

MAP 10.1 The Black Sea and its political division (March 2024)
SOURCE: DARIUSZ RAFAŁ BUGAJSKI

States (Romania, Bulgaria, and Turkey) according to the right of innocent passage. This category also includes navigation up and down the Danube River to all river ports.[63] Navigation through the mentioned waters is not subject to restrictions due to wartime activities and is generally governed solely by the law of maritime neutrality.[64] Therefore, navigation to and from the Ukrainian ports at the mouth of the Danube River in neutral waters may not be blockaded under any circumstances, but navigation from and to the ports of Big Odesa may be. Neutral waters consist of internal waters and territorial waters of neutral States. Neutral airspace is over neutral waters and land territory of neutral States. Belligerent forces may neither enter neutral waters, apart from just for transitory purposes, nor neutral airspace, excluding for transit passage.[65]

The Romanian-Ukrainian border section goes 176 km along the median line of thalweg of the Danube River, including its northern arms, chiefly the Kilia

---

free navigation on the Danube, and of 1921, which resurrected the international regime after the First World War. Europe's acceptance of the principle of free navigation for international rivers was confirmed by the 1815 Act of the Congress of Vienna, the 1831 Mayence Convention, the 1868 Mannheim Convention, the 1856 Treaty of Paris, the 1885 Berlin Treaty, and the 1948 Belgrade Convention. See Ralph W Johnson, 'Freedom of Navigation for International Rivers: What Does It Mean?' (1964), 62(3) Michigan Law Review 465, 466.

63 Raul 'Pete' Pedrozo, 'The Russia-Ukraine Conflict: Blocking Access to the Black Sea' (2022) 75 (4/6) Naval War College Review 37, 42.

64 Ibid, 44–45.

65 Doswald-Beck (n 35) 11.

branch with 60% of the Danube water, which is one of the three main channels of the mouth of the river Danube that forms the Danube Delta.[66] The river part of the border was finally demarcated in 1949.[67] All three arms (the Kilia in the north, the Sulina in the middle, and the St. George branch in the south) are navigational, but the majority of trade goes through the 63-km-long Sulina, which is the most convenient and shortest upstream way for vessels with a maximum draught of 7.32 meters. In the first months of the Russian full-scale invasion and before the liberation of Serpents' Island in June 2022, merchant vessels were restricted to using the Sulina canal, fully under Romanian sovereignty.[68]

The Danube River, with its mouth called Sulina, is defined as an international waterway, in compliance with the 1948 Belgrade Convention, and can, therefore, be used free of charge by navigation, as it is not subject to any navigation dues.[69] Article 1 of the Belgrade Convention provides that, 'navigation on the Danube shall be free and open for the nationals, vessels of commerce and goods of all states, on a footing of equality in regard to port and navigation charges and conditions of merchant shipping'.[70] Beyond this, the northern Kilia and Bystroe arm (formerly Old Stambul), which is not subject to the Belgrade Convention and which falls under the Ukrainian waterway administration, is navigable by river-sea vessels and seagoing vessels with a maximum

66 The Danube is followed into the delta where the boundary coincides with the Kilia arm to Vilkovo and then the Old Stambul (Bystroe) arm to the Black Sea. 'Romania (Rumania) – U.S.S.R. Boundary' (1964) 43(30) International Boundary Study, 2.

67 The demarcation of the frontier was completed, and the final documents were signed by the Joint Russian–Romanian Frontier Commission on 29 September 1949. Several additional treaties on maintenance and settlements of problems (25 November 1949 and 27 February 1961) have been negotiated but they do not affect the general location of the boundary. Ibid, 10–11.

68 Josh Salisbury, 'Ukraine Begins Restoring Danube River Ports in Effort to Beat Black Sea Grain Blockade' The Standard (13 July 2022), available at <www.standard.co.uk/news/world/ukraine-danube-river-black-sea-grain-blockade-b1012041.html> accessed 1 December 2023.

69 The Sulina Canal used almost exclusively by sea-river or seagoing vessels is an exception. The Romanian River Administration of the Lower Danube charges dues calculated per ton deadweight of a vessel for maintenance purposes. 'The Manual on Danube Navigation is a project within the scope of the BMVIT Action Programme for the Danube until 2022' (2019) Viadonau, 171, available at <www.viadonau.org/fileadmin/user_upload/Manual_on_Danube_Navigation.pdf> accessed 15 January 2024.

70 Danube Commission website, available at <www.danubecommission.org/uploads/doc/convention-en.pdf> accessed 16 January 2024.

draught of 5.85 meters, increased up to 6.5 m in early 2023 (with further plans for increasing this to a draught of up to 7.2 meters).[71]

It must be emphasized that the Russian line of 'blockade' extends northward by 0.5 nautical miles from the mouth of the Bystroe arm into the Black Sea. Furthermore, the main Ukrainian arm of the Danube, Kilia, which lies 14 miles further south, was also not being blocked formally. Thus, not the entire coastline and access to only some of the Ukrainian Black Sea ports were 'blockaded' under the Russian navigational warning issued on 25 February 2022.

From the trade security point of view, much more important are the maritime parts of waterways from the Ukrainian ports at the mouth of the Danube, or the ports of Big Odesa. For reaching the territorial sea of Romania, Bulgaria, and Turkey from these Ukrainian ports, the key is Serpents' Island and its reoccupation by Ukrainian forces. Important for the border in this section, apart from demarcation in 1949, is the International Court of Justice judgment on 3 February 2009, in the case concerning Maritime Delimitation in the Black Sea.[72] Despite its small size (662 m × 560 m, 0,214 km^2) the Court considered Serpents' Island to meet the criteria of an island under Article 121(2) of the LOSC.[73]

When Ukraine established, independently, on 10 August 2023, its temporary sea corridors,[74] one of them designed for vessels with a draught of 12 meters went through the territorial sea of Ukraine on the west side of Serpents' Island, and the second for larger ships on the eastern side of the island. It may be pointed out that in the first case there is a strait formed by an island of a State bordering the strait where there exists seaward of the island a route through the high seas or through an exclusive economic zone of similar convenience with respect to navigational and hydrographical characteristics (Article 38(1) of the LOSC).[75] The seaward route through an exclusive economic zone and partially through the territorial sea of Ukraine, being deeper and thus more convenient for larger vessels, is definitely of 'similar convenience' (Article 38(1) of the LOSC) with respect to other navigational and hydrographical

71 Grain Trade website, available at <https://graintrade.com.ua/en/novosti/ukraina-zbilshila-granichne-osidannya-sudiv-po-dunayu-do-65-m-sho-dozvolit-narostiti-ekspo.html> accessed 16 January 2024.

72 *Case concerning Maritime Delimitation in the Black Sea* (Romania v. Ukraine), Judgment, ICJ Reports 2009, p. 61.

73 Ibid.

74 IMO Circular Letter No. 4748 (19 July 2023), available at <www.imo.org/en/MediaCentre/HotTopics/Pages/MaritimeSecurityandSafetyintheBlackSeaandSeaofAzov.aspx> accessed 30 November 2023.

75 Bugajski (n 1) 155.

characteristics. Apart from depth and length, both corridors are navigationally the same, but the landward route (Serpents' Island Passage) is more secure for shipping considering war risks because of direct access to the territorial sea of neutral Romania. Undoubtedly, because of the size of Serpents' Island, even when including its small neighboring shallowness, both routes meet the conventional criteria of similar convenience when compared to the typical case of the Strait of Messina and Sicily.[76] Therefore, international navigation through the Serpents' Island Passage is subject to the right of innocent passage which shall not be suspended.[77] There is no doubt that the right of innocent passage cannot be suspended for neutral ships even during an international armed conflict. The San Remo Manual states that 'the right of innocent passage through international straits […] which exists in peacetime continues to exist for neutral warships in time of armed conflict at sea even though the State bordering a strait […] is a belligerent.'[78]

2 Russia's *De Facto* Naval Blockade in the Black Sea

2.1 *Factual Background and the Notification of the Establishment of the Blockade*

Russia's Navy began to expand its presence in the northwestern areas of the Black Sea early in 2021, undertaking a series of military exercises in Ukrainian

76 Fabio Caffio, *Glossario di Diritto del Mare* (Rivista Marittima 2007) 154; J Ashley Roach and Robert W Smith, 'International Straits', in J Ashley Roach and Robert W Smith, *Excessive Maritime Claims* (US Naval War College 1994) 197; Andrzej Straburzyński, *Status prawny cieśnin morskich* (Koszalin 1995) 61.

77 A solution for island straits, where the strait is formed by an island of a state bordering the strait where there exists seaward of the island a route through the high seas or through an exclusive economic zone of similar convenience with respect to navigational and hydrographical characteristics, was designed (Article 45(1)(a)(2) of the LOSC) for straits such as the Strait of Messina, the Pemba Channel (off the coast of Tanzania), the Corfu Channel, the Læsø passage (Læsø Rende in the Kattegat between Læsø Island and Jutland), the Kea Strait (in the Aegean Sea), the Cheyu Strait (between the island of the same name and the Korean Peninsula), the Pentland Firth (between the Orkneys and Great Britain), the Qiongzhou Strait (South China Sea), the Pentland Firth (between the Orkney islands and the UK), the passage between the Isles of Scilly and the UK, the Kalmar/Kalmarsund Strait (in the Baltic Sea between the island of Oland and the mainland), the Strait of Moonsund/Muhu väin (in the Estonian maritime area), the Le Maire Strait, the Strait of Imroz/Gökçeada, the P'eng-hu (Pescadores) Channel, and many others of lesser local importance for international navigation. Caffio (n 76) 154; Roach and Smith (n 76) 197; Bugajski (n 1) 255–256 and 257–258.

78 Rule 32 of the 1994 San Remo Manual, see Doswald-Beck (n 35) 108.

EEZ and gradually narrowed the area Ukraine could use for trade.[79] The Russian military operation initially was aimed at converting Ukraine into a land-locked State by cutting access to the Black Sea, including the Sea of Azov.[80] This would connect Russia proper and Russian-occupied eastern Ukraine to Transnistria, a Russian controlled region of Moldova.[81] Russia's full-scale invasion of 2022 cut off Ukraine's access to the Sea of Azov by the occupation of its Ukrainian coast, and resulted in a more or less successful and effective blockade of other ports on the western Black Sea.

Following the direct military invasion of Ukraine, Russia's Federal Agency for Maritime and River Transport announced on 24 February 2022 that, 'due to a warning received from the Russian Defense Ministry's Black Sea Fleet, amid the beginning of antiterrorist operations at 4 a.m. on February 24th, navigation in the Sea of Azov was suspended until further notice'.[82] The next day, Russia's Department of Navigation and Oceanography announced a navigational warning that from 25 February 2022, and in the northwestern part of the Black Sea to north of parallel 45°21'N, are declared 'prohibited for navigation due to counterterrorist operations carried out by Russian Navy. Ships and vessels in this area will be regarded as a terrorist threat'.[83]

That same day Ukraine announced, 'in connection with the military aggression of the Russian Federation against Ukraine' for the duration of martial law

79 Cynthia J Parmley and Raul 'Pete' Pedrozo, 'Russia's Illegal Restriction of Navigation in the Black Sea' (27 April 2021) Lawfare, available at <www.lawfaremedia.org/article/russias-illegal-restriction-navigation-black-sea> accessed 30 November 2023.

80 There are at least four arguments supporting the view that the Russians intended to cut off Ukraine from the sea after the launch of the full-scale invasion on 24 February 2022. Firstly, it would be beneficial to unblock the territorially isolated Russian-controlled Transnistria region. Secondly, Russian land forces attacking Crimea, after capturing Kherson, were heading towards Mykolaiv, where they were stopped. Thirdly, in the first days of the war, forces were deployed south of Odesa, intended for an amphibious operation in the port (cancelled due to Ukrainian resistance). Fourthly, Ukraine's Black Sea coast, called Novorossiya, is considered by Russia as Russian for ethnic and historical reasons. See Vladimir Putin, 'On the Historical Unity of Russians and Ukrainians' Press Release (12 July 2021), available at <http://en.kremlin.ru/events/president/news/66181> accessed 24 February 2024.

81 Kraska (n 10) 553.

82 Anonymous, 'Rosmorrechflot confirms suspended navigation in Sea of Azov' Interfax (24 February 2022), available at <https://interfax.com/newsroom/top-stories/73960/> accessed 5 January 2024.

83 A navigational warning available at <https://gcaptain.com/wp-content/uploads/2022/03/Russian-gmdss-warning.jpg> accessed 15 January 2024.

in Ukraine, that 'the ports of Ukraine are closed for entry and exit'.[84] This statement is generally uncontroversial as each country retains the sovereign right to regulate access to its ports.[85]

2.2 *Effectiveness of the Blockade*

Shortly after the start of hostilities, the threat emanating from mine warfare appeared. On 3 March 2022, an Estonian general cargo ship *Helt* sank after colliding with a naval mine off the coast of Odesa.[86] Two weeks after this incident, on 18 March, the Russian coastal station Novorossijsk issued a disturbing maritime shipping communication system Navigational Telex (hereinafter NAVTEX)[87] warning message, stating that mines anchored by Ukrainian naval forces near the port of Odesa, had loose chains due to stormy weather. The Novorossijsk station claimed that about 420 mines were floating on the water and accused Ukraine of violating the provisions of the 1907 Hague Convention VIII.[88] The Russian warning was repeated by other NAVTEX stations (e.g., the Turkish NAVTEX station Samsun).[89] However, according to claims by the Romanian Navy, only 28 mines were detected in the western Black Sea until September 2022, including three mines that were destroyed by Turkey, two mines destroyed by Romania, one mine destroyed by Bulgaria, and 22 mines destroyed by Ukraine.[90] Therefore, it rather appears that the Russian

84 IMO Circular Letter No. 4518 (24 February 2022) available at <https://allaboutshipping.co.uk/2022/04/04/ukraine-imo-information-and-web-page/> accessed 30 November 2023.

85 As for a deterrent from Russian close naval blockade and landing attempts Ukraine mostly counted on towed artillery, multiple launch rocket systems (MLRS), and naval mines. Mining of approaches to the Ukrainian coastline started three days before the Russian invasion on 21 February 2022. Borys Kormych and Tatiana Malyarenko 'From gray zone to conventional warfare: the Russia-Ukraine conflict in the Black Sea' (2023) 34(7) Small Wars and Insurgencies 1235, 1248.

86 Tayfun Ozberk, 'Estonian Cargo Ship Sinks Off The Coast Of Odessa' Naval News (3 March 2022), available at <www.navalnews.com/naval-news/2022/03/estonian-cargo-ship-sinks-off-the-coast-of-odessa/> accessed 18 March 2024.

87 NAVTEX – an international service providing navigational and meteorological warnings and forecasts.

88 Tayfun Ozberk, 'Romanian Minesweeper Hits Sea Mine In The Black Sea' Naval News (11 September 2022), available at <www.navyleaders.com/news/romanian-minesweeper-hits-sea-mine-black-sea> accessed 15 January 2024.

89 Ibid.

90 On 8 September 2022, Romanian minesweeper 'Locotenent Dimitrie Nicolescu' was struck by a floating mine 25 nautical miles (46 km) northeast of the port of Constanța. The detonation left a small hole in the stern of the ship, near the waterline. There were no

navigational warning of March 18 (being a misuse of the NAVTEX system[91]) reporting 420 mines in the western Black Sea was part of a hybrid warfare targeting the coastal States Romania, Bulgaria, and Turkey, and international shipping to create a threat and uncertainty discouraging any support for Ukraine.

On 28 February 2022, Turkey invoked Article 19 of the 1936 Montreux Convention[92] and sealed off the Turkish Straits (the Bosporus and the Dardanelles) to Russian warships not registered to Black Sea home bases and not returning to their ports of origin (see *infra* Chapter 11). This prevented the passage of four Russian warships through the Turkish Straits in late February 2022.[93] To allow safe evacuation of seafarers and to ensure safe passage from the ports of Big Odesa, Kherson, Mykolaiv, and Ochakiv, for merchant vessels, Russia established a humanitarian maritime corridor starting on 27 March 2022.[94]

During the first hours of Russia's full-scale invasion on 24 February 2022, they seized Serpents' Island. Control of this island, situated 35 kilometers off the Ukrainian Black Sea coast, means total control of the naval traffic travelling into and out of Ukraine. The withdrawal of Russia from the grain initiative in July 2023 resulted in almost instant missile and drone attacks on Ukrainian ports of the Big Odesa and the Danube River. Ukraine again found itself *de facto*

---

casualties or injuries, and the minesweeper returned to her homeport of Constanta with the help of the naval tugs. Ibid.

91 In addition to its intentions to obstruct the freedom of navigation, Russia had attempted to legalize the illegally annexed Crimean Peninsula and other territories by taking over the areas of responsibility of NAVAREA-III (the Mediterranean Sea, Black Sea, and the Sea of Azov) under the NAVTEX system. Until 2022, the NAVAREA-III Coordinator (Hydrographic Bureau of the Spanish Navy) had ignored the NAVTEX messages from the port of Novorossijsk, which claimed redistribution of the areas of responsibility of the ports of Odesa and Berdyansk. Oleksandr Khara and Andrii Klymenko, 'Maritime Security and Freedom of Navigation Issues in the Black Sea and the Sea of Azov' (November 2021), available at <https://defence.org.ua/wp-content/uploads/doslidzhennya/CDS-Maritime-Security-and-Freedom-of-Navigation-Issues-eng.pdf> accessed 20 February 2024.

92 Convention regarding the Régime of Straits (opened for signature on 20 July 1936, entered into force 9 November 1936) 173 LNTS 213. The 1936 Montreux Convention gives Turkey control over warships entering the straits and guarantees the free passage of civilian vessels in peacetime. Bugajski (n 1) 242–246; see further *infra* Chapter 11.

93 Sinan Tavsan 'Turkey rejects Russia's request for navy ships to pass Bosporus' Nikkei Assia (2 March 2022), available at <https://asia.nikkei.com/Politics/Ukraine-war/Turkey-rejects-Russia-s-request-for-navy-ships-to-pass-Bosporus> accessed 24 February 2024.

94 The corridor represented an 80-mile long and 3-mile-wide marine traffic lane, with a general course of 200°, operational daily from 8 a.m. to 7 p.m. from the assembly area. IMO Circular Letter No. 4543 (28 March 2022), available at <https://allaboutshipping.co.uk/2022/04/04/ukraine-imo-information-and-web-page/> accessed 30 November 2023.

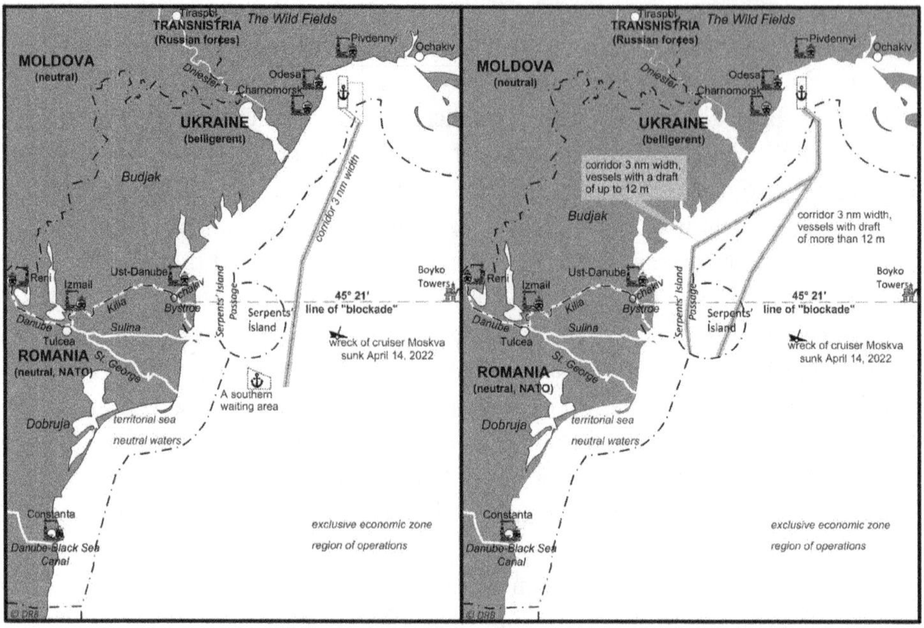

MAP 10.2 The Black Sea Grain Initiative corridor (left map), in force 22 July 2022–17 July 2023. Ukraine declared unilaterally her own temporary sea corridors, in force since 10 August 2023 (right map). Access to the ports of Big Odesa was blocked from 24 February 24 to 21 July 2022.
SOURCE: DARIUSZ RAFAŁ BUGAJSKI

in a naval blockade.[95] Nonetheless, this time in response, and in August 2023, two Ukrainian drones damaged a warship in Novorossijsk Port.[96] Many ships of the Russian Black Sea Fleet withdrew to Novorossijsk from Crimea, which is also a key port for Russian maritime trade. As a result, Russia was forced to relieve its pressure, and on 10 August 2023, Ukraine was able to declare its temporary sea corridors, independent of Moscow (see *supra* Map 10.2).[97]

95 Roman Romaniuk, 'Sea drones, Elon Musk, and high-precision missiles: How Ukraine dominates in the Black Sea' Ukrainska Pravda (1 January 2024), available at <www.pravda.com.ua/eng/articles/2024/01/1/7435326/> accessed 15 January 2024.

96 Olenegorsky Gornyak commissioned in 1976 (Gdańsk, Poland) is a large Ropucha-class landing ship with displacement 2768 t. It was seriously damaged on 4 August 2023. Bill McLoughlin, 'Ukrainian drone strike 'blows hole' in Russian ship at key Black Sea base' The Standard (4 August 2023), available at <www.standard.co.uk/news/world/ukrainian-drone-attack-black-sea-ship-olenegorsky-gornyak-novorossiysk-crimea-b1098717.html> accessed 1 September 2023.

97 Ibid.

While neutral States have a right to continue noncontraband trade at sea, that right is ascribed to neutral flagged vessels and neutral goods but does not guarantee access to belligerent markets. Under the 1856 Paris Declaration, which is accepted as customary law, a neutral flag covers or protects enemy goods from capture and neutral goods may not be seized even if they are carried on enemy merchant ships.[98]

2.3 *A Blockade or a Maritime Exclusion Zone?*

Russia has enforced against Ukraine a 'restricted zone' that is equivalent to 'an exclusion zone' or 'war zone', *de facto* a blockade. Maritime exclusion zones are a lawful method of warfare if they are used to warn merchant and neutral shipping of the hazards inherent in conflict at sea. In any case, before attacking any vessel or aircraft, belligerents must ensure that it is a legitimate military objective. An otherwise protected object does not lose protection by crossing an imaginary line drawn in the sea by a belligerent.[99]

Whether Russia's actions are equivalent to a blockade is a matter of fact and law. In practice, initially, between 24 February and 22 July 2022, when the BSGI began, Russia's operations looked somewhat like a blockade, but the constitutive elements of the blockade have not been met. First of all, it can be agreed that the effectiveness of the notification of a blockade is important, but no specific form (e.g., a diplomatic note) is needed for the notification.[100] Russia misused the NAVTEX system, which is intended solely for transmitting navigation warnings to provide safe navigation, and prohibited vessels from entering parts of the Black Sea, including international waters and the territorial sea of Ukraine. The justification for the prohibition of shipping was to conduct an 'anti-terrorist operation', which, according to Russian political declarations and international practice, can be below the threshold of war. But there is no legal rule in international law that allows to close the international and territorial waters of a foreign State to international navigation in peacetime. Therefore, the Russian declaration has no legal basis, but it is also illogical. If there is no war, there cannot be a naval blockade, and if there is a blockade, there is an international armed conflict.

As a form of economic warfare, naval blockade of enemy ports is designed to sever sea lines of communication and maritime trade between the coastal State and the rest of the world. Although Russia has imposed restrictions in the

98 Articles 2 and 3 of the 1856 Paris Declaration.
99 The Commander's Handbook (n 58) 7–13.
100 Lott (n 11) 78.

Black Sea to prevent the entry or exit of ships from Ukraine, it has not met the legal elements to perfect a *de jure* blockade.

Russia's *de facto* closure of the Sea of Azov and the northwestern part of the Black Sea north of parallel 45°21'N after the invasion in February 2022, was problematic for several reasons. Firstly, the announcement by 'navigational warning'[101] meant that the legal requirements for properly establishing a 'naval blockade' were not met. Moreover, it appears that, while war risks have effectively reduced maritime traffic, Russia has not established an effective naval blockade.[102] As a result, Russia cannot use any belligerent rights derived from a legally established blockade to impose a blockade on vessels. Despite this, there was an attempt to create an illegal naval blockade or *de facto* naval blockade, from at least 24 February until 22 July 2022 which marks the beginning of the BSGI. This assessment cannot be changed even when taking into consideration that Russia allowed since 27 March 2022 vessels and seafarers trapped due to the war to leave Ukrainian ports, which is in conformity with the requirement to establish a period of grace upon the commencement of a blockade.[103]

The closure of navigation in the northern Black Sea must be named a 'maritime exclusion zone' or 'war zone' under international humanitarian law. The establishment of a war zone, however, does not relieve it of its obligation under the law of naval warfare to refrain from attacking vessels and aircraft in the zone that do not constitute military objectives.[104] The institution of a war zone is used to warn vessels and aircraft. A protected vessel or aircraft does not lose its protection from being attacked simply by entering the exclusion zone. As the San Remo Manual states: 'A belligerent cannot be absolved of its duties under international humanitarian law by establishing zones which might adversely affect the legitimate uses of defined areas of the sea'.[105] To the extent that 'a maritime exclusion zone' or 'war zone' serves to warn neutral vessels

---

101 In his communication dated 18th March 2022 the Government of the United Kingdom of Great Britain and Northern Ireland stated: 'We are concerned by the Russian Federation's use of NAVTEX – a maritime shipping communication system – in this way. NAVTEX is a conduit for safety messages enshrined in the Safety of Life at Sea international convention devoted to the perseveration of life at sea. [...] The United Kingdom urges the IMO Member States to condemn the Russian Federation's wholly inappropriate use of NAVTEX.' IMO Circular Letter No. 4537 (21 March 2022), available at <www.imo.org/en/MediaCentre/HotTopics/Pages/Black-Sea-and-Sea-of-Azov-Member-States-Communications.aspx> accessed 15 December 2023.

102 See remarks *supra* in subchapters 2.2. and 2.3.

103 IMO Circular Letter No. 4543 (n 94).

104 Pedrozo (n 11) 25.

105 Rule 105 of the 1994 San Remo Manual, see Doswald-Beck (n 35) 181.

and aircraft away from belligerent activities and thereby reduce their exposure to collateral damage and incidental injury, and to the extent that they do not unreasonably interfere with legitimate neutral commerce, they are lawful.[106] Contrary to this, if a blockade is not, *inter alia*, properly declared or notified or is not effective, then targeting vessels in the area under the guise of breach of blockade may violate the principle of distinction and therefore constitute an offence under international law.[107] Finally, it must be emphasized that the same rules of the law of naval warfare apply inside 'the maritime exclusion zone' which was established by Russia in the Black Sea as outside that zone.[108]

Conclusion

As it is known, hostile powers do not have to take to the battlefield to inflict damage on their adversaries. They can make political and strategic gains in other ways, such as spreading disinformation, launching cyberattacks, and using deception or classic sabotage with the best example being the sabotage of the Nord Stream gas pipeline on 26 September 2022 in the Baltic Sea.[109] These 'hybrid' or 'grey zone' activities blur the line between peace and war and are used to destabilize and undermine affected countries.[110]

In the Black Sea, Russia is conducting a full-scale war that is illegal in itself. The official declaration of the euphemistic 'special military operation' should not obscure the true nature of the ongoing full-scale unprovoked war against

106 The Commander's Handbook (n 58) 7–13.

107 Dale Stephens, 'Wartime Zones', in Michael Schmitt (ed.), *Maritime Operational Zones* (US Naval War College 2013) 4–24.

108 Ibid; Raul 'Pete' Pedrozo, 'Maritime Exclusion Zones in Armed Conflicts' (2022) 99 International Law Studies 527.

109 Three of the four strands of the pipelines, built to provide Russian gas to Germany on the bed of the Baltic Sea, were destroyed by underwater explosions on 26 September 2022 effectively severing the energy link between Russia and Germany. The perpetrator has not been identified, despite three separate national investigations carried out by Germany, Sweden, and Denmark. The vacuum of official information has been filled by speculation variously pinning the blame on the United States, Russia, and the Ukrainian secret services. All three states have denied responsibility. See also *supra* Chapter 5 of Part II. Oliver Moody, 'Ukraine blew up Nord Stream pipelines, Germany believes' The Times (22 May 2023), available at <www.thetimes.co.uk/article/ukraine-blew-up-nord-stream-2-pipeline-german-fbi-2023-95d58fgkv> accessed 17 January 2024.

110 NATO, 'The Secretary General's Annual Report 2019' 29, available at <www.nato.int/nato_static_fl2014/assets/pdf/2020/3/pdf_publications/sgar19-en.pdf> accessed 17 January 2024; Aurel Sari, *Hybrid threats and the law: Building legal resilience* (The European Centre of Excellence for Countering Hybrid Threats 2021).

Ukraine. At the same time, it means that every tool, including a hybrid one, used by Russia which does not violate international law is acceptable under the concept of war itself. Russia is also using some hybrid methods directly against Ukraine which significantly affect other countries. One of them is the threat of naval blockade, and all restrictions interfering with Ukrainian and the neutral countries' navigation in the Black Sea. The indirect targets of those methods are Western societies and countries that are dependent on food imports ('grain as a weapon') from Ukraine and Russia. Another example of Russia's hybrid warfare is the orchestration of an ongoing migration crisis on the Polish-Belarus border.[111] Belarus and Russia are using the existing human rights protection system to exploit vulnerable groups and obtain financial and political benefits. Undoubtedly, by juxtaposing the rights contained in international law of the sea, Russia has the opportunity to create and uphold a confusing and challenging situation in Western societies by influencing food markets and strengthening the migration crises. This is hybrid warfare against Ukraine's allies.[112]

Regardless of whether they are legal or illegal, properly established or not, or effective or not, the Russian 'threat of blockade' and other means and methods of disrupting maritime trade with Ukraine are 'hybrid' in terms of the international consequences directed against the Western allies of Ukraine.

In the current stage of the Russian-Ukrainian war at sea, the only period during which there was an at least partially effective Russian blockade of Ukrainian ports is the period from 24 February to 22 July 2022. It was a *de facto* blockade, but it did not meet the criteria of the law of naval warfare and, therefore, did not give Russia the right to enforce its requirements in respect of shipping. On the contrary, a naval blockade is a method of naval warfare and a part of the maritime *jus in bello*, but blockade as a method of aggression is not legal under *jus ad bellum*.[113] Therefore by declaring and enforcing the blockade, Russia would have been compelled to acknowledge its engagement in warfare, instead of officially disguising its armed aggression against Ukraine as a 'special military operation'.[114]

111 Grzegorz Baziur, 'Operation "Sluice". The so-called migration crisis at the Polish-Belarussian border: an example of hybrid actions taken in the second half of 2021 as documented in the reports of the Polish border guard' (2022) 1 Security Theory and Practice 133.

112 'If the conventional war was conducted only against Ukraine, the hybrid actions and nuclear threat statements were, from the beginning, addressed to Western capitals to diminish their economic and military support of Kiev and cancel the international sanctions against Moscow'. Craisor-Constantin Ionita, 'Conventional and hybrid actions in the Russia's invasion of Ukraine' (2023) 44(4) Security and Defence Quarterly 5.

113 Heinegg (n 8) 204, 212.

114 Lott (n 11) 79.

After 22 July 2022, Russia has only been threatening a blockade. Even though with each passing month of war Russia was losing more and more of their capabilities to implement a blockade, Russia was still able to carry out illegal and indiscriminate attacks on civilian objects, including critical infrastructure such as grain ports. Both the *de facto* blockade and the threat of blockade to international shipping or grain trade are useful means of 'hybrid warfare' directed against the international community, chiefly western supporters of Ukraine. Despite the sustained threat of blockade after two years of war, the only means that could be effectively employed by Russia to enforce a blockade are essentially sea mines and submarines. Under current circumstances, from a military standpoint, such forces cannot ensure the effectiveness required by international law for a blockade along a 130-mile line of the Black Sea, from the mouth of the Danube River to the Crimean Peninsula. However, Russian forces are still capable enough to pose a threat to shipping.

The Russian threat of 'naval blockade' as a method of war is directly aimed against Ukraine, but it is heavily disrupting the international peaceful navigation of formally neutral States. In the case of coastal and maritime trade-dependent nations, they should be well prepared to defend their interests with the support of their allies and partners in international fora, such as the North Atlantic Treaty Organization and the UN. Other 'hybrid tools' at sea that intentionally and not always openly are aimed at impeding the freedom of navigation include excessive protection of underwater cables and pipelines; cyberattacks against shipping; clandestine use of underwater weapons; military exercises disturbing shipping (e.g., shooting areas); declaration of a control zone along a coast, off a port or an island; excessive force protection zones; ship inspection zones; exploitation of disputed maritime areas; detention of foreign-flag vessels or even warships without sufficient legal justification, and a *de facto* naval blockade or maritime exclusion zone, including in choke-points (straits and international canals).

The international law of the sea can be harnessed as a tool to the detriment of security at sea. By juxtaposing the rights contained in the international law, the hybrid actor has the opportunity to create for its victim State(s) a confusing and challenging situation in which it is difficult to form an accurate situational awareness and make the necessary decisions on proper counter-responses in a timely fashion (e.g., a misuse of the NAVTEX system by Russia for disinformation purposes). One of the means used is constant threat of the blockade to create a confusing and challenging situation.

CHAPTER 11

The Montreux Convention and the Ongoing Armed Conflict between Russia and Ukraine

Magne Frostad

Introduction

The ongoing international armed conflict between Russia and Ukraine raises many questions of international law, also in the maritime domain. Examples are the protection of neutral merchant vessels during an international armed conflict,[1] the shipping of non-sanctioned Russian commodities by neutral merchant vessels,[2] and the bilateral agreements entered into by the parties with Turkey and the United Nations on 22 July 2022 regarding the export of grain from Ukraine through the Black Sea.[3]

This paper will begin by considering the geography and history of the relevant Turkish straits, before it addresses certain aspects of the 1936 Convention regarding the Regime of the Straits[4] (hereinafter the Montreux Convention); what constitutes a merchant vessel and a vessel of war, the regulation of peacetime transit of vessels of war, and the regulation of their transit during times of war. Also, some of the classical questions in relation to the Montreux Convention are addressed, as are issues gaining attention in 2022 like whether Turkey may close the Straits to Russian vessels of war, and whether the transportation by Russian owned or flagged merchant vessels of military equipment from Syria to Russian(-held) ports in the Black Sea is in violation of the Montreux

1 Bendik Støren and Gerhard Flaaten, 'Sivile skip løper høy risiko i Svartehavet' Aftenposten (8 March 2022) 10.

2 Bendik Støren, 'Fem norskeide skip har fortsatt å seile til russiske havner' Aftenposten (31 March 2022) 12.

3 Initiative on the Safe Transportation of Grain and Foodstuffs from Ukrainian Ports between Ukraine, Russia, Turkey, and the United Nations (adopted 22 July 2022, entered into force 22 July 2022), available at <https://www.un.org/sites/un2.un.org/files/black_sea_grain_initiative_full_text.pdf> accessed 30 August 2023.

4 Great Britain and Northern Ireland, Australia, Bulgaria, France, Greece, Japan, Roumania, Turkey, Union of Soviet Socialist Republics, Yugoslavia, Convention regarding the Régime of the Straits, with Annexes and Protocol (adopted 20 July 1936, entered into force 9 November 1936) 173 LNTS 213 (No. 4015).

 | DOI:10.1163/9789004707993_013

Convention. The paper will then consider the regulation of amendment and denouncement of the Montreux Convention, before it looks ahead at the future.

On the other hand, this paper will not consider the possibility of suspending the entitlements of Russia under the Montreux Convention as countermeasures or sanctions,[5] nor the enforcement of such responses by foreign coastal States or flag States outside of territorial waters.[6] Also, issues of aerial navigation will not be covered.[7]

1 Geography and History

The use of these two natural waterways, linked by the Sea of Marmara – the Bosporus strait (Istanbul Strait) to the north-east, and the Dardanelles (Çanakkale Strait) to the south-west – has generated much international tension over the centuries. From end to end the Straits cover some 300 km, and vessels today normally navigate them over 16–18 hours. At its most narrow point, the waters are only 700 meters wide.[8]

The relationship between the Russian and the Ottoman Empires has suffered under their often-diverging political interests,[9] and therefore the use

5 As suggested by Mary E O'Connell in a comment to Muhammed E Hayyar, 'Can Turkey Close the Turkish Straits to Russian Warships?' (28 February 2022) EJIL: Talk!, available at <https://www.ejiltalk.org/can-turkey-close-the-turkish-straits-to-russian-warships/> accessed 30 August 2023. On the application of the obligation not to recognize violations of *jus cogens* norms, see also Nilüfer Oral, 'To Close or Not to Close: The Closing of the Turkish Straits under Articles 19 and 21 of the 1936 Montreux Convention Regarding the Regime of the Straits' (4 March 2022) Völkerrechtsblog, available at <10.17176/20220304-120920-0> accessed 29 September 2023.

6 Arguing for NATO inspecting merchant vessels possibly carrying Russian arms, see Yörük Işık, 'Russia is violating the spirit of Montreux by using civilian ships for war' mei.edu (18 May 2022), available at <https://www.mei.edu/publications/russia-violating-spirit-montreux-using-civilian-ships-war> accessed 30 August 2023.

7 See here Mark Nevitt, 'The Russia-Ukraine Conflict, the Black Sea, and the Montreux Convention' (28 February 2022) Just Security, available at <https://www.justsecurity.org/80384/the-russia-ukraine-conflict-the-black-sea-and-the-montreux-convention/> accessed 30 August 2023.

8 The geographical and navigational data are found in Kurtuluş Yücel, *The Legal Regime of the Turkish Straits: Regulation of the Montreux Convention and its Importance on the International Relation safter the Conflict of Ukraine* (PhD thesis at Johann Wolfgang Goethe-University Frankfurt am Main 2019) 185.

9 Ibid, 34–72.

of these waterways has been regulated in a multitude of international agreements – typically bilateral ones – over the centuries.[10]

One clause used for over 300 years was 'the ancient rule', *i.e.* that no foreign ship may pass these straits.[11] Exceptions were granted in bilateral treaties, but even then foreign merchant vessel were not allowed to sail beyond Bosporus.[12] The transit rights for Russian merchant vessels were nevertheless established in the 1774 peace treaty of Kutchuk Kainardji,[13] with similar rights for many other States from 1784 onwards.[14] A general opening of passage for merchant vessels belonging to *any* flag was established as late as in the 1841 London Convention.[15] On the other hand, 'the ancient rule' applied more or less to vessels of war up to 1918.[16]

After World War I Turkey had to consent to large restrictions on her sovereignty in the 1923 Treaty of Lausanne[17] and the 1923 Convention relating to the Regime of the Straits and Turkey (hereinafter the 1923 Lausanne Convention),[18] but over time agreement was reached upon a different regulation where the legitimate concerns of Turkey were better catered for. Here, Turkey argued that

10 A good overview is provided by ibid, 22–72.

11 Ibid, 31. A good description is also found in André Gerolymatos, 'The Turkish Straits: History, Politics and Strategic Dilemmas' (2014) 28 Ocean Yearbook 58–79.

12 Yücel (n 8) 32.

13 Ibid, 40–41. See Treaty of Peace (Küçük Kaynarca) between the Russian Empire and the Ottoman Empire (adopted 21 July 1774), in J C Hurewitz, *Diplomacy in the Near and Middle East. A Documentary Record, 1535–1914*, Vol. I (D. van Nostrand Company 1956) 54–61.

14 Yücel (n 8) 45.

15 Gündüz Aybay and Nilüfer Oral, 'Turkey's Authority to regulate Passage of Vessels through the Turkish Straits' (1998) III (2) Perceptions – Journal of International Affairs 1, 4. See Convention Regarding the Straits: Austria, France, Great Britian, Prussia, and The Ottoman Empire, 13 July 1841, in Hurewitz (n 13) 123.

16 Yücel (n 8) 43. Again, exceptions typically followed in bilateral agreements between the Russian and Ottoman empires, see ibid, 48, 49 and 51.

17 Treaty of Peace and Exchange of War Prisoners with Turkey (adopted 24 July 1923, entered into force 6 August 1924) XXVIII LNTS 12–113 (No. 701). Its Art. 23 states: "The High Contracting Parties are agreed to recognise and declare the principle of freedom of transit and of navigation, by sea and by air, in time of peace as in time of war, in the strait of the Dardanelles, the Sea of Marmora and the Bosporus, as prescribed in the separate Convention signed this day, regarding the regime of the Straits. This Convention will have the same force and effect in so far as the present High Contracting Parties are concerned as if it formed part of the present Treaty".

18 Convention relating to the Regime of the Straits Concluded between the British Empire, France, Italy, Bulgaria, Greece, Rumania, Soviet Russia, Yugoslavia and Turkey (adopted 24 July 1923, entered into force 6 August 1924) XXVIII LNTS 115–137 (No. 702). For an overview of the 1923 Convention, see Nihan Ünlü, *The Legal Regime of the Turkish Straits* (Martinus Nijhoff 2002) 33–38; Yücel (n 8) 89–96.

clausula rebus sic stantibus necessitated a change as the situation in 1936 was very different from that of 1923 when the previous convention was negotiated.[19] The current regime was then established by the 1936 Convention, often named the Montreux Convention after the Swiss city where the text was adopted on 20 July 1936.

Art 27 of the Montreux Convention opens it to accession to all parties to the 1923 Treaty of Lausanne, but due to uncertainty of State succession it is currently uncertain how many States are actually party to the Montreux Convention.[20] That leaves open the question of how the right to transit is to be understood in relation to non-parties to the Montreux Convention – is there a right to such under customary international law?[21] At the very least, the regime has been 'applied *vis-a-vis* the whole world'.[22]

---

19 Ünlü (n 18) 40–41. The underlying issue was the potential inability of the League of Nations to provide security, as illustrated by Japan's invasion of Manchuria in 1931, and Italy's invasion of Ethiopia in 1935; ibid, 40.

20 For the view that there are 9 parties to the Convention, see United Nations Treaty Series Online, available at <https://treaties.un.org/pages/showDetails.aspx?objid=0800000280166981> accessed 30 August 2023 (where admittedly Japan is mentioned without a "Date of Effect"). According to this source, Japan signed, but have not ratified the Convention. Following the 1951 Treaty of San Francisco (the peace treaty between Japan and the Allied Powers) Art. 8 (b) "Japan renounces all such rights and interests as it may derive from being a signatory power of [...] the Straits Agreement of Montreux of July 20, 1936 [...]. For the view that the current parties are Australia, Bulgaria, France, Georgia, Greece, Italy, Japan, Romania, the Russian Federation, Turkey, Ukraine, United Kingdom and Cyprus, see Stefan Birkner, *Die Durchfahrtsrechte von Handels- und Kriegsschiffen durch die türkischen Meerengen* (Duncker & Humblot 2002) 159. On Ukraine becoming a party, see John CK Daly, 'Referee and Goalkeeper of the Turkish Straits: The Relevance and Strategic Implications of the Montreux Convention for Conflict in the Black Sea' jamestown.org (10 May 2022), 11, available at <https://jamestown.org/program/referee-and-goalkeeper-of-the-turkish-straits-the-history-relevance-and-strategic-implications-of-the-montreux-convention-for-conflict-in-the-black-sea/> accessed 30 August 2023. In addition to the parties to the Convention, Turkey has entered into bilateral treaties with Poland and the US that grant vessels of the other party similar entitlements; Ernst Tennstedt, *Die türkischen Meerengen im Zweiten Weltkrieg* (Institut für Internationale Angelegenheiten der Universität Hamburg 1981) 8 (re Poland), and Harry N Howard, 'The United States and the problem of the Turkish Straits: A Reference Article' (1947) 1 Middle East Journal 59, 67–68 (re US).

21 For possibly the view that a right to transit exists in customary international law, see Yücel (n 8) 122, 231.

22 Gerald G Fitzmaurice, 'The Straits Convention of Montreux, 1936' (1937) 18 British Yearbook of International Law 186, 190.

2 The Montreux Convention – an Overview and Selected Topics

2.1 *The Interpretational Context*

The original version of the Montreux Convention is in French, but use will here be made of an English translation published by the League of Nations, and in line with the terminology of the Montreux Convention, the term 'Straits' will refer to both straits mentioned above and the Sea of Marmara.[23]

Following the preamble of the Montreux Convention its intention is to regulate transit and navigation in the Straits in such a way that the principle of Art. 23 of the 1923 Treaty of Lausanne is safeguarded.[24] Also, it explicitly states that this will take into consideration the security of both Turkey and the States bordering the Black Sea.

The right to transit and navigation as such is established in Art 1, where para. 2 states that '[t]he exercise of this freedom shall henceforth be regulated by the provisions of the present Convention.' This is meant to replace the previous 1923 Lausanne Convention,[25] whereas also other legal instruments and customary international law may influence this transit and navigation.[26]

These days, the technical terms used for the vessels covered by the Montreux Convention are warship, auxiliary vessel, and merchant vessel. Of these, the first term is missing in the Montreux Convention, whereas the second type has a diverging definition, as does to some extent the term merchant vessel.[27] This paper will use the terms found in the Montreux Convention.

2.2 *Overview of the Montreux Convention*

The Montreux Convention mirrors to some extent the categories found in the Annex to the 1923 Lausanne Convention. The Montreux Convention is divided into 5 sections, 4 annexes, and 1 protocol. Section I considers merchant vessels, whereas Section II deals with vessels of war, Section III aircraft, Section IV general provisions, and Section V final provisions. Annex I deals with taxes and charges, Annex II with standard displacement and categories of naval vessels, whereas Annex III considers three elderly training ships, and Annex IV the

23 See preamble, 1st paragraph of the Convention.

24 For the text, see n. 17.

25 See also preamble, 2nd paragraph, of the Convention.

26 This well-established frame of interpretation is reflected in the Vienna Convention on the Law of Treaties (adopted 23 May 1969, entered into force 27 January 1980) 1155 UNTS 331, Art 31.

27 Compare here with the definitions found in Rules 13 *litra* g, h, and I of the 1994 San Remo Manual, see Louise Doswald-Beck (ed.), *San Remo Manual on International Law Applicable to Armed Conflicts at Sea* (Cambridge University Press 1995) 9, and 90–91.

calculation of Black Sea tonnage. The protocol allows Turkey to provisionally apply the regime of the Montreux Convention and gives her the right to 'immediately remilitarize the zone of the Straits as defined in the Preamble of the said Convention'.

Before Section I commences, the text includes the preamble and Art 1. In Art 1 the 'principle of freedom of transit and navigation by the sea in the Straits' is recognized,[28] and Section I clarifies what this means for merchant vessels, in peace time and during war. The only restriction here is during a war when Turkey is a belligerent.[29] It is also worthwhile to mention that the definition of vessels of war is found in Section II and Annex II. Section II moreover regulates transit of vessels of war in times of peace and war, and the Montreux Convention has different rules depending on whether Turkey is a belligerent or not. Also, different rules apply to Black Sea powers and non-Black Sea ones. The specifics of Sections III, IV and V (beyond Arts 28 and 29) of the Montreux Convention will not be addressed in this paper.

2.3 *Merchant Vessels*

Merchant vessels are in Art. 7 defined negatively as those vessels not covered by Section II of the Montreux Convention, which is the part that deals with vessels of war. However, Art 8 merely refers further to Annex II.[30] This is a rather technical affair and will be investigated further in chapter 2.4. For now, it suffices to note that merchant vessels are typically privately owned vessels used for primarily trade, but that also yachts and similar are included. The most important characteristic of a merchant vessel under the Montreux Convention is that it does not support the war effort in a way that would have made it at least an auxiliary vessel.

---

28 This was the first time that the freedom of transit and navigation through the Straits was considered a principle of international law; Christos L Rozakis and Petros N Stagos, *The Turkish Straits* (Martinus Nijhoff Publishers 1987) 132 with further references. The phrase "freedom of transit and navigation" is later used in relation to merchant vessels (Arts 2, 4 and 5), whereas the mere reference to "freedom of transit" is used in relation to vessels of war (Arts 10 and 19). Vignes made this observation in Daniel Vignes, '1936 Montreux Convention regarding the Regime of the Straits', in Natalino Ronzitti (ed.), *The Law of Naval Warfare – A Collection of Agreements and Documents with Commentaries* (Martinus Nijhoff Publishers 1988) 435, 473. Admittedly, reference is also made to the first mentioned phrase in Art 28 in the section on final provisions.

29 Art 5 of the Montreux Convention.

30 This Annex is explicitly stated as based on the Treaty for the Limitation of Naval Armament (adopted 25 March 1936, entered into force 31 December 1942) USTS No. 919 (1936 London Naval Treaty).

Although the regulation of transit in the Montreux Convention differs from its predecessor – the 1923 Lausanne Convention – it might nevertheless be worthwhile to note that in para. 1 of the Annex to the 1923 convention the category merchant vessels is held to include hospital ships, yachts and fishing vessels, and non-military aircraft.

Governmentally owned ships not used for war fighting purposes, nor in support of such (as auxiliary vessels), must also be considered as merchant vessels for the purpose of this Convention. Turkey has over time expanded this category to also include passage of ships in tow, as well as other structures in tow like floating docks and drilling platforms that are not normally considered as vessels.[31]

Although the issue of conversion of merchant vessels into vessels of war did arise under one of the previous regimes,[32] it is not addressed by the Montreux Convention. Merchant vessels are under Art 2 entitled to free transit and navigation in times of peace, and this right also exists in times of war as long as Turkey is not one of the parties to the conflict.[33] It is worthwhile to note that this right applies under Art 2 to 'any flag or with any kind of cargo'. That said, transit does not include a right to change cargo with another ship while undertaking transit, and the Turkish restrictions enacted in 1937 in relation to weapons intended for the Spanish civil war shifting hands in the Marmara Sea, should be seen in light of this.[34]

If on the other hand Turkey is a party to a war (belligerent), Art 5 upholds the freedom of transit and navigation to merchant vessels *not* belonging to the state at war with Turkey, as long as 'they do not in any way assist the enemy'. Although no reference is made to pilotage, it would be odd if it could be required in the less dangerous situation to Turkey regulated in Art 6, but not here.[35]

This raises the issue of whether 'belonging' to the other side of the conflict not only covers vessels flagged by that party, but also vessels flagged elsewhere but owned by private or public entities of the enemy State. It would seem natural to apply here the rule found in the 1994 San Remo Manual on International

31 Aybay and Oral (n 15) 6.

32 During the Russo-Japanese war transit of Russian merchant vessels was prohibited through the Straits as long as Russia refused to agree to not convert them into vessels of war; Tennstedt (n 20) 3. The opposite situation occurred in 1902 when four Russian torpedo boats were allowed to transit as merchant vessels after having dismantled their arms and change crew to civilian ones, see ibid, 56–57.

33 Art 4 of the Montreux Convention.

34 Tennstedt (n 20) 10.

35 Birkner (n 20) 191–192.

Law Applicable to Armed Conflicts at Sea, *i.e.* that '[e]nemy character can be determined by registration, ownership, charter or other criteria.'[36] Also, 'not in any way assist the enemy' may seem to *inter alia* constitute a wide notion of contraband.[37] If Turkey has good cause to think that the vessel is assisting the enemy, she may also visit and search the merchant vessel.[38]

The antechamber to being a belligerent is also regulated in the Montreux Convention. The threshold under Art 6 is Turkey being 'threatened with imminent danger of war', but the only additional power granted Turkey, compared to the peace time regime for merchant vessels in Art 2, is that the Straits must then be entered by day, and that transit must follow the route indicated by Turkey. Also, Turkey may make pilotage obligatory, although free of charge.[39]

2.4 *The Definition of Vessels of War*

2.4.1 Some General Issues

As mentioned above, for the definition of vessels of war in Art 8 we are referred to Annex II. Here, a number of different categories of vessels of war are defined; capital ships, aircraft carriers, light surface vessels, submarines, minor war vessels, and auxiliary vessels. If the vessel falls outside of these categories, it is technically considered a merchant vessel for the purpose of this Convention.

The definition of these categories of vessels of war in Annex II is a consequence of a British suggestion based upon Art 1, para. B of the 1936 London Naval Agreement, that was later included in the Montreux Convention itself since not all naval powers were parties to the London Naval Agreement.[40] These two lists, however, diverge as the London Agreement also referred to 'small craft' naval surface vessels under 100 tons – a category excluded from the

36 Rule 117 of the 1994 San Remo Manual, see Doswald-Beck (n 27) 31, 193–195.

37 The 1994 San Remo Manual Rules 146–152 may here be of guidance. They refer to capture of neutral merchant vessels outside of neutral waters, and the territorial and internal waters of the capturing state would be examples of such. However, an argument may be made that a right to "merely" hinder the transit may exist even at a lower "intensity" of cooperation with the enemy than needs to be the case when the outcome may be capture. For the view that "any act contrary to the obligations of a neutral is to be interpreted as "assisting the enemy", see Nicolas Politis as referred to in Ferenc A Váli, *The Turkish Straits and NATO* (Hoover Institution Press 1972) 42, n. d.

38 Rozakis and Stagos (n 28) 207, and Yücel (n 8) 108.

39 On the risks of this subjective determination, see Rozakis and Stagos (n 28) 207. For the view that the restrictions imposed upon transit during World War II was based on this article, see Tennstedt (n 20) 34–35.

40 Cemil Bilsel, 'The Turkish Straits in the Light of Recent Turkish-Soviet Russian Correspondence' (1947) 41 American Journal of International Law 727, 739.

Montreux Convention seemingly due to British strategic considerations,[41] and this no matter their armaments, etc.[42] The 100 tons threshold is found in the definitions of light surface vessels, minor war vessels and auxiliary vessels, and the lack of reference to this threshold in all the other categories, with exception for submarines, is natural as they are capital ships and aircraft carries, inherently heavier than 100 tons already in 1936.

Perhaps counterintuitively, many law enforcement vessels may be expected to qualify as 'merchant vessels', although some coast guard vessels may be challenging to categorize. When they are operated by the armed forces, and armed in a way that would consider them as vessels of war under Annex II, an argument can be made for them not enjoying the transit and navigational benefits of merchant vessels.

A fundamental problem with the categorization of vessels of war under the Montreux Convention is the use of artillery diameter when considering whether a vessel belongs to one category of vessels of war or another.[43] With armaments moving from guns to missiles, many vessels that would otherwise have been considered as vessels of war of a specific category will fall outside of their traditional categories, as they do not mount guns with caliber larger than 203 mm (capital ships and light surface vessels) or 155 mm (some light surface vessels). Also, torpedoes are perhaps not as much used by candidates to the categories of 'minor war vessels' and 'auxiliary vessels' these days as was the case in 1936, and therefore fewer vessels would now be exempted from these categories than would have been the case before. For example, those vessels previously referred to as motor-torpedo boats have – to the extent that their hulls are still used – typically been rearmed with missiles instead of torpedoes. To the extent new classes of vessels have been designed to replace the motor-torpedo boats, these newer vessels typically do not include torpedoes in their armaments.[44]

---

41 Süleyman Seydi and Steven Morewood, 'Turkey's Application of the Montreux Convention in the Second World War' (2005) 41(1) Middle Eastern Studies 79, 88. Bilsel however considers the reasons for this exclusion to be unclear; Bilsel (n 40) 739.

42 For possibly a different view, see Tennstedt (n 20) 62.

43 In the same direction, see Nevitt (n 7).

44 See, e.g. the Norwegian Skjold-class corvette vessels. They are armed with 8 surface Naval Strike Missiles, one 76 mm rapid cannon, and 12,7 mm heavy machine gun and Mistral anti-air missiles (<https://www.forsvaret.no/om-forsvaret/utstyr-og-materiell/sjo> accessed 30 August 2023), and replaced the old Hauk class motor-torpedo boats armed with 6 Penguin-missiles, 2 torpedoes, 40 mm cannon, two 12,7 mm heavy machine guns, and Mistral anti-air missiles (<https://no.wikipedia.org/wiki/Motortorpedob%C3%A5ter_i_Norge> accessed 30 August 2023).

On a related issue, the US argued in relation to Soviet protests in 1968 regarding *USS Dyess* – a destroyer equipped with an 8-missile anti-submarine rocket launcher with a 305mm diameter – that the provisions in Annex II could not apply even by analogy as this class of arms did not exist when the Montreux Convention was negotiated.[45]

The very detailed categorization of classes of vessels of war in Annex II, and presumably also the will of the negotiators and States today, argue against an *abstraction* of the danger potential of these classes of vessels in the 1930s in such a way that newer types of vessels are correspondingly categorized according to what their danger potential is today.[46]

No reference is directly made to armaments in Annex II's treatment of aircraft carriers, where the defining feature is that the vessel is 'designed or adapted *primarily* for the purpose of carrying *and* operating aircraft at sea' (emphasis added). Of course, the weapon is here the aircraft themselves. The mere transport of aircraft is not enough, the vessel must also in theory have a way of making the aircraft airborne – if not the transported ones than at least some other aircraft, beyond mere smaller drones, that the vessel was designed or adapted primarily to cater for. The vessel would also fall outside of this definition if the purpose of carrying and operating aircraft at sea is merely a *secondary* purpose for which it is designed or adapted. Suffice to say, the assessment of such genuine primary or secondary purpose may be a challenging one. It would nevertheless seem odd if the flag State could circumnavigate this category of vessel merely by filling the flight deck of a carrier with e.g. aircraft of a type that needs a longer airfield than the flight deck, and which are only to be used after they have been unloaded from the vessel when it reaches its destination. And although the text refers to 'aircraft', and helicopters were not in use by armed forces in 1936, the proved tactical use of the latter has led to the development of helicopter carriers, and these must presumably be covered by the category of aircraft carries for the purpose of the Montreux Convention. With the introduction of short take-off and vertical landing aircraft, separating the two types of carries will be difficult.

Submarines is another category in Annex II where no specifics are provided regarding armaments. Thus, as with the aircraft/helicopter carriers, technological developments are here unlikely to generate problem in relation to these categories covered by Annex II. The definition even lacks a reference to it being a vessel of war, something that is included for all the other vessels except

45 Rozakis and Stagos (n 28) 132.

46 Birkner (n 20) 178–180.

auxiliary vessels that are referred to as 'naval surface vessels'. This could be held to include civilian – e.g. research – submarines.[47]

None of the categories of vessels of war make any reference to the size of the crew, nor for that sake to the existence of any crew at all. This was naturally interpreted into the term vessel back in 1936, but this now raises the question of how newer autonomous vessels fit into this fold.[48]

Also, the more fundamental question of what criteria need to be met before a vessel constitutes an auxiliary vessel needs to be addressed. These are considered in Annex II as 'naval surface vessels' as opposed to 'surface vessels of war' which is the formulation used for the other categories of vessels of war. Such vessels are not 'specifically built as fighting ships' and they are 'normally employed [...] in some other way than as fighting ships' (the examples of fleet duties and troop transport are given by the provision[49]). There is thus a nexus between what these vessels do and the overall war effort, and their identification as *naval* surface vessels indicate some degree of organizational link to the armed forces. To remain within this category of vessels, they must have limited armaments, not being designed for protection by armor plate, nor designed for greater speed than 28 knots, as well as have little aircraft capacity.[50] Should the vessel fulfill any of the disqualifying criteria of B (6) *litra* a-g, it will instead seemingly be 'upgraded' to minor war vessel, light surface vessel or even capital ship depending on what disqualifying criteria is fulfilled, and the tonnage of the said vessel. The reference to how these vessels are 'normally employed' might seem to exclude from this category merchant vessels that may be used in the future for military purposes, but have not been nor are so used at the present.[51]

Here, help may be found in the 1994 San Remo Manual. In Rule 13 (h) an auxiliary vessel is defined as 'a vessel, other than a warship, that is owned or under the exclusive control of the armed forces of a State *and* used for the

47 For the view that all civilian submarines are included, see Tennstedt (n 20) 47–48. These are then slightly counterintuitively considered as vessels of war due to Art 8's general reference to Annex II.

48 See here Yoram Dinstein and Arne W Dahl (eds.), *Oslo Manual on Select Topics of the Law of Armed Conflict: Rules and Commentary* (Springer Open 2020) 43–53.

49 For an example of what might have to be considered as a merchant vessel due to the reference to "vessels of war" in most of the categories under Annex II, see Tennstedt (n 20) 48.

50 See Annex II, B, (6) of the Montreux Convention.

51 This seems to be the view of the Turkish Minister of Foreign Affairs Numan Menemencioglu on 4 November 1942; 'The Chargé in Turkey (Kelley) to the Secretary of State' (1942) IV The Foreign Relations of the United States: Diplomatic Papers, 809.

time being on government non-commercial service' (emphasis added).[52] Thus, there is no need for the auxiliary vessels to operate together with naval forces, providing seaborn logistics to land and air forces will suffice.

A related issue is how armed merchant vessels are to be considered. The *Kassel* incident in June 1944 – where a *Kriegstransportschiffe*-class ship was found to have onboard the military uniforms of the crew as well as weapons[53] – have by some been seen to exclude them from transit, whereas armed British merchant vessels transited the Straits until 1941 when German control of Greece made transit too dangerous.[54]

Of course, the categorization as either this or that depends on the vessel still fulfilling that function. In other words, when a decommissioned vessel of war is towed to its place of dismantling, there are good reasons to interpret an exception to the otherwise applying rules. Also, Turkish ships are not covered by these restrictions.[55]

2.4.2 Over-Aged Vessels

Earlier, technological advances often meant having to redesign the whole vessel. Thus, the list of 'over-age' in Annex II for such vessels of war made sense in 1936. As seen during both World Wars, older vessels were often easy prey for newer ones. This must be kept in mind in relation to how soon a vessel was to be considered over-aged under the Montreux Convention, ranging from 13 years with submarines to 26 years with capital ships.

If nothing else, the Cold War showed us that hulls may be refitted with new weapon systems, or updates of older ones. For example, USS *Iowa* – a 46,000 ton standard displacement battleship commissioned in 1943 – was only finally decommissioned in 1990, and stricken from the list of US naval ships as late as 2006.[56] If the list in Annex II was to apply, the battleship would have been considered over-age in 1968, when she was admittedly decommissioned, but

---

52 As stated in the commentary to the San Remo Manual, "[a]n auxiliary vessel does not have the rights, duties and obligations of either a warship or a merchant vessel."; Doswald-Beck (n 27) 90. Written originally in 1947, Tennstedt finds that international law requires an organizational connection between the auxiliary vessel and the naval forces, and that mere actual use would not be enough. See Tennstedt (n 20) 71.

53 Tennstedt (n 20) 21, 38–39, 61 and 81, and Seydi and Morewood (n 41) 94. For a list of the German merchant vessels that transited the straits during World War II, as well as Rumanian, Bulgarian, Italian and Hungarian vessels undertaking similar transport for Germany, see Tennstedt (n 20) 41.

54 Tennstedt (n 20) 73–81. See nevertheless Seydi and Morewood (n 41) 92–94.

55 Váli (n 37) 43.

56 See USS Iowa (BB-61), available at <https://en.wikipedia.org/wiki/USS_Iowa_(BB-61)> accessed 30 August 2023.

she was returned to service in 1984 after extensive refitting and equipment modification.[57]

Especially non-intuitive these days are 13 years as threshold for over-aging of submarines, as many modern navies have submarines in service well beyond those 13 years of age. That said, the very concept of over-agedness has a restricted reach within the Montreux Convention. On the one hand, it clearly applies to the assessment of tonnage of Black Sea States under Art 18, as shown by Annex IV, para. 1, i.f.: 'Only those vessels shall be taken into consideration which are not over-age according to the definition contained in the said Annex.' Similarly, over-agedness applies under Annex IV, para. 2 to the information to be provided under Art 18(1)(b). Another clear case is the adjustment of the 15,000 tons limitation in Art 14(1) in relation to transit at the same time of two of the vessels mentioned in Annex III.[58]

The question is then whether the concept of over-agedness relaxes more generally the tonnage limitations of Art 14. This might be argued as the concept is detailed in Annex II where the typification of the vessels of war, including their tonnage, is found. However, beyond the fact that no State has argued this, Art 14(1) provides two explicit exceptions to this tonnage limitation and these are Art 11 and Annex III. Such an explicit list of exceptions should largely be taken as exhaustive, and as over-agedness is the very essence of Annex III, the relationship of this concept to the tonnage limitation in Art 14 has not been overlooked.[59] In short, much space is used in the Annexes on this concept of perhaps limited practical use today.

2.5 *Peacetime Freedom of Transit for Vessels of War*

Art 10 allows for freedom of transit during peacetime for light surface vessels, minor war vessels, and auxiliary vessels, whether they belong to States bordering the Black Sea or not.[60] The main difference between these and merchant vessels regarding transit is the lack of a need to pay the taxes and charges that the latter category is subjected to.[61] Also, these vessels of war need to begin

---

57 Ibid.

58 Art 14 (1) has an explicit reference to Annex III of the Montreux Convention.

59 The use of the concept of over-agedness in the 1936 London Naval Agreement Arts. 1(c) and XXIII does not provide any additional understanding to the inherent meaning of this concept of relevance to how it is to be understood under the Convention, beyond what is already clear from the language used in the Convention itself.

60 The provision even states "whatever their flag", thus presupposing such vessels potentially being flagged with another state than the one owning it.

61 Art 2 and Annex I of the Montreux Convention.

their transit during daylight,[62] as well as provide previous notification under Art 13.[63]

For other vessels of war, *i.e.* capital ships, aircraft carriers, and submarines,[64] the right to transit must abide by the conditions in Arts 11 and 12.[65] Here, a difference is made between vessels belonging to a 'Black Sea Power' and those who do not.

For the first group, they may send their submarines that have been constructed or purchased outside of the Black Sea to the base of the vessel in the Black Sea. These Black Sea submarines may also transit the Straits in order to be repaired 'in dockyards outside the Black Sea', but then 'detailed information on the matter is [to be] given to Turkey'.[66] Art 12 also provides details on how the transit by these submarines is to be undertaken. The provision is intended to be understood as excluding a right to transit for submarines of non-Black Sea States.[67] It would thus seem that the mere sending of Black Sea submarines to patrol on the seas beyond the Straits, i.e. where no dockyard service is at least part of the voyage, would be in violation of the Montreux Convention. As would the Black Sea States sending submarines based elsewhere to the Black Sea for patrolling, etc.

Moreover, the 'Black Sea Powers' are also entitled to send their capital ships through the Straits, as long as these vessels sail singly and are only escorted by two destroyers, without having to consider the tonnage maximum in Art 14.[68] For both groups of States, the use of aircraft carried by a vessel of war is not permitted during transit,[69] and transit shall take no longer than necessary.[70] Also, Art 14 limits the total amount of non-Turkish naval forces that may transit at

62 Ibid, Art 10.

63 See also ibid, Art 24(3)(2). At least earlier, Turkey would seem to enforce these notification requirements strictly; Váli (n 37) 105–106.

64 See the listing of categories of vessels in Annex II of the Montreux Convention.

65 Explicitly stated in ibid, Art 10(2).

66 Ibid, Art 12.

67 For the same view, see Raul 'Pete' Pedrozo, 'Closing the Turkish Straits in Times of War' (3 March 2022) Lieber Institute West Point, available at <https://lieber.westpoint.edu/tag/turkish-straits/> accessed 30 August 2023.

68 Art 11 of the Montreux Convention.

69 Ibid, Art 15.

70 Ibid, Art 16, although it nevertheless makes exception for situations of "damage or peril of the sea".

the same time to 15,000 tons,[71] and no more than 9 vessels.[72] Exceptions to this tonnage limitation are made for naval auxiliary vessels specifically designed for the carriage of fuel – liquid or non-liquid – under Art 9, vessels having suffered damage during their passage[73] – at the very least if they need to undergo repairs in the Straits – and for vessels paying a courtesy visit at the invitation of Turkey to a port in the Straits.[74]

No reference is made in these provisions to aircraft carriers, and the silence is telling as the very category itself is mentioned in Annex II. As these ships are seemingly not considered capital ships since they are listed separately,[75] nor do they belong to any of the other categories mentioned in Art 10, they would not be entitled to ordinary transit rights. Also, the reference to use of aircraft in Art 15 does not refer to aircraft carriers, but rather to other categories of vessels of war that carry aircraft for typically scouting purposes, catapulted from the vessel and later recovered at sea.[76] As held by Starr, '[a]ircraft carriers of any flag are banned outright from the Turkish Straits, in both times of peace and war'.[77] This is also supported by the negotiating history.[78]

That said, State practice has not always been to the letter. Turkey thus allowed from late 1960s onwards transit of the Soviet helicopter cruisers *Moskva* and *Leningrad*, from mid-70s Kiev class carriers,[79] and in 1991 the Kuznetsov class carriers, presumably for political reasons. It would seem that these vessels were intentionally designated as cruisers to circumnavigate the limitations of the Montreux Convention.[80] The carrier-quality of e.g. the Kiev class 'cruiser'

---

71 Exception again made for ibid, Art. 11, as well as for Annex III, *i.e.* in relation to three Japanese over-aged training ships that were scrapped during the late 1940s.

72 For the view that violations of the tonnage limitations "have become routine while complaints have been rather limited", see Rozakis and Stagos (n 28) 132.

73 Art 14(3) of the Montreux Convention.

74 Ibid, Art 14(4). See Arts 14 and 17.

75 For a different view, see Nevitt (n 7).

76 Gary Knight, 'The Kiev and the Turkish Straits' (1977) 71(1) American Journal of International Law 125, 126.

77 Stephen Starr, 'How The 1936 Montreux Convention would Help Russia In A Ukraine War' International Business Times (5 December 2014), available at <https://www.ibtimes.com/how-1936-montreux-convention-would-help-russia-ukraine-war-1582507> accessed 30 August 2023. See also Bilsel (n 40) 738; Vignes (n 28) 473; Birkner (n 20) 181; James Kraska, 'Can Turkey Legally Close Its Straits to Russian Warships? It's Complicated' Foreign Policy (1 March 2022), available at <https://foreignpolicy.com/2022/03/01/turkey-black-sea-straits-russia-ships-ukraine-war/> accessed 30 August 2023.

78 Birkner (n 20) 181.

79 Daly (n 20) 11.

80 See Knight (n 76) 125, 129; Rozakis and Stagos (n 28) 54–55, 132; Vignes (n 28) 478–479; Birkner (n 20) 173.

is illustrated by the 'large, angled flight deck and 25–30 VTOL [vertical takeoff and landing] fighter aircraft designed to provide air cover [that] make it clear that the vessel was designed *primarily* for carrying and operating both the helicopters and the VTOL aircraft and not as a platform for ASW [antisubmarine warfare] missiles.'[81] However, according to Jia, 'only the British government expressed disquiet over the passage, but it raised no protest.'[82]

The US has also sent quasi-helicopter carries through the Straits, as vessels of the Austin and the Harpers Ferry classes have transited multiple times,[83] although these may more easily be excluded from the definition of carrier as the purpose of carrying and operating aircraft at sea is presumably not their *primary* function, as required under the definition in Annex II.

Birkner finds that the lack of protests from interested states to this Soviet/Russian transit of what must be defined as carriers has led to a change of the Montreux Convention by its parties to now allow for the transit of carriers belonging to Black Sea powers, whereas others would seem to hold that this is rather acquiesce in a use that was not meant to establish an entitlement.[84] However, to the extent that larger aircraft carriers can safely navigate the Straits, no legal obstacle under the Montreux Convention would seem to exist for Turkey *inviting* a carrier strike group to visit Istanbul.[85] For those ships to move into the Black Sea, though, the requirements of especially Art 18 must be met. In short, a carrier like USS *Carl Vinson* with a tonnage of 113,500 will always be too heavy to enter the Black Sea, as the non-Black Sea power tonnage of one State must under para. 1 *litra* c not exceed 2/3 of 45,000 tons.[86] Alternatively, and this is submittedly the better view, it may be argued that as such travel into the Black Sea would go beyond a mere courtesy visit to a port in the Straits, the vessel will even have to abide by the relevant tonnage limitation in Art 14.

This tonnage limitation for non-Black Sea States was inserted in order to exclude certain categories of vessels of war in 1936, like German pocket

81 Knight (n 76) 128 (emphasis in the original). See also Birkner (n 20) 182–183.

82 Bing Bing Jia, *The Regime of Straits in International Law* (Clarendon Press 1998) 113 with further differences. Ünlü also refers to the passage in 2001 of the unfinished Ukrainian aircraft carrier *Varyag*, having been sold to China; Ünlü (n 18) 94–95.

83 Birkner (n 20) 175.

84 Ibid, 187 with further reference.

85 For a concurring view, see ibid, 182, n. 35. This might be what took place in 1966 with USS *America* although no details are provided in the source, see Rozakis and Stagos (n 28) 133.

86 Art 18(1) (a)–(c) of the Montreux Convention. As the Soviet Navy increased by more than 10,000 tons since the signing of the Convention, Art 18(1) *litra* a is no longer applicable, having been replaced by the tonnage threshold of *litra* b; Yücel (n 8) 113.

battleships.[87] Annex II thus recognizes that there are capital ships with a 'standard displacement of which exceeds 10,000 tons',[88] but their right to transit is not without restrictions. As mentioned, under Art 11 capital ships of Black Sea States may transit even if they are heavier than the tonnage limitation in Art 14(1) – 15,000 tons.[89] This would seem to mean that capital ships of non-Black Sea States may also transit, but that the said tonnage maximum in Art 14 limits the size of such vessels. The tonnage limitation in Art 14 is admittedly a maximum aggregate tonnage for use typically with more vessels than just one, but it is nevertheless used in Art 11 for the purpose of assessing the tonnage of only one vessel. This is one of the most important differences between forces belonging to States bordering the Black Sea and those States that do not.

Moreover, Art 18(1)(a) and (b) establish a cap on non-Black sea tonnage at 45,000 tons, although under Annex IV *overaged* vessels are not taken into consideration when assessing the Black Sea powers tonnage for the purpose of Art 18. An exception is provided for naval forces of non-Black Sea States sent for 'humanitarian purpose'.[90] During the negotiations, examples given were earthquakes or other natural disasters, and epidemics.[91] However, such forces shall not exceed 8000 tons and will not need to abide by the notification requirements of Art 13,[92] but where such a force will lead to 'foreign' tonnage going beyond 45,000 tons, more is required. In these situations, Turkey will – after having received a request for authorization – 'immediately inform the other Black Sea Powers of the request for authorization, and if the said Powers make no objection within twenty-four hours of having received this information, the Turkish Government shall, within forty-eight hours at the latest, inform the interested Powers of the reply which it has decided to make to their request.' The provision does not explicitly state whether the other Black Sea powers have the right to veto such an authorization, but if that was the case then explicit language to this effect should have been inserted in Art 18.[93]

Vessels of war from such 'foreign' powers are also prohibited from remaining in the Black Sea beyond 21 days 'whatever be the object of their presence

87 Yücel (n 8) 109–110, 122 and 224 with further references.

88 Annex II, Sec. B, para. 1, litra a of the Montreux Convention.

89 Ibid, Art 11 further requires that such capital ships transit singly, although they may be escorted by up to two destroyers.

90 Ibid, Art 18(1)(d).

91 Váli (n 37) 49.

92 Art 18(1)(d) of the Montreux Convention nevertheless establishes a procedural requirement.

93 For a different view, see Yücel (n 8) 114.

there'.[94] This limits the possibility of such powers establishing naval bases for the vessels of war covered by Section II in the Black Sea, e.g. on Romanian or Bulgarian territory.

One issue is similarly regulated in peacetime and war for vessels of war – the need to transit in quarantine and apply necessary prophylactic measures if the vessel has left a port infected by plague, cholera, yellow fever, exanthematic typhus or smallpox 'less than five time twenty-four hours' before passing through the Straits, has had such a case on board within 7 days, or does currently have it.[95] Although the list is formulated in an exhaustive manner, it would seem proper to expand it to also cover newer easily transmitted dangerous deceases like Ebola.

Although the Montreux Convention has regulation for the transit of vessels of war in wartime, non-international armed conflicts (where the high intensity end is often referred to as civil wars) – although the fighting on the ground might be just or even more vicious than in international armed conflicts – will presumably have to be considered under the rubric of peacetime. The defining feature of war as understood by the Montreux Convention is the historical presence of States fighting each other, as opposed to them supporting sides in a non-international armed conflict.[96] This means that Russian vessels of war transiting the Straits in order to support the Syrian authorities after that conflict broke out in 2011 can do so without being restricted by the war time regulations of the Montreux Convention.[97]

An important issue is *how* such transit passage is to be undertaken. Little is found on this in the articles of the Montreux Convention, but the preamble underlines the importance of 'safeguard[ing], within the framework of Turkish security and of the security, in the Black Sea, of the riparian States, the principle enshrined in Art 23 of the Treaty of Peace signed at Lausanne on the 24th July, 1923'.[98] With its emphasis on security, the preamble indicates that the said transit must be undertaken in a way that does not jeopardize the security of *i.a.* Turkey. It would seem that the *travaux préparatoires* also indicates that passage should be 'innocent'.[99] This would seem to put stronger limitations on

94 Art 18(2) of the Montreux Convention.

95 Art 22 of the Montreux Convention.

96 At least until the support reaches such a degree that the rebels are considered to represent the foreign State supporting them.

97 Yücel (n 8) 213–214 provides some data on the increase in Russian military traffic through the Straits after the Syrian non-international armed conflict broke out.

98 The said Art 23 refers to "the principle of freedom of transit and of navigation, by sea and by air, in time of peace as in time of war" of the Straits.

99 Aybay and Oral (n 15) 4, 5.

transit than is the case with transit of international straits under the United Nations Convention on the Law of the Sea[100] (hereinafter LOSC), and is more aligned with that of innocent passage during territorial seas.[101] Thus, the pointing of a rocket launcher at the city of Istanbul during transit – as was done on a Russian vessel of war on 4 December 2015 – is at the very least in violation of the spirit of the Montreux Convention.[102]

2.6 *Vessels of War in Times of War*

2.6.1 When Turkey Is Not a Belligerent

Art 20 was one of the most difficult provisions of the Montreux Convention to agree upon in 1936,[103] and it holds that as long as Turkey is *not* a belligerent, warships generally enjoy the same right to transit that they have during peacetime.[104] There are nevertheless an exception to this.

As stated in Art 20(2), vessels of war belonging to the *belligerent parties* may, as a general rule, *not* transit the Straits. That said, this exception has itself three exceptions. First, if allowing for transit follows from rights and obligations arising from the Covenant of the League of Nations.[105] These days, as will be covered more extensively later, this must be interpreted as referring to such that may arise from the United Nations (hereinafter UN) Charter.[106] Second, when mutual assistance treaties binding on Turkey, and meeting certain procedural requirements,[107] allow for or obligate the transit of vessels of war in assistance of victims of aggression.[108] Third, any vessel of war that has become separated from its base may undertake transit in order to return to its base.[109] Little flexibility exists here as State practice from World War II regarding the

100 United Nations Convention on the Law of the Sea (opened for signature 10 December 1982, entered into force 16 November 1994) 1833 UNTS 3.

101 The prohibition in Art 15 of the Convention on using aircrafts during transit points in this direction, too.

102 Yücel (n 8) 214 with further references.

103 Vignes (n 28) 474.

104 Art 19 of the Montreux Convention.

105 Arts 19(2) and 25 of the Montreux Convention.

106 Yücel (n 8) 115. For a different view, see Ünlü (n 18) 101–106.

107 See Art 20(2) i.f of the Montreux Convention.

108 In the exceptional situations mentioned, "the limitations laid down in Articles 10 to 18 of the present Convention shall not be applicable" (Art 19(3)). For the view that Turkey was obliged under the 1939 Anglo-French-Turkish Treaty of Mutual Assistance to let the vessels of war of these states transit even if they were belligerents, see Vignes (n 28) 475. For the UK view that this treaty gave Turkey the right to become belligerent and that Art 20 would then be the relevant provision, see Tennstedt (n 20) 13.

109 Art 19(4) of the Montreux Convention.

Soviet Union shows that the existence of alternative bases outside of the Black Sea did not allow for transit from the Black Sea under Art 21 for vessels belonging to the Soviet Black Sea fleet.[110]

When transiting in these three exceptional situations, the vessels of war may not undertake visit and search, nor capture or carry out any hostile act.[111] An illustration of the restrictions that Turkey may use in such situations is the use of submarine nets, as was done in the Bosporus strait in 1940 and which remained there for many years.[112]

During 1941, an issue arose in relation to six destroyers that Italy had allegedly sold to Bulgaria. Bulgaria was arguably not a belligerent at the time, and she would as such be able to have her new vessels of war transit the Straits. However, the transaction seemed to be fictitious as there was hardly any Bulgarian Navy, and she thus would have to rely upon the crew being at least partly made up of Italians. The issue was not pressed as Turkey eventually recognized that Bulgaria was a belligerent following exiled Greek and Yugoslav governments declaring war on her. Also, the destroyers never materialized and the rumors where seemingly merely an attempt to disturb Anglo-Turkish relations.[113]

One of the categories of vessels that raised issues during World War II was the more than 200 tons heavy German F barges (*Marinefährprähme*). Following German broadcasts in 1943 of their use as vessels of war, Turkey refused the transit of such barges.[114] Until then, these *Marinefährprähme* transited the Straits after weapons and military personnel had been removed, only to have them added anew at their destination.[115] Beyond the issue of transformation of merchant vessel into vessel of war[116] – or even the three-ways vessel of war to merchant man to vessel of war again – the question is naturally whether the vessel fitted the requirements for being a vessel of war under the Montreux Convention. A description of the essential aspects is mentioned in the definition of auxiliary vessels – 'not specifically built as fighting ships.' Not in existence at the time of the London Naval Agreement, there is naturally no reference to it in Annex II of the Montreux Convention, and it would also seem that the *Marinefährprähme* were multi-purpose vessels rather than specifically built for fighting.[117] Nor were they listed as auxiliary vessels by

110 Hayyar (n 5).
111 Art 19(5) of the Montreux Convention.
112 Aybay and Oral (n 15) 7.
113 The source for this paragraph is Seydi and Morewood (n 41) 82–83.
114 Tennstedt (n 20) 51–59, and Seydi and Morewood (n 41) 91–92.
115 Tennstedt (n 20) 52.
116 Ibid, 54–58, argues for the legality of such transformation.
117 Ibid, 53.

Germany.[118] Nevertheless, their very likely use as vessels of war after the transit took them out of the category of merchant vessels,[119] *i.e.* strong plausibility for such transformation and the close temporal proximity between the transit and the transformation gave the merchant vessel pre-emptively the status as vessel of war.

Naval auxiliary vessels also sought to muddle the divide between vessels of war and merchant vessels during that war. The Italian tankers *Urano* and *Tarvisio* were allowed to sail into the Mediterranean in June 1941 even if they were naval auxiliary vessels.[120] Upon Allied protests, however, Turkey accepted having mistakenly allowed the transit, but she did not stop *Urano* when that vessel made her return journey through the Straits, relying on the unconvincing argument that she was allowed to return home under Art 19 – a provision of relevance to vessels located at the 'wrong' side of the Straits at the time the flag State became a belligerent.[121] When *Tarvision* sought to transit home in August the issue arose anew. She had now been struck from the list of auxiliary vessels, disarmed, and Italy thus held that she was a merchant vessel.[122] The UK held that the possibility of changing the status of the vessel in this way would completely undermine the Montreux Convention – opening for a revolving-door approach to the status of vessels.[123] Turkey thus held that a vessel of war could not, for the purpose of the Montreux Convention, be transformed into a merchant vessel during a war.[124] Again, Turkey sought to avoid becoming a belligerent and let the vessel transit, but as the transit was seen as a breach of the Montreux Convention, pilotage was not provided through the heavily mined Straits.[125] As Turkey held that she had not been informed properly about the character of the vessel by Italy, she also filed a diplomatic protest.[126]

During May 1944 Turkey – upon the insistence of the Allies – conducted a search of smaller German 'merchant vessels' – of the EMS[127] and

118 Seydi and Morewood (n 41) 90.

119 Ibid, 90–92.

120 The facts on this issue differ somewhat between the sources, but the current text bases itself on ibid, 80–82.

121 Seydi and Morewood argues that the reason for this non-fulfilment of her obligations under the Convention might have been Turkey's reluctance to have to resort to measures that might have turned her a belligerent; ibid, 81.

122 Tennstedt (n 20) 36.

123 Seydi and Morewood (n 41) 81.

124 Váli (n 37) 257 and Tennstedt (n 20) 50–51.

125 Seydi and Morewood (n 41) 81. See also Yücel (n 8) 130. Bilsel states that the refusal came in relation to a second attempt at entering the Dardanelles; Bilsel (n 40) 741.

126 Tennstedt (n 20) 36.

127 This term does not seem to have been defined in the sources available to the author.

Kriegstransportschiffe classes[128] – where radar equipment, weapons and naval equipment were found.[129] Consequently, these vessels were not allowed to transit as they were not considered as merchant vessels.[130] It would nevertheless seem odd if the mere existence of military equipment onboard without more would convert a merchant vessel into a vessel of war.[131] A later inspection of a similar vessel – *Kassel* – identified it as a naval auxiliary vessel, with Turkey issuing a formal protest to Germany.[132]

It is doubtful whether there actually existed a category of German vessels referred to as EMS that caught the attention of the Allies in 1944.[133] Tennstedt rather holds that this might refer to armed ships of 40–50 tons that were originally fishing vessels and coastal crafts.[134] As vessels under 100 tons are not covered by Annex II, and it is perceived to be an exhaustive list of what constitutes vessels of war, even heavily armed smaller vessels would technically be 'merchant vessels'. Counterintuitively, admittedly, but required by the logic of the Montreux Convention. Turkey upheld this literal understanding of Annex II in July 1941, when the German *Seefalke* – a 37 tons unarmed motorboat – was not considered as a vessel of war due to her weight.[135] By 1944,

---

128 On these types of vessels in general, see Seydi and Morewood (n 41) 88–95. For the view that some *Kriegstransportschiffe* vessels at the most were built as fighting ships, but not "specifically" so, and that they were not protected by armor plating, see Tennstedt (n 20) 59–61. Some of the *Kriegstransportschiffe* would seem to have been merchant vessels, whereas the others were transformed into merchant vessels for the transit of the Straits; ibid, 61.

129 Seydi and Morewood (n 41) 94.

130 Acer holds that "Turkiye seemed to have considered a merchant ship as a warship simply because a merchant ship would turn into a warship if it was carrying weapons or other war materials"; Yücel Acer, 'Russia's Attack on Ukraine: The Montreux Convention and Turkiye' (2023) 100 International Law Studies 285, 300. Such an assessment by Turkey would seem to ignore the wording of Art 2 ("any kind of cargo").

131 For a different view, see ibid, 305.

132 Yücel (n 8) 131, and Seydi and Morewood (n 41) 94. They seem to have been warships refitted to pose as merchant vessels; Adam Aliano, 'Is Russia Exploiting a Gap in the Montreux Convention?' (14 June 2022) Lawfare, available at <https://www.lawfareblog.com/russia-exploiting-gap-montreux-convention> accessed 30 August 2023. See also Cemil Bilsel, International Law in Turkey, (1944) 38 American Journal of International Law 546, 555, where the vessel's name is given as *Cassel*.

133 Tennstedt (n 20) 61–62. For the Turkish views, see Váli (n 37) 258–259.

134 Tennstedt (n 20) 61–62. Identifying the "MSE" [sic] craft as "smaller vessels of 40–50 tons"; Seydi and Morewood (n 41) 92.

135 Bilsel (n 40) 740–741, and Tennstedt (n 20) 50. For more on the interesting situation that these smaller vessels with potential to become naval assets generated, see Seydi and Morewood (n 41) 88–92. See also Vignes (n 28) 476. As to text of the Turkish note of

however, Turkish practice had changed,[136] and this practice – when accepted by other States – would lead to a change in the regime of the Montreux Convention, basically to include the vessels that the UK had sought to exclude during the negotiations.

Be that as it may, the more general issues raised in the previous subchapter arise here as well. For example, Russia protested about the presence of four vessels of war from neutral NATO Member States in the Black Sea during its invasion of Georgia in the 2008 Russo-Georgian armed conflict – not seemingly against their presence as such, but in their potential violation of the 21 days rule in Art 18(2).[137] Such overstay may occur as a consequence of e.g. engine malfunction, as was the case in February 2014 with *USS Taylor*.[138] This 21 days rule may turn the Straits into a revolving door where leaving vessels merely turn at the gates of the Dardanelles relying on presubmitted notifications.

Also during the Russo-Georgian conflict in 2008, Turkey denied the passage of two US hospital ships – *USNS Mercy* and *USNS Comfort* – that sought to provide humanitarian help[139] to Georgia and weighted all together 140,000 tons, under reference to the tonnage limitation in Art 18.[140] The US instead sent three smaller ships.[141] Strangely, it would not seem that the limitation in Art 14 was central to the discussions.

The issue of tonnage in Art 14 was nevertheless raised when *USS Mount Whitney* transited the Straits and entered the Black Sea on 4 February 2014. Russia protested – as she had not done on the vessel's previous visits to the Black Sea – as she now held that *USS Mount Whitney* was heavier than the 15,000 tons allowed for by Art 14.[142] As *USS Mount Whitney* is an amphibious command ship with a reported displacement of 18,400 tons, fully loaded,[143] there may be

---

22 August 1946 to the Soviet Embassy in Ankara regarding i.a. this vessel, see Váli (n 37) 256–257. The vessel is referred to as *Zeefalke* in Bilsel (n 132) 553.

136 Seydi and Morewood (n 41) 92–94.

137 Yücel (n 8) 211 with further references.

138 Ibid, 219–220, and Selen Baldiran, Dincer Bayer and Hüseyin Gencer, 'The importance of the 1936 Montreux Convention for the Black Sea Security: A Close Look into Russia-NATO Controversy on the Russian-Ukrainian Conflict in 2022' (2022) 51 Information & Security: An International Journal (ISIJ) 11, 17.

139 Russia rather saw this as weapons transports; Yücel (n 8) 212 with further references.

140 Ibid, 211–212.

141 Sinan Ikinci and Peter Schwarz, 'Georgian conflict poses dilemma for Turkey' World Socialist Web Site (9 September 2008), available at <https://www.wsws.org/en/articles/2008/09/turk-s09.html> accessed 30 August 2023.

142 Yücel (n 8) 218–219 with further references.

143 See 'USS Mount Whitney', Wikipedia, available at <https://en.wikipedia.org/wiki/USS_Mount_Whitney_(LCC-20)> accessed 30 August 2023.

some merit to the Russian protest, although the vessel has transited also after this protest.[144] For USS *Mount Whitney* to abide by Art 14, the US will have to argue that the focus should rather be on the tonnage of the vessel without a full load, *i.e.* the 13,957 tons reported in a US diplomatic note.[145] As pointed out by Yücel, '[t]echnological improvements give opportunity to add some extra weapons and other equipment on warships after they were produced. This new equipment can change the aggregate tonnage of warships, and it is difficult to control tonnage during their passage through the Straits.'[146] There is some merit to this.

2.6.2 When Turkey Is a Belligerent

Not surprisingly, more restrictions may be placed on the right to transit when Turkey herself becomes embroiled in war. Here, Art 20 states that the provisions addressing transit for different types of vessels of war are no longer applicable,[147] and that 'the passage of warships shall be left entirely to the discretion of the Turkish Government.'[148] Turkey may thus 'allow the movement of war vessels, presumably friendly ones, both in the straits and the Black Sea, without regard to the balances that [the] Montreux Convention established in its other articles.'[149] Turkey used its entitlement under this article and Art 5 for the first time following her declaration of war upon Germany on 23 February 1945.[150]

2.6.3 When Turkey May Become a Belligerent

Art 21 is similar to Art 6 in the way that both regulate the situation where Turkey is 'threatened with imminent danger of war'. Here, Art 21 allows for the application of the regime under Art 20, *i.e.* a more restrictive regime than that under Art 6. The difference naturally relates to the inherent dangerousness that vessels of war, as opposed to merchant vessels, constitute to Turkey.[151] In such situations Turkey may allow NATO-vessels to transit, but hinder Russian

144 Nevitt (n 7).

145 Yücel (n 8) 218–219, n 696.

146 Ibid, 218, n. 696.

147 Art 20 here refers to Arts 10–18. See also Süha Çubukçuoğlu, 'Russia-Ukraine Crisis and the Turkish Straits' Manara magazine (3 June 2022), available at <https://manaramagazine.org/2022/06/russia-ukraine-crisis-and-the-turkish-straits/> accessed 30 August 2023.

148 Art 20 i.f.

149 Rozakis and Stagos (n 28) 113. See also Váli (n 37) 51.

150 Daly (n 20) 9.

151 For the view that this is a dangerous subjectivity in the implementation of the Convention, see Rozakis and Stagos (n 28) 114.

ones, should she feel threatened by Russia.[152] Vessels of war trapped by measures under Art 21 in waters away from their bases are nevertheless allowed to return, as long as they do not belong to the State 'whose attitude has given rise to the application of' Art 21.

When using the powers under Art 21, Turkey must notify the parties to the Montreux Convention and the Secretary-General of the League of Nations.[153] The Council of the League of Nations may by a 2/3 majority vote, if supported by the majority of the parties to the Montreux Convention, obligate Turkey to discontinue if measures under Art 21 (for the application of this to the UN regime, see *infra* Chapter 2.7.2).[154]

2.7 *The Well-Known Problems*

2.7.1 War

A few well-known issues arise during discussions on the transit of vessels of war during times of war. Among these are when do these war powers apply. Although the issuance of some sort of declaration of war was widespread around the middle of the 1800s[155] – there is even an agreement on this from 1907 that has fallen into *desuetude*[156] – the general consensus holds that a state of war may also exist based upon what takes place between the parties.[157] But even then, we currently hardly have wars as properly understood by international law. Rather, we see instead international or non-international armed conflicts (*jus in bello*), or uses of force or armed attacks under the UN Charter Arts 2(4) and 51 (*jus ad bellum*).

If the war powers only apply when a state of war exists under international law, then the peacetime regime will now mostly replace the war regulation. The relevant political crisis may nevertheless generate the same problems for Turkey and the other Black Sea powers that the existence of war previously did, so there will be a need to apply these powers also to analogical situations that share the fundamental characteristics of the old state of war.

One point of departure is the fact that not all armed conflicts between States around the time when the Montreux Convention was negotiated were

---

152 Nevitt (n 7).

153 Art 21(3) of the Montreux Convention.

154 Ibid, Art 21(4).

155 Stephen C Neff, *War and the Law of Nations* (Cambridge University Press 2005) 110. Its use had however been rather haphazard during the previous times; see ibid, 104, 108, 110.

156 Hague Convention (III) relative to the Opening of Hostilities (adopted 18 October 1907, entered into force 26 January 1910) USTS 263.

157 See already the views held during the 1800s and into the early 1900s; Neff (n 155) 180–183.

considered as war proper.[158] And Turkey would seem to have closed the Straits only once by using the wartime provisions of the Montreux Convention; during World War II to hinder especially German and Italian vessels of war from entering the Black Sea.[159]

Both during the armed conflict in Korea – where Turkey may be held to have been a belligerent – and the many hostilities between Arab States and Israel, the Straits stayed open, and e.g. vessels of war from the United Arab Republic – a short-lived union of Egypt and Syria – were allowed to pass the Straits.[160] During the US Vietnam 'War', upon Soviet Union insistence on US vessels not being entitled to transit due to Art 19, Turkey nevertheless upheld the right to transit by finding the US not to be at war.[161] Similarly, there does not seem to have been discussions on such closing during the 2008 Russo-Georgian armed conflict, nor in relation to the outbreak in 2014 of the Russo-Ukrainian armed conflict.[162]

This may be taken to indicate that 'mere' international armed conflicts do not constitute 'war' for the purpose of the Montreux Convention. Depending on whether Russian vessels of war actually transited or sought to transit the Straits during those periods – for the sake of considering this specific issue we will here focus on the period of hostilities and not on the lingering occupations – it might be argued that no State felt the need to 'upgrade' those conflicts, *i.e.* there was 'acquiesce' in Russian transits. If that is so, did States then ignore the wording of Art 19 to the effect that such vessels of war 'shall not' transit the Straits,[163] or should this instead be seen as the establishment of a rather high threshold for what constitutes war under the Montreux Convention?

Generally, the two alternative 'thresholds' are when an international armed conflict exists under *jus in bello*,[164] or the somewhat higher threshold that

---

158 Hayyar (n 5).

159 Nevitt (n 7).

160 Váli (n 37) 102, and Rozakis and Stagos (n 28) 131. The United Arab Republic even considered itself to be at war with Israel; Birkner (n 20) 191.

161 Rozakis and Stagos (n 28) 131, Birkner (n 20) 172 with further references, and Cornell Overfield, 'Turkey Must Close the Turkish Straits Only to Russian and Ukrainian Warships' (5 March 2022) Lawfare, available at <https://www.lawfareblog.com/turkey-must-close-turkish-straits-only-russian-and-ukrainian-warships> accessed 30 August 2023.

162 Hayyar (n 5) and Nevitt (n 7).

163 As pointed out by Ferhat Ercümen in a comment to Hayyar (n 5).

164 See Common Article 2 of the 1949 Geneva Conventions, and Art 1(4) of the Protocol Additional to the Geneva Conventions of 12 August 1949, and relating to the Protection of Victims of International Armed Conflicts (Protocol I) (adopted 8 June 1977, entered into force 7 December 1978) 1125 UNTS 17512. State practice is well described in ICRC,

seems to be applicable in relation to naval warfare when interfering with the rights of third States.[165] Against the background of State practice it would seem that at the very least the relatively low threshold required to activate the law of international armed conflict is found to be too low for the purpose of the Montreux Convention.[166] Some might nevertheless find the existence of aggression, a *jus ad bellum* term,[167] to be the relevant threshold.[168] Be that as it may, the combined high intensity hostilities *and* official view of Ukraine to the effect that she is at war with Russia allow us to conclude that a war exists for the purpose of the Montreux Convention.[169] After some deliberation, see *infra* Chapter 3.1, Turkey closed the Straits to Russian and Ukrainian vessels of war on 27 February 2022.

As regards the rules applicable to naval warfare during an international armed conflict – beyond the issues regulated by the Montreux Convention[170] – reference may be made to the previously mentioned 1994 San Remo Manual on International Law Applicable to Armed Conflicts at Sea.

Another fundamental question is when a war ends for the purpose of the Montreux Convention. As long as an occupation is continuous, in theory the international armed conflict exists.[171] If that is the case and sole issue of relevance, *i.e.* ignoring the higher threshold for activation that State practice requires, it would have been problematic to allow Russian vessels of war to transit after the five-days war in 2008, as they are still in control of Georgian territories.[172] Similarly with the 2014 Russian invasion of the Crimean peninsula, a part of Ukraine. It is unclear whether a mere cessation of hostilities or a negotiated end to the conflict is required.

Commentary on the first Geneva Convention (Cambridge University Press 2016) 69–125. For seemingly the view that this is the required threshold, see Birkner (n 20) 187–192.

165 See Doswald-Beck (n 27) 74, para 1.3.

166 In this direction, see also Yücel (n 8) 234.

167 Although also an international crime.

168 Perhaps in this direction; Overfield (n 161).

169 Hayyar (n 5). See also Acer (n 130) 303.

170 Von Heinegg may be more inclined than the current author to apply the LOSC rules on transit passage if Turkey is a belligerent, see Wolff Heintschel von Heinegg, 'The Law of Naval Warfare and International Straits' (1998) 71 International Law Studies 263, 264. See, however, ibid, 275.

171 Convention (IV) relative to the Protection of Civilian Persons in Time of War (adopted 12 August 1949, entered into force 21 October 1950) 75 UNTS 973, Art 6(3), and Art 3(b) of the 1977 Additional Protocol.

172 The breakaway provinces of Abkhazia and South Ossetia.

2.7.2 The League of Nations

Also, the Montreux Convention refers to the League of Nations in Arts 18, 19, 21, 24 and 25.[173] E.g., Art 21 requires Turkey to notify *i.a.* the Secretary-General of the League of Nations, and the Council of the League of Nations may by a 2/3 majority vote, if supported by the majority of the parties to the Montreux Convention, obligate Turkey to discontinue its measures under Art 21.[174] To what extent must this now be interpreted as a reference to the United Nations?

The UN General Assembly (hereinafter UNGA) adopted in 1946 resolution 24(I)-I where it declares itself 'willing in principle [...] to assume the exercise of certain functions and powers previously entrusted to the League of Nations [...]'.[175] In relation to 'Functions and Powers under Treaties, International Conventions, Agreements and Other Instruments Having a Political Character', the UNGA states that it 'will itself examine, or will submit to the appropriate organ of the United Nations, any request from the parties that the United Nations should assume the exercise of functions or powers entrusted to the League of Nations by treaties, instrumental conventions, agreements and other instruments having a political character.'[176] The first stop of such a League of Nations issue would then be at the UNGA,[177] and the UNGA is admittedly given some leeway as to whether it wants to consider the issue.[178]

Here, the notification of the UN Secretary General, instead of the Secretary-General of the League of Nations, in Arts 18 and 24 is unproblematic, and Turkish practice in this regard has not met with any protest.[179] Moreover, the registration and publication of treaties of mutual assistance binding Turkey under Art 19(2) would now seem to be understood as having to take place in the UN Treaty Series.[180] Such treaties must be 'concluded within the framework of

---

173 For the view that these provisions "may now be construed as referring to the relevant regulations of the [UN] Charter", see Rozakis and Stagos (n 28) 113.

174 Art 21(4) of the Montreux Convention.

175 League of Nations Committee, 24(I) Transfer of Certain Functions, Activities and Assets of the League of Nations, UN Doc. A/RES/24(I)-I, 12 February 1946, (I)(3).

176 Ibid, (I)(C).

177 Overfield (n 161).

178 Adam Aliano and Russel Spivak, 'Ukraine Symposium – The Montreux Convention and Turkey's Impact on Black Sea Operations' (25 April 2022) Liber Institute West Point, available at <https://lieber.westpoint.edu/montreux-convention-turkeys-impact-black-sea-operations> accessed 30 August 2023.

179 Yücel (n 8) 233.

180 The obligation under the 1919 Covenant of the league of Nations Art 18 is stricter than that of the corresponding UN Charter Art 102.

the Covenant of the League of Nations',[181] and this will presumably – in relation to such treaties entered into by Turkey after the League of Nations folded – have to be conventions established within what the UN Charter allows for, e.g. conventions on collective self-defence like the 1949 NATO Treaty.[182]

The modern stand-in for the Council of the League of Nations would presumably be the UN Security Council (hereinafter UNSC).[183] As any decision on substantive issues by the UNSC is open to the use of the veto, and as the UNSC would be acting in its capacity as such although the 'right' to consider the issue is provided for explicitly by the reference to its predecessor in the Montreux Convention, a 2/3 vote as referred to in Art 21(4) cannot suspend the veto function of a negative vote by a P5. As such, one P5 may torpedo any censuring of Turkey.[184]

Also, the UNSC may override the Montreux Convention should the UNSC agree to use its powers under Chapter VII of the UN Charter and pass a binding resolution.[185]

2.7.3 Tonnage and Caliber of Guns

Not really a matter of disagreement, but it is nevertheless worth pointing out that the tonnage limitations in Art 18(1)(b) is today – and has been for some time – 45,000 tons. Perhaps there is now a wish to lift this tonnage limitation? That said, with the move from guns to missiles, vessels of lesser tonnage are able of inflicting damage way beyond what their tonnage would have indicated in the 1930s.[186]

Also, as many modern vessels have a larger displacement tonnage than was the case in 1936, it might be said that the scheme of the Montreux Convention does not correspond to current realities, and this was recognized by Turkey as far back as in 1947.[187]

---

181 See The Covenant of the League of Nations (adopted 28 June 1919, entered into force 10 January 1920) League of Nations – Official Journal, February 1920, pp. 3–12; Charter of the United Nations (opened for signature 26 June 1945, entered into force 24 October 1945) 1 UNTS XVI.

182 The North Atlantic Treaty (opened for signature 4 April 1949, entered into force 24 August 1949) 34 UNTS 243.

183 In this direction, Acer (n 130) 296.

184 UN Charter Art 27(3). This raises the issue of whether that P5 is a party to the dispute. If so, and the considerations take place under UN Charter chapter VI, that party "shall abstain from voting" (Art 27(3)).

185 See UN Charter Arts 25 and 103.

186 Birkner (n 20) 176.

187 Bilsel (n 40) 741–742.

As remarked earlier, the Montreux Convention also seeks to differentiate between types of vessels by the diameter of its guns, Art 9(2) and Annex II(B), ignoring the change from guns to missiles. Turkey would seem to have accepted in the late 1960s that new types of armament do not change the assessment of the vessel of war as long as these weapons are of a *defensive* nature.[188] However, separating defensive and offensive weapons is a difficult endeavor even at the best of times, and it is probably a better assessment of *de lege lata*, focusing on the lack of protests, that newer weapons are irrelevant for the purposes of categorizing vessels of war under Annex II.[189] It would seem that this also covers nuclear weapons.[190]

3 Recent Issues

3.1 *May Turkey Close the Straits to Russian Vessels of War?*

During early 2022, Turkish authorities tested the waters as to whether they could close the Straits to vessels of war. Not surprisingly, Ukraine sought to have Turkey close the Straits from the very beginning of the new round of the Russo-Ukrainian armed conflict.[191] From having held that she could not legally hinder Russian vessels of war from transiting, on Sunday 27 February the Turkish minister for foreign affairs warned foreign military vessels from sailing the Straits and argued that Turkey would use the Montreux Convention for all that it is worth.[192] Here, uncertainty was introduced as Turkey warned *all* flag states from sending their vessels of war through the Straits.[193]

It is unclear whether this suggested closing of the Straits was based upon Arts 19 or 21, although the better view would seem to be Art 19. The question of what constitutes a 'war' has been addressed earlier in this paper, but an issue here is the right for vessels of war to return to their base, basically allowing vessels in the Black Sea to return to bases beyond the western part of the Straits and *vice versa*. Hayyar finds that '[t]he only practical effect of the closure would be that Russia would no longer be allowed to bring into the Black Sea further warships belonging to its other fleets, i.e. those not themselves based in the Black Sea, which will likely not matter much for the ongoing hostilities.'

188 Váli (n 37) 103–104, and Birkner (n 20) 172.
189 Birkner (n 20) 178–179. For the view that the criterium of defensiveness "gives room for much flexibility and no small measures of subjectivity", see Vignes (n 28) 478.
190 Váli (n 37) 104.
191 See sources mentioned in Hayyar (n 5).
192 See sources in Daly (n 20) 18.
193 Pedrozo (n 67).

Correspondingly, Turkey denied a Russian request to transit four vessels of war into the Black Sea as they were not based at the Sevastopol base and therefore could not apply the exception to the suspension of transit in Art 19(4),[194] although the Russian request stated that only three of these ships were not registered to a base in the Black Sea.[195] Russia would seem to have agreed to this,[196] but it does raise the question of why was the vessel with a base in the Black Sea denied transit. Also, in November 2022 two Russian vessels of war left the Mediterranean, after having stayed there since February of that year, for Vladivostok. That said, it would seem that Russia never requested their transit through the Straits.[197]

In fact, the Montreux Convention functions much like a long-distance quasi-blockade of naval assets of the belligerents, keeping them from entering or leaving the Straits.[198]

3.2 *May Turkey Close the Straits to Vessels of War from Non-belligerent States?*

Although Turkey warned all states from seeking to transit their vessels of war through the Straits on 27 February 2022,[199] the legal basis for this warning has often been held to be wanting.[200] However, the Turkish minister of defense Hulusi Akar is alleged to have stated that 'Turkey will continue to Apply

194 Overfield (n 161) with further references.

195 Anonymous, 'Russia cancelled Black Sea passage bid of four warships: Turkey' Aljazeera (2 March 2022), available at <https://www.aljazeera.com/news/2022/3/2/russia-cancelled-black-sea-passage-bid-warships-turkey> accessed 30 August 2023.

196 Aliano and Spivak (n 178).

197 Ragip Soylu, 'Russia withdraws two war ships after Turkey denies Black Sea access' Middle East Eye (7 November 2022), available at <https://www.middleeasteye.net/news/russia-withdraws-two-war-ships-after-turkey-denies-black-sea-access> accessed 30 August 2023.

198 For Turkey's refusal of navigation of UK-donated minehunter ships to Ukraine, see Huseyin Hayatsever, Jonathan Spicer and Gareth Jones, 'Turkey to block minehunter ships intended for Ukraine' Reuters (2 January 2024), available at <https://www.reuters.com/world/middle-east/turkey-block-uk-minehunter-ships-intended-ukraine-2024-01-02> accessed 3 January 2024.

199 Mumin Atlas, 'Turkiye warns all countries against warships going through Turkish Straits' Anadolu Agency (28 February 2022), available at <https://www.aa.com.tr/en/russia-ukraine-crisis/turkiye-warns-all-countries-against-warships-going-through-turkish-straits/2518827> accessed 30 August 2023, and Tayfun Ozberk, 'Turkey Closes The Dardanelles And Bosphorus To Warships' Naval News (28 February 2022), available at <https://www.navalnews.com/naval-news/2022/02/turkey-closes-the-dardanelles-and-bosphorus-to-warships> accessed 30 August 2023.

200 Aliano and Spivak (n 178).

Articles 19, 20, 21' – seemingly invoking also the powers granted Turkey when she is herself a belligerent or in threat of becoming one.[201]

Many commentators have correctly pointed out that such a general closing of the Strait to non-belligerent vessels of war cannot find its legal source in Art 19 of the Montreux Convention, and that the factual background for a *prima facie* use of Art 21 is lacking.[202] Even if Turkey does not officially close the Straits to such transit, Overfield is correct in considering the warning 'as an attempt to impede and deter traffic, and thus a de facto closure'.[203] It would be in the interest of international society for States to insist on Turkey clarifying the legal and factual basis for its warning, and for them also to respond to this State practice in order to restrict its potential to change the legal regulation of the Montreux Convention.[204]

Admittedly, Art 21 gives Turkey a wide freedom to consider *herself* whether she is 'threatened with imminent danger of war'. Such an assessment must nevertheless be done in good faith.[205] This 'wide latitude to interpret current events unilaterally'[206] is only enhanced by the term 'threatened with imminent danger of war' in Art 21 not corresponding exactly with neither 'armed attack' in the UN Charter Art. 51 nor 'threat or use of force' in the UN Charter Art 2(4).

Be that as it may, and despite views to the contrary,[207] Romanian and Bulgarian warships have transited the Straits since 1 March 2022, so there does not seem to have been a closing of the Straits to such traffic.[208]

3.3 *The Use of Merchant Vessels for Transportation of Military Equipment*

To avoid wartime restrictions on vessels of war, Russia modified such vessels into merchant vessels during the 1904–1905 Russo-Japanese war.[209] Such drastic measures have not been undertaken during the ongoing conflict, but the

---

201 Ozberk (n 199). Here, regretfully, note xiv refers to a source no longer available at the link provided.

202 See e.g. Hayyar (n 5), Kraska (n 77), Pedrozo (n 67), Overfield (n 161), and Aliano (n 132).

203 Overfield (n 161).

204 See also Aliano and Spivak (n 180).

205 See 1969 Vienna Convention on the Law of Treaties, Art 26.

206 Aliano and Spivak (n 180).

207 Aliano (n 132).

208 Anonymous, 'Foreign warships on Bosphorus in 2022' Bosphorus Naval News (19 October 2022), available at <https://turkishnavy.net/foreign-warship-on-bosphorus/foreign-warships-on-bosphorus-in-2022> accessed 30 August 2023.

209 Yücel (n 8) 74.

current use of merchant vessels for transportation of military equipment has raised some issues.

As seen above, there is a discussion on where the dividing line between merchant vessels and vessels of war is to be drawn. It may suffice here to note that unaltered merchant vessels belonging to the belligerent parties during World War II – like *Delchow* and *Larissa* – were allowed to pass. The UK authorities even recognizing that the Montreux Convention did not provide a legal basis to interdict them.[210] This is important, as Turkey held that she had no right to stop merchant vessels 'which claimed merchant status, even if it was carrying any amount of war materials not obviously intended for the armament of the vessels themselves.'[211] That said, seeking to avoid the prohibition of transit of belligerents' vessels of war by e.g. dismantling the vessels and carrying them as cargo onboard merchant vessels would presumably be a violation of the prohibition regarding such vessels of war.[212]

A rather different situation occurs when Turkey has a more direct interest herself in the military hardware being transported on merchant vessels. This was the case in 1994, when Turkey stopped and searched two vessels 'suspected of transporting missile parts in reaction to the Greek-Cypriot Administration's decision to purchase Russia[n] S-300 missiles for targeting against [Turkish aircraft].'[213] By applying the powers under what must have been Art. 21 of the Montreux Convention, Turkey would seem to have acted in accordance with the understanding presented by e.g. the Greek representative at the negotiations in 1936 – Mr. E.B.M. Politis.[214]

After Turkey closed the Strait to vessels of war of the belligerent parties on 27 February 2022, Russia started transporting military equipment on merchant vessels. This is nothing new, though, as Russia has used merchant vessels for transports to e.g. Syria,[215] without it seemingly having raised international protests. Currently, these vessels are also used to transport military material from Syria to Russia.[216]

Işık holds that the use is 'not acceptable and should not be allowed', but adds that this is so even if the use is legal.[217] By looking at the very wording of Art 2 of the Montreux Convention, relevant via Art 4 as Turkey is not a belligerent,

210 Aliano (n 132).
211 Seydi and Morewood (n 41) 85. See also ibid, 95.
212 Tennstedt (n 20) 58–59.
213 Aybay and Oral (n 15) 1, 10.
214 Ibid, 10.
215 Işık (n 6).
216 Aliano (n 132).
217 Işık (n 6).

'[…] merchant vessels shall enjoy complete freedom of transit and navigation […] under any flag and with any kind of cargo […].' This is a very wide-ranging entitlement, that would seem to allow for this Russian 'civilian' sea born logistics system.[218]

Some have criticized Turkey for not stopping the transport of a S-300 missile system on the Russian cargo vessel *Sparta II* in September 2022, although the legal reasoning for such a restriction seems to be related to aggression and crimes against humanity, and not to the Montreux Convention.[219] In other words, and contrary to the view of some,[220] State practice shows that even if a merchant vessel is Russian flagged and carries military equipment, ammunitions, etc., it would be entitled to free transit and navigation through the Straits. The only exception would be if these transports were to be considered as auxiliary vessels. As such vessels need to be 'owned or under the exclusive control of the armed forces of a State and used for the time being on government non-commercial service',[221] chances are that many of these transports do not qualify as such auxiliary vessels.

4 Denouncement and Amendment

The United Kingdom sought through the Montreux Convention to put some restrictions on the access of Soviet naval assets to the Mediterranean, although one of the main effects would seem to have been to protect the Soviet Union against threats, by ensuring Soviet naval dominance in the Black Sea.[222] Some have thus held that the limitations on vessel of war tonnage from non-Black Sea States provides Russia with a strategic advantage during international armed conflicts in the Black Sea,[223] whereas it might also be argued that the current regime prevents the escalations that might otherwise have taken

218 For a similar view, see Aliano (n 132).

219 U.S. Helsinki Commission, 'Helsinki Commission alarmed by reported transport of S-300 missile system by Russia into the Black Sea' (2 September 2022), available at <https://www.csce.gov/international-impact/press-and-media/press-releases/helsinki-commission-alarmed-reported-transport-s> accessed 30 August 2023, and Sunil Tyagi, 'Did Turkey break the 1936 Montreux Convention to help Russia?' Centre for Air Power Studies (9 September 2022), available at <https://capsindia.org/did-turkey-break-the-1936-montreux-convention-to-help-russia> accessed 30 August 2023.

220 Acer (n 130) 305 and 310–311.

221 Rule 13(h) of the 1994 San Remo Manual, see Doswald-Beck (n 27) 9, 90.

222 Ikinci and Schwarz (n 141).

223 Starr (n 77).

place – intentionally or unintentionally – had non-Black Sea States been entitled to move more freely naval assets into this sea via the Straits.[224]

Based on the above-mentioned misalignment of the 'map' of the Montreux Convention with the realities of e.g. the military-technical terrain of our present times, a relevant issue is how to amend or even denounce the Montreux Convention. These issues are now considered in the opposite order.

Under Art 28 the treaty had an original lifespan of 20 years from the date of its entry into force. Denunciation might thus have taken effect on 9 November 1956, but no denunciations have so far been forthcoming, although some discussion for revision took place after World War II.[225] That said, para 2 of Art 28 states that the principle of transit and navigation as 'affirmed' in Art 1 'shall however continue without limit of time'.

As the devil lies in the details, the real question is what this will mean if the Montreux Convention is terminated. What kind of *limitations* does such transit have to undergo, as transit is presumably not intended to be free for all categories of vessels both in times of peace and war. Admittedly, the parties to a new agreement are in no way hindered from establishing a regime that restricts – or even terminates – this right to transit,[226] but this restricted version will then only apply to the parties thereto.

As for other States, the answer to whether there exists an entitlement to transit must be found in customary international law, as Turkey is not a party to LOSC.[227] That said, it is not even certain that the LOSC regulation on international straits – which differ from how the Montreux Convention has regulated it – represents customary international law,[228] if international straits as such exists as a concept in customary international law beyond what the ICJ held in the Corfu Channels case.[229] Also, as both Straits have an inland

224 Yücel (n 8) 222.

225 Rozakis and Stagos (n 28) 127–130, Vignes (n 28) 476–477, and Yücel (n 8) 132–141.

226 As it probably holds no *jus cogens* status.

227 For the list of parties, see United Nations Treaty Collection, available at <https://treaties.un.org/pages/ViewDetailsIII.aspx?src=TREATY&mtdsg_no=XXI-6&chapter=21&Temp=mtdsg3&clang=_en> accessed 30 August 2023. For the views on the application to the different treaty regimes over the years to third parties, see Fitzmaurice (n 22) 189–190.

228 It has been argued that transit passage is more restrictive of coastal states' powers than customary international law up to that point in time; Aybay and Oral (n 15) 3. See also Kentaro Wani, 'Development of the Law of the Sea and the Legal Status of International Straits in Time of International Armed Conflict' (2018) 61 Japanese Yearbook of International Law 39, 72 with further references.

229 See *Corfu Channel Case* (*United Kingdom* v *Albania*), Judgment (Merits), ICJ Reports 1949, p. 4, 29–30. For the view that non-suspendable innocent passage is the applicable regime, see Birkner (n 20) 165–170.

sea – held to be under Turkish sovereignty[230] – at one of their ends – the Sea of Marmara – the geography of the Straits does not fit well the definition of such in Art 37 of the LOSC.[231] That said, there seems nevertheless to be general agreement on the Straits being among the waterways covered by Art 35(c) of the LOSC.[232] An alternative might be a *lex specialis* customary regulation for this specific body of water as opposed to a *lex generalis* regulation reflecting to larger or lesser extent the LOSC regulation.[233] As also non-signatories have sailed their vessels through the Straits for close to 90 years and probably consider themselves entitled to do so, this may be seen as at the very least *prima facie* evidence of such status.[234]

The Montreux Convention further establishes in para 3 of Art 28 a system whereby if no notice of denunciation has been given two years before the said 20-year period passes, any future denunciation would only terminate the application of the Montreux Convention two years after such notice has been given. What is perhaps extraordinary here, is the fact that *one* denunciation will lead to the termination of the whole Convention for *all* parties. In those settings, the parties were to 'be represented at a conference for the purpose of concluding a new Convention.'[235]

This conference may lead to new issues being sought covered by the new agreement, and this might again lead to a slow-moving negotiation process without any guarantee that a new agreement is actually arrived at. Instead of having a suboptimal but largely functioning agreement, the result may then be no treaty agreement at all, leaving us again with the need to establish what international customary law can bring to bear on the issue. Is Russia likely to do this? No, as Yücel is probably right in believing that Russia 'does not seek to

---

230 See e.g. here Aybay and Oral (n 15) 5, and Yüksel Ínan, 'The Current Regime of the Turkish Straits' (2001) VI (1) Journal of International Affairs 2, 5–7.

231 Yücel (n 8) 232.

232 Myron H Nordquist *et al.* (eds.), *United Nations Convention on the Law of the Sea 1982: A Commentary, Vol. II* (Martinus Nijhoff Publishers 1993) 307–308, Jia (n 82) 144, 214 with further differences, von Heinegg (n 170) 290, n. 114, Donald Rothwell and Tim Stephens, *The International Law of the Sea*, 2nd ed. (Hart Publishing 2016) 260; Yoshifumi Tanaka, *The International Law of the Sea*, 4th ed. (Cambridge University Press 2023) 130.

233 Wani holds that "the practice relating to the Turkish Straits in time of war is nothing more than application of the Montreux Convention, and cannot be taken as evidence of customary international law", see Wani (n 228) 42, n 11. For the view that if the Conventions ceased to exist, the navigational freedom "would not be subject to the limitations established by the Montreux Convention", see Rozakis and Stagos (n 28) 106.

234 Yücel (n 8) 182–183 with further references.

235 Art. 28 (4). See here Aybay and Oral (n 15) 4.

change the Montreux Convention because it knows it cannot gain more rights than it has now.'[236]

Another issue is whether a new regulation of the Straits would suffice to be excluded from the reach of the LOSC regulation – leaving aside the fact that Turkey is not a party – as it would no longer be a '*long-standing* international conventions in force specifically relating to such straits'.[237] However, it might be odd if the parties to these *lex specialis* agreements were hindered from adopting the regulation of the relevant waterway to current needs, as such new agreements would still be *lex specialis* regulations, although not as treaty law of long standing, but in a long-standing line of regulation of the said waterway. The issue is nevertheless unclear. That said, such LOSC 'compatible' agreements – if perceived as belonging to preexisting treaties when the LOSC came into effect due to this continuity of their *lex specialis* regulation – will not enjoy protection under Art 311(2) on *sui generis* straits if they add limitations that go beyond the LOSC so that they 'affect the enjoyment by other States Parties of their rights or the performance of their obligations under this Convention'. If that hurdle was overcome, a complicating issue would nevertheless be the uneasy relationship between Art 35(c) and Art 311(2).[238] Little help would moreover be found in newer *inter partes* regulations under Art 311(3), as the new regime has little value unless it is applicable to even non-party flag States.

A less radical change is provided by Art 29, which establishes a rather detailed procedure for amendment of the Montreux Convention. *Inter se*, however, Turkey and some or all of the parties may agree to adopt a different procedure for amendment and the end product will then be binding on the parties thereto. If not all of the current parties to the Montreux Convention become parties to the new agreement, the two regimes will run parallel to the extent that the previous one is not terminated via denunciation.

As regards amendments to the Montreux Convention under Art 29, they require unanimity unless revision relates to Arts 14 and 18. For the latter revisions, typically regarding changes to tonnage-limitations, a majority suffices as

236 Yücel (n 8) 227.

237 LOSC Art 35(c) emphasis added. This might be the view taken by Jia, see Jia (n 82) 144–145. It would also seem to be the understanding held during the negotiations of LOSC, see Nordquist (n 232) 307–308. See also Robin Churchill, Vaughan Lowe and Amy Sander, *The Law of the Sea*, 4th ed. (Manchester University Press 2022) 183, n. 39. For a more nuanced view, see Donald R Rothwell, 'International Straits', in Donald R Rothwell, Alex G Oude Elferink, Karen N Scott and Tim Stephens, *The Oxford Handbook of The Law of the Sea* (Oxford University Press 2015) 114, 127.

238 As to the latter, see Alexander Lott, *The Estonian Straits: Exceptions to the Strait Regime of Innocent or Transit Passage* (Brill 2018) 34–39.

long as it consists of 'three-quarters of the High Contracting Parties which are Black Sea Powers, including Turkey'.[239]

Apropos change, the US would seem to have pushed for Turkey to allow for transit beyond the confines of the Montreux Convention in the buildup before the invasion of Iraq in 2003 and in relation to NATO's Operation Active Endeavour.[240] As a non-party to the Montreux Convention, the US cannot itself activate Art 29, and the US must therefore seek to influence Turkey through other mechanisms.

Although this paper has shown that the Montreux Convention could well do with a 'make-over', it is not clear that the misalignment has gone so far that amendments are necessary. Especially in the current political climate, it might be preferable to abide by the old regulations and rather reconsider the issues when a bit mote 'normalcy' is reestablished, at the very least in Europe and neighboring areas.

This approach would not hinder any adjustment – or even change – from taking place, as State practice and *opinio juris* over the decades may already have amended the Montreux Convention regime. This would be in line with how Art 31 of the 1969 Vienna Convention on the Law of Treaties allows in para 3 *litra* b 'any subsequent practice in the application of the treaty which establishes the agreement of the parties regarding its interpretation'.[241] What 'changes' has Turkey instituted to the regime over the years that have been approved with the required *opinio juris* by the other parties? And what deviations have the other parties than Turkey insisted upon with Turkish acquiescence afterwards? Beyond what has already been mentioned, these issues will not be addressed further by this paper.

Conclusion: Are There Any Clear Hybrid Challenges and What Lies Ahead?

As regards issues of *jus ad bellum*, as long as the use of such hybrid warfare qualifies as use of force under Art. 2(4) of the UN Charter, then any threat thereof will also be covered. Whether hybrid warfare will actually be a violation of this Art. 2(4) or rather the internal affairs part of the sovereignty principle,[242] will depend typically on the use of armed force beyond the law enforcement

239 Art 29 (6).

240 Ikinci and Schwarz (n 141).

241 See also 1969 Vienna Convention on the Law of Treaties Art 31(3)(c).

242 Or even falling below the threshold of violating this part of the principle of sovereignty.

paradigm.[243] Any broadening of the concept of armed attack to also cover some hybrid- or cyberattacks, as done in the 2021 NATO Brussels Summit Communique,[244] has been claimed by some to allow Turkey to activate the war time regime at an earlier point in time that was the case before.[245] However, this must also be seen in connection with the non-use after World War II until 2022 of the wartime regime during 'mere' international armed conflicts.

The Russo-Ukrainian armed conflict has obvious kinetic dimensions, but also includes hybrid warfare. In relation to the Montreux Convention, however, using the room of maneuver provided by the Montreux Convention itself is probably better understood as part of established international law, rather than something that needs to be construed as hybrid warfare. Thus, the transport of military hardware on merchant vessels does support the Russian war effort while conforming to the Montreux Convention, although the transport of smaller naval vessels as cargo onboard such civilian vessels would raise questions of legality under the Montreux Convention. Admittedly, this is a more available solution for Russia than Ukraine due to Russian near-supremacy in the Black Sea, but to label this as hybrid is probably unhelpful, as we would then merely be relabeling activities that have been ongoing in the Straits since World War II. The better question is rather whether the activity is legal or illegal under the Montreux Convention, and how the Montreux Convention must be understood in light of changing circumstances.

On a more theoretical level, the reluctance of Turkish authorities to hold that a war exists for the purpose of the Montreux Convention does nevertheless indicate that non-kinetic activities may run parallel to peacetime application of the Montreux Convention. Any sought undermining of the limitations on the transit of military vessels regime through spoofing either in peace- or wartime, however, will probably be rather unsuccessful as Turkey can easily make visual identification/confirmation of the vessels (allegedly) traveling through the Straits. On the other hand, the threat of or unilateral termination of the Montreux Convention by Russia or Ukraine may be labelled as lawfare by enhancing the uncertainty of what the applicable legal regulation would then become. The problem is nevertheless that it is unclear how this would work to

243 Mary Ellen O'Connell, 'The prohibition of the use of force', in Nigel D White and Christian Henderson (eds.), *Research Handbook on International Conflict and Security Law* (Edward Elgar Publishing 2013) 89, 102.

244 Brussels Summit Communiqué, Issued by the Heads of State and Government participating in the meeting of the North Atlantic Council in Brussels 14 June 2021, para. 31, available at <https://www.nato.int/cps/en/natohq/news_185000.htm> accessed 29 September 2023.

245 Aliano and Spivak (n 180).

Russia's benefit, whereas world society will not appreciate any Ukrainian initiative to terminate the now almost 90-year-old regulation. Perhaps the limited military transit rights under the Montreux Convention are still preferable to the free flow of the international straits regime.

Beyond the wish to gain clarification on the issues raised above – and that does not have to take the form of an amended Convention, nor a new one for that matter – Turkey will also in the future, when considering technological developments and other new circumstances not perceived in 1936, have to balance the exact terms of the Montreux Convention against the presumed spirit of it.[246] A challenging task even at the best of times. That said, it is worthwhile to notice that there are at least four ways whereby States – especially Turkey – may circumnavigate the limitations found in the Montreux Convention.

First, a less practical circumnavigation of the restrictions in the Montreux Convention would be to use the Danube that flows into the Black Sea in Romania and Ukraine.[247] 2415 km of this river is navigable, and it connects ten States.[248] However, being a river, tonnage restrictions apply,[249] as well as there being limited link up possibilities with waterways that run into the Mediterranean. Also, access to the Black Sea may be gained via channels running through Russia for smaller vessels from the White Sea, the Baltic Sea, the Sea of Azov and the Caspian Sea.[250]

Second, the consequences of the canal being constructed parallel to the strait of Bosporus – Canal Istanbul – may undermine the existing regime if transit via it is seen as something different from transit of the Straits under the Montreux Convention.[251] The question is here whether both straits and the sea between need to be transited in order for there to be transit under the Montreux Convention.[252] If that is so, the mere transit of *one* of the straits and the sea may be considered as falling outside of the Montreux regime and its limitations on *inter alia* military vessels. This would presumably have been

246 Seydi and Morewood (n 41) 80.

247 Mentioned in passing by Ikinci and Schwarz (n 141).

248 See the INeS Danube document, 16, available at <http://www.ines-danube.info/goto.php?target=file_1442_download&client_id=ines-5> accessed 30 August 2023.

249 It would seem that maximum draught for the larger vessels is limited to 3,5–3,7 m; See ibid, 105, 107 and 159.

250 Váli (n 37) 111; Rozakis and Stagos (n 28) 55.

251 Yücel (n 8) 244–250, and Tuba Eldem, 'Canal Istanbul: Turkey's controversial megaproject; its likely impacts on the Montreux Convention and regional stability' (2021) 43 Stiftung Wissenschaft und Politik Comment. See also 'The Istanbul Canal', Wikipedia, available at <https://en.wikipedia.org/wiki/Istanbul_Canal> accessed 30 August 2023.

252 For the view that this is not the case, see Daly (n 20) 12.

objected to by the States negotiating the Montreux Convention had they foreseen such a possibility, as it would undermine their joint undertaking, but the issue does not seem to have been raised.

Third, with the current regulation looking like it will remain unchanged well into the future, a *de facto* change that might off-set the balance in the Black Sea would be for NATO to 'reflag' naval assets to Romania, Bulgaria, or Turkey, as has been done with some air surveillance aircraft now registered in Luxemburg.[253] These vessels would then be able to sail through the Straits in the same way as other vessels of the Black Sea States. Whether there is a will to do so – or collectively finance a naval buildup of these three NATO Member States – remains to be seen.

Fourth, as a purely hypothetical scenario, a fundamental change of the power relations in the Black Sea would occur if the US was allowed to buy a small piece of territory from e.g. Ukraine – perhaps as a consequence of extensive US support during the Russian invasion. This would be different from the *de facto* eternal rental agreement with Cuba regarding Guantanamo, and would instead be a microscopic version of the US purchase of Alaska, where it perhaps agreed to 100 years of free use and administration of the corresponding maritime zones by the seller. As a trip-wire regarding further Russian military endeavors – like West-Berlin during the Cold War – the US would then, as a successor to Ukraine's privileges under the Convention for the relevant territory, seemingly be entitled to the same privileges as the other Black Sea powers.

The consequences of the second and third option, and especially the fourth one, would be wide ranging.

---

253 See e.g. Gabrielle Antar, 'NATO AWACS plane over Luxembourg turns heads' Luxembourg Times (23 August 2022), available at <https://www.luxtimes.lu/en/luxembourg/nato-awacs-plane-over-luxembourg-turns-heads-6304cae1de135b9236b2c538> accessed 30 August 2023. See also 'Luxembourg and NATO' nato.int, available at <https://www.nato.int/cps/en/natohq/declassified_162355.htm> accessed 30 August 2023.

CHAPTER 12

Responding to Hybrid Threats in the Japanese Straits

Shin Kawagishi

Introduction

As examined in Chapter 1, there is no universally agreed definition of either hybrid warfare or hybrid threats though a number of definitions have been offered by commentators over the years.[1] In practice, hybrid threats tend to be thought of as having a mix of military and non-military as well as covert and overt activities. For example, in April 2023 the North Atlantic Treaty Organization (hereinafter NATO) described hybrid threats as 'combin[ing] military and non-military as well as covert and overt means, including disinformation, cyber attacks, economic pressure, deployment of irregular armed groups and use of regular forces.'[2]

Understood in this way, hybrid threats have occurred in the Japanese Straits in recent years. In July 2017, a Chinese military vessel passed through the Tsugaru Strait that separates the Japanese islands of Honshu and Hokkaido.[3] While navigating through the waters, the warship entered Japan's territorial

1 Arsalan Bilal, 'Hybrid Warfare: New Threats, Complexity, and 'Trust' as the Antidote' NATO Review (30 November 2021), available at <https://www.nato.int/docu/review/articles/2021/11/30/hybrid-warfare-new-threats-complexity-and-trust-as-the-antidote/index.html> accessed 20 June 2023. For example, Frank G Hoffman provides the definition of hybrid warfare and hybrid threats, according to which they are 'modes of warfare, including conventional capabilities, irregular tactics and formations, terrorist acts including indiscriminate violence and coercion, and criminal disorder.' Frank G Hoffman, *Conflict in the 21st Century: The Rise of Hybrid Wars* (Potomac Institute for Policy Studies 2007) 29; Frank G Hoffman, 'Hybrid Warfare and Challenges' (2009) 52(1) Joint Force Quarterly 34, 36.

2 NATO's response to hybrid threats (4 April 2023), available at <https://www.nato.int/cps/en/natohq/topics_156338.htm#:~:text=NATO's%20strategy%3A%20prepare%2C%20deter%2C%20defend&text=NATO%20will%20ensure%20that%20the,necessary%2C%20will%20defend%20Allies%20concerned> accessed 20 June 2023.

3 Anonymous, 'China dismisses Japanese concerns about warship transiting Tsugaru Strait' Reuters (3 July 2017), available at <https://www.reuters.com/article/us-china-japan-tsugaru-idUSKBN19O1QH/> accessed 10 January 2024.

 | DOI:10.1163/9789004707993_014

sea.[4] Confronted with this unauthorized entry into sovereign territory, the Japanese Ministry of Defense reportedly asked the vessel to leave the territorial sea.[5] But the vessel did not comply and the Chinese Ministry of Foreign Affairs later claimed that the Chinese ship had acted in accordance with international law.[6]

In October 2021, a flotilla of five Chinese warships and five Russian warships passed together through the Tsugaru Strait.[7] After navigating through the waters, some of the ships took part in joint naval exercises in the Sea of Japan.[8] It was the first time that Japan had confirmed the fact of Chinese and Russian warships transiting together through the Tsugaru Strait and jointly conducting naval exercises.[9] This incident caused a rise in tensions between Japan and neighboring States, and especially with China and Russia.[10]

These incidents are primary examples of hybrid threats faced by Japan. The purpose of this chapter is to investigate their implications from a legal point of view. Specifically, it aims to consider what lawful means Japan has at its disposal to respond to the passage of foreign military vessel and naval exercises by foreign warships in the Japanese Straits. The passage of the Chinese military vessel in July 2017 and the naval exercises by Chinese and Russian warships in October 2021 are chosen as the basis of analysis mainly because these incidents took place in close spatial proximity and could be seen as part of a campaign designed to threaten Japan's security.

Against this background, this chapter is constructed as follows: First, it describes the characteristics of the Japanese Straits. Second, it examines how Japan is able to deal with the passage of foreign military vessels through the Straits from the perspective of the law of the sea. Third, the chapter examines how Japan is able to cope with the naval exercises by foreign warships from the perspective of the law on the use of force, namely *Jus ad Bellum*. Finally, this chapter sets out some concluding thoughts on hybrid threats faced by Japan.

---

4 Ibid.

5 Foreign Ministry Spokesperson Gen Shuang's Regular Press Conference (3 July 2017), available at <np.china-embassy.gov.cn/eng/fyrth/201707/t20170704_1595194.htm> accessed 10 January 2024.

6 Ibid.

7 Jesse Johnson, 'Chinese and Russian navies' Tsugaru Strait transit highlights growing defense ties' The Japan Times (19 October 2021), available at <https://www.japantimes.co.jp/news/2021/10/19/national/china-russia-tsugaru-strait/> accessed 1 February 2024.

8 Ibid.

9 Anonymous, 'China, Russia navy ships jointly sail through Japan strait' Reuters (20 October 2021), available at <https://jp.reuters.com/article/us-japan-defence-china-russia-idAFKBN2H905W/> accessed 1 February 2024.

10 Ibid.

1 Characteristics of the Japanese Straits

Traditionally, Japan has consistently considered 3 nautical miles (hereinafter NM) as the limit of the territorial sea under international law.[11] In the First United Nations Conference on the Law of the Sea in 1958, Japan insisted that, 'Japan remained convinced that the three-mile limit was the only established rule of international law and that no reasonable grounds existed for extending the breadth of the territorial sea beyond that limit.'[12] Likewise, in the Second United Nations Conference on the Law of the Sea in 1960, Japan continued to insist that 'the Japanese delegation made it absolutely clear that ... the three-mile breadth for the territorial sea will remain to be the recognized rule of international law.'[13] Although the question of the limit of the territorial sea was extensively discussed among the participating States, it was left unsettled in these two conferences.[14]

However, around the Third United Nations Conference on the Law of the Sea in the 1970s and 1980s, the policy of Japan on the breadth of the territorial sea was shifted.[15] This change was reflected in the contents of the Japanese

---

11 This policy of Japan traced back to the period before World War II. For example, in the Hague Codification Conference in 1930 Japan asserted that '[a]s regards the breadth of territorial waters, the Japanese Government has always maintained the rule of three nautical miles, which is recognized by a number of States in their laws, their practice and their jurisdiction, and in the treaties concluded by them.' League of Nations: Acts of the Conference for the Codification of International Law Held at the Hague from March 13th to April 12th, 1930: Meetings of the Committees, Vol. III Minutes of the Second Committee, p. 21. On the discussion about the breadth of the territorial sea in the Hague Codification Conference in 1930, see, for example, Jesse S Reeves, 'The Codification of the Law of Territorial Waters' (1930) 24(3) American Journal of International Law 486, 486–499; Hunter Miller, 'The Hague Codification Conference' (1930) 24(4) American Journal of International Law 674, 686–693.

12 Official Records of the United Nations Conference on the Law of the Sea, Vol. III (First Committee), p. 149, para 4.

13 Official Records of the Second United Nations Conference on the Law of the Sea (Committee of the Whole), p. 168.

14 On the discussion about the breadth of the territorial sea in these conferences, see, for example, Arthur H Dean, 'The Geneva Conference on the Law of the Sea: What was Accomplished' (1958) 52(4) American Journal of International Law 607, 610–616; Arthur H Dean, 'The Second Geneva Conference on the Law of the Sea: The Fight for Freedom of the Seas' (1960) 54(4) American Journal of International Law 751, 772–777; Shigeru Oda, *International Control of Sea Resources* (Nijhoff 1989) 98–105.

15 See, for example, Shigeru Oda and Hisashi Owada, 'Annual Review of Japanese Practice in International Law X (1971–72)' (1979) 23 Japanese Annual of International Law 73, 90–91.

domestic law, 'the Law on Territorial Sea and Contiguous Zone,'[16] which was enacted in 1977.[17] Article 1 of this law employed a 12 NM, instead of a 3 NM, territorial sea as measured from the baselines.

In the Diet, Takeo Fukuda, the then Prime Minister of Japan, explained why Japan had extended the breadth of the territorial sea to 12 NM. Two of the reasons given merit examination. First, Mr. Fukuda indicated that a great number of States advocated 12 NM as the limit of the territorial sea. This limit, he suggested, was becoming a global trend that Japan found it necessary to follow.[18] Second, he suggested that foreign fishing fleets had begun operating close as Japan's coast. As a consequence, Japan felt compelled to reconsider its 3 NM limit and extend the territorial sea out to 12 NM in order to protect Japan's coastal fisheries.[19]

As a result of this change, most of the Japanese Straits were now covered by Japan's territorial sea. However, Japan acknowledged an exception to the general rule. Japan did not employ a 12 NM territorial sea in relation to its five straits, i.e., the Soya Strait, the Tsugaru Strait, the Tsushima Eastern Channel, the Tsushima Western Channel, and the Osumi Strait. The second paragraph of the Supplementary Provisions ('extent of the territorial sea pertaining to the designated areas') of 'the Law on Territorial Sea and Contiguous Zone' stipulated as follows:

> For the time being, *the provisions of article 1 shall not apply to the Soya Kaikyo, the Tsugaru Kaikyo, the Tsushima Kaikyo Higashi Suido, the Tsushima*

16 The Law on the Territorial Sea and the Contiguous Zone (Law No. 30 of 1977, as amended by Law No. 73 of 1996).

17 On the outline of this law, see Shunji Yanai and Kuniaki Asomura, 'Japan and the Emerging Order of the Sea: Two Maritime Laws of Japan' (1977) 21 Japanese Annual of International Law 48, 49–65.

18 'Nowadays, about 60 countries have set 12 NM as the breadth of the territorial sea. In the Third United Nations Conference on the Law of the Sea, there was a controversy among the participating States about the passage regime in international straits, but they scarcely objected to the position to set 12 NM as the limit of the territorial sea…Taking into account these situations, we submit this law to the Diet and then extend the breadth of the territorial sea to 12 NM.' Statement of Takeo Fukuda, Prime Minister, 80th Diet, House of Representatives, Plenary Meeting, No. 16 (7 April 1977), p. 3 (translated into English by the present author).

19 'In recent years, our coastal fisheries have been considerably affected by foreign fishing fleets' operations in Japanese coastal waters. For example, our fishing vessels and implements have been frequently damaged and our coastal fisheries' operations have been seriously restricted … Taking into account these situations, we submit this law to the Diet and then extend the breadth of the territorial sea to 12 NM.' Ibid (translated into English by the present author).

> *Kaikyo Nishi Suido, and the Osumi Kaikyo* (... hereinafter referred to as 'the designated areas').[20]

As a result of maintaining a 3 NM territorial sea, a corridor of high seas, nowadays within the exclusive economic zone (hereinafter EEZ), was created in these five straits. This paragraph continued:

> The territorial sea pertaining to the designated areas shall be respectively the areas of the sea extending from the baseline to *the line 3 nautical miles seaward thereof* and to the line drawn connecting with the said line.[21]

From this perspective, the Japanese Straits can be divided into two.[22] The first category is a strait covered by the territorial sea as a result of Japan extending the breadth of the territorial sea to 12 NM. Most of the Japanese Straits belong to this category. In contrast, the second category is a strait in which a corridor of high seas, now an EEZ, is created by maintaining a 3 NM territorial sea. The five straits, namely the Soya Strait,[23] the Tsugaru Strait,[24] the Tsushima Eastern Channel,[25] the Tsushima Western Channel,[26] and the Osumi Strait[27] are classified under this category. These five straits are referred to as 'the designated areas.'

---

20 The Law on the Territorial Sea and the Contiguous Zone (n 16) (emphasis added).

21 Ibid (emphasis added).

22 Tadao Kuribayashi, 'The Basic Structure of the New Regime of Passage through International Straits: An Emerging Trend in the Third UNCLOS and Japan's Situation' (1977) 21 Japanese Annual of International Law 29, 43.

23 Map of the Soya Strait published on 16 June 2005 by the Japan Coast Guard, available at <https://www.un.org/depts/los/LEGISLATIONANDTREATIES/PDFFILES/MAPS/JPN_MZN61_2008_00174.jpg> accessed 17 January 2024.

24 Map of the Tsugaru Strait published on 1 November 2007 by the Japan Coast Guard, available at <https://www.un.org/depts/los/LEGISLATIONANDTREATIES/PDFFILES/MAPS/JPN_MZN61_2008_00140.jpg> accessed 17 January 2024.

25 Map of the Tsushima Eastern Channel published on 18 December 2003 by the Japan Coast Guard, available at <https://www.un.org/depts/los/LEGISLATIONANDTREATIES/PDFFILES/MAPS/JPN_MZN61_2008_00184.jpg> accessed 17 January 2024.

26 Map of the Tsushima Western Channel published on 18 December 2003 by the Japan Coast Guard, available at <https://www.un.org/depts/los/LEGISLATIONANDTREATIES/PDFFILES/MAPS/JPN_MZN61_2008_00184.jpg> accessed 17 January 2024.

27 Map of the Osumi Strait published on 16 August 2001 by the Japan Coast Guard, available at <https://www.un.org/depts/los/LEGISLATIONANDTREATIES/PDFFILES/MAPS/JPN_MZN61_2008_00187.jpg> accessed 17 January 2024.

2 The Law of the Sea and Hybrid Threats Faced by Japan

2.1 *The Legal Regime of the Japanese Straits in 'the Designated Areas'*

As explained in the introduction, in July 2017 a Chinese military vessel passed through the Tsugaru Strait, which separated the Japanese island of Hokkaido from that of Honshu. The Japanese Ministry of Defense announced that on 2 July 2017, a Chinese People's Liberation Army-Navy Type 815 *Dongdiao*-class auxiliary general intelligence (hereinafter AGI) vessel was found in the Tsugaru Strait.[28] It claimed that, while navigating through the waters, the AGI vessel entered the Japan's territorial sea for a period of 90 minutes.[29]

However, the Chinese Ministry of Defense stressed that '[t]he activities of China's warship are in line with international law.'[30] In response to Japan's claim, the Chinese Ministry of Defense insisted that '[i]n accordance with the UN Convention on the Law of the Sea and geographic condition of the Strait, all ships passing the Strait have *the right of transit passage*.'[31] These demonstrate that China regards the Tsugaru Strait as a strait to which the regime of transit passage applies.

How should we evaluate China's position that the Tsugaru Strait, one of 'the designated areas', is regarded as a strait to which the regime of transit passage applies? The starting point for our discussion is Article 37 of Section 2 ('transit passage') of Part III ('straits used for international navigation') in the United Nations Convention on the Law of the Sea (hereinafter LOSC),[32] according to which '[t]his section applies to straits which are used for international navigation between one part of the high seas or an exclusive economic zone and another part of the high seas or an exclusive economic zone.'

---

28 Ankit Panda, 'Chinese Navy Type 815 Intelligence Ship Transits Tsugaru Strait in Northern Japan' The Diplomat (4 July 2017), available at <https://thediplomat.com/2017/07/chinese-navy-type-815-intelligence-ship-transits-tsugaru-strait-in-northern-japan/> accessed 27 June 2023.

29 Ibid.

30 Ibid.

31 Ibid (emphasis added). Strictly speaking, the Chinese Ministry of Defense insisted that '[t]he Tsugaru Strait is a non-territorial strait and therefore, international ships such as naval ships have the rights of navigation.' Ibid. According to the media, the Chinese Ministry of Defense's justification for their transit in the Tsugaru Strait was quite similar to language used by Geng Shuang, the then Chinese Foreign Ministry spokesperson, in 2015 when People's Liberation Army-Navy vessels transited through the Strait of Tanaga in the Aleutian chain off Alaska. Ibid.

32 United Nations Convention on the Law of the Sea (opened for signature 10 December 1982, entered into force 16 November 1994) 1833 UNTS.

Article 37 defines a strait to which the regime of transit passage applies in terms of two conditions. The first condition is geographical.[33] A strait to which the regime of transit passage applies is one 'between one part of the high seas or an exclusive economic zone and another part of the high seas or an exclusive economic zone.' The second condition is functional.[34] A strait which is 'used for international navigation' is one to which the regime of transit passage applies. Although it is difficult to determine how this condition can be fulfilled, it is often argued that a strait has to be actually used for international navigation and that its potential utility for international navigation is not enough.[35]

At first sight, the Tsugaru Strait might be thought of as meeting these two conditions. However, it must not be ignored that LOSC acknowledges several straits to which the regime of transit passage does not apply. One is a strait in which there is a route through the high seas or through an EEZ.[36] Article 36 of the LOSC thus provides that, '[t]his Part [Part III] does not apply to a strait used for international navigation if there exists through the strait a route through the high seas or through an exclusive economic zone of similar convenience with respect to navigational and hydrographical characteristics.'[37]

'The designated areas', including the Tsugaru Strait, fall under Article 36 of the LOSC because a corridor of an EEZ is created by maintaining a 3 NM

33 Yoshifumi Tanaka, *The International Law of the Sea* (Cambridge University Press 2015) 99.

34 Ibid.

35 See, for example, Daniel Patrick O'Connell, *The International Law of the Sea: Vol. I* (Oxford University Press 1982) 314; Bing Bing Jia, *The Regime of Straits in International Law* (Clarendon Press 1998) 49–52.

36 Horace B Robertson, 'Passage Through International Straits: A Right Preserved in the Third United Nations Conference on the Law of the Sea' (1980) 20(4) Virginia Journal of International Law 801, 827–828.

37 In addition to Article 36 of the LOSC described in the text, we can exemplify the following straits to which the regime of transit passage does not apply. First, according to Article 38(1) of the LOSC, the regime of transit passage shall not apply to straits which are formed by an island of a State bordering the strait and its mainland, in which a route exists seaward of the island through the high seas or through an EEZ. Second, under Article 45(1)(b) of the LOSC, the regime of innocent passage, rather than the regime of transit passage, shall apply to straits connecting the high seas or an EEZ with the territorial sea of a third State. Third, Article 35(c) of the LOSC provides that the regime of transit passage shall not affect the rules applicable under long-standing international conventions which govern passage through particular straits. In this context, the 1936 Convention regarding the Régime of the Straits (the Turkish Straits), the Treaty for the Redemption of the Sound Dues between Denmark and European States of 14 March 1857 (the Danish Belt and the Sound), the 1881 Treaty between Argentina and Chile (the Strait of Magellan), the 1912 Treaty between France and Spain regarding Morocco (the Strait of Gibraltar), and the 1921 Convention on the Non-Fortification and Neutrality of the Åland Islands and the 1940 Agreement on the demilitarization of the islands (the Åland Strait) can be mentioned.

territorial sea.[38] This means that 'the designated areas', including the Tsugaru Strait, are excluded from the scope of applicability of the regime of transit passage.[39] Hence, China's position that the Tsugaru Strait is regarded as a strait to which the regime of transit passage applies is legally unsustainable. Japan's reasons for creating a corridor of an EEZ in 'the designated areas' and precluding the application of the regime of transit passage are examined next.

2.2 *The Reasons for Creating an EEZ Corridor in 'the Designated Areas'*

2.2.1 Security Considerations

On 10 August 2011, Rintaro Ogata, the then member of the House of Representatives, asked the Japanese government why Japan maintained a 3 NM territorial sea in 'the designated areas':

> States are currently able to extend the breadth of the territorial sea to 12 NM. Indeed, in 'the Law on Territorial Sea and Contiguous Zone' of 1977, Japan extended the limit of the territorial sea to 12 NM in principle. However, the Supplementary Provisions to this law provide for the exception in 'the designated areas.' In other words, the breadth of the territorial sea is restricted to 3 NM in the Soya Strait, the Tsugaru Strait, the Tsushima Eastern Channel, the Tsushima Western Channel, and the Osumi Strait. *Why did Japan adopt such a policy?*'[40]

In answering this question, Yasumasa Nagamine, the then Director-General of International Legal Affairs Bureau in the Ministry of Foreign Affairs, emphasized the importance of the security of Japan. He replied:

> If 'the designated areas' are covered by territorial sea, the regime of transit passage provided for in the law of the sea convention might be

---

38 On the drafting history of Article 36 of the LOSC, see Satya N Nandan and David H Anderson, 'Straits used for International Navigation: A Commentary on Part III of the United Nations Convention on the Law of the Sea 1982' (1990) 60 The British Yearbook of International Law 159, 176–178.

39 See, for example, Ana G López Martin, *International Straits: Concept, Classification and Rules of Passage* (Springer 2010) 83; Hugo Caminos and Vincent P Cogliati-Bantz, *The Legal Regime of Straits: Contemporary Challenges and Solutions* (Cambridge University Press 2014) 44; Alexander Lott, *Hybrid Threats and the Law of the Sea: Use of Force and Discriminatory Navigational Restrictions in Straits* (Brill 2022) 10.

40 Statement of Rintaro Ogata, member of the House of Representatives, 177th Diet, House of Representatives, Special Committee on the Response to Piracy, the Prevention of International Terrorism, and Japan's Cooperation, No. 2 (10 August 2011), p. 3 (translated into English by the present author) (emphasis added).

> applied to these areas … *We believe that if this regime is introduced in these areas, a variety of careful measures are required from the perspective of our security* … Hence, at this moment we will not change the Japanese government's position to maintain 3 NM as the limit of the territorial sea in these areas.[41]

According to Mr. Nagamine, security considerations led Japan to create a corridor of high seas, later to be replaced with the regime of an EEZ, in 'the designated areas' and preclude the application of the regime of transit passage.[42] Indeed, the regime of transit passage enables the freedom of navigation and overflight and therefore threatens the coastal State's security.[43] Under Article 38(2) of the LOSC, transit passage is defined as 'the exercise in accordance with this Part [Part III] of the freedom of navigation and overflight solely for the purpose of continuous and expeditious transit.' In this context, it is important to realize that the regime of transit passage is more liberal for navigation and overflight than that of innocent passage in several respects.

First, Article 38(1) of the LOSC provides that '[i]n straits referred to in article 37, all ships and aircraft enjoy the right of transit passage, which shall not be impeded.' This article makes it clear that all ships including military vessels, and all aircraft including military aircraft, enjoy the freedom of navigation and overflight in a strait.[44] Unlike the right of transit passage, the right of innocent passage ensures only navigational rights subject to the coastal State's control, not the freedom of navigation nor the freedom of overflight which applies only in the high seas or in straits subject to the regime of transit passage. In fact,

---

41 Statement of Yasumasa Nagamine, Director-General of International Legal Affairs Bureau in the Ministry of Foreign Affairs, 177th Diet, House of Representatives, Special Committee on the Response to Piracy, the Prevention of International Terrorism, and Japan's Cooperation, No. 2 (10 August 2011), p. 4 (translated into English by the present author) (emphasis added).

42 We can find out other similar statements by the Japanese government. For example, Yutaka Banno, the then Senior Vice-Minister for Foreign Affairs, stressed the importance of the security of Japan as follows: 'Taking into considerations the basic issues in territorial sea and strait and *the change of security environment surrounding our country*, we will carefully and constantly address the issue of the breadth of the territorial sea in "the designated areas".' Statement of Yutaka Banno, Senior Vice-Minister for Foreign Affairs, 177th Diet, House of Representatives, Special Committee on the Response to Piracy, the Prevention of International Terrorism, and Japan's Cooperation, No. 2 (10 August 2011), p. 4 (translated into English by the present author) (emphasis added).

43 Frank Nolta, 'Passage Through International Straits: Free or Innocent? The Interests at Stake' (1974) 11(3) San Diego Law Review 815, 828.

44 Robin Churchill, Vaughan Lowe and Amy Sander, *The Law of the Sea* (Manchester University Press 2022) 177.

Article 17 of the LOSC reflects this by merely stipulating that 'ships of all States, whether coastal or land-locked, enjoy the right of innocent passage through the territorial sea.'

Second, according to Article 44 of the LOSC, coastal States cannot suspend transit passage.[45] Contrary to transit passage, innocent passage in the territorial sea can be suspended temporarily by coastal States in certain circumstances. Indeed, Article 25(3) of the LOSC accepts this by stipulating that '[t]he coastal State may, without discrimination in form or in fact among foreign ships, suspend temporarily in specified areas of its territorial sea the innocent passage of foreign ships if such suspension is essential for the protection of its security, including weapons exercises.'

Third, Article 39(1) of the LOSC provides that while exercising the right of transit passage, ships and aircraft shall 'refrain from any activities other than those incident to their normal modes of continuous and expeditious transit.' Generally speaking, the normal mode of transit for submarines and other underwater vehicles is to submerge.[46] Article 20 of the LOSC stipulates that while exercising the right of innocent passage, '[i]n the territorial sea, submarines and other underwater vehicles are required to navigate on the surface and to show their flag.' In contrast, the LOSC does not provide for the obligation for submarines and other underwater vehicles to navigate on the surface and to show their flag while exercising the right of transit passage. Given this difference, the dominant view is that submarines and other underwater vehicles can submerge while exercising the right of transit passage.[47]

This illustrates that the regime of transit passage enables the freedom of navigation and overflight and therefore presents a threat to the security of coastal States. To summarize, because of security considerations, Japan created initially high seas corridors which were later superseded by EEZ corridors in 'the designated areas' to preclude the application of the regime of transit

45 Ibid, 175.

46 William T Burke, 'Submerged Passage through Straits: Interpretations of the Proposed Law of the Sea Treaty Text' (1977) 52(2) Washington Law Review 193, 214; Elliot L Richardson, 'Law of the Sea: Navigation and Other Traditional National Security Considerations' (1982) 19(3) San Diego Law Review 553, 565. Arguably, the argument that the normal mode of transit for submarine and other underwater vehicles is not necessarily to submerge has been made by some scholars. See, for example, Michael Reisman, 'The Regime of Straits and National Security: An Appraisal of International Lawmaking' (1980) 74(1) American Journal of International Law 48, 71–75.

47 Churchill, Lowe and Sander (n 44) 177.

passage.[48] However, the reasons for creating an EEZ corridor in 'the designated areas' are not confined to the importance of the security of Japan, as is now explored.[49]

2.2.2 Uncertainties on the Regime of Transit Passage

On 7 April 1977, when submitting the draft 'Law on Territorial Sea and Contiguous Zone' in the Diet, Takeo Fukuda, the then Prime Minister of Japan, explained why Japan maintained a 3 NM territorial sea in 'the designated areas.' Notably, he stressed that this policy is provisional:

> The current trend in discussions in the Third United Nations Conference on the Law of the Sea is towards recognizing a more liberal passage regime in international straits than innocent passage regime. *Considering that it is desirable in view of our national interests to wait until the issue of a passage is resolved internationally in line with such a trend, we decide that, for the time being, the limit of the territorial sea is maintained as the status quo in straits in question.*[50]

According to this statement, he deemed it preferable for Japan to freeze a 3 NM territorial sea in 'the designated areas' until the Third United Nations Conference on the Law of the Sea settles the issue of a passage in international straits. To put it another way, he seemed to desire that Japan decide its own future position on the extent of the territorial sea in 'the designated areas' after the

48 Alexander Lott, 'Maritime Security in the Baltic and Japanese Straits From the Perspective of EEZ Corridors' (2023) 54(3) Ocean Development and International Law 327, 327–348.

49 In connection with security considerations, it has been often said that the Non-Nuclear Principles are also one of the reasons for Japan to create the high seas/EEZ corridors in the straits in question. The Non-Nuclear Principles mean that the Japanese government will not possess, produce, or permit the introduction of nuclear weapons into Japan. Since 1960s, the Japanese government upheld it as Japan's policy. It has been often argued that the Japanese government wants to keep the high seas/EEZ corridors to allow United States (hereinafter US) warships with nuclear weapons to pass through sea routes without violating the Non-Nuclear Principles. However, the Japanese government did not officially admit this reasoning. See, for example, statement of Takeo Miki, Minister of Foreign Affairs, 58th Diet, House of Representatives, Committee on Foreign Affairs, No. 12 (17 April 1968), p. 8; statement of Takeo Fukuda, Prime Minister, 80th Diet, House of Representatives, Plenary Meeting, No. 16 (7 April 1977), p. 3. On this topic, see Yurika Ishii, *Japanese Maritime Security and Law of the Sea* (Brill 2022) 97–98.

50 Statement of Takeo Fukuda, Prime Minister, 80th Diet, House of Representatives, Plenary Meeting, No. 16 (7 April 1977), p. 3 (translated into English by the present author).

issue of a passage in international straits is fixed in the Third United Nations Conference on the Law of the Sea.[51]

After the LOSC was adopted in 1982, Japan still maintained a 3 NM territorial sea in 'the designated areas.' When Japan finally ratified the LOSC in 1996, deliberations on this issue took place once again in the Diet. On 10 May 1996, Shigefumi Matsuzawa, the then member of the House of Representatives, objected to Japan's policy as follows:

> *Why does not the Japanese government extend the limit of the territorial sea to 12 NM in 'the designated areas'?* I have doubts about Japan's policy.[52]

In response to this objection, Ryutaro Hashimoto, the then Prime Minister of Japan, explained why Japan maintained a 3 NM territorial sea in 'the designated areas':

> The Part III of the law of the sea convention has provisions on the regime of transit passage in international straits. However, *until now there remain uncertainties on the regime of transit passage because State practice has not been sufficiently accumulated on that regime* … Hence, we will not change the current situation of the five straits.[53]

---

51 In other words, he seemed to signal Japan's intent to keep all options on the table and signal that Japan might abolish the high seas/EEZ corridors when it so wishes. Similar statements have been expressed by the Japanese government. For example, on 23 February 1977, Zenko Suzuki, the then Minister of Agriculture, Forestry and Fisheries, announced as follows: 'In expanding the breadth of the territorial sea to 12 NM, an important question is that of the regime of passage through international straits. This question is now considered in the Third United Nations Conference on the Law of the Sea, which is likely to adopt a regime of passage through international straits more liberal than that of the innocent passage in the territorial sea … It is desirable for Japan to wait until this question is resolved internationally. On the basis of these considerations, we will for the time being as a provisional measure maintain the present status of waters which might be termed international straits.' Statement of Zenko Suzuki, the Minister of Agriculture, Forestry and Fisheries, 80th Diet, House of Representatives, Committee of Budget, No. 12 (23 February 1977), p. 5 (translated into English by the present author).

52 Statement of Shigefumi Matsuzawa, member of the House of Representatives, 136th Diet, House of Representatives, Plenary Meeting, No. 23 (10 May 1996), p. 10 (translated into English by the present author) (emphasis added).

53 Statement of Ryutaro Hashimoto, Prime Minister, 136th Diet, House of Representatives, Plenary Meeting, No. 23 (10 May 1996), p. 10 (translated into English by the present author) (emphasis added).

The meaning of this statement is not entirely clear. This statement does not specify in which aspects the regime of transit passage is uncertain. However, he seemed to think that although Japan's policy to freeze a 3 NM territorial sea in 'the designated areas' is provisional, it is still too early for Japan to abandon this policy because of uncertainties on some aspects of the regime of transit passage.

Although it is unclear if Japan was worried about the customary status of the regime of transit passage, this status is one of the uncertain aspects of the regime of transit passage. It is difficult to argue that, at the time of the adoption of the LOSC, the right of transit passage would have formed part of customary international law. Indeed, when closing the plenary meeting of the Third United Nations Conference on the Law of the Sea, its president opined that '[t]he argument that, except for Part XI, the Convention codifies customary law or reflects existing international practice is factually incorrect and legally insupportable,' adding that '[t]he regime of transit passage through straits used for international navigation and the regime of archipelagic sea lanes passage are only two examples of the many new concepts in the Convention.'[54]

However, since the adoption of the LOSC some States have taken the view that the right of transit passage is part of customary international law. For example, the US endorsed this position by suggesting that 'the regimes of ... transit passage, as reflected in the Convention, are clearly based on customary practice of long standing and reflect the balance of rights and interests among all States, regardless of whether they signed or ratified the Convention.'[55] In light of these different opinions, it is still uncertain if the regime of transit passage forms customary international law.[56]

54 Official Records of the Third United Nations Conference on the Law of the Sea, Vol. XVII (Plenary Meetings, Summary Records and Verbatim Records, as well as Documents of the Conference, Resumed Eleventh Session and Final Part Eleventh Session and Conclusion), pp. 135–136, para 48.

55 J Ashley Roach and Robert W Smith, *Excessive Maritime Claims* (Nijhoff 2012) 294–295.

56 Although some States have advocated that the regime of transit passage forms part of customary international law, a number of scholars have still objected to this status. See, for example, Kathryn Surace-Smith, 'United States Activity Outside of the Law of the Sea Convention: Deep Seabed Mining and Transit Passage' (1984) 84(4) Columbia Law Review 1032, 1054–1058; Said Mahmoudi, 'Passage of warships through the Strait of Hormuz' (1991) 15(5) Marine Policy 338, 339; James Kraska, 'Legal Vortex in the Strait of Hormuz' (2013) 54(2) Virginia Journal of International Law 324, 360.

3 The Law on the Use of Force and Hybrid Threats Faced by Japan

3.1 *Naval Exercises by Chinese and Russian Warships*

As noted in the introduction, in October 2021 a group of ten Chinese and Russian warships sailed through the Tsugaru Strait.[57] After transiting through the Tsugaru Strait, some of these ships participated in joint naval exercises in the Sea of Japan.[58] This was the first time that Chinese and Russian warships had passed through the Tsugaru Strait together and then jointly carried out naval exercises.[59]

China sent five warships through the Strait, one of which was the People's Liberation Army Navy Type 055 destroyer *Nanchang*, a 10,000 ton-class large destroyer.[60] Likewise, Russia sent five warships, including the Russian Navy's Project 20380 corvettes *Hero of Russia Aldar Tsydenzhapov* and *Gromsky* (Steregushchiy-class).[61] During the naval exercises, Chinese and Russian warships practiced communications, sea mine countermeasures, air defense, live-fire shooting at maritime targets, joint maneuvering and joint anti-submarine missions.[62] They started the naval exercises without any rehearsal, making the exercises closer to real combat.[63]

When conducting joint naval exercises in the Sea of Japan, China and Russia emphasized the maintenance of stability in the region. The Chinese Ministry of Defense announced that the aim of joint naval exercises was to 'enhance the joint action capabilities of both parties and jointly maintain international and regional strategic stability.'[64] Similarly, the Russian Ministry of Defense expressed the view that '[t]he tasks of the patrols were the demonstration of

57 Anonymous, 'Russian, Chinese warships hold first joint patrols in the Pacific' Reuters (24 October 2021), available at <https://www.reuters.com/world/russian-chinese-warships-hold-first-joint-patrols-pacific-2021-10-23/> accessed 8 February 2024.

58 Ibid.

59 Ibid.

60 Anonymous, 'Video: Russia-China Combined Naval Drills In Sea Of Japan' Naval News (18 October 2021), available at <https://www.navalnews.com/naval-news/2021/10/video-russia-china-combined-naval-drills-in-sea-of-japan/> accessed 8 February 2024.

61 Ibid.

62 Guo Yuandan and Liu Xuanzun, 'China, Russia hold joint naval drill in Sea of Japan, display 'higher level of trust, capability'' Global Times (14 October 2021), available at <https://www.globaltimes.cn/page/202110/1236294.shtml#:~:text=With%20China's%20advanced%20Type%20055,of%20strategic%20mutual%20mutual%20trust%2C%20but> accessed 8 February 2024.

63 Ibid.

64 Anonymous (n 57).

the Russian and Chinese state flags, maintaining of peace and stability in the Asia-Pacific region.'[65]

In the face of this incident, Japan was on guard against joint naval exercises. Yoshihiko Isozaki, the then Deputy Chief Cabinet Secretary, announced that '[t]he government is closely watching Chinese and Russian naval vessels' activities around Japan like this one with high interest.'[66] Nevertheless, shortly after the first joint naval exercises, in September 2022 Chinese and Russian warships again sailed together through the Osumi Strait[67] and in December 2022 they jointly conducted naval exercises.[68] During the naval exercises, a flotilla of Chinese and Russian warships held a demonstration with a number of aircraft carriers, one of which was the *Liaoning* aircraft carrier, and destroyers, including the *Marshal Shaposhnikov* destroyer.[69] In response to this incident, Yasukazu Hamada, the then Minister of Defense, seemed to consider these joint naval exercises as the threat or use of force by indicating that '[i]t was clearly meant as a show of force and we regard it a serious concern.'[70]

This illustrates the reality that international tensions between Japan and the neighboring States have been heightened by recent naval exercises by Chinese and Russian warships.[71] What is more, the exercises by the warships potentially threatened the security of Japan. How should we evaluate them under the law on the use of force? To put it another way, if a coastal State seeks to resort to the use of force in self-defence in response to naval exercises by foreign warships, how can it be justified under the law on the use of force? The

65 Ibid.

66 Anonymous (n 9).

67 Keoni Everington, '7 Chinese, Russian warships tracked around Japan' Taiwan News (30 September 2022), available at <https://www.taiwannews.com.tw/en/news/4673032> accessed 8 February 2024.

68 Helen Davidson, 'Surge in China's military operations reflects 'new normal' under Xi Jinping' The Guardian (22 December 2022), available at <https://www.theguardian.com/world/2022/dec/22/surge-china-military-operations-new-normal-xi-jinping>, accessed 9 February 2024.

69 Ibid.

70 Anonymous, 'Russian warships pass through Tsushima Strait' The Japan News (1 October 2022), available at <https://japannews.yomiuri.co.jp/politics/defense-security/20221001-61697/> accessed 8 February 2024.

71 Although the naval exercises by Chinese and Russian warships in October 2021 was the first time, Chinese warships had previously sailed through the Japanese Straits and conducted operations such as scouting, signaling, and gatekeeping. See in detail Peter A Dutton, 'Scouting, Signaling, and Gatekeeping: Chinese Naval Operations in Japanese Waters and the International Law Implications' (2009) 2 China Maritime Studies Institute Red Books 1, 1–32.

aim of this section is to answer this question by means of using the naval exercises by Chinese and Russian warships in October 2021 as a case study.

3.2 *The Use of Force in Self-Defence in Response to Naval Exercises by Foreign Warships*

3.2.1 Self-Defence in Case of Naval Exercises by Foreign Warships

The naval exercises by Chinese and Russian warships in October 2021 did not attack Japan but rather presented potential threats to its security. Given this character, they clearly did not amount to the occurrence of an 'armed attack' triggering the right of self-defence under Article 51 of the United Nations (hereinafter UN) Charter.[72] However, as is well-known, a number of scholars have advocated the lawfulness of anticipatory self-defence, according to which a State is entitled to exercise the right of self-defence against imminent threats.[73] For example, Thomas Franck endorsed it by stating that 'States seem willing to accept strong evidence of the imminence of an overpowering attack as tantamount to the attack itself, allowing a demonstrably threatened state to respond under Article 51 [of the UN Charter].'[74]

However, the present author believes that the lawfulness of anticipatory self-defence is legally untenable under the law on the use of force.[75] Two reasons

---

72 Charter of the United Nations (opened for signature 26 June 1945, entered into force 24 October 1945) 1 UNTS XVI.

73 For example, Humphrey Waldock, 'The Regulation of the Use of Force by Individual States in International Law' (1951) 81 Collected Courses of the Hague Academy of International Law 451, 497–498; Derek Bowett, *Self-Defence in International Law* (Manchester University Press 1958) 188–189; Gerald Fitzmaurice, 'The General Principles of International Law Considered from the Standpoint of the Rule of Law' (1957) 92 Collected Courses of the Hague Academy of International Law 1, 171; Stephen Schwebel, 'Aggression, Intervention and Self-Defence in Modern International Law' (1972) 136 Collected Courses of the Hague Academy of International Law 411, 478–481; Rosalyn Higgins, *Problems and Process: International Law and How We Use It* (Clarendon Press 1994) 242–243; Thomas M Franck, *Recourse to Force: State Action Against Threats and Armed Attacks* (Cambridge University Press 2002) 107; Christopher Greenwood, 'International Law and the Pre-emptive Use of Force: Afghanistan, Al-Qaida and Iraq' (2003) 4 San Diego International Law Journal 7, 13.

74 Franck (n 73) 107.

75 As is well-known, a number of scholars have insisted that the lawfulness of anticipatory self-defence is legally unsustainable under the law on the use of force. For example, Hans Kelsen, *The Law of the United Nations: A Critical Analysis of Its Fundamental Problems* (Stevens and Sons 1950) 797–798; Ian Brownlie, *International Law and the Use of Force by States* (Oxford University Press 1963) 257–258; Josef L Kunz, *The Changing Law of Nations: Essays on International Law* (Ohio State University Press 1968) 571; Louis Henkin, *How Nations Behave: Law and Foreign Policy* (Columbia University Press 1979) 141–144; Albrecht Randelzhofer, 'Article 51', in Bruno Simma (ed.), *The Charter of the United Nations: A Commentary* (Oxford University Press 2002) 803; Christine Gray, 'A Crisis of Legitimacy for

merit examination. First, the International Court of Justice (hereinafter ICJ) seems to implicitly deny the lawfulness of anticipatory self-defence. The judgment in the *Military and Paramilitary Activities in and against Nicaragua case*[76] has been often considered as refraining from pronouncing on the lawfulness of anticipatory self-defence. For example, Tom Ruys evaluates that 'the Court has indeed refrained from taking sides in the long-standing academic row regarding pre-emptive action.'[77] In fact, the Court decided as follows:

> [R]eliance is placed by the Parties only on the right of self-defence in the case of an armed attack which has already occurred, and *the issue of the lawfulness of a response to the imminent threat of armed attack has not been raised. Accordingly, the Court expresses no view on that issue.*[78]

Nevertheless, in the subsequent paragraph the Court referred to the need for a State exercising the right of self-defence to have been actually the casualty of an 'armed attack':

> In the case of individual self-defence, *the exercise of this right is subject to the State concerned having been the victim of an armed attack.*[79]

This part of the judgment can be interpreted as implying that the Court seems unwilling to accept the lawfulness of anticipatory self-defence.[80] For example, Olivier Corten assesses that '[a]ll of these statements seem to denote a reluctant attitude of the Court ... in respect of any form of preventive war conducted

the UN Security System?' (2007) 56(1) International and Comparative Law Quarterly 157, 160–161.

76 *Military and Paramilitary Activities in and against Nicaragua* (Nicaragua v. United States of America), Judgment, ICJ Reports 1986.

77 Tom Ruys, *'Armed Attack' and Article 51 of the UN Charter: Evolution in Customary Law and Practice* (Cambridge University Press 2010) 263.

78 *Military and Paramilitary Activities in and against Nicaragua* (n 76) p. 103, para 194 (emphasis added). Similarly, the Court held that '[t]he possible lawfulness of a response to the imminent threat of an armed attack which has not yet taken place has not been raised.' Ibid, pp. 27–28, para 35.

79 Ibid, p. 103, para 195 (emphasis added).

80 Unlike this interpretation, this part of the judgment was read as suggesting that 'such pronouncements of the Court were made in relation to the arguments presented before it in each case.' James A Green, *The International Court of Justice and Self-Defence in International Law* (Hart 2009) 29.

without Security Council authorization.'[81] Hence, although the Court decided not to address the issue of anticipatory self-defence, there is a room for interpreting its part of the judgment as substantially excluding the lawfulness of anticipatory self-defence.[82]

Second, we can acquire an important guidance on the lawfulness of anticipatory self-defence from the debates in the UN General Assembly World Summit in September 2005.[83] Kofi Annan, the then Secretary-General of the UN, submitted the report ('In Larger Freedom: towards development, security and human rights for all'), according to which a State is entitled to exercise the right of self-defence against imminent threats under Article 51 of the UN Charter:

---

81 Olivier Corten, *The Law Against War: The Prohibition of the Use of Force in Contemporary International Law* (Hart 2021) 435.

82 Gennadit M Danilenko, 'The Principle of Non-Use of Force in the Practice of the International Court of Justice', in William E Butler (ed.), *The Non-Use of Force in International Law* (Brill 1989) 105–106. The same holds true for the judgment in the *Armed Activities on the Territory of Congo case. Armed Activities on the Territory of the Congo* (Democratic Republic of the Congo v. Uganda), Judgment, ICJ Reports 2005. The Court decided not to address the issue of anticipatory self-defence by stating as follows: '[T]he Court recalls that Uganda has insisted in this case that operation "Safe Haven" was not a use of force against an anticipated attack. As was the case also in the *Military and Paramilitary Activities in and against Nicaragua* (*Nicaragua v. United States of America*) case, "reliance is placed by the Parties only on the right of self-defence in the case of an armed attack which has already occurred, and the issue of the lawfulness of a response to the imminent threat of armed attack has not been raised" (*I.C.J. Reports 1986*, p. 103, para. 194). The Court there found that "[a]ccordingly [it] expresses no view on that issue". So it is in the present case.' Ibid, p. 222, para 143. Nevertheless, following this ruling the Court opined that '[a]rticle 51 of the [UN] Charter may justify a use of force in self-defence only within the strict confines there laid down,' adding that '[i]t does not allow the use of force by a State to protect perceived security interests beyond these parameters.' Ibid, pp. 223–224, para 148. This part of the judgment also can be interpreted as substantially excluding the lawfulness of anticipatory self-defence. See, for example, Philippa Webb, *International Judicial Integration and Fragmentation* (Oxford University Press 2013) 121–122; Christine Gray, *International Law and the Use of Force* (Oxford University Press 2018) 252; Robert Kolb, *International Law on the Maintenance of Peace: Jus Contra Bellum* (Edward Elgar 2018) 386–387; Stuart Casey-Maslen, *Jus ad Bellum: The Law on Inter-State Use of Force* (Hart 2020) 66.

83 In the UN General Assembly World Summit, the issue of the lawfulness of self-defence against non-imminent threats was also raised. This chapter does not deal with this issue because it concentrates on the lawfulness of self-defence against imminent threats. It suffices to note that in the UN General Assembly World Summit, the lawfulness of self-defence against non-imminent threats was explicitly or implicitly rejected by the Secretary-General's report as well as a significant number of States. See Ruys (n 77) 327–342; Corten (n 81) 419–427; Gray (n 82) 248–253.

> *Imminent threats are fully covered by Article 51* [of the UN Charter], which safeguards the inherent right of sovereign States to defend themselves against armed attack. Lawyers have long recognized that this covers an imminent attack as well as one that has already happened.[84]

During the debates in the UN General Assembly, a small number of States endorsed this position.[85] For example, the US observed that '[t]he Secretary-General's report makes the key point that a State need not wait until it is actually attacked in order to use force in self-defence, which is to say that there is a right of anticipatory self-defence in appropriate circumstances,' adding that '[a]nticipatory action is an element of the inherent right of self-defence that remains lawful under the United Nations Charter.'[86]

However, a significant number of States took a different position to that of the Secretary-General in his report.[87] For example, Iran opposed it by asserting that 'Article 51 [of the UN Charter] in no way covers imminent threats, and international law does not confer any legitimacy on the dangerous doctrine of pre-emption.'[88]

As a consequence, the UN General Assembly World Summit deleted the part on self-defence against imminent threats and there was no mention of it in the text of the Outcome. This indicates that a significant number of States were reluctant to support self-defence against imminent threats.[89] As Christine Gray evaluates, '[t]he General Assembly debates on *In Larger Freedom* showed that most states were not willing to accept anticipatory, let alone pre-emptive, self-defence.'[90]

Taking into consideration the judgment of the ICJ in the *Military and Paramilitary Activities in and against Nicaragua case* and a majority of State practice in the UN General Assembly World Summit, the lawfulness of anticipatory self-defence is legally unsustainable under the law on the use of force. Hence, if we apply this analysis to the naval exercises by Chinese and Russian warships in October 2021, Japan could not have resorted to the use of force in

84 UN Doc. A/59/2005, p. 33, para 124 (emphasis added).

85 For example, UN Doc. A/59/PV. 85, p. 26 (the United Kingdom); A/59/PV. 87, p. 23 (the US).

86 UN Doc. A/59/PV. 87, p. 23.

87 For example, UN Doc. A/59/PV. 86, p. 5 (Pakistan), p. 9 (Algeria), p. 18 (Morocco); A/59/PV. 87, p. 17 (Iran); A/59/PV. 89, p. 14 (Cuba), p. 22 (Vietnam); A/59/PV. 90, p. 24 (India).

88 UN Doc. A/59/PV. 87, p. 17.

89 Ruys (n 77) 341; Corten (n 81) 426–427; Gray (n 82) 251.

90 Gray (n 82) 251.

self-defence if there would have been a need to react to the joint military exercises of China and Russia.

3.2.2 Self-Defence in Case of Naval Exercises by Foreign Warships Involving an Attack on a Coastal State Vessel

Given that the naval exercises by Chinese and Russian warships in October 2021 comprised activities such as live-fire shooting at maritime targets, as a hypothetical scenario there might be a possibility that the shots would target – intentionally or by accident – a Japanese vessel. In this hypothetical scenario, can Japan be entitled to exercise the right of self-defence? In answering this question, one of the most crucial issues is whether an attack on a warship or merchant vessel is able to reach the threshold of an 'armed attack.'

In this context, the judgment of the ICJ in the *Oil Platforms case*[91] is of great relevance. The Court opined that an 'armed attack' is the most grave form of the use of force. This means that an 'armed attack' needs to have a higher threshold than for other prohibited uses of force under Article 2(4) of the UN Charter:

> As the Court observed in the case concerning *Military and Paramilitary Activities in and against Nicaragua*, it is necessary to distinguish "*the most grave forms of the use of force* (*those constituting an armed attack*) from other less grave forms."[92]

Nevertheless, in assessing the mining of the *USS Samuel B. Roberts* the Court admitted the possibility that the mining of even a single military vessel could be characterized as an 'armed attack':

> [T]he Court does not exclude the possibility that *the mining of a single military vessel might be sufficient to bring into play the 'inherent right of self-defence'*.[93]

Taking into account this line of reasoning, one may consider that although the Court categorized an 'armed attack' as the most grave form of the use of force, it applied the *de minimis* threshold of an 'armed attack' in a flexible manner.[94]

---

91 *Oil Platforms* (Islamic Republic of Iran v. United States of America), Judgment, ICJ Reports 2003.

92 Ibid, p. 187, para 51 (emphasis added).

93 Ibid, p. 195, para 72 (emphasis added).

94 See, for example, Olivier Corten, 'Judge Simma's Separate Opinion in the Oil Platforms Case: To What Extent Are Armed 'Proportionate Defensive Measures' Admissible in Contemporary International Law?', in Ulrich Fastenrath *et al.* (eds.), *From Bilateralism*

As Olivier Corten observes, 'by not excluding the possibility that the mining of a single military vessel could be sufficient to trigger the right of self-defence, the Court made a very important statement confirming the great flexibility of the 'gravity criteria.''[95]

Can the same reasoning be adopted by the Court to an attack on a single merchant vessel?[96] Regrettably, the Court did not expressly address this issue.[97] The Court's final ruling was that the attacks under consideration could not be regarded as an 'armed attack' against the US. The Court opined that 'even taken cumulatively, and reserving, as already noted, the question of Iranian responsibility, these incidents do not seem to the Court to constitute an armed attack on the United States, of the kind that the Court in the case concerning *Military and Paramilitary Activities in and against Nicaragua*, qualified as a 'most grave' form of the use of force.'[98] However, we must clarify the line of reasoning by which the Court finally ruled that the attacks under consideration could not be considered as an 'armed attack' against the US.

In this context, the part of the judgment on the attack on the *Texaco Caribbean* has great importance. The ICJ emphasized the fact that this merchant vessel did not fly a US flag. The Court decided as follows:

> [T]he *Texaco Caribbean*, whatever its ownership, *was not flying a United States flag, so that an attack on the vessel is not in itself to be equated with an attack on that State.*[99]

In this part of the judgment, the Court examined whether the attack on the *Texaco Caribbean* could be regarded as an 'armed attack' against the US. The reason why the Court did not consider the attack on the *Texaco Caribbean* as an 'armed attack' against the US was that this merchant vessel did not fly a US flag. Taking into consideration this line of reasoning, the Court left room

---

to Community Interest: Essays in Honour of Judge Bruno Simma (Oxford University Press 2011) 852; Claus Kreβ, 'The International Court of Justice and the 'Principle of Non-Use of Force'', in Marc Weller (ed.), *The Oxford Handbook of the Use of Force in International Law* (Oxford University Press 2015) 582.

95 Corten (n 94) 852.

96 The present author has already examined this question. See Alexander Lott and Shin Kawagishi, 'The Legal Regime of the Strait of Hormuz and Attacks against Oil Tankers: Law of the Sea and Law on the Use of Force Perspectives' (2022) 53(2–3) Ocean Development and International Law 123, 123–146.

97 See, for example, Webb (n 82) 119.

98 *Oil Platforms* (n 91) pp. 191–192, para 64.

99 Ibid (emphasis added).

for the possibility that the attack on the *Texaco Caribbean* could potentially reach the threshold of an 'armed attack' against the flag State. To put it another way, the implication of this part of the judgment is that an attack on a single merchant vessel could potentially reach the threshold of an 'armed attack.' As Claus Kreβ assesses, 'the Court ... did not seem to exclude the possibility of an armed attack being directed against a *merchant* vessel of a state.'[100]

Therefore, it is possible that an attack on even a single warship or merchant vessel could be characterized as an 'armed attack.' On the other hand, as regards the attack on the *Sea Isle City*, the Court emphasized that it could not have been specifically aimed at this merchant vessel:

> The Court notes first that the *Sea Isle City* was in Kuwaiti waters at the time of the attack on it, and that *a Silkworm missile fired from (it is alleged) more than 100 km away could not have been aimed at the specific vessel*, but simply programmed to hit some target in Kuwaiti waters.[101]

This part of the judgment indicates that a specific intention to attack a particular target is required for triggering an 'armed attack.'[102] Taking into account this criterion, the Court seemed to acknowledge the possibility that an intentional attack on a single warship or merchant vessel could trigger an 'armed attack' under Article 51 of the UN Charter.[103] Hence, if we apply this analysis to our hypothetical scenario, assuming that naval exercises of foreign warships would involve an intentional attack on a single warship or merchant vessel of the coastal State, then the latter can resort to the use of force in self-defence subject to the other requirements of self-defence, especially the principles of necessity and proportionality.[104]

---

100 Kreβ (n 94) 582 (emphasis original).

101 *Oil Platforms* (n 91) pp. 191–192, para 64 (emphasis added).

102 The same holds true for another part of the judgment in the *Oil Platform case*. As regards the attack on the *Bridgeton*, the Court also emphasized that it did not involve the specific intention of attacking this particular merchant vessel. The ICJ opined that 'similarly it has not been established that the mine struck by the *Bridgeton* was laid with the specific intention of harming that ship.' Ibid, p. 192, para 64. However, this position has been criticized by some scholars. See, for example, William H Taft, 'Self-defence and the Oil Platforms Decision' (2004) 29(2) Yale Journal of International Law 295, 302–303. According to this position, a victim State subject to an indiscriminate attack could not respond in self-defence. Ibid.

103 See, for example, Dominic Raab, ''Armed Attack' After the Oil Platforms Case' (2004) 17(4) Leiden Journal of International Law 719, 728; James A Green, 'Self-Defence: A State of Mind for States?' (2008) 55(2) Netherlands International Law Review 181, 202–203.

104 Needless to say, the conduct of the members of armed forces in Chinese and Russian warships can be attributed to China and Russia respectively. It is firmly established under

Conclusion

The passage of foreign military vessels through the Japanese Straits and recent naval exercises by foreign warships are of great relevance in the context of hybrid threats to Japan. This chapter examined how Japan can respond to the passage of foreign warships and their naval exercises in the Japanese Straits. The law of the sea and the law on the use of force enable to ensure stability in the Japanese Straits in the face of hybrid threats.

For protecting its maritime security in view of the passage of foreign military vessels through its straits, Japan adopted a 3 NM territorial sea and thereby created a corridor of high seas/an EEZ in 'the designated areas', including the Tsugaru Strait. As a consequence, the application of the regime of transit passage provided for in the LOSC, can be precluded in these straits. Hence, although in a corridor of high seas/an EEZ, foreign military vessels can enjoy the freedom of navigation, in the 3 NM territorial sea it must navigate through in accordance with the regime of innocent passage. To summarize, Japan's policy to create a corridor of high seas/an EEZ by maintaining 3 NM as the breadth of the territorial sea in 'the designated areas' enables this country to preclude the application of the regime of transit passage and thereby exercise more control over the passage of foreign military vessels in the Japanese Straits.

The naval exercises of foreign warships in and around the Japanese Straits present potential threats to the security of Japan. Depending on the circumstances, should the naval exercises of foreign warships involve an intentional attack on a single Japanese warship or merchant vessel, the possibility that the military exercises could potentially trigger an 'armed attack' within the meaning of Article 51 of the UN Charter is not excluded. In such a hypothetical scenario, it might be possible for a coastal State to resort to the use of force in self-defence.

---

customary international law that the conduct of any State organ is attributed to that State. Article 4 of the International Law Commission's Articles on State Responsibility provides that: 'The conduct of any State organ shall be considered as act of that State under international law, whether the organ exercises legislative, executive, judicial or any other functions, whatever position it holds in the organization of the State, and whatever its character as an organ of the central Government or of a territorial unit of the State.' James Crawford, *The International Law Commission's Articles on State Responsibility: Introduction, Text and Commentaries* (Cambridge University Press 2002) 94.

Concluding Observations on the Nature of Hybrid Warfare at Sea and Its Implications to the Safety of Offshore Infrastructure and International Navigation

Alexander Lott

This book concluded that hybrid warfare implies a combination of regular and irregular military operations, with the addition of non-military means. Hybrid warfare employs a wide array of methods, such as sabotage, cyberattacks, gunboat diplomacy, terrorism, propaganda, and espionage. It is aimed at influencing the adversary's mind. This research showed that hybrid warfare relies on the indeterminacy of the law as the aggressor tends to exploit gaps in the relevant legal framework.

Arguably, the concept of hybrid warfare is not useful for assessing the legality of a State's actions in the maritime domain. As a political concept, hybrid warfare makes sense. Thévenin opined that the concept of hybrid warfare can be used as a tool to describe problematic incidents prior to making a legal determination on it. Yet, legally speaking, this book confirmed the hypothesis that States should be able to classify any incidents of hybrid warfare under either the ramifications of armed conflict, or peacetime military activities at sea or law enforcement operations.

Thus, hybrid warfare at sea merely implies the indeterminacy (grey areas) of the classification of a particular incident between the legal concepts of law enforcement operations, military activities at sea, and naval warfare. Different from the concepts of law enforcement and military activities at sea, naval warfare means the existence of an international armed conflict. Law enforcement is mostly understood as peacetime measures aimed at countering a threat to public order or the elimination of a breach of public order. According to Thévenin, military activities at sea designates the peacetime activities conducted by a warship, which are neither passage nor law enforcement activities. He notes that, in the territorial sea, military activities are banned, whereas elsewhere they are allowed if the flag State refrains from the threat or use of force and pays due regard to the sovereign rights of the coastal States. In this context, Thévenin suggests that the Baltic States could adopt guidelines for ensuring the peaceful navigation and overflight in and over the Baltic Sea based on the

 | DOI:10.1163/9789004707993_015

success of the guidelines developed in the beginning of this century in the Asia-Pacific region.

In her contribution to this book, Anna Petrig focuses on the threshold of applicability of the law of naval warfare. Based on a review of recent incidents, she finds that hybrid adversaries know how to exploit this threshold by engaging in conduct which is difficult to assess in terms of the applicability of various bodies of law. Petrig argues that this strips a 'law-compliant state' from the possibility to rely on the more permissive wartime rules, effectively resulting in the 'instrumentalization of legal thresholds' in the context of hybrid warfare. In an instance of hybrid warfare (e.g., the Kerch Strait incident of 2018 and incidents in the Red Sea involving the Houthi militia), it tends to be unclear whether a particular attack of a hybrid adversary has a sufficient nexus to an on-going nearby armed conflict for triggering the applicability of the law of naval warfare. Petrig explains that such nexus is determinative of whether the law of armed conflict applies in hybrid warfare.

The authors of this book agreed that the concept of hybrid warfare is intertwined with the threshold of an armed conflict since the methods of hybrid warfare are commonly designed to remain just below it. As explained by Casey-Maslen, Dahl, Galani and myself, the threshold of armed conflict is crossed when one of the parties to an incident abandons the law enforcement paradigm, where minimum force necessary is used against persons that represent an imminent and local threat, as opposed to a military paradigm where maximum force against enemy combatant personnel is employed irrespective of whether they constitute any threat. Petrig explains that, in the context of the proportionality principle in naval warfare, 'the target as such is not covered by the principle; what is more, civilian persons on board a targetable vessel are generally not taken into account in the proportionality assessment'. In conclusion, the law of armed conflict enables the victim State to respond to an attack of a hybrid adversary more effectively as under the peacetime maritime law enforcement paradigm.

In most cases, the threshold of armed conflict is crossed as soon as the use of force against a State reaches the level of an armed attack under Article 51 of the United Nations (hereinafter UN) Charter in response to which that State uses her right of self-defence. The right of self-defence must be exercised subject to the principles of necessity and proportionality. Casey-Maslen explains that necessity means that no pacific alternatives, such as seizing the UN Security Council of the affair or referring the case to the International Court of Justice, reasonably exist to respond to the armed attack. In the context of *jus ad bellum*, the principle of proportionality has a different meaning as compared to the peacetime law enforcement or the law of the armed conflict paradigms as it places a ceiling on what kind of forcible action may be taken in response to an armed attack.

Hybrid warfare tends to imply a clandestine and/or rather minimal use of force against the target. This puts the victim State in her response to such an incident in a difficult position. In its case law, the International Court of Justice has set the threshold of an armed attack relatively high. Furthermore, as argued by Casey-Maslen, the need for unequivocal attribution of responsibility means that, in many instances, there will be no right to use force in self-defence in response to hybrid warfare. Casey-Maslen points out that, in such cases, law enforcement measures, but also such countermeasures that do not involve the use of force can serve as the possible responses to hybrid warfare.

Based on a review of recent incidents concerning suspected sabotage against submarine cables and pipelines located in the exclusive economic zone (hereinafter EEZ) or the high seas it was concluded that these important pathways of energy and telecommunications are highly vulnerable to hybrid warfare at sea. As potential measures for increasing the safety of submarine cables and pipelines in the EEZ in the face of sabotage, I proposed that:

- States can consider establishing safety zones around these objects of critical infrastructure following the practice of Denmark. Despite its controversiality, the establishment of safety zones provides an effective measure for the coastal States to address a legal gap in the United Nations Convention on the Law of the Sea (hereinafter LOSC) in relation to the protection of submarine cables and pipelines outside the limits of the territorial sea against acts of sabotage;
- States need to complement the establishment of such safety zones with preparedness to take rapid enforcement measures, including by way of an active use of the right of hot pursuit, against any violations in the safety zones;
- States should uphold the legal concept of neutral submarine cables and grant them a higher standard of protection under the law of naval warfare;
- Belligerent States must meet the requirement of due regard for the rights and duties of neutral States as well as the protection and preservation of the marine environment when conducting belligerent operations in the neutral States' EEZ and on their continental shelf against submarine cables and pipelines.

I find that States should stop drawing a clear legal boundary between attacks against critical offshore infrastructure within and beyond the outer limits of the territorial sea. Instead, States should assert that sabotage against critical offshore infrastructure may amount to an armed attack if conducted not only within, but also outside the sovereign territory of a coastal State. An attack against a coastal State's underwater road or rail tunnel, wind farm, oil or gas platform, submarine pipeline or cable may have equally grave consequences if carried out in the EEZ or on the continental shelf instead of its territorial sea.

However, for claiming the right of self-defence, the victim State first needs to know whom to blame for the attack. The suspected acts of sabotage against critical offshore infrastructure in the past couple of years have shown that, in the maritime domain, it can be very challenging to identify the actor responsible for the damage to submarine cables or pipelines. Commercial ships such as fishing trawlers and container ships can be effectively weaponized by States for sabotaging critical offshore infrastructure. In this context, the limits of the coastal State's right of ship interdiction are of critical importance.

This led this book to address legal problems related to the interdiction of foreign-flagged ships suspected of having inflicted damage to a pipeline outside the limits of the territorial sea. In a co-authored chapter, Ringbom and I find that this is an area of law which includes many legal gaps. These gaps need to be overcome, either by way of a dynamic interpretation of the relevant treaty provisions or by way of developing new treaty law. We argue that the more coastal States manage to close such grey areas, the less room there is for hybrid warfare against critical offshore infrastructure.

Since the success of State actors to deliberately target pipelines and cables as a means of hybrid warfare depends on the caution exercised by victim States in not taking actions which are not explicitly authorized in the relevant international conventions, a cautious response may even promote hybrid warfare against critical offshore infrastructure in the future. Ringbom and I conclude that for deterring sabotage against offshore critical infrastructure and for taking enforcement action against the suspected ship in the EEZ, the coastal States may adopt the following measures:

- The amendment of domestic legislation to provide more flexibility for enforcing the domestic laws against a suspected ship by way of not making in this context a sharp distinction between maritime areas within and beyond the territorial sea, thereby reducing the jurisdictional grey zones;
- Effective monitoring and surveying of submarine cables and pipelines at the surface and on the seafloor to increase the coastal State's maritime domain awareness and readiness to take enforcement against suspected acts of sabotage;
- Making the fullest use of the zonal approach of the LOSC, including by way of introducing navigational restrictions near pipelines, such as non-anchoring zones and full-scale mandatory areas to be avoided;
- Developing new treaty law for granting universal enforcement jurisdiction in respect of ships suspected of damaging submarine pipelines or cables

outside the limits of the territorial sea similar to the universal jurisdiction granted over piracy and unauthorized broadcasting under the LOSC;

- A more proactive stance to taking proportionate enforcement measures against the suspected offenders based on a dynamic interpretation of the LOSC, while being open to the idea that the legality of the enforcement action might end up being assessed by an international court or tribunal.

As an important lesson learned from the Balticconnector incident, we find that it would be counterproductive to expect a specific legal basis for any enforcement action against hybrid warfare, since the latter by definition targets grey zones in the legal system.

In a similar vein, Koivurova and Winkel find that building resilience against hybrid warfare is crucial in the legal domain, since otherwise the legal gaps are abused by an aggressor State for strategic purposes. In my view, Koivurova's and Winkel's chapter underlines the trend towards the securitization of international environmental law in an era of great power competition. In order to achieve one's geopolitical aims by means of advancing or resisting the weaponization of energy and its means of transportation (including submarine cables and pipelines), it has become increasingly important to be able to speak the 'language' of environmental law. In the context of lawfare, this inevitably implies the so-to-say instrumentalization of international environmental law.

In a hindsight, Koivurova and Winkel appear to find that the completion of the Nord Stream project and the almost successful completion of its extension project (Nord Stream 2) show that liberal-democratic societies in Europe tend to neglect the implications of lawfare by interpreting the relevant law too narrowly. In the case of the Nord Stream project, politics-wise financial gain was prioritized at the expense of security considerations. Koivurova and Winkel show how Russia successfully used the European Union law, international law, and the relevant regional and domestic institutions as instruments of lawfare to eventually damage European security. They emphasize the vast impact that the law had in legitimizing the Nord Stream projects as they conclude that, 'the law enabled the Nord Stream project to proceed and facilitate the strategic objectives of a hybrid actor, where energy matters turned into a tool of manipulation, all while being veiled as an economic project. /…/ Russia was nearly able to fulfil its geopolitical objectives based on a clever, yet cynical manipulation of the law.' Notably, since its full-scale invasion of Ukraine Russia has increasingly employed methods of lawfare. To some extent, this has enabled her to evade Western sanctions.

In the chapter on Russia's shadow fleet, Parlov and Sverdrup show how Russia continues to manipulate with the applicable law to limit the effectiveness of the Oil Price Cap regime that was imposed by Western States on Russia in reaction to its invasion of Ukraine in 2022. By way of essentially decoupling itself from the mostly Western-controlled liability insurance system and by establishing a shadow fleet of uninsured and unsafe tankers, Russia's shipment of oil primarily to such Asian markets which are not part of the sanctions regime has continued largely unabated. A similar scheme has been used by Iran and Venezuela for decades.

The size of global shadow fleet has risen sharply since 2022 and now accounts for up to a fifth of international oil shipments. This recent development has significantly increased threats to the environment and safety of life at sea, not least because these mostly substandard ships switch off their automatic identification system (hereinafter AIS) when undertaking environmentally risky ship-to-ship transfers of oil on the high seas. The phenomenon of shadow fleet is problematic from the perspective of rules-based order of maritime trade, the main guarantor of which is the International Maritime Organization (hereinafter IMO).

Parlov and Sverdrup indicate that the primary concern here is the potential decoupling of shipping to the extent that the existing maritime governance system reaches its breaking point. To prevent this, they suggest that the IMO needs to 'encourage States to adopt a more robust due diligence regime with clear procedural steps to be followed in screening the financial strength of the providers of financial security to vessels carrying oil and dangerous cargo, probably along the more robust procedures for ship registration.' Parlov and Sverdrup are hopeful that the full disintegration of the current shipping system can be avoided.

In the context of hybrid warfare, authoritarian States have weaponized not only critical offshore infrastructure and shipping, but also mass migration as a means to weaken the security of European States. Galani finds that while the orchestration of mass migration against another State does not amount to an armed conflict, it generates a grey zone in relation to the measures that a State may adopt in response to mass immigration. Galani stresses the importance of upholding human rights obligations towards migrants regardless of whether migration is treated as a hybrid threat. Galani finds that 'no exceptions or derogation rules arise out of this 'grey zone' that would permit States to deviate from their human rights obligations under international law'. Galani proposes that European States should focus on building cyberspace resilience to protect their citizens from disinformation campaigns and fake news concerning migrants. She argues that the maritime environment cannot be used as a legitimate reason for creating any exceptional conditions that would permit derogation from human rights obligations despite the significant number of boat migrants reaching Europe.

Bugajski's chapter focuses on the question of the existence of naval blockade of Ukraine's Black Sea ports in the light of international law. Due to the relevance and controversy of this topic, I would like to complement Bugajski's analysis with a couple of points for future scholarly discussions. In my view, the effectiveness of a blockade should be the quintessential criterion based on which one should determine its existence.

In the spring and summer of 2022, I was a frequent visitor to the Marine Traffic website. The AIS data showed that international navigation in the Sea of Azov had stopped since the end of February and resumed only in late spring and early summer of 2022. If Russia, hypothetically, allowed some ships to enter or leave its ports in the Sea of Azov and navigate through the Kerch Strait, then this did not render the blockade against Ukraine's coast on the Sea of Azov ineffective. It is doubtful that any ships from the Ukrainian ports of Berdyansk or Mariupol (both are now occupied) were allowed to leave the Sea of Azov as the war progressed. Yet even if such exceptional instances occurred, then it would not necessarily render Russia's blockade ineffective. Article 7 of the 1909 London Declaration stipulates that: "In circumstances of distress, acknowledged by an officer of the blockading force, a neutral vessel may enter a place under blockade and subsequently leave it, provided that she has neither discharged nor shipped any cargo there." Thus, if Russia allowed some commercial ships to leave – but not to enter – the Sea of Azov in the end of February 2022, as claimed by some reports, then it should be at least questioned if it had a real impact on the overall effectiveness of the blockade against the Ukrainian coast on the Sea of Azov, or indeed in the Black Sea proper. Notably, it is a standard practice that upon the commencement of a blockade, the blockading force provides a period of grace for neutral ships to leave the blockaded area.

Bugajski discusses the customary international law applicable to a naval blockade and comes to the conclusion that Russia's actions in the Black Sea amount to a *de facto* blockade. Like many other scholars before him, Bugajski finds that Russia's blockade does not satisfy the legal requirements of declaration and notification. Bugajski concludes that:

> Although Russia has imposed restrictions in the Black Sea to prevent the entry or exit of ships from Ukraine, it has not met the legal elements to perfect a *de jure* blockade. The rules governing blockade are codified in the 1909 London Declaration. Blockades are confined to the ports and coasts belonging to or occupied by the enemy. Notification and declaration of blockade is required to place all states on notice. The belligerent imposing the blockade must communicate the date the order begins, the geographic limits of the coastline subject to the order, and the period of time within which neutrals may exist in the area (period of grace).

Yet there remains a certain degree of ambiguity and controversy in relation to the conclusion that Russia's actions in the Black Sea in 2022 did not amount to a naval blockade legally. In my view, the contemporary meaning of the criteria of declaration and notification of a blockade should be explored critically. The requirements of declaration and notification are still being assessed on the basis of the criteria that were developed in the late 19th century and early 20th century. That was an era of mostly declared wars. Nowadays, in an era of undeclared wars, the criteria of declaration and notification of a blockade could be interpreted dynamically to ensure the relevance and viability of the rules of blockade to contemporary armed conflicts. For example, Russia internationally communicated its announcements of 24 February 2022 that 'due to a warning received from the Russian Defense Ministry's Black Sea Fleet, amid the beginning of antiterrorist operations at 4 a.m. on February 24th, navigation in the Sea of Azov was suspended until further notice' and of 25 February 2022 that the northwestern part of Black Sea to north of parallel 45°21'N is 'prohibited for navigation due to counterterrorist operations carried out by Russian Navy. Ships and vessels in this area will be regarded as a terrorist threat'. In my view, these announcements should satisfy the requirements of declaration and notification. Notably, the 1856 Paris Declaration did not make any reference to these two criteria. It simply stated that: 'Blockades, in order to be binding, must be effective, that is to say, maintained by a force sufficient really to prevent access to the coast of the enemy.'

By contrast, according to the San Remo Manual, a blockade needs to be declared and notified to all belligerents as well as neutral States and the declaration has to specify the commencement, duration, location, and extent of the blockade and the period within which vessels of neutral States may leave the blockaded coastline (Rules 93 and 94). The Newport Manual on the Law of Naval Warfare further specifies that:

> All aspects of the blockade (geographic extent, date of commencement, general scope of measures employed) must be declared and notified in a Notice to Mariners (for a maritime blockade) and/or a Notice to Airmen (where the blockade is also operative against aircraft), or some other official declaration or announcement, by the belligerent State establishing the blockade. (Section 7.4.2)

In the relevant legal literature, most authors seem to limit themselves to simply noting that Russia did not make a formal declaration of a naval blockade in the wake of its full-scale invasion of Ukraine and thus a naval blockade was not established. However, in my view, a clear declaration of a blockade would have been incompatible with Russia's official position that it is not at war with

Ukraine and instead had launched a "special military operation". In this context, from the aggressor State Russia's perspective, the declaration of blockade would have been non-sensical given that the blockade of the ports or coasts of a State by the armed forces of another State qualifies automatically for an act of aggression under Article 3(c) of the General Assembly Resolution 3314 *Definition of Aggression.*

The law has mostly adapted to the reality of undeclared wars by determining the existence of an armed conflict based on the objective facts. Should not the same approach be adopted for determining the existence of a naval blockade? It is widely accepted that the San Remo Manual reflects the customary international law applicable to naval warfare, including the rules of blockade. The on-going revision of the San Remo Manual as well as the Newport Manual on the Law of Naval Warfare 2.0 revision process provide potential avenues to address this matter. Bugajski concludes that Russia's actions in the Black Sea amount to the use of maritime exclusion zones (see Rules 105 to 108 of the San Remo Manual) and not to a naval blockade. But does this concept really offer a meaningful alternative to a naval blockade? After all, the legal concept of a blockade provides under the law of naval warfare significant protection to the population of the State against which the blockade is enforced. According to the San Remo Manual, the shipment of humanitarian supplies to the blockaded conflict zone is explicitly permitted (Rules 103 and 104).

In this context, I would recommend revising the Newport Manual to the extent that it provides differently from the San Remo Manual that '[t]here is no exemption from blockade enforcement for vessels carrying humanitarian materials intended for the civilian population of a blockaded area' and that the passage of food, medical supplies and other objects essential for human survival depends on the goodwill of the blockading State that 'may make and declare arrangements for the provision of humanitarian support to a blockaded area' (Section 7.4.5). The use of the word 'may' in the above quote suggests that this decision is subject to the complete discretion of the blockading State. To accept such complete discretion means that the civilian population in a blockaded area is exposed to a significant risk of starvation and inhuman treatment by the blockading State. As demonstrated by the markedly different approach adopted by the San Remo Manual, the guidelines of the Newport Manual on this matter could hardly be in accordance with the aims of the international humanitarian law that seeks to avoid the unnecessary suffering of the civilian population in an armed conflict.

By contrast, legally speaking, maritime exclusion zones have essentially nothing to offer to the belligerents, the civilian population, and neutral States.

Maritime exclusion zones are of rather declaratory value as they do not have an impact on the rights and duties of belligerents and neutral States.

In my view, it would be rather useless to wait for the aggressor State to declare a blockade when it clearly has no intention to do so, but still blocks, harasses, and attacks neutral international navigation. Were China to launch its anticipated "special military operation" against Taiwan, it would presumably establish a blockade in all but name against the island. In a potential scenario involving a great maritime power's invasion of a small island State (e.g., Cyprus), a partly enclaved State (e.g., Estonia) or isolated regions (e.g., Gaza, Taiwan) and where third States would decide not to directly intervene militarily (as in the case of Russia's invasion of Ukraine in 2022), the third States would still be entitled, under the rules of blockade, to freely send foodstuffs and other essential supplies (such as medicines) to the blockaded area (San Remo Manual, Rules 103–104). However, if what seems to be the majority's legal view about the non-existence of Russia's naval blockade against Ukraine continues to be applied *mutatis mutandis* to analogous cases in the future, then third States would be stripped from a right to send seaborne humanitarian relief shipments to the area which has been subject to a *de facto* blockade. It would be rather arbitrary to provide the blockading force the complete discretionary right to decide over whether its actions amount to a blockade legally based on its interest in this legal categorization. In my view, international humanitarian law should not be allowed to be held hostage of the aggressor State's intentional manipulations with the law. It should not suffice for an aggressor State to evade the rules of blockade simply by branding its aggression as a "special military operation" and defying the existence of an armed conflict against objective facts.

These considerations lead me to disagree with Bugajski's conclusion as well as with the dominant view in the legal literature on this matter. In my view, it would enable to better ensure the viability of the rules of blockade if Russia's actions in the Black Sea in the spring and summer of 2022 would be classified as a blockade also legally. After all, the rules of blockade were drafted over a century ago when States were used to declared wars. It seems to me that the alternative is to accept the risk that the legal concept of a naval blockade becomes largely irrelevant because it becomes detached from the reality of contemporary naval warfare that does not necessarily correspond to its 19th/early 20th Century meaning. States should consider reinterpreting the meaning of the criteria of declaration and notification under the rules of naval blockade in order to ensure its relevancy in future international armed conflicts, but also in the context of less intense hybrid warfare.

Similar to Galani, Frostad is also cautious of the idea of broadening the legal concept of armed attack under Article 51 of the UN Charter to include hybrid warfare or cyberattacks, as done in the 2021 Brussels Summit Communique of the North Atlantic Treaty Organization. He finds that this could have implications to the passage regime through one of the most widely known major shipping routes, i.e. the Turkish Straits (the Dardanelles and the Bosporus Strait), as it could possibly allow Turkey to activate the war-time passage regime through the Turkish Straits more flexibly.

However, Frostad notes that not all armed conflicts between States around the time when the 1936 Montreux Convention was negotiated were considered as war proper and that prior to the full-scale Russian invasion of Ukraine in 2022 Turkey seems to have closed the Bosporus and the Dardanelles only once, that is during World War II. Frostad distils from this that the existence of an armed conflict does not necessarily activate the war-time passage regime under the Montreux Convention. Hence, the existence of hybrid warfare that ranks even lower on the scale of aggression than an armed conflict could not alter the peacetime passage regime in the Turkish Straits. Thereby, the Montreux Convention appears to contribute to ensuring stability in this major shipping route in the context of hybrid warfare.

The combined high-intensity hostilities and official view of Ukraine to the effect that she is at war with Russia allows Frostad to conclude that Turkey rightly took the position that a 'war' exists for the purpose of the Montreux Convention. Frostad concludes that as soon as the war-time passage regime is activated in respect of the Turkish Straits, the Montreux Convention functions like a long-distance quasi-blockade, keeping the naval assets of the belligerents from entering or leaving the Turkish Straits.

The focus of Kawagishi's chapter is also on straits. Kawagishi finds that the severity of maritime security threats (or hybrid threats) led Japan to alter the passage regime that would have been otherwise applicable to some of the most important straits located in her maritime area. Japan decided to preclude the freedom of navigation of foreign warships and overflight of military aircraft in and over Japan's territorial sea under the right of transit passage for maritime security considerations. To achieve this purpose, Japan decided, in 1977, to establish EEZ corridors in the five designated areas of Japanese Straits (these corridors functioned as high seas corridors prior to the adoption of the EEZ regime under the LOSC). In the EEZ corridors, the freedom of navigation and overflight applies, whereas in the rest of the maritime area that comprise the territorial sea in the relevant straits, the right of innocent passage of ships and permit-based overflight of aircraft is applicable. This enables Japan to exercise control over the activities of foreign ships and aircraft in and above its territorial sea. In essence, this deters potential hybrid threats emanating from the passage of foreign ships and aircraft or from foreign military exercises adjacent to Japan's coast. However, if such threats emerge, then the coastal State can, depending on the circumstances, employ the law on the use of force if the aggressor has launched an attack against it. For example, Kawagishi found that if the naval exercises lead to an intentional attack on a single warship or merchant vessel, then this can potentially trigger an 'armed attack' within the meaning of Article 51 of the UN Charter. The occurrence of such an armed attack would permit the flag State to resort to the use of force in self-defence.

Index

www.ingramcontent.com/pod-product-compliance
Lightning Source LLC
Chambersburg PA
CBHW071231230926
51849CB00001B/69